Toyota Camry and Lexus ES 350 Automotive Repair Manual

by Jeff Killingsworth and John H Haynes

Member of the Guild of Motoring Writers

Models covered:

Toyota Camry and Avalon,
and Lexus ES 350 models
2007 through 2015

Does not include information specific to hybrid models

(92009 - 10U3)

ABCDE
FGHIJ
KL

Haynes Publishing Group
Sparkford Nr Yeovil
Somerset BA22 7JJ England

Haynes North America, Inc
859 Lawrence Drive
Newbury Park
California 91320 USA
www.haynes.com

Acknowledgements

Wiring diagrams provided exclusively for Haynes North America, Inc. by Valley Forge Technical Information Services.

© **Haynes North America, Inc. 2011, 2016**

With permission from J.H. Haynes & Co. Ltd.

A book in the Haynes Automotive Repair Manual Series

Printed in Malaysia

ISBN-10: 1-62092-271-1
ISBN-13: 978-1-62092-271-2

Library of Congress Control Number 2016955149

16-336

Contents

Haynes mechanic and author with a 2010 Camry

About this manual

Its purpose

The purpose of this manual is to help you get the best value from your vehicle. It can do so in several ways. It can help you decide what work must be done, even if you choose to have it done by a dealer service department or a repair shop; it provides information and procedures for routine maintenance and servicing; and it offers diagnostic and repair procedures to follow when trouble occurs.

We hope you use the manual to tackle the work yourself. For many simpler jobs, doing it yourself may be quicker than arranging an appointment to get the vehicle into a shop and making the trips to leave it and pick it up. More importantly, a lot of money can be saved by avoiding the expense the shop must pass on to you to cover its labor and overhead costs. An added benefit is the sense of satisfaction and accomplishment that you feel after doing the job yourself.

Using the manual

The manual is divided into Chapters. Each Chapter is divided into numbered Sections, which are headed in bold type between horizontal lines. Each Section consists of consecutively numbered paragraphs.

At the beginning of each numbered Section you will be referred to any illustrations which apply to the procedures in that Section. The reference numbers used in illustration captions pinpoint the pertinent Section and the Step within that Section. That is, illustration 3.2 means the illustration refers to Section 3 and Step (or paragraph) 2 within that Section.

Procedures, once described in the text, are not normally repeated. When it's necessary to refer to another Chapter, the reference will be given as Chapter and Section number. Cross references given without use of the word "Chapter" apply to Sections and/or paragraphs in the same Chapter. For example, "see Section 8" means in the same Chapter.

References to the left or right side of the vehicle assume you are sitting in the driver's seat, facing forward.

Even though we have prepared this manual with extreme care, neither the publisher nor the author can accept responsibility for any errors in, or omissions from, the information given.

NOTE

A **Note** provides information necessary to properly complete a procedure or information which will make the procedure easier to understand.

CAUTION

A **Caution** provides a special procedure or special steps which must be taken while completing the procedure where the Caution is found. Not heeding a Caution can result in damage to the assembly being worked on.

WARNING

A **Warning** provides a special procedure or special steps which must be taken while completing the procedure where the Warning is found. Not heeding a Warning can result in personal injury.

Introduction to the Toyota Camry, Avalon and Lexus ES 350

This manual covers the Toyota Camry and Avalon, and Lexus ES 350 models. All models are four-door sedans.

The transversely mounted inline four-cylinder (Camry models only) and V6 engines (available on all models) are equipped with electronic port fuel injection.

The engine drives the front wheels through either a five-speed manual or a five- or six-speed automatic transaxle via independent driveaxles.

Independent suspension, featuring coil spring/strut damper units, is used on all four wheels. The power-assisted rack-and-pinion steering unit is mounted behind the engine.

The brakes are disc-type at the front and rear, with power assist standard. All models are equipped with anti-lock brakes (ABS).

Vehicle identification numbers

Modifications are a continuing and unpublicized process in vehicle manufacturing. Since spare parts manuals and lists are compiled on a numerical basis, the individual vehicle numbers are essential to correctly identify the component required.

Vehicle Identification Number (VIN)

This very important identification number is stamped on a plate attached to the dashboard inside the windshield on the driver's side of the vehicle (see illustration). It can also be found on the certification label located on the driver's side door post. The VIN also appears on the Vehicle Certificate of Title and Registration. It contains information such as where and when the vehicle was manufactured, the model year and the body style.

Manufacturer's Certification Regulation label

The certification label is attached to the end of the driver's door post (see illustration). The plate contains the name of the manufacturer, the month and year of production, the Gross Vehicle Weight Rating (GVWR), the Gross Axle Weight Rating (GAWR) and the certification statement.

VIN model year code

Counting from the left, the model year code letter designation is the 10th character. **On all models covered by this manual the model year codes are:**

7	2007
8	2008
9	2009
A	2010
B	2011
C	2012
D	2013
E	2014
F	2015

Engine numbers

The engine code number can be found in a variety of locations, depending on engine type (see illustrations). Camry models can be equipped with either the 2AZ-FE four-cylinder (through 2009), the 2AR-FE four-cylinder (2010 and later) or the 2GR-FE V6. Avalon and Lexus ES 350 models are only available with the 2GR-FE V6 engine.

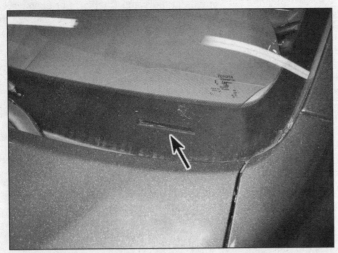

The Vehicle Identification Number (VIN) is located on a plate on top of the dash (visible through the windshield)

The vehicle certification label is located at the rear of the driver's door opening

The engine serial number on the four-cylinder engine is located on the front side of the block below the cylinder head, adjacent to the transaxle

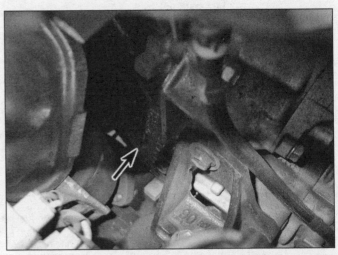

The V6 engine serial number is located on the front side of the block, adjacent to the transaxle

Recall information

Vehicle recalls are carried out by the manufacturer in the rare event of a possible safety-related defect. The vehicle's registered owner is contacted at the address on file at the Department of Motor Vehicles and given the details of the recall. Remedial work is carried out free of charge at a dealer service department.

If you are the new owner of a used vehicle which was subject to a recall and you want to be sure that the work has been carried out, it's best to contact a dealer service department and ask about your individual vehicle - you'll need to furnish them your Vehicle Identification Number (VIN).

The table below is based on information provided by the National Highway Traffic Safety Administration (NHTSA), the body which oversees vehicle recalls in the United States. The recall database is updated constantly. **Note:** *This a partial list containing only the Toyota dealer recalls. There are additional aftermarket recalls available.* For the latest information on vehicle recalls, check the NHTSA website at www.nhtsa.gov, or call the NHTSA hotline at 1-888-327-4236.

Recall date	Recall campaign number	Model(s) affected	Concern
MAR 28, 2006	06V096000	2007 Toyota Camry	On certain passenger vehicles, due to improper assembly of the airbag inflator, which is used in the side airbag, the curtain shield airbag, and the knee airbag assembly, some inflators were produced with an insufficient amount of the heating agents necessary for proper airbag deployment. In this condition, the expansion force of the gas may be insufficient to properly inflate the airbag when the SRS system is activated during a crash. This may increase the risk of injury to the occupant in the involved seating position in the event of a crash.
DEC 14, 2006	06V488000	2007 Toyota Camry	On certain vehicles equipped with curtain side airbags (CSA), the CSA tether strap located in the front pillars may have been incorrectly routed during the assembly process. If the tether strap is not correctly routed, the front side of the CSA may not deploy as designed, which may result in insufficient occupant protection during a side impact crash or rollover event.
SEP 26, 2007	07E082000	2007, 2008 Toyota Camry and Lexus ES350	On some models equipped with optional all weather floor mats (AWFM), if the AWFM is not secured by itself or if it is placed on top of an existing carpeting floor mat, the mat could move forward during vehicle usage and it may interfere with the accelerator pedal. The accelerator pedal may temporarily become stuck in a partially depressed position when returning to the idle position. If this condition occurs, it may increase the possibility of a crash.

Recall date	Recall campaign number	Model(s) affected	Concern
OCT 5, 2009	09V388000	2007, 2008, 2009, 2010 Toyota Camry, Avalon and Lexus ES350	On certain models the accelerator pedal can get stuck in the wide open position due to its being trapped by an unsecured or incompatible driver's floor mat. A stuck-open accelerator pedal may result in very high vehicle speeds and make it difficult to stop the vehicle, which could cause a crash, serious injury or death.
JAN 21, 2010	10V017000	2007, 2008, 2009, 2010 Toyota Camry and Avalon	On some models, due to the manner in which the friction lever interacts with the sliding surface of the accelerator pedal inside the pedal sensor assembly, the sliding surface of the lever may become smooth during vehicle operation. In this condition, if condensation occurs on the surface, as may occur from heater operation (without a/c) when the pedal assembly is cold, the friction when the accelerator pedal is operated may increase, which may result in the accelerator pedal becoming harder to depress, slower to return, or, in the worst case, mechanically stuck in a partially depressed position, increasing the risk of a crash.
JAN 26, 2010	10V035000	2007, 2008, 2009, 2010 Toyota Camry and Avalon	Certain models fail to comply with the requirements of Federal Motor Vehicle Safety Standard No. 110, "tire selection and rims." These vehicles were sold without the requisite load carrying capacity modification labels. This does not meet the standard requirements.
FEB 9, 2010	10V040000	2010 Toyota Camry	On some models the length of the power steering pressure hose on vehicles equipped with the 4-cylinder (2AR-FE) engine may be insufficient, such that the gap between the crimp on the pressure hose and the brake tube for the left rear brake may be insufficient. Under these circumstances the brake tube may interfere with the crimp and may wear and perforate. A brake tube perforation may result in brake fluid leakage. A leak in brake fluid may impact braking performance increasing the risk of a crash.
JAN 16, 2013	13V442000	2012, 2013 Camry 2012, 2013 Avalon	A drain hose for the air conditioner condenser may become clogged and cause water to accumulate in the bottom of the condenser unit. This water may leak onto the airbag control module creating a short circuit which could disable the airbags or cause an inadvertent deployment. An inoperative airbag increases the risk of severe injury in a crash. An inadvertently deployed airbag can increase the risk of injury or the possibility of a crash. The power steering could also become inoperable and increase the steering effort which also increases the risk of a crash.

JAN 16, 2013	13V014000	2009, 2010, 2011, 2012 Camry 2009, 2010 Avalon	In certain models that were modified to include accessories such as leather seat covers, seat heaters or headrest DVD systems, the passenger seat occupant sensing system may not have been calibration tested. Consequently, the occupant sensing system may not operate as designed. If this system is out of calibration, the front passenger airbags may not deploy or it may inappropriately deploy for the passenger's size and position. This could increase the risk of personal injury in the event of a crash.
OCT 17, 2013	13V505000	2013, 2014 Camry 2013, 2014 Avalon	On some models, the windshield wiper switch may short circuit. This could reduce driver visibility and increase the risk of a crash.
OCT 17, 2013	13V442000	2012, 2013 Camry 2012, 2013 Avalon	A drain hose for the air conditioner condenser may become clogged and cause water to accumulate in the bottom of the condenser unit. This water may leak onto the airbag control module creating a short circuit which could disable the airbags or cause an inadvertent deployment. An inoperative airbag increases the risk of severe injury in a crash. An inadvertently deployed airbag can increase the risk of injury or the possibility of a crash. The power steering could also become inoperable and increase the steering effort which can increase the risk of a crash.
SEP 19, 2014	14V576000	2014 Camry 2014 Avalon	Fuel may leak from one of the fuel delivery pipes in the engine compartment which increases the risk of fire in the affected models.
NOV 7, 2014	14V715000	2014 Camry 2014 Avalon	On affected models with 16-inch or 17-inch rims, the front suspension lower arm on the left side may have been incorrectly manufactured. Consequently, the lower arm may not have enough clamping surface area for one of the bolts that secures the lower arm to the lower ball joint. This insufficient clamping force may cause the lower arm to separate from the ball joint which increases the risk of a crash.
JAN 28, 2015	15V047000	2011, 2012 Avalon	On some models, the sub-woofer in the speaker located in the trunk may intermittently short out which could damage the integrated circuit in the audio amplifier. This could result in a constant flow of electrical current to the sub-woofer which could increase the risk of fire.
MAR 13, 2015	15V144000	2015 Camry	A component in the electric power steering electronic control unit (ECU) may have been damaged during manufacturing. Over time, this may result in a failure of the electric power steering system. The unexpected loss of power steering increases the risk of a crash.
NOV 03, 2015	15V728000	2013, 2014, 2015 Avalon 2013, 2014, 2015 ES350	In affected models with an optional Pre-Collision System (PCS), the system may unexpectedly activate and apply the brakes when the radar detects a steel joint or plate in the roadway. The unexpected application of the brake increases the risk of a crash.

Buying parts

Replacement parts are available from many sources, which generally fall into one of two categories - authorized dealer parts departments and independent retail auto parts stores. Our advice concerning these parts is as follows:

Retail auto parts stores: Good auto parts stores will stock frequently needed components which wear out relatively fast, such as clutch components, exhaust systems, brake parts, tune-up parts, etc. These stores often supply new or reconditioned parts on an exchange basis, which can save a considerable amount of money. Discount auto parts stores are often very good places to buy materials and parts needed for general vehicle maintenance such as oil, grease, filters, spark plugs, belts, touch-up paint, bulbs, etc. They also usually sell tools and general accessories, have convenient hours, charge lower prices and can often be found not far from home.

Authorized dealer parts department: This is the best source for parts which are unique to the vehicle and not generally available elsewhere (such as major engine parts, transmission parts, trim pieces, etc.).

Warranty information: If the vehicle is still covered under warranty, be sure that any replacement parts purchased - regardless of the source - do not invalidate the warranty!

To be sure of obtaining the correct parts, have engine and chassis numbers available and, if possible, take the old parts along for positive identification.

Maintenance techniques, tools and working facilities

Maintenance techniques

There are a number of techniques involved in maintenance and repair that will be referred to throughout this manual. Application of these techniques will enable the home mechanic to be more efficient, better organized and capable of performing the various tasks properly, which will ensure that the repair job is thorough and complete.

Fasteners

Fasteners are nuts, bolts, studs and screws used to hold two or more parts together. There are a few things to keep in mind when working with fasteners. Almost all of them use a locking device of some type, either a lockwasher, locknut, locking tab or thread adhesive. All threaded fasteners should be clean and straight, with undamaged threads and undamaged corners on the hex head where the wrench fits. Develop the habit of replacing all damaged nuts and bolts with new ones. Special locknuts with nylon or fiber inserts can only be used once. If they are removed, they lose their locking ability and must be replaced with new ones.

Rusted nuts and bolts should be treated with a penetrating fluid to ease removal and prevent breakage. Some mechanics use turpentine in a spout-type oil can, which works quite well. After applying the rust penetrant, let it work for a few minutes before trying to loosen the nut or bolt. Badly rusted fasteners may have to be chiseled or sawed off or removed with a special nut breaker, available at tool stores.

If a bolt or stud breaks off in an assembly, it can be drilled and removed with a special tool commonly available for this purpose. Most automotive machine shops can perform this task, as well as other repair procedures, such as the repair of threaded holes that have been stripped out.

Flat washers and lockwashers, when removed from an assembly, should always be replaced exactly as removed. Replace any damaged washers with new ones. Never use a lockwasher on any soft metal surface (such as aluminum), thin sheet metal or plastic.

Fastener sizes

For a number of reasons, automobile manufacturers are making wider and wider use of metric fasteners. Therefore, it is important to be able to tell the difference between standard (sometimes called U.S. or SAE) and metric hardware, since they cannot be interchanged.

All bolts, whether standard or metric, are sized according to diameter, thread pitch and length. For example, a standard 1/2 - 13 x 1 bolt is 1/2 inch in diameter, has 13 threads per inch and is 1 inch long. An M12 - 1.75 x 25 metric bolt is 12 mm in diameter, has a thread pitch of 1.75 mm (the distance between threads) and is 25 mm long. The two bolts are nearly identical, and easily confused, but they are not interchangeable.

In addition to the differences in diameter, thread pitch and length, metric and standard bolts can also be distinguished by examining the bolt heads. To begin with, the distance across the flats on a standard bolt head is measured in inches, while the same dimension on a metric bolt is sized in millimeters (the same is true for nuts). As a result, a standard wrench should not be used on a metric bolt and a metric wrench should not be used on a standard bolt. Also, most standard bolts have slashes radiating out from the center of the head to denote the grade or strength of the bolt, which is an indication of the amount of torque that can be applied to it. The greater the number of slashes, the greater the strength of the bolt. Grades 0 through 5 are commonly used on automobiles. Metric bolts have a property class (grade) number, rather than a slash, molded into their heads to indicate bolt strength. In this case, the higher the number, the stronger the bolt. Property class numbers 8.8, 9.8 and 10.9 are commonly used on automobiles.

Strength markings can also be used to distinguish standard hex nuts from metric hex nuts. Many standard nuts have dots stamped into one side, while metric nuts are marked with a number. The greater the number of

dots, or the higher the number, the greater the strength of the nut.

Metric studs are also marked on their ends according to property class (grade). Larger studs are numbered (the same as metric bolts), while smaller studs carry a geometric code to denote grade.

It should be noted that many fasteners, especially Grades 0 through 2, have no distinguishing marks on them. When such is the case, the only way to determine whether it is standard or metric is to measure the thread pitch or compare it to a known fastener of the same size.

Standard fasteners are often referred to as SAE, as opposed to metric. However, it should be noted that SAE technically refers to a non-metric fine thread fastener only. Coarse thread non-metric fasteners are referred to as USS sizes.

Since fasteners of the same size (both standard and metric) may have different

strength ratings, be sure to reinstall any bolts, studs or nuts removed from your vehicle in their original locations. Also, when replacing a fastener with a new one, make sure that the new one has a strength rating equal to or greater than the original.

Tightening sequences and procedures

Most threaded fasteners should be tightened to a specific torque value (torque is the twisting force applied to a threaded component such as a nut or bolt). Overtightening the fastener can weaken it and cause it to break, while undertightening can cause it to eventually come loose. Bolts, screws and studs, depending on the material they are made of and their thread diameters, have specific torque values, many of which are noted in the Specifications at the beginning of each Chapter. Be sure to follow the torque recommendations closely. For fasteners not assigned a

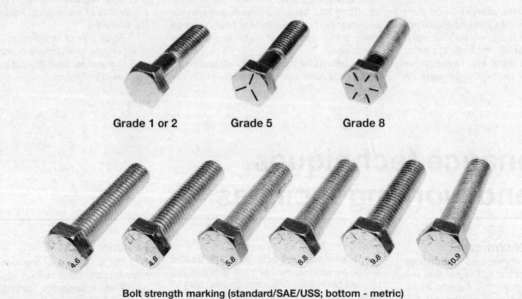

Grade 1 or 2   Grade 5   Grade 8

Bolt strength marking (standard/SAE/USS; bottom - metric)

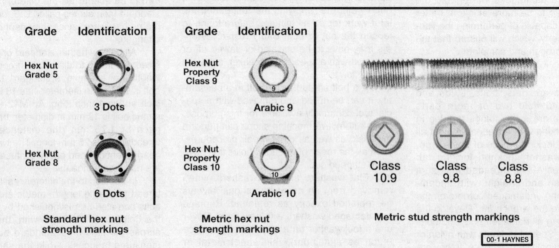

Grade	Identification
Hex Nut Grade 5	3 Dots
Hex Nut Grade 8	6 Dots

Standard hex nut strength markings

Grade	Identification
Hex Nut Property Class 9	Arabic 9
Hex Nut Property Class 10	Arabic 10

Metric hex nut strength markings

Class 10.9   Class 9.8   Class 8.8

Metric stud strength markings

specific torque, a general torque value chart is presented here as a guide. These torque values are for dry (unlubricated) fasteners threaded into steel or cast iron (not aluminum). As was previously mentioned, the size and grade of a fastener determine the amount of torque that can safely be applied to it. The figures listed here are approximate for Grade 2 and Grade 3 fasteners. Higher grades can tolerate higher torque values.

Fasteners laid out in a pattern, such as cylinder head bolts, oil pan bolts, differential cover bolts, etc., must be loosened or tightened in sequence to avoid warping the component. This sequence will normally be shown in the appropriate Chapter. If a specific pattern is not given, the following procedures can be used to prevent warping.

Initially, the bolts or nuts should be assembled finger-tight only. Next, they should be tightened one full turn each, in a criss-cross or diagonal pattern. After each one has been tightened one full turn, return to the first one and tighten them all one-half turn, following the same pattern. Finally, tighten each of them one-quarter turn at a time until each fastener has been tightened to the proper torque. To loosen and remove the fasteners, the procedure would be reversed.

Component disassembly

Component disassembly should be done with care and purpose to help ensure that

Metric thread sizes

Metric thread sizes	Ft-lbs	Nm
M-6	6 to 9	9 to 12
M-8	14 to 21	19 to 28
M-10	28 to 40	38 to 54
M-12	50 to 71	68 to 96
M-14	80 to 140	109 to 154

Pipe thread sizes

Pipe thread sizes		
1/8	5 to 8	7 to 10
1/4	12 to 18	17 to 24
3/8	22 to 33	30 to 44
1/2	25 to 35	34 to 47

U.S. thread sizes

U.S. thread sizes		
1/4 - 20	6 to 9	9 to 12
5/16 - 18	12 to 18	17 to 24
5/16 - 24	14 to 20	19 to 27
3/8 - 16	22 to 32	30 to 43
3/8 - 24	27 to 38	37 to 51
7/16 - 14	40 to 55	55 to 74
7/16 - 20	40 to 60	55 to 81
1/2 - 13	55 to 80	75 to 108

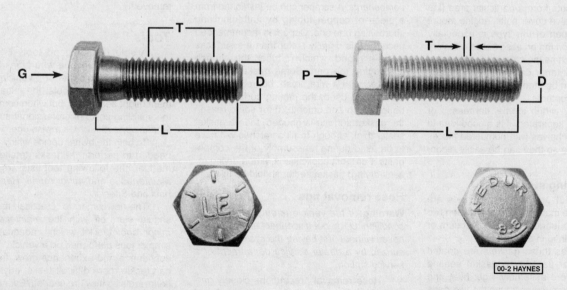

00-2 HAYNES

Standard (SAE and USS) bolt dimensions/grade marks

G	Grade marks (bolt strength)
L	Length (in inches)
T	Thread pitch (number of threads per inch)
D	Nominal diameter (in inches)

Metric bolt dimensions/grade marks

P	Property class (bolt strength)
L	Length (in millimeters)
T	Thread pitch (distance between threads in millimeters)
D	Diameter

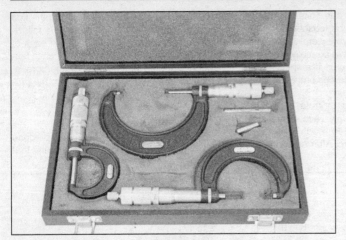

Micrometer set

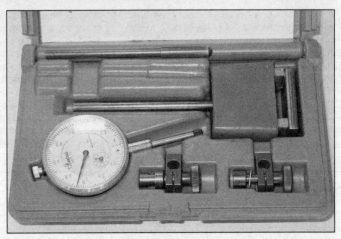

Dial indicator set

the parts go back together properly. Always keep track of the sequence in which parts are removed. Make note of special characteristics or marks on parts that can be installed more than one way, such as a grooved thrust washer on a shaft. It is a good idea to lay the disassembled parts out on a clean surface in the order that they were removed. It may also be helpful to make sketches or take instant photos of components before removal.

When removing fasteners from a component, keep track of their locations. Sometimes threading a bolt back in a part, or putting the washers and nut back on a stud, can prevent mix-ups later. If nuts and bolts cannot be returned to their original locations, they should be kept in a compartmented box or a series of small boxes. A cupcake or muffin tin is ideal for this purpose, since each cavity can hold the bolts and nuts from a particular area (i.e. oil pan bolts, valve cover bolts, engine mount bolts, etc.). A pan of this type is especially helpful when working on assemblies with very small parts, such as the carburetor, alternator, valve train or interior dash and trim pieces. The cavities can be marked with paint or tape to identify the contents.

Whenever wiring looms, harnesses or connectors are separated, it is a good idea to identify the two halves with numbered pieces of masking tape so they can be easily reconnected.

Gasket sealing surfaces

Throughout any vehicle, gaskets are used to seal the mating surfaces between two parts and keep lubricants, fluids, vacuum or pressure contained in an assembly.

Many times these gaskets are coated with a liquid or paste-type gasket sealing compound before assembly. Age, heat and pressure can sometimes cause the two parts to stick together so tightly that they are very difficult to separate. Often, the assembly can be loosened by striking it with a soft-face hammer near the mating surfaces. A regular hammer can be used if a block of wood is placed between the hammer and the part. Do

not hammer on cast parts or parts that could be easily damaged. With any particularly stubborn part, always recheck to make sure that every fastener has been removed.

Avoid using a screwdriver or bar to pry apart an assembly, as they can easily mar the gasket sealing surfaces of the parts, which must remain smooth. If prying is absolutely necessary, use an old broom handle, but keep in mind that extra clean up will be necessary if the wood splinters.

After the parts are separated, the old gasket must be carefully scraped off and the gasket surfaces cleaned. Stubborn gasket material can be soaked with rust penetrant or treated with a special chemical to soften it so it can be easily scraped off. **Caution:** *Never use gasket removal solutions or caustic chemicals on plastic or other composite components.* A scraper can be fashioned from a piece of copper tubing by flattening and sharpening one end. Copper is recommended because it is usually softer than the surfaces to be scraped, which reduces the chance of gouging the part. Some gaskets can be removed with a wire brush, but regardless of the method used, the mating surfaces must be left clean and smooth. If for some reason the gasket surface is gouged, then a gasket sealer thick enough to fill scratches will have to be used during reassembly of the components. For most applications, a non-drying (or semi-drying) gasket sealer should be used.

Hose removal tips

Warning: *If the vehicle is equipped with air conditioning, do not disconnect any of the A/C hoses without first having the system depressurized by a dealer service department or a service station.*

Hose removal precautions closely parallel gasket removal precautions. Avoid scratching or gouging the surface that the hose mates against or the connection may leak. This is especially true for radiator hoses. Because of various chemical reactions, the rubber in hoses can bond itself to the metal spigot that the hose fits over. To remove

a hose, first loosen the hose clamps that secure it to the spigot. Then, with slip-joint pliers, grab the hose at the clamp and rotate it around the spigot. Work it back and forth until it is completely free, then pull it off. Silicone or other lubricants will ease removal if they can be applied between the hose and the outside of the spigot. Apply the same lubricant to the inside of the hose and the outside of the spigot to simplify installation.

As a last resort (and if the hose is to be replaced with a new one anyway), the rubber can be slit with a knife and the hose peeled from the spigot. If this must be done, be careful that the metal connection is not damaged.

If a hose clamp is broken or damaged, do not reuse it. Wire-type clamps usually weaken with age, so it is a good idea to replace them with screw-type clamps whenever a hose is removed.

Tools

A selection of good tools is a basic requirement for anyone who plans to maintain and repair his or her own vehicle. For the owner who has few tools, the initial investment might seem high, but when compared to the spiraling costs of professional auto maintenance and repair, it is a wise one.

To help the owner decide which tools are needed to perform the tasks detailed in this manual, the following tool lists are offered: *Maintenance and minor repair, Repair/overhaul* and *Special.*

The newcomer to practical mechanics should start off with the *maintenance and minor repair* tool kit, which is adequate for the simpler jobs performed on a vehicle. Then, as confidence and experience grow, the owner can tackle more difficult tasks, buying additional tools as they are needed. Eventually the basic kit will be expanded into the *repair and overhaul* tool set. Over a period of time, the experienced do-it-yourselfer will assemble a tool set complete enough for most repair and overhaul procedures and will add tools from the special category when it is felt that the expense is justified by the frequency of use.

Dial caliper

Hand-operated vacuum pump

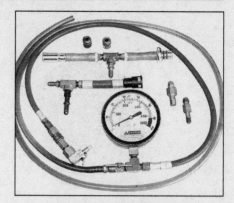

Fuel pressure gauge set

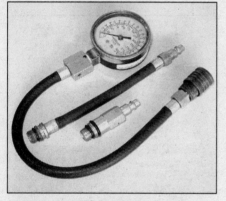

Compression gauge with spark plug
hole adapter

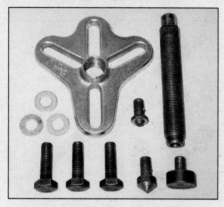

Damper/steering wheel puller

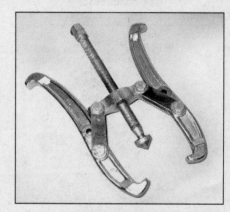

General purpose puller

Hydraulic lifter removal tool

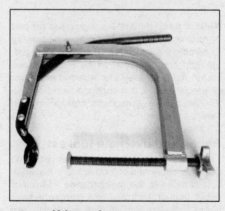

Valve spring compressor

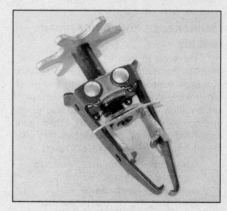

Valve spring compressor

Ridge reamer

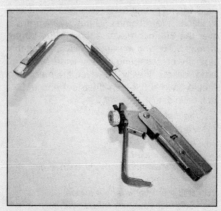

Piston ring groove cleaning tool

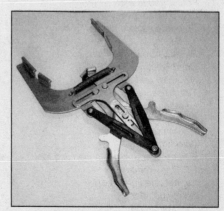

Ring removal/installation tool

Ring compressor

Cylinder hone

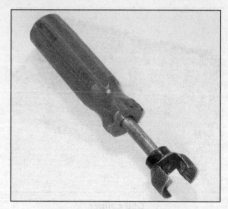

Brake hold-down spring tool

Torque angle gauge

Clutch plate alignment tool

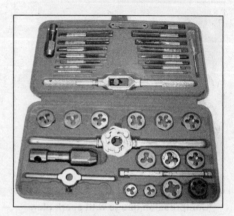

Tap and die set

Maintenance and minor repair tool kit

The tools in this list should be considered the minimum required for performance of routine maintenance, servicing and minor repair work. We recommend the purchase of combination wrenches (box-end and open-end combined in one wrench). While more expensive than open end wrenches, they offer the advantages of both types of wrench.

> Combination wrench set (1/4-inch to 1 inch or 6 mm to 19 mm)
> Adjustable wrench, 8 inch
> Spark plug wrench with rubber insert
> Spark plug gap adjusting tool
> Feeler gauge set
> Brake bleeder wrench
> Standard screwdriver (5/16-inch x 6 inch)
> Phillips screwdriver (No. 2 x 6 inch)
> Combination pliers - 6 inch
> Hacksaw and assortment of blades
> Tire pressure gauge
> Grease gun
> Oil can
> Fine emery cloth
> Wire brush
> Battery post and cable cleaning tool
> Oil filter wrench
> Funnel (medium size)
> Safety goggles
> Jackstands (2)
> Drain pan

Note: *If basic tune-ups are going to be part of routine maintenance, it will be necessary to purchase a good quality stroboscopic timing light and combination tachometer/dwell meter. Although they are included in the list of special tools, it is mentioned here because they are absolutely necessary for tuning most vehicles properly.*

Repair and overhaul tool set

These tools are essential for anyone who plans to perform major repairs and are in addition to those in the maintenance and minor repair tool kit. Included is a comprehensive set of sockets which, though expensive, are invaluable because of their versatility, especially when various extensions and drives are available. We recommend the 1/2-inch drive over the 3/8-inch drive. Although the larger drive is bulky and more expensive, it has the capacity of accepting a very wide range of large sockets. Ideally, however, the mechanic should have a 3/8-inch drive set and a 1/2-inch drive set.

> Socket set(s)
> Reversible ratchet
> Extension - 10 inch
> Universal joint
> Torque wrench (same size drive as sockets)
> Ball peen hammer - 8 ounce
> Soft-face hammer (plastic/rubber)
> Standard screwdriver (1/4-inch x 6 inch)

> Standard screwdriver (stubby - 5/16-inch)
> Phillips screwdriver (No. 3 x 8 inch)
> Phillips screwdriver (stubby - No. 2)
> Pliers - vise grip
> Pliers - lineman's
> Pliers - needle nose
> Pliers - snap-ring (internal and external)
> Cold chisel - 1/2-inch
> Scribe
> Scraper (made from flattened copper tubing)
> Centerpunch
> Pin punches (1/16, 1/8, 3/16-inch)
> Steel rule/straightedge - 12 inch
> Allen wrench set (1/8 to 3/8-inch or 4 mm to 10 mm)
> A selection of files
> Wire brush (large)
> Jackstands (second set)
> Jack (scissor or hydraulic type)

Note: *Another tool which is often useful is an electric drill with a chuck capacity of 3/8-inch and a set of good quality drill bits.*

Special tools

The tools in this list include those which are not used regularly, are expensive to buy, or which need to be used in accordance with their manufacturer's instructions. Unless these tools will be used frequently, it is not very economical to purchase many of them. A consideration would be to split the cost and use between yourself and a friend or friends. In addition, most of these tools can be obtained from a tool rental shop on a temporary basis.

This list primarily contains only those tools and instruments widely available to the public, and not those special tools produced by the vehicle manufacturer for distribution to dealer service departments. Occasionally, references to the manufacturer's special tools are included in the text of this manual. Generally, an alternative method of doing the job without the special tool is offered. However, sometimes there is no alternative to their use. Where this is the case, and the tool cannot be purchased or borrowed, the work should be turned over to the dealer service department or an automotive repair shop.

> *Valve spring compressor*
> *Piston ring groove cleaning tool*
> *Piston ring compressor*
> *Piston ring installation tool*
> *Cylinder compression gauge*
> *Cylinder ridge reamer*
> *Cylinder surfacing hone*
> *Cylinder bore gauge*
> *Micrometers and/or dial calipers*
> *Hydraulic lifter removal tool*
> *Balljoint separator*
> *Universal-type puller*
> *Impact screwdriver*
> *Dial indicator set*
> *Stroboscopic timing light (inductive*
> *   pick-up)*
> *Hand operated vacuum/pressure pump*
> *Tachometer/dwell meter*
> *Universal electrical multimeter*
> *Cable hoist*
> *Brake spring removal and installation*
> *   tools*
> *Floor jack*

Buying tools

For the do-it-yourselfer who is just starting to get involved in vehicle maintenance and repair, there are a number of options available when purchasing tools. If maintenance and minor repair is the extent of the work to be done, the purchase of individual tools is satisfactory. If, on the other hand, extensive work is planned, it would be a good idea to purchase a modest tool set from one of the large retail chain stores. A set can usually be bought at a substantial savings over the individual tool prices, and they often come with a tool box. As additional tools are needed, add-on sets, individual tools and a larger tool box can be purchased to expand the tool selection. Building a tool set gradually allows the cost of the tools to be spread over a longer period of time and gives the mechanic the freedom to choose only those tools that will actually be used.

Tool stores will often be the only source of some of the special tools that are needed, but regardless of where tools are bought, try to avoid cheap ones, especially when buying screwdrivers and sockets, because they won't last very long. The expense involved in replacing cheap tools will eventually be greater than the initial cost of quality tools.

Care and maintenance of tools

Good tools are expensive, so it makes sense to treat them with respect. Keep them clean and in usable condition and store them properly when not in use. Always wipe off any dirt, grease or metal chips before putting them away. Never leave tools lying around in the work area. Upon completion of a job, always check closely under the hood for tools that may have been left there so they won't get lost during a test drive.

Some tools, such as screwdrivers, pliers, wrenches and sockets, can be hung on a panel mounted on the garage or workshop wall, while others should be kept in a tool box or tray. Measuring instruments, gauges, meters, etc. must be carefully stored where they cannot be damaged by weather or impact from other tools.

When tools are used with care and stored properly, they will last a very long time. Even with the best of care, though, tools will wear out if used frequently. When a tool is damaged or worn out, replace it. Subsequent jobs will be safer and more enjoyable if you do.

How to repair damaged threads

Sometimes, the internal threads of a nut or bolt hole can become stripped, usually from overtightening. Stripping threads is an all-too-common occurrence, especially when working with aluminum parts, because aluminum is so soft that it easily strips out.

Usually, external or internal threads are only partially stripped. After they've been cleaned up with a tap or die, they'll still work. Sometimes, however, threads are badly damaged. When this happens, you've got three choices:

1) *Drill and tap the hole to the next suitable oversize and install a larger diameter bolt, screw or stud.*
2) *Drill and tap the hole to accept a threaded plug, then drill and tap the plug to the original screw size. You can also buy a plug already threaded to the original size. Then you simply drill a hole to the specified size, then run the threaded plug into the hole with a bolt and jam nut. Once the plug is fully seated, remove the jam nut and bolt.*
3) *The third method uses a patented thread repair kit like Heli-Coil or Slimsert. These easy-to-use kits are designed to repair*

damaged threads in straight-through holes and blind holes. Both are available as kits which can handle a variety of sizes and thread patterns. Drill the hole, then tap it with the special included tap. Install the Heli-Coil and the hole is back to its original diameter and thread pitch.

Regardless of which method you use, be sure to proceed calmly and carefully. A little impatience or carelessness during one of these relatively simple procedures can ruin your whole day's work and cost you a bundle if you wreck an expensive part.

Working facilities

Not to be overlooked when discussing tools is the workshop. If anything more than routine maintenance is to be carried out, some sort of suitable work area is essential.

It is understood, and appreciated, that many home mechanics do not have a good workshop or garage available, and end up removing an engine or doing major repairs outside. It is recommended, however, that the overhaul or repair be completed under the cover of a roof.

A clean, flat workbench or table of comfortable working height is an absolute necessity. The workbench should be equipped with a vise that has a jaw opening of at least four inches.

As mentioned previously, some clean, dry storage space is also required for tools, as well as the lubricants, fluids, cleaning solvents, etc. which soon become necessary.

Sometimes waste oil and fluids, drained from the engine or cooling system during normal maintenance or repairs, present a disposal problem. To avoid pouring them on the ground or into a sewage system, pour the used fluids into large containers, seal them with caps and take them to an authorized disposal site or recycling center. Plastic jugs, such as old antifreeze containers, are ideal for this purpose.

Always keep a supply of old newspapers and clean rags available. Old towels are excellent for mopping up spills. Many mechanics use rolls of paper towels for most work because they are readily available and disposable. To help keep the area under the vehicle clean, a large cardboard box can be cut open and flattened to protect the garage or shop floor.

Whenever working over a painted surface, such as when leaning over a fender to service something under the hood, always cover it with an old blanket or bedspread to protect the finish. Vinyl covered pads, made especially for this purpose, are available at auto parts stores.

Jacking and towing

Jacking

The jack supplied with the vehicle should only be used for raising the vehicle for changing a tire or placing jackstands under the frame. **Warning:** *Never crawl under the vehicle or start the engine when the jack is being used as the only means of support.*

All vehicles are supplied with a scissors-type jack. When jacking the vehicle, it should be engaged with the seam notch, between the two dimples **(see illustration)**.

The vehicle should be on level ground with the wheels blocked and the transaxle in Park (automatic) or Reverse (manual). Pry off the hub cap (if equipped) using the tapered end of the lug wrench. Loosen the lug nuts one-half turn and leave them in place until the wheel is raised off the ground.

Place the jack under the side of the vehicle in the indicated position. Use the supplied wrench to turn the jackscrew clockwise until the wheel is raised off the ground. Remove the lug nuts, pull off the wheel and replace it with the spare.

With the beveled side in, replace the lug nuts and tighten them until snug. Lower the vehicle by turning the jackscrew counterclockwise. Remove the jack and tighten the nuts in a diagonal pattern to the torque listed in the Chapter 1 Specifications. If a torque wrench is not available, have the torque checked by a service station as soon as possible. Replace the hubcap by placing it in position and using the heel of your hand or a rubber mallet to seat it.

Towing

Manual transaxle-equipped vehicles can be towed with all four wheels on the ground. Automatic transaxle-equipped models should only be towed with all four wheels on the ground if speeds do not exceed 35 mph and the distance is not over 50 miles, otherwise transaxle damage can result.

Towing equipment specifically designed for this purpose should be used and should be attached to the main structural members of the vehicle, not the bumper or brackets.

Safety is a major consideration when towing and all applicable state and local laws must be obeyed. A safety chain system must be used for all towing.

While towing, the parking brake should be released and the transaxle should be in Neutral. The steering must be unlocked (ignition switch in the Off position). Remember that power steering and power brakes will not work with the engine off.

Traction control

On models equipped with Traction-Control system, push in the TRAC switch (on the dashboard or floor console, depending on model) anytime the vehicle is on a "rolling road" tester such as a speedometer test machine or chassis dynamometer. The TRAC OFF indicator light should illuminate when the system is turned off.

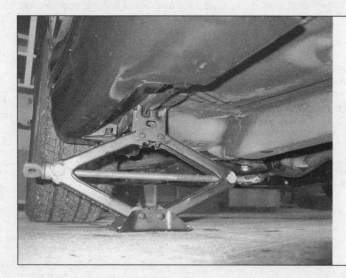

The jack fits over the rocker panel flange, between the two notches (there are two jacking points on each side of the vehicle)

Booster battery (jump) starting

Observe these precautions when using a booster battery to start a vehicle:

a) *Before connecting the booster battery, make sure the ignition switch is in the Off position.*
b) *Turn off the lights, heater and other electrical loads.*
c) *Your eyes should be shielded. Safety goggles are a good idea.*
d) *Make sure the booster battery is the same voltage as the dead one in the vehicle.*
e) *The two vehicles MUST NOT TOUCH each other!*
f) *Make sure the transaxle is in Neutral (manual) or Park (automatic).*
g) *If the booster battery is not a maintenance-free type, remove the vent caps and lay a cloth over the vent holes.*

Connect the red jumper cable to the positive (+) terminals of each battery **(see illustration)**.

Connect one end of the black jumper cable to the negative (-) terminal of the booster battery. The other end of this cable should be connected to a good ground on the vehicle to be started, such as a bolt or bracket on the body.

Start the engine using the booster battery, then, with the engine running at idle speed, disconnect the jumper cables in the reverse order of connection.

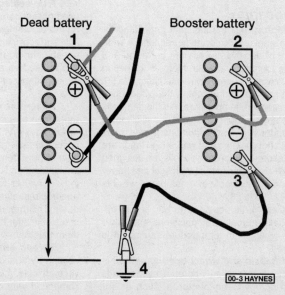

Dead battery   Booster battery

00-3 HAYNES

Make the booster battery cable connections in the numerical order shown (note that the negative cable of the booster battery is NOT attached to the negative terminal of the dead battery)

Automotive chemicals and lubricants

A number of automotive chemicals and lubricants are available for use during vehicle maintenance and repair. They include a wide variety of products ranging from cleaning solvents and degreasers to lubricants and protective sprays for rubber, plastic and vinyl.

Cleaners

Carburetor cleaner and choke cleaner is a strong solvent for gum, varnish and carbon. Most carburetor cleaners leave a dry-type lubricant film which will not harden or gum up. Because of this film it is not recommended for use on electrical components.

Brake system cleaner is used to remove brake dust, grease and brake fluid from the brake system, where clean surfaces are absolutely necessary. It leaves no residue and often eliminates brake squeal caused by contaminants.

Electrical cleaner removes oxidation, corrosion and carbon deposits from electrical contacts, restoring full current flow. It can also be used to clean spark plugs, carburetor jets, voltage regulators and other parts where an oil-free surface is desired.

Demoisturants remove water and moisture from electrical components such as alternators, voltage regulators, electrical connectors and fuse blocks. They are non-conductive and non-corrosive.

Degreasers are heavy-duty solvents used to remove grease from the outside of the engine and from chassis components. They can be sprayed or brushed on and, depending on the type, are rinsed off either with water or solvent.

Lubricants

Motor oil is the lubricant formulated for use in engines. It normally contains a wide variety of additives to prevent corrosion and reduce foaming and wear. Motor oil comes in various weights (viscosity ratings) from 0 to 50. The recommended weight of the oil depends on the season, temperature and the demands on the engine. Light oil is used in cold climates and under light load conditions. Heavy oil is used in hot climates and where high loads are encountered. Multi-viscosity oils are designed to have characteristics of both light and heavy oils and are available in a number of weights from 0W-20 to 20W-50.

Gear oil is designed to be used in differentials, manual transmissions and other areas where high-temperature lubrication is required.

Chassis and wheel bearing grease is a heavy grease used where increased loads and friction are encountered, such as for wheel bearings, balljoints, tie-rod ends and universal joints.

High-temperature wheel bearing grease is designed to withstand the extreme temperatures encountered by wheel bearings in disc brake equipped vehicles. It usually contains molybdenum disulfide (moly), which is a dry-type lubricant.

White grease is a heavy grease for metal-to-metal applications where water is a problem. White grease stays soft under both low and high temperatures (usually from -100 to +190-degrees F), and will not wash off or dilute in the presence of water.

Assembly lube is a special extreme pressure lubricant, usually containing moly, used to lubricate high-load parts (such as main and rod bearings and cam lobes) for initial start-up of a new engine. The assembly lube lubricates the parts without being squeezed out or washed away until the engine oiling system begins to function.

Silicone lubricants are used to protect rubber, plastic, vinyl and nylon parts.

Graphite lubricants are used where oils cannot be used due to contamination problems, such as in locks. The dry graphite will lubricate metal parts while remaining uncontaminated by dirt, water, oil or acids. It is electrically conductive and will not foul electrical contacts in locks such as the ignition switch.

Moly penetrants loosen and lubricate frozen, rusted and corroded fasteners and prevent future rusting or freezing.

Heat-sink grease is a special electrically non-conductive grease that is used for mounting electronic ignition modules where it is essential that heat is transferred away from the module.

Sealants

RTV sealant is one of the most widely used gasket compounds. Made from silicone, RTV is air curing, it seals, bonds, waterproofs, fills surface irregularities, remains flexible, doesn't shrink, is relatively easy to remove, and is used as a supplementary sealer with almost all low and medium temperature gaskets.

Anaerobic sealant is much like RTV in that it can be used either to seal gaskets or to form gaskets by itself. It remains flexible, is solvent resistant and fills surface imperfections. The difference between an anaerobic sealant and an RTV-type sealant is in the curing. RTV cures when exposed to air, while an anaerobic sealant cures only in the absence of air. This means that an anaerobic sealant cures only after the assembly of parts, sealing them together.

Thread and pipe sealant is used for sealing hydraulic and pneumatic fittings and vacuum lines. It is usually made from a Teflon compound, and comes in a spray, a paint-on liquid and as a wrap-around tape.

Chemicals

Anti-seize compound prevents seizing, galling, cold welding, rust and corrosion in fasteners. High-temperature ant-seize, usually made with copper and graphite lubricants, is used for exhaust system and exhaust manifold bolts.

Anaerobic locking compounds are used to keep fasteners from vibrating or working loose and cure only after installation, in the absence of air. Medium strength locking compound is used for small nuts, bolts and screws that may be removed later. High-strength locking compound is for large nuts, bolts and studs which aren't removed on a regular basis.

Oil additives range from viscosity index improvers to chemical treatments that claim to reduce internal engine friction. It should be noted that most oil manufacturers caution against using additives with their oils.

Gas additives perform several functions, depending on their chemical makeup. They usually contain solvents that help dissolve gum and varnish that build up on carburetor, fuel injection and intake parts. They also serve to break down carbon deposits that form on the inside surfaces of the combustion chambers. Some additives contain upper cylinder lubricants for valves and piston rings, and others contain chemicals to remove condensation from the gas tank.

Miscellaneous

Brake fluid is specially formulated hydraulic fluid that can withstand the heat and pressure encountered in brake systems. Care must be taken so this fluid does not come in contact with painted surfaces or plastics. An opened container should always be resealed to prevent contamination by water or dirt.

Weatherstrip adhesive is used to bond weatherstripping around doors, windows and trunk lids. It is sometimes used to attach trim pieces.

Undercoating is a petroleum-based, tar-like substance that is designed to protect metal surfaces on the underside of the vehicle from corrosion. It also acts as a sound-deadening agent by insulating the bottom of the vehicle.

Waxes and polishes are used to help protect painted and plated surfaces from the weather. Different types of paint may require the use of different types of wax and polish. Some polishes utilize a chemical or abrasive cleaner to help remove the top layer of oxidized (dull) paint on older vehicles. In recent years many non-wax polishes that contain a wide variety of chemicals such as polymers and silicones have been introduced. These non-wax polishes are usually easier to apply and last longer than conventional waxes and polishes.

Conversion factors

Length (distance)

Inches (in)	X 25.4	= Millimeters (mm)	X 0.0394	= Inches (in)
Feet (ft)	X 0.305	= Meters (m)	X 3.281	= Feet (ft)
Miles	X 1.609	= Kilometers (km)	X 0.621	= Miles

Volume (capacity)

Cubic inches (cu in; in³)	X 16.387	= Cubic centimeters (cc; cm³)	X 0.061	= Cubic inches (cu in; in³)
Imperial pints (Imp pt)	X 0.568	= Liters (l)	X 1.76	= Imperial pints (Imp pt)
Imperial quarts (Imp qt)	X 1.137	= Liters (l)	X 0.88	= Imperial quarts (Imp qt)
Imperial quarts (Imp qt)	X 1.201	= US quarts (US qt)	X 0.833	= Imperial quarts (Imp qt)
US quarts (US qt)	X 0.946	= Liters (l)	X 1.057	= US quarts (US qt)
Imperial gallons (Imp gal)	X 4.546	= Liters (l)	X 0.22	= Imperial gallons (Imp gal)
Imperial gallons (Imp gal)	X 1.201	= US gallons (US gal)	X 0.833	= Imperial gallons (Imp gal)
US gallons (US gal)	X 3.785	= Liters (l)	X 0.264	= US gallons (US gal)

Mass (weight)

Ounces (oz)	X 28.35	= Grams (g)	X 0.035	= Ounces (oz)
Pounds (lb)	X 0.454	= Kilograms (kg)	X 2.205	= Pounds (lb)

Force

Ounces-force (ozf; oz)	X 0.278	= Newtons (N)	X 3.6	= Ounces-force (ozf; oz)
Pounds-force (lbf; lb)	X 4.448	= Newtons (N)	X 0.225	= Pounds-force (lbf; lb)
Newtons (N)	X 0.1	= Kilograms-force (kgf; kg)	X 9.81	= Newtons (N)

Pressure

Pounds-force per square inch (psi; lbf/in²; lb/in²)	X 0.070	= Kilograms-force per square centimeter (kgf/cm²; kg/cm²)	X 14.223	= Pounds-force per square inch (psi; lbf/in²; lb/in²)
Pounds-force per square inch (psi; lbf/in²; lb/in²)	X 0.068	= Atmospheres (atm)	X 14.696	= Pounds-force per square inch (psi; lbf/in²; lb/in²)
Pounds-force per square inch (psi; lbf/in²; lb/in²)	X 0.069	= Bars	X 14.5	= Pounds-force per square inch (psi; lbf/in²; lb/in²)
Pounds-force per square inch (psi; lbf/in²; lb/in²)	X 6.895	= Kilopascals (kPa)	X 0.145	= Pounds-force per square inch (psi; lbf/in²; lb/in²)
Kilopascals (kPa)	X 0.01	= Kilograms-force per square centimeter (kgf/cm²; kg/cm²)	X 98.1	= Kilopascals (kPa)

Torque (moment of force)

Pounds-force inches (lbf in; lb in)	X 1.152	= Kilograms-force centimeter (kgf cm; kg cm)	X 0.868	= Pounds-force inches (lbf in; lb in)
Pounds-force inches (lbf in; lb in)	X 0.113	= Newton meters (Nm)	X 8.85	= Pounds-force inches (lbf in; lb in)
Pounds-force inches (lbf in; lb in)	X 0.083	= Pounds-force feet (lbf ft; lb ft)	X 12	= Pounds-force inches (lbf in; lb in)
Pounds-force feet (lbf ft; lb ft)	X 0.138	= Kilograms-force meters (kgf m; kg m)	X 7.233	= Pounds-force feet (lbf ft; lb ft)
Pounds-force feet (lbf ft; lb ft)	X 1.356	= Newton meters (Nm)	X 0.738	= Pounds-force feet (lbf ft; lb ft)
Newton meters (Nm)	X 0.102	= Kilograms-force meters (kgf m; kg m)	X 9.804	= Newton meters (Nm)

Vacuum

Inches mercury (in. Hg)	X 3.377	= Kilopascals (kPa)	X 0.2961	= Inches mercury
Inches mercury (in. Hg)	X 25.4	= Millimeters mercury (mm Hg)	X 0.0394	= Inches mercury

Power

Horsepower (hp)	X 745.7	= Watts (W)	X 0.0013	= Horsepower (hp)

Velocity (speed)

Miles per hour (miles/hr; mph)	X 1.609	= Kilometers per hour (km/hr; kph)	X 0.621	= Miles per hour (miles/hr; mph)

Fuel consumption*

Miles per gallon, Imperial (mpg)	X 0.354	= Kilometers per liter (km/l)	X 2.825	= Miles per gallon, Imperial (mpg)
Miles per gallon, US (mpg)	X 0.425	= Kilometers per liter (km/l)	X 2.352	= Miles per gallon, US (mpg)

Temperature

Degrees Fahrenheit = (°C x 1.8) + 32

Degrees Celsius (Degrees Centigrade; °C) = (°F - 32) x 0.56

*It is common practice to convert from miles per gallon (mpg) to liters/100 kilometers (l/100km), where mpg (Imperial) x l/100 km = 282 and mpg (US) x l/100 km = 235

0-22

DECIMALS to MILLIMETERS

Decimal	mm	Decimal	mm
0.001	0.0254	0.500	12.7000
0.002	0.0508	0.510	12.9540
0.003	0.0762	0.520	13.2080
0.004	0.1016	0.530	13.4620
0.005	0.1270	0.540	13.7160
0.006	0.1524	0.550	13.9700
0.007	0.1778	0.560	14.2240
0.008	0.2032	0.570	14.4780
0.009	0.2286	0.580	14.7320
		0.590	14.9860
0.010	0.2540		
0.020	0.5080		
0.030	0.7620		
0.040	1.0160	0.600	15.2400
0.050	1.2700	0.610	15.4940
0.060	1.5240	0.620	15.7480
0.070	1.7780	0.630	16.0020
0.080	2.0320	0.640	16.2560
0.090	2.2860	0.650	16.5100
		0.660	16.7640
0.100	2.5400	0.670	17.0180
0.110	2.7940	0.680	17.2720
0.120	3.0480	0.690	17.5260
0.130	3.3020		
0.140	3.5560		
0.150	3.8100		
0.160	4.0640	0.700	17.7800
0.170	4.3180	0.710	18.0340
0.180	4.5720	0.720	18.2880
0.190	4.8260	0.730	18.5420
		0.740	18.7960
0.200	5.0800	0.750	19.0500
0.210	5.3340	0.760	19.3040
0.220	5.5880	0.770	19.5580
0.230	5.8420	0.780	19.8120
0.240	6.0960	0.790	20.0660
0.250	6.3500		
0.260	6.6040		
0.270	6.8580	0.800	20.3200
0.280	7.1120	0.810	20.5740
0.290	7.3660	0.820	20.8280
		0.830	21.0820
0.300	7.6200	0.840	21.3360
0.310	7.8740	0.850	21.5900
0.320	8.1280	0.860	21.8440
0.330	8.3820	0.870	22.0980
0.340	8.6360	0.880	22.3520
0.350	8.8900	0.890	22.6060
0.360	9.1440		
0.370	9.3980		
0.380	9.6520		
0.390	9.9060	0.900	22.8600
0.400	10.1600	0.910	23.1140
0.410	10.4140	0.920	23.3680
0.420	10.6680	0.930	23.6220
0.430	10.9220	0.940	23.8760
0.440	11.1760	0.950	24.1300
0.450	11.4300	0.960	24.3840
0.460	11.6840	0.970	24.6380
0.470	11.9380	0.980	24.8920
0.480	12.1920	0.990	25.1460
0.490	12.4460	1.000	25.4000

FRACTIONS to DECIMALS to MILLIMETERS

Fraction	Decimal	mm	Fraction	Decimal	mm
1/64	0.0156	0.3969	33/64	0.5156	13.0969
1/32	0.0312	0.7938	17/32	0.5312	13.4938
3/64	0.0469	1.1906	35/64	0.5469	13.8906
1/16	0.0625	1.5875	9/16	0.5625	14.2875
5/64	0.0781	1.9844	37/64	0.5781	14.6844
3/32	0.0938	2.3812	19/32	0.5938	15.0812
7/64	0.1094	2.7781	39/64	0.6094	15.4781
1/8	0.1250	3.1750	5/8	0.6250	15.8750
9/64	0.1406	3.5719	41/64	0.6406	16.2719
5/32	0.1562	3.9688	21/32	0.6562	16.6688
11/64	0.1719	4.3656	43/64	0.6719	17.0656
3/16	0.1875	4.7625	11/16	0.6875	17.4625
13/64	0.2031	5.1594	45/64	0.7031	17.8594
7/32	0.2188	5.5562	23/32	0.7188	18.2562
15/64	0.2344	5.9531	47/64	0.7344	18.6531
1/4	0.2500	6.3500	3/4	0.7500	19.0500
17/64	0.2656	6.7469	49/64	0.7656	19.4469
9/32	0.2812	7.1438	25/32	0.7812	19.8438
19/64	0.2969	7.5406	51/64	0.7969	20.2406
5/16	0.3125	7.9375	13/16	0.8125	20.6375
21/64	0.3281	8.3344	53/64	0.8281	21.0344
11/32	0.3438	8.7312	27/32	0.8438	21.4312
23/64	0.3594	9.1281	55/64	0.8594	21.8281
3/8	0.3750	9.5250	7/8	0.8750	22.2250
25/64	0.3906	9.9219	57/64	0.8906	22.6219
13/32	0.4062	10.3188	29/32	0.9062	23.0188
27/64	0.4219	10.7156	59/64	0.9219	23.4156
7/16	0.4375	11.1125	15/16	0.9375	23.8125
29/64	0.4531	11.5094	61/64	0.9531	24.2094
15/32	0.4688	11.9062	31/32	0.9688	24.6062
31/64	0.4844	12.3031	63/64	0.9844	25.0031
1/2	0.5000	12.7000	1	1.0000	25.4000

Safety first!

Regardless of how enthusiastic you may be about getting on with the job at hand, take the time to ensure that your safety is not jeopardized. A moment's lack of attention can result in an accident, as can failure to observe certain simple safety precautions. The possibility of an accident will always exist, and the following points should not be considered a comprehensive list of all dangers. Rather, they are intended to make you aware of the risks and to encourage a safety conscious approach to all work you carry out on your vehicle.

Essential DOs and DON'Ts

DON'T rely on a jack when working under the vehicle. Always use approved jackstands to support the weight of the vehicle and place them under the recommended lift or support points.

DON'T attempt to loosen extremely tight fasteners (i.e. wheel lug nuts) while the vehicle is on a jack - it may fall.

DON'T start the engine without first making sure that the transmission is in Neutral (or Park where applicable) and the parking brake is set.

DON'T remove the radiator cap from a hot cooling system - let it cool or cover it with a cloth and release the pressure gradually.

DON'T attempt to drain the engine oil until you are sure it has cooled to the point that it will not burn you.

DON'T touch any part of the engine or exhaust system until it has cooled sufficiently to avoid burns.

DON'T siphon toxic liquids such as gasoline, antifreeze and brake fluid by mouth, or allow them to remain on your skin.

DON'T inhale brake lining dust - it is potentially hazardous (see *Asbestos* below).

DON'T allow spilled oil or grease to remain on the floor - wipe it up before someone slips on it.

DON'T use loose fitting wrenches or other tools which may slip and cause injury.

DON'T push on wrenches when loosening or tightening nuts or bolts. Always try to pull the wrench toward you. If the situation calls for pushing the wrench away, push with an open hand to avoid scraped knuckles if the wrench should slip.

DON'T attempt to lift a heavy component alone - get someone to help you.

DON'T *rush or take unsafe shortcuts to finish a job.*

DON'T allow children or animals in or around the vehicle while you are working on it.

DO wear eye protection when using power tools such as a drill, sander, bench grinder, etc. and when working under a vehicle.

DO keep loose clothing and long hair well out of the way of moving parts.

DO make sure that any hoist used has a safe working load rating adequate for the job.

DO get someone to check on you periodically when working alone on a vehicle.

DO carry out work in a logical sequence and make sure that everything is correctly assembled and tightened.

DO keep chemicals and fluids tightly capped and out of the reach of children and pets.

DO remember that your vehicle's safety affects that of yourself and others. If in doubt on any point, get professional advice.

Steering, suspension and brakes

These systems are essential to driving safety, so make sure you have a qualified shop or individual check your work. Also, compressed suspension springs can cause injury if released suddenly - be sure to use a spring compressor.

Airbags

Airbags are explosive devices that can **CAUSE** injury if they deploy while you're working on the vehicle. Follow the manufacturer's instructions to disable the airbag whenever you're working in the vicinity of airbag components.

Asbestos

Certain friction, insulating, sealing, and other products - such as brake linings, brake bands, clutch linings, torque converters, gaskets, etc. - may contain asbestos or other hazardous friction material. Extreme care must be taken to avoid inhalation of dust from such products, since it is hazardous to health. If in doubt, assume that they do contain asbestos.

Fire

Remember at all times that gasoline is highly flammable. Never smoke or have any kind of open flame around when working on a vehicle. But the risk does not end there. A spark caused by an electrical short circuit, by two metal surfaces contacting each other, or even by static electricity built up in your body under certain conditions, can ignite gasoline vapors, which in a confined space are highly explosive. Do not, under any circumstances, use gasoline for cleaning parts. Use an approved safety solvent.

Always disconnect the battery ground (-) cable at the battery before working on any part of the fuel system or electrical system. Never risk spilling fuel on a hot engine or exhaust component. It is strongly recommended that a fire extinguisher suitable for use on fuel and electrical fires be kept handy in the garage or workshop at all times. Never try to extinguish a fuel or electrical fire with water.

Fumes

Certain fumes are highly toxic and can quickly cause unconsciousness and even death if inhaled to any extent. Gasoline vapor falls into this category, as do the vapors from some cleaning solvents. Any draining or pouring of such volatile fluids should be done in a well ventilated area.

When using cleaning fluids and solvents, read the instructions on the container carefully. Never use materials from unmarked containers.

Never run the engine in an enclosed space, such as a garage. Exhaust fumes contain carbon monoxide, which is extremely poisonous. If you need to run the engine, always do so in the open air, or at least have the rear of the vehicle outside the work area.

The battery

Never create a spark or allow a bare light bulb near a battery. They normally give off a certain amount of hydrogen gas, which is highly explosive.

Always disconnect the battery ground (-) cable at the battery before working on the fuel or electrical systems.

If possible, loosen the filler caps or cover when charging the battery from an external source (this does not apply to sealed or maintenance-free batteries). Do not charge at an excessive rate or the battery may burst.

Take care when adding water to a non maintenance-free battery and when carrying a battery. The electrolyte, even when diluted, is very corrosive and should not be allowed to contact clothing or skin.

Always wear eye protection when cleaning the battery to prevent the caustic deposits from entering your eyes.

Household current

When using an electric power tool, inspection light, etc., which operates on household current, always make sure that the tool is correctly connected to its plug and that, where necessary, it is properly grounded. Do not use such items in damp conditions and, again, do not create a spark or apply excessive heat in the vicinity of fuel or fuel vapor.

Secondary ignition system voltage

A severe electric shock can result from touching certain parts of the ignition system (such as the spark plug wires) when the engine is running or being cranked, particularly if components are damp or the insulation is defective. In the case of an electronic ignition system, the secondary system voltage is much higher and could prove fatal.

Hydrofluoric acid

This extremely corrosive acid is formed when certain types of synthetic rubber, found in some O-rings, oil seals, fuel hoses, etc. are exposed to temperatures above 750-degrees F (400-degrees C). The rubber changes into a charred or sticky substance containing the acid. *Once formed, the acid remains dangerous for years. If it gets onto the skin, it may be necessary to amputate the limb concerned.*

When dealing with a vehicle which has suffered a fire, or with components salvaged from such a vehicle, wear protective gloves and discard them after use.

Troubleshooting

Contents

This section provides an easy reference guide to the more common problems which may occur during the operation of your vehicle. These problems and their possible causes are grouped under headings denoting various components or systems, such as Engine, Cooling system, etc. They also refer you to the chapter and/or section which deals with the problem.

Remember that successful troubleshooting is not a mysterious art practiced only by professional mechanics. It is simply the result of the right knowledge combined with an intelligent, systematic approach to the problem. Always work by a process of elimination, starting with the simplest solution and working through to the most complex - and never overlook the obvious. Anyone can run the gas tank dry or leave the lights on overnight, so don't assume that you are exempt from such oversights.

Finally, always establish a clear idea of why a problem has occurred and take steps to ensure that it doesn't happen again. If the electrical system fails because of a poor connection, check the other connections in the system to make sure that they don't fail as well. If a particular fuse continues to blow, find out why - don't just replace one fuse after another. Remember, failure of a small component can often be indicative of potential failure or incorrect functioning of a more important component or system.

Engine

1 Engine will not rotate when attempting to start

1   Battery terminal connections loose or corroded (Chapter 1).
2   Battery discharged or faulty (Chapter 1).
3   Automatic transaxle not completely engaged in Park (Chapter 7) or clutch not completely depressed (Chapter 8).
4   Broken, loose or disconnected wiring in the starting circuit (Chapters 5 and 12).
5   Starter motor pinion jammed in flywheel ring gear (Chapter 5).
6   Starter solenoid faulty (Chapter 5).
7   Starter motor faulty (Chapter 5).
8   Ignition switch faulty (Chapter 12).
9   Starter pinion or flywheel teeth worn or broken (Chapter 5).

2 Engine rotates but will not start

1   Fuel tank empty.
2   Battery discharged (engine rotates slowly) (Chapter 5).
3   Battery terminal connections loose or corroded (Chapter 1).
4   Leaking fuel injector(s), faulty fuel pump, pressure regulator, etc. (Chapter 4).
5   Fuel not reaching fuel rail (Chapter 4).

6   Ignition system problem (Chapter 5).
7   Worn, faulty or incorrectly gapped spark plugs (Chapter 1).
8   Faulty camshaft or crankshaft position sensor (Chapter 6).

3 Engine hard to start when cold

1   Battery discharged or low (Chapter 1).
2   Malfunctioning fuel system (Chapter 4).
3   Injector(s) leaking (Chapter 4).
4   Faulty coolant temperature sensor (Chapter 6).

4 Engine hard to start when hot

1   Air filter clogged (Chapter 1).
2   Fuel not reaching the fuel injection system (Chapter 4).
3   Corroded battery connections, especially ground (Chapter 1).

5 Starter motor noisy or excessively rough in engagement

1   Pinion or flywheel gear teeth worn or broken (Chapter 5).
2   Starter motor mounting bolts loose or missing (Chapter 5).

6 Engine starts but stops immediately

1   Loose or faulty electrical connections at coil(s) or alternator (Chapter 5).
2   Insufficient fuel reaching the fuel injector(s) (Chapters 1 and 4).
3   Vacuum leak at the gasket between the intake manifold/plenum and throttle body (Chapters 1 and 4).

7 Oil puddle under engine

1   Oil pan gasket and/or oil pan drain bolt washer leaking (Chapter 2).
2   Oil pressure sending unit leaking (Chapter 2).
3   Valve covers leaking (Chapter 2).
4   Engine oil seals leaking (Chapter 2).
5   Oil pump housing leaking (Chapter 2).

8 Engine lopes while idling or idles erratically

1   Vacuum leakage (Chapters 2 and 4).
2   Air filter clogged (Chapter 1).
3   Fuel pump not delivering sufficient fuel to the fuel injection system (Chapter 4).
4   Leaking head gasket (Chapter 2).
5   Timing chain and/or sprockets worn (Chapter 2).
6   Camshaft lobes worn (Chapter 2).

9 Engine misses at idle speed

1   Spark plugs worn or not gapped properly (Chapter 1).
2   Vacuum leaks (Chapter 1).
3   Fault in engine management system (Chapter 6).
4   Uneven or low compression (Chapter 2).

10 Engine misses throughout driving speed range

1   Fuel filter clogged and/or impurities in the fuel system (Chapter 1).
2   Faulty injector(s) (Chapter 4).
3   Faulty or incorrectly gapped spark plugs (Chapter 1).
4   Faulty ignition coil(s) (Chapter 5).
5   Fault in engine management system (Chapter 6).
6   Faulty emission system components (Chapter 6).
7   Low or uneven cylinder compression pressures (Chapter 2).
8   Faulty ignition system (Chapter 5).
9   Vacuum leak in intake manifold/plenum, air control valve or vacuum hoses (Chapter 4).

11 Engine stumbles on acceleration

1   Spark plugs fouled (Chapter 1).
2   Fuel injection system faulty (Chapter 4).
3   Fuel filter clogged (Chapter 4).
4   Fault in engine management system (Chapter 6).
5   Intake manifold or plenum air leak (Chapters 2 and 4).

12 Engine surges while holding accelerator steady

1   Intake air leak (Chapter 4).
2   Fuel pump faulty (Chapter 4).
3   Defective ECM or information sensor (Chapter 6).

13 Engine stalls

1   Idle speed incorrect (Chapter 1).
2   Fuel filter clogged and/or water and impurities in the fuel system (Chapter 4).
3   Ignition system problem (Chapter 5).
4   Faulty emissions system components (Chapter 6).
5   Faulty or incorrectly gapped spark plugs (Chapter 1).
6   Vacuum leak in the intake manifold or vacuum hoses (Chapters 2 and 4).
8   Valve clearances incorrectly set (2009 and earlier four-cylinder models only) (Chapter 1).

14 Engine lacks power

1   Fault in engine management system (Chapter 6).
2   Faulty or incorrectly gapped spark plugs (Chapter 1).
3   Fuel injection system malfunction (Chapter 4).
4   Faulty coil(s) (Chapter 5).
5   Brakes dragging (Chapter 9).
6   Automatic transaxle fluid level incorrect (Chapter 1).
7   Clutch slipping (Chapter 8).
8   Fuel filter clogged and/or impurities in the fuel system (Chapter 4).
9   Emissions control systems not functioning properly (Chapter 6).
10   Low or uneven cylinder compression pressures (Chapter 2).
11   Obstructed exhaust system (Chapter 4).

15 Engine backfires

1   Emission control system not functioning properly (Chapter 6).
2   Fault in engine management system (Chapter 6).
3   Faulty secondary ignition system (cracked spark plug insulator or ignition coil) (Chapters 1 and 5).
4   Fuel injection system malfunction (Chapter 4).
5   Vacuum leak at fuel injector(s), intake manifold, air control valve or vacuum hoses (Chapters 2 and 4).
6   Valve clearances incorrectly set and/or valves sticking (Chapter 1).

16 Pinging or knocking engine sounds during acceleration or uphill

1   Incorrect grade of fuel.
2   Fault in engine management system (Chapter 6).
3   Fuel injection system faulty (Chapter 4).
4   Improper or damaged spark plugs or wires (Chapter 1).
5   Vacuum leak (Chapters 2 and 4).
6   Defective knock sensor (Chapter 6).

17 Engine runs with oil pressure light on

1   Low oil level (Chapter 1).
2   Faulty oil pressure sender (Chapter 2).
3   Worn engine bearings and/or oil pump (Chapter 2).

18 Engine diesels (continues to run) after switching off

1   Faulty ignition switch (Chapter 12), Powertrain Control Module (PCM) (Chapter 6), or Body Control Module (BCM).
2   Leaking fuel injector(s) (Chapter 4).

Engine electrical system

19 Battery will not hold a charge

1   Drivebelt or tensioner defective (Chapter 1).
2   Battery electrolyte level low (Chapter 1).
3   Battery terminals loose or corroded (Chapter 1).
4   Alternator not charging properly (Chapter 5).
5   Loose, broken or faulty wiring in the charging circuit (Chapter 5).
6   Internally defective battery (Chapters 1 and 5).

20 Alternator light fails to go out

1   Faulty alternator or charging circuit (Chapter 5).
2   Alternator drivebelt or tensioner defective (Chapter 1).
3   Alternator voltage regulator inoperative (Chapter 5).

21 Alternator light fails to come on when key is turned on

1   Warning light bulb defective (Chapter 12).
2   Fault in the printed circuit, dash wiring or bulb holder (Chapter 12).

Fuel system

22 Excessive fuel consumption

1   Dirty or clogged air filter element (Chapter 1).
2   Fault in engine management system (Chapter 6).
3   Emissions systems not functioning properly (Chapter 6).
4   Fuel injection system not functioning properly (Chapter 4).
5   Low tire pressure or incorrect tire size (Chapter 1).

23 Fuel leakage and/or fuel odor

1   Leaking fuel line (Chapters 1 and 4).
2   Tank overfilled.
3   Evaporative canister filter clogged (Chapters 1 and 6).
4   Fuel injection system not functioning properly (Chapter 4).

Cooling system

24 Overheating

1   Insufficient coolant in system (Chapter 1).
2   Water pump defective (Chapter 3).
3   Radiator core blocked or grille restricted (Chapter 3).
4   Thermostat faulty (Chapter 3).
5   Electric coolant fan blades broken or cracked (Chapter 3).
6   Radiator cap not maintaining proper pressure (Chapter 3).
7   Fault in engine management system (Chapter 6).

25 Overcooling

1   Faulty thermostat (Chapter 3).
2   Temperature gauge defective.

26 External coolant leakage

1   Deteriorated/damaged hoses; loose clamps (Chapters 1 and 3).
2   Water pump defective (Chapter 3).
3   Leakage from radiator core or coolant reservoir bottle (Chapter 3).
4   Engine drain or water jacket core plugs leaking.
5   Too much coolant in system (Chapter 1)

27 Internal coolant leakage

1   Leaking cylinder head gasket (Chapter 2).
2   Cracked cylinder bore or cylinder head (Chapter 2).

28 Coolant loss

1   Coolant boiling away because of overheating (Chapter 3).
2   Internal or external leakage (Chapter 3).
3   Faulty radiator cap (Chapter 3).

29 Poor coolant circulation

1   Inoperative water pump (Chapter 3).
2   Restriction in cooling system (Chapters 1 and 3).
3   Water pump drivebelt defective/out of adjustment (Chapter 1).
4   Thermostat sticking (Chapter 3).

Clutch

30 Pedal travels to floor - no pressure or very little resistance

1   Master or release cylinder faulty (Chapter 8).
2   Hose/pipe burst or leaking (Chapter 8).
3   Connections leaking (Chapter 8).
4   No fluid in reservoir (Chapter 8).
5   If fluid level in reservoir rises as pedal is depressed, master cylinder center valve seal is faulty (Chapter 8).
6   If there is fluid on dust seal at master cylinder, piston primary seal is leaking (Chapter 8).
7   Broken release bearing or fork (Chapter 8).

31 Fluid in area of master cylinder dust cover and on pedal

Rear seal failure in master cylinder (Chapter 8).

32 Fluid on release cylinder

Release cylinder plunger seal faulty (Chapter 8).

33 Pedal feels spongy when depressed

Air in system (Chapter 8).

34 Unable to select gears

1   Faulty transaxle (Chapter 7).
2   Faulty clutch disc (Chapter 8).
3   Release lever and bearing not assembled properly (Chapter 8).
4   Faulty pressure plate (Chapter 8).
5   Pressure plate-to-flywheel bolts loose (Chapter 8).

35 Clutch slips (engine speed increases with no increase in vehicle speed)

1   Clutch plate worn (Chapter 8).
2   Clutch plate is oil soaked by leaking rear main seal (Chapters 2 and 8).
3   Clutch plate not seated. It may take 30 or 40 normal starts for a new one to seat.
4   Warped pressure plate or flywheel (Chapter 8).
5   Weak diaphragm spring (Chapter 8).
6   Clutch plate overheated. Allow to cool.

36 Grabbing (chattering) as clutch is engaged

1   Oil on clutch plate lining, burned or glazed facings (Chapter 8).
2   Worn or loose engine or transaxle mounts (Chapters 2 and 7).
3   Worn splines on clutch plate hub (Chapter 8).
4   Warped pressure plate or flywheel (Chapter 8).
5   Burned or smeared resin on flywheel or pressure plate (Chapter 8).

37 Transaxle rattling (clicking)

1   Release lever loose (Chapter 8).
2   Clutch plate damper spring failure (Chapter 8).

38 Noise in clutch area

1   Faulty release bearing (Chapter 8).
2   Loose pressure plate bolts.

39 Clutch pedal stays on floor

1   Clutch master cylinder piston binding in bore (Chapter 8).
2   Broken release bearing or fork (Chapter 8).

40 High pedal effort

1   Piston binding in bore (Chapter 8).
2   Pressure plate faulty (Chapter 8).
3   Incorrect size master or release cylinder (Chapter 8).

Manual transaxle

41 Knocking noise at low speeds

1   Worn driveaxle constant velocity (CV) joints (Chapter 8).
2   Worn side gear shaft counterbore in differential case (Chapter 7A).*

42 Noise most pronounced when turning

Differential gear noise (Chapter 7A).*

43 Clunk on acceleration or deceleration

1   Loose engine or transaxle mounts (Chapters 2 and 7A).
2   Worn differential pinion shaft in case.*
3   Worn side gear shaft counterbore in differential case (Chapter 7A).*
4   Worn or damaged driveaxle inner CV joints (Chapter 8).

44 Clicking noise in turns

Worn or damaged outer CV joint (Chapter 8).

45 Vibration

1   Rough wheel bearing (Chapter 10).
2   Damaged driveaxle (Chapter 8).
3   Out of round tires (Chapter 1).
4   Tire out of balance (Chapters 1 and 10).
5   Worn CV joint (Chapter 8).

46 Noisy in neutral with engine running

1   Damaged input gear bearing (Chapter 7A).*
2   Damaged clutch release bearing (Chapter 8).

47 Noisy in one particular gear

1   Damaged or worn constant mesh gears (Chapter 7A).*
2   Damaged fourth speed gear or output gear (Chapter 7A).*
3   Worn or damaged reverse idler gear or idler bushing (Chapter 7A).*

48 Noisy in all gears

1 Insufficient lubricant (Chapters 1 and 7A).
2 Damaged or worn bearings (Chapter 7A).*
3 Worn or damaged input gear shaft and/or output gear shaft (Chapter 7A).*
4 Worn or damaged reverse idler gear or idler bushing (Chapter 7A).*

49 Slips out of gear

1 Worn or improperly adjusted cable(s) (Chapter 7A).
2 Shift linkage does not work freely, binds (Chapter 7A).
3 Input gear bearing retainer broken or loose (Chapter 7A).*
4 Dirt between clutch cover and engine housing (Chapter 7A).
5 Worn shift fork (Chapter 7A).*

50 Leaks lubricant

1 Driveaxle seals worn (Chapter 7B).
2 Excessive amount of lubricant in transaxle (Chapters 1 and 7A).
3 Loose or broken input gear shaft bearing retainer (Chapter 7A).*
4 Input gear bearing retainer O-ring and/or lip seal damaged (Chapter 7A).*

51 Locked in gear

Lock pin or interlock pin missing (Chapter 7A).*

Although the corrective action necessary to remedy the symptoms described is beyond the scope of this manual, the above information should be helpful in isolating the cause of the condition so that the owner can communicate clearly with a professional mechanic.

Automatic transaxle

Note: *Due to the complexity of the automatic transaxle, it is difficult for the home mechanic to properly diagnose and service this component. For problems other than the following, the vehicle should be taken to a dealer or transmission shop.*

52 Fluid leakage

1 Automatic transaxle fluid is a deep red color. Fluid leaks should not be confused with engine oil, which can easily be blown onto the transaxle by air flow.
2 To pinpoint a leak, first remove all built-up dirt and grime from the transaxle housing with degreasing agents and/or steam cleaning.

Then drive the vehicle at low speeds so air flow will not blow the leak far from its source. Raise the vehicle and determine where the leak is coming from. Common areas of leakage are:

a) *Pan (Chapters 1 and 7)*
b) *Dipstick tube (Chapters 1 and 7)*
c) *Transaxle oil lines (Chapter 7)*
d) *Speed sensor (Chapter 7)*
e) *Differential drain plug (Chapters 1 and 7B)*

53 Transaxle fluid brown or has a burned smell

Transaxle fluid overheated (Chapter 1).

54 General shift mechanism problems

1 Chapter 7, Part B, deals with checking and adjusting the shift cable on automatic transaxles. Common problems which may be attributed to poorly adjusted cable are:

a) *Engine starting in gears other than Park or Neutral.*
b) *Indicator on shifter pointing to a gear other than the one actually being used.*
c) *Vehicle moves when in Park.*

2 Refer to Chapter 7B for the shift cable adjustment procedure.

55 Transaxle will not downshift with accelerator pedal pressed to the floor

Since these transmissions are electronically controlled, check for any diagnostic trouble codes stored in the PCM. The actual repair will most likely have to be performed by a qualified repair shop with the proper equipment.

56 Engine will start in gears other than Park or Neutral

Park/Neutral Position switch malfunctioning (Chapter 7B).

57 Transaxle slips, shifts roughly, is noisy or has no drive in forward or reverse gears

There are many probable causes for the above problems, but the home mechanic should be concerned with only one possibility - fluid level. Before taking the vehicle to a repair shop, check the level and condition of the fluid as described in Chapter 1. Correct the fluid level as necessary or change the fluid

and filter if needed. If the problem persists, have a professional diagnose the cause.

Driveaxles

58 Clicking noise in turns

Worn or damaged outboard CV joint (Chapter 8).

59 Shudder or vibration during acceleration

1 Excessive toe-in (Chapter 10).
2 Worn or damaged inboard or outboard CV joints (Chapter 8).
3 Sticking inboard CV joint assembly (Chapter 8).

60 Vibration at highway speeds

1 Out of balance front wheels and/or tires (Chapters 1 and 10).
2 Out of round tires (Chapters 1 and 10).
3 Worn CV joint(s) (Chapter 8).

Brakes

Note: *Before assuming that a brake problem exists, make sure that:*
a) *The tires are in good condition and properly inflated (Chapter 1).*
b) *The front end alignment is correct (Chapter 10).*
c) *The vehicle is not loaded with weight in an unequal manner.*

61 Vehicle pulls to one side during braking

1 Incorrect tire pressures (Chapter 1).
2 Front end out of alignment (have the front end aligned).
3 Front, or rear, tires not matched to one another.
4 Restricted brake lines or hoses (Chapter 9).
5 Malfunctioning caliper assembly (Chapter 9).
6 Loose suspension parts (Chapter 10).
7 Excessive wear of pad material or disc on one side.

62 Noise (high-pitched squeal when the brakes are applied)

Front and/or rear disc brake pads worn out. The noise comes from the wear sensor rubbing against the disc (does not apply to all vehicles). Replace pads with new ones immediately (Chapter 9).

63 Brake roughness or chatter (pedal pulsates)

1   Excessive lateral runout (Chapter 9).
2   Uneven pad wear (Chapter 9).
3   Defective disc (Chapter 9).

64 Excessive brake pedal effort required to stop vehicle

1   Malfunctioning power brake booster (Chapter 9).
2   Partial system failure (Chapter 9).
3   Excessively worn pads or shoes (Chapter 9).
4   Piston in caliper stuck or sluggish (Chapter 9).
5   Brake pads contaminated with oil, grease or brake fluid (Chapter 9).
6   New pads installed and not yet seated. It will take a while for the new material to seat against the disc.

65 Excessive brake pedal travel

1   Partial brake system failure (Chapter 9).
2   Insufficient fluid in master cylinder (Chapters 1 and 9).
3   Air trapped in system (Chapters 1 and 9).

66 Dragging brakes

1   Incorrect adjustment of brake light switch (Chapter 9).
2   Master cylinder pistons not returning correctly (Chapter 9).
3   Restricted brakes lines or hoses (Chapters 1 and 9).
4   Incorrect parking brake adjustment (Chapter 9).

67 Grabbing or uneven braking action

Contaminated pad lining material (Chapter 9).

68 Brake pedal feels spongy when depressed

1   Air in hydraulic lines (Chapter 9).
2   Master cylinder mounting nuts loose (Chapter 9).
3   Master cylinder defective (Chapter 9).

69 Brake pedal travels to the floor with little resistance

1   Little or no fluid in the master cylinder reservoir caused by leaking caliper piston(s) (Chapter 9).
2   Loose, damaged or disconnected brake lines (Chapter 9).

70 Parking brake does not hold

Parking brake linkage improperly adjusted (Chapters 1 and 9).

Suspension and steering systems

Note: *Before attempting to diagnose the suspension and steering systems, perform the following preliminary checks:*

a) *Tires for wrong pressure and uneven wear.*
b) *Steering universal joints from the column to the rack and pinion for loose connectors or wear.*
c) *Front and rear suspension and the rack and pinion assembly for loose or damaged parts.*
d) *Out-of-round or out-of-balance tires, bent rims and loose and/or rough wheel bearings.*

71 Vehicle pulls to one side

1   Mismatched or uneven tires (Chapter 10).
2   Broken or sagging springs (Chapter 10).
3   Wheel alignment (Chapter 10).
4   Front brake dragging (Chapter 9).

72 Abnormal or excessive tire wear

1   Wheel alignment (Chapter 10).
2   Sagging or broken springs (Chapter 10).
3   Tire out of balance (Chapter 10).
4   Worn strut damper (Chapter 10).
5   Overloaded vehicle.
6   Tires not rotated regularly.

73 Wheel makes a thumping noise

1   Blister or bump on tire (Chapter 10).
2   Improper strut damper action (Chapter 10).

74 Shimmy, shake or vibration

1   Tire or wheel out-of-balance or out-of-round (Chapter 10).
2   Worn wheel bearings (Chapters 10).

3   Worn tie-rod ends (Chapter 10).
4   Worn balljoints (Chapters 1 and 10).
5   Excessive wheel runout (Chapter 10).
6   Blister or bump on tire (Chapter 10).

75 Hard steering

1   Worn balljoints or tie-rod ends (Chapter 10).
2   Front wheel alignment incorrect (Chapter 10).
3   Low tire pressure(s) (Chapters 1 and 10).

76 Poor returnability of steering to center

1   Worn balljoints or tie-rod ends (Chapter 10).
2   Binding in steering column (Chapter 10).
3   Front wheel alignment incorrect (Chapter 10).

77 Abnormal noise at the front end

1   Worn balljoints or tie-rod ends (Chapter 10).
2   Damaged strut mounting (Chapter 10).
3   Worn control arm bushings or tie-rod ends (Chapter 10).
4   Loose stabilizer bar or worn bushing (Chapter 10).
5   Loose wheel nuts (Chapters 1 and 10).
6   Loose suspension bolts (Chapter 10)

78 Wander or poor steering stability

1   Mismatched or uneven tires (Chapter 10).
2   Worn balljoints or tie-rod ends (Chapter 10).
3   Worn strut assemblies (Chapter 10).
4   Loose stabilizer bar (Chapter 10).
5   Broken or sagging springs (Chapter 10).
6   Wheels out of alignment (Chapter 10).

79 Erratic steering when braking

1   Wheel bearings worn (Chapter 10).
2   Broken or sagging springs (Chapter 10).
3   Defective brake caliper (Chapter 10).
4   Warped brake discs (Chapter 10).

80 Excessive pitching and/or rolling around corners or during braking

1   Loose stabilizer bar (Chapter 10).
2   Worn strut dampers or mountings (Chapter 10).
3   Broken or sagging springs (Chapter 10).
4   Overloaded vehicle.

81 Suspension bottoms

1   Overloaded vehicle.
2   Worn strut dampers (Chapter 10).
3   Incorrect, broken or sagging springs (Chapter 10).

82 Cupped tires

1   Front wheel or rear wheel alignment (Chapter 10).
2   Worn strut dampers (Chapter 10).
3   Wheel bearings worn (Chapter 10).
4   Excessive tire or wheel runout (Chapter 10).
5   Worn balljoints (Chapter 10).

83 Excessive tire wear on outside edge

1   Inflation pressures incorrect (Chapter 1).
2   Excessive speed in turns.

3   Front end alignment incorrect (excessive toe-in). Have professionally aligned.
4   Suspension arm bent (Chapter 10).

84 Excessive tire wear on inside edge

1   Inflation pressures incorrect (Chapter 1).
2   Front end alignment incorrect (toe-out). Have professionally aligned.
3   Loose or damaged steering components (Chapter 10).

85 Tire tread worn in one place

1   Tires out of balance.
2   Damaged or buckled wheel. Inspect and replace if necessary.
3   Defective tire (Chapter 1).

86 Excessive play or looseness in steering system

1   Wheel bearing(s) worn (Chapter 10).
2   Tie-rod end loose (Chapter 10).
3   Steering gear loose (Chapter 10).
4   Worn or loose steering intermediate shaft (Chapter 10).

87 Rattling or clicking noise in steering gear

1   Steering gear loose (Chapter 10).
2   Steering gear defective.

Chapter 1
Tune-up and routine maintenance

Contents

Specifications

Recommended lubricants and fluids

Note: *Listed here are manufacturer recommendations at the time this manual was written. Manufacturers occasionally upgrade their fluid and lubricant specifications, so check with your auto parts store for current recommendations.*

Engine oil
Type .... API "certified for gasoline engines"
   Viscosity
      2011 and earlier models (2012 Avalon and ES350 models)
         Four-cylinder engines .... SAE 0W-20 (preferred), 5W-20
         V6 engine .... SAE 5W-30 (preferred), 10W-30
      2012 and later models except 2012 Avalon and ES350 models .. SAE 0W20 (preferred), 5W-20
Fuel
   Four-cylinder engines .... Unleaded fuel, 87 octane or higher
   V6 engine .... Unleaded fuel, 91 octane or higher
      2011 and earlier models .... Unleaded fuel, 91 octane or higher
      2012 and later models .... Unleaded fuel, 87 octane or higher
Coolant .... Toyota Genuine Long Life Coolant (SLLC) or equivalent.

Caution: *In order to avoid damage to the engine cooling system and other problems, only use TOYOTA SLLC or similar high quality ethylene glycol based non-silicate, non-amine, non-nitrite, non-borate coolant with long-life hybrid organic acid technology.*

Recommended lubricants and fluids (continued)

Automatic transaxle fluid type..	Toyota ATF WS automatic transmission fluid
Manual transaxle lubricant type...	API GL-4 or GL-5 75W-90 gear oil
Brake fluid type..	DOT 3 brake fluid
Clutch fluid type...	DOT 3 brake fluid
Power steering system fluid (2011 and earlier models)...........	DEXRON III automatic transmission fluid

Capacities*

Engine oil (including filter)
Four-cylinder engines
2AZ-FE (2009 and earlier models).....................	4.3 qts
2AR-FE (2010 and later models).........................	4.6 qts
V6 engine..	6.4 qts

Coolant
Four-cylinder engines
2AZ-FE (2009 and earlier models).....................	6.6 qts
2AR-FE (2010 and later models).........................	7.5 qts

V6 engine
2011 and earlier models...	7.9 qts
2012 and later models..	9.7 qts

Transaxle
Automatic
U250E (2009 and earlier four-cylinder models, drain and refill) ...	3.7 qts
U760E (2010 and later four-cylinder models, dry fill**)................	6.9 qts
U660E (V6 models, dry fill**)	6.94 qts
Manual (EB62)...	2.6 qts

*All capacities approximate. Add as necessary to bring up to appropriate level.

**Since this is a dry-fill specification, the amount required during a routine fluid change will be substantially less. The best way to determine the amount of fluid to add during a routine fluid change is to measure the amount drained. Begin the refill procedure by initially adding 1/3 of the amount drained. Then, with the engine running, add 1/2-pint at a time (cycling the shifter through each gear position between additions) until the level is correct on the dipstick. It is important to not overfill the transaxle.

Ignition system

Spark plug
Type
Four-cylinder engines
2AZ-FE (2009 and earlier models)..	SK20R11 (DENSO)
2AR-FE (2010 and later models)...	SK16HR11 (DENSO)
V6 engine..	FK20HBR11 (DENSO)
Gap...	0.043 inch

Engine firing order
Four-cylinder engines...	1-3-4-2
V6 engine..	1-2-3-4-5-6

Cylinder numbering - four-cylinder engines

Valve clearance (engine cold) - four-cylinder engines (2007 through 2009 models only)

Intake...	0.008 to 0.011 inch
Exhaust..	0.015 to 0.018 inch

Clutch

Clutch pedal freeplay..	0.197 to 0.591 inch
Pedal height...	6.252 to 6.645 inches
Pushrod play at pedal top...	0.039 to 0.197 inch

Brakes

Disc brake pad lining thickness (minimum)	1/16 inch
Parking brake shoe lining thickness (minimum)	1/16 inch

Brake pedal
Freeplay	0.04 to 0.24 inch

Free height
2011 and earlier models	5.673 to 6.067 inches
2012 and later models	5.46 to 5.84 inches

Brake light switch clearance
2012 and earlier models (except 2012 Avalon and 2013 ES350).	0.060 to 0.098 inch
2012 Avalon and 2013 ES350 models...................................	0.023 to 0.102 inch

Cylinder numbering - V6 engine

Brakes (continued)

Pedal reserve height
    Manual transaxle .... 2.48 inches
    Automatic transaxle
        2011 and earlier models .... 2.43 inches
        2012 and later models (at 112 lbs force) .... more than 3.78 inches
Parking brake adjustment
    Cable adjustment
        Hand lever type.. 7 to 9 clicks to firm apply
        Foot pedal type .... 7 to 10 clicks to firm apply
    Shoe adjustment (rear disc brakes) .... Back off 8 notches from shoe contact

Suspension and steering

Steering wheel freeplay limit.. 1-3/16 inches (1.18 in)
Balljoint allowable movement .... 0.0 inch

Torque specifications   **Ft-lbs** (unless otherwise indicated)

Note: *One foot-pound (ft-lb) of torque is equivalent to 12 inch-pounds (in-lbs) of torque. Torque values below approximately 15 foot-pounds are expressed in inch-pounds, because most foot-pound torque wrenches are not accurate at these smaller values.*

Engine oil drain plug
    Four-cylinder engines
        2AZ-FE (2009 and earlier models) .... 80 in-lbs
        2AR-FE (2010 and later models)................................. 30
    V6 engine 30
Engine oil filter (2010 and later four-cylinder [2AR-FE] and all V6 engines)
    Filter cap 18
    Filter cap drain plug
        All models except 2013 ES350................................... 120 in-lbs
        2013 ES350 models .... 108 in-lbs
Automatic transaxle
    Pan bolts .... 62 in-lbs
    Strainer bolts
        U250E transaxle .... 96 in-lbs
        U660E/U760E transaxles .... 85 in-lbs
    Drain/fill plugs... 36
    Overflow plug (U660E/U760E transaxles) 30
Manual transaxle drain and filler plugs 29
Drivebelt idler pulley bolts
    Idler pulley no. 1 bolt.. 40
    Idler pulley no. 2 bolt
        2011 and earlier models 29
        2012 and later models 40
Drivebelt tensioner mounting bolts (2012 and later models) 32
Chassis and body
    Front seat mounting bolts.. 27
    Front suspension subframe-to-body nuts/bolts.............. See Chapter 2C
    Rear suspension crossmember-to-body nuts/bolts........ See Chapter 10
Spark plugs
    Four-cylinder engine
        2011 and earlier models .... 168 in-lbs
        2012 and later models 18
    V6 engine.. 156 in-lbs
Wheel lug nuts.. 76

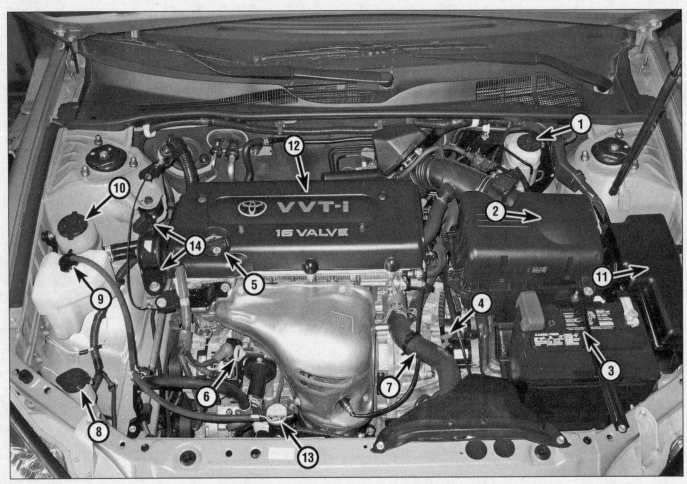

Four-cylinder engine compartment layout - 2009 and earlier models

1 Brake fluid reservoir	6 Engine oil dipstick	11 Engine compartment fuse/relay box
2 Air filter housing	7 Radiator hose	12 Engine cover (remove for access to
3 Battery	8 Windshield washer fluid reservoir	spark plugs)
4 Automatic transaxle fluid dipstick	9 Engine coolant reservoir	13 Radiator cap
5 Engine oil filler cap	10 Power steering fluid reservoir	14 Upper control rod and bracket

Four-cylinder engine compartment layout - 2010 and later models

1	Brake fluid reservoir	6	Radiator cap
2	Air filter housing	7	Engine oil dipstick
3	Engine compartment fuse/relay box	8	Windshield washer fluid reservoir
4	Battery	9	Engine coolant reservoir
5	Radiator hose		

1 Brake fluid reservoir
2 Air filter housing
3 Engine compartment fuse/relay box
4 Battery
5 Radiator hose

6 Radiator cap
7 Engine oil dipstick
8 Windshield washer fluid reservoir
9 Engine coolant reservoir

10 Power steering fluid reservoir
11 Engine oil filler cap
12 Ignition coils (spark plugs underneath)
13 Upper control rod and bracket

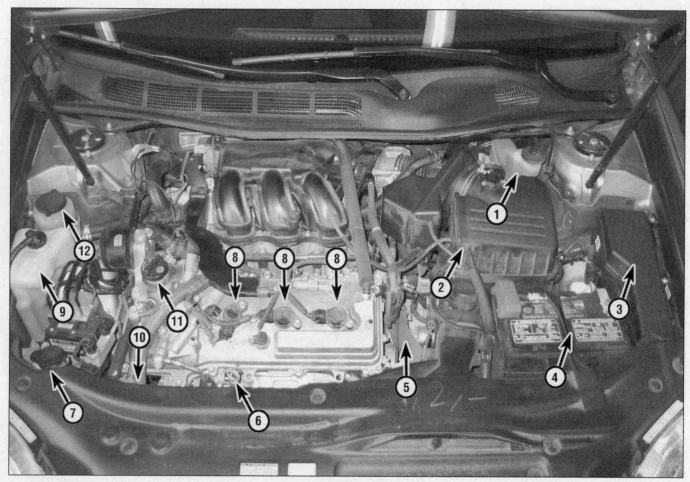

V6 engine compartment layout

1	Brake fluid reservoir	6	Engine oil dipstick	9	Engine coolant reservoir
2	Air filter housing	7	Windshield washer fluid reservoir	10	Cooling system pressure cap
3	Engine compartment fuse/relay box	8	Ignition coils (spark plugs underneath;	11	Engine oil filler cap
4	Battery		rear bank spark plugs under the upper	12	Power steering fluid reservoir
5	Radiator hose		intake manifold)		

Typical 2009 and earlier four-cylinder model front underside components

1 Engine oil drain plug
2 Front brake calipers
3 Outer driveaxle boots
4 Balljoints

5 Automatic transaxle drain plug
   (U250F transaxle)
6 Exhaust pipe

7 Inner driveaxle boots
8 Brake hoses
9 Engine oil filter

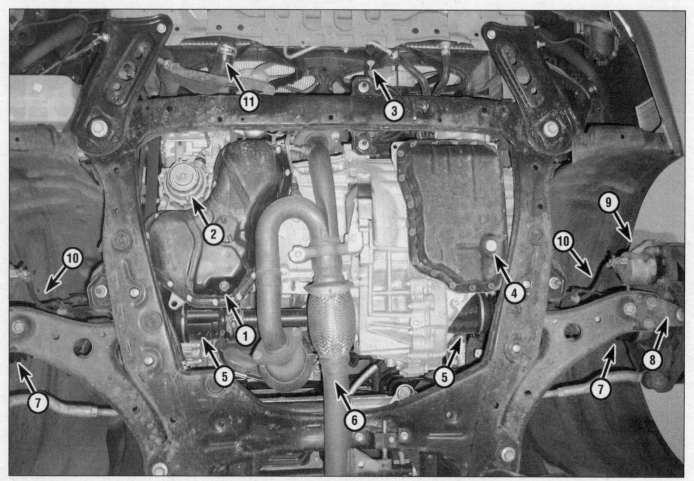

Typical V6 engine model front underside components

1	Engine oil drain plug	5	Inner CV joint and boots	9	Front brake caliper
2	Oil filter housing	6	Exhaust pipe	10	Brake hoses
3	Radiator drain	7	Outer driveaxle boots	11	Lower radiator hose
4	Automatic transaxle fluid overflow (level check) plug (U660E transaxle)	8	Balljoint		

Typical rear underside components

1 Rear brake calipers	4 Exhaust pipe	6 Brake disc and parking brake (drum)
2 Shock and spring assembly	5 Mufflers	7 Parking brake cables
3 Fuel tank		

1 Toyota Camry and Avalon, and Lexus ES 350, Maintenance schedule

The maintenance intervals in this manual are provided with the assumption that you, not the dealer, will be doing the work. These are the minimum maintenance intervals recommended by the factory for vehicles that are driven daily. If you wish to keep your vehicle in peak condition at all times, you may wish to perform some of these procedures even more often. Because frequent maintenance enhances the efficiency, performance and resale value of your car, we encourage you to do so. If you drive in dusty areas, tow a trailer, idle or drive at low speeds for extended periods or drive for short distances (less than four miles) in below freezing temperatures, shorter intervals are also recommended.

When your vehicle is new, it should be serviced by a factory authorized dealer service department to protect the factory warranty. In many cases, the initial maintenance check is done at no cost to the owner.

Every 250 miles or weekly, whichever comes first

Check the engine oil level (Section 4)
Check the engine coolant level (Section 4)
Check the windshield washer fluid level (Section 4)
Check the brake and clutch fluid levels (Section 4)
Check the power steering fluid level (Section 4)
Check the tires and tire pressures (Section 5)

Every 3000 miles or 3 months, whichever comes first

All items listed above plus:
Change the engine oil and oil filter (Section 6)

Every 5000 miles or 6 months, whichever comes first

All items listed above plus:
Check installation of driver's floor mat
Check the automatic transaxle fluid level (2009 and earlier four-cylinder models) (Section 7)
Inspect the windshield wiper blades (Section 8)
Check and service the battery (Section 9)

Inspect all underhood hoses (Section 10)
Check the cooling system (Section 11)
Rotate the tires (Section 12)
Inspect the brake system (Section 13)

Every 15,000 miles or 18 months, whichever comes first

All items listed above plus:
Inspect the suspension and steering components and drive-axle boots (Section 14)*
Inspect the exhaust system (Section 15)
Check the engine drivebelt(s) (Section 27) (after the initial 60,000-mile or 72-month check)

Every 30,000 miles or 36 months, whichever comes first

All items listed above plus:
Check the automatic transaxle fluid level (2010 and later four-cylinder models and all V6 models) (Section 7
Replace the air filter (Section 16)*
Inspect the fuel system (Section 17)
Check the manual transaxle lubricant level (Section 18)**
Replace the cabin air filter (Section 19)
Check the clutch pedal for proper freeplay and height (Section 20)
Inspect the evaporative emissions control system (Section 23)
Check and tighten critical chassis and body fasteners (Section 24)*

Every 50,000 miles or 60 months, whichever comes first

Service the cooling system (drain, flush and refill) (Section 29) (after the initial 100,000-mile or 120-month service)

Every 60,000 miles or 72 months, whichever comes first

All items listed above plus:
Check and replace if necessary the fuel tank cap gasket
  (Section 21)
Check and replace if necessary the PCV valve (Section 22)
Change the automatic transaxle fluid (Section 25)**
Change the manual transaxle lubricant (Section 25)**
Check and replace if necessary the engine drivebelts
  (Section 27)
Inspect and if necessary adjust the valve clearances (2009
  and earlier four-cylinder engines) (Section 28)

100,000 miles or 120 months, whichever comes first - every 50,000 miles or 60 months thereafter, whichever comes first

Service the cooling system (drain, flush and refill)
  (Section 29)

Every 120,000 miles or 144 months, whichever comes first

Replace the spark plugs (Section 30)
*   This item is affected by "severe" operating conditions
    as described below. If your vehicle is operated under
    "severe" conditions, inspect all maintenance indicated
    with an asterisk (*) at 5000 mile/6 month intervals and
    perform maintenance or replace parts as necessary.
    Severe conditions are indicated if you mainly operate
    your vehicle under one or more of the following condi-
    tions:
Operating in dusty areas
Idling for extended periods and/or low speed operation
Operating when outside temperatures remain below freez-
    ing and when most trips are less than 4 miles
** If used for trailer towing, change the automatic transaxle
    fluid or manual transaxle lubricant every 30,000 miles
    (Section 25 or Section 26)

2   Introduction

This Chapter is designed to help the home mechanic maintain his vehicle for peak performance, economy, safety and long life.

Included is a master maintenance schedule, followed by sections dealing specif-ically with each item on the schedule. Visual checks, adjustments, component replace-ment and other helpful items are included. Refer to the **accompanying illustrations** of the engine compartment and the underside of the vehicle for the location of various compo-nents.

Servicing your vehicle in accordance with the mileage/time maintenance schedule and the following Sections will provide it with a planned maintenance program that should result in a long and reliable service life. This is a comprehensive plan, so maintaining some items but not others at the specified service intervals won't produce the same results.

As you service your vehicle, you will dis-cover that many of the procedures can - and should - be grouped together because of the nature of the particular procedure you're per-forming or because of the close proximity of two otherwise unrelated components to one another.

For example, if the vehicle is raised for any reason, you should inspect the exhaust, suspension, steering and fuel systems while you're under the vehicle. When you're rotating the tires, it makes good sense to check the brakes and wheel bearings since the wheels are already removed.

Finally, let's suppose you have to borrow or rent a torque wrench. Even if you only need to tighten the spark plugs, you might as well check the torque of as many critical fasteners as time allows.

The first step of this maintenance pro-gram is to prepare yourself before the actual work begins. Read through all sections perti-nent to the procedures you're planning to do, then make a list of and gather together all the parts and tools you will need to do the job. If it looks as if you might run into problems during a particular segment of some procedure, seek advice from your local parts man or dealer service department.

3   Tune-up general information

The term tune-up is used in this manual to represent a combination of individual oper-ations rather than one specific procedure.

If, from the time the vehicle is new, the routine maintenance schedule is followed closely and frequent checks are made of fluid levels and high wear items, as suggested throughout this manual, the engine will be kept in relatively good running condition and the need for additional work will be minimized.

More likely than not, however, there will be times when the engine is running poorly due to lack of regular maintenance. This is even more likely if a used vehicle, which has not received regular and frequent mainte-nance checks, is purchased. In such cases, an engine tune-up will be needed outside of the regular routine maintenance intervals.

The first step in any tune-up or engine diagnosis to help correct a poor running engine would be a cylinder compression check. A check of the engine compression (see Chapter 2C) will give valuable informa-tion regarding the overall performance of many internal components and should be used as a basis for tune-up and repair proce-dures. If, for instance, a compression check indicates serious internal engine wear, a con-ventional tune-up will not help the running condition of the engine and would be a waste of time and money. Also in Chapter 2, Part C is information on checking engine vacuum, which also gives information on the engine's state-of-tune and condition.

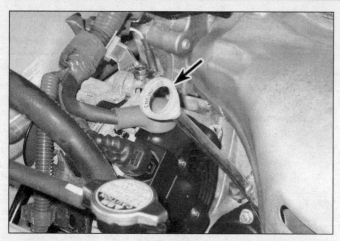

4.2 The engine oil dipstick is located on the front (radiator) side of the engine

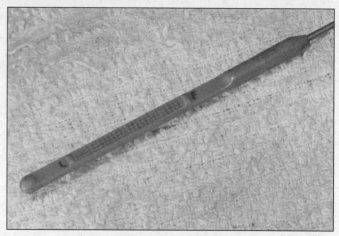

4.4 The oil level should be at or near the F mark on the dipstick - if it isn't, add enough oil to bring the level to or near the F mark (it takes about one quart to raise the level from the L to F mark)

The following series of operations are those most often needed to bring a generally poor-running engine back into a proper state of tune.

Minor tune-up

Check all engine related fluids (Section 4)
Clean, inspect and test the battery (Section 9)
Check all underhood hoses (Section 10)
Check the cooling system (Section 11)
Check the air filter (Section 16)
Check the drivebelts (Section 27)

Major tune-up

All items listed under Minor tune-up, plus . . .

Replace the air filter (Section 16)
Check the fuel system (Section 17)
Replace the spark plugs (Section 30)
Check the charging system (Chapter 5)

4.6 The threaded oil filler cap is located on the valve cover - to prevent dirt from contaminating the engine, always make sure the area around this opening is clean before removing the cap (engine cover removed)

4   Fluid level checks (every 250 miles or weekly)

1   Fluids are an essential part of the lubrication, cooling, brake, clutch and other systems. Because these fluids gradually become depleted and/or contaminated during normal operation of the vehicle, they must be periodically replenished. See *Recommended lubricants and fluids* and *Capacities* in this Chapter's Specifications before adding fluid to any of the following components. **Note:** *The vehicle must be on level ground before fluid levels can be checked.*

Engine oil

Refer to illustrations 4.2, 4.4 and 4.6

2   The engine oil level is checked with a dipstick located at the front side of the engine **(see illustration)**.
3   The oil level should be checked before the vehicle has been driven, or about 5 minutes after the engine has been shut off. If the oil is checked immediately after driving the vehicle, some of the oil will remain in the upper engine components, producing an inaccurate reading on the dipstick.
4   Pull the dipstick from the tube and wipe all the oil from the end with a clean rag or paper towel. Insert the clean dipstick all the way back into its metal tube and pull it out again. Observe the oil at the end of the dipstick. At its highest point, the level should be between the L and F marks **(see illustration)**.
5   It takes about one quart of oil to raise the level from the L mark to the F mark on the dipstick. Do not allow the level to drop below the L mark or oil starvation may cause engine damage. Conversely, overfilling the engine (adding oil above the F mark) may cause oil-fouled spark plugs, oil leaks or oil seal failures.
6   Remove the threaded cap from the valve

cover to add oil **(see illustration)**. Use a funnel to prevent spills. After adding the oil, install the filler cap hand tight. Start the engine and look carefully for any small leaks around the oil filter or drain plug. Stop the engine and check the oil level again after it has had sufficient time to drain from the upper block and cylinder head galleys.
7   Checking the oil level is an important preventive maintenance step. A continually dropping oil level indicates oil leakage through damaged seals, from loose connections, or past worn rings or valve guides. If the oil looks milky in color or has water droplets in it, a cylinder head gasket may be blown. The engine should be checked immediately. The condition of the oil should also be checked. Each time you check the oil level, slide your thumb and index finger up the dipstick before wiping off the oil. If you see small dirt or metal particles clinging to the dipstick, the oil should be changed (see Section 6).

Engine coolant

Refer to illustration 4.8

Warning: *Do not allow antifreeze to come in contact with your skin or painted surfaces of the vehicle. Flush contaminated areas immediately with plenty of water. Don't store new coolant or leave old coolant lying around where it's accessible to children or pets - they're attracted by its sweet smell. Ingestion of even a small amount of coolant can be fatal! Wipe up garage floor and drip pan spills immediately. Keep antifreeze containers covered and repair cooling system leaks as soon as they're noticed.*

8   All models covered by this manual are equipped with a coolant recovery system. The coolant reservoir is located in the front corner of the engine compartment and is connected by a hose to the base of the coolant filler cap **(see illustration)**. If the coolant heats up past a certain point during engine operation, cool-

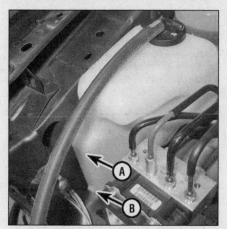

4.8 Make sure the coolant level is between the Full (A) and Low (B) lines - if it's below the Low line, add a sufficient quantity of the specified mixture of antifreeze and water

4.14 The windshield washer fluid reservoir is located at the passenger's side front corner of the engine compartment

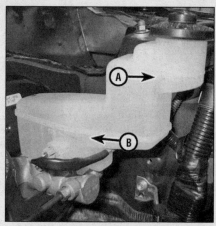

4.16 The brake fluid should be kept between the Max (A) and Min (B) marks on the reservoir

ant can escape through the pressurized filler cap and connecting hose into the reservoir. As the engine cools, the coolant is automatically drawn back into the cooling system to maintain the correct level.

9   The coolant level should be checked regularly. It must be between the Full and Low lines on the tank. The level will vary with the temperature of the engine. When the engine is cold, the coolant level should be at or slightly above the Low mark on the tank. Once the engine has warmed up, the level should be at or near the Full mark. If it isn't, allow the fluid in the tank to cool, then remove the cap from the reservoir and add coolant to bring the level up to the Full line. Use only ethylene/glycol type coolant and water in the mixture ratio recommended by your owner's manual. Do not use supplemental inhibitors or additives. If only a small amount of coolant is required to bring the system up to the proper level, water can be used. However, repeated additions of water will dilute the recommended antifreeze and water solution. In order to maintain the proper ratio of antifreeze and water, it is advisable to top up the coolant level with the correct mixture. Refer to your owner's manual for the recommended ratio.

10   If the coolant level drops within a short time after replenishment, there may be a leak in the system. Inspect the radiator, hoses, engine coolant filler cap, drain plugs, air bleeder plugs and water pump. If no leak is evident, have the radiator cap pressure tested. **Warning:** *Never remove the radiator pressure cap when the engine is running or has just been shut down, because the cooling system is hot. Escaping steam and scalding liquid could cause serious injury.*

11   If it is necessary to open the radiator cap, wait until the system has cooled completely, then wrap a thick cloth around the cap and turn it to the first stop. If any steam escapes,

wait until the system has cooled further, then remove the cap.

12   When checking the coolant level, always note its condition. It should be relatively clear. If it is brown or rust colored, the system should be drained, flushed and refilled. Even if the coolant appears to be normal, the corrosion inhibitors wear out with use, so it must be replaced at the specified intervals.

13   Do not allow antifreeze to come in contact with your skin or painted surfaces of the vehicle. Flush contacted areas immediately with plenty of water.

Windshield washer fluid

Refer to illustration 4.14

14   Fluid for the windshield washer system is stored in a plastic reservoir which is located at the right front corner of the engine compartment **(see illustration)**. In milder climates, plain water can be used to top up the reservoir, but the reservoir should be kept no more than two-thirds full to allow for expansion should the water freeze. In colder climates, the use of a specially designed windshield washer fluid, available at your dealer and any auto parts store, will help lower the freezing point of the fluid. Mix the solution with water in accordance with the manufacturer's directions on the container. Do not use regular antifreeze. It will damage the vehicle's paint.

Brake and clutch fluid

Refer to illustration 4.16

15   The brake master cylinder is mounted on the front of the power booster unit in the engine compartment. The clutch cylinder, used with a manual transaxle, is located next to the master cylinder.

16   To check the fluid level of the brake

master cylinder reservoir, simply look at the MAX and MIN marks on the reservoir **(see illustration)**. To check the fluid level of the clutch master cylinder reservoir, note whether the fluid level is even with the maximum level line.

17   If the level is low for either reservoir, wipe the top of the reservoir cover with a clean rag to prevent contamination of the brake or clutch system before removing the cap.

18   Add only the specified brake fluid to the brake or clutch reservoir (refer to *Recommended lubricants and fluids* in this Chapter's Specifications or to your owner's manual). Mixing different types of brake fluid can damage the system. **Warning:** *Use caution when filling either reservoir - brake fluid can harm your eyes and damage painted surfaces. Do not use brake fluid that has been opened for more than one year or has been left open. Brake fluid absorbs moisture from the air. Excess moisture can cause a dangerous loss of braking.*

19   While the reservoir cap is removed, inspect the master cylinder reservoir for contamination. If deposits, dirt particles or water droplets are present, the system should be drained and refilled.

20   After filling the reservoir to the proper level, make sure the lid is properly seated to prevent fluid leakage and/or system pressure loss.

21   The brake fluid in the master cylinder will drop slightly as the brake pads at each wheel wear down during normal operation.

22   If the master cylinder requires repeated replenishing to keep it at the proper level, this is an indication of leakage in the brake system, which should be corrected immediately. Check all brake lines and connections, along with the calipers and booster (see Section 13 for more information).

4.26 The power steering fluid reservoir is located on the right side of the engine compartment - the reservoir is translucent so the fluid level can be checked either hot or cold without removing the cap

5.2 Use a tire tread depth gauge to monitor tire wear - they are available at auto parts stores and service stations and cost very little

Power steering fluid level check

Refer to illustration 4.26

23   Unlike manual steering, the power steering system relies on fluid which may, over a period of time, require replenishing.

24   The fluid reservoir for the power steering pump is located on the right (passenger's side) inner fender panel near the front of the engine.

25   For the check, the front wheels should be pointed straight ahead and the engine should be off.

26   The reservoir is translucent plastic and the fluid level can be checked visually **(see illustration)**.

27   If additional fluid is required, pour the specified type directly into the reservoir, using a funnel to prevent spills.

28   If the reservoir requires frequent fluid additions, all power steering hoses, hose connections, the power steering pump and the rack and pinion assembly should be carefully checked for leaks.

5   Tire and tire pressure checks (every 250 miles or weekly)

Refer to illustrations 5.2, 5.3, 5.4a, 5.4b and 5.8

1   Periodic inspection of the tires may spare you from the inconvenience of being stranded with a flat tire. It can also provide you with vital information regarding possible problems in the steering and suspension systems before major damage occurs.

2   Normal tread wear can be monitored with a simple, inexpensive device known as a tread depth indicator **(see illustration)**. When the tread depth reaches the specified minimum, replace the tire(s).

3   Note any abnormal tread wear **(see illustration)**. Tread pattern irregularities such as cupping, flat spots and more wear on one side than the other are indications of front end alignment and/or balance problems. If any of these conditions are noted, take the vehicle to a tire shop or service station to correct the problem.

UNDERINFLATION

CUPPING

Cupping may be caused by:
- Underinflation and/or mechanical irregularities such as out-of-balance condition of wheel and/or tire, and bent or damaged wheel.
- Loose or worn steering tie-rod or steering idler arm.
- Loose, damaged or worn front suspension parts.

OVERINFLATION

INCORRECT TOE-IN OR EXTREME CAMBER

FEATHERING DUE TO MISALIGNMENT

5.3 This chart will help you determine the condition of the tires, the probable cause(s) of abnormal wear and the corrective action necessary

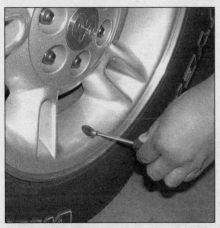

5.4a If a tire loses air on a steady basis, check the valve core first to make sure it's snug (a special inexpensive wrench is commonly available at auto parts stores)

5.4b If the valve core is tight, raise the corner of the vehicle with the low tire and spray a soapy water solution onto the tread as the tire is turned slowly - leaks will cause small bubbles to appear

5.8 To extend the life of the tires, check the air pressure at least once a week with an accurate gauge (don't forget the spare)

4   Look closely for cuts, punctures and embedded nails or tacks. Sometimes a tire will hold its air pressure for a short time or leak down very slowly even after a nail has embedded itself into the tread. If a slow leak persists, check the valve stem core to make sure it is tight **(see illustration)**. Examine the tread for an object that may have embedded itself into the tire or for a plug that may have begun to leak (radial tire punctures are repaired with a plug that is fitted in a puncture). If a puncture is suspected, it can be easily verified by spraying a solution of soapy water onto the puncture area **(see illustration)**. The soapy solution will bubble if there is a leak. Unless the puncture is inordinately large, a tire shop or gas station can usually repair the punctured tire.
5   Carefully inspect the inner sidewall of each tire for evidence of brake fluid leakage. If you see any, inspect the brakes immediately.
6   Correct tire air pressure adds miles to the lifespan of the tires, improves mileage and enhances overall ride quality. Tire pressure cannot be accurately estimated by looking at a tire, particularly if it is a radial. A tire pressure gauge is therefore essential. Keep an accurate gauge in the glove box. The pressure gauges fitted to the nozzles of air hoses at gas stations are often inaccurate.
7   Always check tire pressure when the tires are cold. "Cold," in this case, means the vehicle has not been driven over a mile in the three hours preceding a tire pressure check. A pressure rise of four to eight pounds is not uncommon once the tires are warm.
8   Unscrew the valve cap protruding from the wheel or hubcap and push the gauge firmly onto the valve **(see illustration)**. Note the reading on the gauge and compare this figure to the recommended tire pressure shown on the tire placard in the glove box. Be sure to reinstall the valve cap to keep dirt and mois-

ture out of the valve stem mechanism. Check all four tires and, if necessary, add enough air to bring them up to the recommended pressure levels.
9   Don't forget to keep the spare tire inflated to the specified pressure (consult your owner's manual). Note that the air pressure specified for a compact spare is significantly higher than the pressure of the regular tires.

6   Engine oil and oil filter change (every 3000 miles or 3 months)

Refer to illustrations 6.2 and 6.7
1   Frequent oil changes are the best preventive maintenance the home mechanic can give the engine, because aging oil becomes diluted and contaminated, which leads to premature engine wear.
2   Make sure that you have all the necessary tools before you begin this procedure **(see illustration)**. You should also have plenty of rags or newspapers handy for mopping up any spills.
3   Park the vehicle on a level spot. Start the engine and allow it to reach its normal operating temperature (the needle on the temperature gauge should be at least above the bottom mark). Warm oil and sludge will flow out more easily. Turn off the engine when it's warmed up.
4   Remove the filler cap in the rear cam cover.
5   Raise the vehicle and support it securely on jackstands. **Warning:** *To avoid personal injury, never get beneath the vehicle when it is supported by only by a jack. The jack provided with your vehicle is designed solely for raising the vehicle to remove and replace the wheels. Always use jackstands to support the vehicle when it becomes necessary to place*

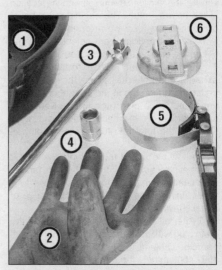

6.2 These tools are required when changing the engine oil and filter

1   *Drain pan* - It should be fairly shallow in depth, but wide to prevent spills
2   *Rubber gloves* - When removing the drain plug and filter, you will get oil on your hands (the gloves will prevent burns)
3   *Breaker bar* - Sometimes the oil drain plug is tight, and a long breaker bar is needed to loosen it
4   *Socket* - To be used with the breaker bar or a ratchet (must be the correct size to fit the drain plug)
5   *Filter wrench* - This is a metal band-type wrench, which requires clearance around the filter to be effective
6   *Filter wrench* - This type fits on the bottom of the filter and can be turned with a ratchet or breaker bar (different-size wrenches are available for different types of filters)

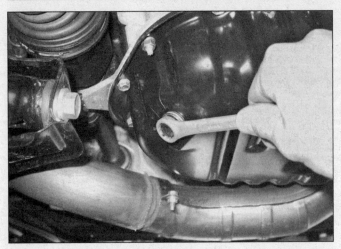

6.7   Use the proper size box-end wrench or socket to remove the oil drain plug without rounding off the corners

6.12   Location of the oil filter on 2009 and earlier four-cylinder models

your body underneath the vehicle.

6   If this is your first oil change, get under the vehicle and familiarize yourself with the location of the oil drain plug. The engine and exhaust components will be warm during the actual work, so try to anticipate any potential problems before the engine and accessories are hot.

7   Being careful not to touch the hot exhaust components, place the drain pan under the drain plug in the bottom of the pan and remove the plug **(see illustration)**. You may want to wear gloves while unscrewing the plug the final few turns if the engine is really hot.

8   Allow the old oil to drain into the pan. It may be necessary to move the pan farther under the engine as the oil flow slows to a trickle. Inspect the old oil for the presence of metal shavings and chips.

9   After all the oil has drained, wipe off the drain plug with a clean rag. Even minute metal particles clinging to the plug would immediately contaminate the new oil.

10   Clean the area around the drain plug opening, reinstall the plug and tighten it to the torque listed in this Chapter's Specifications.

11   Move the drain pan into position under the oil filter.

2009 and earlier four-cylinder models

Refer to illustrations 6.12 and 6.14

12   Loosen the oil filter **(see illustration)** by turning it counterclockwise with the filter wrench. Any standard filter wrench should work. Once the filter is loose, use your hands to unscrew it from the block. Just as the filter is detached from the block, immediately tilt the open end up to prevent the oil inside the filter from spilling out. **Warning:** *The engine exhaust manifold may still be hot, so be careful.*

13   With a clean rag, wipe off the mounting surface on the block. If a residue of old oil is allowed to remain, it will smoke when the block is heated up. It will also prevent the new filter from seating properly. Also make sure that none of the old gasket remains stuck to

the mounting surface. It can be removed with a scraper if necessary.

14   Compare the old filter with the new one to make sure they are the same type. Smear some engine oil on the rubber gasket of the new filter and screw it into place **(see illustration)**.

15   Because over-tightening the filter will damage the gasket, do not use a filter wrench to tighten the filter. Tighten it by hand until the gasket contacts the seating surface, then seat the filter by giving it an additional 3/4-turn. Lower the vehicle and proceed to Step 19.

2010 and later four-cylinder and all V6 models

Refer to illustrations 6.16a, 6.16b and 6.16c

16   Use a ratchet with an extension to remove the plug from the bottom of the oil filter housing, being careful to minimize the inevitable spillage **(see illustration)**. You can then use a blunt tool to push up the inner valve and allow the canister to drain **(see illustration)**.

6.14   Lubricate the oil filter gasket with clean engine oil before installing the filter on the engine

6.16a   Use a 3/8-inch drive extension to remove the oil filter housing drain plug - the entire filter housing can be removed instead, but it creates more spillage

6.16b   The filter housing can be drained by inserting a blunt tool to lift the drain valve - be sure to have the drain pan centered under the filter

6.16c The main filter housing can usually be unscrewed by hand - if it's stuck you'll have to use an oil filter wrench, but be careful as the housing can be easily damaged

7.4 On 2009 and earlier four-cylinder models, the automatic transaxle dipstick is located next to the battery

7.6 If the automatic transaxle fluid is cold, the level should be between the lower two notches; if it's at normal operating temperature, the level should be between the upper notches on the dipstick (2009 and earlier four-cylinder models)

Note: *A special tool is available for this that includes a drain hose in order to make the job as clean as possible.* Unscrew the main oil filter housing. If it's too tight to be removed by hand, you can use an oil filter wrench (**see illustration**).

17   Remove the filter element and the large O-ring from the housing. **Note:** *Don't use a metal tool to remove the O-ring, as this may scratch the soft housing.*

18   Carefully clean all components and the engine block sealing area. Install a new O-ring and filter, then screw the assembly back onto the engine. Tighten it to the torque listed in this Chapter's Specifications. If you removed the drain plug, clean it thoroughly, install a new O-ring and tighten the plug to the torque listed in this Chapter's Specifications. Lower the vehicle.

All models

19   Add new oil to the engine through the oil filler cap in the valve cover. Use a funnel to prevent oil from spilling onto the top of the engine. Pour four (four-cylinder engines) or five (V6 engine) quarts of fresh oil into the engine. Wait a few minutes to allow the oil to drain into the pan, then check the level on the oil dipstick (see Section 4 if necessary). If the oil level is at or near the F mark, install the filler cap hand tight, start the engine and allow the new oil to circulate.

20   Allow the engine to run for about a minute. While the engine is running, look under the vehicle and check for leaks at the oil pan drain plug and around the oil filter. If either is leaking, stop the engine and tighten the plug or filter slightly.

21   Wait a few minutes to allow the oil to trickle down into the pan, then recheck the level on the dipstick and, if necessary, add enough oil to bring the level to the F mark.

22   During the first few trips after an oil change, make it a point to check frequently for leaks and proper oil level.

23   The old oil drained from the engine cannot be reused in its present state and should be discarded. Oil reclamation centers, auto garages and gas stations will normally accept the oil, which can be refined and used again. After the oil has cooled, it can be drained into a suitable container (capped plastic jugs, topped bottles, milk cartons, etc.) for transport to one of these disposal sites.

Service reminder light resetting

24   Turn the ignition key to the On position and depress the button to the right of the speedometer until the odometer is displayed.

25   Turn the ignition key to the Off position.

26   Depress the button again and hold it, then turn the ignition key to the On position. Hold the button in the depressed position for five seconds.

27   The odometer should indicate "000000" and the MAINT REQD light should turn off.

---

7   Automatic transaxle fluid level check (see *Maintenance schedule* for service interval)

---

1   The level of the automatic transaxle fluid should be carefully maintained. Low fluid level can lead to slipping or loss of drive, while overfilling can cause foaming, loss of fluid and transaxle damage.

2   The transaxle fluid level should only be checked when the transaxle is hot (at its normal operating temperature). If the vehicle has just been driven over 10 miles (15 miles in a frigid climate), and the fluid temperature

is 160 to 175-degrees F, the transaxle is hot. **Caution:** *If the vehicle has just been driven for a long time at high speed or in city traffic in hot weather, or if it has been pulling a trailer, an accurate fluid level reading cannot be obtained. Allow the fluid to cool down for about 30 minutes.*

3   If the vehicle has not been driven, park the vehicle on level ground, set the parking brake, then start the engine and bring it to operating temperature. While the engine is idling, deprss the brake pedal and move the selector lever through all the gear ranges, beginning and ending in Park.

2009 and earlier four-cylinder models (U250E transaxle)

Refer to illustrations 7.4 and 7.6

4   With the engine still idling, remove the dipstick from its tube (**see illustration**). Check the level of the fluid on the dipstick and note its condition. Refer to the underhood photographs at the beginning of this Chapter for the exact location of the automatic transaxle dipstick.

5   Wipe the fluid from the dipstick with a clean rag and reinsert it back into the filler tube until the cap seats.

6   Pull the dipstick out again and note the fluid level (**see illustration**). If the transmission is cold, the level should be in the COOL range on the dipstick. If it is hot, the fluid level should be in the HOT range. If the level is at the low side of either range, add the specified automatic transmission fluid through the dipstick tube with a funnel.

7   Add just enough of the recommended fluid to fill the transmission to the proper level. It takes about one pint to raise the level from the low mark to the high mark when the fluid is hot, so add the fluid a little at a time and keep checking the level until it is correct. Proceed to Step 12.

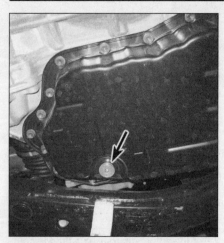

7.8 Transaxle fluid overflow plug (U660E/
U760E transaxles)

8.5 Pull up the tab to release the wiper
blade frame assembly from the wiper arm

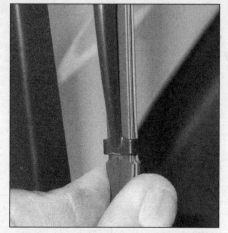

8.6 Squeeze the end of the wiper element
and pull it straight out of the frame

2010 and later four-cylinder models and all V6 models

Refer to illustration 7.8

Note: *These models are not equipped with an automatic transaxle fluid dipstick.*

Note: *The vehicle must be level for this check. If there is not enough room to crawl under the vehicle, raise both ends and support it securely on jackstands.*

Note: *The fluid temperature must be between 95 to 113-degrees F (35 to 45-degrees C) on four-cylinder (U760E) and 104 to 113-degrees F (40 to 45-degrees C) on V6 (U660E) models to perform this check.*

8   Set the parking brake and block the rear wheels. With the engine idling, remove the overflow plug from the bottom of the transaxle fluid pan (**see illustration**).

9   If the fluid runs out of the hole, allow it to drip until it stops. If no fluid comes out of the hole, remove the fill plug, located on the side of the transaxle housing, near the rear.

10   Add the proper type of transmission fluid (see this Chapter's Specifications) until fluid flows from the overflow hole in the bottom

of the pan. When the flow of fluid slows to a trickle, install the overflow plug and tighten it to the torque listed in this Chapter's Specifications.

11   Tighten the fill plug to the torque listed in this Chapter's Specifications.

All models

12   The condition of the fluid should also be checked along with the level. If the fluid at the end of the dipstick (if equipped) is black or a dark reddish brown color, or if it emits a burned smell, the fluid should be changed (see Section 25). If you are in doubt about the condition of the fluid, purchase some new fluid and compare the two for color and smell.

---

8   Windshield wiper blade inspection and replacement (every 5000 miles or 6 months)

Refer to illustrations 8.5, 8.6, 8.7 and 8.8

1   The windshield wiper and blade assembly should be inspected periodically for dam-

age, loose components and cracked or worn blade elements.

2   Road film can build up on the wiper blades and affect their efficiency, so they should be washed regularly with a mild detergent solution.

3   The action of the wiping mechanism can loosen bolts, nuts and fasteners, so they should be checked and tightened, as necessary, at the same time the wiper blades are checked.

4   If the wiper blade elements are cracked, worn or warped, or no longer clean adequately, they should be replaced with new ones.

5   Lift the arm assembly away from the glass, then flip up the tab to release the wiper blade frame assembly from the wiper arm (**see illustration**).

6   Squeeze the end of the wiper element and pull it out of the frame (**see illustration**).

7   Insert the end of the new element without cutouts into the end of the frame (**see illustration**).

8   Work the rubber along the slot in the blade frame until the cutouts are locked into place by the wiper frame claw (**see illustration**).

---

9   Battery check, maintenance and charging (every 5000 miles or 6 months)

Warning: *Certain precautions must be followed when checking and servicing the battery. Hydrogen gas, which is highly flammable, is always present in the battery cells, so keep lighted tobacco and all other open flames and sparks away from the battery. The electrolyte inside the battery is actually dilute sulfuric acid, which will cause injury if splashed on your skin or in your eyes. It will also ruin clothes and painted surfaces. When removing the battery cables, always detach the negative cable first and hook it up last!*

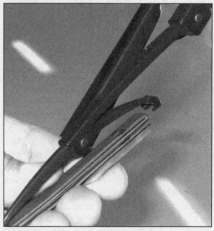

8.7 Insert the end without the cutout into
the frame

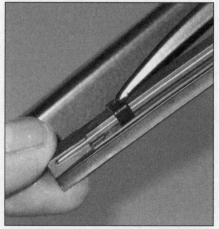

8.8 Slide the element into place until the
cutouts seat into the locking claw

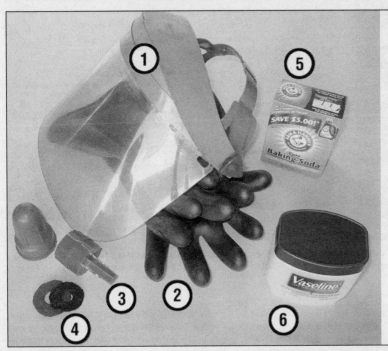

9.1 Tools and materials required for battery maintenance

1   *Face shield/safety goggles - When removing corrosion with a brush, the acidic particles can easily fly up into your eyes*
2   *Rubber gloves - Another safety item to consider when servicing the battery; remember that's acid inside the battery!*
3   *Battery post/cable cleaner - This wire brush cleaning tool will remove all traces of corrosion from the battery posts and cable clamps*
4   *Treated felt washers - Placing one of these on each post, directly under the cable clamps, will help prevent corrosion*
5   *Baking soda - A solution of baking soda and water can be used to neutralize corrosion*
6   *Petroleum jelly - A layer of this on the battery posts will help prevent corrosion*

Check

Refer to illustration 9.1

1   A routine preventive maintenance program for the battery in your vehicle is the only way to ensure quick and reliable starts. But before performing any battery maintenance, make sure that you have the proper equipment necessary to work safely around the battery **(see illustration)**.

2   There are also several precautions that should be taken whenever battery maintenance is performed. Before servicing the battery, always turn the engine and all accessories off and disconnect the cable from the negative terminal of the battery.

3   The battery produces hydrogen gas, which is both flammable and explosive. Never create a spark, smoke or light a match around the battery. Always charge the battery in a ventilated area.

4   Electrolyte contains poisonous and corrosive sulfuric acid. Do not allow it to get in your eyes, on your skin or your clothes. Never ingest it. Wear protective safety glasses when working near the battery. Keep children away from the battery.

5   Note the external condition of the battery. If the positive terminal and cable clamp on your vehicle's battery is equipped with a rubber protector, make sure that it's not torn or damaged. It should completely cover the terminal. Look for any corroded or loose connections, cracks in the case or cover, or loose hold-down clamps. Also check the entire length of each cable for cracks and frayed conductors.

6   Some models with sealed batteries have a battery condition indicator on top of the bat-

tery. Compare the color showing in the window to the condition color chart on the battery. You may catch a low-charge battery condition before it strands you on the roadside. If the color indicates a low state of charge, charge the battery and examine the charging system (see Chapter 5 and this Section).

Maintenance

Refer to illustrations 9.7a, 9.7b, 9.8a, 9.8b and 9.13

7   If corrosion, which looks like white, fluffy deposits **(see illustration)** is evident, particularly around the terminals, the battery should be removed for cleaning. Loosen the cable clamp bolts with a wrench, being careful to remove the negative cable first, and slide them off the terminals **(see illustration)**. Then

9.7a Battery terminal corrosion usually appears as light, fluffy powder

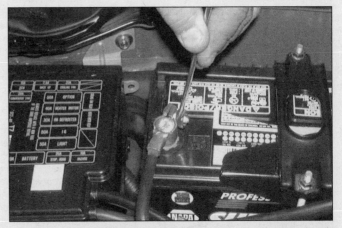

9.7b Loosen the battery cable clamp bolt with a wrench - sometimes special battery pliers are required for this procedure if corrosion has deteriorated the hex nut - always remove the negative cable first and reconnect it last!

9.8a When cleaning the cable clamps, all corrosion must be removed (the inside of the clamp is tapered to match the taper on the post, so don't remove too much material)

9.8b Regardless of the type of tool used on the battery posts, a clean, shiny surface should be the result

disconnect the hold-down clamp bolt and nut, remove the clamp and lift the battery from the engine compartment.

8   Clean the cable clamps thoroughly with a battery brush or a terminal cleaner and a solution of warm water and baking soda. Wash the terminals and the top of the battery case with the same solution but make sure that the solution doesn't get into the battery. When cleaning the cables, terminals and battery top, wear safety goggles and rubber gloves to prevent any solution from coming in contact with your eyes or hands. Wear old clothes too - even diluted, sulfuric acid splashed onto clothes will burn holes in them. If the terminals have been extensively corroded, clean them up with a terminal cleaner **(see illustrations)**. Thoroughly wash all cleaned areas with plain water.

9   Whenever the battery is removed for cleaning or charging, inspect the battery carrier before reinstalling the battery in the engine compartment. If the carrier is dirty or covered with corrosion, clean it in the same solution of warm water and baking soda. Inspect the metal brackets which support the carrier to make sure that they are not covered with

9.13 Make sure the battery hold-down nuts are tight

corrosion. If they are, wash them off. If corrosion is extensive, sand the brackets down to bare metal and spray them with a zinc-based primer (available in spray cans at auto paint and body supply stores).

10   Reinstall the battery back into the engine compartment. Make sure that no parts or wires are laying on the carrier during installation of the battery. Information on removing and installing the battery can be found in Chapter 5. Information on jump starting can be found at the front of this manual. For more detailed battery checking procedures, refer to the *Haynes Automotive Electrical Manual*.

11   Install a pair of specially-treated felt washers around the terminals (available at auto parts stores), then coat the terminals and the cable clamps with petroleum jelly or grease to prevent further corrosion. Install the cable clamps and tighten the nuts, being careful to install the negative cable last.

12   Install the hold-down clamp and nuts. Tighten the nuts only enough to hold the battery firmly in place. Overtightening these nuts can crack the battery case.

13   Make sure that the battery tray is in good condition and the hold-down clamp bolts are tight **(see illustration)**. If the battery is removed from the tray, make sure no parts remain in the bottom of the tray when the battery is reinstalled. When reinstalling the hold-down clamp bolts, do not overtighten them.

Charging

Warning: *When batteries are being charged, hydrogen gas, which is very explosive and flammable, is produced. Do not smoke or allow open flames near a charging or a recently charged battery. Wear eye protection when near the battery during charging. Also, make sure the charger is unplugged before connecting or disconnecting the battery from the charger.*

14   Slow-rate charging is the best way to restore a battery that's discharged to the point where it will not start the engine. It's also a good way to maintain the battery charge in a

vehicle that's only driven a few miles between starts. Maintaining the battery charge is particularly important in the winter when the battery must work harder to start the engine and electrical accessories that drain the battery are in greater use.

15   It's best to use a one or two-amp battery charger (sometimes called a "trickle" charger). They are the safest and put the least strain on the battery. They are also the least expensive. For a faster charge, you can use a higher amperage charger, but don't use one rated more than 1/10th the amp/hour rating of the battery. Rapid boost charges that claim to restore the power of the battery in one to two hours are hardest on the battery and can damage batteries not in good condition. This type of charging should only be used in emergency situations.

16   The average time necessary to charge a battery should be listed in the instructions that come with the charger. As a general rule, a trickle charger will charge a battery in 12 to 16 hours.

10   Underhood hose check and replacement (every 5000 miles or 6 months)

Caution: *Replacement of air conditioning hoses must be left to a dealer service department or air conditioning shop that has the equipment to depressurize the system safely. Never remove air conditioning components or hoses until the system has been evacuated and the refrigerant recovered by a dealer service department or air conditioning shop.*

General

1   High temperatures in the engine compartment can cause the deterioration of the rubber and plastic hoses used for engine, accessory and emission systems operation. Periodic inspection should be made for cracks, loose clamps, material hardening and leaks.

2   Information specific to the cooling system hoses can be found in Section 11.

3   Some, but not all, hoses are secured to the fittings with clamps. Where clamps are used, check to be sure they haven't lost their tension, allowing the hose to leak. If clamps aren't used, make sure the hose has not expanded and/or hardened where it slips over the fitting, allowing it to leak.

Vacuum hoses

4   It's quite common for vacuum hoses, especially those in the emissions system, to be color coded or identified by colored stripes molded into them. Various systems require hoses with different wall thickness, collapse resistance and temperature resistance. When replacing hoses, be sure the new ones are made of the same material.

5   Often the only effective way to check a hose is to remove it completely from the vehicle. If more than one hose is removed, be sure to label the hoses and fittings to ensure correct installation.

6   When checking vacuum hoses, be sure to include any plastic T-fittings in the check. Inspect the fittings for cracks and the hose where it fits over the fitting for distortion, which could cause leakage.

7   A small piece of vacuum hose (1/4-inch inside diameter) can be used as a stethoscope to detect vacuum leaks. Hold one end of the hose to your ear and probe around vacuum hoses and fittings, listening for the hissing sound characteristic of a vacuum leak. **Warning:** *When probing with the vacuum hose stethoscope, be very careful not to come into contact with moving engine components such as the drivebelts, cooling fan, etc.*

Fuel hose

Warning: *There are certain precautions which must be taken when inspecting or servicing fuel system components. Work in a well ventilated area and do not allow open flames (cigarettes, appliance pilot lights, etc.) or bare light bulbs near the work area. Mop up any spills immediately and do not store fuel soaked rags where they could ignite.*

8   Check all rubber fuel lines for deterioration and chafing. Check especially for cracks in areas where the hose bends and just before fittings, such as where a hose attaches to the fuel filter.

9   High quality fuel line should be used for fuel line replacement. Never, under any circumstances, use unreinforced vacuum line, clear plastic tubing or water hose for fuel lines.

10   Spring-type clamps are commonly used on fuel lines. These clamps often lose their tension over a period of time, and can be sprung during removal. Replace all spring-type clamps with screw clamps whenever a hose is replaced.

Metal lines

11   Sections of metal line are often used for fuel line between the fuel pump and fuel injec-tion unit. Check carefully to be sure the line has not been bent or crimped and that cracks have not started in the line.

12   If a section of metal fuel line must be replaced, only seamless steel tubing should be used, since copper and aluminum tubing don't have the strength necessary to withstand normal engine vibration.

13   Check the metal brake lines where they enter the master cylinder and brake proportioning unit (if used) for cracks in the lines or loose fittings. Any sign of brake fluid leakage calls for an immediate thorough inspection of the brake system.

---

11   Cooling system check (every 5000 miles or 6 months)

Refer to illustration 11.4

1   Many major engine failures can be attributed to a faulty cooling system. If the vehicle is equipped with an automatic transaxle, the cooling system also cools the transaxle fluid and thus plays an important role in prolonging transaxle life.

2   The cooling system should be checked with the engine cold. Do this before the vehicle is driven for the day or after the engine has been shut off for at least three hours. **Warning:** *Never remove the radiator pressure cap when the engine is running or has just been shut down, because the cooling system is hot. Escaping steam and scalding liquid could cause serious injury.*

3   Remove the radiator pressure cap by turning it to the left until it reaches a stop. If you hear a hissing sound (indicating there is still pressure in the system), wait until it stops. Press down on the cap with the palm of your hand and continue turning to the left until the cap can be removed. Thoroughly clean the cap, inside and out, with clean water. Also clean the filler neck on the radiator. All traces of corrosion should be removed. The coolant inside the radiator should be relatively transparent. If it's rust colored, the system should be drained and refilled (see Section 29). If the coolant level isn't up to the top, add additional antifreeze/coolant mixture (see Section 4).

4   Carefully check the large upper and lower radiator hoses along with the smaller diameter heater hoses which run from the engine to the bulkhead. Inspect each hose along its entire length, replacing any hose which is cracked, swollen or shows signs of deterioration. Cracks may become more apparent if the hose is squeezed **(see illustration)**. Regardless of condition, it's a good idea to replace hoses with new ones every two years.

5   Make sure that all hose connections are tight. A leak in the cooling system will usually show up as white or rust colored deposits on the areas adjoining the leak. If wire-type clamps are used at the ends of the hoses, it may be a good idea to replace them with more secure screw-type clamps.

6   Use compressed air or a soft brush to

Check for a chafed area that could fail prematurely.

Check for a soft area indicating the hose has deteriorated inside.

Overtightening the clamp on a hardened hose will damage the hose and cause a leak.

Check each hose for swelling and oil-soaked ends. Cracks and breaks can be located by squeezing the hose.

11.4 Hoses, like drivebelts, have a habit of failing at the worst possible time - to prevent the inconvenience of a blown radiator or heater hose, inspect them carefully as shown here

remove bugs, leaves, etc. from the front of the radiator or air conditioning condenser. Be careful not to damage the delicate cooling fins or cut yourself on them.

7   Every other inspection, or at the first indication of cooling system problems, have the cap and system pressure tested. If you don't have a pressure tester, most gas stations and garages will do this for a minimal charge.

---

12   Tire rotation (every 5000 miles or 6 months)

Refer to illustrations 12.2a and 12.2b

1   The tires should be rotated at the specified intervals and whenever uneven wear is noticed. Since the vehicle will be raised and the tires removed anyway, check the brakes (see Section 13) at this time.

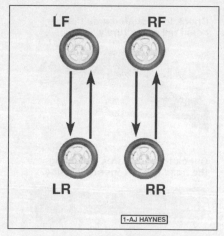

12.2a The recommended tire rotation pattern for directional tires

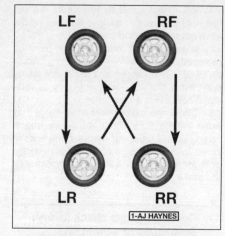

12.2b The recommended tire rotation pattern for non-directional tires

13.6 You'll find an inspection hole like this in each caliper through which you can view the inner brake pad lining

2   Radial tires must be rotated in a specific pattern **(see illustrations)**. Most models are equipped with non-directional tires, but some sport models may be equipped with directional tires, which have a specific rotational pattern. When choosing replacement tires, examine the sidewalls. Directional tires have arrows on the sidewall that indicate the direction they must turn, and a set of these tires includes two left-side tires and two right-side tires. The left and right side tires must not be rotated to the other side.

3   Refer to the information in *Jacking and towing* at the front of this manual for the proper procedures to follow when raising the vehicle and changing a tire. If the brakes are to be checked, do not apply the parking brake as stated. Make sure the tires are blocked to prevent the vehicle from rolling.

4   Preferably, the entire vehicle should be raised at the same time. This can be done on a hoist or by jacking up each corner and then lowering the vehicle onto jackstands placed under the frame rails. Always use four jackstands and make sure the vehicle is firmly supported.

5   After rotation, check and adjust the tire pressures as necessary and be sure to check the wheel lug nut torque.

6   For further information on the wheels and tires, refer to Chapter 10.

---

13   Brake check (every 5000 miles or 6 months)

Warning: *Dust created by the brake system is harmful to your health. Never blow it out with compressed air and don't inhale any of it. An approved filtering mask should be worn when working on the brakes. Do not, under any circumstances, use petroleum-based solvents to clean brake parts. Use brake system cleaner only!*
Note: *For detailed photographs of the brake system, refer to Chapter 9.*

1   In addition to the specified intervals, the brakes should be inspected every time the wheels are removed or whenever a defect is suspected. Any of the following symptoms could indicate a potential brake system defect: The vehicle pulls to one side when the brake pedal is depressed; the brakes make squealing or dragging noises when applied; brake travel is excessive; the pedal pulsates; brake fluid leaks, usually onto the inside of the tire or wheel.

2   The disc brake pads have built-in wear indicators which should make a high pitched squealing or scraping noise when they are worn to the replacement point. When you hear this noise, replace the pads immediately or expensive damage to the discs can result.

3   Loosen the wheel nuts.

4   Raise the vehicle and place it securely on jackstands.

5   Remove the wheels (see *Jacking and towing* at the front of this book, or your owner's manual, if necessary).

Disc brakes

Refer to illustration 13.6

6   There are two pads - an outer and an inner - in each caliper. The inner pad lining material is visible through inspection holes in each caliper **(see illustration)**.

7   Check the pad thickness by looking at each end of the caliper and through the inspection hole in the caliper body. If the lining material is less than the thickness listed in this Chapter's Specifications, replace the pads. **Note:** *Keep in mind that the lining material is riveted or bonded to a metal backing plate and the metal portion is not included in this measurement.*

8   If it is difficult to determine the exact thickness of the remaining pad material by the above method, or if you are at all concerned about the condition of the pads, remove the caliper(s), then remove the pads from the calipers for further inspection (see Chapter 9).

9   Once the pads are removed from the

calipers, clean them with brake cleaner and re-measure them with a small steel pocket ruler or a vernier caliper.

10   Measure the disc thickness with a micrometer to make sure that it still has service life remaining. If any disc is thinner than the specified minimum thickness, replace it (see Chapter 9). Even if the disc has service life remaining, check its condition. Look for scoring, gouging and burned spots. If these conditions exist, remove the disc and have it resurfaced (see Chapter 9).

11   Before installing the wheels, check all brake lines and hoses for damage, wear, deformation, cracks, corrosion, leakage, bends and twists, particularly in the vicinity of the rubber hoses at the calipers. Check the clamps for tightness and the connections for leakage. Make sure that all hoses and lines are clear of sharp edges, moving parts and the exhaust system. If any of the above conditions are noted, repair, reroute or replace the lines and/or fittings as necessary (see Chapter 9).

Rear parking brake shoes

Refer to illustration 13.15

12   Rear disc brakes incorporate a drum-type parking brake into the rear discs.

13   To check the parking brake shoe lining thickness without removing the brake discs, remove the rubber plug from the front of the disc and use a flashlight to inspect the linings. For a more thorough brake inspection, follow the procedure below.

14   Refer to Chapter 9 and remove the rear brake caliper and disc. **Warning:** *Brake dust produced by lining wear and deposited on brake components is hazardous to your health. DO NOT blow it out with compressed air and DO NOT inhale it!*

15   Note the thickness of the lining material on the rear parking brake shoes **(see illustration)**. If the lining material is within 1/16-inch of the recessed rivets or metal shoes, replace the parking brake shoes with new ones. The shoes should also be replaced if they are

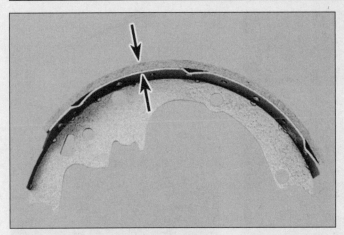

13.15 If the lining is bonded to the brake shoe, measure the lining thickness from the outer surface to the metal shoe; if the lining is riveted to the shoe, measure from the lining outer surface to the rivet head

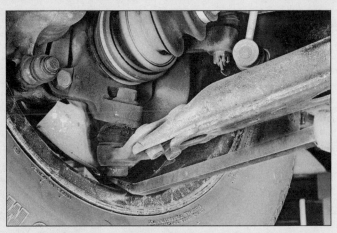

14.7 To check the balljoints, attempt to move the lower arm up and down with a prybar to make sure there is no play in the balljoint (if there is, replace it)

cracked, glazed (shiny lining surfaces) or contaminated. See Chapter 9 for the replacement procedure.

16   Check the shoe return and hold-down springs and the adjusting mechanism to make sure they're fitted correctly and in good condition. Deteriorated or distorted springs, if not replaced, could allow the linings to drag and wear prematurely.

17   Check the drum side of the brake discs for cracks, score marks, deep scratches and hard spots, which will appear as small discolored areas. If imperfections cannot be removed with emery cloth, the discs must be resurfaced by an automotive machine shop (see Chapter 9 for more detailed information).

18   Refer to Chapter 9 and install the brake rotors and calipers.

19   Install the wheels and snug the wheel nuts finger tight.

20   Remove the jackstands and lower the vehicle.

21   Tighten the wheel nuts to the torque listed in this Chapter's Specifications.

Brake booster check

22   Sit in the driver's seat and perform the following sequence of tests.

23   With the brake fully depressed, start the engine - the pedal should move down a little when the engine starts.

24   With the engine running, depress the brake pedal several times - the travel distance should not change.

25   Depress the brake, stop the engine and hold the pedal in for about 30 seconds - the pedal should neither sink nor rise.

26   Restart the engine, run it for about a minute and turn it off. Then firmly depress the brake several times - the pedal travel should decrease with each application.

27   If your brakes do not operate as described above when the preceding tests are performed, the brake booster is either in need of repair or has failed. Refer to Chapter 9 for the removal procedure.

Parking brake

28   Slowly pull up on the parking brake handle or push down on the parking brake pedal and count the number of clicks you hear until the handle is up (or the pedal down) as far as it will go. The adjustment is correct if you hear the specified number of clicks. If you hear more or fewer clicks, it's time to adjust the parking brake (see Chapter 9).

29   An alternative method of checking the parking brake is to park the vehicle on a steep hill with the parking brake set and the transaxle in Neutral. If the parking brake cannot prevent the vehicle from rolling, it is in need of adjustment (see Chapter 9).

---

14   Steering, suspension and driveaxle boot check (every 15,000 miles or 18 months)

Steering check

Note: *For detailed illustrations of the steering and suspension components, refer to Chapter 10.*

1   With the vehicle on the ground and the front wheels pointed straight ahead, rock the steering wheel gently back and forth. If freeplay is excessive, a front wheel bearing, main shaft yoke, intermediate shaft yoke, lower arm balljoint or steering system joint is worn or the steering gear is out of adjustment or broken. Steering wheel freeplay is the amount of travel (measured at the rim of the steering wheel) between the initial steering input and the point at which the front wheels begin to turn (indicated by slight resistance). Refer to Chapter 10 for the appropriate repair procedure.

2   Other symptoms, such as excessive vehicle body movement over rough roads, swaying (leaning) around corners and binding as the steering wheel is turned, may indicate faulty steering and/or suspension components.

Suspension check

Refer to illustrations 14.7 and 14.8

3   Check the shock absorbers by pushing down and releasing the vehicle several times at each corner. If the vehicle does not come back to a level position within one or two bounces, the shocks/struts are worn and must be replaced. When bouncing the vehicle up and down, listen for squeaks and noises from the suspension components. Additional information on suspension components can be found in Chapter 10.

4   Raise the vehicle with a floor jack and support it securely on jackstands. See *Jacking and towing* at the front of this book for the proper jacking points.

5   Check the tires for irregular wear patterns and proper inflation. See Section 5 in this Chapter for information regarding tire wear and Chapter 10 for the wheel bearing replacement procedures.

6   Inspect the universal joint between the steering shaft and the steering gear housing. Check the steering gear housing for lubricant leakage or oozing. Make sure that the dust seals and boots are not damaged and that the boot clamps are not loose. Check the steering linkage for looseness or damage. Check the tie-rod ends for excessive play. Look for loose bolts, broken or disconnected parts and deteriorated rubber bushings on all suspension and steering components. While an assistant turns the steering wheel from side to side, check the steering components for free movement, chafing and binding. If the steering components do not seem to be reacting with the movement of the steering wheel, try to determine where the slack is located.

7   Check the balljoints for wear by trying to move each lower arm up and down with a prybar **(see illustration)** to ensure that its balljoint has no play. If any balljoint does have play, replace it. See Chapter 10 for the balljoint replacement procedure.

14.8 Push on the balljoint boot to check for tears and grease leaks

14.10 Flex the driveaxle boots by hand to check for tears, cracks and leaking grease

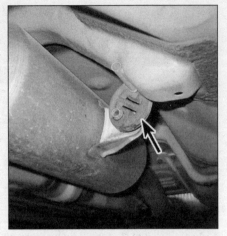

15.2 Check the exhaust system for damage, or worn rubber hangers

8   Inspect the balljoint boots for damage and leaking grease **(see illustration)**. Replace the balljoints with new ones if they are damaged (see Chapter 10).

Driveaxle boot check

Refer to illustration 14.10

9   The driveaxle boots are very important because they prevent dirt, water and foreign material from entering and damaging the constant velocity (CV) joints.

10   Inspect the boots for tears and cracks as well as loose clamps **(see illustration)**. If there is any evidence of cracks or leaking lubricant, they must be replaced as described in Chapter 8.

15   Exhaust system check (every 15,000 miles or 18 months)

Refer to illustration 15.2

1   With the engine cold (at least three hours

after the vehicle has been driven), check the complete exhaust system from its starting point at the engine to the end of the tailpipe. This should be done on a hoist where unrestricted access is available.

2   Check the pipes and connections for evidence of leaks, severe corrosion or damage. Make sure that all brackets and hangers are in good condition and tight **(see illustration)**.

3   At the same time, inspect the underside of the body for holes, corrosion, open seams, etc. which may allow exhaust gases to enter the passenger compartment. Seal all body openings with silicone or body putty.

4   Rattles and other noises can often be traced to the exhaust system, especially the mounts and hangers. Try to move the pipes, silencer and catalytic converter. If the components can come in contact with the body or suspension parts, secure the exhaust system with new mounts.

5   Check the running condition of the engine by inspecting inside the end of the tailpipe. The exhaust deposits here are an indi-

cation of engine state-of-tune. If the pipe is black and sooty or coated with white deposits, the engine is in need of a tune-up, including a thorough fuel system inspection.

16   Air filter replacement (every 30,000 miles or 36 months)

Refer to illustrations 16.1a, 16.1b and 16.2

1   The air filter is located inside a housing at the left (driver's) side of the engine compartment. On four-cylinder models, unscrew the bolts retaining the two halves of the air cleaner housing **(see illustration)**; on V6 models, release the spring clips that keep the two halves together **(see illustration)**.

2   Lift the cover up and remove the air filter element **(see illustration)**.

3   Inspect the outer surface of the filter element. If it is dirty, replace it. If it is only moderately dusty, it can be reused by blow-

16.1a Unscrew the two bolts securing the air filter housing lid - four cylinder models

16.1b Unlatch the clips securing the air filter housing lid - V6 models

16.2 Lift the cover up and remove the filter

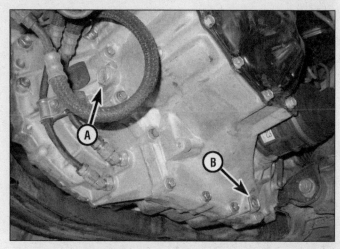

18.1 Remove the fill plug to check the manual transaxle lubricant level - the level should be at the bottom of the hole

| A | Check/fill plug | B | Drain plug |

ing it clean from the back to the front surface with compressed air. **Warning:** *Always wear eye protection when using compressed air!* Because it is a pleated paper type filter, it cannot be washed or oiled. If it cannot be cleaned satisfactorily with compressed air, discard and replace it. **Caution:** *Never drive the vehicle with the air cleaner removed. Excessive engine wear could result and backfiring could even cause a fire under the hood.*

4   Installation is the reverse of removal. Make sure the hinge tabs on the housing cover engage properly with the lower part of the housing.

17 Fuel system check (every 30,000 miles or 36 months)

Warning: *Certain precautions should be observed when inspecting or servicing the fuel system components. Work in a well-ventilated area and do not allow open flames (cigarettes, appliance pilot lights, etc.) near the work area. Mop up spills immediately and do not store fuel-soaked rags where they could ignite. It is a good idea to keep a dry chemical (Class B) fire extinguisher near the work area any time the fuel system is being serviced.*

1   If you smell fuel while driving or after the vehicle has been sitting in the sun, inspect the fuel system immediately.

2   Remove the fuel filler cap and inspect if for damage and corrosion. The gasket should have an unbroken sealing imprint. If the gasket is damaged, remove it and install a new one (see Section 21).

3   Inspect the fuel feed and return lines for cracks. Make sure that the threaded flare nut type connectors (which secure the metal fuel lines to the fuel injection system) and the

banjo bolts (which secure the banjo fittings to the in-line fuel filter) are tight.

4   Since some components of the fuel system - the fuel tank and part of the fuel feed line, for example - are underneath the vehicle, they can be inspected more easily with the vehicle raised on a hoist. If that's not possible, raise the vehicle and support it securely on jackstands.

5   With the vehicle raised and safely supported, inspect the fuel tank and filler neck for punctures, cracks and other damage. The connection between the filler neck and the tank is particularly critical. Sometimes a rubber filler neck will leak because of loose clamps or deteriorated rubber. These are problems a home mechanic can usually rectify. **Warning:** *Do not, under any circumstances, try to repair a fuel tank (except rubber components). A welding torch or any open flame can easily cause fuel vapors inside the tank to explode.*

6   Carefully check all rubber hoses and metal lines leading away from the fuel tank. Check for loose connections, deteriorated hoses, crimped lines and other damage. Carefully inspect the lines from the tank to the fuel injection system. Repair or replace damaged sections as necessary (see Chapter 4).

18 Manual transaxle lubricant level check (every 30,000 miles or 36 months)

Refer to illustration 18.1

1   The manual transaxle does not have a dipstick. To check the fluid level, raise the vehicle and support it securely on jackstands. On the lower front side of the transaxle housing, you will see a plug **(see illustration)**

- remove it. If the lubricant level is correct, it should be up to the lower edge of the hole.

2   If the transaxle needs more lubricant (if the level is not up to the hole), use a syringe or a gear oil pump to add more. Stop filling the transaxle when the lubricant begins to run out the hole.

3   Install the plug and tighten it securely. Drive the vehicle a short distance, then check for leaks.

19 Cabin air filter replacement (every 30,000 miles or 36 months)

Refer to illustrations 19.3 and 19.4

1   There is an air filter in the blower housing that cleans the air before it enters the passenger compartment.

2   Remove the glove box (see Chapter 11).

3   Depress the filter cover retaining tabs and remove the cover **(see illustration)**.

19.3 Push in the cabin air filter cover tabs and remove the cover

19.4 Slide the filter out from the housing

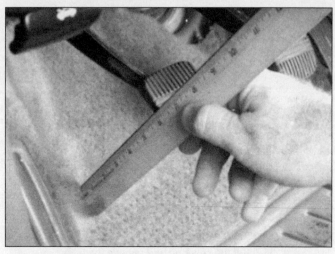

20.1 To check the pedal height, measure the distance between the natural resting place of the pedal and the floor

4   Remove the air filter element **(see illustration)**.
5   Installation is the reverse of removal.

20   Clutch/brake pedal height and freeplay - check and adjustment (every 30,000 miles or 36 months)

Pedal height

Refer to illustrations 20.1 and 20.2

1   The height of the clutch or brake pedal is the distance the pedal sits off the floor **(see illustration)**. If the pedal height is not within Specifications, it must be adjusted.
2   To adjust the brake pedal, loosen the locknut and back the pushrod out for clearance. Turn the pushrod to adjust the pedal height in the middle of the specified range, then retighten the locknut **(see illustration)**.

3   At the clutch pedal, loosen the locknut on the clutch switch and retract the switch. Before measuring the clutch pedal height, make sure the pedal is in the fully-returned position. Measure the pedal height and adjust if necessary (see Step 2).
4   Adjust the brake pedal switch by turning it clockwise until the switch body just contacts the pedal arm. Rotate it counterclockwise to gain the clearance listed in this Chapter's Specifications and tighten the switch locknut.

Pedal freeplay

Refer to illustration 20.5

5   Freeplay is the pedal slack, or the distance the pedal can be depressed before it begins to have any effect on the clutch or brake system **(see illustration)**. If the pedal freeplay is not within the specified range, it must be adjusted.
6   To adjust the clutch pedal freeplay,

loosen the locknut on the clutch pushrod. Back out the pushrod to adjust the freeplay to the specified range, then retighten the locknut.
7   Before adjusting brake pedal freeplay, depress the brake pedal several times (with the engine off). Measure the freeplay and adjust if necessary. Loosen the locknut on the pushrod, then back off the pushrod to adjust the pedal freeplay to the specified range and retighten the locknut.

Brake pedal reserve distance

8   With the parking brake released and the engine running, depress the pedal with normal braking effort and have an assistant measure the distance from the center of the pedal pad to the floor. If the distance is less than specified, refer to Chapter 9 and troubleshoot the brake system.

20.2 Loosen the pedal pushrod locknut, then adjust the pushrod to achieve proper pedal height

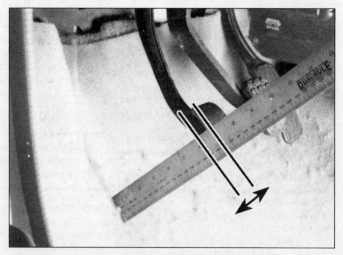

20.5 Pedal freeplay is the distance between the natural resting point of the pedal to the point at which resistance is felt

21   Fuel tank cap gasket inspection and replacement (every 30,000 miles or 36 months)

Refer to illustration 21.2

1   Remove the tank cap and inspect the rubber gasket for cracks or tears.
2   If replacement is necessary, carefully pry the old gasket out of the recess **(see illustration)**. Be very careful not to damage the sealing surface inside the cap.
3   Work the new gasket into the cap recess.
4   Install the cap, then remove it and make sure the gasket seals all the way around.

22   Positive Crankcase Ventilation (PCV) valve check and replacement (every 30,000 miles or 36 months)

1   The PCV valve and hose are located in the valve cover on all models except 2010 and later four-cylinder models. **Note:** *On 2010 and later four-cylinder models, the PCV valve and hose are located on the back side of the engine underneath the intake manifold. The intake manifold must be removed to replace the PCV valve or hose (see Chapter 2A).*
2   Disconnect the hose, unscrew the PCV valve from the cover, then reconnect the hose.
3   With the engine idling at normal operating temperature, place your finger over the valve opening. If there's no vacuum at the valve, check for a plugged hose or valve. Replace any plugged or deteriorated hoses.
4   Turn off the engine. Remove the PCV valve from the hose. Blow through the valve from the valve cover (cylinder head) end. If air will not pass through the valve in this direc-

21.2 Use a small screwdriver to carefully pry out the old gasket - take care not to damage the cap

tion, replace it with a new one.
5   When purchasing a replacement PCV valve, make sure it's for your particular vehicle and engine size. Compare the old valve with the new one to make sure they're the same.

23   Evaporative emissions control system check (every 30,000 miles or 36 months)

Refer to illustration 23.2

1   The function of the evaporative emissions control system is to draw fuel vapors from the fuel tank and fuel system, store them in a charcoal canister, then burn them during normal engine operation.
2   The most common symptom of a fault in the evaporative emissions system is a strong fuel odor in or around the vehicle. If a fuel

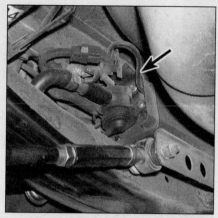

23.2 Check the charcoal canister for damage and the hose connections for cracks and damage; the canister is located at the rear of the vehicle, above the suspension crossmember (typical)

odor is detected, inspect the charcoal canister. Check the canister and all hoses for damage and deterioration **(see illustration)**.
3   The evaporative emissions control system is explained in more detail in Chapter 6.

24   Chassis and body fastener check (every 30,000 miles or 36 months)

Refer to illustrations 24.1a and 24.1b

Tighten the following fasteners to the torque values listed in this Chapter's Specifications:

a) *Front seat mounting bolts.*
b) *Both front and rear suspension member-to-body mounting bolts and nuts (left and right sides)* **(see illustrations)**.

24.1a Periodically check the tightness of the nuts and bolts on each side of the front suspension subframe . . .

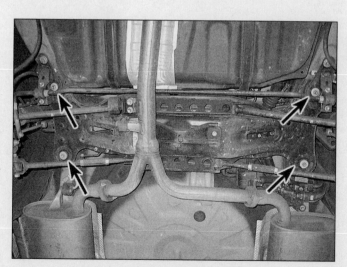

24.1b . . . and rear suspension mounts

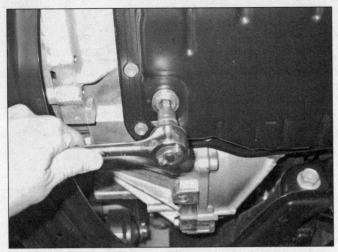

25.6 Remove the automatic transaxle drain plug (2009 and earlier four-cylinder models)

25.7a After loosening the front bolts, remove the rear pan bolts . . .

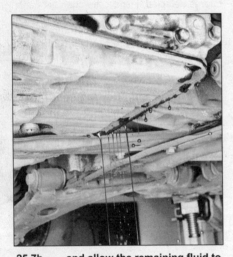

25.7b . . . and allow the remaining fluid to drain out

25 Automatic transaxle fluid change (every 60,000 miles or 72 months)

Refer to illustrations 25.6, 25.7a, 25.7b, 25.8 and 25.11

1   At the specified time intervals, the automatic transaxle fluid should be drained and replaced. **Note:** *Although the manufacturer doesn't specify it, it is a good idea to clean the transaxle fluid strainer periodically to remove accumulated dirt and metal particles.*

2   Before beginning work, purchase the specified transaxle fluid (see *Recommended lubricants and fluids* in this Chapter's Specifications).

3   The fluid should be drained immediately after the vehicle has been driven. Hot fluid is more effective than cold fluid at removing built up sediment. **Warning:** *Fluid temperature can exceed 350-degrees F in a hot transaxle. Wear protective gloves.*

4   Raise the vehicle and support it securely on jackstands.

5   Move the necessary equipment under the vehicle, being careful not to touch any of the hot exhaust components.

6   **2009 and earlier four-cylinder models:** Place the drain pan under the drain plug in the transaxle pan and remove the drain plug **(see illustration)**. Be sure the drain pan is in position, as fluid will come out with some force. Once the fluid is drained, reinstall the drain plug securely. If you aren't going to clean the strainer, proceed to Step 14.

7   Remove the front transaxle pan bolts, then loosen the rear bolts and carefully pry the pan loose with a screwdriver and allow the remaining fluid to drain **(see illustrations)**. Once the fluid had drained, remove the bolts and lower the pan. **Warning:** *On models with the U660E or U760E transaxle (and no drain plug), the pan will be full of fluid.*

8   Remove the strainer retaining bolts, disconnect the clip (some models) and lower the strainer from the transaxle **(see illustration)**. Be careful when lowering the strainer as it

25.8 Remove the strainer bolts and lower the strainer (be careful, there will be some residual fluid)

25.11 Noting their locations, remove the magnets and wash them and the pan in solvent before installing them

contains residual fluid.

9   Clean the strainer thoroughly.

10   Place the strainer in position, connect the clip (if equipped) and install the bolts. Tighten the bolts to the torque listed in this Chapter's Specifications.

11   Carefully clean the gasket surfaces of the fluid pan, removing all traces of old gasket material. Remove the magnets, noting their locations. Wash the pan in clean solvent and dry it with compressed air. **Warning:** *Always wear eye protection when using compressed air! Be sure to clean and reinstall the magnets in the pan* (**see illustration**).

12   Install a new gasket, place the fluid pan in position and install the bolts in their original positions. Tighten the bolts to the torque listed in this Chapter's Specifications.

2009 and earlier four-cylinder models

13   Lower the vehicle.

14   With the engine off, add new fluid to the transaxle through the dipstick tube (see this Chapter's Specifications for the recommended fluid type and capacity). Use a funnel to prevent spills. It is best to add a little fluid at a time, continually checking the level with the dipstick (see Section 7). Allow the fluid time to drain into the pan.

15   Start the engine and shift the shifter into all positions from P through L, then place the shifter into P and apply the parking brake.

16   With the engine idling, check the fluid level. Add fluid up to the Cool level on the dipstick.

All V6 models, 2010 and later four-cylinder models

17   Lower the vehicle.

18   Refer to Section 7 for the refilling procedure.

19   Check under the vehicle for leaks during the first few trips. Check the fluid level again when the transaxle is hot (see Section 7).

26   Manual transaxle lubricant change - when the vehicle is used for towing (every 60,000 miles or 72 months)

1   The lubricant should be drained immediately after the vehicle has been driven. Hot lubricant is more effective than cold fluid at removing built up sediment.

2   After the vehicle has been driven to warm up the fluid, raise it and place it on jackstands for access to the drain plug.

3   Remove the fill plug, then remove the drain plug and drain the lubricant (see Section 18).

4   Reinstall the drain plug securely.

5   Add new lubricant until it begins to run out of the filler hole. See *Recommended lubricants and fluids* for the specified lubricant type.

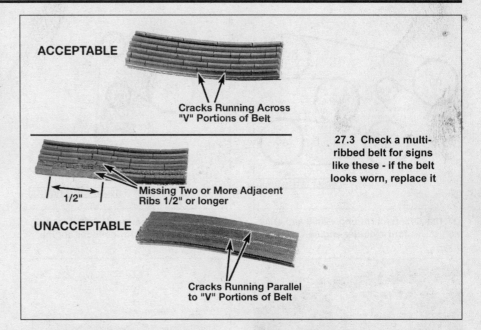

27.3 Check a multi-ribbed belt for signs like these - if the belt looks worn, replace it

ACCEPTABLE

Cracks Running Across "V" Portions of Belt

1/2" Missing Two or More Adjacent Ribs 1/2" or longer

UNACCEPTABLE

Cracks Running Parallel to "V" Portions of Belt

27   Drivebelt check and replacement (60,000 miles or 72 months and every 15,000 miles and 18 months thereafter)

Check

Refer to illustration 27.3

1   The drivebelts are located at the front of the engine and play an important role in the operation of the vehicle and its components. Due to their function and material makeup, belts are prone to failure after a period of time and should be inspected and adjusted periodically to prevent major damage.

2   All V6 and 2009 and earlier four-cylinder models use a single serpentine belt. 2010 and later four-cylinder models use two serpentine belts; one for the power steering pump and the other belt for the alternator, water pump and air conditioning compressor. No adjustment is necessary because an automatic tensioner(s) is used.

3   With the engine turned off, open the hood and locate the drivebelt(s) at the front of the engine. Use a flashlight to carefully check for a severed core, separation of the adhesive rubber on both sides of the core and for core separation from the belt side. Inspect the ribs for separation from the adhesive rubber and for cracking or separation of the ribs, torn or worn ribs or cracks in the inner ridges of the ribs (**see illustration**). Also check for fraying and glazing, which gives the belt a shiny appearance. Inspect both sides of the belt by twisting the belt to check the underside. Use your fingers to feel the belt where you can't see it. If any of the above conditions are evident, replace the belt(s). **Note:** *The drivebelt inspection can be made easier by removing the under-vehicle splash shield.*

Replacement

Note: *Take the old belt with you when purchasing new ones in order to make a direct comparison for length, width and design.*

4   Disconnect the negative cable from the battery (see Chapter 5).

Four-cylinder engine

Refer to illustrations 27.8, 27.10a, 27.10b and 27.10c

5   Remove the right front wheel.

6   Remove the right side fender apron seal.

7   Remove the right side engine cover assembly.

8   Place a box-end wrench on the tensioner pulley bolt (2009 and earlier models) or on the hex-shaped lug (2010 and later models), slowly turn the drivebelt tensioner away from the belt, remove the belt and slowly release the tensioner (**see illustration**).

27.8 Rotate the drivebelt tensioner so the tensioner pulley moves away from the belt - 2010 four-cylinder engine shown (alternator/water pump/air conditioning compressor belt)

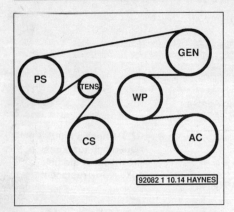

27.10a Drivebelt routing - 2009 and erlier four-cylinder engine

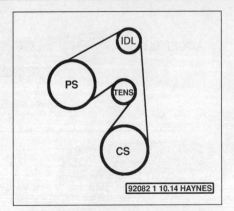

27.10b Power steering drivebelt routing - 2010 and later four-cylinder engine

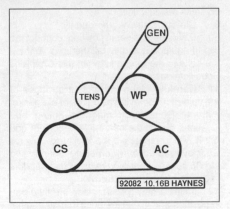

27.10c Alternator and A/C drivebelt routing - 2010 and later four-cylinder engine

27.11 Using a wrench on the center bolt of the tensioner, rotate the tensioner to loosen the belt

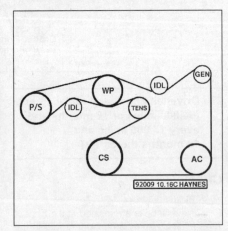

27.14a Drivebelt routing – V6 engine, 2011 and earlier models/ 2012 Avalon and ES350 models

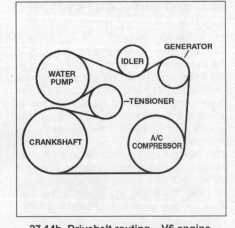

27.14b Drivebelt routing – V6 engine, 2012 and later Camry models/2013 and later Avalon and ES350 models

27.16a The drivebelt tensioner on 2009 and earlier four-cylinder engines is retained by a nut and a bolt (2010 and later models similar)

27.16b Remove the alternator drivebelt tensioner on 2010 and later four-cylinder models by removing the mounting bolt and tensioner; the power steering drivebelt tensioner removal is similar

9   2010 and later models: If you are replacing the power steering pump belt, you will have to remove the alternator/water pump/air conditioning compressor belt first because of the way they are arranged on the crankshaft

pulley. Because of this and because belts tend to wear out more or less together, it is a good idea to replace both belts at the same time. Mark each belt and its appropriate pulley groove so the replacement belts can be fitted

in their proper positions.
10   Install the new belt and rotate the tensioner to allow the belt to slip over it, then release the tensioner slowly until it contacts the drivebelt. Make sure the drivebelt is centered on all of the pulleys **(see illustrations)**.

V6 engine

Refer to illustrations 27.11 and 27.14

11   Place a wrench on the bolt in the center of the tensioner pulley and rotate it away from the belt to release tension on the belt **(see illustration)**. Remove the belt and slowly release the tensioner.
12   Before installing the drivebelt, lock the tensioner as follows: rotate the tensioner, align the two holes on the tensioner assembly and insert a 0.24-inch dowel pin or drill bit through the two holes.
13   Install the drivebelt. Be sure to route it correctly. Remove the dowel pin or drill bit and tension the belt. Make sure that the belt is centered on all of the pulleys.
14   Route the new belt over the pulleys **(see illustration)**, again rotating the tensioner to allow the belt to be installed, then release the belt tensioner. **Note:** *New belts are difficult to place into position. It may be easiest to slip*

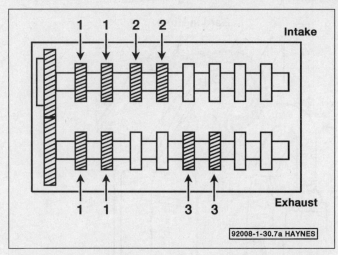

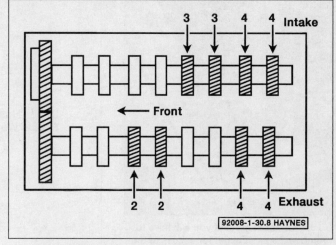

28.6 When the no. 1 piston is at TDC on the compression stroke, the valve clearance for the no. 1 and no. 3 cylinder exhaust valves and the no. 1 and no. 2 cylinder intake valves can be measured

28.7 When the no. 4 piston is at TDC on the compression stroke, the valve clearance for the no. 2 and no. 4 exhaust valves and the no. 3 and no. 4 intake valves can be measured

the belt over the tensioner pulley and the idler pulley last as you turn the tensioner pulley.

15　Make sure the belt is properly centered in the pulleys **(see illustration 27.14)**.

Drivebelt tensioner replacement

Refer to illustrations 27.16a and 27.16b

Warning: *Disconnect the cable from the negative terminal of the battery before performing this procedure (see Chapter 5, Section 3).*

16　To replace a tensioner that can't properly tension the belt, or one that exhibits binding or a worn-out bearing/pulley, remove the drivebelt, then unscrew the mounting fastener(s) **(see illustrations)**.

17　Installation is the reverse of the removal procedure, be sure the locking pin is seated into the housing. Tighten the fasteners to the torque values listed in this Chapter's Specifications.

18　Install the drivebelt.

28　Valve clearance check and adjustment (2009 and earlier four-cylinder models) (every 60,000 miles or 48 months)

Warning: *These models are equipped with airbags. Always disable the airbag system before working in the vicinity of any airbag system component to avoid the possibility of accidental deployment of the airbag(s), which could cause personal injury (see Chapter 12).*
Note: *All V6 engines and 2010 and later four-cylinder engines have hydraulic lash adjusters that don't require checking or adjustment.*

Check

Refer to illustrations 28.6 and 28.7

1　Disconnect the negative cable from the battery (see Chapter 5).

2　Remove the ignition coils (see Chapter 5) and any other components that will interfere with valve cover removal.

3　Blow out the recessed area around the spark plug openings with compressed air, if available, to remove any debris that might fall into the cylinders, then remove the spark plugs (see Section 30).

4　Remove the valve cover (see Chapter 2A).

5　Refer to Chapter 2A and position the number 1 piston at TDC on the compression stroke.

6　Measure the clearances of the indicated valves with feeler gauges **(see illustration)**. Record the measurements which are out of specification. They will be used later to determine the required replacement lifters.

7　Turn the crankshaft one complete revolution and realign the timing marks. Measure the remaining valves **(see illustration)**.

Adjustment

Refer to illustration 28.9

8　If any of the valve clearances were out of adjustment, remove the camshaft(s) from over the lifter(s) that was/were out of the specified clearance range (see Chapter 2A).

9　Measure the thickness of the lifter with a micrometer **(see illustration)**. To calculate the correct thickness of a replacement lifter that will place the valve clearance within the specified value, use the following formula:

$$N = T + (A - V)$$

T = thickness of the old lifter
A = valve clearance measured
N = thickness of the new lifter
V = desired valve clearance (see this Chapter's Specifications)

10　Select a lifter with a thickness as close as possible to the valve clearance calculated. The lifters are available in 35 sizes in increments of 0.0008-inch (0.020 mm), ranging in size from 0.1992-inch (5.060 mm) to 0.2260-

28.9 Measure the thickness of the lifter head with a micrometer

inch (5.740 mm).

11　Install the proper thickness lifter(s) in position, making sure to lubricate them with camshaft installation lube first. **Note:** *Apply the lubricant to the underside of the lifter where it contacts the valve stem, the walls of the lifter and the face of the lifter.*

12　Install the camshaft(s) (see Chapter 2A).

13　The remainder of installation is the reverse of removal.

29　Cooling system servicing (draining, flushing and refilling) (at 100,000 miles or 120 months and every 50,000 miles or 60 months thereafter)

Warning: *Wait until the engine is completely cool before beginning this procedure.*
Warning: *Do not allow engine coolant (antifreeze) to come in contact with your skin or painted surfaces of the vehicle. Rinse off spills immediately with plenty of water. Antifreeze*

29.4 On most models you will have to remove a splash panel for access to the drain fitting located at the bottom of the radiator

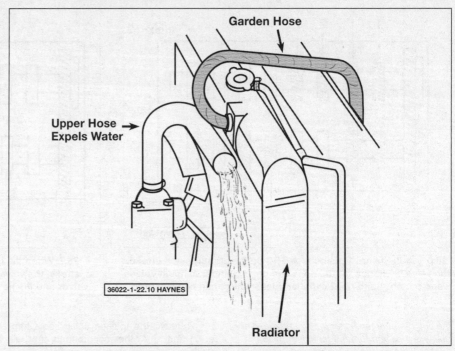

29.10 With the thermostat removed, disconnect the upper radiator hose and flush the radiator and engine block with a garden hose

is highly toxic if ingested. Never leave antifreeze laying around in an open container or in puddles on the floor; children and pets are attracted by it's sweet smell and may drink it. Check with local authorities about disposing of used antifreeze. Many communities have collection centers which will see that antifreeze is disposed of safely.

1   Periodically, the cooling system should be drained, flushed and refilled to replenish the antifreeze mixture and prevent formation of rust and corrosion, which can impair the performance of the cooling system and cause engine damage. When the cooling system is serviced, all hoses and the radiator cap should be checked and replaced if necessary.

Draining

Refer to illustration 29.4

2   Apply the parking brake and block the wheels. If the vehicle has just been driven, wait several hours to allow the engine to cool down before beginning this procedure.
3   Once the engine is completely cool, remove the radiator cap.
4   Move a large container under the radiator drain to catch the coolant. Attach a length of hose to the drain fitting to direct the coolant into the container (some models are already equipped with a hose), then open the drain fitting (a pair of pliers may be required to turn it) **(see illustration)**.
5   After the coolant stops flowing out of the radiator, move the container under the engine block drain plug(s). Loosen the plug(s) and allow the coolant in the block to drain. On 2011 and earlier four-cylinder models, the block drain plug is on the front side of the engine block. Block drain plugs are not used on 2012 and later 4-cylinder models. On V6 models, a block drain plug is on each side of the block.
6   While the coolant is draining, check the condition of the radiator hoses, heater hoses

and clamps (see Section 11 if necessary).
7   Replace any damaged clamps or hoses (see Chapter 3).

Flushing

Refer to illustration 29.10

8   Once the system is completely drained, remove the thermostat from the engine (see Chapter 3). Then reinstall the thermostat housing without the thermostat. This will allow the system to be flushed.
9   Reinstall the engine block drain plugs and tighten the radiator drain plug. Turn your heating system controls to Hot, so that the heater core will be flushed at the same time as the rest of the cooling system.
10   Disconnect the upper radiator hose from the radiator. Place a garden hose in the upper radiator inlet, turn the water on and flush the system until the water runs clear out of the upper radiator hose **(see illustration)**.
11   In severe cases of contamination or clogging of the radiator, remove the radiator (see Chapter 3) and have a radiator repair facility clean and repair it if necessary. Many deposits can be removed by the chemical action of a cleaner available at auto parts stores. Follow the procedure outlined in the manufacturer's instructions. **Note:** *When the coolant is regularly drained and the system refilled with the correct antifreeze/water mixture, there should be no need to use chemical cleaners or descalers.*
12   After flushing, drain the radiator and remove the block drain plug(s) once again to drain the water from the system.

Refilling

13   Close and tighten the radiator drain. Install and tighten the block drain plug(s).
14   Place the heater temperature control in the maximum heat position.
15   Slowly add new coolant to the radiator until it's full. Add coolant to the reservoir up to the Full mark.
16   Install the radiator cap off and run the engine in a well-ventilated area until the thermostat opens (coolant will begin flowing through the radiator and the upper radiator hose will become hot).
17   Turn the engine off and let it cool completely. Add more coolant mixture to bring the level back up to the lip on the radiator filler neck.
18   Squeeze the upper radiator hose to expel air, then add more coolant mixture if necessary. Reinstall the radiator cap.
19   If necessary, add more coolant to the reservoir until it's up to the Full mark.
20   Start the engine, allow it to reach normal operating temperature and check for leaks.

30 Spark plug check and replacement (every 120,000 miles or 144 months)

Refer to illustrations 30.1, 30.4, 30.6, 30.8, 30.10a and 30.10b

1   Spark plug replacement requires a spark plug socket, an extension and a ratchet. This socket is lined with a rubber grommet to pro-

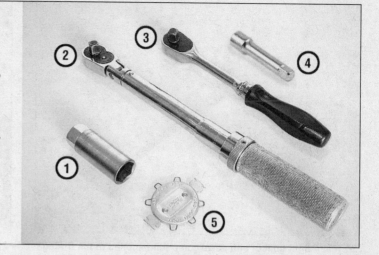

30.1 Tools required for changing spark plugs

1   **Spark plug socket** - This will have special padding inside to protect the spark plug's porcelain insulator
2   **Torque wrench** - Although not mandatory, using this tool is the best way to ensure the plugs are tightened properly
3   **Ratchet** - Standard hand tool to fit the spark plug socket
4   **Extension** - Depending on model and accessories, you may need special extensions and universal joints to reach one or more of the plugs
5   **Spark plug gap gauge** - This gauge for checking the gap comes in a variety of styles. Make sure the gap for your engine is included

tect the porcelain insulator of the spark plug and to hold the plug while you insert it into the spark plug hole. You will also need a wire-type feeler gauge to check and adjust the spark plug gap and a torque wrench to tighten the new plugs to the specified torque **(see illustration)**.

2   If you are replacing the plugs, purchase the new plugs, adjust them to the proper gap and then replace each plug one at a time.

3   Inspect each of the new plugs for defects. If there are any signs of cracks in the porcelain insulator of a plug, don't use it.

4   Check the gap by inserting the wire gauge of the proper thickness between the electrodes at the tip of the plug **(see illustration)**. The gap between the electrodes should be identical to that listed in this Chapter's Specifications or on the VECI label. If the gap is incorrect, replace the spark plug. **Note:** *Do not adjust the gap on iridium spark plugs. Using a gapping tool on*

them could damage the iridium plating on the electrodes. These spark plugs are pre-gapped by the manufacturer.

5   Remove the engine cover(s) and disconnect any hoses or components that would interfere with access and move them out of the way.

6   Remove the bolts and detach each ignition coil assembly from the spark plugs **(see illustration)**. **Note:** *On all V6 models, the upper intake manifold must be removed to gain access to the rear plugs (see Chapter 2B).*

7   If compressed air is available, blow any dirt or foreign material away from the spark plug area before proceeding (a common bicycle pump will also work). **Warning:** *Always wear eye protection when using compressed air!*

8   Remove the spark plug **(see illustration)**.

30.4 Spark plug manufacturers recommend using a wire-type gauge when checking the gap - if the wire does not slide between the electrodes with a slight drag, spark plug replacement is required

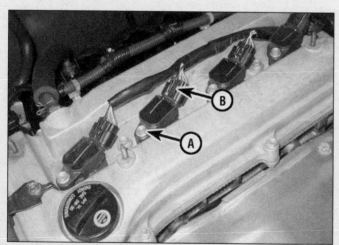

30.6 Remove the retaining bolt (A), disconnect the electrical connector (B) and detach the individual coils to reach the front spark plugs (four-cylinder models shown, V6 models similar)

30.8 Because they are deeply recessed, the proper spark plug socket and an extension will be required when removing or installing the spark plugs

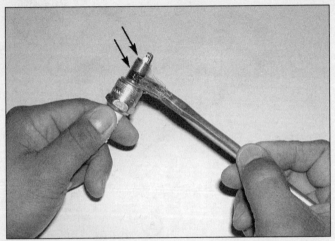

30.10a A light coat of anti-seize compound applied to the threads of the spark plugs will keep the threads in the cylinder head from being damaged the next time the plugs are removed. Don't get any near the lower threads

30.10b A section of rubber hose will aid in getting the spark plug threads started

9   Whether you are replacing the plugs at this time or intend to re-use the old plugs, compare each old spark plug with those shown on the inside of the back cover to determine the overall running condition of the engine.

10   Apply a small amount of anti-seize compound to the spark plug threads **(see illustration)**. It's often difficult to insert spark plugs into their holes without cross-threading them. To avoid this possibility, fit a short piece of rubber hose over the end of the spark plug **(see illustration)**. The flexible hose acts as a universal joint to help align the plug with the spark plug hole. Should the plug begin to cross-thread, the hose will slip on the spark plug, prevent-ing thread damage. Tighten the plug to the torque listed in this Chapter's Specifica-tions.

11   Install the ignition coil.

12   Follow the above procedure for the remaining spark plugs, replacing them one at a time to prevent mixing up the spark plug wires.

Notes

Notes

Chapter 2 Part A
Four-cylinder engines

Contents

Specifications

General

Engine designation
2009 and earlier	2AZ-FE
2010 and later	2AR-FE

Displacement
2AZ-FE	144.2 cubic inches (2.4 liters)
2AR-FE	152.2 cubic inches (2.5 liters)
Cylinder numbers (drivebelt end-to-transaxle end)	1-2-3-4
Firing order	1-3-4-2

Cylinder numbering diagram

Cylinder head

Warpage limit

2009 and earlier
Cylinder block side	0.0031 inch
Intake and exhaust manifold sides	0.0031 inch

2010 and later
Cylinder block side	0.0197 inch
Intake and exhaust manifold sides	0.0394 inch

Timing chain

Timing chain sprocket wear limit **(see illustration 6.27b)**	
2009 and earlier	
Camshaft sprocket(s) (w/chain)	3.831 inches
Crankshaft sprocket (w/chain)	2.031 inches
2010 and later	
Camshaft sprocket(s) (w/chain)	Not available
Crankshaft sprocket (w/chain)	2.36 inches
Timing chain stretch limit **(see illustration 6.27a)**	
2009 and earlier	
No. 1 chain (15 pins)	4.508 inches
No. 2 sub chain (15 pins)	4.024 inches
2010 and later (15 pins)	5.42 inches
Timing chain guide wear limit	0.039 inch
No. 1 chain vibration damper wear limit	0.039 inch

Camshaft and lifters

Journal diameter	
2009 and earlier No. 1 journal	1.4162 to 1.4167 inches
2010 and later No. 1 journal	1.356 to 1.357 inches
All others	0.904 to 0.905 inch
Bearing oil clearance	
No.1 journal	
Intake	
2009 and earlier	0.0003 to 0.0015 inch
2010 and later	0.0014 to 0.0028 inch
Exhaust	
2009 and earlier	0.0016 to 0.0031 inch
2010 and later	0.0019 to 0.0034 inch
All others	0.0010 to 0.0024 inch
Runout limit	0.0012 inch
Thrust clearance (endplay)	
2009 and earlier	
Intake	
Standard	0.0016 to 0.0037 inch
Maximum	0.0043 inch
Exhaust	
Standard	0.0035 to 0.0057 inch
Maximum	0.006 inch
2010 and later	
Standard	0.0023 to 0.006 inch
Maximum	0.007 inch
Lobe height	
2009 and earlier	
Intake camshaft	
Standard	1.8624 to 1.8664 inches
Service limit (minimum)	1.8581 inches
Exhaust camshaft	
Standard	1.8135 to 1.8174 inches
Service limit (minimum)	1.8092 inches
2010 and later	
Intake camshaft	
Standard	1.739 to 1.744 inches
Service limit (minimum)	1.733 inches
Exhaust camshaft	
Standard	1.738 to 1.744 inches
Service limit (minimum)	1.732 inches
Valve lifter (2009 and earlier models)	
Diameter	1.2191 to 1.2195 inches
Bore diameter	1.2208 to 1.2215 inches
Lifter oil clearance (2009 and earlier models)	
Standard	0.0013 to 0.0023 inch
Service limit	0.0031 inch

Oil pump

2009 and earlier models	
Drive chain sprocket wear limit (w/chain)	1.898 inches
Drive chain stretch limit, 15 pins	2.063 inches
Drive chain guide wear limit	0.039 inch
2010 and later models	Not available

Torque specifications

Ft-lbs (unless otherwise indicated)

Note: *One foot-pound (ft-lb) of torque is equivalent to 12 inch-pounds (in-lbs) of torque. Torque values below approximately 15 foot-pounds are expressed in inch-pounds, because most foot-pound torque wrenches are not accurate at these smaller values.*

Camshaft bearing cap bolts	
2009 and earlier models	
Journal No.1 (intake and exhaust)	22
All others	80 in-lbs
2010 and later models	144 in-lbs
Camshaft housing and large bearing cap bolts	
(2010 and later models)	20
Camshaft sprocket bolts	
2009 and earlier models	40
2010 and later models	63
Crankshaft pulley/vibration damper bolt	
2009 and earlier models	133
2010 and later models	184
Cylinder head bolts (in sequence - **see illustrations 10.24a and 10.24b**)	
2009 and earlier models	
Step 1	52
Step 2	Tighten an additional 90-degrees
2010 and later models	
Step 1	27
Step 2	27
Step 3	Tighten an additional 90-degrees
Step 4	Tighten an additional 90-degrees
Drivebelt tensioner	
2009 and earlier models	44
2010 and later models	
Alternator tensioner bolt	15
Power steering pump tensioner bolts	84 in-lbs
Engine balancer assembly	
2009 and earlier models	
Step 1	16
Step 2	Tighten an additional 90-degrees
2010 and later models	18
Exhaust manifold nuts/bolts	27
Exhaust manifold brace bolts	32
Exhaust manifold heat shield bolts	108 in-lbs
Exhaust pipe-to-exhaust manifold bolts	
2009 and earlier models	46
2010 and later models	40
Flywheel/driveplate bolts	
Manual transaxle	96
Automatic transaxle	72
Intake manifold nuts/bolts	
2009 and earlier models	22
2010 and later models	15
Lower crankcase-to-engine block bolts	See Chapter 2C
Oil pump (2009 and earlier models)	
Oil pump bolts	14
Oil pump drive chain tensioner	108 in-lbs
Oil pump sprocket bolt	22
Oil pan bolts	
2011 and earlier models	80 in-lbs
2012 and later models	89 in-lbs
Timing chain guide bolts (stationary)	
2009 and earlier models	80 in-lbs
2010 and later models	15
Timing chain tensioner pivot arm bolt	
2009 and earlier models	14
2010 and later models	15
Timing chain cover bolts/nuts	
2009 and earlier models (**see illustration 6.40**)	
Bolt A (10 mm head)	80 in-lbs
Bolts B (12 mm head)	18
Bolts C (14 mm head)	41
Nuts D	96 in-lbs

Torque specifications (continued)   **Ft-lbs** (unless otherwise indicated)

Note: *One foot-pound (ft-lb) of torque is equivalent to 12 inch-pounds (in-lbs) of torque. Torque values below approximately 15 foot-pounds are expressed in inch-pounds, because most foot-pound torque wrenches are not accurate at these smaller values.*

Timing chain cover bolts/nuts (continued)

    2010 and later models **(see illustrations 6.57a and 6.57b)**

        Bolts A (8 mm head) 16

        Bolts B (10 mm head) 41

        Bolt C (8 mm head) 16

        Nuts D 16

Timing chain tensioner

    2009 and earlier models (nuts) .... 80 in-lbs

    2010 and later models (bolts) .... 90 in-lbs

Upper timing chain guide bolt (2010 and later models) 15

Valve cover

    2009 and earlier models

        Perimeter bolts .... 86 in-lbs

        Center bolts .... 120 in-lbs

        Nuts .... 86 in-lbs

    2010 and later models (bolts) .... 108 in-lbs

1   General information

This Part of Chapter 2 is devoted to repair procedures for the four-cylinder engine, with the exception of overhaul. Information concerning engine removal, installation and overhaul can be found in Part C of this Chapter.

2009 and earlier four-cylinder engines are designated 2AZ-FE (2.4L); 2010 and later four-cylinder engines are designated 2AR-FE (2.5L). These engines incorporate an aluminum cylinder block with a lower crankcase to strengthen the lower half of the block. Although the cylinder head utilizes the usual dual overhead camshafts (DOHC) with four valves per cylinder as in previous model years, it is of new design also. The camshafts are driven from a single timing chain off the crankshaft, and a Variable Valve Timing (VVT-i) system is incorporated on the intake camshaft on 2AZ-FE engines and intake and exhaust camshafts on the 2AR-FE engines to increase horsepower and decrease emissions.

2   Repair operations possible with the engine in the vehicle

Many major repair operations can be accomplished without removing the engine from the vehicle.

Clean the engine compartment and the exterior of the engine with some type of degreaser before any work is done. It will make the job easier and help keep dirt out of the internal areas of the engine.

Depending on the components involved, it may be helpful to remove the hood to improve access to the engine as repairs are performed (refer to Chapter 11 if necessary). Cover the fenders to prevent damage to the paint. Special pads are available, but an old bedspread or blanket will also work.

If vacuum, exhaust, oil or coolant leaks develop, indicating a need for gasket or seal replacement, the repairs can generally be made with the engine in the vehicle. The intake and exhaust manifold gaskets, oil pan gasket, crankshaft oil seals and cylinder head gasket (2009 and earlier models only) are all accessible with the engine in place.

Exterior engine components, such as the intake and exhaust manifolds, the oil pan, the oil pump (2009 and earlier models only), the water pump, the starter motor, the alternator and the fuel system components can be removed for repair with the engine in place.

Since the cylinder head can be removed without pulling the engine (2009 and earlier models only), camshaft and valve component servicing can also be accomplished with the engine in the vehicle. Replacement of the timing chain and sprockets is also possible with the engine in the vehicle (2009 and earlier models only).

3.5 A compression gauge can be used in the number one spark plug hole to assist in finding TDC

3   Top Dead Center (TDC) for number one piston - locating

Refer to illustrations 3.5 and 3.8

1   Top Dead Center (TDC) is the highest point in the cylinder that each piston reaches as it travels up the cylinder bore. Each piston reaches TDC on the compression stroke and again on the exhaust stroke, but TDC generally refers to piston position on the compression stroke.

2   Positioning the piston(s) at TDC is an essential part of many procedures such as valve adjustment and camshaft and timing chain/sprocket removal.

3   Before beginning this procedure, be sure to place the transmission in Neutral and apply the parking brake or block the rear wheels. If method b) in the next Step will be used to rotate the engine, disable the fuel system (see Chapter 4, Section 3), then disconnect the electrical connectors from the ignition coils (see Chapter 5).

4   In order to bring any piston to TDC, the crankshaft must be turned using one of the methods outlined below. When looking at the front of the engine, normal crankshaft rotation is clockwise.

   a) *The preferred method is to turn the crankshaft with a socket and ratchet attached to the bolt threaded into the front of the crankshaft. Turn the bolt in a clockwise direction only.*

   b) *If an assistant is available to turn the ignition switch to the Start position in short bursts, you can get the piston close to TDC without a remote starter switch. Make sure your assistant is out of the vehicle, away from the ignition switch, then use a socket and ratchet as described in Paragraph a) to complete the procedure.*

5   Remove the spark plugs (see Chapter 1) and install a compression gauge in the number one spark plug hole **(see illustration)**. It should be a gauge with a screw-in fitting and

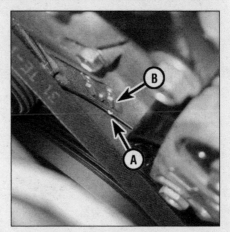

3.8 Align the groove in the damper (A) with the "0" mark on the timing chain cover (B)

a hose at least six inches long.

6   Rotate the crankshaft using one of the methods described above while observing for pressure on the compression gauge. The moment the gauge shows pressure indicates that the number one cylinder has begun the compression stroke.

7   Once the compression stroke has begun, TDC for the compression stroke is reached by bringing the piston to the top of the cylinder.

8   On 2011 and earlier models, continue turning the crankshaft until the notch in the crankshaft damper is aligned with the "TDC" or the "0" mark on the timing chain cover **(see illustration)**. On 2012 and later models, continue turning the crankshaft pulley until the notch on the pulley aligns with the "0" mark on the timing chain cover. At this point, the number one cylinder is at TDC on the compression stroke. If the marks are aligned but there was no compression, the piston was on the exhaust stroke; continue rotating the crankshaft 360-degrees (1-turn). **Note:** *If a compression gauge is not available, you can simply place a blunt object over the spark plug hole and listen for compression as the engine is rotated. Once compression at the No.1 spark plug hole is noted the remainder of the Step is the same.*

9   After the number one piston has been positioned at TDC on the compression stroke, TDC for any of the remaining cylinders can be located by turning the crankshaft 180 degrees and following the firing order (refer to the Specifications). Rotating the engine 180 degrees past TDC #1 will put the engine at TDC compression for cylinder #3.

4   Valve cover - removal and installation

Removal

Refer to illustrations 4.2a, 4.2b and 4.6

1   Disconnect the cable from the negative battery terminal (see Chapter 5).

4.2a Engine cover mounting nuts and retainers - 2009 and earlier models

4.2b Lift the cover up from the rear, off the ballstuds, then detach the front, and remove the cover - 2010 and later models

Installation

Refer to illustrations 4.7a, 4.7b and 4.8

7   Remove the valve cover gasket from the valve cover and clean the mating surfaces with brake system cleaner. On 2010 and later models, remove the O-rings from the cylinder head **(see illustration)**. Install a new rubber gasket (and O-rings on 2010 and later models), pressing it evenly into the grooves around the underside of the valve cover. **Note:** *Make sure the spark plug tube seals are in place on the underside of the valve cover before reinstalling it* **(see illustration)**. The mating surfaces of the timing chain cover, the cylinder head and valve cover must be perfectly clean when the valve cover is installed. If there's residue or oil on the mating surfaces when the valve cover is installed, oil leaks may develop.

8   Apply RTV sealant at the timing chain cover-to-cylinder head joint, then install the valve cover and fasteners **(see illustration)**.

9   Tighten the nuts/bolts to the torque listed in this Chapter's Specifications in three or four equal steps.

2   On 2009 and earlier models, remove the engine cover mounting fasteners and remove the cover **(see illustration)**. On 2010 and later models, lift the cover up from the back off of the ballstuds, then from the front, and remove the cover **(see illustration)**.

3   Disconnect the electrical connectors from the ignition coils, remove the nuts securing the wiring harness to the valve cover and position the ignition coil wiring harness aside. Then remove the ignition coil pack from each of the spark plugs (see Chapter 5).

4   Detach the breather hoses from the valve cover.

5   On 2010 and later models, disconnect the camshaft timing control valve assemblies and camshaft position sensor electrical connectors. Remove the mounting bolts for the control valves and sensors (see Chapter 6).

6   Remove the valve cover mounting fasteners, then detach the valve cover and gasket from the cylinder head **(see illustration)**. If the valve cover is stuck to the cylinder head, bump the end with a wood block and a hammer to jar it loose. If that doesn't work, try to slip a flexible putty knife between the cylinder

head and valve cover to break the seal. **Caution:** *Don't pry at the valve cover-to-cylinder head joint or damage to the sealing surfaces may occur, leading to oil leaks after the valve cover is reinstalled.*

4.6 Valve cover fastener locations (2009 and earlier model shown, 2010 and later models similar)

4.7a Replace the O-ring gaskets in the cylinder head

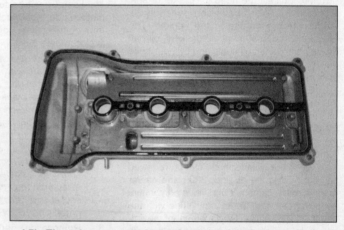

4.7b The valve cover gasket and the spark plug tube seals are incorporated into a single rubber O-ring-like seal. Press the gasket evenly into the grooves around the underside of the valve cover and the spark plug openings (2009 and earlier models)

4.8 Apply sealant at the timing chain cover-to-cylinder head joint before installing the valve cover

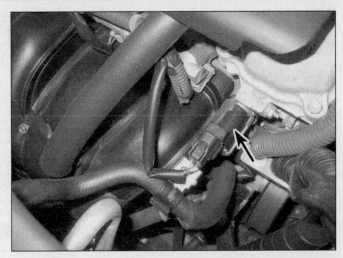

5.2a On 2009 and earlier models, the Variable Valve Timing (VVT) oil control valve is located at the rear of the cylinder

10   Reinstall the remaining parts, run the engine and check for oil leaks.

5   Variable Valve Timing (VVT and VVT-i) system - description

Refer to illustrations 5.2a, 5.2b, 5.4a and 5.4b

1   The VVT system varies intake or exhaust camshaft timing by directing oil pressure to advance or retard the camshaft sprocket/actuator assembly. Changing the camshaft timing during certain engine conditions increases engine power output, fuel economy and reduces emissions.

2   System components include the Powertrain Control Module (PCM), the VVT oil control valve (OCV) and the intake camshaft sprocket/actuator assembly on all models and the exhaust camshaft on 2010 and later models **(see illustrations)**.

3   The PCM uses inputs from the following sensors to turn the oil control valve ON or OFF:

a) *Vehicle Speed Sensor (VSS)*
b) *Throttle Position Sensor (TPS)*
c) *Mass Airflow (MAF) sensor*
d) *Engine Coolant Temperature (ECT) sensor*

4   Once the VVT oil control valve is actuated by the PCM, it directs the specified amount of oil pressure from the engine to advance or retard the intake or exhaust camshaft sprocket/actuator assembly **(see illustrations)**.

5   The camshaft sprocket/actuator assembly is equipped with an inner hub that is attached to the camshaft. The inner hub consists of a series of fixed vanes that use oil pressure as a wedge against the vanes to rotate the camshaft. The higher the oil pressure (or flow), the more the actuator assembly will rotate, thereby advancing or retarding the camshaft.

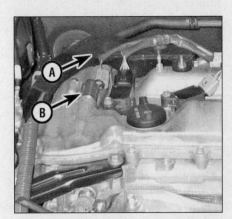

5.2b On 2010 and later models, there are two Variable Valve Timing (VVT) oil control valves located in the valve cover

A   *Intake camshaft VVT oil control valve*
B   *Exhaust camshaft VVT oil control valve*

5.4a Location of the intake camshaft actuator assembly on 2009 and earlier models

5.4b Locations of the intake (A) and exhaust (B) camshaft actuators on 2010 and later models

6.7a Verify the engine is at TDC by observing the position of the camshaft sprocket marks (lower arrows) - they must be aligned with the marks on the camshaft bearing caps (upper arrows) (2009 and earlier models)

6   When oil is applied to the advance or retard side of the vanes, the actuator can advance or retard the camshaft timing. The PCM can also send a signal to the oil control valve to stop oil flow to both (advance and retard) passages to hold camshaft(s) in its current position.

6   Timing chain and sprockets - removal, inspection and installation

Note: *If you're working on a 2010 or later model, the manufacturer recommends removing the engine and transaxle assembly to perform this procedure (see Chapter 2C).*

Removal

Refer to illustrations 6.7a and 6.7b

Warning: *Wait until the engine is completely cool before beginning this procedure.*

Caution: *The timing system is complex, and severe engine damage will occur if you make any mistakes. Do not attempt this procedure unless you are highly experienced with this type of repair. If you are at all unsure of your abilities, be sure to consult an expert. Double-check all your work and be sure everything is correct before you attempt to start the engine.*

1   Disconnect the cable from the negative battery terminal (see Chapter 5).

2   Remove the drivebelt (see Chapter 1) and the alternator (see Chapter 5).

3   Remove the valve cover (see Section 4) and the ABS actuator, if equipped (see Chapter 9). **Note:** *On 2010 and later models, remove the three gaskets from the camshaft bearing caps.*

4   With the parking brake applied and the rear wheels blocked, loosen the right front wheel lug nuts, then raise the front of the vehicle and support it securely on jackstands. Remove the right front wheel and the right splash shield from the wheelwell.

5   Drain the cooling system (see Chapter 1).

6   While the coolant is draining, remove the power steering pump from the engine without disconnecting the fluid lines (see Chapter 10). Tie the power steering pump to the body with a piece of wire and position it out of the way.

7   Position the number one piston at TDC on the compression stroke (see Section 3). Confirm the engine is at TDC on the compression stroke by verifying that the timing mark on the crankshaft pulley/vibration damper is aligned with the "0" mark on the timing chain cover **(see illustration 3.8)** and the camshaft sprocket marks are aligned with the marks on the camshaft front bearing caps **(see illustrations)**. **Note:** *There are two sets of marks on the camshaft sprockets. The marks that align at TDC are for TDC reference only; the other two marks are used to align the sprockets with the timing chain during installation.*

8   Remove the crankshaft pulley/vibration damper, being careful not to rotate the engine from TDC (see Section 11). If the engine rotates off TDC during this step, reposition the engine back to TDC before proceeding.

9   Support the engine from above using an engine support fixture (available at rental yards), or from below using a floor jack. Use a wood block between the floor jack and the engine to prevent damage.

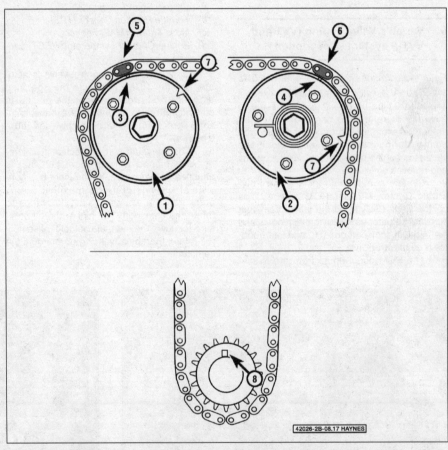

6.7b Camshafts and crankshaft TDC timing chain mark locations - 2010 and later models

1	Intake camshaft sprocket	6	Timing chain "yellow" colored link - exhaust
2	Exhaust camshaft sprocket	7	Index mark, not a timing mark
3	Intake camshaft sprocket timing mark	8	Crankshaft "TDC" keyway at 12 o'clock position
4	Exhaust camshaft sprocket timing mark		
5	Timing chain "yellow" colored link - intake		

10   Remove the passenger side engine mount and movement control rod (see Section 17).

11   Remove the drivebelt tensioner(s) (see Chapter 1) and the crankshaft position sensor (see Chapter 6) from the timing chain cover. Also remove the bolt securing the crankshaft position sensor wiring harness to the timing chain cover.

12   Remove the steel oil pan (see Section 13).

2009 and earlier models

Refer to illustrations 6.13a, 6.13b, 6.14a, 6.14b, 6.14c, 6.14d, 6.15 and 6.16

13   Detach the main wiring harness junction and remove the timing chain tensioner from the rear side of the timing chain cover (**see illustrations**).

14   Remove the timing chain cover fasteners and pry the cover off the engine (**see illustrations**).

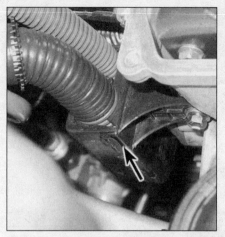

6.13a Remove the fasteners securing the main harness to the timing chain cover and position the harness aside - 2009 and earlier models

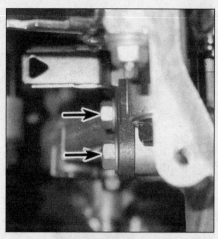

6.13b Timing chain tensioner mounting nuts - 2009 and earlier models

6.14a Timing chain cover upper fasteners

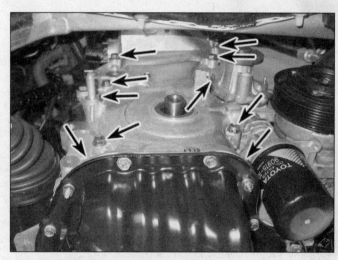

6.14b Timing chain cover lower fasteners; make a note of the fastener sizes, locations and lengths as they are removed, as they must be installed back in their original positions (2009 and earlier models)

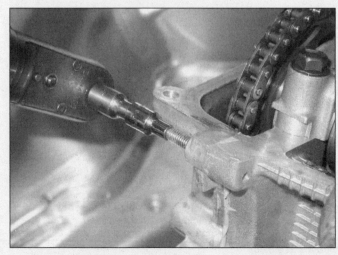

6.14c It will be necessary to remove the timing chain cover studs . . .

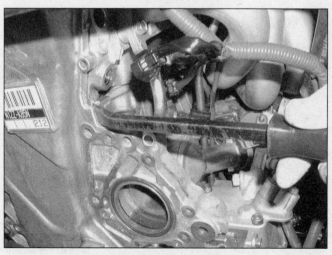

6.14d . . . before prying the timing chain cover off the engine - 2009 and earlier models

6.15 Slide the crankshaft position sensor reluctor ring off the crankshaft - note the "F" mark on the front (it must be facing outward upon installation) (2009 and earlier models)

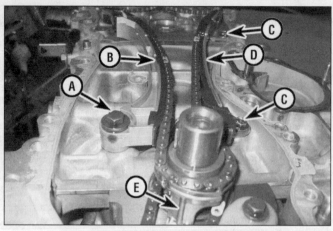

6.16 Timing chain guide mounting details - 2009 and earlier models

A   Pivot bolt
B   Tensioner pivot arm/chain guide
C   Stationary chain guide mounting bolts
D   Stationary chain guide
E   Lower timing chain guide

15   Slide the crankshaft position sensor reluctor ring off the crankshaft **(see illustration)**.
16   Remove the timing chain tensioner pivot arm/chain guide and the lower chain guide **(see illustration)**.
17   Lift the timing chain off the camshaft sprockets and remove the timing chain and the crankshaft sprocket as an assembly from the engine. The crankshaft sprocket should slip off the crankshaft by hand. If not, carefully pry the sprocket off the crankshaft. **Note:** *If you intend to reuse the timing chain, use white paint or chalk to make a mark indicating the front of the chain. If a used timing chain is reinstalled with the wear pattern in the opposite direction, noise and increased wear may occur.*
18   Remove the stationary timing chain guide **(see illustration 6.16)**.

2010 and later models

Refer to illustrations 6.21 and 6.22

19   Remove the movement control rod mounting bracket from the front of the timing chain cover **(see illustration 6.58)**, then remove the timing chain cover fasteners and carefully pry the cover off the engine from several locations. **Note:** *The timing chain cover has several different size mounting bolts; take note of each bolt's location so they can be returned to the same locations on reassembly.*
20   Once the cover is off, remove the O-rings from the crankcase.
21   Remove the top chain guide mounting bolt and guide **(see illustration)**.
22   Let the tensioner plunger extend until a 0.06 inch (1.5 mm) pin can be inserted into the alignment holes **(see illustration)** of the

stopper plate and the tensioner. Release the tensioner and make sure the pin is secured.
23   Remove the mounting bolts and the timing chain tensioner.
24   Remove the timing chain tensioner pivot arm/chain guide and the stationary timing chain guide.
25   Lift the timing chain off the camshaft sprockets and remove the timing chain and the crankshaft sprocket as an assembly from the engine. The crankshaft sprocket should slip off the crankshaft by hand. If not, carefully pry the sprocket off the crankshaft. **Note:** *If you intend to reuse the timing chain, use white paint or chalk to make a mark indicating the front of the chain. If a used timing chain is reinstalled with the wear pattern in the opposite direction, noise and increased wear may occur.*

All models

Refer to illustration 6.26

26   To remove the camshaft sprockets, loosen the bolts while holding the hex on the camshaft with a wrench **(see illustration)**. Note the identification marks on the camshaft sprockets before removal, then remove the bolts. Pull on the sprockets by hand until they slip off the dowels. If necessary, use a small puller, with the legs inserted in the relief holes, to pull the sprockets off. **Note:** *These models are equipped with variable valve timing, which consists of an actuator assembly attached to the intake camshaft sprocket (and exhaust camshaft on 2010 and later models). When removing the intake camshaft sprocket (and exhaust camshaft sprocket on 2010 and later models), only loosen and remove the center bolt, which fastens the sprocket to the camshaft. Do not loosen the outer four bolts that secure the actuator to the sprocket.*

6.21 Top chain guide, mounting bolt and locating pin

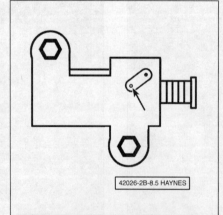

6.22 Align the hole on the lock with the hole in the tensioner, then insert a 0.06 inch (1.5 mm) pin or drill bit through both components to lock the tensioner

6.26 Hold the hex-shaped lug on the camshaft with a wrench to keep it from rotating as the sprocket bolts are loosened - when loosening the camshaft sprocket, loosen only the center bolt which secures the sprocket to the camshaft (2010 and later shown, earlier models similar)

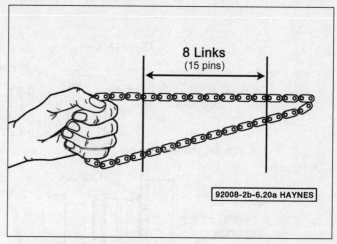

6.27a Timing chain stretch is measured by checking the length of the chain between 8 links (15 pins) at 3 or more places (selected randomly) around the chain - if chain stretch exceeds the specifications between any 8 links, the chain must be replaced

Inspection

Refer to illustrations 6.27a, 6.27b and 6.28

27 Visually inspect all parts for wear and damage. Check the timing chain for loose pins, cracks, worn rollers and side plates. Check the sprockets for hook-shaped, chipped and broken teeth. Also check the timing chain for stretching and the diameter of the timing sprockets for wear with the chain assembled on the sprockets **(see illustrations)**. Be sure to measure across the chain rollers when checking the sprocket diameter and to measure chain stretch at three or more places around the chain. Maximum chain elongation and minimum sprocket diameter (with chain) should not exceed the amount listed in this Chapter's Specifications. Replace the timing chain and sprockets as a set if the engine has

high mileage or fails inspection.

28 Check the chain guides for excessive wear **(see illustration)**. Replace the chain guides if scoring or wear exceeds the amount listed in this Chapter's Specifications. Note that some scoring of the timing chain guide shoes is normal. If excessive wear is indicated, it will also be necessary to inspect the chain guide oil hole on the front of the block for clogging **(see illustration 14.5d)**.

Installation

Refer to illustration 6.30

Caution: *Before starting the engine, carefully rotate the crankshaft by hand through at least two full revolutions (use a socket and breaker bar on the crankshaft pulley center bolt). If*

you feel any resistance, STOP! There is something wrong - most likely, valves are contacting the pistons. You must find the problem before proceeding.

29 Remove all traces of old sealant from the timing chain cover and the mating surfaces of the engine block and cylinder head.

30 Make sure the camshafts are positioned with the dowel pins at the top in the 12 o'clock position, then install both camshaft sprockets in their original locations by aligning the dowel pin hole on the rear of the sprockets with the dowel pin on the camshaft. Apply medium-strength thread locking compound to the camshaft sprocket bolt threads and make sure the washers are in place. Hold the camshaft from turning as described in Step 26 and tighten the bolts to the torque listed in this Chapter's Specifications. Make sure the camshaft

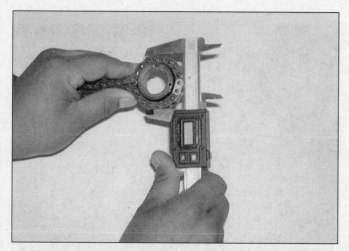

6.27b Wrap the chain around each of the timing sprockets and measure the diameter of the sprockets across the chain rollers - if the measurement is less than the minimum sprocket diameter, the chain and the timing sprockets must be replaced

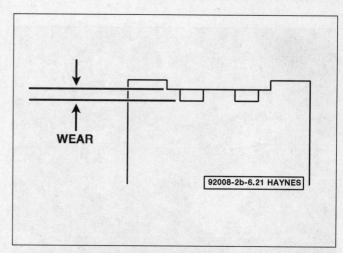

6.28 Timing chain guide wear is measured from the top of the chain contact surface to the bottom of the wear grooves

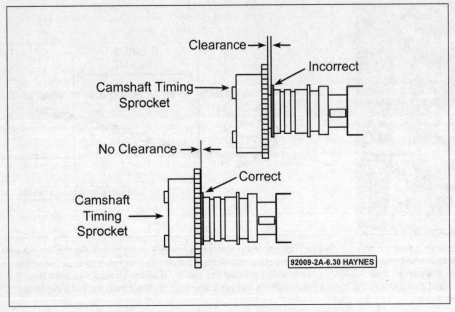

6.30 Camshaft timing sprocket installation details

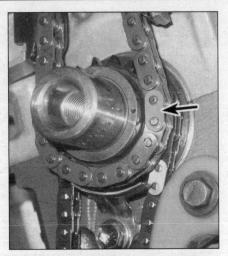

6.34 Loop the timing chain around the crankshaft sprocket and align the No.1 colored link with the mark on the crankshaft sprocket. Install the chain and crankshaft sprocket as an assembly on the engine and install the lower chain guide

sprocket is fully seated against the camshaft flange (see illustration).

2009 and earlier models

Refer to illustrations 6.34, 6.35, 6.36, 6.39a, 6.39b, 6.40, 6.41, 6.42 and 6.44

31   Make sure the TDC marks on the camshaft sprockets are still in alignment (see illustration 6.7a).

32   If the crankshaft has been rotated off TDC during this procedure, it will be necessary to rotate the crankshaft until the keyway is pointing straight up in the 12 o'clock position with the centerline of the cylinder bores.

33   Install the stationary timing chain guide (see illustration 6.16).

34   Loop the timing chain around the crank-shaft sprocket and align the No.1 colored link with the mark on the crankshaft sprocket. Install the chain and crankshaft sprocket as an assembly on the engine, then install the lower timing chain guide (see illustration). **Note:** *There are three colored links on the timing chain. The No.1 colored link is the link farthest away from the two colored links that are closest together.*

35   Slip the timing chain into the lip of the stationary timing chain guide and over the exhaust camshaft sprocket, then around the intake camshaft sprocket, making sure to align the remaining two colored links with the marks on the camshaft sprockets (see illustration). Make sure to remove all slack from the right side of the chain when performing this step.

36   Use one hand to remove the slack from the left side of the chain and install the timing chain tensioner pivot arm/chain guide. Tighten the pivot bolt to the torque listed in this Chapter's Specifications. After installation, make sure the tab on the pivot arm can't move past the stopper on the cylinder head (see illustration).

37   Reconfirm that the number one piston is still at TDC on the compression stroke and that the timing marks on the crankshaft and camshaft sprockets are aligned with the colored links on the chain.

38   Install the crankshaft position sensor reluctor ring with the "F" mark facing outward (see illustration 6.15).

39   Apply a bead of RTV sealant to the tim-

6.35 Loop the timing chain up over the exhaust camshaft and around the intake camshaft, while aligning the remaining two colored links with the marks on the camshaft sprockets

6.36 After the tensioner pivot arm is installed, make sure the tab on the pivot arm can't move past the stopper on the cylinder head

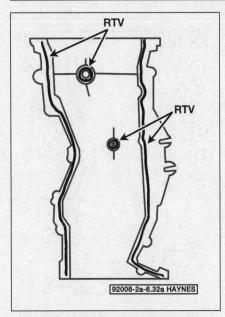

6.39a Timing chain cover sealant installation details

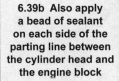

6.39b Also apply a bead of sealant on each side of the parting line between the cylinder head and the engine block

ing chain cover sealing surfaces (see illustrations). Place the timing chain cover in position on the engine and install the bolts in their original locations.

40 Tighten the bolts evenly in several steps to the torque listed in this Chapter's Specifications. Be sure to follow the sealant manufacturer's recommendations for assembly and sealant curing times (see illustration).

41 Reload and lock the timing chain tensioner to its zero position as follows:

a) Raise the ratchet pawl and push the plunger inward until it bottoms out (see illustration).

b) Engage the hook on the tensioner body with the pin on the tensioner plunger to lock the plunger in place.

42 Lubricate the tensioner O-ring with a small amount of oil and install the tensioner into the timing chain cover with the hook facing up (see illustration).

43 Install the crankshaft pulley/vibration damper (see Section 11).

44 Rotate the engine counterclockwise slightly to set the chain tension (see illustration). As the engine is rotated, the hook on the tensioner body should release itself from the pin on the plunger and allow the plunger to spring out and apply tension to the timing chain. If the plunger does not spring outward and apply tension to the timing chain, press downward on the pivot arm and release the hook with a screwdriver. Proceed to Step 60.

2010 and later models

Refer to illustrations 6.46, 6.57a, 6.57b and 6.58

45 Temporarily install the crankshaft pulley bolt and rotate the crankshaft counterclockwise until the keyway is pointing to the 10 o'clock position.

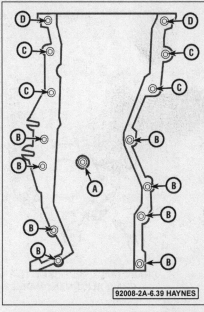

6.40 Timing chain cover bolt tightening guide - 2009 and earlier models (refer to the Specifications for the torque settings)

6.41 Raise the ratchet pawl and push the plunger inward until the hook on the tensioner body can be engaged with the pin on the plunger to lock the plunger in place

6.42 Apply a small amount of oil to the tensioner O-ring and insert the tensioner into the timing chain cover with the hook facing upward

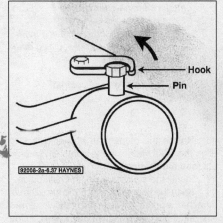

6.44 Rotate the engine counterclockwise to disengage the hook from the plunger pin on the tensioner, then rotate it clockwise and confirm that the plunger has extended outward against the pivot arm/chain guide

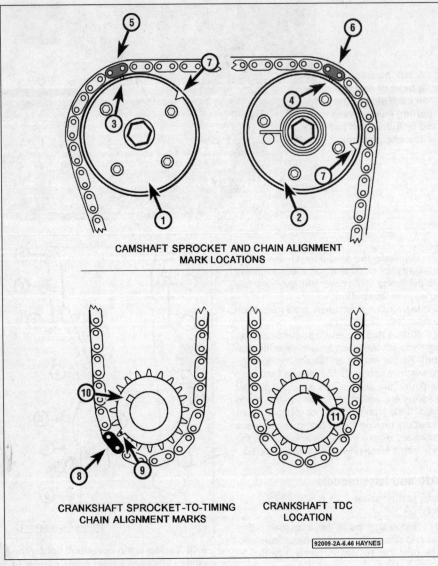

CAMSHAFT SPROCKET AND CHAIN ALIGNMENT
MARK LOCATIONS

CRANKSHAFT SPROCKET-TO-TIMING
CHAIN ALIGNMENT MARKS

CRANKSHAFT TDC
LOCATION

92009-2A-6.46 HAYNES

6.46 2010 and later timing chain alignment details

1   Intake camshaft sprocket
2   Exhaust camshaft sprocket
3   Intake camshaft sprocket timing mark
4   Exhaust camshaft sprocket timing mark
5   Timing chain "yellow" colored
    link - intake
6   Timing chain "yellow" colored
    link - exhaust
7   Index mark, not a timing mark
8   Timing chain "pink" colored link -
    crankshaft
9   Crankshaft sprocket timing mark
10 Crankshaft keyway 10 o'clock position
11 Crankshaft "TDC" keyway at 12
    o'clock position

46   Rotate the camshafts as necessary to align the TDC marks on the camshaft sprockets **(see illustration)**.
47   Install the stationary timing chain guide.
48   Loop the timing chain around the exhaust camshaft sprocket. Align the yellow colored link with the exhaust camshaft sprocket timing mark. **Note:** *There are three colored links on the timing chain. The pink colored link is the link farthest away from the two yellow colored links that are closest together.*
49   Guide the chain into the stationary chain guide and align the crankshaft sprocket with

the pink colored link and the mark on the crankshaft sprocket. **Note:** *Once the timing mark on the crankshaft sprocket and the colored link have been aligned, it may be necessary to tie the chain to the sprocket to prevent it from falling off during installation.*
50   Slip the timing chain around the intake camshaft sprocket but not onto the teeth of the sprocket. Using a wrench on the lug on the intake camshaft, rotate the camshaft counterclockwise to align the timing mark on the intake camshaft sprocket and the chain colored link. Once the camshaft sprocket and

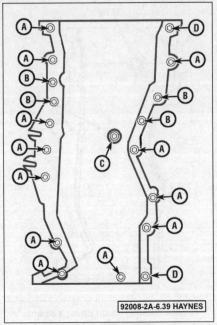

92008-2A-6.39 HAYNES

6.57a Timing chain cover bolt identification - 2010 and later models (refer to the Specifications for the torque settings)

colored link are aligned, install the chain on to the teeth of the camshaft sprocket. **Caution:** *Do not let go of the wrench holding the intake camshaft sprocket in place until the tensioner is installed.*
51   Using your free hand, remove the string holding the chain to the crankshaft sprocket. Rotate just the crankshaft clockwise until the keyway is pointing to the 12 o'clock position and all the slack is removed.
52   Install the tensioner guide and mounting bolt, then tighten the bolt to the torque listed in this Chapter's Specifications.
53   Install a new gasket and the tensioner with the mounting bolts. Tighten the tensioner mounting bolts to the torque listed in this Chapter's Specifications, then remove the pin and allow the plunger to contact the tensioner guide.
54   Confirm that the number one piston is still at TDC on the compression stroke and that the timing marks on the crankshaft and camshaft sprockets are aligned with the colored links on the chain **(see illustration 6.46)**.
55   Install the top chain guide mounting bolt and guide.
56   Apply a bead of RTV sealant to the timing chain cover sealing surfaces. Place the timing chain cover in position on the engine and install the bolts in their original locations.
57   Tighten the bolts a little at time, in the proper sequence, to the torque listed in this Chapter's Specifications **(see illustrations)**. Be sure to follow the sealant manufacturer's recommendations for assembly and sealant curing times.
58   Install the movement control rod mounting bracket **(see illustration)** to the front of the timing chain cover and tighten the bolts in

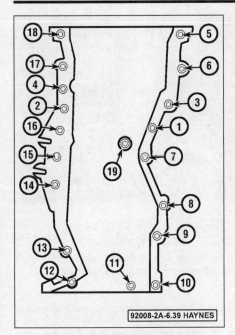

6.57b Timing chain cover bolt tightening sequence - 2010 and later models (refer to the Specifications for the torque settings)

6.58 Movement control rod mounting bracket bolt tightening sequence (use the reverse sequence for removal)

sequence to the torque listed in this Chapter's Specifications.

59 Install the crankshaft pulley/vibration damper (see Section 11).

All models

Caution: *Carefully rotate the crankshaft by hand through at least two full revolutions (use a socket and breaker bar on the crankshaft pulley center bolt). If you feel any resistance, STOP! There is something wrong - most likely, valves are contacting the pistons. You must find the problem before proceeding.*

60 Rotate the engine clockwise at least two revolutions and reposition the number one piston at TDC on the compression stroke (see Section 3). Visually confirm that the timing mark on the crankshaft pulley/vibration damper is aligned with the "0" mark on the timing chain cover and the camshaft sprocket marks are aligned and parallel with the top of the timing chain cover as shown in **illustrations 6.7a or 6.7b**.

61 The remainder of installation is the reverse of removal.

---

7 Camshafts and lifters - removal, inspection and installation

---

Note: *The camshafts should be thoroughly inspected before installation and camshaft endplay should be checked prior to camshaft removal (see Step 20).*

Removal

Refer to illustration 7.7

1 Disconnect the cable from the negative battery terminal (see Chapter 5).
2 Remove the valve cover (see Section 4).
3 Place the engine at TDC on the compression stroke for number 1 cylinder (see Section 3).
4 With the engine set to TDC on the compression stroke for number 1 cylinder, apply a dab of paint to the timing chain links where they meet the timing marks on the camshaft sprockets.
5 Using a wrench to hold the camshafts from turning, loosen the camshaft sprocket bolts several turns **(see illustration 6.26)**.
6 On 2009 and earlier models, remove the timing chain tensioner from the timing chain cover **(see illustrations 6.13a and 6.13b)** and the camshaft position sensor from the cylinder head (see Chapter 6). On 2010 and later models, remove the timing chain cover and tensioner (see Section 6, Steps 19 through 25).

7 Remove the camshaft sprocket retaining bolts. Disengage the timing chain from the sprockets and remove the camshaft sprockets from the engine. Make sure to note that the Variable Valve Timing (VVT) actuator is installed on the intake camshaft on all models (and the exhaust camshaft on 2010 and later models). On 2009 and earlier models, after removing the sprockets, hang the timing chain up with a piece of wire and attach it to an object on the firewall **(see illustration)**. This will prevent the timing chain from falling into the engine as the remaining steps in this procedure are performed. Also place a rag into the opening of the timing chain cover to prevent any foreign objects from falling into the engine.

2009 and earlier models

Refer to illustrations 7.8, 7.11a and 7.11b

8 Verify the markings on the camshaft bearing caps. The caps should be marked from 1 to 5 with an "I" or an "E" mark on the cap indicating whether they're for the intake

7.7 With the camshaft sprockets removed, hang the timing chain out of the way with a piece of wire and place a shop rag in the timing chain cover opening to prevent foreign objects from falling into the engine

7.8 The camshaft bearing caps are numbered and have an arrow that should face the timing chain end of the engine

7.11a Mark the lifters (I for intake, E for exhaust, and number their location) and remove them with a magnetic retrieval tool

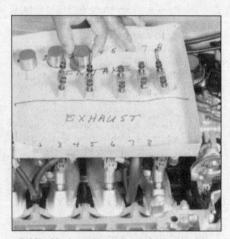

7.11b Mark up a cardboard box to store the lifters and bearing caps in order

7.20 Mount a dial indicator as shown to measure camshaft endplay - pry the camshaft forward and back and read the endplay on the dial

Clean the camshaft housing mounting surface and the mating surface on the cylinder head.

17   Remove the rocker arms from the cylinder head. **Caution:** *Keep the rocker arms in order. They must go back in the position from which they were removed.*

18   Remove the lash adjusters from the cylinder head. **Caution:** *Keep the lash adjusters in order. They must go back in the position from which they were removed.*

19   Inspect the camshafts, camshaft bearings, camshaft housing, rockers and lash adjusters as described below. Also inspect the camshaft sprockets for wear on the teeth. Inspect the chains for cracks or excessive wear of the rollers, and for stretching (see Section 6). If any of the components show signs of excessive wear, they must be replaced.

Inspection

Refer to illustrations 7.20, 7.21, 7.22, 7.23, 7.25 and 7.26

20   Before the camshafts are removed from the engine, check the camshaft endplay by placing a dial indicator with the stem in line with the camshaft and touching the snout **(see illustration)**. Push the camshaft all the way to the rear and zero the dial indicator. Next, pry the camshaft to the front as far as possible and check the reading on the dial indicator. The distance it moves is the endplay. If the endplay for the intake camshaft is greater than the Specifications listed in this Chapter, check the thrust surfaces of the No.1 journal bearing for wear. If the thrust surface is worn, the bearings must be replaced. If the endplay for the exhaust camshaft is greater than the Specifications listed in this Chapter, the camshaft or the cylinder head (or both) may need to be replaced.

21   With the camshafts removed, visually check the camshaft bearing surfaces in the cylinder head for pitting, score marks, galling and abnormal wear. On 2009 and earlier models, if the bearing surfaces are damaged, the

---

or exhaust camshaft **(see illustration)**.

9   Loosen the camshaft bearing caps in two or three steps, in the reverse order of the tightening sequence **(see illustration 7.29). Caution:** *Keep the caps in order. They must go back in the same location they were removed from.*

10   Detach the bearing caps, then remove the camshaft(s) from the cylinder head. Mark the camshaft(s) "Intake" or "Exhaust" to avoid mixing them up. **Note:** *When looking at the engine from the front of the vehicle, the forward facing cam is the exhaust camshaft and the cam nearest the firewall is the intake camshaft. It is very important that the camshafts are returned to their original locations during installation.*

11   Remove the lifters from the cylinder head, keeping them in order with their respective valve and cylinder **(see illustrations). Caution:** *Keep the lifters in order. They must go back in the position from which they were removed.*

12   Inspect the camshafts, camshaft bear-

ings and lifters (see Steps 20 through 26). Also inspect the camshaft sprockets for wear on the teeth. Inspect the chains for cracks or excessive wear of the rollers, and for stretching (see Section 6). If any of the components show signs of excessive wear, they must be replaced.

2010 and later models

13   Loosen the camshaft housing bearing cap bolts in sequence in two or three steps, in the reverse order of the tightening sequence **(see illustration 7.38).**

14   Remove the camshaft housing by prying between the cylinder head and camshaft housing with a screwdriver. **Note:** *Be careful not to damage the cylinder head and camshaft housing.*

15   Loosen the camshaft bearing cap bolts in sequence in two or three steps, in the reverse order of the tightening sequence **(see illustration 7.42).**

16   Remove the bearing caps, oil control filter and camshafts from the camshaft housing.

7.21 Inspect the No. 2 through No. 5 cam bearing surfaces in the cylinder head for pits, score marks and abnormal wear - if wear or damage is noted, the cylinder head (2009 and earlier models) or the camshaft housing (2010 and later models) must be replaced

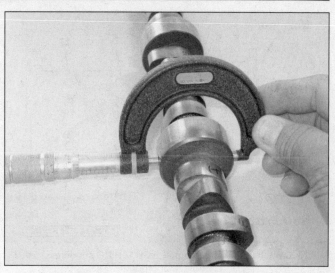

7.22 Measure each journal diameter with a micrometer - if any journal measures less than the specified limit, replace the camshaft

cylinder head or the No.1 journal bearings of the intake camshaft may have to be replaced **(see illustration)** On 2010 and later models, the camshaft housing or camshaft(s) will need to be replaced.

22 Measure the outside diameter of each camshaft bearing journal and record your measurements **(see illustration)**. Compare them to the journal outside diameter specified in this Chapter, then measure the inside diameter of each corresponding camshaft bearing and record the measurements. Subtract each cam journal outside diameter from its respective cam bearing bore inside diameter to determine the oil clearance for each bearing. Compare the results to the specified journal-to-bearing clearance. If any of the measurements fall outside the standard specified wear limits in this Chapter, either the camshaft or the cylinder head (or both) must be replaced.

Note: *If precision measuring tools are not available, Plastigage may be used to determine the bearing journal oil clearance.*

23 Using a micrometer, measure the height of each camshaft lobe **(see illustration)**. Compare your measurements with this Chapter's Specifications. If the height for any one lobe is less than the specified minimum, replace the camshaft.

24 Check the camshaft runout by placing the camshaft back into the cylinder head and set up a dial indicator on the center journal. Zero the dial indicator. Turn the camshaft slowly and note the dial indicator readings. Runout should not exceed 0.0012 inch (0.03 mm). If the measured runout exceeds the specified runout, replace the camshaft.

25 Inspect the lifters for scuffing and score marks **(see illustration)**. On 2010 and later models, inspect each rocker as well.

26 Measure the outside diameter of each lifter **(see illustration)** and the corresponding lifter bore inside diameter. Subtract the lifter diameter from the lifter bore diameter to determine the oil clearance. Compare it to this Chapter's Specifications. If the oil clearance is excessive, a new cylinder head and/or new lifters will be required.

Installation
2009 and earlier models
Refer to illustration 7.29

27 If the No.1 journal bearings were removed, install them into the cylinder head and the bearing cap now. Apply camshaft installation lubricant to the camshaft lobes and journals and install the camshaft into the cylinder head with the No.1 cylinder camshaft lobes pointing outward away from each other

7.23 Measure the lobe heights on each camshaft - if any lobe height is less than the specified allowable minimum, replace that camshaft

7.25 Wipe off the oil and inspect each lifter for wear and scuffing - 2009 and earlier model shown

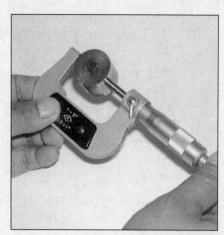

7.26 Measure the outside diameter of each lifter and the inside diameter of each lifter bore to determine the oil clearance measurement (2009 and earlier models)

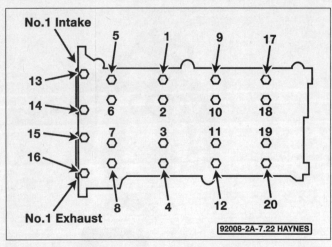

7.29 Camshaft bearing cap bolt TIGHTENING sequence - 2009 and earlier models

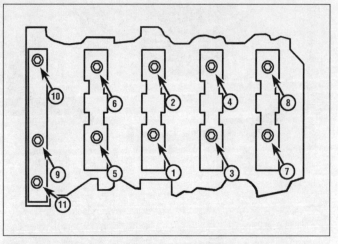

7.38 Camshaft bearing cap bolt TIGHTENING sequence - 2010 and later models

(at an approximately 30-degree angle), and the dowel pins facing upward.

28   Install the bearing caps and bolts and tighten them hand tight.

29   Tighten the bearing cap bolts in several equal steps, to the torque listed in this Chapter's Specifications, using the proper tightening sequence **(see illustration)**.

30   Engage the camshaft sprocket teeth with the timing chain links so that the match marks made during removal align with the upper timing marks on the sprockets, then position the sprockets over the dowels on the camshaft hubs and install the camshaft sprocket bolts finger tight. The mark on the crankshaft pulley should be aligned with the "0" mark on the timing chain cover, the

camshaft sprocket TDC marks should be aligned and parallel with the top of the timing chain cover, and the timing chain match marks should be aligned with the upper timing sprocket marks with all of the slack in the chain positioned towards the tensioner side of the engine.

31   Double check that the timing sprockets are returned to the proper camshaft and tighten the camshaft sprocket bolts to the torque listed in this Chapter's Specifications.

32   Install the timing chain tensioner as described in Section 6, Steps 41 and 42.

33   The remainder of installation is the reverse of removal.

2010 and later models

Refer to illustrations 7.38 and 7.42

34   Coat the lash adjusters with engine oil and install them into the cylinder head in the same locations from which they were removed.

35   Apply oil to the rocker arms and install them, making sure each rocker arm is seated to its lash adjuster.

36   Install the camshaft bearings and oil control valve filter into the camshaft housing.

37   Apply camshaft installation lubricant to the camshaft lobes and journals and install the camshaft into the camshaft housing.

38   Install the camshaft bearing caps to the camshaft housing and tighten the bearing cap bolts in several equal steps, to the torque listed in this Chapter's Specifications, using the proper tightening sequence **(see illustration)**.

39   Check that the rocker arms are installed properly and have not moved.

40   Position the dowel pins facing upwards; the intake camshaft dowel pin should be at a 17-degree angle and the exhaust pin should be at a 2-degree angle (counterclockwise from the 12 o'clock position).

41   Apply a 1/4-inch wide bead of Toyota Genuine Seal Packing Black, Three Bond 1207B (or equivalent) to the camshaft housing-to-cylinder head contact surface. **Note:** *The camshaft housing must be installed within 3 minutes, and the bolts must be tightened within 10 minutes after applying seal packing.*

42   Install the camshaft housing to the cylinder head, install the mounting bolts and tighten the bolts in several equal steps, to the torque listed in this Chapter's Specifications, using the proper tightening sequence **(see illustration)**. **Note:** *Do not add oil or try to start the engine for at least 4 hours after installation or the seal packing will leak.*

43   Install the camshaft sprockets, timing chain and timing chain cover (see Section 6).

44   The remainder of installation is the reverse of removal.

7.42 Camshaft housing bolt TIGHTENING sequence - 2010 and later models

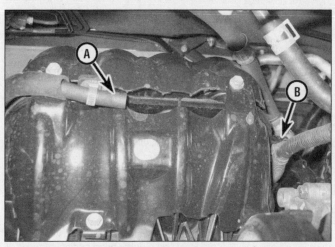

8.4 Label and disconnect the vacuum hoses (A) and the wire harness retainers (B) from the intake manifold

8.5 Intake manifold lower fastener locations

8 Intake manifold - removal and installation

Warning: *Wait until the engine is completely cool before beginning this procedure.*

Removal

1 Relieve the fuel system pressure (see Chapter 4), then disconnect the cable from the negative battery terminal (see Chapter 5).

2 Remove the air intake duct and resonator (see Chapter 4), then remove the cowl cover assembly (see Chapter 11).

2009 and earlier models

Refer to illustrations 8.4, 8.5 and 8.6

3 Remove the fuel rail and injectors as an assembly. Also remove the throttle linkage and the throttle body from the intake manifold (see Chapter 4).

4 Label and detach the PCV and vacuum hoses connected to the rear of the intake manifold **(see illustration)**.

5 Raise the vehicle and support it securely on jackstands. Working below the vehicle, remove the manifold lower mounting bolts **(see illustration)**.

6 Working from above, remove the intake manifold upper mounting nuts and bolts. Remove the manifold, the gasket and the manifold insulator from the engine **(see illustration)**.

2010 and later models

Refer to illustration 8.13

7 Remove the engine cover **(see illustration 4.2b)**.

8 Disconnect the vacuum hoses and ventilation tubes from the intake manifold.

9 Remove the throttle body from the intake manifold (see Chapter 4).

10 Disconnect the fuel inlet line to the fuel rail (see Chapter 4).

11 Disconnect the electrical connectors from the fuel rail, remove the harness mounting fasteners and set the harness to the side.

12 Disconnect and remove the main harness connector to the intake manifold and tumble control valves. **Note:** *The tumble control valve harness connector is located just below the throttle body.*

13 Using test leads, apply battery voltage to terminal no. 8 of the tumble control valve electrical connector and ground the no. 4 terminal **(see illustration)**; this will close the tumble control valve to prevent it from being damaged when the manifold is removed. Don't apply voltage longer than three seconds. **Caution:** *If the voltage is applied longer than three seconds, or any other terminals are touched, the actuator may be damaged.*

14 Remove the intake manifold support bracket and disconnect the vacuum switching valve assembly electrical connector.

8.6 Intake manifold upper fastener locations

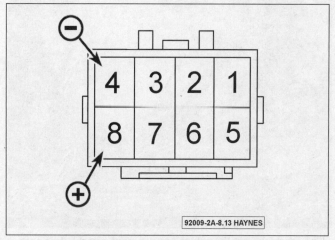

8.13 Tumble control valve connector pin identification - DO NOT apply voltage longer than three seconds or touch any other terminals or the actuator may be damaged.

8.17 Press the gasket into the groove on the intake manifold

15   Unscrew the intake manifold mounting fasteners and remove the manifold.

Installation

Refer to illustration 8.17

16   Clean the mating surfaces of the intake manifold and the cylinder head mounting surface. If the gasket shows signs of leaking, check the manifold for warpage with a straightedge and feeler gauges. If the manifold is warped, it must be replaced.
17   Press a new gasket into the grooves on the intake manifold **(see illustration)**. Install the manifold and gasket over the studs on the cylinder head.
18   Tighten the manifold-to-cylinder head nuts/bolts in three or four equal steps to the torque listed in this Chapter's Specifications. Work from the center out towards the ends to avoid warping the manifold.
19   Install the remaining parts in the reverse order of removal. Check the coolant level, adding as necessary (see Chapter 1).
20   Before starting the engine, check the throttle linkage for smooth operation.

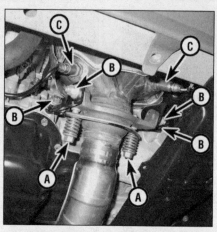

9.3 Working below the vehicle, remove the exhaust pipe-to-manifold mounting bolts (A) and lower the front exhaust pipe. Be careful not to damage the oxygen sensors (C) - (B) indicates the mounting fasteners for the exhaust manifold lower brace

21   Run the engine and check for coolant and vacuum leaks.

9   Exhaust manifold - removal and installation

Warning: *The engine must be completely cool before beginning this procedure.*

Removal

Refer to illustrations 9.3, 9.5 and 9.6

1   Disconnect the cable from the negative battery terminal (see Chapter 5).
2   Raise the front of the vehicle and support it securely on jackstands. Working below the vehicle, remove the lower splash shields.
3   Apply penetrating oil to the bolts retaining the exhaust pipe to the manifold. After the bolts have soaked, remove the bolts retaining

the exhaust pipe to the manifold **(see illustration)**. Separate the front exhaust pipe from the manifold.
4   Unbolt the lower exhaust manifold braces and remove them from the engine. Also disconnect the oxygen sensor connectors.
5   Working in the engine compartment, remove the upper heat shield from the manifold **(see illustration)**. **Note:** *There is also a lower heat shield, but it is attached to the manifold from underneath and does not need to be removed.*
6   Remove the nuts/bolts and detach the manifold and gasket **(see illustration)**.

Installation

7   Use a scraper to remove all traces of old gasket material and carbon deposits from the manifold and cylinder head mating surfaces. If the gasket shows signs of leaking, check the manifold for warpage with a straight edge. If the manifold is warped, it must be replaced. **Note:** *If the manifold is being replaced with a new one, it will be necessary to remove the lower heat shield and fasten it to the new manifold.*
8   Position a new gasket over the cylinder head studs, noting any directional marks or arrows on the gasket which may be present.
9   Install the manifold and thread the mounting nuts into place.
10   Working from the center out, tighten the nuts/bolts to the torque listed in this Chapter's Specifications in three or four equal steps.
11   Reinstall the remaining parts in the reverse order of removal.
12   Run the engine and check for exhaust leaks.

10   Cylinder head - removal and installation

Warning: *The engine must be completely cool before beginning this procedure.*

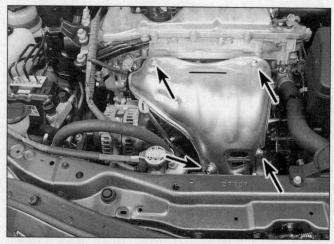

9.5 Working from the engine compartment, remove the upper heat shield mounting bolts . . .

9.6 . . . and the exhaust manifold retaining nuts, then pull the manifold off the studs on the cylinder head and remove from above

Caution: *New cylinder head bolts should be used when installing the cylinder head.*
Note: *If you're working on a 2010 or later model, the manufacturer recommends removing the engine and transaxle assembly to perform this procedure (see Chapter 2C).*

Removal

Refer to illustration 10.11

1   Relieve the fuel system pressure (see Chapter 4), then disconnect the cable from the negative terminal of the battery.
2   Drain the engine coolant (see Chapter 1).
3   Remove the drivebelt and the alternator (see Chapter 5).
4   Remove the valve cover (see Section 4).
5   Remove the throttle body, fuel injectors and fuel rail (see Chapter 4).
6   Remove the intake manifold (see Section 8).
7   Remove the exhaust manifold (see Section 9).
8   Remove the timing chain and camshaft sprockets (see Section 6).
9   On 2010 and later models, remove the camshafts, lifters and camshaft housing (see Section 7).
10   Remove the variable valve timing control valve **(see illustration 5.2a or 5.2b)**.
11   Label and remove the coolant hoses and electrical connections from the cylinder head **(see illustration)**.
12   Using a 10 mm hex-head socket bit and a breaker bar, loosen the cylinder head bolts in 1/4-turn increments until they can be removed by hand. Loosen the cylinder head bolts in the reverse order of the recommended tightening sequence **(see illustration 10.24a or 10.24b)** to avoid warping or cracking the cylinder head.
13   Lift the cylinder head off the engine block. If it's stuck, very carefully pry up at the transaxle end, beyond the gasket.
14   Remove any remaining external components from the cylinder head to allow for thorough cleaning and inspection.

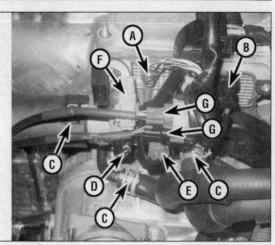

10.11 Disconnect the following components from the driver's side of the cylinder head and position the electrical wiring harness aside - 2009 and earlier models shown

A   Ground straps
B   Camshaft position sensor
C   Coolant hoses
D   Oil pressure sending unit
E   Coolant temperature sensor
F   Radio noise suppressor
G   Oxygen sensor connector

Installation

Refer to illustrations 10.24a and 10.24b

15   The mating surfaces of the cylinder head and block must be perfectly clean when the cylinder head is installed.
16   Use a gasket scraper to remove all traces of carbon and old gasket material, then clean the mating surfaces with brake system cleaner. If there's oil on the mating surfaces when the cylinder head is installed, the gasket may not seal correctly and leaks could develop. When working on the block, stuff the cylinders with clean shop rags to keep out debris.
17   Use a vacuum cleaner to remove material that falls into the cylinders.
18   Check the block and cylinder head mating surfaces for nicks, deep scratches and other damage. If damage is slight, it can be removed with a file; if it's excessive, machining may be the only alternative.
19   Use a tap of the correct size to chase the threads in the cylinder head bolt holes, then clean the holes with compressed air - make sure that nothing remains in the holes. **Warning:** *Wear eye protection when using compressed air!*

20   Install the components that were removed from the cylinder head.
21   Position the new gasket over the dowel pins in the block, then apply RTV sealant to the ends of the cylinder head gasket on the timing chain cover side.
22   Carefully set the cylinder head on the block without disturbing the gasket.
23   Before installing the cylinder head bolts, apply a small amount of clean engine oil to the threads and under the bolt heads.
24   Install the new cylinder head bolts and tighten them finger tight. Following the recommended sequence, tighten the bolts to the torque listed in this Chapter's Specifications **(see illustrations)**.
25   The remainder of installation is the reverse of removal. **Caution:** *Wait at least four hours before adding oil and coolant and starting the engine.*
26   On 2009 and earlier models, check and adjust the valves as necessary (see Chapter 1).
27   Change the engine oil and filter (see Chapter 1).
28   Refill the cooling system (see Chapter 1), run the engine and check for leaks.

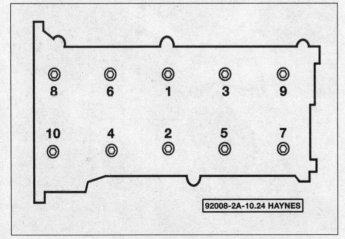

10.24a Cylinder head bolt TIGHTENING sequence - 2009 and earlier models

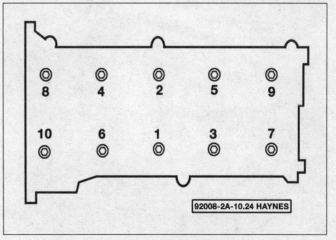

10.24b Cylinder head bolt TIGHTENING sequence - 2010 and later models

11.4 A puller base and several spacers can be mounted to the center hub of the pulley to keep the crankshaft from turning as the pulley retaining bolt is loosened - install the socket over the crankshaft bolt head before installing the puller, then insert the extension through the center hole of the puller

11.5 When using a puller on the crankshaft pulley, be sure to use the proper adapter between the puller screw and the nose of the crankshaft

11   Crankshaft pulley/vibration damper - removal and installation

Refer to illustrations 11.4 and 11.5

1   Disconnect the cable from the negative battery terminal (see Chapter 5).

2   Remove the drivebelt (see Chapter 1).

3   With the parking brake applied and the shifter in Park (automatic) or in gear (manual), loosen the lug nuts from the right front wheel, then raise the front of the vehicle and support it securely on jackstands. Remove the right front wheel and the right splash shield from the wheelwell.

4   Remove the bolt from the front of the crankshaft. A breaker bar will probably be necessary, since the bolt is very tight (**see illustration**).

5   Using a puller that bolts to the crankshaft hub, remove the crankshaft pulley from the crankshaft (**see illustration**). **Note:** *Depending on the type of puller you have it may be necessary to support the engine from above, remove the right side engine mount and lower to engine to gain sufficient clearance to use the puller.* **Caution:** *Do not use a jaw-type puller - it will damage the pulley/damper assembly.*

6   To install the crankshaft pulley, slide the pulley onto the crankshaft as far as it will slide on, then use a vibration damper installation tool to press the pulley onto the crankshaft. Note that the slot (keyway) in the hub must be aligned with the Woodruff key in the end of the crankshaft and that the crankshaft bolt can also be used to press the crankshaft pulley into position.

7   Tighten the crankshaft bolt to the torque listed in this Chapter's Specifications.

8   The remainder of installation is the reverse of removal.

12   Crankshaft front oil seal - replacement

Refer to illustrations 12.2 and 12.3

1   Remove the crankshaft pulley (see Section 11).

2   Note how the seal is installed - the new one must be installed to the same depth and facing the same way. Carefully pry the oil seal out of the cover with a seal puller or a large screwdriver (**see illustration**). Be very careful not to distort the cover or scratch the crankshaft!

3   Apply clean engine oil or multi-purpose grease to the outer edge of the new seal, then install it in the cover with the lip (spring side) facing IN. Drive the seal into place with a seal driver or a large socket and a hammer (**see illustration**). Make sure the seal enters the bore squarely and stop when the front face is at the proper depth.

12.2 Carefully pry the old seal out of the timing chain cover - don't damage the crankshaft in the process

12.3 Drive the new seal into place with a large socket and hammer

13.6a Oil pan mounting bolts

13.6b Pry the oil pan loose with a screwdriver or putty knife - be careful not to damage the mating surfaces of the pan and block or oil leaks may develop

4   Check the surface on the pulley hub that the oil seal rides on. If the surface has been grooved from long-time contact with the seal, the pulley should be replaced.
5   Lubricate the pulley hub with clean engine oil and reinstall the crankshaft pulley (see Section 11).
6   Install the crankshaft pulley retaining bolt and tighten it to the torque listed in this Chapter's Specifications.
7   The remainder of installation is the reverse of removal.

13 Oil pan - removal and installation

Removal

Refer to illustrations 13.6a and 13.6b

1   Disconnect the cable from the negative battery terminal (see Chapter 5).
2   Set the parking brake and block the rear wheels.
3   Raise the front of the vehicle and support it securely on jackstands.
4   Remove the two plastic splash shields under the engine, if equipped.
5   Drain the engine oil and remove the oil filter (see Chapter 1). Remove the oil dipstick.
6   Remove the bolts and detach the oil pan. If it's stuck, pry it loose very carefully with a small screwdriver or putty knife **(see illustrations)**. Don't damage the mating surfaces of the pan and block or oil leaks could develop.

Installation

7   Use a scraper to remove all traces of old sealant from the block and oil pan. Clean the mating surfaces with brake system cleaner.
8   Make sure the threaded bolt holes in the block are clean.
9   Check the oil pan flange for distortion, particularly around the bolt holes. Remove

14.2a Rotate the engine 90-degrees counterclockwise (from TDC) and set the crankshaft key to the left horizontal position (A), then remove the oil pump drive chain tensioner and bolt (B)

14.2b Using a screwdriver to lock the lower gear in place, loosen the retaining bolt and remove the drive chain and lower gear and from the engine

any nicks or burrs as necessary.
10   Inspect the oil pump pick-up tube assembly for cracks and a blocked strainer. If the pick-up was removed, clean it thoroughly and install it now, using a new gasket. Tighten the nuts/bolts to the torque listed in this Chapter's Specifications.
11   Apply a 3/16-inch wide bead of RTV sealant to the mating surface of the oil pan. **Note:** *Be sure follow the sealant manufacturers recommendations for assembly and sealant curing times.*
12   Carefully position the oil pan on the engine block and install the oil pan-to-engine block bolts loosely.
13   Working from the center out, tighten the oil pan-to-engine block bolts to the torque listed in this Chapter's Specifications in three or four steps.
14   The remainder of installation is the reverse of removal. Be sure to wait at least one hour before adding oil to allow the sealant

to properly cure.
15   Run the engine and check for oil pressure and leaks.

14 Oil pump - removal and installation

Note: *On 2010 and later models, the oil pump is not serviceable separately from the timing chain cover. If the oil pump is defective, the timing chain cover and pump must be replaced as a unit (see Section 6).*

Removal

Refer to illustrations 14.2a, 14.2b, 14.3, 14.5a and 14.5b

1   Remove the timing chain and the crankshaft sprocket (see Section 6).
2   Remove the oil pump drive chain and sprockets **(see illustrations)**.

14.3 Oil pump mounting bolts

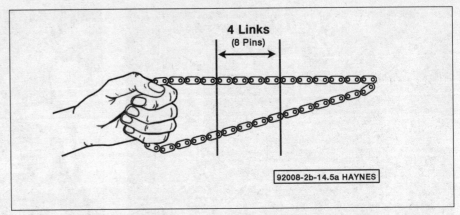

14.5a Oil pump drive chain stretch is measured by checking the length of the chain between 4 links (8 pins) at 3 or more places (selected randomly) around the chain - if chain stretch exceeds the specifications between any 4 links, the chain must be replaced

3   Remove the three bolts and detach the oil pump body from the engine (see illustration). You may have to pry carefully between the front of the block and the pump body with a screwdriver to remove it.

4   Use a scraper to remove all traces of sealant and old gasket material from the pump body and engine block, then clean the mating surfaces with brake system cleaner.

5   Inspect the oil pump and chain for wear and damage. If the oil pump shows signs of wear or you're in doubt about its condition it is simply best to replace it. Oil pump drive chain stretch is measured by checking the length of the chain between 4 links (8 pins) at 3 or more places (selected randomly) around the chain - if chain stretch exceeds the specifications between any 4 links, the chain must be replaced (see illustration). Wrap the chain around each of the oil pump drive sprockets and measure the diameter of the sprockets across the chain rollers (see illustration 6.27b) - if the measurement is less than the minimum sprocket diameter, the chain and the sprockets must be replaced. Oil pump chain guide wear is measured from the top of the chain contact surface to the bottom of the wear grooves (see illustration 6.28). Also check the oil jet for blockage (see illustration).

Installation

Refer to illustration 14.9

6   Lubricate the pump cavity by pouring a small amount of clean engine oil into the inlet side of the oil pump and turning the drive gear shaft.

7   Position the oil pump and a new gasket against the block and install the mounting bolts.

8   Tighten the bolts to the torque listed in this Chapter's Specifications in several steps. Follow a criss-cross pattern to avoid warping the body.

9   Install the drive chain and sprockets so that the colored links on the chain align with the alignment marks on the drive gears (see illustration).

10   Tighten the lower drive sprocket retaining bolt to the torque listed in this Chapter's Specifications.

14.5b Check that the oil jet is free of debris - a blockage here will lead to an excessively worn timing chain, oil pump drive chain and guides

11   Reinstall the remaining parts in the reverse order of removal.

12   Add oil to the proper level, start the engine and check for oil pressure and leaks.

15   Flywheel/driveplate - removal and installation

Removal

Refer to illustrations 15.3 and 15.5

1   Remove the transaxle (see Chapter 7). If it's leaking, now would be a very good time to replace the front pump seal/O-ring (automatic transaxle only).

2   Remove the pressure plate and clutch disc (see Chapter 8) (manual transaxle equipped vehicles). Now is a good time to check/replace the clutch components.

3   Use a center punch or paint to make alignment marks on the flywheel/driveplate and crankshaft to ensure correct alignment during reinstallation (see illustration).

4   Remove the bolts that secure the flywheel/driveplate to the crankshaft. If the

14.9 Install the oil pump drive chain with the colored links aligned with the marks on the sprockets

crankshaft turns, wedge a screwdriver in the ring gear teeth to jam the flywheel.

5   Remove the flywheel/driveplate from the crankshaft. Since the flywheel is fairly heavy, be sure to support it while removing the last bolt. Automatic transaxle equipped vehicles have spacers on both sides of the driveplate (see illustration). Keep them with the driveplate.

Installation

6   Clean the flywheel to remove grease and oil. Inspect the surface for cracks, rivet grooves, burned areas and score marks. Light scoring can be removed with emery cloth. Check for cracked and broken ring gear teeth. Lay the flywheel on a flat surface and use a straightedge to check for warpage.

7   Clean and inspect the mating surfaces of the flywheel/driveplate and the crankshaft. If the crankshaft rear seal is leaking, replace it before reinstalling the flywheel/driveplate.

8   Position the flywheel/driveplate against the crankshaft. Be sure to align the marks made during removal. Note that some engines have an alignment dowel or staggered bolt holes to ensure correct installation. Before installing the bolts, apply thread locking compound to the threads.

15.3 Mark the flywheel/driveplate and the crankshaft so they can be reassembled in the same relative positions - most models will have eight flywheel bolts

15.5 On vehicles with an automatic transaxle, there is a spacer plate on each side of the driveplate; when installing, line up the spacers with the locating pin (arrow)

9   Wedge a screwdriver in the ring gear teeth to keep the flywheel/driveplate from turning and tighten the bolts to the torque listed in this Chapter's Specifications. Follow a criss-cross pattern and work up to the final torque in three or four steps.

10   The remainder of installation is the reverse of the removal procedure.

16   Rear main oil seal - replacement

1   Remove the engine/transaxle assembly (see Chapter 2C), then separate the transaxle from the engine (see Chapter 7A or 7B).

2   Remove the flywheel/driveplate (see Section 15).

3   Pry the oil seal from the rear of the engine with a screwdriver. Be careful not to nick or scratch the crankshaft or the seal bore. Be sure to note how far it's recessed into the bore before removal so the new seal can be installed to the same depth. Thoroughly clean the seal bore in the block with a shop towel. Remove all traces of oil and dirt.

4   Lubricate the outside diameter of the seal and install the seal over the end of the crankshaft. Make sure the lip of the seal points toward the engine. Preferably, a seal installation tool (available at most auto parts store) is needed to press the new seal back into place. If the proper seal installation tool is unavailable, use a large socket, section of pipe or a blunt tool and carefully drive the new seal squarely into the seal bore and flush with the edge of the engine block.

5   Install the flywheel/driveplate (see Section 15).

6   Install the transaxle to the engine (see Chapter 7A or 7B), then install the engine/transaxle assembly (see Chapter 2C).

17   Powertrain mounts - check and replacement

1   Powertrain mounts seldom require attention, but broken or deteriorated mounts should be replaced immediately or the added strain placed on driveline components may cause damage or wear.

Check

2   During the check, the engine (or transaxle) must be raised slightly to remove the weight from the mounts.

3   Raise the vehicle and support it securely on jackstands, then remove the splash shields under the engine and position a jack under the engine oil pan. Place a large block of wood between the jack and the oil pan, then carefully raise the engine just enough to take the weight off the mounts. Do not position the wood block under the oil drain plug. **Warning:** *DO NOT place any part of your body under the engine when it is supported only by a jack!*

4   Check the mounts to see if the rubber is cracked, hardened or separated from the bushing in the center of the mount.

5   Check for relative movement between the mount plates and the engine or frame (use a large screwdriver or pry bar to attempt to move the mounts). If movement is noted, lower the engine and tighten the mount fasteners.

6   Rubber preservative should be applied to the mounts to slow deterioration.

Replacement

Refer to illustrations 17.8, 17.11, 17.14 and 17.20

7   Disconnect the cable from the negative battery terminal (see Chapter 5), then

17.8 Right-hand engine mount details

A   *Engine mount nuts*
B   *Engine mount bracket fasteners (under the plastic plug covers)*

raise the vehicle and support it securely on jackstands, if not already done. Support the engine as described in Step 3. **Note:** *If several mounts need replacement, only replace one at a time and tighten them as you go. Do not remove all the mounts at once.*

Passenger's side (right-hand) engine mount

8   Working below the vehicle, remove the nuts securing the mount to the upper and lower brackets (**see illustration**).

9   Remove the bolts securing the mount to the frame, then raise the transaxle enough to allow removal of the mount.

10   Installation is the reverse of the removal. Use thread-locking compound on the bolts and be sure to tighten them securely.

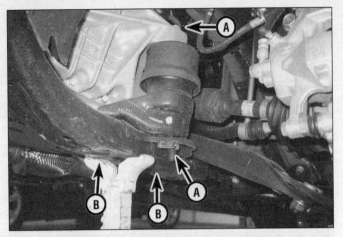

17.11 Left-hand transaxle mount details

A   *Transaxle/engine mount nuts*
B   *Transaxle/engine mount bracket fasteners (under the plastic plug covers)*

17.14 Front mount details

A   *Transaxle/engine mount*
B   *Transaxle/engine upper mounting bracket*
C   *Mount upper fastener*

Driver's side (left-hand) transaxle mount

11   Working below the vehicle, remove the nut securing the mount to the upper and lower brackets **(see illustration)**.

12   Remove the bolts securing the mount to the frame, then raise the engine enough to allow removal of the mount.

13   Installation is the reverse of the removal. Use thread-locking compound on the bolts and be sure to tighten them securely.

Front engine mount

14   Working from the top, remove the fastener securing the mount to the bracket **(see illustration)**.

15   Working below the vehicle, remove the bolts securing the mount to the frame, then raise the engine enough to allow removal of the mount.

16   Installation is the reverse of the removal. Use thread-locking compound on the bolts

and be sure to tighten them securely.

Rear engine mount

17   Working below the vehicle, remove the mount nut and slide the through bolt out of the insulator.

18   Remove the bolts securing the mount to the frame, then raise the engine enough to allow removal of the mount.

19   Installation is the reverse of the removal. Use thread-locking compound on the bolts and be sure to tighten them securely.

Engine movement control rod

20   Working in the engine compartment, remove the bolts securing the engine movement control rod and its bracket **(see illustration)**.

21   Installation is the reverse of the removal. Use thread-locking compound on the bolts and be sure to tighten them securely.

18 Engine balancer assembly - removal and installation

2AR-FE engine (2010 and later models)

Refer to illustrations 18.8, 18.9 and 18.10

1   Position the engine at TDC compression for cylinder No. 1 (see Section 3). Disconnect the negative battery cable (see Chapter 5).

2   Remove the engine oil pan (see Section 13), then remove the oil strainer mounting bolts and remove the strainer.

3   Remove the oil baffle plate mounting bolts and remove the baffle plate.

4   Remove the balancer assembly mounting bolts and lift the assembly off.

5   Before installing the balancer assembly, check that the alignment line mark of the balance shaft damper cover and dot on the bal-

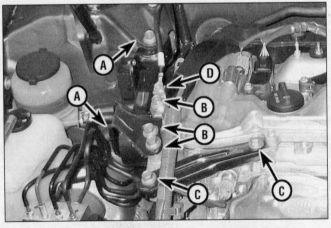

17.20 Engine movement control rod details

A   *Control rod mounting bolts*
B   *Engine mounting bracket and bolts*
C   *Support bracket and bolts*
D   *Engine ground strap*

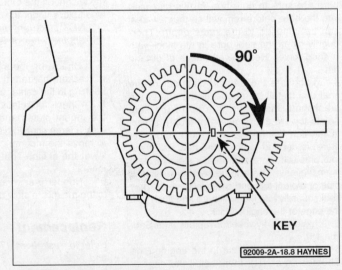

18.8 Before installing the engine balancer, turn the crankshaft 90-degrees clockwise from its TDC position . . .

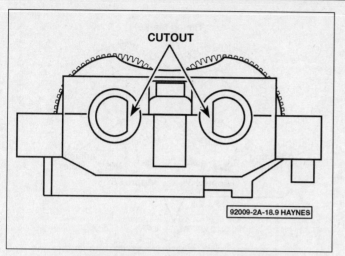

18.9 . . . and make sure the cutouts at the rear ends of the balancer shafts are facing each other like this

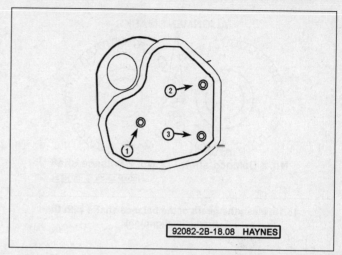

18.10 Engine balancer assembly bolt TIGHTENING sequence - 2010 and later models

ance shaft driven gear are aligned.

6   If the alignment marks are not aligned, place a wrench on the rear cutout of the No. 2 balance shaft and hold the assembly.

7   Rotate the balance shaft gear of the No. 1 balance shaft counterclockwise to align the alignment dot of the balance shaft gear with the alignment mark line of the balance shaft damper cover. Make sure the balance shafts stay in this position until the assembly is installed.

8   Turn the crankshaft 90-degrees clockwise so the keyway is aligned with the bottom of the cylinder block **(see illustration)**.

9   Check to make sure the cutouts at the rear ends of the shafts are facing each other **(see illustration)**.

10   Install the engine balancer and tighten the bolts in the proper sequence **(see illustration)** to the torque listed in this Chapter's Specifications.

2AZ-FE engine (2009 and earlier models)

Refer to illustrations 18.16, 18.17, 18.18

Note: *It is recommended to remove the engine to perform this procedure (see Chapter 2C). Additionally, it is important to note that in the following procedure, the orientation of the components and timing marks are shown with the engine inverted (as if mounted on an engine stand).*

11   Disconnect the negative battery cable (see Chapter 5).

12   Remove the oil pan and the oil pump (see Sections 13 and 14).

13   Remove the balance shaft housing bolts, in the order opposite that of the tightening sequence **(see illustration 18.20)**.

14   Remove the balance shafts.

15   Remove the balance shaft bearing shells from the housing and the lower crankcase and install new ones. Lubricate the bearing faces with engine assembly lube.

16   Turn the driven gear of balance shaft no. 1 counterclockwise until it hits its stop. Make sure the matchmarks on the no. 1 driven gear and the no. 2 driven gear are in alignment **(see illustration)**.

17   Turn the crankshaft so the balance shaft drive gear timing mark on the crankshaft must be approximately 16-degrees before the 12 o'clock position **(see illustration)**.

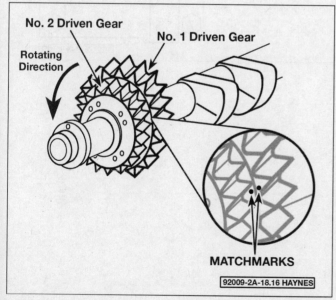

18.16 Align the matchmarks of the driven gears on the No. 1 balance shaft

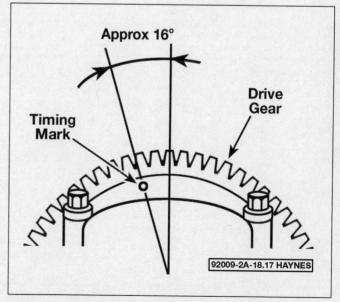

18.17 The timing mark on the balance shaft drive gear must be approximately 16-degrees before the 12 o'clock position (engine shown inverted)

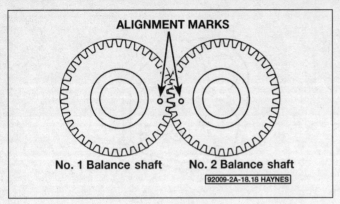

18.18 Mesh the gears of the balance shafts with the marks in alignment

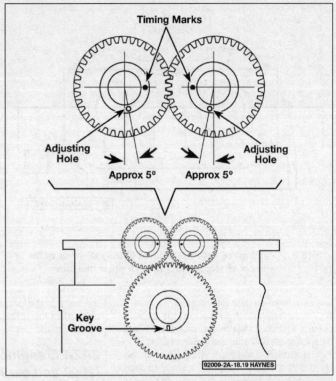

18.19 When installed, the balance shaft markings and the key groove in the nose of the crankshaft must be positioned like this

18   Mesh the gears of the balance shafts, aligning the matchmarks **(see illustration)**.
19   Install the balance shafts in the crankcase with the timing marks and adjusting holes aligned as shown **(see illustration)**.
20   Install the balance shaft housing and tighten the bolts, in sequence **(see illustration)**, to the torque listed in this Chapter's Specifications.

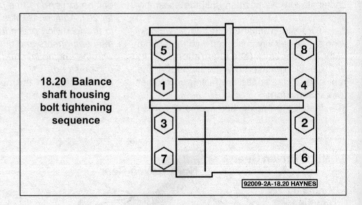

18.20 Balance shaft housing bolt tightening sequence

Chapter 2 Part B
V6 engine

Contents

Specifications

General

Engine designation	2GR-FE
Displacement	
2011 and earlier models	213 cubic inches (3.5 liters)
2012 and later models	210.9 cubic inches (3.456 liters)
Cylinder numbers (timing chain end-to-transmission end)	
Rear cylinder bank	1-3-5
Front cylinder bank	2-4-6
Firing order	1-2-3-4-5-6

Warpage limits

Cylinder head	
Cylinder-to-block surface	0.0020 inch
Intake and exhaust manifold surfaces	0.0031 inch
Maximum	0.0039 inch
Intake manifold	
Intake plenum side	0.031 inch
Cylinder head side	0.008 inch
Exhaust manifolds	0.028 inch

92007-2b-SPECS HAYNES

Cylinder locations

Camshaft and related components

Valve clearance .... Hydraulic, non-adjustable

Camshaft journal diameter
    Journal no. 1 .... 1.4152 to 1.4157 inches
    All other journals .... 1.0220 to 1.0226 inches

Bearing oil clearance
    Standard
        No. 1 journal
            2011 and earlier models .... 0.0016 to 0.0031 inch
            2012 and later models .... 0.0013 to 0.0024 inch
        Others .... 0.0010 to 0.0024 inch
    Service limit
        No. 1 journal .... 0.0039 inch
        Others .... 0.0035 inch

Lobe height
    Intake
        Standard .... 1.7447 to 1.7487 inches
        Service limit .... 1.7388 inches
    Exhaust
        Standard
            2011 and earlier models .... 1.7551 to 1.7591 inches
            2012 and later models .... 1.7426 to 1.7465 inches
        Service limit .... 1.7367 inches

Thrust clearance (endplay)
    Standard .... 0.0031 to 0.0051 inch
    Service limit .... 0.06 inch
Runout limit (total indicator reading) .... 0.0016 inch

Timing chain

Timing chain (No. 1) stretch limit (between 15 pins) .... 5.390 inches
Timing chain (No. 2) stretch limit .... 5.417 inches
Timing chain sprocket wear limit (with No. 1 chain installed) ... 2.417 inches
Idler sprocket wear limits
    With No. 1 chain installed .... 2.417 inches
    Idler sprocket collar diameter .... 0.9050 to 0.9055 inch
    Idler sprocket inside diameter .... 0.9063 to 0.9067 inch
    Oil clearance
        Standard .... 0.0008 to 0.0017 inch
        Maximum .... 0.0017 inch
Chain tensioner No. 2 wear limit .... 0.039 inch
Chain tensioner slipper wear limit .... 0.039 inch
Vibration damper No. 1 and No. 2 wear limit .... 0.039 inch

Oil pump

Driven rotor-to-pump body clearance
    Standard .... 0.0098 to 0.0128 inch
    Service limit .... 0.0128 inch
Rotor tip clearance
    Standard .... 0.0024 to 0.0063 inch
    Service limit .... 0.0063 inch
Rotor side clearance
    Standard .... 0.0012 to 0.0035 inch
    Service limit .... 0.0035 inch

Torque specifications   **Ft-lbs** (unless otherwise indicated)

Note: *One foot-pound (ft-lb) of torque is equivalent to 12 inch-pounds (in-lbs) of torque. Torque values below approximately 15 ft-lbs are expressed in inch-pounds, since most foot-pound torque wrenches are not accurate at these smaller values*

Intake manifold assembly
    Upper intake manifold bolts .... 156 in-lbs
    Upper intake manifold nuts .... 144 in-lbs
    Lower intake manifold bolts 15
Valve cover fasteners
    Small bolts .... 84 in-lbs
    Large bolts 15
Exhaust manifold nuts 15

Torque specifications (continued)

Ft-lbs (unless otherwise indicated)

Note: *One foot-pound (ft-lb) of torque is equivalent to 12 inch-pounds (in-lbs) of torque. Torque values below approximately 15 ft-lbs are expressed in inch-pounds, since most foot-pound torque wrenches are not accurate at these smaller values*

Crankshaft pulley bolt
    2011 and earlier models, 2012 and later Camry and ES350 models,
        and 2012 through 2014 Avalon models 184
    2015 Avalon models
        Pulley bolt with No. 11 grade markings.. 192
        Pulley bolt with No. 10 grade marking 184
Timing chain cover bolts/nuts - in sequence **(see illustration 7.40)**
    Bolt in center of upper vee 32
    All others 15
Drivebelt idler pulley bolts
    Idler pulley No. 1 bolt (lower left of engine)..................................... See Chapter 1
    Idler pulley No. 2 bolt .... See Chapter 1
Drivebelt tensioner mounting bolts .... See Chapter 1
Camshaft housing bolts - in sequence
(see illustration 9.18a or 9.18b)... 21
Camshaft timing sprocket bolt 74
Camshaft bearing cap bolts - in sequence **(see illustration 9.19a or 9.19b)**
    2011 and earler models.. 84 in-lbs
    2012 and later models
        Step 1 .... 84 in-lbs
        Step 2 .... 144 in-lbs
Cylinder head bolts, in sequence **(see illustrations 10.12a and 10.12b)**
    Step 1 27
    Step 2 .... Tighten an additional 90-degrees
    Step 3 .... Tighten an additional 90-degrees
Left cylinder head (two front 14 mm-head bolts) 22
Oil pan bolts/nuts
    Oil pan No. 1 (to engine block and front cover)
        2 small bolts... 84 in-lbs
        Other bolts.. 15
    Oil pan No. 2 (to oil pan No. 1) nuts and bolts .... 84 in-lbs
Oil pan-to-transmission.. 27
Oil pick-up tube nuts .... 84 in-lbs
Oil pump assembly
    Oil pump cover bolts .... 81 in-lbs
    Oil pump relief valve plug... 37
Driveplate-to-crankshaft bolts... 61
Engine rear oil seal retainer.. 84 in-lbs
Timing chain tensioner bolts
    Chain tensioner No. 1 .... 84 in-lbs
    Chain tensioner No. 2 15
    Chain tensioner No. 3 15
Timing chain guide bolts.. 17
Timing chain idler sprocket shaft.. 44

1   General information

This Part of Chapter 2 is devoted to the 3.5L (2GR-FE) V6 engine. Information concerning engine removal and installation and engine overhaul can be found in Part C of this Chapter.

Most of the repair procedures are based on the assumption that the engine is installed in the vehicle. If the engine has been removed from the vehicle and mounted on a stand, many of the steps outlined in this Part of Chapter 2 will not apply.

2   Repair operations possible with the engine in the vehicle

1   Some major repair operations can be accomplished without removing the engine from the vehicle. Clean the engine compartment and the exterior of the engine with some type of degreaser before any work is done. It will make the job easier and help keep dirt out of the internal areas of the engine.

2   Depending on the components involved, it may be helpful to remove the hood to improve access to the engine as repairs are performed (refer to Chapter 11 if necessary). Cover the fenders to prevent damage to the paint. Special pads are available, but an old bedspread or blanket will also work.

3   The cowl assembly is removable and must be taken out for access to any components in the upper rear of the engine compartment. Refer to Section 4.

4   If vacuum, exhaust, oil or coolant leaks develop, indicating a need for gasket or seal replacement, the repairs can sometimes be made with the engine in the vehicle.

5   Although some major components can be removed with the engine in place, it is usually easier to first lower the engine/transaxle assembly out of the vehicle. Because of this, most procedures in this Section do not have details for in-the-vehicle service.

3   Top Dead Center (TDC) for number one piston - locating

Refer to illustration 3.6

1   Top Dead Center (TDC) is the highest point in the cylinder that each piston reaches as it travels up the cylinder bore. Each piston reaches TDC on the compression stroke and again on the exhaust stroke, but TDC generally refers to piston position on the compression stroke.

2   Positioning the piston(s) at TDC is an essential part of many procedures such as valve adjustment and camshaft and timing chain/sprocket removal.

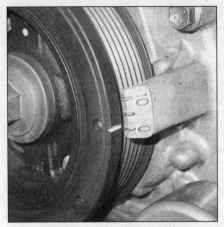

3.6 Turn the crankshaft until the notch in the pulley aligns with the zero on the timing plate

3   Before beginning this procedure, be sure to place the transmission in Neutral and apply the parking brake or block the wheels. If method b) in the next Step will be used to rotate the engine, disable the fuel system (see Chapter 4, Section 3), then disconnect the electrical connectors from the ignition coils (see Chapter 5).

4   In order to bring any piston to TDC, the crankshaft must be turned using one of the methods outlined below. When looking at the front of the engine, normal crankshaft rotation is clockwise.

a) *The preferred method is to turn the crankshaft with a socket and ratchet attached to the bolt threaded into the front of the crankshaft. Turn the bolt in a clockwise direction only.*

b) *If an assistant is available to turn the ignition switch to the Start position in short bursts, you can get the piston close to TDC without a remote starter switch. Make sure your assistant is out of the vehicle, away from the ignition switch, then use a socket and ratchet as described in Paragraph (a) to complete the procedure.*

5   Install a compression pressure gauge in the number one spark plug hole (see Chapter 2C). It should be a gauge with a screw-in fitting and a hose at least six inches long.

6   Rotate the crankshaft using one of the methods described above while observing the compression gauge. When TDC for the compression stroke of number one cylinder is reached, compression pressure will show on the gauge as the marks on the crankshaft pulley are beginning to line up **(see illustration)**. If you go past the marks, release the gauge pressure and rotate the crankshaft around two more revolutions.

7   After the number one piston has been positioned at TDC on the compression stroke, TDC for the next cylinder in the firing order can be located by turning the crankshaft another 120-degrees (refer to the firing order in this Chapter's Specifications).

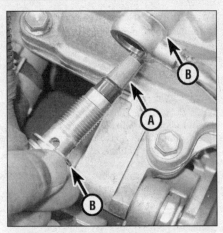

4.9 Take care with the oil filter (A) and the sealing washers (B) when disconnecting the oil line from the valve cover

4   Valve covers - removal and installation

Refer to illustrations 4.9, 4.10 and 4.11

1   Disconnect the cable from the negative terminal of the battery (see Chapter 5).

2   Remove the windshield wiper arms, side seals and plastic cowl (see Chapter 12).

3   Remove the wiper motor and linkage (see Chapter 12).

4   Remove the cowl assembly (see Chapter 11).

5   Pull up on the front side of the engine top cover to detach it from the two front retainers. After the front is detached, pull up on the back retainer and remove the engine cover. **Caution:** *Do not pull up on the front and rear at the same time or the cover can be damaged.*

6   Disconnect the hose from the PCV valve.

7   Remove the upper intake manifold (see Chapter 4).

8   Remove the ignition coils (see Chapter 5). Disconnect the wiring from the sensors and actuators and secure the wiring harnesses out of the way.

9   Disconnect the oil line from the end of each valve cover **(see illustration)**. Carefully set aside the oil control valve filter when you remove the upper banjo bolt from the valve cover. The sealing washers should be replaced with new ones if they're worn.

10   Remove the valve cover bolts and remove the valve cover **(see illustration)**.

11   Check the three small round interior gaskets as well as the large perimeter gasket **(see illustration)**. They should be replaced with new ones if they show signs of deterioration.

12   Installation is the reverse of removal. Thoroughly clean all sealing surfaces prior to putting the new gaskets in place.

13   Apply dabs of RTV sealant to the joints where the timing chain cover meets the cylinder heads.

14   Evenly tighten the valve cover nuts and

4.10 The valve cover is retained with 11 perimeter bolts (A) and a central bolt (B)

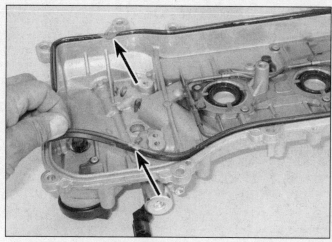

4.11 Make sure that the gasket is fully seated into the valve cover groove, and that the spark plug tube seals are seated as well; arrows indicate areas where sealant was applied on the joint between the timing chain cover and the cylinder head - clean old sealant from the gasket before reusing it

bolts to the torque listed in this Chapter's Specifications.

15   Start the engine and check for oil leaks around the edges of the valve cover.

5   Intake manifold - removal and installation

Warning: *Wait until the engine is completely cool before beginning this procedure.*

Upper intake manifold

Refer to illustrations 5.6 and 5.7

Note: *Toyota refers to the upper intake manifold as the intake air surge tank. If you're buying a gasket for the upper intake manifold at a dealer parts department, use the Toyota terminology.*

1   Disconnect the cable from the negative terminal of the battery (see Chapter 5). **Warning:** *If you plan on removing the lower intake manifold, relieve the fuel system pressure before disconnecting the battery (see Chapter 4, Section 2).*

2   Disconnect all hoses and the wiring from the throttle body (see Chapter 4). The coolant hoses can be pinched off to avoid draining the cooling system. Label the hoses to avoid confusion later.

3   Disconnect the air intake tube from the throttle body.

4   Remove the throttle body bracket and the upper intake manifold brace.

5   Disconnect all wiring and hoses from the manifold.

6   Remove the intake manifold mounting fasteners and remove the upper intake manifold **(see illustration)**.

7   Check the condition of the upper intake manifold gasket **(see illustration)**. If it isn't cracked, hardened or flattened, it can be reused.

8   Installation is the reverse of removal. Be sure to tighten the upper intake manifold mounting bolts and nuts to the torque listed in this Chapter's Specifications.

Lower intake manifold

Refer to illustration 5.13

Note: *Toyota refers to the lower intake manifold as simply the "intake manifold." If you're buying a gasket for the lower intake manifold at a dealer parts department, use the Toyota terminology.*

9   Remove the upper intake manifold (see Steps 1 through 7).

10   If you're removing the lower intake manifold to replace it, remove the fuel rail now (see Chapter 4).

11   If you're just removing the lower intake manifold to replace the gaskets, it's not necessary to remove the fuel rail, but you'll have

5.6 Upper intake manifold fasteners

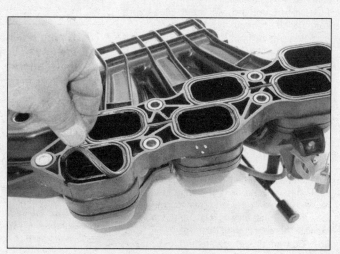

5.7 Check the condition of the upper intake manifold gasket, replacing it if necessary

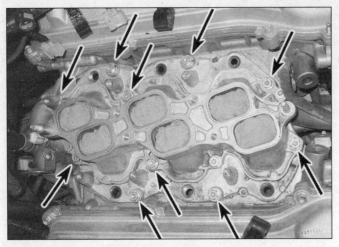

5.13 **Lower intake manifold mounting bolts**

7.3a **Hold the crankshaft pulley with a pin spanner while removing the bolt**

to disconnect the fuel line connection (see Chapter 4).

12   Remove the interfering brace.

13   Unscrew the bolts and remove the lower intake manifold **(see illustration)**.

14   Remove and discard the old lower intake manifold gaskets. Clean off all traces of old gasket material from the mating surfaces of the manifold and cylinder heads, then wipe the surfaces with brake system cleaner.

15   Installation is the reverse of removal. Be sure to use new gaskets and tighten the lower intake manifold bolts a little at a time, in a criss-cross pattern working from the center bolts outward, to the torque listed in this Chapter's Specifications.

6   Exhaust manifolds - removal and installation

Warning: *The engine must be completely cool before beginning this procedure.*

Note: *The following procedure applies to either exhaust manifold.*

1   Disconnect the electrical connectors from the left upstream oxygen sensor.

2   Remove the bolts that secure the exhaust manifold support bracket and remove it.

3   Disconnect any interfering wire clamps.

4   Remove the heat shield from the front exhaust manifold.

5   Evenly loosen the nuts that secure each exhaust manifold and remove the exhaust manifold.

6   Remove and discard the old exhaust manifold gasket.

7   Installation is the reverse of removal. Be sure to use a new gasket and install it with the oval-shaped protruding tip facing in the correct direction. For the left (driver's side) manifold, the tip must face to the rear; on the right manifold, it must face to the front.

8   Tighten the exhaust manifold nuts a little at a time, working from the center nuts outward, to the torque listed in this Chapter's Specifications.

7.3b **If the crankshaft pulley can't be removed by hand, use a puller that bolts to the hub of the pulley, not a jaw-type puller. Also, be sure to use the correct adapter between the nose of the crankshaft and the puller screw, so as not to damage the threads in the crankshaft**

7   Timing chains and sprockets - removal, inspection and installation

Removal

Refer to illustrations 7.3a, 7.3b, 7.6, 7.8a, 7.8b, 7.8c, 7.8d and 7.9

Warning: *Wait until the engine is completely cool before beginning this procedure.*

Caution: *The timing system is complex, and severe engine damage will occur if you make any mistakes. Do not attempt this procedure unless you are highly experienced with this type of repair. If you are at all unsure of your abilities, be sure to consult an expert. Double-check all your work and be sure everything is correct before you attempt to start the engine.*

Note: *The manufacturer recommends remov-*

7.6 **The timing chain cover can be pried loose at the lower corners and at the upper corners; prying anywhere else may damage the cover**

ing the engine and transaxle assembly to perform this procedure (see Chapter 2C).

1   Remove the engine/transaxle assembly (see Chapter 2C).

2   Remove the drivebelt, unbolt the drivebelt tensioner (see *Drivebelt check and replacement* in Chapter 1), remove the idler pulley bolts and remove the two idler pulleys.

3   Set the engine to TDC (see Section 3). Remove the crankshaft pulley **(see illustrations)**.

4   Remove the four timing chain cover bolts from the front of the upper oil pan.

5   Remove the water inlet (see Chapter 3). Remove the O-ring and gasket from the water inlet and discard them.

6   Remove the timing chain cover mounting fasteners and remove the timing chain cover. **Note:** *There are three different sized bolts used on the timing chain cover* **(see illustration 7.40)**. There are only a few spots where you can safely pry the cover off without damaging it **(see illustration)**. Do NOT pry the timing chain cover loose at any other spot

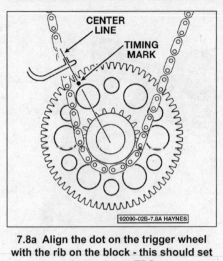

7.8a Align the dot on the trigger wheel with the rib on the block - this should set the engine at TDC

7.8b The exhaust camshaft sprocket of the left (front) cylinder head with the engine at TDC

7.8c The intake camshaft sprocket of the left (front) cylinder head with the engine at TDC

or you will damage the sealing surface of the cover.

7 After removing the timing chain cover, carefully pry out the old crankshaft seal with a screwdriver (see Section 8). Make sure that you don't scratch the seal bore. If you want to inspect or replace any oil pump parts, refer to Section 12. **Note:** *Keep track of the locations of all of the bolts. They are of different lengths and can't be interchanged.*

8 Verify that the piston in the No. 1 cylinder is near TDC on its compression stroke. If not, install the crankshaft pulley bolt, then rotate the crankshaft until the dot on the crankshaft position trigger wheel (the toothed wheel behind the lower crankshaft sprocket) is at the 11 o'clock position and is aligned with the rib on the engine block **(see illustration)**. You can also temporarily install the front cover and the crankshaft pulley and set the pulley at the 0 degree mark. Verify that the timing marks on the camshaft timing sprockets are aligned with their correspond-

ing marks on top of the front camshaft bearing caps **(see illustrations)**. If the marks are not aligned, rotate the crankshaft another 360-degrees and recheck the marks.

9 Turn the stopper plate on the No. 1 tensioner clockwise and push in the tensioner plunger **(see illustration)**. **Note:** *The No. 1 tensioner is the tensioner for the main timing chain.* To lock the plunger in this position, turn the stopper plate counterclockwise and insert a drill or pin (2011 and earlier models: 0.138-inch diameter/2012 and later models: 0.050-inch diameter) through the holes in the stopper plate and the tensioner body. Remove the tensioner mounting bolts and the No. 1 tensioner.

10 Remove the chain tensioner slipper.

11 Using a 10 mm hex wrench, unscrew the idler sprocket shaft and remove the idler shaft, sprocket and collar. Note which side of the sprocket faces out.

12 Remove the chain vibration dampers.

13 Note the positions of the timing marks on each camshaft sprocket and the crankshaft

sprocket. Make sketches or take pictures. Remove the No. 1 (main) timing chain. **Caution:** *While the No. 1 timing chain is removed, DO NOT ROTATE THE CRANKSHAFT!*

14 Remove the crankshaft timing chain sprocket.

15 Compress chain tensioner No. 2 and insert a drill bit or punch (0.039-inch diameter) into the hole. **Note:** *Timing chain No. 2 and the No. 2 chain tensioner are on the right (rear) cylinder head. Timing chain No. 3 and the No. 3 tensioner are on the left (front) cylinder head.*

16 Hold the hex on the exhaust camshaft with a wrench and unscrew the two bolts that secure the camshaft timing sprockets to the camshafts. Remove the sprockets and chain as an assembly. Keep the components in a resealable plastic bag to ensure that none of these components is mixed with the other timing chain set. **Caution:** *Don't attempt to disassemble the adjustable intake sprocket assembly. If disassembled, it will have to be replaced.*

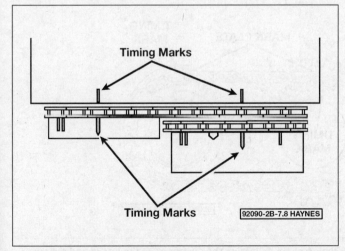

7.8d Alignment marks for the right (rear) camshaft sprockets

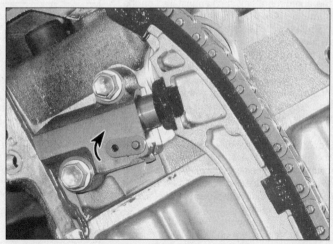

7.9 To lock the tensioner in the retracted position, rotate the stopper plate clockwise and push the plunger in, then rotate the stopper plate counterclockwise and insert a pin through the hole in the stopper plate and the tensioner body

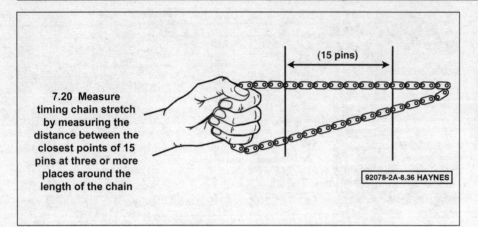

7.20 Measure timing chain stretch by measuring the distance between the closest points of 15 pins at three or more places around the length of the chain

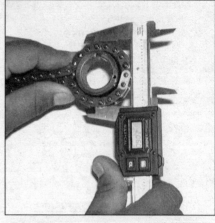

7.21 Wrap the chain around each of the timing chain sprockets and measure the diameter of the sprockets across the chain rollers. If the measurement is less than the minimum sprocket diameter, replace the chain and the timing sprockets

17   Remove the chain tensioner No. 2 mounting bolt and remove chain tensioner No. 2. Store the tensioner in the plastic bag with the other No. 2 timing chain components.
18   To remove the No. 3 timing chain and tensioner, repeat these Steps. Again, store the components in a resealable plastic bag. **Caution:** *While the timing chains are removed, DO NOT ROTATE THE CRANKSHAFT!*

Inspection

Refer to illustrations 7.20 and 7.21

19   Inspect all parts of the timing chain assembly for wear and damage. Inspect the three timing chains for loose pins, cracks, and worn rollers and side plates. Inspect the sprockets for hook-shaped, chipped and/or broken teeth.
20   Inspect timing chain No. 1 for stretching. To measure timing chain stretch, measure the distance between 15 pins at three or more places around the length of the chain **(see illustration)**. Measure between the inside of the rollers and compare your measurements with the distance listed in this Chapter's Specifications.
21   Measure the diameter of each timing chain sprocket and idler sprocket with the appropriate timing chain installed on the sprocket **(see illustration)**. The sprocket diameter, with the chain in place, should not exceed the dimensions listed in this Chapter's Specifications.
22   Measure the idler sprocket oil clearance as follows. First, measure the diameter of the idler sprocket collar with a micrometer and record your measurement. Then measure the inside diameter of the idler sprocket and record that measurement as well. Subtract the idler sprocket collar diameter from the inside diameter of the idler sprocket and compare the result with the clearance listed in this Chapter's Specifications. If the clearance is excessive, replace the idler sprocket and/or collar, as necessary.
23   Some scoring and wear of the timing chain tensioners and vibration dampers is normal, but excessive wear will increase chain noise, accelerate chain and sprocket wear and could damage the engine if a chain jumps timing. Inspect chain tensioners No. 2

and 3, the timing chain tensioner slipper and the timing chain vibration dampers for excessive wear. If the measured chain wear for any of these components exceeds the depth listed in this Chapter's Specifications, replace the component.
24   Check the chain tensioners for correct operation. On the No. 1 tensioner, raise the ratchet pawl and verify that the plunger moves smoothly in and out of the tensioner, then release the ratchet pawl and verify that it prevents the plunger from sliding back into the tensioner. Also verify that the plungers on the No. 2 and No. 3 tensioners move in and out smoothly.

Installation

Refer to illustrations 7.26, 7.28, 7.33a, 7.33b and 7.40

Caution: *Before starting the engine, carefully rotate the crankshaft by hand through at least two full revolutions (use a socket and breaker bar on the crankshaft pulley center bolt). If you feel any resistance, STOP! There is something wrong - most likely, valves are contacting the pistons. You must find the problem before proceeding.*

25   Push in the tensioner plunger on chain tensioner No. 2 and insert a drill or punch (0.039 inch diameter) into the hole of the tensioner to lock the plunger in the retracted position. Install the tensioners and tighten the mounting bolts to the torque listed in this Chapter's Specifications.
26   Install the No. 2 (right bank inner) timing chain on the camshaft sprockets. Make sure that the yellow mark links on the chain are aligned with the single timing dots or lines on the camshaft sprockets **(see illustration)**.
27   Align the yellow links on the No. 2 timing chain with the timing marks on the bearing caps and install timing chain No. 2 and the camshaft sprockets as an assembly. Install the two bolts that secure the timing sprockets to the camshafts. Immobilize the hex on the exhaust camshaft with an adjustable wrench

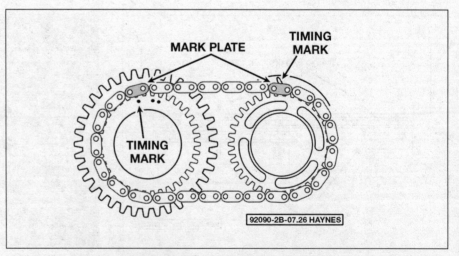

7.26 The small No. 2 timing chain maintains the alignment of the intake and exhaust camshaft sprockets of the right (rear) cylinder head; set the yellow links on the single line and single dot of the camshaft sprockets

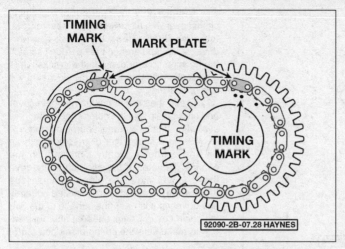

7.28 Set the yellow links of the No. 3 timing chain of the left (front) cylinder head on the double lines and double dots of the camshaft sprockets

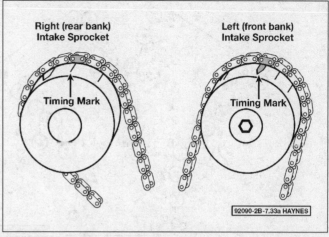

7.33a The orange links of the No. 1 (main) timing chain must align with the correct marks on each intake sprocket - the rear single line on the right (rear bank) head and the large arrowhead on the left (front bank) head

and tighten these two bolts to the torque listed in this Chapter's Specifications. Remove the drill or punch that was used to lock the tensioner plunger in its retracted position and verify that the plunger tensions the chain.

28 Install the other inner timing chain by repeating Steps 25 through 27. Align the yellow links with the double line or dot marks on the sprockets **(see illustration)**. Also align its yellow links with the marks on the bearing caps.

29 Install the chain guides and tighten the bolts to the torque listed in this Chapter's Specifications.

30 Install the crankshaft timing sprocket on the crankshaft. Be sure to align the timing sprocket keyway with the keys on the crankshaft.

31 Apply a light coat of engine oil to the bearing surface of the idler sprocket collar. Install the idler sprocket collar, sprocket and shaft. Make sure that the teeth on the idler sprocket are facing forward. Tighten the idler sprocket shaft to the torque listed in this Chapter's Specifications.

32 Verify that the timing marks on the camshaft timing sprockets are aligned with their corresponding marks on top of the front camshaft bearing caps.

33 Install the long timing chain (No. 1) on the camshaft timing sprockets and on the idler sprocket. Turn the camshaft sprockets to remove the slack in the upper part of the chain, then install the chain over the crankshaft sprocket. Make sure that the yellow link is aligned with the timing dot on the crankshaft timing sprocket (it's near the 3 o'clock position) and that the orange links are aligned with the timing marks on the intake camshaft sprockets **(see illustrations)**. There is a dot on the crankshaft position trigger wheel (the toothed wheel behind the lower crankshaft sprocket) that must be at the 11 o'clock position and aligned with the rib on the engine block **(see illustration 7.8a)**.

34 Turn the stopper plate on the No. 1 tensioner clockwise and push in the tensioner plunger. To lock the plunger in this position, turn the stopper plate counterclockwise and insert a drill or punch (0.138-inch diameter) through the holes in the stopper plate and the tensioner. Install the tensioner and tighten the tensioner mounting bolts to the torque listed in this Chapter's Specifications. Remove the drill or punch that you inserted into chain tensioner No. 1 and verify that it tensions timing chain No. 1. **Caution:** *Carefully rotate the crankshaft by hand through at least two full revolutions (use a socket and breaker bar on the crankshaft pulley center bolt). If you feel any resistance, STOP! There is something*

wrong - most likely, valves are contacting the pistons. You must find the problem before proceeding.

35 Remove all old RTV sealant from the gasket mating surfaces of the timing chain cover and from the front of the cylinder heads and engine block.

36 Install a new crankshaft oil seal in the timing chain cover (see Section 8).

37 Install a new O-ring on the left cylinder head.

38 Apply gray RTV sealant on the timing chain cover in all areas where the cover seals to the engine block and oil pan. These beads should be about 1/8 to 3/16-inch (3 to 4.5 mm) wide. **Caution:** *Once you have installed the*

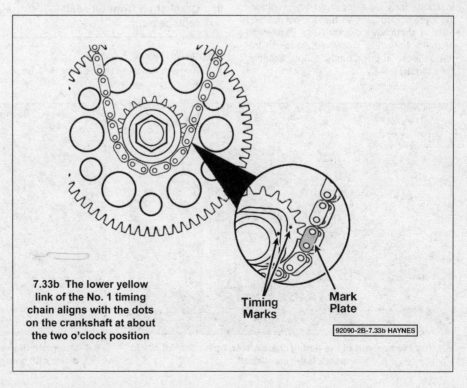

7.33b The lower yellow link of the No. 1 timing chain aligns with the dots on the crankshaft at about the two o'clock position

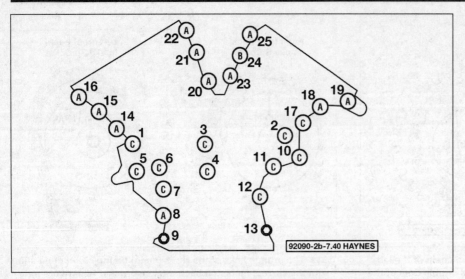

7.40 Timing chain cover bolt length and tightening sequence

A   Bolt A 0.98-inches (25 mm) length
B   Bolt B 2.17-inches (55 mm) length
C   Bolt C 1.57-inches (40 mm) length

sealant on the engine and timing chain cover you have three minutes to install the cover. If you take longer than that, the sealant might not set up properly, so you'll have to remove the sealant and re-apply it. Be sure to get sealant into the corners where the oil pan meets the engine block and avoid getting any on the O-rings.

39   Rotate the flats on the oil drive rotor to align it with the square part of the crankshaft timing sprocket and slide the timing chain cover into place.

40   Install all of the cover bolts in the same locations they were removed from, tightening them as you go. **Caution:** *Do not put long bolts in short holes or vice versa.* Tighten all of the bolts in the proper sequence to the torque listed in this Chapter's Specifications **(see illustration).**

41   Install and tighten the four oil pan bolts that go into the timing chain cover.
42   The remainder of installation is the reverse of removal.
43   Install the engine/transaxle assembly (see Chapter 2C).
44   Refill the engine with oil and coolant (see Chapter 1).
45   Reconnect the cable to the negative terminal of the battery (see Chapter 5).
46   Start the engine and check for leaks.

8   Crankshaft front oil seal - replacement

Refer to illustrations 8.2 and 8.4

1   Remove the crankshaft pulley (see Section 7).

2   Carefully pry the seal out of the timing chain cover with a screwdriver or seal removal tool **(see illustration).** If you use a screwdriver, wrap tape around the tip - don't scratch the housing bore or damage the crankshaft (if the crankshaft is damaged, the new seal will end up leaking).

3   Clean the bore in the timing chain cover and coat the lip and the outer edge of the new seal with engine oil or multi-purpose grease.

4   Using a seal driver or a socket with an outside diameter slightly smaller than the outside diameter of the seal, carefully drive the new seal into place with a hammer **(see illustration).** Make sure it's installed squarely and driven in flush with the surface of the timing chain cover. Check the seal after installation to make sure the spring didn't pop out of place.

5   Reinstall the crankshaft pulley, tightening the bolt to the torque listed in this Chapter's Specifications.

6   Run the engine and check for oil leaks at the front seal.

9   Camshafts, rocker arms and valve adjusters - removal, inspection and installation

Removal

Note: *The manufacturer recommends removing the engine and transaxle assembly to perform this procedure (see Chapter 2C).*

Note: *The following procedure is not for beginners. Please read the entire procedure carefully before deciding whether this is a job that you want to tackle at home.*

1   Remove the engine and transaxle (see Chapter 2C).
2   Drain the engine oil and coolant (see Chapter 1).
3   Remove the timing chains and sprockets (see Section 7).
4   Before removing the camshafts from the right (rear bank) cylinder head, check to make

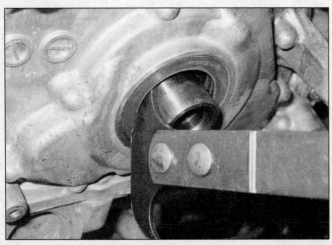

8.2 Pry the seal out of the timing chain cover, being careful not to scratch the crankshaft

8.4 Lubricate the seal lip and drive the new crankshaft seal into place with a large socket or piece of pipe and a hammer

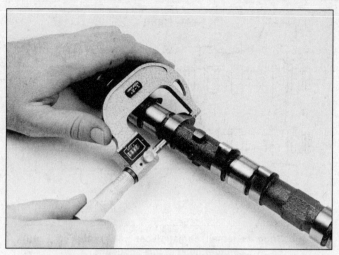

9.12 Measure the lobe heights on each camshaft - if any lobe height is less than the specified allowable minimum, replace that camshaft

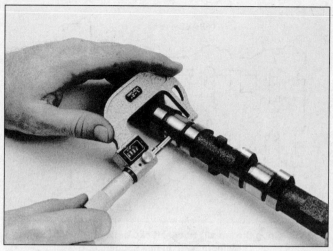

9.13 Measure each journal diameter with a micrometer - if any journal measures less than the specified limit, replace the camshaft

sure that the nose of the intake cam lobe for the No. 1 cylinder is facing toward 12 o'clock, and the nose of the exhaust cam lobe is facing approximately 3 o'clock (the locating pins at the front of the camshaft should be at 12 o'clock for the exhaust cam and approximately 1:30 for the intake cam).

5   Gradually loosen and remove the 8 (smaller) bearing cap bolts in the reverse of the tightening sequence **(see illustrations 9.19a and 9.19b)**.

6   Gradually loosen and remove the remaining 12 housing bolts in the reverse of the tightening sequence **(see illustrations 9.18a and 9.18b)**.

7   Remove all five bearing caps and remove the intake and exhaust camshafts. Be sure to keep all of the components in the correct order. One way to do this is to put them in a box and label the cap numbers with a utility marker pen.

8   Carefully pry the camshaft housing from

9.14 Compare the width of the crushed Plastigage to the scale on the envelope to determine the oil clearance

the top of the cylinder head. **Caution:** *Use a screwdriver wrapped with tape to avoid scratching the parts.*

9   Remove all of the rocker arms and lash adjusters and put them in the same box with the cam bearing caps. Every component should be marked or labeled so that it can be returned to its original location.

10   If you're removing the camshafts from the front bank cylinder head, repeat Steps 5 through 9. Make sure that the front camshaft lobes on the intake cam are positioned at 9 o'clock and the exhaust cam at 1 o'clock (the locating pins at the front of the camshaft should be at 12 o'clock for both cams). **Caution:** *While the timing chains and camshafts are removed, DO NOT ROTATE THE CRANKSHAFT!*

Inspection

Refer to illustrations 9.12, 9.13 and 9.14

11   Inspect each rocker and lash adjuster arm for wear.

12   Visually examine the cam lobes and bearing journals for score marks, pitting, galling and evidence of overheating (blue, discolored areas). Look for flaking away of the hardened surface layer of each lobe. Using a micrometer, measure the height of each camshaft lobe **(see illustration)**. Compare your measurements with this Chapter's Specifications. If the height for any one lobe is less than the specified minimum, replace the camshaft.

13   Using a micrometer, measure the diameter of each journal at several points **(see illustration)**. Compare your measurements with this Chapter's Specifications. If the diameter of any one journal is less than specified, replace the camshaft.

14   Check the oil clearance for each camshaft journal as follows:

a) *Clean the bearing caps and the camshaft journals with brake system cleaner.*

b) *Carefully lay the camshaft(s) in place in the cylinder head. Don't install the lifters and don't use any lubrication.*

c) *Lay a strip of Plastigage on each journal.*

d) *Install the bearing caps with the arrows pointing toward the front (timing chain end) of the engine.*

e) *Tighten the bolts to the torque listed in this Chapter's Specifications in 1/4-turn increments.* **Note:** *Don't turn the camshaft while the Plastigage is in place.*

f) *Remove the bolts and detach the caps.*

g) *Compare the width of the crushed Plastigage (at its widest point) to the scale on the Plastigage envelope* **(see illustration)**.

h) *If the clearance is greater than specified, replace the camshaft and/or cylinder head.*

i) *Scrape off the Plastigage with your fingernail or the edge of a credit card - don't scratch or nick the journals or bearing caps.*

Installation

Refer to illustrations 9.16a, 9.16b, 9.18a, 9.18b, 9.19a and 9.19b

15   Lightly lubricate the lash adjuster bores and the adjusters themselves with clean engine oil, then install them in the same bores from which they were removed. Install the rocker arms in their original positions, oiling all wear points as you do so.

16   Right side (rear cylinder bank): Lubricate the camshaft journals and lobes with camshaft installation lubricant. Install the camshafts on the right camshaft housing so that the locating pin of the exhaust camshaft is at 12 o'clock and the intake camshaft's locating pin is rotated approximately 45 degrees to 1:30. Apply a light coat of engine oil to the upper bearing caps, then install them in their correct locations. Tighten the bolts snug at

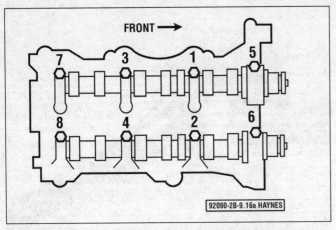

9.16a Snug the (small) camshaft cap bolts of the right (rear) cylinder head in this sequence

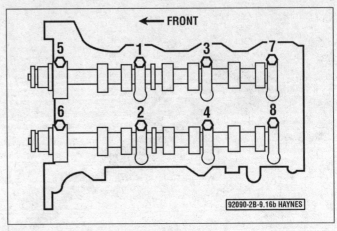

9.16b Snug the (small) camshaft cap bolts of the left (front) cylinder head in this sequence

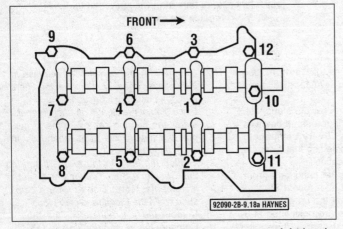

9.18a Camshaft housing bolt tightening sequence - right (rear) cylinder head

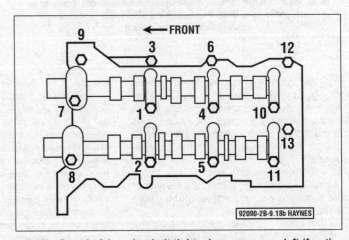

9.18b Camshaft housing bolt tightening sequence - left (front) cylinder head

this time in the correct sequence (see illustrations).

17   Thoroughly clean the sealing surfaces of the bottom of the camshaft bearing support and the top of the cylinder head. Apply a continuous 1/8-inch to 3/16-inch bead of RTV silicone sealer to the surface of the top of the cylinder head that mates with the camshaft bearing housing.

18   Set the camshaft housing assembly into place. Install the 12 mounting bolts and tighten them in the correct sequence to the torque listed in this Chapter's Specifications (see illustrations).

19   Install the remaining (smaller) bearing cap bolts, then tighten them in the correct sequence to the torque listed in this Chapter's Specifications (see illustrations).

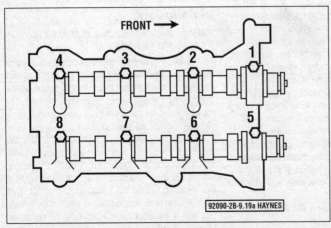

9.19a Camshaft bearing cap bolt tightening sequence - small bolts - for the right (rear) cylinder head

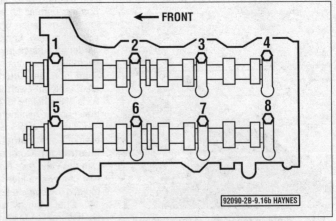

9.19b Camshaft cap bolt tightening sequence - small bolts - for the left (front) cylinder head

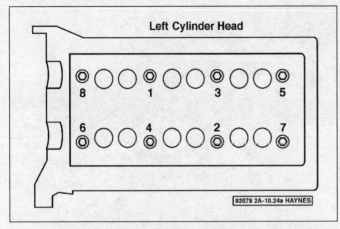
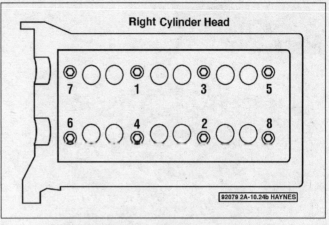

**10.12a Cylinder head bolt tightening sequence -
left (front bank) cylinder head**

**10.12b Cylinder head bolt tightening sequence -
right (rear bank) cylinder head**

20 Left side (front cylinder bank): Lightly lubricate the camshaft journals with camshaft installation lubricant. Install the camshafts on the left cylinder head so that the locating pin of each camshaft is in the 12 o'clock position. Proceed as with the right cylinder head. **Note:** *There are 13 bolts in the camshaft housing instead of 12.*

21 The remainder of installation is the reverse of removal. Install the timing chains, the timing chain cover and all of the components attached to the cover (see Section 7). **Caution:** *Carefully rotate the crankshaft by hand through at least two full revolutions (use a socket and breaker bar on the crankshaft pulley center bolt). If you feel any resistance, STOP! There is something wrong - most likely valves are contacting the pistons. You must find the problem before proceeding.*

22 Refill the engine with oil and coolant (see Chapter 1), reconnect the cable to the negative battery terminal, start the engine and check for leaks. **Note:** *It may take a few minutes for lifter clatter to disappear.*

10 Cylinder heads - removal and installation

Warning: *The engine must be completely cool before starting this procedure.*
Caution: *New cylinder head bolts should be used when installing the cylinder head.*
Note: *This procedure applies to either cylinder head.*
Note: *The manufacturer recommends removing the engine and transaxle assembly to perform this procedure (see Chapter 2C).*

Removal

1 Remove the camshafts and the camshaft housings (see Section 9).
2 Remove the exhaust manifolds (see Section 6).
3 If you're removing the left cylinder head, gradually loosen and remove the two front bolts.

4 Remove the cylinder head bolts gradually and evenly, in the order opposite that of the tightening sequence, then remove the cylinder head from the engine block.
5 Remove and discard the old cylinder head gasket.

Installation

Refer to illustrations 10.12a, 10.12b and 10.14
6 The mating surfaces of the cylinder heads and the block must be perfectly clean as the heads are installed.
7 Use a gasket scraper to remove all traces of carbon and old gasket material, then clean the mating surfaces with brake system cleaner. If there's oil on the mating surfaces when the head is installed, the gasket may not seal correctly and leaks could develop.
8 When working on the block, stuff the cylinders with clean shop rags to keep out debris. Use a vacuum cleaner to remove material that falls into the cylinders.
9 Check the block and head mating surfaces for nicks, deep scratches and other damage. If damage is slight, it can be removed with a file; if it's excessive, machining may be the only alternative.
10 Use a tap of the correct size to chase the threads in the cylinder head bolt holes, then clean them with compressed air - make sure that nothing remains in the holes. **Warning:** *Wear eye protection when using compressed air!*
11 Position the cylinder head gasket on the engine block so that the lot number stamp is on the center upper edge of the gasket facing up. Carefully place the cylinder head on the head gasket.
12 Apply a light coat of oil to the new cylinder head bolts, then install and tighten them (don't forget the washers!) gradually and evenly, in the proper sequence **(see illustrations)**, to the initial torque listed in this Chapter's Specifications.
13 After tightening all eight bolts to the initial torque, put a paint mark on the front edge of each bolt (the edge facing toward

the front of the engine), then retighten each bolt, in the same sequence, another 90-degrees. Repeat this one more time so that the bolts have turned 180-degrees from the initial torque. Make sure to use the proper sequence.
14 If you're installing the left cylinder head, install the two front head bolts and tighten them in the correct sequence to the torque listed in this Chapter's Specifications **(see illustration)**.
15 If you removed both cylinder heads, install the other cylinder head now.
16 Install the intake and exhaust camshafts (see Section 9).
17 Install the camshaft timing oil control valve, the oil control valve filter and the VVT-i sensor (see *Variable Valve Timing-intelligent (VVT-i) - description and component replacement* in Chapter 6).
18 Install the timing chains, the timing chain cover and all components attached to the cover (see Section 7).
19 The remainder of installation is the reverse of removal.
20 Install the engine/transaxle assembly

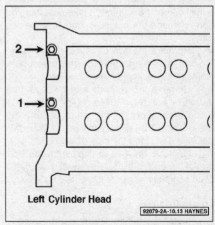

10.14 After you've tightened the other bolts of the left cylinder head, tighten these two in this order

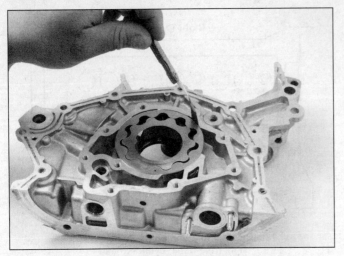

12.6a Measure the driven rotor-to-body clearance with a feeler gauge

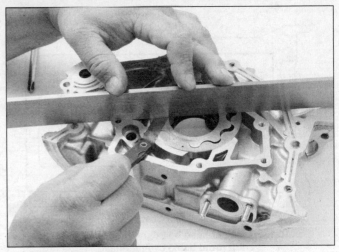

12.6b Measure the rotor side clearance with a precision straightedge and feeler gauge

(see Chapter 2C). Refill the engine with oil and coolant (see Chapter 1).
21   Reconnect the cable to the negative battery terminal, start the engine and check for leaks.

11   Oil pan - removal and installation

Note: *The manufacturer recommends removing the engine and transaxle assembly to perform this procedure (see Chapter 2C).*

Removal

1   Drain the engine oil (see Chapter 1).
2   Remove the bolts and nuts that secure oil pan No. 2 (the smaller stamped steel pan) to the larger cast aluminum oil pan.
3   Oil pan No. 2 will probably be stuck to the oil pan with RTV sealant. Try tapping it loose with a rubber-tipped mallet. If you're unable to knock it loose, carefully cut the sealant with a putty knife and a hammer. Make sure that you don't damage the mating surfaces of the two pans.
4   Remove the two oil pump pickup tube/ strainer mounting nuts and the brace bolt. Remove the pickup/strainer assembly.
5   Remove the 16 bolts and two nuts that secure oil pan No. 1 to the engine block.
6   Carefully pry the oil pan loose from the engine block. **Caution:** *Only pry in the small cutout areas along the side of the pan.*
7   Remove the two O-rings from the bottom of the engine block. The sheet metal baffle plate can be removed at this time if necessary.

Installation

8   Install the baffle plate if you removed it. Tighten the fasteners to the torque listed in this Chapter's Specifications.
9   Use a scraper to remove all traces of old

sealant from the block and oil pan. Clean the mating surfaces with brake system cleaner.
10   Make sure the threaded holes in the block are clean. Install new O-rings to the block, holding them in place with clean grease if required.
11   Check the flange of the steel oil pan for distortion around the bolt holes. If necessary, place it on a wood block and use a hammer to flatten and restore the gasket surface.
12   Inspect the strainer for cracks or blockage. Clean it with solvent and install it using a new gasket. Tighten the fasteners to the torque listed in this Chapter's Specifications.
13   Apply a 1/8-inch bead of RTV sealant to the upper oil pan flange.
14   Position the pan onto the block and install the fasteners. Working from the center out, tighten the fasteners to the torque listed in this Chapter's Specifications in several steps.
15   After you have installed the aluminum portion of the oil pan, apply a bead of RTV sealant to the flange of the No. 2 oil pan, carefully position it on the upper oil pan and install the bolts. Working from the center out, tighten them to the torque listed in this Chapter's Specifications in several steps.
16   The remainder of installation is the reverse of removal. Add oil and install a new filter (see Chapter 1). Run the engine and check for leaks.

12   Oil pump - removal, inspection and installation

Removal

1   Remove the timing chain cover (see Section 7). The oil pump is on the inside of the cover.
2   Remove the relief valve plug using a 27

mm socket. Slide out the spring and the relief valve.
3   Remove the oil pump cover bolts and remove the oil pump cover. Remove the oil pump drive rotor and driven rotor.

Inspection

Refer to illustrations 12.6a, 12.6b and 12.6c

4   Clean all components with solvent, then inspect them for wear and damage. Check that the oiled relief valve falls easily through its bore without sticking.
5   Check the oil pressure relief valve sliding surface and valve spring. If either the spring or the valve is damaged, they must be replaced as a set.
6   Check the clearance of the following components with a feeler gauge and compare the measurements to this Chapter's Specifications **(see illustrations)**:

  a) *Driven rotor-to-oil pump body*
  b) *Rotor side clearance*
  c) *Rotor tip clearance*

7   Replace any worn parts or replace the entire oil pump assembly.

Installation

8   Pry the old crankshaft seal out of the timing chain cover with a screwdriver.
9   Apply multi-purpose grease or engine oil to the outer edge of the new crank seal and carefully drive it into place with a deep socket and a hammer. Apply multi-purpose grease or engine oil to the seal lip.
10   Apply a coat of petroleum jelly to the pump drive and driven rotors, then place the two rotors into position in the timing chain cover. Make sure that the pump marks (dimples) are facing out, toward the pump cover and away from the timing chain cover.
11   Pack the pump cavity with petroleum jelly (this will help to prime the pump) and

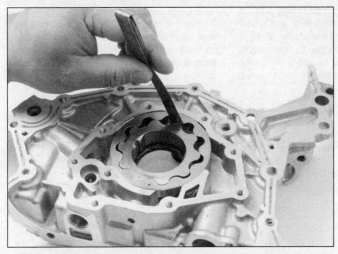

12.6c Measure the rotor tip clearance with a feeler gauge - note the rotor marks are facing out (when the pump body cover is installed, the marks will be against the cover)

14.4 Drive the new seal into the retainer with a wood block or a section of pipe - make sure that you don't cock the seal in the retainer bore

install the cover. Tighten the cover bolts to the torque listed in this Chapter's Specifications.

12 Lubricate the oil pressure relief valve with clean engine oil and insert the valve, then the spring, into the pump cover. Screw in the plug and tighten it to the torque listed in this Chapter's Specifications.

13 Install the timing chain cover (see Section 7).

14 The remainder of installation is the reverse of removal. Add oil and install a new filter (see Chapter 1). Run the engine and check for leaks.

13 Driveplate - removal and installation

Removal

1 Remove the engine/transmission assembly from the vehicle (see Chapter 2C), then remove the transaxle from the engine (see Chapter 7).

2 Make alignment marks on the driveplate and crankshaft to ensure correct alignment during reinstallation.

3 Remove and discard the old bolts securing the driveplate to the crankshaft. If the crankshaft turns, wedge a screwdriver in the ring gear teeth to hold the driveplate.

4 Remove the driveplate from the crankshaft. Be sure to support it while removing the last bolt. Automatic transmission equipped vehicles have spacers on both sides of the driveplate. Keep them with the driveplate.

Installation

5 Clean the driveplate to remove grease and oil. Inspect the surface for cracks. Check for cracked or broken ring gear teeth.

6 Clean and inspect the mating surfaces of the driveplate and the crankshaft. If the crank-

shaft rear seal is leaking, replace it before reinstalling the driveplate (see Section 14).

7 Position the driveplate against the crankshaft. Be sure to align the marks made during removal. Note that some engines have an alignment dowel or staggered bolt holes to ensure correct installation. Before installing the new bolts, apply thread-locking compound to the threads.

8 Wedge a screwdriver in the ring gear teeth to keep it from turning and tighten the bolts to the torque listed in this Chapter's Specifications. Follow a criss-cross pattern and work up to the final torque in three or four steps.

9 The remainder of installation is the reverse of removal.

14 Rear main oil seal - replacement

Refer to illustration 14.4

Note: *This procedure assumes that the engine has been removed from the vehicle.*

1 Remove the engine/transmission assembly from the vehicle (see Chapter 2C), then remove the transaxle from the engine (see Chapter 7). Remove the driveplate (see Section 13).

2 The seal can be replaced without removing the oil pan or seal retainer. The easiest method involves using a seal-removal tool. If this tool isn't available, you can use a sharp knife to cut the lip off the old seal while carefully avoiding scratching the crankshaft. With the lip gone, use a screwdriver wrapped with tape to pry the seal out.

3 Lubricate the crankshaft seal journal and the lip of the new seal with multi-purpose grease.

4 Evenly drive the new seal into the retainer with a wood block or a section of pipe

slightly smaller in diameter than the outside diameter of the seal **(see illustration)**. The new seal should be approximately flush with the surface of the retainer.

5 The remainder of installation is the reverse of removal.

15 Engine mounts - check and replacement

1 Engine mounts seldom require attention, but broken or deteriorated mounts should be replaced immediately or the added strain placed on the driveline components may cause damage or wear.

Check

2 During the check, the engine must be raised slightly to remove the weight from the mounts.

3 Raise the vehicle and support it securely on jackstands, then position a jack under the engine oil pan. Place a large wood block between the jack head and the oil pan, then carefully raise the engine just enough to take the weight off the mounts. Do not position the wood block under the drain plug. **Warning:** *DO NOT place any part of your body under the engine when it's supported only by a jack!*

4 Check the mounts to see if the rubber is cracked, hardened or separated from the metal plates. Sometimes the rubber will separate from the bushing in the center of the mount.

5 Check for relative movement between the mount plates and the engine or frame (use a large screwdriver or prybar to attempt to move the mounts).

6 If movement is noted, lower the engine and tighten the mount fasteners.

Replacement

7   Raise the vehicle and support it securely on jackstands (if not already done). Support the engine as described in Step 3.

8   To remove an engine mount, remove the fasteners, raise the engine and detach the mount. The engine can be raised with an engine hoist, or with a floor jack and wood block placed under the oil pan. **Note:** *Even if only one mount is being replaced, remove the mount-to-engine bracket nut from the other mount (this will allow the engine to be raised far enough for mount removal).*

9   Installation is the reverse of removal. Use non-hardening thread locking compound on the mount bolts/nuts and be sure to tighten them securely.

Chapter 2 Part C
General engine overhaul procedures

Contents

Specifications

General

Engine designation
  Four-cylinder engines
    2009 and earlier.......... 2AZ-FE
    2010 and later.......... 2AR-FE
  V6 engine.......... 2GR-FE
Displacement
  2AZ-FE.......... 144.2 cubic inches (2.4 liters)
  2AR-FE.......... 152.2 cubic inches (2.5 liters)
  2GR-FE.......... 210.9 cubic inches (3.5 liters)
Bore and stroke
  2AZ-FE.......... 3.48 x 3.78 inches (88.5 x 96.0 mm)
  2AR-FE.......... 3.54 x 3.86 inches (90.0 x 98.0 mm)
  2GR-FE.......... 3.70 x 3.27 inches (94.0 x 83.0 mm)
Cylinder compression pressure @ 250 rpm
  2AZ-FE engine
    Standard.......... 184 to 196 psi (13.0 to 13.8 kg/cm^2) or more
    Minimum.......... 142 psi (10 kg/cm^2)
    Difference between cylinders.......... 15 psi (1.0 kg/cm^2) or less
  2AR-FE engine
    Standard.......... 210 psi (14.7 kg/cm^2) or more
    Minimum.......... 142 psi (10 kg/cm^2)
    Difference between cylinders
      2011 and earlier models.......... 29 psi (2.0 kg/cm^2) or less
      2012 and later models.......... 15 psi (1.0 kg/cm^2)

General (continued)

Cylinder compression pressure @ 250 rpm (continued)
    2GR-FE engine
        Standard
            All except 2012 Avalon and ES350 models............................ 189 (13.0 to 14.0 kg/cm^2) or more
            2012 Avalon and ES350 models .... 199 psi (13 kg/cm^2)
        Minimum .... 142 psi (10 kg/cm^2)
        Difference between cylinders.. 15 psi (1.0 kg/cm^2) or less
Oil pressure (engine warm)
    2AZ-FE engines
        At idle... 4.3 psi minimum
        At 3000 rpm.. 22 to 44 psi
    2AR-FE engine
        At idle... 4.3 psi minimum
        At 4000 rpm.. 38 psi minimum
    2GR-FE engine
        2011 and earlier models
            At idle .... 11.6 psi minimum
            At 3000 rpm... 55.5 psi minimum
        2012 and later Camry models and 2013 and later Avalon and ES350 models
            At idle .... 4.4 psi minimum
            At 3000 rpm... 29 psi minimum
        2012 Avalon and ES350 models
            At idle .... 11.6 psi minimum
            At 6000 rpm... 55.5 psi minimum

Torque specifications   **Ft-lbs** (unless otherwise indicated)

Connecting rod bearing cap bolts
    2AZ-FE engine
        Step 1 18
        Step 2 .... Tighten an additional 90-degrees
    2AR-FE engine
        Step 1 30
        Step 2 .... Tighten an additional 90-degrees
    2GR-FE engine
        Step 1 18
        Step 2 .... Tighten an additional 90-degrees
Main bearing cap bolts
    Four-cylinder engines
        Step 1 15
        Step 2
            2009 and earlier 29
            2010 and later 30
        Step 3 .... Tighten an additional 90-degrees
    V6 engines
        Step 1 45
        Step 2 .... Tighten an additional 90-degrees
        Side bolts.. 38
Lower crankcase bolts
    2AZ-FE engine **(see illustration 11.2b)** 18
    2AR-FE engine **(see illustration 11.2c)**
        Bolts "A"... 18
        All others.. 32

1.1 An engine block being bored. An engine rebuilder will use special machinery to recondition the cylinder bores

1.2 If the cylinders are bored, the machine shop will normally hone the engine on a machine like this

1 General information - engine overhaul

Refer to illustrations 1.1, 1.2, 1.3, 1.4, 1.5 and 1.6

Included in this portion of Chapter 2 are general information and diagnostic testing procedures for determining the overall mechanical condition of your engine.

The information ranges from advice concerning preparation for an overhaul and the purchase of replacement parts and/or components to detailed, step-by-step procedures covering removal and installation.

The following Sections have been written to help you determine whether your engine needs to be overhauled and how to remove and install it once you've determined it needs to be rebuilt. For information concerning in-vehicle engine repair, see Chapter 2A or 2B.

The Specifications included in this Part are general in nature and include only those necessary for testing the oil pressure and checking the engine compression. Refer to Chapter 2A or 2B for additional engine Specifications.

It's not always easy to determine when, or if, an engine should be completely overhauled, because a number of factors must be considered.

High mileage is not necessarily an indication that an overhaul is needed, while low mileage doesn't preclude the need for an overhaul. Frequency of servicing is probably the most important consideration. An engine that's had regular and frequent oil and filter changes, as well as other required maintenance, will most likely give many thousands of miles of reliable service. Conversely, a neglected engine may require an overhaul very early in its service life.

Excessive oil consumption is an indication that piston rings, valve seals and/or valve guides are in need of attention. Make sure that oil leaks aren't responsible before deciding that the rings and/or guides are bad. Perform a cylinder compression check to deter-

1.3 A crankshaft having a main bearing journal ground

mine the extent of the work required (see Section 3). Also check the vacuum readings under various conditions (see Section 4).

Check the oil pressure with a gauge installed in place of the oil pressure sending unit and compare it to this Chapter's Specifications (see Section 2). If it's extremely low, the bearings and/or oil pump are probably worn out.

Loss of power, rough running, knocking or metallic engine noises, excessive valve train noise and high fuel consumption rates may also point to the need for an overhaul, especially if they're all present at the same time. If a complete tune-up doesn't remedy the situation, major mechanical work is the only solution.

An engine overhaul involves restoring the internal parts to the specifications of a new engine. During an overhaul, the piston rings are replaced and the cylinder walls are reconditioned (rebored and/or honed) **(see illustrations 1.1 and 1.2)**. If a rebore is done by an automotive machine shop, new oversize pistons will also be installed. The main bearings, connecting rod bearings and camshaft bearings are generally replaced with new ones and, if necessary, the crankshaft may be

1.4 A machinist checks for a bent connecting rod, using specialized equipment

reground to restore the journals **(see illustration 1.3)**. Generally, the valves are serviced as well, since they're usually in less-than-perfect condition at this point. While the engine is being overhauled, other components, such as the starter and alternator, can be rebuilt as well. The end result should be similar to a new engine that will give many trouble free miles. **Note:** *Critical cooling system components such as the hoses, drivebelts, thermostat and water pump should be replaced with new parts when an engine is overhauled. The radiator should be checked carefully to ensure that it isn't clogged or leaking (see Chapter 3). If you purchase a rebuilt engine or short block, some rebuilders will not warranty their engines unless the radiator has been professionally flushed. Also, we don't recommend overhauling the oil pump - always install a new one when an engine is rebuilt.*

Overhauling the internal components on today's engines is a difficult and time-consuming task which requires a significant amount of specialty tools and is best left to a professional engine rebuilder **(see illustrations 1.4, 1.5 and 1.6)**. A competent engine

1.5 A bore gauge being used to check the main bearing bore

1.6 Uneven piston wear like this indicates a bent connecting rod

2.2a On four-cylinder models, the oil pressure sending unit is located at the end of the cylinder head on the driver's side of the vehicle

rebuilder will handle the inspection of your old parts and offer advice concerning the reconditioning or replacement of the original engine; never purchase parts or have machine work done on other components until the block has been thoroughly inspected by a professional machine shop. As a general rule, time is the primary cost of an overhaul, especially since the vehicle may be tied up for a minimum of two weeks or more. Be aware that some engine builders only have the capability to rebuild the engine you bring them while other rebuilders have a large inventory of rebuilt exchange engines in stock. Also be aware that many machine shops could take as much as two weeks time to completely rebuild your engine depending on shop workload. Sometimes it makes more sense to simply exchange your engine for another engine that's already rebuilt to save time.

2   Oil pressure check

Refer to illustrations 2.2a and 2.2b

1   Low engine oil pressure can be a sign of an engine in need of rebuilding. A low oil pressure indicator (often called an "idiot light") is not a test of the oiling system. Such indicators only come on when the oil pressure is dangerously low. Even a factory oil pressure gauge in the instrument panel is only a relative indication, although much better for driver information than a warning light. A better test is with a mechanical (not electrical) oil pressure gauge.

2   Locate the oil pressure indicator sending unit:

a) *On four-cylinder models, the oil pressure sending unit is located at the end of the cylinder head* **(see illustration)**.

b) *On V6 engine models, the oil pressure sending unit is located next to the oil filter* **(see illustration)**.

2.2b Location of the oil pressure sending unit - V6 models

3   Remove the oil pressure sending unit and install a fitting which will allow you to directly connect your hand-held, mechanical oil pressure gauge. Use Teflon tape or sealant on the threads of the adapter and the fitting on the end of your gauge's hose.

4   Connect an accurate tachometer to the engine, according to the tachometer manufacturer's instructions.

5   Check the oil pressure with the engine running (normal operating temperature) at the specified engine speed, and compare it to this Chapter's Specifications. If it's extremely low, the bearings and/or oil pump are probably worn out.

3   Cylinder compression check

Refer to illustration 3.6

1   A compression check will tell you what mechanical condition the upper end of your engine (pistons, rings, valves, head gaskets) is in. Specifically, it can tell you if the com-

3.6 A compression gauge with a threaded fitting for the spark plug hole is preferred over the type that requires hand pressure to maintain the seal - be sure to block open the throttle valve as far as possible during the compression check

pression is down due to leakage caused by worn piston rings, defective valves and seats or a blown head gasket. **Note:** *The engine must be at normal operating temperature and the battery must be fully charged for this check.*

2   Disable the fuel pump circuit (see Chapter 4, Section 3).

3   Clean the area around the spark plugs before you remove them (compressed air should be used, if available). The idea is to prevent dirt from getting into the cylinders as the compression check is being done.

4   Remove all of the spark plugs from the engine (see Chapter 1).

5   Block the throttle wide open.

6   Install the compression gauge in the spark plug hole **(see illustration)**.

7   Crank the engine over at least seven compression strokes and watch the gauge. The compression should build up quickly in a

4.4 A simple vacuum gauge can be handy in diagnosing engine condition and performance

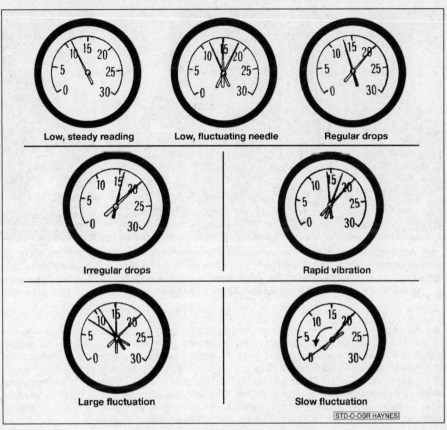

Low, steady reading

Low, fluctuating needle

Regular drops

Irregular drops

Rapid vibration

Large fluctuation

Slow fluctuation

STD-O-OBR HAYNES

4.6 Typical vacuum gauge readings

healthy engine. Low compression on the first stroke, followed by gradually increasing pressure on successive strokes, indicates worn piston rings. A low compression reading on the first stroke, which doesn't build up during successive strokes, indicates leaking valves or a blown head gasket (a cracked head could also be the cause). Deposits on the undersides of the valve heads can also cause low compression. Record the highest gauge reading obtained.

8   Repeat the procedure for the remaining cylinders and compare the results to this Chapter's Specifications.

9   Add some engine oil (about three squirts from a plunger-type oil can) to each cylinder, through the spark plug hole, and repeat the test.

10   If the compression increases after the oil is added, the piston rings are definitely worn. If the compression doesn't increase significantly, the leakage is occurring at the valves or head gasket. Leakage past the valves may be caused by burned valve seats and/or faces or warped, cracked or bent valves.

11   If two adjacent cylinders have equally low compression, there's a strong possibility that the head gasket between them is blown. The appearance of coolant in the combustion chambers or the crankcase would verify this condition.

12   If one cylinder is slightly lower than the others, and the engine has a slightly rough idle, a worn lobe on the camshaft could be the cause.

13   If the compression is unusually high, the combustion chambers are probably coated with carbon deposits. If that's the case, the cylinder head(s) should be removed and decarbonized.

14   If compression is way down or varies greatly between cylinders, it would be a good idea to have a leak-down test performed by an automotive repair shop. This test will pinpoint exactly where the leakage is occurring and how severe it is.

15   After all of the cylinders have been

checked, unblock the throttle and restore the ignition and fuel system functions.

4   Vacuum gauge diagnostic checks

Refer to illustrations 4.4 and 4.6

1   A vacuum gauge provides valuable information about what is going on in the engine at a low-cost. You can check for worn rings or cylinder walls, leaking head or intake manifold gaskets, incorrect carburetor adjustments, restricted exhaust, stuck or burned valves, weak valve springs, improper ignition or valve timing and ignition problems.

2   Unfortunately, vacuum gauge readings are easy to misinterpret, so they should be used in conjunction with other tests to confirm the diagnosis.

3   Both the absolute readings and the rate of needle movement are important for accurate interpretation. Most gauges measure vacuum in inches of mercury (in-Hg). The following references to vacuum assume the diagnosis is being performed at sea level. As elevation increases (or atmospheric pressure decreases), the reading will decrease. For every 1,000 foot increase in elevation above approximately 2000 feet, the gauge readings will decrease about one inch of mercury.

4   Connect the vacuum gauge directly to intake manifold vacuum, not to ported (throttle

body) vacuum **(see illustration)**. Be sure no hoses are left disconnected during the test or false readings will result.

5   Before you begin the test, allow the engine to warm up completely. Block the wheels and set the parking brake. With the transmission in Park, start the engine and allow it to run at normal idle speed. **Warning:** *Keep your hands and the vacuum gauge clear of the fans.*

6   Read the vacuum gauge; an average, healthy engine should normally produce about 17 to 22 in-Hg with a fairly steady needle **(see illustration)**. Refer to the following vacuum gauge readings and what they indicate about the engine's condition:

7   A low steady reading usually indicates a leaking gasket between the intake manifold and cylinder head(s) or throttle body, a leaky vacuum hose, late ignition timing or incorrect camshaft timing. Check ignition timing with a timing light and eliminate all other possible causes, utilizing the tests provided in this Chapter before you remove the timing chain cover to check the timing marks.

8   If the reading is three to eight inches below normal and it fluctuates at that low reading, suspect an intake manifold gasket leak at an intake port or a faulty fuel injector.

9   If the needle has regular drops of about two-to-four inches at a steady rate, the valves are probably leaking. Perform a compression check or leak-down test to confirm this.

6.1 After tightly wrapping water-vulnerable components, use a spray cleaner on everything, with particular concentration on the greasiest areas, usually around the valve cover and lower edges of the block. If one section dries out, apply more cleaner

6.2 Depending on how dirty the engine is, let the cleaner soak in according to the directions and hose off the grime and cleaner. Get the rinse water down into every area you can get at; then dry important components with a hair dryer or paper towels

10   An irregular drop or down-flick of the needle can be caused by a sticking valve or an ignition misfire. Perform a compression check or leak-down test and read the spark plugs.

11   A rapid vibration of about four in-Hg vibration at idle combined with exhaust smoke indicates worn valve guides. Perform a leak-down test to confirm this. If the rapid vibration occurs with an increase in engine speed, check for a leaking intake manifold gasket or head gasket, weak valve springs, burned valves or ignition misfire.

12   A slight fluctuation, say one inch up and down, may mean ignition problems. Check all the usual tune-up items and, if necessary, run the engine on an ignition analyzer.

13   If there is a large fluctuation, perform a compression or leak-down test to look for a weak or dead cylinder or a blown head gasket.

14   If the needle moves slowly through a wide range, check for a clogged PCV system, incorrect idle fuel mixture, carburetor/throttle body or intake manifold gasket leaks.

15   Check for a slow return after revving the engine by quickly snapping the throttle open until the engine reaches about 2,500 rpm and let it shut. Normally the reading should drop to near zero, rise above normal idle reading (about 5 in-Hg over) and then return to the previous idle reading. If the vacuum returns slowly and doesn't peak when the throttle is snapped shut, the rings may be worn. If there is a long delay, look for a restricted exhaust system (often the muffler or catalytic converter). An easy way to check this is to temporarily disconnect the exhaust ahead of the suspected part and redo the test.

5   Engine rebuilding alternatives

The do-it-yourselfer is faced with a number of options when purchasing a rebuilt engine. The major considerations are cost, warranty, parts availability and the time

required for the rebuilder to complete the project. The decision to replace the engine block, piston/connecting rod assemblies and crankshaft depends on the final inspection results of your engine. Only then can you make a cost effective decision whether to have your engine overhauled or simply purchase an exchange engine for your vehicle.

Some of the rebuilding alternatives include:

Individual parts - If the inspection procedures reveal that the engine block and most engine components are in reusable condition, purchasing individual parts and having a rebuilder rebuild your engine may be the most economical alternative. The block, crankshaft and piston/connecting rod assemblies should all be inspected carefully by a machine shop first.

Short block - A short block consists of an engine block with a crankshaft and piston/connecting rod assemblies already installed. All new bearings are incorporated and all clearances will be correct. The existing camshafts, valve train components, cylinder head and external parts can be bolted to the short block with little or no machine shop work necessary.

Long block - A long block consists of a short block plus an oil pump, oil pan, cylinder head, valve cover, camshaft and valve train components, timing sprockets and chain or gears and timing cover. All components are installed with new bearings, seals and gaskets incorporated throughout. The installation of manifolds and external parts is all that's necessary.

Low mileage used engines - Some companies now offer low mileage used engines which is a very cost effective way to get your vehicle up and running again. These engines often come from vehicles which have been in totaled in accidents or come from other countries which have a higher vehicle turn over rate. A low mileage used engine also

usually has a similar warranty like the newly remanufactured engines.

Give careful thought to which alternative is best for you and discuss the situation with local automotive machine shops, auto parts dealers and experienced rebuilders before ordering or purchasing replacement parts.

6   Engine removal - methods and precautions

Refer to illustrations 6.1, 6.2, 6.3 and 6.4

If you've decided that an engine must be removed for overhaul or major repair work, several preliminary steps should be taken. Read all removal and installation procedures carefully prior to committing to this job.

Locating a suitable place to work is extremely important. Adequate work space, along with storage space for the vehicle, will be needed. If a shop or garage isn't available, at the very least a flat, level, clean work surface made of concrete or asphalt is required.

Cleaning the engine compartment and engine before beginning the removal procedure will help keep tools clean and organized **(see illustrations 6.1 and 6.2)**.

An engine hoist will also be necessary. Make sure the hoist is rated in excess of the combined weight of the engine and transaxle. Safety is of primary importance, considering the potential hazards involved in removing the engine from the vehicle.

A vehicle hoist will be necessary for engine removal, since on these models the subframe must be removed and the engine/transaxle assembly must be lowered from the engine compartment, then the vehicle is raised and the powertrain unit is removed from under the vehicle. If the necessary equipment is not available, the engine will have to be removed by a qualified automotive repair facility.

If you're a novice at engine removal, get

6.3 Get an engine stand sturdy enough to firmly support the engine while you're working on it. Stay away from three-wheeled models: they have a tendency to tip over more easily, so get a four-wheeled unit

6.4 A clutch alignment tool is necessary if you plan to install a rebuilt engine mated to a manual transaxle

at least one helper. One person cannot easily do all the things you need to do to remove a big heavy engine and transaxle assembly from the engine compartment. Also helpful is to seek advice and assistance from someone who's experienced in engine removal.

Plan the operation ahead of time. Arrange for or obtain all of the tools and equipment you'll need prior to beginning the job **(see illustrations 6.3 and 6.4)**. Some of the equipment necessary to perform engine removal and installation safely and with relative ease are (in addition to a vehicle hoist and an engine hoist) a heavy duty floor jack (preferably fitted with a transaxle jack head adapter), complete sets of wrenches and sockets as described in the front of this manual, wooden blocks, plenty of rags and cleaning solvent for mopping up spilled oil, coolant and gasoline.

Plan for the vehicle to be out of use for quite a while. A machine shop can do the work that is beyond the scope of the home mechanic. Machine shops often have a busy schedule, so before removing the engine, consult the shop for an estimate of how long it will take to rebuild or repair the components that may need work.

7 Engine - removal and installation

Warning: *The models covered by this manual are equipped with Supplemental Restraint Systems (SRS), more commonly known as airbags. Always disable the airbag system before working in the vicinity of airbag system components to avoid the possibility of accidental deployment of the airbag, which could cause personal injury (see Chapter 12).*
Warning: *Gasoline is extremely flammable, so take extra precautions when you work on any part of the fuel system. Don't smoke or allow open flames or bare light bulbs near the work area, and don't work in a garage where a gas-type appliance (such as a water heater or a clothes dryer) is present. Since gasoline is carcinogenic, wear fuel-resistant gloves when*

there's a possibility of being exposed to fuel, and, if you spill any fuel on your skin, rinse it off immediately with soap and water. Mop up any spills immediately and do not store fuel-soaked rags where they could ignite. The fuel system is under constant pressure, so, if any fuel lines are to be disconnected, the fuel pressure in the system must be relieved first (see Chapter 4 for more information). When you perform any kind of work on the fuel system, wear safety glasses and have a Class B type fire extinguisher on hand.
Note: *Engine removal on these models is a difficult job, especially for the do-it-yourself mechanic working at home. Because of the vehicle's design, the manufacturer states that the engine and transaxle have to be removed as a unit from the bottom of the vehicle, not the top. With a floor jack and jackstands, the vehicle can't be raised high enough and supported safely enough for the engine/transaxle assembly to slide out from underneath. The manufacturer recommends that removal of the engine/transaxle assembly only be performed on a vehicle hoist.*

Removal

Refer to illustrations 7.14, 7.30 and 7.33

1   Park the vehicle on a frame-contact type vehicle hoist. The pads of the hoist arms must contact the body welt along each side of the vehicle (see *Jacking and towing* at the front of this manual).
2   Relieve the fuel system pressure (see Chapter 4), then disconnect the negative cable from the battery.
3   Place protective covers on the fenders and cowl and remove the hood (see Chapter 11).
4   Remove the air filter housing (see Chapter 4).
5   Remove the cowl cover assembly and the vent tray (see Chapter 11).
6   Disconnect the battery cables, then remove the battery and the battery tray (see Chapter 5).
7   Remove the windshield wiper assembly (see Chapter 12).

8   Loosen the front wheel lug nuts and the driveaxle/hub nuts, then raise the vehicle on the hoist.
9   Drain the cooling system and engine oil (see Chapter 1).
10   Drain the transaxle fluid (see Chapter 1).
11   If equipped with a manual transaxle, disconnect the clutch slave cylinder and accumulator lines and cap the lines and ports.
Caution: *Don't allow brake fluid to come into contact with paint, as it will damage the finish.*
12   Remove the drivebelt(s) (see Chapter 1).
13   Remove the right side engine mount stay mounting fasteners and stay (see Chapter 2).
14   Clearly label, then disconnect all vacuum lines, radiator hoses, heater hoses, oil cooler hoses and emissions hoses, wiring harness connectors, ground straps and fuel lines. Masking tape and/or a touch up paint applicator work well for marking items **(see illustration)**. Take photos or sketch the locations of components and brackets.
15   Remove the engine movement control rod fasteners and the rod with the bracket.
16   Remove the engine wiring harness connectors from the engine compartment junc-

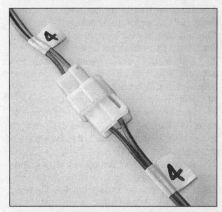

7.14 Label both ends of each wire and hose before disconnecting it

7.30 With the chain or sling attached securely to the engine, take up the slack until there is slight tension on the chain

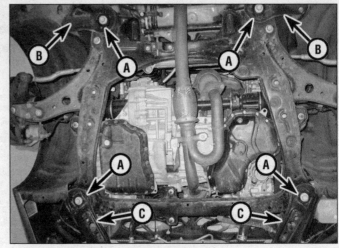

7.33 Subframe and bracket details - V6 shown, four-cylinder models similar

A   *Subframe mounting bolts*   C   *Front subframe brackets*
B   *Rear subframe brackets*

tion box. On four-cylinder models, detach the wiring harness connectors from the PCM and remove the PCM from the engine compartment (see Chapter 6).

17   Disconnect the shift linkage from the transaxle, then detach the cables from the front crossmember (see Chapter 7A or 7B). Also disconnect any wiring harness connectors from the transaxle.

18   Remove all fuel lines and/or emission control components that might be damaged during engine removal (see Chapters 4 and 6).

19   Remove the alternator and the starter (see Chapter 5).

20   Remove the power steering pump (see Chapter 10).

21   Remove the cooling fan(s), shroud(s) and radiator (see Chapter 3). **Note:** *This step is not absolutely necessary, but it will help avoid damage to the cooling fans and radiator as the engine is lowered out of the vehicle. If the radiator is not removed, it will still be necessary to detach the transaxle oil cooler lines from the bottom of the radiator on automatic transaxle equipped vehicles.*

22   Disconnect the air conditioning clutch electrical connector, then unbolt the air conditioning compressor and set it aside. Do not disconnect the refrigerant hoses.

23   Detach the front exhaust pipe from the exhaust manifold(s) (see Chapter 4) and remove the support bracket.

24   Remove the driveaxles (see Chapter 8).

25   Detach the stabilizer bar links from the bar (see Chapter 10) and remove the fasteners securing the lower balljoints to the lower control arms (see Chapter 10).

26   Disconnect the front speed sensor connectors (see Chapter 9).

27   Detach the tie rods from the steering knuckles (see Chapter 10).

28   Remove the driveplate-to-torque converter bolts (see Chapter 7B).

29   Disconnect the steering shaft u-joint from the steering gear.

30   Attach a lifting sling or chain to the engine **(see illustration)**. Position an engine hoist and connect the sling to it. Take up the slack until there is slight tension on the sling or chain. Position the chain on the hoist so it balances the engine and the transaxle level with the vehicle.

31   Recheck to be sure nothing except the mounts are still connecting the engine/transaxle to the vehicle.

32   Disconnect and label anything still remaining.

33   Remove the subframe front and rear mounting bolts and brackets **(see illustration)**.

34   Slowly lower the engine/transaxle from the vehicle. **Note:** *Placing a sheet of hardboard or paneling between the engine and the floor makes moving the powertrain easier.*

35   Once the powertrain is on the floor, disconnect the engine lifting hoist and raise the vehicle hoist until the powertrain can be slid out from underneath. **Note:** *A helper will be needed to move the powertrain.*

36   Reconnect the chain or sling and take up the slack with the engine hoist. Remove the front and rear engine mount fasteners, raise the engine/transaxle assembly, then slide the crossmember out from under the engine. Lower the engine back to the ground and separate the engine from the transaxle (see Chapter 7). Disregard any steps that do not apply since the transaxle is already removed from the vehicle.

37   Remove the flywheel/driveplate and mount the engine on a stand.

Installation

38   Check the engine/transaxle mounts. If they're worn or damaged, replace them.

39   On manual transaxle equipped models, inspect the clutch components (see Chap-

ter 8). **Note:** *On 2010 and later models, the manufacturer recommends replacing the slave cylinder and throw out bearing unit when the transaxle is removed.* On automatic transaxle models, inspect the converter seal and bushing.

40   On manual transaxle equipped vehicles, apply a dab of high temperature grease to the splines of the input shaft. On automatic transaxle equipped models, apply a dab of grease to the nose of the torque converter.

41   Carefully guide the transaxle into place, following the procedure outlined in Chapter 7. **Caution:** *Do not use the bolts to force the engine and transaxle into alignment. It may crack or damage major components.*

42   Install the transaxle-to-engine bolts and tighten them securely.

43   Raise the engine/transaxle assembly and slide the subframe into place. Lower the engine/transaxle and reconnect the mounts to the subframe. Raise the assembly, move it into position under the vehicle and disconnect the engine hoist. Slowly lower the vehicle over the powertrain, being very careful to ensure that nothing on the vehicle makes contact with the powertrain as this is done.

44   Roll the engine hoist into position, attach the chain or sling in a position that will allow a good balance and slowly raise the powertrain/subframe assembly until the subframe-to-chassis bolts and brackets can be installed. **Warning:** *Support each side of the subframe with a floor jack while installing the bolts.* Tighten the bolts securely.

45   Reinstall the remaining components in the reverse order of removal.

46   Add coolant, oil, power steering and transmission fluids as needed (see Chapter 1).

47   Run the engine and check for proper operation and leaks. Shut off the engine and recheck the fluid levels.

9.1 Before you try to remove the pistons from engines with very worn cylinders, use a ridge reamer to remove the raised material (ridge) from the top of the cylinders

9.3 Checking the connecting rod endplay (side clearance)

9.4 If the connecting rods and caps are not marked, use a center punch or numbered impression stamps to mark the caps to the rods by cylinder number (for example, this would be the No. 4 connecting rod)

8 Engine overhaul - disassembly sequence

1   It's much easier to remove the external components if the engine is mounted on a portable engine stand. A stand can often be rented quite cheaply from an equipment rental yard. Before the engine is mounted on a stand, the flywheel/driveplate should be removed from the engine.

2   If a stand isn't available, it's possible to remove the external engine components with it blocked up on the floor. Be extra careful not to tip or drop the engine when working without a stand.

3   If you're going to obtain a rebuilt engine, all external components must come off first, to be transferred to the replacement engine. These components include:

    Emissions control components
    Ignition coils
    Thermostat and housing cover
    Water pump
    Water bypass tube
    EFI components
    Intake/exhaust manifolds
    Oil filter
    Engine mount brackets
    Clutch and flywheel/driveplate

Note: *When removing the external components from the engine, pay close attention to details that may be helpful or important during installation. Note the installed position of gaskets, seals, spacers, pins, brackets, washers, bolts and other small items.*

4   If you're obtaining a short block, which consists of the engine block, crankshaft, pistons and connecting rods all assembled, then the timing belt or chain, the cylinder head, the oil pan, the oil pump, the lower crankcase, will have to be removed as well from your engine so that your short block can be turned in to

the rebuilder as a core (see Chapter 2A or 2B). See *Engine rebuilding alternatives* for additional information regarding the different possibilities to be considered.

9 Pistons and connecting rods - removal and installation

Caution: *New connecting rod cap bolts should be used when reinstalling the pistons/connecting rods.*

Removal

Refer to illustrations 9.1, 9.3 and 9.4

Note: *Prior to removing the piston/connecting rod assemblies, remove the cylinder head and oil pan, and, on 2010 and later four-cylinder engines, the balance shaft assembly (see Chapter 2A or 2B).*

1   Use your fingernail to feel if a ridge has formed at the upper limit of ring travel (about 1/4-inch down from the top of each cylinder). If carbon deposits or cylinder wear have produced ridges, they must be completely removed with a special tool **(see illustration)**. Follow the manufacturer's instructions provided with the tool. Failure to remove the ridges before attempting to remove the piston/connecting rod assemblies may result in piston breakage. **Caution:** *2010 and later model four-cylinder engines have a removable cylinder block water jacket and should not be machined. If service is needed to the water jacket, the block should be taken to a dealer service department or qualified machine shop.*

2   After the cylinder ridges have been removed, turn the engine so the crankshaft is facing up.

3   Before the connecting rods are removed, check the connecting rod endplay with feeler gauges. Slide them between the first con-

necting rod and the crankshaft throw until the play is removed **(see illustration)**. Repeat this procedure for each connecting rod. The endplay is equal to the thickness of the feeler gauge(s). Check with an automotive machine shop for the endplay service limit. If the play exceeds the service limit, new connecting rods will be required. If new rods (or a new crankshaft) are installed, the endplay may fall under the minimum allowable clearance. If it does, the rods will have to be machined to restore it. If necessary, consult an automotive machine shop for advice.

4   Check the connecting rods and caps for identification marks **(see illustration)**. If they aren't plainly marked, use a small center-punch to make the appropriate number of indentations on each rod and cap (1, 2, 3, etc., depending on the cylinder they're associated with).

5   Loosen each of the connecting rod cap bolts 1/2-turn at a time until they can be removed by hand. Remove the number one connecting rod cap and bearing insert. Don't drop the bearing insert out of the cap.

6   Remove the bearing insert and push the connecting rod/piston assembly out through the top of the engine. Use a wooden or plastic hammer handle to push on the upper bearing surface in the connecting rod. If resistance is felt, double-check to make sure that the entire ridge was removed from the cylinder.

7   Repeat the procedure for the remaining cylinders.

8   Reassemble the connecting rod caps and bearing inserts in their respective connecting rods and install the cap bolts finger tight. Leaving the old bearing inserts in place until reassembly will help prevent the connecting rod bearing surfaces from being accidentally nicked or gouged.

9   The pistons and connecting rods are now ready for inspection and overhaul at an automotive machine shop.

9.12 Install the piston ring into the cylinder, then push it down into position using a piston so the ring will be square in the cylinder

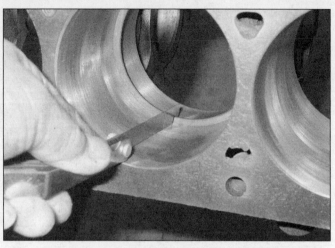

9.13 With the ring square in the cylinder, measure the ring end gap with a feeler gauge

Piston ring installation

Refer to illustrations 9.12, 9.13, 9.14, 9.18a, 9.18b and 9.21

10   Before installing the new piston rings, the ring end gaps must be checked. It's assumed that the piston ring side clearance has been checked and verified correct.

11   Lay out the piston/connecting rod assemblies and the new ring sets so the ring sets will be matched with the same piston and cylinder during the end gap measurement and engine assembly.

12   Insert the top (number one) ring into the first cylinder and square it up with the cylinder walls by pushing it in with the top of the piston **(see illustration)**. The ring should be near the bottom of the cylinder, at the lower limit of ring travel.

13   To measure the end gap, slip feeler gauges between the ends of the ring until a gauge equal to the gap width is found **(see illustration)**. The feeler gauge should slide between the ring ends with a slight amount of drag. Check with an automotive machine shop for the correct end gap for your engine. If the gap is larger or smaller than specified, double-check to make sure you have the correct rings before proceeding.

14   If the gap is too small, it must be enlarged or the ring ends may come in contact with each other during engine operation, which can cause serious damage to the engine. The end gap can be increased by filing the ring ends very carefully with a fine file. Mount the file in a vise equipped with soft jaws, slip the ring over the file with the ends contacting the file face and slowly move the ring to remove material from the ends. When performing this operation, file only by pushing the ring from the outside end of the file towards the vise **(see illustration)**. Be sure to remove all raised material.

15   Excess end gap isn't critical unless it's greater than approximately 0.040-inch. Again, double-check to make sure you have the correct ring type and that you are referencing the correct section and category of specifications.

16   Repeat the procedure for each ring that will be installed in the first cylinder and for each ring in the remaining cylinders. Remember to keep rings, pistons and cylinders matched up.

17   Once the ring end gaps have been checked/corrected, the rings can be installed on the pistons.

18   The oil control ring (lowest one on the piston) is usually installed first. It's composed of three separate components. Slip the spacer/expander into the groove **(see illustration)**. If an anti-rotation tang is used, make sure it's inserted into the drilled hole in the ring groove. Next, install the upper side rail in the same manner **(see illustration)**. Don't use a piston ring installation tool on the oil ring side rails, as they may be damaged. Instead, place one

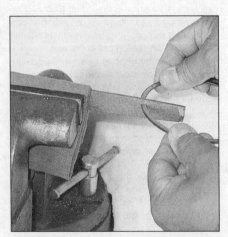

9.14 If the ring end gap is too small, clamp a file in a vise and file the piston ring ends - file from the outside of the ring inward only

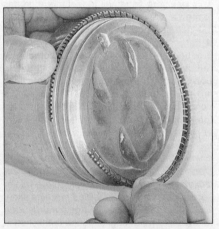

9.18a Installing the spacer/expander in the oil ring groove

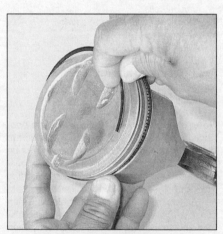

9.18b DO NOT use a piston ring installation tool when installing the oil control side rails

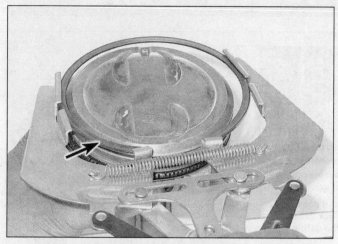

9.21 Use a piston ring installation tool to install the number 2 and the number 1 (top) rings - be sure the directional mark on the piston ring(s) is facing toward the top of the piston

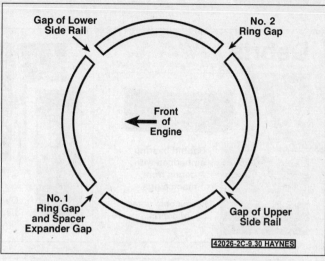

9.28 Position the piston ring end gaps as shown

end of the side rail into the groove between the spacer/expander and the ring land, hold it firmly in place and slide a finger around the piston while pushing the rail into the groove. Finally, install the lower side rail.

19   After the three oil ring components have been installed, check to make sure that both the upper and lower side rails can be rotated smoothly inside the ring grooves.

20   The number two (middle) ring is installed next. It's usually stamped with a mark which must face up, toward the top of the piston. Do not mix up the top and middle rings, as they have different cross-sections. **Note:** *Always follow the instructions printed on the ring package or box - different manufacturers may require different approaches.*

21   Use a piston ring installation tool and make sure the identification mark is facing the top of the piston, then slip the ring into the middle groove on the piston **(see illustration).** Don't expand the ring any more than necessary to slide it over the piston.

22   Install the number one (top) ring in the same manner. Make sure the mark is facing up. Be careful not to confuse the number one and number two rings.

23   Repeat the procedure for the remaining pistons and rings.

Installation

24   Before installing the piston/connecting rod assemblies, the cylinder walls must be perfectly clean, the top edge of each cylinder bore must be chamfered, and the crankshaft must be in place.

25   Remove the cap from the end of the number one connecting rod (refer to the marks made during removal). Remove the original bearing inserts and wipe the bearing surfaces of the connecting rod and cap with a

clean, lint-free cloth. They must be kept spotlessly clean.

Connecting rod bearing oil clearance check

Refer to illustrations 9.28, 9.33, 9.36 and 9.40

26   Clean the back side of the new upper bearing insert, then lay it in place in the connecting rod. Make sure the tab on the bearing fits into the recess in the rod. Don't hammer the bearing insert into place and be very careful not to nick or gouge the bearing face. Don't lubricate the bearing at this time.

27   Clean the back side of the other bearing insert and install it in the rod cap. Again, make sure the tab on the bearing fits into the recess in the cap, and don't apply any lubricant. It's critically important that the mating surfaces of the bearing and connecting rod are perfectly clean and oil free when they're assembled.

28   Position the piston ring gaps at 90-degree intervals around the piston as shown **(see illustration).**

29   Lubricate the piston and rings with clean engine oil and attach a piston ring compressor to the piston. Leave the skirt protruding about 1/4-inch to guide the piston into the cylinder. The rings must be compressed until they're flush with the piston.

30   Rotate the crankshaft until the number one connecting rod journal is at BDC (bottom dead center) and apply a liberal coat of engine oil to the cylinder walls.

31   With the mark (cavity) on top of the piston facing the front of the engine, gently insert the piston/connecting rod assembly into the number one cylinder bore and rest the bottom edge of the ring compressor on the engine block.

32   Tap the top edge of the ring compressor to make sure it's contacting the block around its entire circumference.

33   Gently tap on the top of the piston with the end of a wooden or plastic hammer handle **(see illustration)** while guiding the end of the connecting rod into place on the crankshaft journal.

34   The piston rings may try to pop out of the ring compressor just before entering the cylinder bore, so keep some downward pressure on the ring compressor. Work slowly, and if any resistance is felt as the piston enters the cylinder, stop immediately. Find out what's hanging up and fix it before proceeding. Do not, for any reason, force the piston into the cylinder - you might break a ring and/or the piston.

35   Once the piston/connecting rod assembly is installed, the connecting rod bearing oil clearance must be checked before the rod cap is permanently installed.

36   Cut a piece of the appropriate size Plastigage slightly shorter than the width of the con-

9.33 Use a plastic or wooden hammer handle to push the piston into the cylinder

ENGINE BEARING ANALYSIS

Debris

Babbitt bearing embedded with debris from machinings

Microscopic detail of debris

Microscopic detail of gouges

Overplated copper alloy bearing gouged by cast iron debris

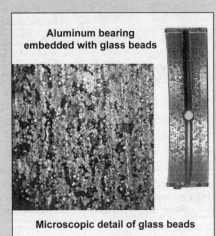

Aluminum bearing embedded with glass beads

Microscopic detail of glass beads

Damaged lining caused by dirt left on the bearing back

Misassembly

Result of a lower half assembled as an upper - blocking the oil flow

Excessive oil clearance is indicated by a short contact arc

Polished and oil-stained backs are a result of a poor fit in the housing bore

Result of a wrong, reversed, or shifted cap

Overloading

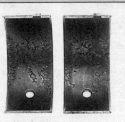

Damage from excessive idling which resulted in an oil film unable to support the load imposed

Damaged upper connecting rod bearings caused by engine lugging; the lower main bearings (not shown) were similarly affected

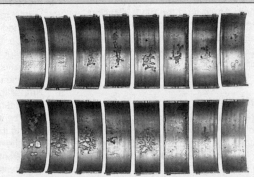

The damage shown in these upper and lower connecting rod bearings was caused by engine operation at a higher-than-rated speed under load

Misalignment

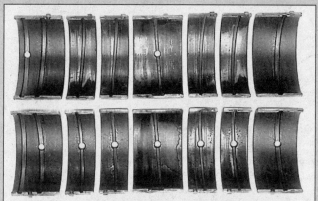

A warped crankshaft caused this pattern of severe wear in the center, diminishing toward the ends

A poorly finished crankshaft caused the equally spaced scoring shown

A tapered housing bore caused the damage along one edge of this pair

A bent connecting rod led to the damage in the "V" pattern

Lubrication

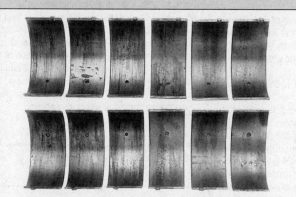

Result of dry start: The bearings on the left, farthest from the oil pump, show more damage

Result of a low oil supply or oil starvation

Severe wear as a result of inadequate oil clearance

Corrosion

Microscopic detail of corrosion

Corrosion is an acid attack on the bearing lining generally caused by inadequate maintenance, extremely hot or cold operation, or inferior oils or fuels

Microscopic detail of cavitation

Example of cavitation - a surface erosion caused by pressure changes in the oil film

Damage from excessive thrust or insufficient axial clearance

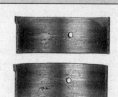

Bearing affected by oil dilution caused by excessive blow-by or a rich mixture

9.36 Place Plastigage on each connecting rod bearing journal parallel to the crankshaft centerline

9.40 Use the scale on the Plastigage package to determine the bearing oil clearance - be sure to measure the widest part of the Plastigage and use the correct scale; it comes with both standard and metric scales

necting rod bearing and lay it in place on the number one connecting rod journal, parallel with the journal axis **(see illustration)**.

37   Clean the connecting rod cap bearing face and install the rod cap. Make sure the mating mark on the cap is on the same side as the mark on the connecting rod.

38   Install the old rod bolts at this time, and tighten them to the torque listed in this Chapter's Specifications, working up to it in three steps. **Note:** *Use a thin-wall socket to avoid erroneous torque readings that can result if the socket is wedged between the rod cap and the bolt. If the socket tends to wedge itself between the fastener and the cap, lift up on it slightly until it no longer contacts the cap. DO NOT rotate the crankshaft at any time during this operation.*

39   Remove the fasteners and detach the rod cap, being very careful not to disturb the Plastigage.

40   Compare the width of the crushed Plastigage to the scale printed on the Plastigage envelope to obtain the oil clearance **(see illustration)**. The connecting rod oil clearance is usually about 0.002 inch. Consult an automotive machine shop for the clearance specified for the rod bearings on your engine.

41   If the clearance is not as specified, the bearing inserts may be the wrong size (which means different ones will be required). Before deciding that different inserts are needed, make sure that no dirt or oil was between the bearing inserts and the connecting rod or cap when the clearance was measured. Also, recheck the journal diameter. If the Plastigage was wider at one end than the other, the journal may be tapered. If the clearance still exceeds the limit specified, the bearing will have to be replaced with an undersize bearing. **Caution:** *When installing a new crankshaft, always use a standard size bearing.*

Final installation

42   Carefully scrape all traces of the Plastigage material off the rod journal and/or bearing face. Be very careful not to scratch the bearing - use your fingernail or the edge of a plastic card.

43   Make sure the bearing faces are perfectly clean, then apply a uniform layer of clean moly-base grease or engine assembly lube to both of them. You'll have to push the piston into the cylinder to expose the face of the bearing insert in the connecting rod. **Caution:** *Recheck the diameter of the connecting rod bolts at this time, making sure that none of them have stretched so much as to cause the necked-down area of the bolt to fall under the minimum allowable diameter listed in this Chapter's Specifications.*

44   Slide the connecting rod back into place on the journal, install the rod cap, install the **NEW** bolts and tighten them to the torque listed in this Chapter's Specifications. Again, work up to the torque in three steps.

45   Repeat the entire procedure for the remaining pistons/connecting rods.

46   The important points to remember are:

a) *Keep the back sides of the bearing inserts and the insides of the connecting rods and caps perfectly clean when assembling them.*

b) *Make sure you have the correct piston/ rod assembly for each cylinder.*

c) *The mark on the piston must face the front of the engine.*

d) *Lubricate the cylinder walls liberally with clean oil.*

e) *Lubricate the bearing faces when installing the rod caps after the oil clearance has been checked.*

47   After all the piston/connecting rod assemblies have been correctly installed, rotate the crankshaft a number of times by

hand to check for any obvious binding.

48   As a final step, check the connecting rod endplay again. If it was correct before disassembly and the original crankshaft and rods were reinstalled, it should still be correct. If new rods or a new crankshaft were installed, the endplay may be inadequate. If so, the rods will have to be removed and taken to an automotive machine shop for resizing.

10   Crankshaft - removal and installation

Caution: *New main bearing cap bolts should be used when reinstalling the crankshaft.*

Removal

Refer to illustrations 10.1 and 10.3

Note: *The crankshaft can be removed only after the engine has been removed from the vehicle. It's assumed that the driveplate, crankshaft pulley, timing belt or chain, oil pan, oil pump body, balance shaft assembly (2010 and later four-cylinder engines), piston oil jet nozzles, and piston/connecting rod assemblies have already been removed. The rear main oil seal retainer must be unbolted and separated from the block before proceeding with crankshaft removal.*

1   Before the crankshaft is removed, measure the endplay. Mount a dial indicator with the indicator in line with the crankshaft and touching the end of the crankshaft **(see illustration)**.

2   Pry the crankshaft all the way to the rear and zero the dial indicator. Next, pry the crankshaft to the front as far as possible and check the reading on the dial indicator. The distance traveled is the endplay. A typical crankshaft

10.1 Checking crankshaft endplay with a dial indicator

10.3 Checking crankshaft endplay with feeler gauges at the thrust bearing journal

endplay will fall between 0.003 to 0.010-inch. If it's greater than that, check the crankshaft thrust surfaces for wear after it's removed. If no wear is evident, new main bearings should correct the endplay.

3   If a dial indicator isn't available, feeler gauges can be used. Gently pry the crankshaft all the way to the front of the engine. Slip feeler gauges between the crankshaft and the front face of the thrust bearing or washer to determine the clearance **(see illustration)**.

4   Loosen the main bearing cap bolts 1/4-turn at a time each, until they can be removed by hand. **Note:** *On V6 engines, first remove the main bearing cap side bolts in the order opposite that of the tightening sequence* **(see illustration 10.19c)**

5   Gently tap the main bearing cap(s) with a soft-face hammer. Pull the main bearing cap(s) straight up and off the cylinder block. Try not to drop the bearing inserts if they come out with the assembly.

6   Carefully lift the crankshaft out of the engine. It may be a good idea to have an assistant available, since the crankshaft is quite heavy and awkward to handle. With the bearing inserts in place inside the engine block and main bearing caps, reinstall the main bearing cap assembly onto the engine block and tighten the bolts finger tight. Make sure you install the main bearing cap(s) with the arrow facing the front end of the engine.

Installation

7   Crankshaft installation is the first step in engine reassembly. It's assumed at this point that the engine block and crankshaft have been cleaned, inspected and repaired or reconditioned.

8   Position the engine block with the bottom facing up.

9   Remove the mounting bolts and lift off the main bearing caps.

10   If they're still in place, remove the original bearing inserts from the block and from the main bearing cap(s). Wipe the bearing surfaces of the block and main bearing cap(s) with a clean, lint-free cloth. They must be kept spotlessly clean. This is critical for determining the correct bearing oil clearance.

Main bearing oil clearance check

Refer to illustrations 10.17, 10.19a, 10.19b, 10.19c and 10.21

11   Without mixing them up, clean the back sides of the new upper main bearing inserts (with grooves and oil holes) and lay one in each main bearing saddle in the block. Each upper bearing has an oil groove and oil hole in it. **Caution:** *The oil holes in the block must line up with the oil holes in the upper bearing inserts.* The thrust washer on four-cylinder models is located on the number 3 crankshaft journal. The thrust washer on V6 models is located on the number 2 crankshaft journal. Install the thrust washers with the grooved side facing out, with one set located in the block and the other set with the main bearing cap. Clean the back sides of the lower main bearing inserts (without grooves) and lay them in the corresponding main bearing caps. Make sure the tab on the bearing insert fits into the recess in the block or main bearing cap. **Caution:** *Do not hammer the bearing insert into place and don't nick or gouge the bearing faces. DO NOT apply any lubrication at this time.*

12   Clean the faces of the bearing inserts in the block and the crankshaft main bearing journals with a clean, lint-free cloth.

13   Check or clean the oil holes in the crankshaft, as any dirt here can go only one way - straight through the new bearings.

10.17 Place the Plastigage onto the crankshaft bearing journal as shown

14   Once you're certain the crankshaft is clean, carefully lay it in position in the cylinder block.

15   Before the crankshaft can be permanently installed, the main bearing oil clearance must be checked.

16   Cut several strips of the appropriate size of Plastigage (they must be slightly shorter than the width of the main bearing journal).

17   Place one piece on each crankshaft main bearing journal, parallel with the journal axis **(see illustration)**.

18   Clean the faces of the bearing inserts in the main bearing caps. Hold the bearing inserts in place and install the caps onto the crankshaft and cylinder block. DO NOT disturb the Plastigage. Make sure you install the main bearing cap assembly with the arrow facing the front of the engine.

19   Apply clean engine oil to all bolt threads prior to installation, then install all bolts finger-tight. **Note:** *Use the old main bearing cap*

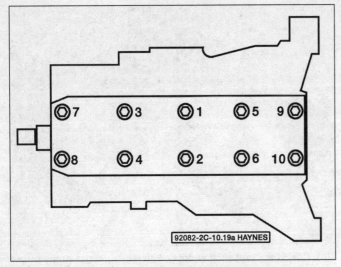

10.19a Main bearing cap bolt tightening sequence (four-cylinder engine)

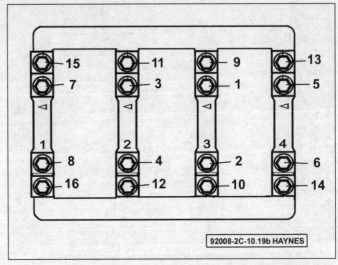

10.19b Main bearing cap bolt tightening sequence (V6 engine)

bolts for the oil clearance checking procedure. Tighten the main bearing cap bolts in the sequences shown **(see illustrations)**, progressing in two steps, to the torque listed in this Chapter's Specifications. DO NOT rotate the crankshaft at any time during this operation. **Note:** *On V6 engines, tighten the main bearing cap bolts first, then the main bearing cap side bolts.* **Note:** *The side bolts labeled 4 and 7 in* **illustration 10.19c** *are longer than the other bolts; make sure they are installed into the correct locations.*

20   Remove the bolts a little at a time (and in the *reverse* order of the tightening sequence) and carefully lift the main bearing caps straight up and off the block. Do not disturb the Plastigage or rotate the crankshaft. If a main bearing cap is difficult to remove, tap it gently from side-to-side with a soft-face hammer to loosen it.

21   Compare the width of the crushed Plastigage on each journal to the scale printed on the Plastigage envelope to determine the main bearing oil clearance **(see illustration)**. A typical main bearing oil clearance should fall between 0.0015 to 0.0023-inch. Check with an automotive machine shop for the clearance specified for your engine.

22   If the clearance is not as specified, the bearing inserts may be the wrong size (which means different ones will be required). Before deciding if different inserts are needed, make sure that no dirt or oil was between the bearing inserts and the cap assembly or block when the clearance was measured. If the Plastigage was wider at one end than the other, the crankshaft journal may be tapered. If the clearance still exceeds the limit specified, the bearing insert(s) will have to be

replaced with an undersize bearing insert(s). **Caution:** *When installing a new crankshaft, always install a standard bearing insert set.*

23   Carefully scrape all traces of the Plastigage material off the main bearing journals and/or the bearing insert faces. Be sure to remove all residue from the oil holes. Use your fingernail or the edge of a plastic card - don't nick or scratch the bearing faces.

Final installation

24   Carefully lift the crankshaft out of the cylinder block.

25   Clean the bearing insert faces in the cylinder block, then apply a thin, uniform layer of moly-base grease or engine assembly lube to each of the bearing surfaces. Be sure to coat the thrust faces as well as the journal face of the thrust bearing.

26   Make sure the crankshaft journals are clean, then lay the crankshaft back in place in the cylinder block.

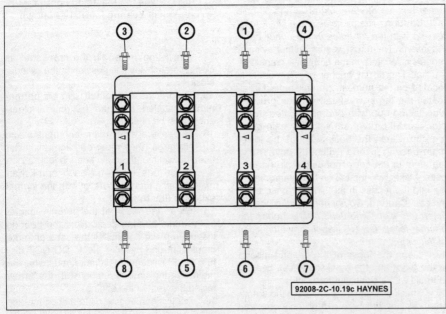

10.19c Main bearing cap side bolt tightening sequence (V6 engine)

10.21 Use the scale on the Plastigage package to determine the bearing oil clearance - be sure to measure the widest part of the Plastigage and use the correct scale; it comes with both standard and metric scales

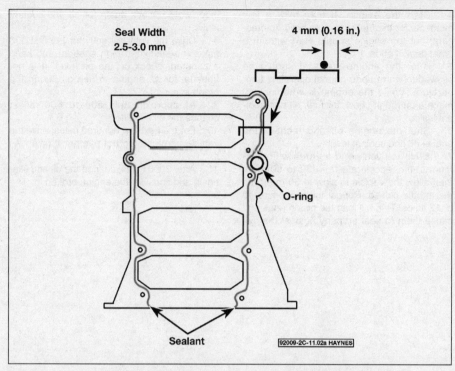

11.2a Cylinder block-to-lower crankcase sealant installation details

34 Recheck crankshaft endplay with a feeler gauge or a dial indicator. The endplay should be correct if the crankshaft thrust faces aren't worn or damaged and if new bearings have been installed.

35 Rotate the crankshaft a number of times by hand to check for any obvious binding. It should rotate with a running torque of 50 in-lbs or less. If the running torque is too high, correct the problem at this time.

36 Install the new rear main oil seal (see Chapter 2A or 2B).

11 Engine overhaul - reassembly sequence

Refer to illustrations 11.2a, 11.2b and 11.2c

1 Before beginning engine reassembly, make sure you have all the necessary new parts, gaskets and seals as well as the following items on hand:
Common hand tools
A 1/2-inch drive torque wrench
New engine oil
Gasket sealant
Thread locking compound

2 If you obtained a short block it will be necessary to install the cylinder head, the oil pump, the timing belt or chain, the lower crankcase (**see illustrations**), the front covers, the oil pan and the valve cover (see Chapter 2A or 2B). In order to save time and avoid problems, the external components must be installed in the following general order:
Thermostat and housing cover
Water pump
Water by pass tube
Intake/exhaust manifolds
EFI components
Emissions control components
Ignition coils
Oil filter
Engine mount brackets
Clutch and flywheel/driveplate

27 Clean the bearing insert faces and apply the same lubricant to them.

28 Hold the bearing inserts in place and install the main bearing caps on the crankshaft and cylinder block. Tap the bearing caps into place with a brass punch or a soft-face hammer.

29 Apply clean engine oil to the **new** bolt threads, wipe off any excess oil and install the bolts finger-tight.

30 Tighten the main bearing cap bolts in the indicated sequence (**see illustration 10.19a or 10.19b**) to 10 or 12 foot-pounds.

31 Push the crankshaft forward using a screwdriver or prybar to seat the thrust bearing. Once the crankshaft is pushed fully forward to seat the thrust bearing, leave the screwdriver in position so that pressure stays on the crankshaft until after all main bearing cap bolts have been tightened.

32 Tighten the main bearing cap bolts in the indicated sequence to the torque and angle of rotation listed in this Chapter's Specifications (**see illustrations 10.19a and 10.19b**).

33 On V6 engines, install and tighten the main bearing cap side bolts, in the correct sequence, to the torque listed in this Chapter's Specifications (**see illustration 10.19c**).

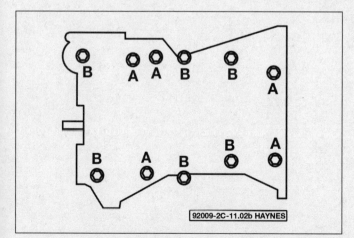

11.2b Lower crankcase bolt locations - (A) indicates the location of the long bolts and (B) indicates the location of the short bolts (2009 and earlier four-cylinder engines)

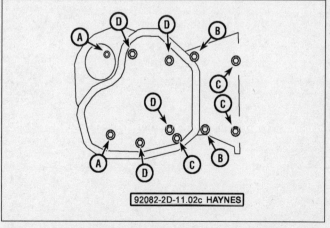

11.2c Lower crankcase bolt locations - four different length bolts are used (2010 and later four-cylinder engines)

A 2.56 inches (65 mm) long	C 4.92 inches (125 mm) long
B 1.38 inches (35 mm) long	D 6.50 inches (165 mm) long

12   Initial start-up and break-in after installation

Warning: *Have a fire extinguisher handy when starting the engine for the first time.*

1   Once the engine has been installed in the vehicle, double-check the engine oil and coolant levels.

2   With the spark plugs out of the engine and the ignition system and fuel pump disabled (see Chapter 4, Section 3), crank the engine until oil pressure registers on the gauge or the light goes out.

3   Install the spark plugs, hook up the plug wires and restore the ignition system and fuel pump functions.

4   Start the engine. It may take a few moments for the fuel system to build up pressure, but the engine should start without a great deal of effort.

5   After the engine starts, it should be allowed to warm up to normal operating temperature. While the engine is warming up, make a thorough check for fuel, oil and coolant leaks.

6   Shut the engine off and recheck the engine oil and coolant levels.

7   Drive the vehicle to an area with minimum traffic, accelerate from 30 to 50 mph, then allow the vehicle to slow to 30 mph with the throttle closed. Repeat the procedure 10 or 12 times. This will load the piston rings and cause them to seat properly against the cyl-

inder walls. Check again for oil and coolant leaks.

8   Drive the vehicle gently for the first 500 miles (no sustained high speeds) and keep a constant check on the oil level. It is not unusual for an engine to use oil during the break-in period.

9   At approximately 500 to 600 miles, change the oil and filter.

10   For the next few hundred miles, drive the vehicle normally. Do not pamper it or abuse it.

11   After 2000 miles, change the oil and filter again and consider the engine broken in.

COMMON ENGINE OVERHAUL TERMS

B

Backlash - The amount of play between two parts. Usually refers to how much one gear can be moved back and forth without moving gear with which it's meshed.

Bearing Caps - The caps held in place by nuts or bolts which, in turn, hold the bearing surface. This space is for lubricating oil to enter.

Bearing clearance - The amount of space left between shaft and bearing surface. This space is for lubricating oil to enter.

Bearing crush - The additional height which is purposely manufactured into each bearing half to ensure complete contact of the bearing back with the housing bore when the engine is assembled.

Bearing knock - The noise created by movement of a part in a loose or worn bearing.

Blueprinting - Dismantling an engine and reassembling it to EXACT specifications.

Bore - An engine cylinder, or any cylindrical hole; also used to describe the process of enlarging or accurately refinishing a hole with a cutting tool, as to bore an engine cylinder. The bore size is the diameter of the hole.

Boring - Renewing the cylinders by cutting them out to a specified size. A boring bar is used to make the cut.

Bottom end - A term which refers collectively to the engine block, crankshaft, main bearings and the big ends of the connecting rods.

Break-in - The period of operation between installation of new or rebuilt parts and time in which parts are worn to the correct fit. Driving at reduced and varying speed for a specified mileage to permit parts to wear to the correct fit.

Bushing - A one-piece sleeve placed in a bore to serve as a bearing surface for shaft, piston pin, etc. Usually replaceable.

C

Camshaft - The shaft in the engine, on which a series of lobes are located for operating the valve mechanisms. The camshaft is driven by gears or sprockets and a timing chain. Usually referred to simply as the cam.

Carbon - Hard, or soft, black deposits found in combustion chamber, on plugs, under rings, on and under valve heads.

Cast iron - An alloy of iron and more than two percent carbon, used for engine blocks and heads because it's relatively inexpensive and easy to mold into complex shapes.

Chamfer - To bevel across (or a bevel on) the sharp edge of an object.

Chase - To repair damaged threads with a tap or die.

Combustion chamber - The space between the piston and the cylinder head, with the piston at top dead center, in which air-fuel mixture is burned.

Compression ratio - The relationship between cylinder volume (clearance volume) when the piston is at top dead center and cylinder volume when the piston is at bottom dead center.

Connecting rod - The rod that connects the crank on the crankshaft with the piston. Sometimes called a con rod.

Connecting rod cap - The part of the connecting rod assembly that attaches the rod to the crankpin.

Core plug - Soft metal plug used to plug the casting holes for the coolant passages in the block.

Crankcase - The lower part of the engine in which the crankshaft rotates; includes the lower section of the cylinder block and the oil pan.

Crank kit - A reground or reconditioned crankshaft and new main and connecting rod bearings.

Crankpin - The part of a crankshaft to which a connecting rod is attached.

Crankshaft - The main rotating member, or shaft, running the length of the crankcase, with offset throws to which the connecting rods are attached; changes the reciprocating motion of the pistons into rotating motion.

Cylinder sleeve - A replaceable sleeve, or liner, pressed into the cylinder block to form the cylinder bore.

D

Deburring - Removing the burrs (rough edges or areas) from a bearing.

Deglazer - A tool, rotated by an electric motor, used to remove glaze from cylinder walls so a new set of rings will seat.

E

Endplay - The amount of lengthwise movement between two parts. As applied to a crankshaft, the distance that the crankshaft can move forward and back in the cylinder block.

F

Face - A machinist's term that refers to removing metal from the end of a shaft or the face of a larger part, such as a flywheel.

Fatigue - A breakdown of material through a large number of loading and unloading cycles. The first signs are cracks followed shortly by breaks.

Feeler gauge - A thin strip of hardened steel, ground to an exact thickness, used to check clearances between parts.

Free height - The unloaded length or height of a spring.

Freeplay - The looseness in a linkage, or an assembly of parts, between the initial application of force and actual movement. Usually perceived as slop or slight delay.

Freeze plug - See Core plug.

G

Gallery - A large passage in the block that forms a reservoir for engine oil pressure.

Glaze - The very smooth, glassy finish that develops on cylinder walls while an engine is in service.

H

Heli-Coil - A rethreading device used when threads are worn or damaged. The device is installed in a retapped hole to reduce the thread size to the original size.

I

Installed height - The spring's measured length or height, as installed on the cylinder head. Installed height is measured from the spring seat to the underside of the spring retainer.

J

Journal - The surface of a rotating shaft which turns in a bearing.

K

Keeper - The split lock that holds the valve spring retainer in position on the valve stem.

Key - A small piece of metal inserted into matching grooves machined into two parts fitted together - such as a gear pressed onto a shaft - which prevents slippage between the two parts.

Knock - The heavy metallic engine sound, produced in the combustion chamber as a result of abnormal combustion - usually detonation. Knock is usually caused by a loose or worn bearing. Also referred to as detonation, pinging and spark knock. Connecting rod or main bearing knocks are created by too much oil clearance or insufficient lubrication.

L

Lands - The portions of metal between the piston ring grooves.

Lapping the valves - Grinding a valve face and its seat together with lapping compound.

Lash - The amount of free motion in a gear train, between gears, or in a mechanical assembly, that occurs before movement can begin. Usually refers to the lash in a valve train.

Lifter - The part that rides against the cam to transfer motion to the rest of the valve train.

M

Machining - The process of using a machine to remove metal from a metal part.

Main bearings - The plain, or babbit, bearings that support the crankshaft.

Main bearing caps - The cast iron caps, bolted to the bottom of the block, that support the main bearings.

O

O.D. - Outside diameter.

Oil gallery - A pipe or drilled passageway in the engine used to carry engine oil from one area to another.

Oil ring - The lower ring, or rings, of a piston; designed to prevent excessive amounts of oil from working up the cylinder walls and into the combustion chamber. Also called an oil-control ring.

Oil seal - A seal which keeps oil from leaking out of a compartment. Usually refers to a dynamic seal around a rotating shaft or other moving part.

O-ring - A type of sealing ring made of a special rubberlike material; in use, the O-ring is compressed into a groove to provide the sealing action.

Overhaul - To completely disassemble a unit, clean and inspect all parts, reassemble it with the original or new parts and make all adjustments necessary for proper operation.

P

Pilot bearing - A small bearing installed in the center of the flywheel (or the rear end of the crankshaft) to support the front end of the input shaft of the transmission.

Pip mark - A little dot or indentation which indicates the top side of a compression ring.

Piston - The cylindrical part, attached to the connecting rod, that moves up and down in the cylinder as the crankshaft rotates. When the fuel charge is fired, the piston transfers the force of the explosion to the connecting rod, then to the crankshaft.

Piston pin (or wrist pin) - The cylindrical and usually hollow steel pin that passes through the piston. The piston pin fastens the piston to the upper end of the connecting rod.

Piston ring - The split ring fitted to the groove in a piston. The ring contacts the sides of the ring groove and also rubs against the cylinder wall, thus sealing space between piston and wall. There are two types of rings: Compression rings seal the compression pressure in the combustion chamber; oil rings scrape excessive oil off the cylinder wall.

Piston ring groove - The slots or grooves cut in piston heads to hold piston rings in position.

Piston skirt - The portion of the piston below the rings and the piston pin hole.

Plastigage - A thin strip of plastic thread, available in different sizes, used for measuring clearances. For example, a strip of plastigage is laid across a bearing journal and mashed as parts are assembled. Then parts are disassembled and the width of the strip is measured to determine clearance between journal and bearing. Commonly used to measure crankshaft main-bearing and connecting rod bearing clearances.

Press-fit - A tight fit between two parts that requires pressure to force the parts together. Also referred to as drive, or force, fit.

Prussian blue - A blue pigment; in solution, useful in determining the area of contact between two surfaces. Prussian blue is commonly used to determine the width and location of the contact area between the valve face and the valve seat.

R

Race (bearing) - The inner or outer ring that provides a contact surface for balls or rollers in bearing.

Ream - To size, enlarge or smooth a hole by using a round cutting tool with fluted edges.

Ring job - The process of reconditioning the cylinders and installing new rings.

Runout - Wobble. The amount a shaft rotates out-of-true.

S

Saddle - The upper main bearing seat.

Scored - Scratched or grooved, as a cylinder wall may be scored by abrasive particles moved up and down by the piston rings.

Scuffing - A type of wear in which there's a transfer of material between parts moving against each other; shows up as pits or grooves in the mating surfaces.

Seat - The surface upon which another part rests or seats. For example, the valve seat is the matched surface upon which the valve face rests. Also used to refer to wearing into a good fit; for example, piston rings seat after a few miles of driving.

Short block - An engine block complete with crankshaft and piston and, usually, camshaft assemblies.

Static balance - The balance of an object while it's stationary.

Step - The wear on the lower portion of a ring land caused by excessive side and back-clearance. The height of the step indicates the ring's extra side clearance and the length of the step projecting from the back wall of the groove represents the ring's back clearance.

Stroke - The distance the piston moves when traveling from top dead center to bottom dead center, or from bottom dead center to top dead center.

Stud - A metal rod with threads on both ends.

T

Tang - A lip on the end of a plain bearing used to align the bearing during assembly.

Tap - To cut threads in a hole. Also refers to the fluted tool used to cut threads.

Taper - A gradual reduction in the width of a shaft or hole; in an engine cylinder, taper usually takes the form of uneven wear, more pronounced at the top than at the bottom.

Throws - The offset portions of the crankshaft to which the connecting rods are affixed.

Thrust bearing - The main bearing that has thrust faces to prevent excessive endplay, or forward and backward movement of the crankshaft.

Thrust washer - A bronze or hardened steel washer placed between two moving parts. The washer prevents longitudinal movement and provides a bearing surface for thrust surfaces of parts.

Tolerance - The amount of variation permitted from an exact size of measurement. Actual amount from smallest acceptable dimension to largest acceptable dimension.

U

Umbrella - An oil deflector placed near the valve tip to throw oil from the valve stem area.

Undercut - A machined groove below the normal surface.

Undersize bearings - Smaller diameter bearings used with re-ground crankshaft journals.

V

Valve grinding - Refacing a valve in a valve-refacing machine.

Valve train - The valve-operating mechanism of an engine; includes all components from the camshaft to the valve.

Vibration damper - A cylindrical weight attached to the front of the crankshaft to minimize torsional vibration (the twist-untwist actions of the crankshaft caused by the cylinder firing impulses). Also called a harmonic balancer.

W

Water jacket - The spaces around the cylinders, between the inner and outer shells of the cylinder block or head, through which coolant circulates.

Web - A supporting structure across a cavity.

Woodruff key - A key with a radiused backside (viewed from the side).

Chapter 3
Cooling, heating and air conditioning systems

Contents

Specifications

General

Radiator cap pressure rating
   Four-cylinder engine
      2009 and earlier.. 13.5 to 17.8 psi
      2010 and later... 13.6 to 17 psi
   V6 engine.. 13.5 to 17.8 psi
Thermostat rating
   Opens .... 176 to 183-degrees F
   Fully open.. 203-degrees F

Torque specifications

Ft-lbs (unless otherwise indicated)

Note: *One foot-pound (ft-lb) of torque is equivalent to 12 inch-pounds (in-lbs) of torque. Torque values below approximately 15 foot-pounds are expressed in inch-pounds, because most foot-pound torque wrenches are not accurate at these smaller values.*

Receiver/drier Allen plug... 26 in-lbs
Thermostat housing bolts
   Four-cylinder engine
      2009 and earlier.. 80 in-lbs
      2010 and later... 84 in-lbs
   V6 engine.. 84 in-lbs
Water pump bolts/nuts
   Four-cylinder engine.. 80 in-lbs
   V6 engine **(see illustration 7.24)**
      Bolt "A".. 15
      Bolt "B".. 81 in-lbs
      Bolt "C".. 81 in-lbs
Water pump pulley
   Four-cylinder engine
      2009 and earlier.. 19
      2010 and later... 15
   V6 engine.. 15

1   General information

Warning: *Do not allow antifreeze to come in contact with your skin or painted surfaces of the vehicle. Rinse off spills immediately with plenty of water. Antifreeze is highly toxic if ingested. Never leave antifreeze lying around in an open container or in puddles on the floor; children and pets are attracted by it's sweet smell and may drink it. Check with local authorities about disposing of used antifreeze. Many communities have collection centers which will see that antifreeze is disposed of safely. Never dump used antifreeze on the ground or pour it into drains.*

Engine cooling system

All modern vehicles employ a pressurized engine cooling system with thermostatically controlled coolant circulation. The cooling system consists of a radiator, an expansion tank or coolant reservoir, a pressure cap (located on the expansion tank or radiator), a thermostat, a cooling fan, and a water pump.

The water pump circulates coolant through the engine. The coolant flows around each cylinder and around the intake and exhaust ports, near the spark plug areas and in close proximity to the exhaust valve guides.

A thermostat controls engine coolant temperature. During warm up, the closed thermostat prevents coolant from circulating through the radiator. As the engine nears normal operating temperature, the thermostat opens and allows hot coolant to travel through the radiator, where it's cooled before returning to the engine.

Heating system

The heating system consists of a blower fan and heater core located in a housing under the dash, the hoses connecting the heater core to the engine cooling system and the heater/air conditioning control head on the dashboard. Hot engine coolant is circulated through the heater core. When the heater mode is activated, a flap door in the housing opens to expose the heater core to the passenger compartment through air ducts. A fan switch on the control head activates the blower motor, which forces air through the core, heating the air.

Air conditioning system

The air conditioning system consists of a condenser mounted in front of the radiator, an evaporator mounted adjacent to the heater core, a compressor mounted on the engine, a receiver-drier or accumulator and the plumbing connecting all of the above components.

A blower fan forces the warmer air of the passenger compartment through the evaporator core (sort of a radiator-in-reverse), transferring the heat from the air to the refrigerant. The liquid refrigerant boils off into low pressure vapor, taking the heat with it when it leaves the evaporator.

2   Troubleshooting

Coolant leaks

Refer to illustration 2.2

1   A coolant leak can develop anywhere in the cooling system, but the most common causes are:

 a) A loose or weak hose clamp
 b) A defective hose
 c) A faulty pressure cap
 d) A damaged radiator
 e) A bad heater core
 f) A faulty water pump
 g) A leaking gasket at any joint that carries coolant

2   Coolant leaks aren't always easy to find. Sometimes they can only be detected when the cooling system is under pressure. Here's where a cooling system pressure tester comes in handy. After the engine has cooled completely, the tester is attached in place of the pressure cap, then pumped up to the pressure value equal to that of the pressure cap rating **(see illustration)**. Now, leaks that only exist when the engine is fully warmed up will become apparent. The tester can be left connected to locate a nagging slow leak.

Coolant level drops, but no external leaks

Refer to illustrations 2.5a and 2.5b

3   If you find it necessary to keep adding coolant, but there are no external leaks, the probable causes include:

 a) A blown head gasket
 b) A leaking intake manifold gasket (only on engines that have coolant passages in the manifold)
 c) A cracked cylinder head or cylinder block

4   Any of the above problems will also usually result in contamination of the engine oil, which will cause it to take on a milkshake-like appearance. A bad head gasket or cracked head or block can also result in engine oil contaminating the cooling system.

5   Combustion leak detectors (also known as block testers) are available at most auto parts stores. These work by detecting exhaust gases in the cooling system, which indicates a compression leak from a cylinder into the coolant. The tester consists of a large bulb-type syringe and bottle of test fluid **(see illustration)**. A measured amount of the fluid is added to the syringe. The syringe is placed over the cooling system filler neck and, with the engine running, the bulb is squeezed and a sample of the gases present in the cooling system are drawn up through the test fluid **(see illustration)**. If any combustion gases are present in the sample taken, the test fluid will change color.

6   If the test indicates combustion gas is present in the cooling system, you can be sure that the engine has a blown head gasket or a crack in the cylinder head or block, and will require disassembly to repair.

Pressure cap

Refer to illustration 2.8

Warning: *Wait until the engine is completely cool before beginning this check.*

7   The cooling system is sealed by a spring-loaded cap, which raises the boiling point of the coolant. If the cap's seal or spring are worn out, the coolant can boil and escape past the cap. With the engine completely cool, remove the cap and check the seal; if it's cracked, hardened or deteriorated in any way, replace it with a new one.

8   Even if the seal is good, the spring might not be; this can be checked with a cooling system pressure tester **(see illustration)**. If the cap can't hold a pressure within approximately 1-1/2 lbs of its rated pressure (which is marked on the cap), replace it with a new one.

9   The cap is also equipped with a vacuum relief spring. When the engine cools off, a vacuum is created in the cooling system. The vacuum relief spring allows air back into the system, which will equalize the pressure and prevent damage to the radiator (the radiator tanks could collapse if the vacuum is great enough). If, after turning the engine off and

2.2 The cooling system pressure tester is connected in place of the pressure cap, then pumped up to pressurize the system

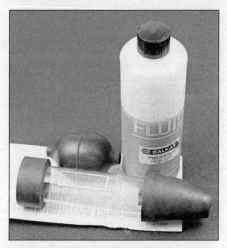

2.5a The combustion leak detector consists of a bulb, syringe and test fluid

2.5b Place the tester over the cooling system filler neck and use the bulb to draw a sample into the tester

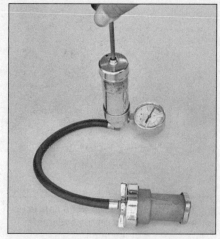

2.8 Check the cooling system pressure cap with a cooling system pressure tester

allowing it to cool down you notice any of the cooling system hoses collapsing, replace the pressure cap with a new one.

Thermostat

Refer to illustration 2.10

10   Before assuming the thermostat **(see illustration)** is responsible for a cooling system problem, check the coolant level (see Chapter 1), drivebelt tension (see Chapter 1) and temperature gauge (or light) operation.

11   If the engine takes a long time to warm up (as indicated by the temperature gauge or heater operation), the thermostat is probably stuck open. Replace the thermostat with a new one.

12   If the engine runs hot or overheats, a thorough test of the thermostat should be performed.

13   Definitive testing of the thermostat can only be made when it is removed from the vehicle. If the thermostat is stuck in the open position at room temperature, it is faulty and must be replaced. **Caution:** *Do not drive the vehicle without a thermostat. The computer*

may stay in open loop and emissions and fuel economy will suffer.

14   To test a thermostat, suspend the (closed) thermostat on a length of string or wire in a pot of cold water.

15   Heat the water on a stove while observing thermostat. The thermostat should fully open before the water boils.

16   If the thermostat doesn't open and close as specified, or sticks in any position, replace it.

Cooling fan

Electric cooling fan

17   If the engine is overheating and the cooling fan is not coming on when the engine temperature rises to an excessive level, unplug the fan motor electrical connector(s) and connect the motor directly to the battery with fused jumper wires. If the fan motor doesn't come on, replace the motor.

18   If the radiator fan motor is okay, but it isn't coming on when the engine gets hot, the fan relay might be defective. A relay is used to control a circuit by turning it on and off in

response to a control decision by the Powertrain Control Module (PCM). These control circuits are fairly complex, and checking them should be left to a qualified automotive technician. Sometimes, the control system can be fixed by simply identifying and replacing a bad relay.

19   Locate the fan relays in the engine compartment fuse/relay box.

20   Test the relay (see Chapter 12).

21   If the relay is okay, check all wiring and connections to the fan motor. Refer to the wiring diagrams at the end of Chapter 12. If no obvious problems are found, the problem could be the Engine Coolant Temperature (ECT) sensor or the Powertrain Control Module (PCM). Have the cooling fan system and circuit diagnosed by a dealer service department or repair shop with the proper diagnostic equipment. **Note:** *These models are equipped with a cooling fan motor resistor. Have the resistor checked if the fan motor does not respond to the speed variations signaled by the PCM.*

Belt-driven cooling fan

22   Disconnect the cable from the negative terminal of the battery and rock the fan back and forth by hand to check for excessive bearing play.

23   With the engine cold (and not running), turn the fan blades by hand. The fan should turn freely.

24   Visually inspect for substantial fluid leakage from the clutch assembly. If problems are noted, replace the clutch assembly.

25   With the engine completely warmed up, turn off the ignition switch and disconnect the negative battery cable from the battery. Turn the fan by hand. Some drag should be evident. If the fan turns easily, replace the fan clutch.

Water pump

26   A failure in the water pump can cause serious engine damage due to overheating.

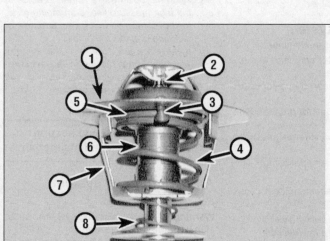

2.10 Typical thermostat:

1   *Flange*
2   *Piston*
3   *Jiggle valve*
4   *Main coil spring*
5   *Valve seat*
6   *Valve*
7   *Frame*
8   *Secondary coil spring*

2.28 The water pump weep hole is generally located on the underside of the pump

Drivebelt-driven water pump

Refer to illustration 2.28

27   There are two ways to check the operation of the water pump while it's installed on the engine. If the pump is found to be defective, it should be replaced with a new or rebuilt unit.

28   Water pumps are equipped with weep (or vent) holes **(see illustration)**. If a failure occurs in the pump seal, coolant will leak from the hole.

29   If the water pump shaft bearings fail, there may be a howling sound at the pump while it's running. Shaft wear can be felt with the drivebelt removed if the water pump pulley is rocked up and down (with the engine off). Don't mistake drivebelt slippage, which causes a squealing sound, for water pump bearing failure.

Timing chain or timing belt-driven water pump

30   Water pumps driven by the timing chain or timing belt are located underneath the timing chain or timing belt cover.

31   Checking the water pump is limited because of where it is located. However, some basic checks can be made before deciding to remove the water pump. If the pump is found to be defective, it should be replaced with a new or rebuilt unit.

32   One sign that the water pump may be failing is that the heater (climate control) may not work well. Warm the engine to normal operating temperature, confirm that the coolant level is correct, then run the heater and check for hot air coming from the ducts.

33   Check for noises coming from the water pump area. If the water pump impeller shaft or bearings are failing, there may be a howling sound at the pump while the engine is running. **Note:** *Be careful not to mistake drivebelt noise (squealing) for water pump bearing or shaft failure.*

34   It you suspect water pump failure due to noise, wear can be confirmed by feeling for play at the pump shaft. This can be done by rocking the drive sprocket on the pump shaft up and down. To do this you will need to

remove the tension on the timing chain or belt as well as access the water pump.

All water pumps

35   In rare cases or on high-mileage vehicles, another sign of water pump failure may be the presence of coolant in the engine oil. This condition will adversely affect the engine in varying degrees. **Note:** *Finding coolant in the engine oil could indicate other serious issues besides a failed water pump, such as a blown head gasket or a cracked cylinder head or block.*

36   Even a pump that exhibits no outward signs of a problem, such as noise or leakage, can still be due for replacement. Removal for close examination is the only sure way to tell. Sometimes the fins on the back of the impeller can corrode to the point that cooling efficiency is diminished significantly.

Heater system

37   Little can go wrong with a heater. If the fan motor will run at all speeds, the electrical part of the system is okay. The three basic heater problems fall into the following general categories:
 a) *Not enough heat*
 b) *Heat all the time*
 c) *No heat*

38   If there's not enough heat, the control valve or door is stuck in a partially open position, the coolant coming from the engine isn't hot enough, or the heater core is restricted. If the coolant isn't hot enough, the thermostat in the engine cooling system is stuck open, allowing coolant to pass through the engine so rapidly that it doesn't heat up quickly enough. If the vehicle is equipped with a temperature gauge instead of a warning light, watch to see if the engine temperature rises to the normal operating range after driving for a reasonable distance.

39   If there's heat all the time, the control valve or the door is stuck wide open.

40   If there's no heat, coolant is probably not reaching the heater core, or the heater core is plugged. The likely cause is a collapsed or plugged hose, core, or a frozen heater control valve. If the heater is the type that flows coolant all the time, the cause is a stuck door or a broken or kinked control cable.

Air conditioning system

41   If the cool air output is inadequate:
 a) *Inspect the condenser coils and fins to make sure they're clear*
 b) *Check the compressor clutch for slippage.*
 c) *Check the blower motor for proper operation.*
 d) *Inspect the blower discharge passage for obstructions.*
 e) *Check the system air intake filter for clogging.*

42   If the system provides intermittent cooling air:
 a) *Check the circuit breaker, blower switch and blower motor for a malfunction.*
 b) *Make sure the compressor clutch isn't slipping.*

 c) *Inspect the plenum door to make sure it's operating properly.*
 d) *Inspect the evaporator to make sure it isn't clogged.*
 e) *If the unit is icing up, it may be caused by excessive moisture in the system, incorrect super heat switch adjustment or low thermostat adjustment.*

43   If the system provides no cooling air:
 a) *Inspect the compressor drivebelt. Make sure it's not loose or broken.*
 b) *Make sure the compressor clutch engages. If it doesn't, check for a blown fuse.*
 c) *Inspect the wire harness for broken or disconnected wires.*
 d) *If the compressor clutch doesn't engage, bridge the terminals of the A/C pressure switch(es) with a jumper wire; if the clutch now engages, and the system is properly charged, the pressure switch is bad.*
 e) *Make sure the blower motor is not disconnected or burned out.*
 f) *Make sure the compressor isn't partially or completely seized.*
 g) *Inspect the refrigerant lines for leaks.*
 h) *Check the components for leaks.*
 i) *Inspect the receiver-drier/accumulator or expansion valve/tube for clogged screens.*

44   If the system is noisy:
 a) *Look for loose panels in the passenger compartment.*
 b) *Inspect the compressor drivebelt. It may be loose or worn.*
 c) *Check the compressor mounting bolts. They should be tight.*
 d) *Listen carefully to the compressor. It may be worn out.*
 e) *Listen to the idler pulley and bearing and the clutch. Either may be defective.*
 f) *The winding in the compressor clutch coil or solenoid may be defective.*
 g) *The compressor oil level may be low.*
 h) *The blower motor fan bushing or the motor itself may be worn out.*
 i) *If there is an excessive charge in the system, you'll hear a rumbling noise in the high pressure line, a thumping noise in the compressor, or see bubbles or cloudiness in the sight glass.*
 j) *If there's a low charge in the system, you might hear hissing in the evaporator case at the expansion valve, or see bubbles or cloudiness in the sight glass.*

---

3   Air conditioning and heating system - check and maintenance

---

Air conditioning system

Refer to illustration 3.1

Warning: *The air conditioning system is under high pressure. Do not loosen any hose fittings or remove any components until after the system has been discharged. Air conditioning*

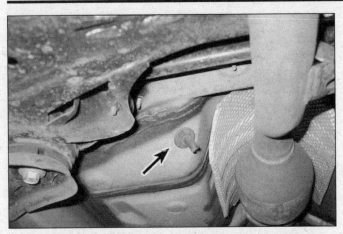

3.1 Evaporator drain hose is located under the vehicle on the passenger's side

3.9 Insert a thermometer in the center vent, turn on the air conditioning system and wait for it to cool down; depending on the humidity, the output air should be 35 to 40 degrees cooler than the ambient air temperature

refrigerant should be properly discharged into an EPA-approved recovery/recycling unit at a dealer service department or an automotive air conditioning repair facility. Always wear eye protection when disconnecting air conditioning system fittings.

Caution 1: *All models covered by this manual use environmentally friendly R-134a. This refrigerant (and its appropriate refrigerant oils) are not compatible with R-12 refrigerant system components and must never be mixed or the components will be damaged.*

Caution 2: *When replacing entire components, additional refrigerant oil should be added equal to the amount that is removed with the component being replaced. Be sure to read the can before adding any oil to the system, to make sure it is compatible with the R-134a system.*

1   The following maintenance checks should be performed on a regular basis to ensure that the air conditioning continues to operate at peak efficiency.

a) *Inspect the condition of the compressor drivebelt. If it is worn or deteriorated, replace it (see Chapter 1).*

b) *Check the drivebelt tension (see Chapter 1).*

c) *Inspect the system hoses. Look for cracks, bubbles, hardening and deterioration. Inspect the hoses and all fittings for oil bubbles or seepage. If there is any evidence of wear, damage or leakage, replace the hose(s).*

d) *Inspect the condenser fins for leaves, bugs and any other foreign material that may have embedded itself in the fins. Use a fin comb or compressed air to remove debris from the condenser.*

e) *Make sure the system has the correct refrigerant charge.*

f) *If you hear water sloshing around in the dash area or have water dripping on the carpet, check the evaporator housing drain tube (see illustration) and insert a piece of wire into the opening to check for blockage.*

2   It's a good idea to operate the system for about ten minutes at least once a month. This is particularly important during the winter months because long term non-use can cause hardening, and subsequent failure, of the seals. Note that using the Defrost function operates the compressor.

3   If the air conditioning system is not working properly, proceed to Step 6 and perform the general checks outlined below.

4   Because of the complexity of the air conditioning system and the special equipment necessary to service it, in-depth troubleshooting and repairs beyond checking the refrigerant charge and the compressor clutch operation are not included in this manual. However, simple checks and component replacement procedures are provided in this Chapter. For more complete information on the air conditioning system, refer to the *Haynes Automotive Heating and Air Conditioning Manual.*

5   The most common cause of poor cooling is simply a low system refrigerant charge. If a noticeable drop in system cooling ability occurs, one of the following quick checks will help you determine if the refrigerant level is low.

Checking the refrigerant charge

Refer to illustration 3.9

6   Warm the engine up to normal operating temperature.

7   Place the air conditioning temperature selector at the coldest setting and put the blower at the highest setting.

8   After the system reaches operating temperature, feel the larger pipe exiting the evaporator at the firewall. The outlet pipe should be cold (the tubing that leads back to the compressor). If the evaporator outlet pipe is warm, the system probably needs a charge.

9   Insert a thermometer in the center air distribution duct **(see illustration)** while operating the air conditioning system at its maximum setting - the temperature of the output air should be 35 to 40 degrees F below the ambient air temperature (down to approximately 40 degrees F). If the ambient (outside) air temperature is very high, say 110 degrees F, the duct air temperature may be as high as 60 degrees F, but generally the air conditioning is 35 to 40 degrees F cooler than the ambient air.

10   Further inspection or testing of the system requires special tools and techniques and is beyond the scope of the home mechanic.

Adding refrigerant

Refer to illustrations 3.11 and 3.13

Caution: *Make sure any refrigerant, refrigerant oil or replacement component you purchase is designated as compatible with R-134a systems.*

11   Purchase an R-134a automotive charging kit at an auto parts store **(see illustration)**. A charging kit includes a can of refrigerant, a tap valve and a short section of hose that can be attached between the tap valve and the system low side service valve. **Caution:** *Never add more than one can of refrigerant to the system. If more refrigerant than that is required, the system should be evacuated and leak tested.*

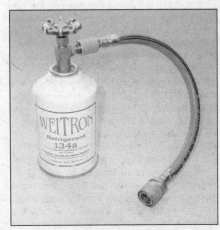

3.11 R-134a automotive air conditioning charging kit

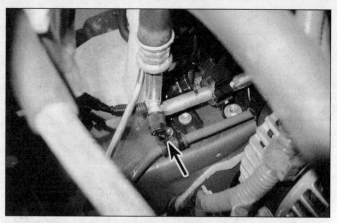

3.13 Location of the low-side charging port (in the right-front corner of the engine compartment)

3.24 Remove the cabin air filter (see Chapter 1) and insert the hose of the disinfectant can into the opening (don't allow it to contact the blower fan)

12   Back off the valve handle on the charging kit and screw the kit onto the refrigerant can, making sure first that the O-ring or rubber seal inside the threaded portion of the kit is in place. **Warning:** *Wear protective eyewear when dealing with pressurized refrigerant cans.*

13   Remove the dust cap from the low-side charging port and attach the hose's quick-connect fitting to the port **(see illustration)**. **Warning:** *DO NOT hook the charging kit hose to the system high side! The fittings on the charging kit are designed to fit **only** on the low side of the system.*

14   Warm up the engine and turn On the air conditioning. Keep the charging kit hose away from the fan and other moving parts. **Note:** *The charging process requires the compressor to be running. If the clutch cycles off, you can put the air conditioning switch on High and leave the car doors open to keep the clutch on and compressor working. The compressor can be kept on during the charging by removing the connector from the pressure switch and bridging it with a paper clip or jumper wire during the procedure.*

15   Turn the valve handle on the kit until the stem pierces the can, then back the handle out to release the refrigerant. You should be able to hear the rush of gas. Keep the can upright at all times, but shake it occasionally. Allow stabilization time between each addition. **Note:** *The charging process will go faster if you wrap the can with a hot-water-soaked rag to keep the can from freezing up.*

16   If you have an accurate thermometer, you can place it in the center air conditioning duct inside the vehicle and keep track of the output air temperature. A charged system that is working properly should cool down to approximately 40 degrees F. If the ambient (outside) air temperature is very high, say 110 degrees F, the duct air temperature may be as high as 60 degrees F, but generally the air conditioning is 35 to 40 degrees F cooler than the ambient air.

17   When the can is empty, turn the valve handle to the closed position and release the connection from the low-side port. Reinstall the dust cap.

18   Remove the charging kit from the can and store the kit for future use with the piercing valve in the UP position, to prevent inadvertently piercing the can on the next use.

Heating systems

19   If the carpet under the heater core is damp, or if antifreeze vapor or steam is coming through the vents, the heater core is leaking. Remove it (see Section 11) and install a new unit (most radiator shops will not repair a leaking heater core).

20   If the air coming out of the heater vents isn't hot, the problem could stem from any of the following causes:

a)   *The thermostat is stuck open, preventing the engine coolant from warming up enough to carry heat to the heater core. Replace the thermostat (see Section 4).*

b)   *There is a blockage in the system, preventing the flow of coolant through the heater core. Feel both heater hoses at the firewall. They should be hot. If one of them is cold, there is an obstruction in one of the hoses or in the heater core, or the heater control valve is shut. Detach the hoses and back flush the heater core with a water hose. If the heater core is clear but circulation is impeded, remove the two hoses and flush them out with a water hose.*

c)   *If flushing fails to remove the blockage from the heater core, the core must be replaced (see Section 11).*

Eliminating air conditioning odors

Refer to illustration 3.24

21   Unpleasant odors that often develop in air conditioning systems are caused by the growth of a fungus, usually on the surface of the evaporator core. The warm, humid environment there is a perfect breeding ground for mildew to develop.

22   The evaporator core on most vehicles is difficult to access, and factory dealerships have a lengthy, expensive process for elimi-

nating the fungus by opening up the evaporator case and using a powerful disinfectant and rinse on the core until the fungus is gone. You can service your own system at home, but it takes something much stronger than basic household germ-killers or deodorizers.

23   Aerosol disinfectants for automotive air conditioning systems are available in most auto parts stores, but remember when shopping for them that the most effective treatments are also the most expensive. The basic procedure for using these sprays is to start by running the system in the RECIRC mode for ten minutes with the blower on its highest speed. Use the highest heat mode to dry out the system and keep the compressor from engaging by disconnecting the wiring connector at the compressor.

24   The disinfectant can usually comes with a long spray hose. Insert the nozzle into an intake port inside the cabin, and spray according to the manufacturer's recommendations **(see illustration)**. Try to cover the whole surface of the evaporator core, by aiming the spray up, down and sideways. Follow the manufacturer's recommendations for the length of spray and waiting time between applications.

25   Once the evaporator has been cleaned, the best way to prevent the mildew from coming back again is to make sure your evaporator housing drain tube is clear **(see illustration 3.1)**.

Automatic heating and air conditioning systems

26   Some vehicles are equipped with an optional automatic climate control system. This system has its own computer that receives inputs from various sensors in the heating and air conditioning system. This computer, like the PCM, has self-diagnostic capabilities to help pinpoint problems or faults within the system. Vehicles equipped with automatic heating and air conditioning systems are very complex and considered beyond the scope of the home mechanic. Vehicles equipped with automatic heating and air conditioning systems should be taken to

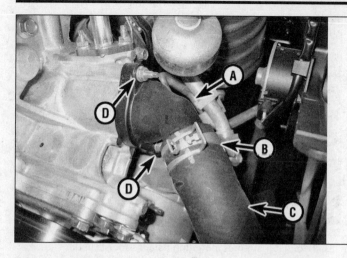

4.5 Typical four-cylinder thermostat details

A   Thermostat housing
B   Radiator hose spring clamp
C   Radiator hose
D   Thermostat mounting nuts

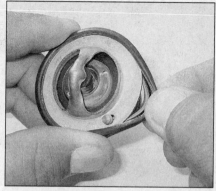

4.7 The thermostat gasket, which is actually a grooved sealing ring, fits around the edge of the thermostat

dealer service department or other qualified facility for repair.

4   Thermostat - replacement

Warning: *Wait until the engine is completely cool before beginning this procedure.*
Warning: *Do not allow antifreeze to come in contact with your skin or painted surfaces of the vehicle. Rinse off spills immediately with plenty of water. Antifreeze is highly toxic if ingested. Never leave antifreeze lying around in an open container or in puddles on the floor; children and pets are attracted by its sweet smell and may drink it. Check with local authorities on disposing of used antifreeze. Many communities have collection centers, which will see that antifreeze is disposed of safely. Never dump used antifreeze on the ground or into drains.*

1   Disconnect the cable from the negative battery terminal (see Chapter 5).
2   Raise the front of the vehicle and support it securely on jackstands, then remove the lower engine covers and the lower inner fender corner splash shield(s).
3   Drain the engine coolant (see Chapter 1). Disconnect the radiator hose from the thermostat housing or water inlet pipe.

Four-cylinder engines

Refer to illustrations 4.5 and 4.7

4   On 2010 and later models, remove the alternator (see Chapter 5).
5   Disconnect the radiator hose from the thermostat housing **(see illustration)**, then unbolt the thermostat housing from the engine.
6   Remove the thermostat, noting the direction in which it was installed in the housing, and thoroughly clean the sealing surfaces.
7   Install a new gasket to the thermostat **(see illustration)**. Make sure it is evenly fitted all the way around.
8   Install the thermostat into the engine, with the jiggle valve positioned at the highest point. Install the thermostat housing and proceed to Step 15.

V6 engines

9   Remove the front engine mount bracket and control rod assembly (see Chapter 2B).
10   Remove the drivebelt (see Chapter 1).
11   Remove the idler pulley assembly (see Chapter 2B).
12   Disconnect the radiator hose from the thermostat housing.
13   Remove the thermostat housing mounting fasteners and housing from the coolant inlet housing. Remove the thermostat, noting the direction in which it was installed in the housing, and thoroughly clean the sealing surfaces.
14   Install a new gasket to the thermostat **(see illustration 4.7)**. Install the thermostat into the inlet housing, with the jiggle valve positioned at the highest point. Install the thermostat housing and proceed to the next Step.

All models

15   Tighten the housing fasteners to the torque listed in this Chapter's Specifications and reinstall the remaining components in the reverse order of removal.
16   Refill the cooling system (see Chapter 1). Run the engine and check for leaks and proper operation.

5   Engine cooling fans - removal and installation

Refer to illustrations 5.3 and 5.4
Warning: *Wait until the engine is completely cool before beginning this procedure.*
Warning: *Do not allow antifreeze to come in contact with your skin or painted surfaces of the vehicle. Rinse off spills immediately with plenty of water. Antifreeze is highly toxic if ingested. Never leave antifreeze lying around in an open container or in puddles on the floor; children and pets are attracted by its sweet smell and may drink it. Check with local authorities on disposing of used antifreeze. Many communities have collection centers, which will see that antifreeze is disposed of safely. Never dump used antifreeze on the ground or into drains.*

1   Remove the radiator and fan/shroud from the vehicle (see Section 6).
2   Disconnect the fan shroud clips and lift the fan/shroud from the radiator.
3   Hold the fan blades and remove the fan retaining nut **(see illustration)**.
4   Unbolt the fan motor from the shroud **(see illustration)**.
5   Installation is the reverse of removal. Refill the cooling system (see Chapter 1).

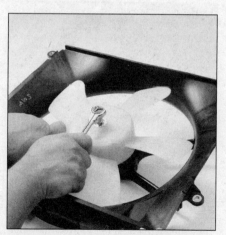

5.3 Remove the fan from the motor

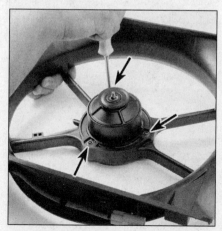

5.4 Remove the screws and separate the motor from the shroud

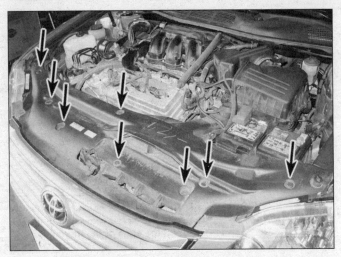

6.6 Remove the hood seal clips and hood seal

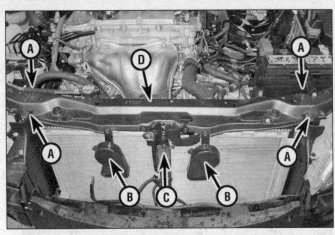

6.9 Radiator support mounting details - four-cylinder shown, V6 similar

A	Radiator support fasteners	C	Hood latch support fastener
B	Horns	D	Radiator support

6   Radiator and coolant reservoir - removal and installation

Warning: *Wait until the engine is completely cool before beginning this procedure.*

Warning: *Do not allow antifreeze to come in contact with your skin or painted surfaces of the vehicle. Rinse off spills immediately with plenty of water. Antifreeze is highly toxic if ingested. Never leave antifreeze lying around in an open container or in puddles on the floor; children and pets are attracted by its sweet smell and may drink it. Check with local authorities on disposing of used antifreeze. Many communities have collection centers, which will see that antifreeze is disposed of safely. Never dump used antifreeze on the ground or into drains.*

Radiator
Removal

Refer to illustrations 6.6 and 6.9

1   Disconnect the cable from the negative battery terminal (see Chapter 5).

2   Raise the front of the vehicle and support it securely on jackstands, then remove the lower engine covers and the lower inner fender corner splash shield(s).

3   Drain the cooling system (see Chapter 1).

4   Detach the upper and lower radiator hoses from the radiator.

5   Disconnect the reservoir hose from the radiator filler neck.

6   Remove the upper engine covers (and on V6 models, remove the engine seal cover clips and seal), then remove the air inlet assembly fasteners and air inlet **(see illustration)**.

7   Remove the air cleaner inlet duct (see Chapter 4).

8   Remove the front bumper (see Chapter 11).

9   Disconnect the electrical connectors to the horns, and remove the hood latch support mounting fasteners and the radiator support **(see illustration)**.

10   Remove the radiator support mounting fasteners and lift the support out.

11   If equipped with an automatic transaxle, disconnect the cooler lines from the radiator. Place a drip pan to catch the fluid and cap the fittings.

12   Remove the condenser mounting fasteners (see Section 14) and wire the condenser up to prevent it from falling once the radiator is removed.

13   Lift out the radiator and fan shroud assembly. Be aware of dripping fluids and the sharp fins. Separate the fan/shroud from the radiator (see Section 5).

14   With the radiator removed, it can be inspected for leaks, damage and internal blockage. If in need of repairs, have a professional radiator shop perform the work, as special techniques are required.

15   Bugs and dirt can be cleaned from the radiator with compressed air and a soft brush. Don't bend the cooling fins as this is done. **Warning:** *Wear eye protection.*

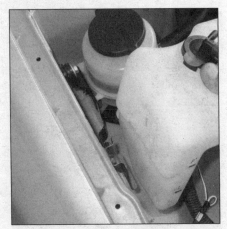

6.20 Pull the coolant reservoir up and out of its bracket to remove it

7.3 Using a pin spanner to hold the water pump pulley, remove the pulley mounting bolts

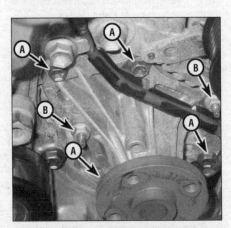

7.6 The water pump on 2009 and earlier four-cylinder models is retained by four bolts (A, one lower bolt not seen in this photo) and two nuts (B)

7.13 Water pump mounting details - 2010 and later four-cylinder models

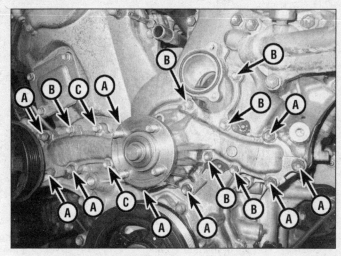

7.24 Locations of the different length water pump mounting bolts - V6 models

Installation

16   Installation is the reverse of the removal procedure. Be sure the rubber mounts are in place.

17   After installation, refill the cooling system (see Chapter 1).

18   Start the engine and check for leaks. Allow the engine to reach normal operating temperature, indicated by the upper radiator hose becoming hot. Recheck the coolant level and add more if required.

19   On automatic transaxle equipped models, check and add fluid as needed (see Chapter 1).

Coolant reservoir removal and installation

Refer to illustration 6.20

20   On most models, the coolant reservoir simply pulls up and out of the bracket on the fenderwell **(see illustration)**.

21   Pour the coolant into a container. Wash out the reservoir and inspect it for cracks and chafing. Replace it if damaged.

22   Installation is the reverse of removal.

7   Water pump - replacement

Warning: *Wait until the engine is completely cool before beginning this procedure.*

Warning: *Do not allow antifreeze to come in contact with your skin or painted surfaces of the vehicle. Rinse off spills immediately with plenty of water. Antifreeze is highly toxic if ingested. Never leave antifreeze lying around in an open container or in puddles on the floor; children and pets are attracted by its sweet smell and may drink it. Check with local authorities on disposing of used antifreeze. Many communities have collection centers, which will see that antifreeze is disposed of safely. Never dump used antifreeze on the ground or into drains.*

1   Disconnect the cable from the negative battery terminal (see Chapter 5) and drain the cooling system (see Chapter 1).

2009 and earlier four-cylinder models

Refer to illustrations 7.3 and 7.6

2   Remove the engine covers, radiator support trim cover and coolant reservoir (see Section 6).

3   Loosen the water pump pulley bolts **(see illustration)**, then remove the drivebelt and tensioner (see Chapter 1). Now unscrew the bolts and remove the pulley. **Note:** *If the drivebelt doesn't prevent the pulley from turning when loosening the bolts, use a pin spanner to immobilize it.*

4   Remove the alternator (see Chapter 5).

5   Remove the wiring harness from the clamp on the water pump and harness bracket.

6   Remove the water pump mounting fasteners **(see illustration)** and pry the water pump from the housing.

7   Thoroughly clean all sealing surfaces, removing all traces of old gasket material.

8   Installation is the reverse of removal. Be sure to tighten the fasteners to the torque listed in this Chapter's Specifications.

9   Refill the cooling system (see Chapter 1), run the engine and check for leaks and proper operation.

2010 and later four-cylinder models

Refer to illustration 7.13

10   Remove the engine covers, radiator support trim cover and coolant reservoir (see Section 6).

11   Remove the drivebelts (see Chapter 1).

12   Remove the alternator (see Chapter 5)

and tensioner for the alternator belt (see Chapter 1).

13   Remove the water pump mounting fasteners, then remove the water pump from the housing **(see illustration)**.

14   Thoroughly clean all sealing surfaces, removing all traces of old gasket.

15   Installation is the reverse of removal. Be sure to tighten the fasteners to the torque listed in this Chapter's Specifications.

16   Refill the cooling system (see Chapter 1), run the engine and check for leaks and proper operation.

V6 models

Refer to illustrations 7.24, 7.26 and 7.27

17   Remove the engine/transaxle assembly (see Chapter 2C).

18   Remove the alternator (see Chapter 5).

19   Remove the six bolts and the upper front engine mount bracket.

20   Remove both the front and rear drivebelt idler pulley assemblies. Keep them in order and note that the larger of the washers goes under the head of the pulley bolt. The smaller goes between the pulley and the engine block.

21   Remove the five bolts and the drivebelt tensioner.

22   Remove the thermostat housing (see Section 4).

23   Hold the water pump pulley with a special pin-spanner wrench. If you don't have one, you can use a chain wrench or strap wrench instead, Remove the pulley mounting bolts and pulley.

24   Remove the water pump mounting bolts **(see illustration)**, then remove the water pump and gasket. **Note:** *The bolts that secure the water pump are of three different lengths. Make note of where each bolt is located so it may be reinstalled in the same location.*

25   Thoroughly clean all sealing surfaces, removing all traces of old gasket and sealer.

7.26 Be sure to install a new gasket and clean the surface of the timing chain cover thoroughly

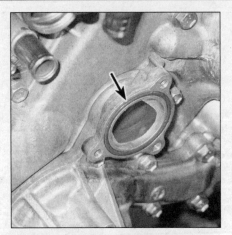

7.27 After installing the water pump, be sure to replace the inlet housing O-ring with a new one

9.4 The blower motor is located under the right end of the instrument panel

A   *Blower motor connector*
B   *Blower motor mounting screws*

9.5 Use pliers to release and remove the clip, then lift the blower fan off the motor shaft

26   Install a new gasket to the water pump **(see illustration)**. Install the water pump and tighten the bolts and nuts to the torque listed in this Chapter's Specifications.
27   Install new gasket and O-ring to the water inlet housing **(see illustration)**.
28   Installation is the reverse of removal. Tighten the bolts to the torque listed in this Chapter's Specifications.
29   Install the engine/transaxle assembly (see Chapter 2C). Refill the cooling system (see Chapter 1) and run the engine, checking for leaks and proper operation.

8   Coolant temperature indicator system - check

Warning: *Wait until the engine is completely cool before beginning this procedure.*
1   The coolant temperature indicator system consists of a temperature gauge on the dash and a sensor mounted on the engine.

On all models, an Engine Coolant Temperature (ECT) sensor (see Chapter 6), which is an information sensor for the Powertrain Control Module (PCM), provides a signal to the PCM which controls and actuates the temperature gauge.
2   If an overheating indication has occurred, first check the coolant level and mixture in the system (see Chapter 1). Refer to Section 2 before assuming that the temperature indicator is faulty.
3   Start the engine and warm it up for 10 minutes. If the temperature gauge has not moved from the C position, check the wiring harness connections going to the instrument cluster.
4   If there is a problem with the ECT sensor, it is very likely that the Malfunction Indicator Lamp will be illuminated and the sensor or circuit will need repair (see Chapter 6).

9   Blower motor - removal and installation

Refer to illustrations 9.4 and 9.5
Warning: *The models covered by this manual are equipped with Supplemental Restraint Systems (SRS), more commonly known as airbags. Always disarm the airbag system before working in the vicinity of any airbag system component to avoid the possibility of accidental deployment of the airbag, which could cause personal injury (see Chapter 12).*
1   Disconnect the cable from the negative battery terminal (see Chapter 5).
2   The blower unit is located in the passenger compartment above the right front footwell.
3   Remove the glove compartment liner, the glove compartment door and the right lower dash panel (see Chapter 11).
4   To remove the blower, remove the blower unit retaining screws and lower the unit from the housing **(see illustration)**.

5   If the motor is being replaced, transfer the fan to the new motor prior to installation **(see illustration)**.
6   Installation is the reverse of removal. Check for proper operation.

10   Heater and air conditioning control assembly - removal and installation

Refer to illustrations 10.3 and 10.4
Warning: *The models covered by this manual are equipped with Supplemental Restraint Systems (SRS), more commonly known as airbags. Always disarm the airbag system before working in the vicinity of any airbag system component to avoid the possibility of accidental deployment of the airbag, which could cause personal injury (see Chapter 12).*
1   Disconnect the cable from the negative battery terminal (see Chapter 5).
2   Remove the center console (see Chapter 11).

10.3 On Camry and Lexus models, carefully pry the center register out of the instrument panel

10.4 On Avalon models, the register and control panel are one unit, carefully pry each side to release the clips and remove the assembly

11.4 Remove the heater hose spring clamps and heater hoses

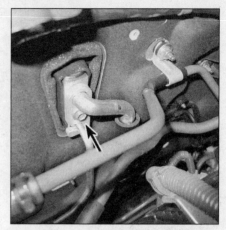

11.5 Remove the refrigerant line-to-evaporator core mounting bolt and separate the line

3   On Camry and Lexus models, use a trim tool to carefully pry the center register out **(see Illustration)** from each side, disengaging the clips from each side of the instrument panel.

4   On Avalon models, the center register and control panel are one piece; remove the center instrument panel trim panels (see Chapter 11). Use a trim tool to carefully pry the control assembly out **(see Illustration)** from each side, disengaging the clips from each side of the instrument panel. Disconnect the electrical connectors and remove the assembly.

5   Remove the audio/navigation unit (see Chapter 12) if equipped.

6   Remove the mounting brackets from each side of the audio/navigation unit.

7   Hold the audio/navigation unit and slide the a/c control assembly from left to right, releasing the retaining clips and control assembly.

8   Installation is the reverse of the removal procedure.

9   Run the engine and check for proper functioning of the heater and air conditioning.

11   Heater core - removal and installation

Refer to illustrations 11.4, 11.5, 11.19 and 11.20

Warning: *The models covered by this manual are equipped with Supplemental Restraint Systems (SRS), more commonly known as airbags. Always disarm the airbag system before working in the vicinity of any airbag system components to avoid the possibility of accidental deployment of the airbag, which could cause personal injury (see Chapter 12).*

Warning: *Do not allow antifreeze to come*

in contact with your skin or painted surfaces of the vehicle. Rinse off spills immediately with plenty of water. Antifreeze is highly toxic if ingested. Never leave antifreeze lying around in an open container or in puddles on the floor; children and pets are attracted by it's sweet smell and may drink it. Check with local authorities about disposing of used antifreeze. Many communities have collection centers which will see that antifreeze is disposed of safely. Never dump used antifreeze on the ground or pour it into drains.

Warning: *The air conditioning system is under high pressure. Do not loosen any hose fittings or remove any components until the system has been discharged. Air conditioning refrigerant should be properly discharged into an EPA-approved recovery/recycling unit by a dealer service department or an automotive air conditioning repair facility. Always wear eye protection when disconnecting air conditioning system fittings.*

Warning: *The engine must be completely cool before draining the cooling system.*

Note: *The manufacturer recommends removal of the entire instrument panel to remove the heater core as detailed in Chapter 11. This involves disconnecting numerous electrical connectors and there is the potential for breakage of delicate plastic tabs on various components. This is a difficult job for the average home mechanic.*

1   Have the air conditioning system discharged by a licensed automotive air conditioning technician.

2   Disconnect the cable from the negative terminal of the battery (see Chapter 5).

3   Wait until the engine is completely cool, then drain the cooling system (see Chapter 1). Remove the cowl assembly (see Chapter 11).

4   Working in the engine compartment, disconnect the heater hoses at the firewall **(see illustration)**. Push the rubber seal

around the hoses toward the inside of the vehicle, releasing it from the sheetmetal. Plug the heater core pipes to prevent leakage when it is removed. **Note:** *The manufacturer recommends removing the complete cowl assembly to have better access to the hoses and fasteners at the firewall (see Chapter 11).*

5   Disconnect the refrigerant lines from the evaporator lines at the firewall **(see illustration)**.

6   Remove the instrument panel (see Chapter 11).

7   Remove the Powertrain Control Module (PCM) (see Chapter 6) and the mounting bracket.

8   Remove the air conditioning amplifier module.

9   Working on the left side of the interior, remove the left side defroster nozzle duct and the heater-to-register duct.

10   Working on the right side of the interior, remove the right side defroster nozzle duct and the heater-to-register duct.

11   Remove the left side floor duct and the right side floor duct.

12   Pull the carpet back and remove the carpet mounting bracket and the reinforcement brace mounting brackets at the center console.

13   Remove the center console duct box and the left and right side air ducts.

14   Detach the steering column from the reinforcement brace (see Chapter 10).

15   Remove the fuse and relay box from the left side of the interior.

16   Release the wiring harness clamps and mounting bolts and carefully separate the harness from the reinforcement brace.

17   Remove the reinforcement brace mounting nuts and mounting bolts.

18   Lift the reinforcement brace and the air conditioning/heater assembly from the passenger compartment. **Caution:** *Work slowly and carefully to avoid breaking any plastic components during removal.*

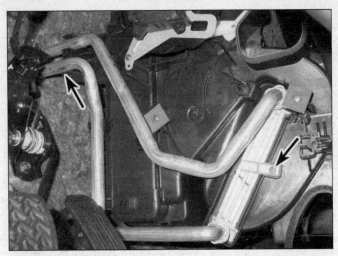

11.19 Release the clip near the firewall and remove the screw on the retaining strap at the housing

11.20 Carefully slide the heater core from the housing

19   Remove the mounting bolt from the heater core inlet and outlet pipe bracket **(see illustration)**.

20   Slide the heater core from the air conditioning/heater housing **(see illustration)**.

21   Installation is the reverse order of removal.

22   Refill the cooling system (see Chapter 1), reconnect the battery and run the engine. Check for leaks and proper system operation.

23   Have the air conditioning system recharged by the shop that discharged it.

12   Air conditioning receiver/drier - removal and installation

Refer to illustration 12.3

Warning: *The air conditioning system is under high pressure. Do not loosen any hose fittings or remove any components*

12.3 After the system has been discharged, remove the Allen plug and pull the receiver/drier from the tube on the condenser

until the system has been discharged. Air conditioning refrigerant must be properly discharged into an EPA-approved recovery/ recycling unit by a dealer service department or an automotive air conditioning repair facility. Always wear eye protection when disconnecting air conditioning system fittings.

1   Have the refrigerant discharged by an air conditioning technician.

2   Disconnect the cable from the negative battery terminal (see Chapter 5).

3   Remove the condenser (see Section 14). Using an Allen wrench, detach the end plug **(see illustration)** and remove the receiver/ drier from the condenser.

4   Installation is the reverse of removal. Be sure to tighten the end plug to the torque listed in this Chapter's Specifications.

5   Have the system evacuated, charged and leak tested by the shop that discharged it. If the receiver/drier was replaced, have them add the proper amount of refrigeration oil to the compressor. Use only compressor oil compatible with R-134a refrigerant.

13   Air conditioning compressor - removal and installation

Warning: *The air conditioning system is under high pressure. Do not loosen any hose fittings or remove any components until the system has been discharged. Air conditioning refrigerant must be properly discharged into an EPA-approved recovery/recycling unit by a dealer service department or an automotive air conditioning repair facility. Always wear eye protection when disconnecting air conditioning system fittings.*

Warning: *The engine must be completely cool before draining the cooling system.*

Caution: *The receiver/drier should be replaced whenever the compressor is replaced.*

1   Have the refrigerant discharged by an automotive air conditioning technician.

2   Disconnect the cable from the negative battery terminal (see Chapter 5).

3   Raise the front of the vehicle and support it securely on jackstands, then remove the passenger's side front wheel and the lower inner fender corner splash shield(s).

4   Drain the cooling system (see Chapter 1).

5   Remove the drivebelt from the compressor (see Chapter 1).

6   Remove the alternator (see Chapter 5).

2009 and earlier four-cylinder models

7   Detach the upper radiator hose from the thermostat housing.

8   Remove the clamp that supports the refrigerant lines.

2010 and later four cylinder models and all V6 models

9   Remove the air cleaner assembly and air inlet duct (see Chapter 4).

10   Remove the front bumper (see Chapter 11).

11   Remove the radiator (see Section 6).

All models

Refer to illustration 13.12

12   Detach the electrical connector and the refrigerant lines **(see illustration)**.

13   Unbolt the compressor and lift it from the vehicle.

14   If a new or rebuilt compressor is being installed, follow the directions which come with it regarding the proper level of oil prior to installation.

15   Installation is the reverse of removal. Replace any O-rings with new ones specifically made for the purpose and lubricate them with refrigerant oil.

16   Have the system evacuated, recharged and leak tested by the shop that discharged it.

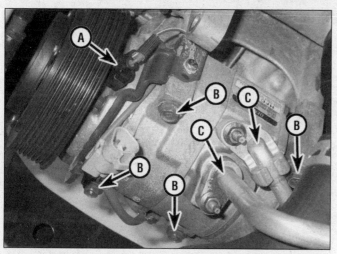

13.12 Compressor details - 2009 and earlier four-cylinder models (shown with alternator removed), other models similar

A   *Electrical connector*   C   *Refrigerant lines*
B   *Mounting bolts*

14.7 Remove the bolts holding the refrigerant lines to the right side of the condenser - on some models, the line is clamped to the side of the condenser as well

14 Air conditioning condenser - removal and installation

Refer to illustrations 14.7 and 14.8

Warning: *The air conditioning system is under high pressure. Do not loosen any hose fittings or remove any components until the system has been discharged. Air conditioning refrigerant must be properly discharged into an EPA-approved recovery/recycling unit by a dealer service department or an automotive air conditioning repair facility. Always wear eye protection when disconnecting air conditioning system fittings.*

Caution: *The receiver/drier should be replaced whenever the condenser is replaced.*

1   Have the refrigerant discharged by an air conditioning technician.
2   Remove the engine covers (see Chapter 2).
3   Remove the air cleaner assembly and air inlet duct (see Chapter 4).
4   Remove the front bumper (see Chapter 11).
5   Remove the radiator support (see Section 6).
6   Remove the hood lock support mounting

14.8 Remove the fasteners for the condenser upper and lower mounting brackets

fasteners and support.
7   Disconnect the inlet and outlet fittings **(see illustration)**. Cap the open fittings immediately to keep moisture and dirt out of the system.
8   Remove the mounting nuts/bolts **(see illustration),** then pull the condenser up and out of the vehicle.
9   Install the condenser, brackets and bolts,

making sure the rubber cushions fit on the mounting points properly.
10   Reconnect the refrigerant lines, using new O-rings where needed.
11   Reinstall the remaining parts in the reverse order of removal.
12   Have the system evacuated, charged and leak tested by the shop that discharged it.

Notes

Chapter 4
Fuel and exhaust systems

Contents

Specifications

Fuel system

Fuel system pressure
All except 2012 Avalon and ES350 models	44 to 50 psi
2012 Avalon and ES350 models	55 to 61 psi
Fuel system hold pressure (after five minutes)	21 psi minimum
Injector resistance (approximate)	11.3 to 12.4 ohms

Torque specifications

Ft-lbs (unless otherwise indicated)

Note: *One foot-pound (ft-lb) of torque is equivalent to 12 inch-pounds (in-lbs) of torque. Torque values below approximately 15 foot-pounds are expressed in inch-pounds, because most foot-pound torque wrenches are not accurate at these smaller values.*

Fuel rail mounting bolts	15
Fuel pulsation damper bolts	
2011 and earlier models	80 In-lbs
2012 and later models	89 in-lbs
Fuel pump retainer ring	53 in-lbs
Fuel tank strap bolts	29
Intake Air Control valve (2010 and 2011 four-cylinder models)	53 in-lbs
Intake air control valve actuator (2012 and later four-cylinder models)	80 in-lbs
Vacuum switching valve (2012 and later V6 models)	30 in-lbs
Throttle body mounting bolts	
2011 and earlier models	
Four-cylinder engines	80 in-lbs
V6 engines	84 in-lbs
2012 and later models	89 in-lbs

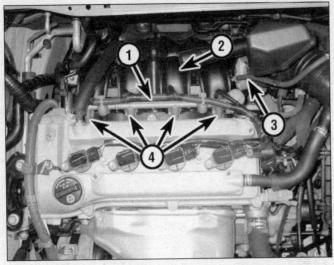

**Fuel system components - 2AZ-FE four-cylinder engine
(2009 and earlier models)**

1	Fuel rail	3	Throttle body
2	Intake manifold	4	Fuel injectors

**Fuel system components - 2AR-FE four-cylinder engine
(2010 and later models)**

1	Intake manifold	3	Fuel injectors (mounted
2	Throttle body		on the back side of the
			cylinder head)

1 General information

Fuel system warnings

Gasoline is extremely flammable and repairing fuel system components can be dangerous. Consider your automotive repair knowledge and experience before attempting repairs which may be better suited for a professional mechanic.

- Don't smoke or allow open flames or bare light bulbs near the work area
- Don't work in a garage with a gas-type appliance (water heater, clothes dryer)
- Use fuel-resistant gloves. If any fuel spills on your skin, wash it off immediately with soap and water
- Clean up spills immediately
- Do not store fuel-soaked rags where they could ignite
- Prior to disconnecting any fuel line, you must relieve the fuel pressure (see Section 3)
- Wear safety glasses
- Have a proper fire extinguisher on hand

Fuel system

The fuel system consists of the fuel tank, electric fuel pump/fuel level sending unit (located in the fuel tank), fuel rail and fuel injectors. The fuel injection system is a multi-port system; multi-port fuel injection uses timed impulses to inject the fuel directly into the intake port of each cylinder. The Powertrain Control Module (PCM) controls the injectors. The PCM monitors various engine parameters and delivers the exact amount of fuel required into the intake ports.

Fuel is circulated from the fuel pump to the fuel rail through fuel lines running along the underside of the vehicle. Various sections of the fuel line are either rigid metal or nylon, or flexible fuel hose. The various sections of the fuel hose are connected either by quick-connect fittings or threaded metal fittings.

Exhaust system

The exhaust system consists of the exhaust manifold(s), catalytic converter(s),

Fuel system components - 2GR-FE V6 engine

1	Fuel rail	4	Fuel injectors (the remaining three are
2	Upper intake manifold		under the upper intake manifold)
3	Throttle body		

2.2 The EFI No. 1 fuse (A) is located in the engine compartment fuse/relay box; (B) is the EFI MAIN relay

2.9 An automotive stethoscope is used to listen to the fuel injectors in operation

muffler(s), tailpipe and all connecting pipes, flanges and clamps. The catalytic converters are an emission control device added to the exhaust system to reduce pollutants.

2 Troubleshooting

Fuel pump

Refer to illustration 2.2

1   The fuel pump is located inside the fuel tank. Sit inside the vehicle with the windows closed, turn the ignition key to ON (not START) and listen for the sound of the fuel pump as it's briefly activated. You will only hear the sound for a second or two, but that sound tells you that the pump is working. Alternatively, have an assistant listen at the fuel filler cap.

2   If the pump does not come on, check the fuel pump fuse labeled "EFI no. 1" and relay labeled "EFI main" **(see illustration)**. If the fuse and relay are okay, check the wiring back to the fuel pump. If the fuse, relay and wiring are okay, the fuel pump is probably defective. If the pump runs continuously with the ignition key in the ON position, the Powertrain Control Module (PCM) is probably defective. Have the PCM checked by a professional mechanic.

Fuel injection system

Refer to illustration 2.9

Note: *The following procedure is based on the assumption that the fuel pump is working and the fuel pressure is adequate (see Section 4).*

3   Check all electrical connectors that are related to the system. Check the ground wire connections for tightness.

4   Verify that the battery is fully charged (see Chapter 5).

5   Inspect the air filter element (see Chapter 1).

6   Check all fuses related to the fuel system (see Chapter 12).

7   Check the air induction system between the throttle body and the intake manifold for air leaks. Also inspect the condition of all vacuum hoses connected to the intake manifold and to the throttle body.

8   Remove the air intake duct from the throttle body and look for dirt, carbon, varnish, or other residue in the throttle body, particularly around the throttle plate. If it's dirty, clean it with carb cleaner, a toothbrush and a clean shop towel.

9   With the engine running, place an automotive stethoscope against each injector, one at a time, and listen for a clicking sound that indicates operation **(see illustration)**. **Warning:** *Stay clear of the drivebelt and any rotating or hot components.*

10   If you can hear the injectors operating, but the engine is misfiring, the electrical circuits are functioning correctly, but the injectors might be dirty or clogged. Try a commercial injector cleaning product (available at auto parts stores). If cleaning the injectors doesn't help, replace the injectors.

11   If an injector is not operating (it makes no sound), disconnect the injector electrical connector and measure the resistance across the injector terminals with an ohmmeter. Compare this measurement to the other injectors. If the resistance of the non-operational injector is quite different from the other injectors, replace it.

12   If the injector is not operating, but the resistance reading is within the range of resistance of the other injectors, the PCM or the circuit between the PCM and the injector might be faulty.

3 Fuel pressure relief procedure

Warning: *Gasoline is extremely flammable. See **Fuel system warnings** in Section 1.*

1   Remove the fuel filler cap to relieve any pressure built-up in the fuel tank.

2   Remove the rear seat cushion (see Chapter 11).

3   Disconnect the electrical connector from the fuel pump **(see illustration 7.5)**.

4   Start the engine and allow it to run until it dies.

5   Operate the starter motor once again to make sure the engine doesn't start (indicating that the fuel pressure has been relieved).

6   If the engine did not start, the fuel pressure is now relieved. Disconnect the cable from the negative terminal of the battery before performing any work on the fuel system (see Chapter 5).

7   Although the fuel pressure is relieved, be prepared for fuel spillage whenever disconnecting any part of the fuel system. Properly dispose of any fuel-soaked rags.

4 Fuel pressure - check

Refer to illustrations 4.1a and 4.1b

Warning: *Gasoline is extremely flammable. See **Fuel system warnings** in Section 1.*

Note: *The following procedure assumes that the fuel pump is receiving voltage and runs.*

Note: *In order to perform the fuel pressure test, you will need to obtain a fuel pressure gauge capable of measuring high fuel pressure and the proper adapter set for the specific fuel injection system.*

1   Relieve the fuel system pressure (see Section 3). Disconnect the fuel line from the fuel rail, then use the proper adapter to con-

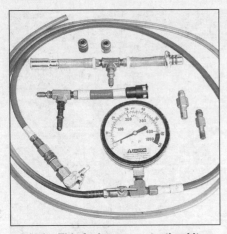

4.1a This fuel pressure testing kit contains all the necessary fittings and adapters, along with the fuel pressure gauge, to test most automotive fuel systems

4.1b Attach the fuel pressure gauge between the two sides of the quick-connect fitting; turn the ignition key ON and check the fuel pressure

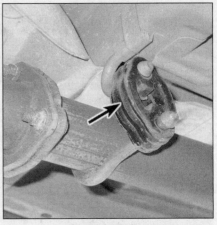

6.1 A typical exhaust system hanger. Inspect regularly and replace at the first sign of damage or deterioration

nect the pressure gauge between the fuel line and fuel rail **(see illustrations)**.

2   Turn all the accessories Off and switch the ignition key On. The fuel pump should run for about two seconds; note the reading on the gauge. After the pump stops running, the pressure should hold steady. After five minutes it should not drop below the minimum listed in this Chapter's Specifications.

3   Start the engine and let it idle. The pressure should remain the same. If all the pressure readings are within the limits listed in this Chapter's Specifications, the system is operating properly.

4   If the fuel pressure is not within specifications, check the following:

   a) *If the pressure is higher than specified, replace the fuel pressure regulator (see Section 8).*

   b) *If the pressure is lower than specified, check the fuel filter and fuel lines from the fuel rail to the fuel tank for restrictions or damage. Check the fuel injectors for leaks. If the pressure is still low, most likely the fuel pressure regulator and/or the fuel pump is defective. In this situation, it is recommended that both the fuel pressure regulator and fuel pump are replaced to prevent any future fuel pressure problems.*

5   After the testing is done, relieve the fuel pressure (see Section 3) and remove the fuel pressure gauge.

5   Fuel lines and fittings - general information

Warning: *Gasoline is extremely flammable. See* **Fuel system warnings** *in Section 1.*

1   Relieve the fuel pressure before servicing fuel lines or fittings (see Section 3), then disconnect the cable from the negative battery terminal (see Chapter 5) before proceeding.

2   The fuel supply line connects the fuel pump in the fuel tank to the fuel rail on the engine. The Evaporative Emission (EVAP) system lines connect the fuel tank to the EVAP canister and connect the canister to the intake manifold.

3   Whenever you're working under the vehicle, be sure to inspect all fuel and evaporative emission lines for leaks, kinks, dents and other damage. Always replace a damaged fuel or EVAP line immediately.

4   If you find signs of dirt in the lines during disassembly, disconnect all lines and blow them out with compressed air. Inspect the fuel strainer on the fuel pump pick-up unit for damage and deterioration.

Steel tubing

5   It is critical that the fuel lines be replaced with lines of equivalent type and specification.

6   Some steel fuel lines have threaded fittings. When loosening these fittings, hold the stationary fitting with a wrench while turning the tube nut.

Plastic tubing

7   When replacing fuel system plastic tubing, use only original equipment replacement plastic tubing. **Caution:** *When removing or installing plastic fuel line tubing, be careful not to bend or twist it too much, which can damage it. Also, plastic fuel tubing is NOT heat resistant, so keep it away from excessive heat.*

Flexible hoses

8   When replacing fuel system flexible hoses, use only original equipment replacements.

9   Don't route fuel hoses (or metal lines) within four inches of the exhaust system or within ten inches of the catalytic converter. Make sure that no rubber hoses are installed

directly against the vehicle, particularly in places where there is any vibration. If allowed to touch some vibrating part of the vehicle, a hose can easily become chafed and it might start leaking. A good rule of thumb is to maintain a minimum of 1/4-inch clearance around a hose (or metal line) to prevent contact with the vehicle underbody.

6   Exhaust system servicing - general information

Refer to illustration 6.1

Warning: *Allow exhaust system components to cool before inspection or repair. Also, when working under the vehicle, make sure it is securely supported on jackstands.*

1   The exhaust system consists of the exhaust manifolds, catalytic converter, muffler, tailpipe and all connecting pipes, flanges and clamps. The exhaust system is isolated from the vehicle body and from chassis components by a series of rubber hangers **(see illustration)**. Periodically inspect these hangers for cracks or other signs of deterioration, replacing them as necessary.

2   Conduct regular inspections of the exhaust system to keep it safe and quiet. Look for any damaged or bent parts, open seams, holes, loose connections, excessive corrosion or other defects which could allow exhaust fumes to enter the vehicle. Do not repair deteriorated exhaust system components; replace them with new parts.

3   If the exhaust system components are extremely corroded, or rusted together, a cutting torch is the most convenient tool for removal. Consult a properly-equipped repair shop. If a cutting torch is not available, you can use a hacksaw, or if you have compressed air, there are special pneumatic cutting chisels that can also be used. Wear

Disconnecting Fuel Line Fittings

Two-tab type fitting; depress both tabs with your fingers, then pull the fuel line and the fitting apart

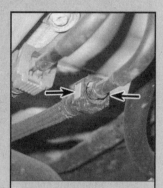

On this type of fitting, depress the two buttons on opposite sides of the fitting, then pull it off the fuel line

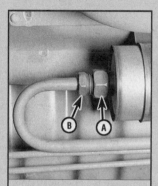

Threaded fuel line fitting; hold the stationary portion of the line or component (A) while loosening the tube nut (B) with a flare-nut wrench

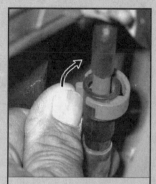

Plastic collar-type fitting; rotate the outer part of the fitting

Metal collar quick-connect fitting; pull the end of the retainer off the fuel line and disengage the other end from the female side of the fitting . . .

. . . insert a fuel line separator tool into the female side of the fitting, push it into the fitting and pull the fuel line off the pipe

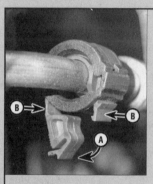

Some fittings are secured by lock tabs. Release the lock tab (A) and rotate it to the fully-opened position, squeeze the two smaller lock tabs (B) . . .

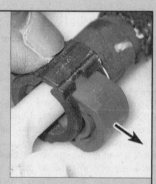

. . . then push the retainer out and pull the fuel line off the pipe

Spring-lock coupling; remove the safety cover, install a coupling release tool and close the tool around the coupling . . .

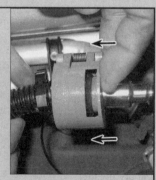

. . . push the tool into the fitting, then pull the two lines apart

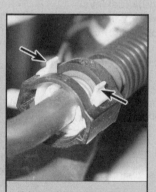

Hairpin clip type fitting: push the legs of the retainer clip together, then push the clip down all the way until it stops and pull the fuel line off the pipe

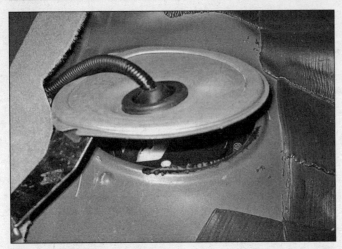

7.4 Pry the fuel access cover up - the adhesive is very sticky and will stain the carpet or seats

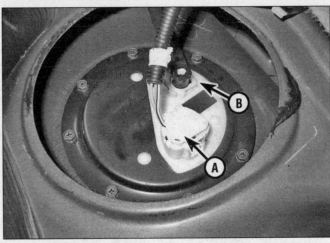

7.5 Disconnect the electrical connector (A), then pull the fuel line retaining clip (B) back and remove the fuel hose

safety goggles to protect your eyes from metal chips and wear work gloves to protect your hands.

4   Here are some simple guidelines to follow when repairing the exhaust system:

a) *Work from the back to the front when removing exhaust system components.*

b) *Apply penetrating oil to the exhaust system component fasteners to make them easier to remove.*

c) *Use new gaskets, hangers and clamps.*

d) *Apply anti-seize compound to the threads of all exhaust system fasteners during reassembly.*

e) *Be sure to allow sufficient clearance between newly installed parts and all points on the underbody to avoid over-heating the floor pan and possibly damaging the interior carpet and insulation. Pay particularly close attention to the catalytic converter and heat shield.*

7   Fuel pump module/fuel level sending unit - removal, component replacement and installation

Warning: *Gasoline is extremely flammable, so take extra precautions when you work on any part of the fuel system. See the* **Fuel system warnings** *in Section 1.*

Removal

Refer to illustrations 7.4 and 7.5

1   Relieve the fuel system pressure (see Section 3).

2   Disconnect the cable from the negative terminal of the battery (see Chapter 5).

3   Remove the rear seat cushion (see Chapter 11).

4   Carefully pry up the fuel pump module/fuel level sending unit access cover **(see illustration)**.

5   Disconnect the electrical connector(s)

and the fuel line from the top of the fuel pump unit **(see illustration)**. Using a small screwdriver, pull the yellow clip back to release the fuel line.

6   Remove the fuel pump module/fuel level sending unit retaining bolts.

7   Carefully withdraw the fuel pump module/fuel level sending unit assembly from the fuel tank.

8   The components of the fuel pump assembly are modular and all attach to the main housing.

Fuel level sending unit

Refer to illustration 7.10

9   Disconnect the fuel sender electrical connector **(see Illustration 7.14b)**.

10   Depress the fuel sender plastic locking tab **(see illustration)** and slide it out to remove the unit.

11   Installation is the reverse of removal.

Fuel pump module

12   Remove fuel pump module/fuel level sending unit from the tank as described.

13   Remove the fuel level sending unit as previously described.

Four-cylinder models (2011 and earlier models)

Refer to illustrations 7.14a, 7.14b and 7.20

14   Disconnect the fuel pump electrical connector from the fuel suction plate **(see illustrations)**.

15   Using needle-nose pliers remove the spring E-clip, then disengage the suction support mounting clips and separate the band bracket from the fuel filter assembly. **Caution:** *Do not try to disconnect the fuel tube line between the fuel suction plate and the top plate. The tube and suction plate will be damaged.*

16   Remove the spring from the fuel suction plate.

17   Using a screwdriver, disengage the clips from the fuel suction support and separate the support from the fuel pump.

18   Pull the fuel pump out from the filter assembly.

19   Disconnect and remove the fuel pump electrical harness.

20   Disengage the clips securing the inlet strainer to the pump **(see illustration)**.

21   Remove the strainer and inspect it for contamination. If it is dirty, replace it.

7.10 Disconnect the electrical connector (A) and pry the fuel level sending unit from the clips (B)

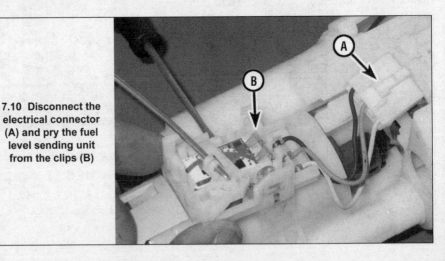

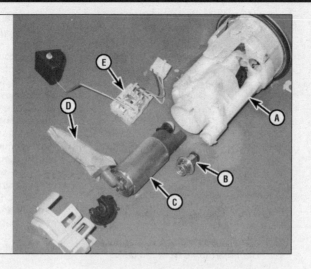

7.14a Exploded view of the fuel pump/fuel level sending unit module - four-cylinder models

A   Fuel filter
B   Fuel pressure regulator
C   Fuel pump
D   Strainer
E   Fuel level sending unit

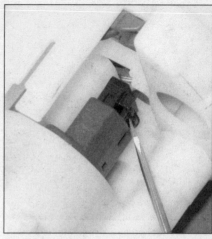

7.14b Release the electrical connector at the top of the fuel pump assembly

V6 models, and 2012 and later 4-cylinder models

Refer to illustration 7.22

22   Using a screwdriver, pry the sub-tank from the base of the assembly **(see Illustration)**.
23   Remove the rubber cushion from the bottom of the fuel pump. **Note:** *At the time of writing, the fuel strainer is permanently attached to the fuel pump.*
24   Disconnect the fuel pump electrical connector and disengage the fuel suction plate mounting clips.
25   Disconnect and remove the fuel pump electrical harness.
26   Pull the fuel pump up and out from the filter assembly.
27   Remove the clip securing the inlet strainer to the pump.
28   Remove the strainer and inspect it for contamination. If it is dirty, replace it.

Installation

29   Reassemble the fuel pump module in the reverse order of disassembly.
30   Install the fuel pump/sending unit assembly in the fuel tank. Connect the fuel line and

electrical connector. If equipped with a quick-connect fitting, see Section 5.
31   The remainder of installation is the reverse of removal.

8   Fuel pressure regulator - removal and installation

Refer to illustration 8.4

Warning: *Gasoline is extremely flammable, so take extra precautions when you work on*

any part of the fuel system. See the **Fuel system warnings** *in Section 1.*
1   Relieve the fuel system pressure (see Section 3). Disconnect the cable from the negative battery terminal (see Chapter 5).
2   Remove the fuel pump/fuel level sending unit from the fuel tank (see Section 7).
3   Remove the sub-tank from the fuel pump assembly (see Section 7).

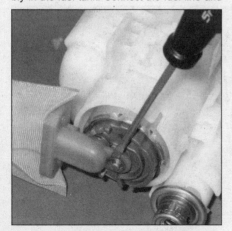

7.20 Carefully use a screwdriver to remove the clip securing the fuel sock filter to the pump

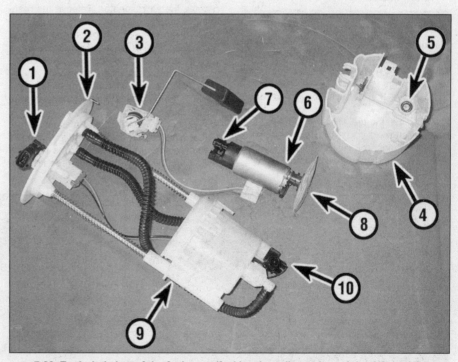

7.22 Exploded view of the fuel pump/fuel level sending unit module - V6 models

1   Main harness connector
2   Mounting flange
3   Fuel level sending unit
4   Fuel pump sub-tank
5   O-ring (always replace)
6   Fuel pump
7   Fuel pump spacer
8   Strainer (fuel pump inlet filter)
9   Fuel filter assembly (sealed, cannot be replaced separately from the housing)
10 Fuel pressure regulator

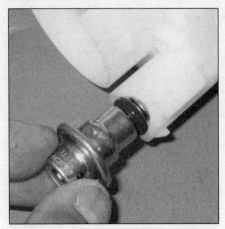

8.4 The fuel pressure regulator is a push fit in the fuel pump/sending unit assembly, make sure the O-ring comes out with it

4   Twist the fuel pressure regulator from the assembly **(see illustration)**. **Note:** *It may be necessary to use a screwdriver to pry the pressure regulator from the filter assembly.*
5   Installation is the reverse of removal. Be sure to install a new O-ring(s) on the fuel pressure regulator.

9   Fuel tank - removal and installation

Refer to illustrations 9.9 and 9.11
Warning: *Gasoline is extremely flammable, so take extra precautions when you work on any part of the fuel system. See the* **Fuel system warnings** *in Section 1.*
1   Relieve the fuel system pressure (see Section 3).
2   Remove the fuel filler cap to relieve fuel tank pressure.
3   Disconnect the cable from the negative terminal of the battery (see Chapter 5).

9.9 Loosen the clamp and disconnect the fuel filler hose from the tank

4   If the tank is full or nearly full, siphon the fuel into an approved container using a siphoning kit (available at most auto parts stores). **Warning:** *Do not start the siphoning action by mouth!*
5   Remove the rear seat cushion (see Chapter 11).
6   Raise the vehicle and place it securely on jackstands. Disconnect the parking brake cable mounting fasteners (see Chapter 9).
7   If necessary on 2012 and later V6 models, remove the No. 1 air inlet and then remove the air resonator. Release the resonator clamp, turn out the mounting bolts, and remove the resonator. Note the location of any vacuum line or electrical connectors.
8   Remove the lower floor pan cover mounting fasteners and covers, if equipped.
9   Remove the exhaust system from the center exhaust pipe completely to the rear of the vehicle.
10   Refer to Section 7 and disconnect the electrical connector and fuel line from the fuel pump module, then disconnect the fuel filler hose from the fuel tank fittings **(see illustra-**

tion). **Note:** *Be sure to plug the hoses to prevent leakage and contamination of the fuel system.*
11   Remove the rear stabilizer bar mounting brackets and move the bar away from the tank.
12   Remove the four fasteners securing the exhaust heat shield below the fuel tank **(see illustration)**.
13   Support the fuel tank with a floor jack. Place a sturdy plank between the jack head and the fuel tank to protect the tank.
14   Remove the bolts from the fuel tank retaining straps.
15   Disconnect the vent hose at the rear of the tank and any other hoses or wiring harnesses that are attached to the tank.
16   Remove the tank from the vehicle.
17   Installation is the reverse of removal.

10   Air filter housing - removal and installation

Refer to illustrations 10.4, 10.5 and 10.6
1   Disconnect the air filter vent hose, canister purge line hose clamp, the mass air flow and vacuum switching valve electrical connectors.
2   Disconnect the throttle body inlet hose clamp and separate the air filter hose from the throttle body.
3   Remove the air filter cover mounting fasteners or unsnap the retainer clips, then remove the air filter cover and duct as an assembly (see Chapter 1). Remove the filter element.
4   Remove the radiator support cover retaining push pins, then remove the cover. **(see illustration)**. On V6 models, mark and disconnect any vacuum lines and electrical connectors.
5   Remove the fresh air inlet fasteners and pull the inlet out of the housing **(see illustration)**.

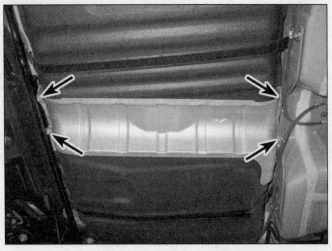

9.11 Remove the four bolts and the exhaust heat shield

10.4 Remove the radiator support cover mounting pins and cover

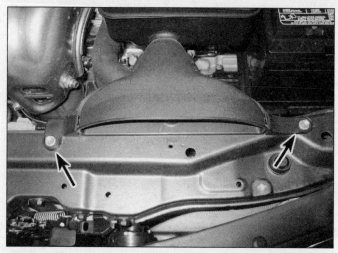

10.5 Remove the fresh air inlet fasteners and inlet from the air filter housing

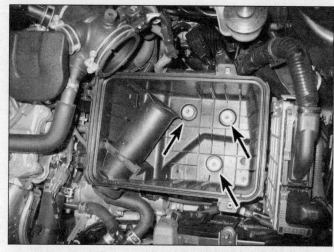

10.6 Air filter housing bolts (four-cylinder model shown)

6   Remove the housing mounting fasteners **(see illustration)**, then remove the air filter assembly from the engine compartment.

7   Installation is the reverse of removal.

11 Throttle body - removal and installation

Refer to illustrations 11.7a and 11.7b

Warning: *Gasoline is extremely flammable, so take extra precautions when you work on any part of the fuel system. See the* **Fuel system warnings** *in Section 1.*

Warning: *Wait until the engine is completely cool before beginning this procedure.*

1   Disconnect the cable from the negative battery terminal (see Chapter 5, Section 3).

2   Remove the engine cover(s).

3   Loosen the air intake duct clamps, then remove the air intake duct and air filter housing (see Section 10).

4   Disconnect the electrical connector from the throttle control motor.

5   Clamp-off the coolant hoses leading to the throttle body.

6   Clearly label, then detach, all vacuum and coolant hoses from the throttle body. Plug the coolant hoses to prevent coolant leakage. **Caution:** *Make sure no coolant is allowed to drain into the intake manifold.*

7   Remove the throttle body mounting nuts/bolts **(see illustrations)**.

8   Detach the throttle body and gasket from the intake manifold.

9   Installation of the throttle body is the reverse of removal. Use a new gasket between the throttle body and the intake manifold.

10   Be sure to tighten the throttle body mounting bolts to the torque listed in this Chapter's Specifications.

11   Check the coolant level and add some, if necessary, to bring it to the appropriate level (see Chapter 1).

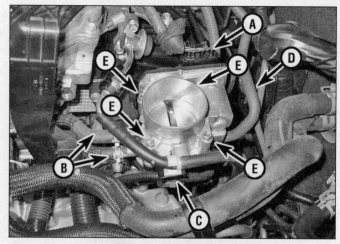

11.7a Throttle body mounting details (2AR-FE four-cylinder engine)

A   Throttle position sensor and control motor connector
B   Coolant hoses
C   Harness and fuel line retaining clip
D   Vapor hose
E   Throttle body mounting bolts

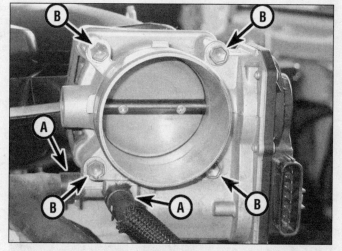

11.7b Throttle body mounting details (2GR-FE V6 engine)

A   Coolant hoses

B   Throttle body mounting bolts

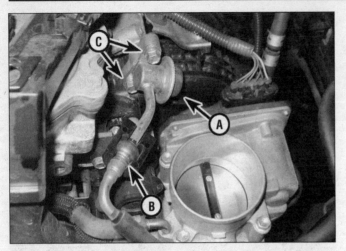

12.6 Fuel pulsation damper details - four-cylinder engine

A   *Fuel pulsation damper*
B   *Fuel line quick-connect coupling*
C   *Mounting bolts*

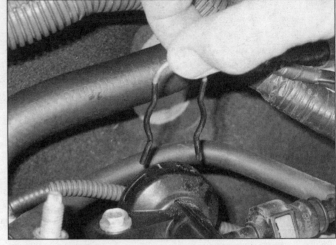

12.10a   To remove the fuel pulsation damper from the fuel rail on V6 models, remove the retainer clip . . .

12   Fuel pulsation damper - replacement

Warning: *Gasoline is extremely flammable, so take extra precautions when you work on any part of the fuel system. See the* **Fuel system warnings** *in Section 1.*

1   Remove the engine cover(s).
2   Relieve the fuel pressure (see Section 3).
3   Disconnect the cable from the negative battery terminal (see Chapter 5).
4   Disconnect the fuel line connector where it joins the pipe from the fuel pulsation damper at the end of the fuel rail (see *Disconnecting fuel line fittings*).
5   Remove the air filter housing (see Section 10).

Four-cylinder models

Refer to illustration 12.6

6   Remove the two damper mounting bolts at the fuel rail **(see illustration)** and the damper.
7   Installation is the reverse of removal. Be sure to install a new O-ring and tighten the bolts to the torque listed in this Chapter's Specifications.

V6 models

Refer to illustrations 12.10a, 12.10b and 12.11

8   Remove the upper intake manifold (see Chapter 2B).
9   Disconnect the vacuum line to the damper.
10   Pull the locking clip out from the base of the damper and separate the damper from the fuel rail **(see illustrations)**.
11   Installation is the reverse of removal. Be

sure to install a new O-ring onto the damper **(see illustration)**.

13   Fuel rail and injectors - removal and installation

Warning: *Gasoline is extremely flammable, so take extra precautions when you work on any part of the fuel system. See the* **Fuel system warnings** *in Section 1.*

Removal

1   Relieve the fuel pressure (see Section 3).
2   Disconnect the cable from the negative battery terminal (see Chapter 5).
3   Remove the engine covers.
4   Remove the cowl assembly (see Chapter 11).

12.10b   . . . then pull the pulsation damper out of the fuel rail

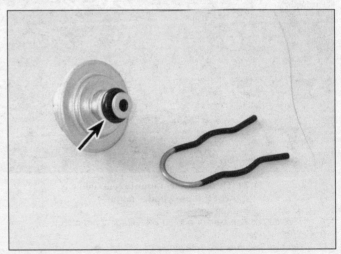

12.11   Remove the old O-ring from the fuel pressure pulsation damper and replace it (V6 models)

13.7 Remove the fuel rail mounting bolts - four-cylinder models

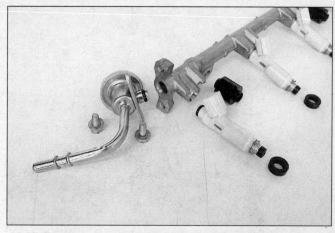

13.11 Be sure to install new O-rings on the injectors and the fuel pulsation damper

Four-cylinder models

Refer to illustrations 13.7 and 13.11

5   Remove the air filter housing (see Section 10).

6   Remove the wiring harness mounting clips.

7   Disconnect the injector electrical connectors and remove the fuel rail mounting bolts **(see illustration)**.

8   Disconnect the fuel line from the fuel rail (see Section 5).

9   Remove the fuel rail with the fuel injectors attached.

10   Remove the fuel injector(s) from the fuel rail and set them aside in a clearly labeled storage container. **Note:** *Remove the spacers and injector grommets from the cylinder head if they didn't come off when the fuel rail was removed.*

11   If you intend to re-use the same injectors, replace the grommets and O-rings **(see illustration)**.

V6 models

Refer to illustrations 13.15a, 13.15b, 13.16, 13.17 and 13.18

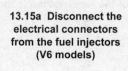

13.15a Disconnect the electrical connectors from the fuel injectors (V6 models)

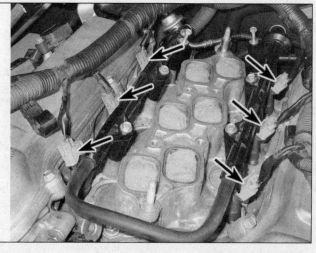

12   Remove the air filter housing (see Section 10).

13   Remove the upper intake manifold (see Chapter 2B).

14   Disconnect the fuel lines from the fuel rail (see Section 5).

15   Disconnect the fuel injector electrical connectors **(see illustration)** and remove the fuel rail mounting fasteners **(see illustration)**.

16   Remove the fuel rail with the fuel injectors attached **(see illustration)**.

17   Remove the fuel injector(s) from the fuel

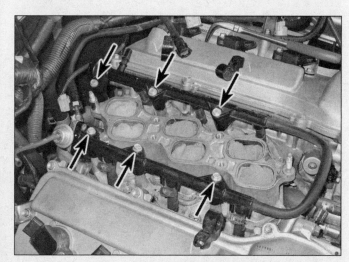

13.15b To detach the fuel rail from a V6 engine, remove these bolts

13.16 Remove the fuel rail and injectors as a single assembly (V6 models)

13.17 Remove each injector from the fuel rail (V6 models)

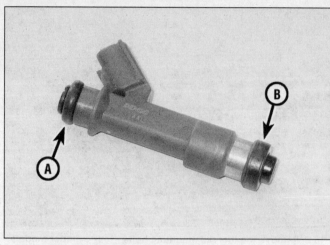

13.18 Remove the O-ring (A) and insulator (B) from each injector and discard them (always use a new ones when installing an injector) (V6 models)

rail and set them aside in a clearly labeled storage container **(see illustration)**.

18   If you intend to re-use the same injectors, replace the grommets and O-rings **(see illustration)**.

Installation

19   Installation of the fuel injectors is the reverse of removal.

20   Tighten the fuel rail mounting bolts to the torque listed in this Chapter's Specifications.

Chapter 5
Engine electrical systems

Contents

Specifications

Charging system

Charging voltage	13.5 to 15.0 volts
Standard amperage	
No load	10 amps or less
With load	30 amps or more

1 General information and precautions

General information

Ignition system

The electronic ignition system consists of the Crankshaft Position (CKP) sensor, the Camshaft Position (CMP) sensor, the Knock Sensor (KS), the Powertrain Control Module (PCM), the ignition switch, the battery, the individual ignition coils, and the spark plugs. For more information on the CKP, CMP and KS sensors, as well as the PCM, refer to Chapter 6.

Charging system

The charging system includes the alternator (with an integral voltage regulator), the Powertrain Control Module (PCM), the Body Control Module (BCM), a charge indicator light on the dash, the battery, a fuse or fusible link and the wiring connecting all of these components. The charging system supplies electrical power for the ignition system, the lights, the radio, etc. The alternator is driven by a drivebelt.

Starting system

The starting system consists of the battery, the ignition switch, the starter relay, the Powertrain Control Module (PCM), the Body Control Module (BCM), the Transmission Range (TR) switch, the starter motor and solenoid assembly, and the wiring connecting all of the components.

Precautions

Always observe the following precautions when working on the electrical system:

a) *Be extremely careful when servicing engine electrical components. They are easily damaged if checked, connected or handled improperly.*

b) *Never leave the ignition switched on for long periods of time when the engine is not running.*

c) *Never disconnect the battery cables while the engine is running.*

d) *Maintain correct polarity when connecting battery cables from another vehicle during jump starting - see the "Booster battery (jump) starting" Section at the front of this manual.*

e) *Always disconnect the cable from the negative battery terminal before working on the electrical system, but read the battery disconnection procedure first (see Section 3).*

It's also a good idea to review the safety-related information regarding the engine electrical systems located in the *Safety first!* Section at the front of this manual before beginning any operation included in this Chapter.

Electrical system components - four-cylinder models

1 Battery
2 Alternator
3 Starter (under air inlet housing)

4 Ignition coils
5 Underhood fuse/relay block

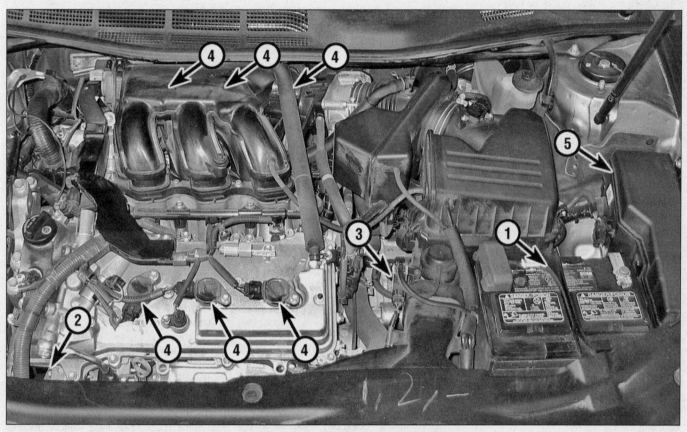

Electrical system components - V6 models

1   Battery
2   Alternator
3   Starter (under air inlet duct and air
    filter housing)

4   Ignition coils (back three under intake
    plenum)
5   Underhood fuse/relay block

2   Troubleshooting

Ignition system

1   If a malfunction occurs in the ignition system, do not immediately assume that any particular part is causing the problem. First, check the following items:

a) *Make sure that the cable clamps at the battery terminals are clean and tight.*
b) *Test the condition of the battery (see Steps 21 through 24). If it doesn't pass all the tests, replace it.*
c) *Check the ignition coil or coil pack connections.*
d) *Check any relevant fuses in the engine compartment fuse and relay box (see Chapter 12). If they're burned, determine the cause and repair the circuit.*

Check

Refer to illustration 2.3

Warning: *Because of the high voltage generated by the ignition system, use extreme care when performing a procedure involving ignition components.*

Note 1: *The ignition system components on these vehicles are difficult to diagnose. In the event of ignition system failure that you can't diagnose, have the vehicle tested at a dealer service department or other qualified auto repair facility.*

Note 2: *You'll need a spark tester for the following test. Spark testers are available at most auto supply stores.*

2   If the engine turns over but won't start, verify that there is sufficient ignition voltage to fire the spark plugs as follows.

3   On models with a coil-over-plug type ignition system, remove a coil and install the tester between the boot at the lower end of the coil and the spark plug **(see illustration)**. On models with spark plug wires, disconnect a spark plug wire from a spark plug and install the tester between the spark plug wire boot and the spark plug.

4   Crank the engine and note whether or not the tester flashes. **Caution:** *Do NOT crank the engine or allow it to run for more than five seconds; running the engine for more than five seconds may set a Diagnostic Trouble Code (DTC) for a cylinder misfire.*

Models with a coil-over-plug type ignition system

5   If the tester flashes during cranking, the coil is delivering sufficient voltage to the spark plug to fire it. Repeat this test for each cylinder to verify that the other coils are OK.

6   If the tester doesn't flash, remove a coil from another cylinder and swap it for the one being tested. If the tester now flashes, you know that the original coil is bad. If the tester still doesn't flash, the PCM or wiring harness is probably defective. Have the PCM checked out by a dealer service department or other qualified repair shop (testing the PCM is beyond the scope of the do-it-your-

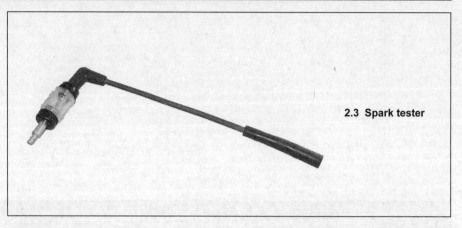

2.3 Spark tester

selfer because it requires expensive special tools).

7   If the tester flashes during cranking but a misfire code (related to the cylinder being tested) has been stored, the spark plug could be fouled or defective.

Models with spark plug wires

8   If the tester flashes during cranking, sufficient voltage is reaching the spark plug to fire it.

9   Repeat this test on the remaining cylinders.

10   Proceed on this basis until you have verified that there's a good spark from each spark plug wire. If there is, then you have verified that the coils in the coil pack are functioning correctly and that the spark plug wires are OK.

11   If there is no spark from a spark plug wire, then either the coil is bad, the plug wire is bad or a connection at one end of the plug wire is loose. Assuming that you're using new plug wires or known good wires, then the coil is probably defective. Also inspect the coil pack electrical connector. Make sure that it's clean, tight and in good condition.

12   If all the coils are firing correctly, but the engine misfires, then one or more of the plugs might be fouled. Remove and check the spark plugs or install new ones (see Chapter 1).

13   No further testing of the ignition system is possible without special tools. If the problem persists, have the ignition system tested by a dealer service department or other qualified repair shop.

Charging system

14   If a malfunction occurs in the charging system, do not automatically assume the alternator is causing the problem. First check the following items:

a) *Check the drivebelt tension and condition, as described in Chapter 1. Replace it if it's worn or deteriorated.*
b) *Make sure the alternator mounting bolts are tight.*
c) *Inspect the alternator wiring harness and the connectors at the alternator and voltage regulator. They must be in good condition, tight and have no corrosion.*

d) *Check the fusible link (if equipped) or main fuse in the underhood fuse/relay box. If it is burned, determine the cause, repair the circuit and replace the link or fuse (the vehicle will not start and/or the accessories will not work if the fusible link or main fuse is blown).*
e) *Start the engine and check the alternator for abnormal noises (a shrieking or squealing sound indicates a bad bearing).*
f) *Check the battery. Make sure it's fully charged and in good condition (one bad cell in a battery can cause overcharging by the alternator).*
g) *Disconnect the battery cables (negative first, then positive). Inspect the battery posts and the cable clamps for corrosion. Clean them thoroughly if necessary (see Chapter 1). Reconnect the cables (positive first, negative last).*

Alternator - check

15   Use a voltmeter to check the battery voltage with the engine off. It should be at least 12.6 volts **(see illustration 2.21)**.

16   Start the engine and check the battery voltage again. It should now be approximately 13.5 to 15 volts.

17   If the voltage reading is more or less than the specified charging voltage, the voltage regulator is probably defective, which will require replacement of the alternator (the voltage regulator is not replaceable separately). Remove the alternator and have it bench tested (most auto parts stores will do this for you).

18   The charging system (battery) light on the instrument cluster lights up when the ignition key is turned to ON, but it should go out when the engine starts.

19   If the charging system light stays on after the engine has been started, there is a problem with the charging system. Before replacing the alternator, check the battery condition, alternator belt tension and electrical cable connections.

20   If replacing the alternator doesn't restore voltage to the specified range, have the charging system tested by a dealer service department or other qualified repair shop.

2.21 To test the open circuit voltage of the battery, touch the black probe of the voltmeter to the negative terminal and the red probe to the positive terminal of the battery; a fully charged battery should be at least 12.6 volts

2.23 Connect a battery load tester to the battery and check the battery condition under load following the tool manufacturer's instructions

Battery - check

Refer to illustrations 2.21 and 2.23

21   Check the battery state of charge. Visually inspect the indicator eye on the top of the battery (if equipped with one); if the indicator eye is black in color, charge the battery as described in Chapter 1. Next perform an open circuit voltage test using a digital voltmeter. **Note:** *The battery's surface charge must be removed before accurate voltage measurements can be made. Turn on the high beams for ten seconds, then turn them off and let the vehicle stand for two minutes.* With the engine and all accessories Off, touch the negative probe of the voltmeter to the negative terminal of the battery and the positive probe to the positive terminal of the battery **(see illustration)**. The battery voltage should be 12.6 volts or slightly above. If the battery is less than the specified voltage, charge the battery before proceeding to the next test. Do not proceed with the battery load test unless the battery charge is correct.

22   Disconnect the negative battery cable, then the positive cable from the battery.

23   Perform a battery load test. An accurate check of the battery condition can only be performed with a load tester **(see illustration)**. This test evaluates the ability of the battery to operate the starter and other accessories during periods of high current draw. Connect the load tester to the battery terminals. Load test the battery according to the tool manufacturer's instructions. This tool increases the load demand (current draw) on the battery.

24   Maintain the load on the battery for 15 seconds and observe that the battery voltage does not drop below 9.6 volts. If the battery condition is weak or defective, the tool will indicate this condition immediately. **Note:** *Cold temperatures will cause the minimum voltage reading to drop slightly. Follow the chart given in the manufacturer's instructions to compensate for cold climates. Minimum load voltage for freezing temperatures (32 degrees F) should be approximately 9.1 volts.*

Starting system

The starter rotates, but the engine doesn't

25   Remove the starter (see Section 8). Check the overrunning clutch and bench test the starter to make sure the drive mechanism extends fully for proper engagement with the flywheel ring gear. If it doesn't, replace the starter.

26   Check the flywheel ring gear for missing teeth and other damage. With the ignition turned off, rotate the flywheel so you can check the entire ring gear.

The starter is noisy

27   If the solenoid is making a chattering noise, first check the battery (see Steps 21 through 24). If the battery is okay, check the cables and connections.

28   If you hear a grinding, crashing metallic sound when you turn the key to Start, check for loose starter mounting bolts. If they're tight, remove the starter and inspect the teeth on the starter pinion gear and flywheel ring gear. Look for missing or damaged teeth.

29   If the starter sounds fine when you first turn the key to Start, but then stops rotating the engine and emits a zinging sound, the problem is probably a defective starter drive that's not staying engaged with the ring gear. Replace the starter.

The starter rotates slowly

30   Check the battery (see Steps 21 through 24).

31   If the battery is okay, verify all connections (at the battery, the starter solenoid and motor) are clean, corrosion-free and tight. Make sure the cables aren't frayed or damaged.

32   Check that the starter mounting bolts are tight so it grounds properly. Also check the pinion gear and flywheel ring gear for evidence of a mechanical bind (galling, deformed gear teeth or other damage).

The starter does not rotate at all

33   Check the battery (see Steps 21 through 24).

34   If the battery is okay, verify all connections (at the battery, the starter solenoid and motor) are clean, corrosion-free and tight. Make sure the cables aren't frayed or damaged.

35   Check all of the fuses in the underhood fuse/relay box.

36   Check that the starter mounting bolts are tight so it grounds properly.

37   Check for voltage at the starter solenoid "S" terminal when the ignition key is turned to the start position. If voltage is present, replace the starter/solenoid assembly. If no voltage is present, the problem could be the starter relay, the Transmission Range (TR) switch (see Chapter 6) or clutch start switch (see Chapter 8), or with an electrical connector somewhere in the circuit (see the wiring diagrams at the end of Chapter 12). Also, on many modern vehicles, the Powertrain Control Module (PCM) and the Body Control Module (BCM) control the voltage signal to the starter solenoid; on such vehicles a special scan tool is required for diagnosis.

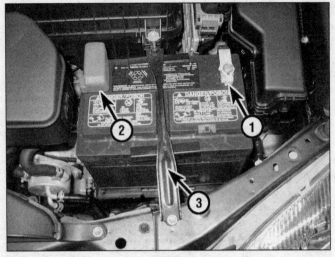

4.2 Battery details:

1   Negative battery cable   3   Battery hold-down clamp
2   Positive battery cable

**6.2   Remove the engine cover from the ballstuds by pulling up
from the rear, then the front**

3   Battery - disconnection and reconnection

Caution: *Always disconnect the cable from the negative battery terminal FIRST and hook it up LAST or the battery may be shorted by the tool being used to loosen the cable clamps.*

Caution: *Once the ignition switch is turned Off, always wait at least 90 seconds before disconnecting the negative battery cable. Several systems (the radio, time display, navigation system, parking assist, etc.) need this time to record memory and various settings before the power is disconnected.*

1   Some systems on the vehicle require battery power to be available at all times, either to maintain continuous operation (alarm system, power door locks, etc.), or to maintain control unit memory (radio station presets, Powertrain Control Module and other control units). When the battery is disconnected, the power that maintains these systems is cut. So, before you disconnect the battery, please note that on a vehicle with power door locks, it's a wise precaution to remove the key from the ignition and to keep it with you, so that it does not get locked inside if the power door locks should engage accidentally when the battery is reconnected!

2   Devices known as "memory-savers" can be used to avoid some of these problems. Precise details vary according to the device used. The typical memory saver is plugged into the cigarette lighter and is connected to a spare battery. Then the vehicle battery can be disconnected from the electrical system. The memory saver will provide sufficient current to maintain audio unit security codes, PCM memory, etc. and will provide power to always hot circuits such as the clock and radio memory circuits. **Warning:** *Some memory savers deliver a considerable amount of current in order to keep vehicle systems operational after the main battery is disconnected. If you're using a memory saver, make sure that the circuit concerned is actually open before servicing it.* **Warning:** *If you're going to work near any of the airbag system components, the battery MUST be disconnected and a memory saver must NOT be used. If a memory saver is used, power will be supplied to the airbag, which means that it could accidentally deploy and cause serious personal injury.*

3   To disconnect the battery for service procedures requiring power to be cut from the vehicle, loosen the cable end bolt and disconnect the cable from the negative battery terminal. Isolate the cable end to prevent it from coming into accidental contact with the battery terminal.

4   Several relearn procedures must be performed on certain models after the battery is reconnected. These include:

• Correcting steering angle neutral point
• Power window initialization
• Sunroof initialization
• Smart access
• Power trunk lid operation

Correcting steering angle neutral point (2012 and later Camry models, and 2013 and later Avalon and ES350 models)

5   Start the car and park it on a level surface.
6   Set the parking brake and move the shift lever to the P position.
7   Turn the steering wheel to the fully right position and then to the fully left position.

Power window initialization (2012 Avalon models)

8   Turn the ignition switch to On position.
9   If the window is fully closed, open it.
10   Pull up and hold the Auto Up switch, and completely close the window. Continue to hold up the Auto Up switch for at least 1 second after the window completely closes and then release the Auto Up switch.

Sunroof Initialization and check (2012 Avalon models)

11   Turn the ignition switch to the On position.
12   Operate the sunroof by holding the Tilt Up switch until the roof glass complete tilts upward.

Smart Access Learning (2012 and later ES350 models)

13   Activate the main body ECU by performing a wireless door unlock or lock operation.
14   If the battery had been completely discharged, initialize the steering lock system by performing Steps 18 through 20.
15   Move the shift lever to the P position.
16   Turn the engine switch off, and open the driver's side door.
17   Depress the brake pedal, and press the START STOP switch.
18   To start the engine after the battery is reconnected, open and closed the driver's side door. Wait 10 seconds or more, and then try to start the engine.

Note: *The first start attempt will fail. This is normal. The steering lock ECU must learn the steering lock position. The engine can be started upon the second or subsequent start attempt.*

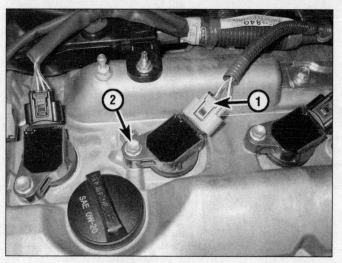

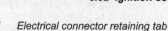

6.5a Ignition coil details

1   *Electrical connector retaining tab*
2   *Mounting bolt*

6.5b The individual ignition coil boot directly mounts over each spark plug

Power Lid Reset (2013 and later ES350 models)

Note: *Initialization is not necessary if the luggage compartment door was closed when the negative battery terminal was disconnected.*
19   Manually close the luggage compartment door once.
20   Press the luggage door open switch, and confirm that the door opens.
21   Insert a piece of wood or some other object into the trunk, and press the door control switch. Confirm that the luggage compartment door immediately reverses direction once it contacts the wood.

4   Battery - removal and installation

Refer to illustration 4.2
1   If equipped, remove the fasteners securing the battery cover, then remove the cover and set it aside.
2   Disconnect the cable from the negative battery terminal first, then disconnect the cable from the positive battery terminal **(see illustration)**.
3   Remove the battery hold-down clamp.
4   Lift out the battery. Be careful - it's heavy.
Note: *Battery straps and handlers are available at most auto parts stores for reasonable prices. They make it easier to remove and carry the battery.*
5   If you are replacing the battery, make sure you get one that's identical, with the same dimensions, amperage rating, cold cranking rating, etc.
6   Installation is the reverse of removal. Be sure to connect the positive cable first and the negative cable last.

5   Battery cables - replacement

1   When removing the cables, always disconnect the cable from the negative battery terminal first and hook it up last, or you might accidentally short out the battery with the tool you're using to loosen the cable clamps. Even if you're only replacing the cable for the positive terminal, be sure to disconnect the negative cable from the battery first.
2   Disconnect the old cables from the battery, then trace each of them to their opposite ends and disconnect them. Be sure to note the routing of each cable before disconnecting it to ensure correct installation.
3   If you are replacing any of the old cables, take them with you when buying new cables. It is vitally important that you replace the cables with identical parts.
4   Clean the threads of the solenoid or ground connection with a wire brush to remove rust and corrosion. Apply a light coat of battery terminal corrosion inhibitor or petroleum jelly to the threads to prevent future corrosion.
5   Attach the cable to the solenoid or ground connection and tighten the mounting nut/bolt securely.
6   Before connecting a new cable to the battery, make sure that it reaches the battery post without having to be stretched.
7   Connect the cable to the positive battery terminal first, *then* connect the ground cable to the negative battery terminal.

6   Ignition coil(s) - replacement

1   Disconnect the cable from the negative battery terminal (see Section 3).

Four-cylinder engines

Refer to illustration 6.2
2   On 2009 and earlier models, remove the engine cover mounting fasteners and lift the engine cover off. On 2010 and later models, lift the engine cover up from the rear, then the front and remove the cover from the mounting pins **(see illustration)**.

V6 engines

3   Pry the engine cover up from the rear and remove the cover from the mounting pins.
4   Remove the upper intake manifold (see Chapter 2B) to access the rear ignition coils.

All models

Refer to illustrations 6.5a and 6.5b
5   Each ignition coil/igniter assembly is secured by one bolt **(see illustration)**. Unscrew the bolt, disconnect the electrical connector and pull the coil/igniter assembly straight up, using a twisting motion **(see illustration)**.
6   Installation is the reverse of removal.

7   Alternator - removal and installation

1   Disconnect the cable from the negative battery terminal (see Section 3).

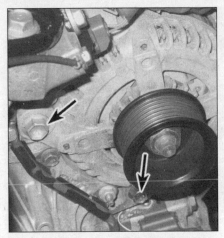

7.5 Alternator mounting bolt locations - four-cylinder model shown

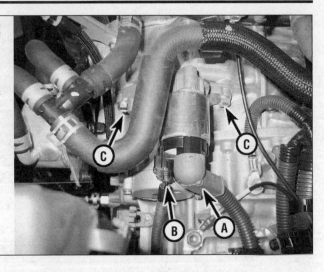

8.4 Starter motor details

A   Positive battery cable connection
B   Solenoid electrical connection
C   Starter mounting bolts 9.47 Short-pin fuse location

Four-cylinder engines

Refer to illustration 7.5

2   Raise the vehicle and support it securely on jackstands.
3   Remove the drivebelt (see Chapter 1).
4   Detach the electrical connectors from the alternator.
5   Remove the alternator mounting bolts and harness clamps **(see illustration)**.
6   Remove the alternator from the mounting bracket.

V6 engines

7   Loosen the right-front wheel lug nuts, then raise the vehicle and support it securely on jackstands.
8   Remove the right front wheel.
9   Remove the lower engine cover(s).
10   Remove the fender inner liner (see Chapter 11).
11   Remove the drivebelt (see Chapter 1).
12   Remove the upper engine covers.
13   Remove the air cleaner and inlet assembly (see Chapter 4).
14   Remove the front bumper assembly (see Chapter 11).
15   Drain the engine coolant.
16   Remove the coolant expansion tank mounting fasteners and set the tank to the side (see Chapter 3).
17   Remove the radiator (see Chapter 3).
18   Detach the electrical connectors from the alternator.
19   Remove the alternator mounting bolts and harness clamps.
20   Remove the alternator from the mounting bracket.

Installation

21   If you are replacing the alternator, take the old alternator with you when purchasing a replacement unit. Make sure that the new/rebuilt unit is identical to the old alternator. Look at the terminals - they should be the same in number, size and locations as the terminals on the old alternator. Finally, look at the

identification markings - they will be stamped in the housing or printed on a tag or plaque affixed to the housing. Make sure that these numbers are the same on both alternators.
22   Many new/rebuilt alternators do not have a pulley installed, so you may have to switch the pulley from the old unit to the new/rebuilt one. When buying an alternator, find out the shop's policy regarding installation of pulleys - some shops will perform this service free of charge.
23   Installation is the reverse of removal.
24   Check the charging voltage to verify proper operation of the alternator (see Section 2).

8   Starter motor - removal and installation

Refer to illustration 8.4

1   Disconnect the cable from the negative battery terminal (see Section 3).
2   Remove the engine cover(s).
3   Remove the air filter housing and air inlet duct (see Chapter 4).
4   Detach the electrical connectors from the starter/solenoid assembly **(see illustration)**.
5   Remove the starter motor mounting bolts. Remove the starter motor assembly from the engine compartment.
6   Installation is the reverse of removal.

9   Repair Initialization (2012 and later models)

1   When certain parts are replaced or serviced, the system that controls or monitors those parts must be initialized before the vehicle is returned to service. During initialization, controllers relearn particular settings so they can effectively operate the parts in question. To initialize a particular system, find that system in this section, locate the replaced part(s) and/or the problem that was repaired, and perform the indicated procedure.

Note: *On 2012 and later models, electrical power is turned on or off by either an ignition switch or an engine switch. Once initialization has started, do not turn off the ignition switch or the engine switch until initialization has been completed. Doing so interrupts the process. You will have to start again.*

Power Window Control System Initialization

2   The power window control system must be initialized whenever a door window regulator assembly, power window regulator motor, door glass, or door-glass run has been replaced or reinstalled.
3   A diagnostic trouble code is set whenever a power window regulator motor has been replaced. Clear the DTC after initialization is completed.
4   During initialization, use the power window switch of each door to initialize each power window.
5   Park the vehicle on a level surface, and turn off all electrical systems before beginning initialization.

Power window regulator motor replacement or when the window glass unexpectedly reverses or stops

6   Connect the battery, and turn on the ignition switch or the engine switch.
7   Completely open the window by pressing and holding the multiplex network master switch, power window regulator switch or the rear power window regulator switch. Continue to hold the switch for at least 1 second after the window has completely opened.
8   Completely close the window by lifting and holding the multiplex network master switch, power window regulator switch or the rear power window regulator switch. Continue to hold the switch for at least 1 second after the window has completely closed. This resets the glass position and completes initialization for the first door. Repeat for each of the remaining doors.

Power window regulator motor removal/installation; door glass or glass run removal/ installation or replacement

9   Connect the battery, and turn on the ignition switch or the engine switch.

10   Completely close the window by lifting and holding the multiplex network master switch, power window regulator switch or the rear power window regulator switch. Continue to hold the switch for at least 6 seconds after the window has completely closed.

11   Completely open the window by pressing and holding the multiplex network master switch, power window regulator switch or the rear power window regulator switch. Continue to hold the switch for at least 1 second after the window has completely opened.

12   Release the multiplex network master switch, power window regulator switch or the rear power window regulator switch, and then press and hold the switch down for 4 seconds or more.

13   Completely close the window by lifting and holding the multiplex network master switch, power window regulator switch or the rear power window regulator switch. Continue to hold the switch for at least 1 second after the window has completely closed. This resets the glass position and completes initialization for the first door. Repeat for each remaining door.

Sunroof ECU Initialization

14   The sunroof ECU must be initialized whenever the roof glass or roof drive cable subassembly is adjusted or removed and installed, or when the sliding roof drive gear is replaced.

Auto slide open and close/tilt up and down functions do not operate

15   Turn on the ignition switch or the engine switch.

All 2012 and later models except 2013 and later ES350 models with a glass roof

16   Completely close the roof, and release the roof switch.

17   Press and hold the close or up switch. The roof should tilt up, pause for 1 second, tilt down, slide open and then slide closed. Once the system completes this operation, release the switch. The initialization is completed.

18   Confirm that the sliding roof auto function works normally.

2013 and later ES350 models with a glass roof

19   Press and hold the close or down switch. The roof should slide to its fully closed position.

20   Continue to hold the close or down switch, and confirm that the roof opens and stops again at the fully closed position.

Release the close or down switch. The initialization is completed.

21   Confirm that the sliding roof auto function works properly.

If the roof automatically moves but does not stop at the correct position or the roof reverses direction during tilt down operation

22   Turn the on ignition switch or the engine switch.

All 2012 and later models except 2013 and later ES350 models with a glass roof

23   Press and hold the up switch until the roof slides to the fully tilted up position and release the switch.

24   Again press the hold the up switch. The roof should pause for approximately 10 seconds or more, tilt inching motion, pause for 1 second, tilt down, slide open and then slide to the closed position. Release the up switch. The initialization is completed.

25   Confirm that the sliding roof auto function works properly.

2013 and later ES350 models with a glass roof

26   Press and hold the close or down switch. The roof should tilt down, move in the reverse direction, pause for approximately 10 seconds or more, tilt down, and stop at its fully closed position.

27   Continue to hold the close or down switch, and confirm that the roof opens and stops again at the fully closed position. Release the close or down switch. The initialization process is completed.

28   Confirm that the sliding roof auto function works properly.

The roof automatically moves, but reverses direction during the close operation

29   Turn on the ignition switch or the engine switch.

All 2012 and later models except 2013 and later ES350 models with a glass roof

30   Press and hold the close switch until the roof slides closed, moves in the reverse direction, pauses for approximately 10 seconds or more, slides closed, tilts up, pauses for 1 second, tilts down, slides open and finally slides fully closed. Release the close switch. The initialization process is completed.

31   Confirm that the sliding roof auto function works properly.

2013 and later ES350 models with a glass roof

32   Press and hold the down switch. When the roof stops sliding, release the switch.

33   Press and hold the down switch. The roof pauses for approximately 10 seconds or more and then stops at the fully closed position. Once the roof stops, confirm that the roof move again and stops at the fully closed position. The initialization process is completed.

34   Confirm that the sliding roof auto function works properly.

Drive parts or roof glass removed and installed or replaced (2012 ES350 models)

35   When replacing the sliding roof drive gear, initialize the roof ECU by turning the engine switch On and performing Steps 19 through 21.

36   When replacing drive parts and the roof glass without replacing the sliding roof drive gear and the sliding roof glass works automatically, initialize the roof ECU by turning the engine switch on and performing Steps 26 through 28. If the glass does not work automatically, perform the Steps 19 through 21.

Headlight leveling ECU (All 2012 and later Camry models and 2013 and later Avalon and ES350 models)

37   Initialize the headlight leveling ECU whenever the headlight leveling ECU assembly has been replaced, after the vehicle height has changed due to replacement or service of suspension components, and after the removal/installation or replacement of the rear height control sensor subassembly.

Pre-initialization preparation

38   Unload the vehicle and the trunk. Make sure no one is in the vehicle, and confirm that the spare tire, jack and tools are in their original positions in the trunk.

39   Park the vehicle on a level surface and confirm that the headlights are turned off.

40   Turn on the ignition switch or the engine switch, and check the headlight leveling system indicator light.

a) *If the headlight leveling ECU assembly has been replaced, the indicator light should repeatedly flash 6 times at a rate of 2 cycles per second.*

b) *If the rear height control sensor subassembly has been serviced or replaced or if a suspension part has been replaced, the indicator light should turn on for approximately 3 seconds and then turn off.*

41   Also note the position of the needle on the fuel gauge. During initialization, you must turn the light switch on and off a certain number of times. The position of the fuel gauge needle determines that number. If the needle indicates less than empty, turn the light switch on and off once during initialization. If the needle sits between empty and ¼ full, cycle the switch on and off twice; if the needle sits between ¼ and ½ full, cycle the switch on and off 3 times; cycle the switch 4 times if the

needle sits between ½ and ¾ full, and cycle the light switch on and off 5 times if the needle sits between ¾ full and full.

Initialization

42   Use a jumper wire to connect terminals 4 (CG) and 8 (LVL) of the data link connector (DLC3).

43 While standing outside the vehicle, use the light switch to turn the low beams on and off the number of times indicated by the fuel gauge needle (see Step 41). Start within 20 seconds after connecting the data link terminals, and cycle the switch on and off at less than 3 second intervals.

44   Check the headlight leveling system indicator light. If the headlight leveling ECU assembly has been replaced, the indicator light should repeatedly flash 6 times at a rate of 2 cycles per second and then repeatedly flash the same number of times that the low beam switch was cycled on and off. If the rear height control sensor subassembly has been serviced or replaced or if vehicle height has changed because a suspension part was replaced, the indicator light should remain off and then repeatedly flash the same number of times that the low beam switch was cycled on and off.

45 Initialization is completed.

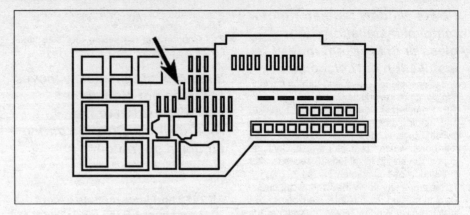

9.47 Short-pin fuse location (2012 ES350 models)

Steering lock ECU (2012 ES350 models)

46   On 2012 ES350 models with a smart access system and also a push-button start function, the starter may not operate after the battery has been charged or if the vehicle was jump-started. If either has occurred, initialize the steering lock ECU by performing the following.

47   Confirm that the short-pin fuse has been installed in the engine compartment fuse/ relay box **(see illustration)**. If it is not, install it now.

48   Move the shift lever to the P position, turn the engine switch Off, and open the driver's door. The initialization process has begun.

49   Press the brake pedal, and press the start/stop switch.

50   Initialization is completed.

Notes

Notes

Chapter 6
Emissions and engine control systems

Contents

1 General information

To prevent pollution of the atmosphere from incompletely burned and evaporating gases, and to maintain good driveability and fuel economy, a number of emission control systems are incorporated. They include the:

Catalytic converter

A catalytic converter is an emission control device in the exhaust system that reduces certain pollutants in the exhaust gas stream. There are two types of converters: oxidation converters and reduction converters.

Oxidation converters contain a monolithic substrate (a ceramic honeycomb) coated with the semi-precious metals platinum and palla-dium. An oxidation catalyst reduces unburned hydrocarbons (HC) and carbon monoxide (CO) by adding oxygen to the exhaust stream as it passes through the substrate, which, in the presence of high temperature and the catalyst materials, converts the HC and CO to water vapor (H_2O) and carbon dioxide (CO_2).

Reduction converters contain a monolithic substrate coated with platinum and rhodium. A reduction catalyst reduces oxides of nitrogen (NOx) by removing oxygen, which in the presence of high temperature and the catalyst material produces nitrogen (N) and carbon dioxide (CO_2).

Catalytic converters that combine both types of catalysts in one assembly are known as "three-way catalysts" or TWCs. A TWC can reduce all three pollutants.

Evaporative Emissions Control (EVAP) system

The Evaporative Emissions Control (EVAP) system prevents fuel system vapors (which contain unburned hydrocarbons) from escaping into the atmosphere. On warm days, vapors trapped inside the fuel tank expand until the pressure reaches a certain threshold. Then the fuel vapors are routed from the fuel tank through the fuel vapor vent valve and the fuel vapor control valve to the EVAP canister, where they're stored temporarily until the next time the vehicle is operated. When the conditions are right (engine warmed up, vehicle up to speed, moderate or heavy load on the engine, etc.) the PCM opens the canister purge valve, which allows fuel vapors to be drawn from the canister into the intake manifold. Once in the intake manifold, the fuel vapors mix with incoming air before being drawn through the intake ports into the combustion chambers where they're burned up with the rest of the air/fuel mixture. The EVAP system is complex and virtually impossible to troubleshoot without the right tools and training.

Exhaust Gas Recirculation (EGR) system

The EGR system reduces oxides of nitrogen by recirculating exhaust gases from the exhaust manifold, through the EGR valve and intake manifold, then back to the combustion chambers, where it mixes with the incoming air/fuel mixture before being consumed. These recirculated exhaust gases dilute the incoming air/fuel mixture, which cools the combustion chambers, thereby reducing NOx emissions.

The EGR system consists of the Powertrain Control Module (PCM), the EGR valve, the EGR valve position sensor and various other information sensors that the PCM uses to determine when to open the EGR valve. The degree to which the EGR valve is opened is referred to as "EGR valve lift." The PCM is programmed to produce the ideal EGR valve lift for varying operating conditions. The EGR valve position sensor, which is an integral part of the EGR valve, detects the amount of EGR valve lift

and sends this information to the PCM. The PCM then compares it with the appropriate EGR valve lift for the operating conditions. The PCM increases current flow to the EGR valve to increase valve lift and reduces the current to reduce the amount of lift. If EGR flow is inappropriate to the operating conditions (idle, cold engine, etc.) the PCM simply cuts the current to the EGR valve and the valve closes.

Secondary Air Injection (AIR) system

Some models are equipped with a secondary air injection (AIR) system. The secondary air injection system is used to reduce tailpipe emissions on initial engine start-up. The system uses an electric motor/pump assembly, relay, vacuum valve/solenoid, air shut-off valve, check valves and tubing to inject fresh air directly into the exhaust manifolds. The fresh air (oxygen) reacts with the exhaust gas in the catalytic converter to reduce HC and CO levels. The air pump and solenoid are controlled by the PCM through the AIR relay. During initial start-up, the PCM energizes the AIR relay, the relay supplies battery voltage to the air pump and the vacuum valve/solenoid, engine vacuum is applied to the air shut-off valve which opens and allows air to flow through the tubing into the exhaust manifolds. The PCM will operate the air pump until closed loop operation is

reached (approximately four minutes). During normal operation, the check valves prevent exhaust backflow into the system.

Powertrain Control Module (PCM)

The Powertrain Control Module (PCM) is the brain of the engine management system. It also controls a wide variety of other vehicle systems. In order to program the new PCM, the dealer needs the vehicle as well as the new PCM. If you're planning to replace the PCM with a new one, there is no point in trying to do so at home because you won't be able to program it yourself.

Positive Crankcase Ventilation (PCV) system

The Positive Crankcase Ventilation (PCV) system reduces hydrocarbon emissions by scavenging crankcase vapors, which are rich in unburned hydrocarbons. A PCV valve or orifice regulates the flow of gases into the intake manifold in proportion to the amount of intake vacuum available.

The PCV system generally consists of the fresh air inlet hose, the PCV valve or orifice and the crankcase ventilation hose (or PCV hose). The fresh air inlet hose connects the air intake duct to a pipe on the valve cover. The crankcase ventilation hose (or PCV hose) connects the PCV valve or orifice in the valve cover to the intake manifold.

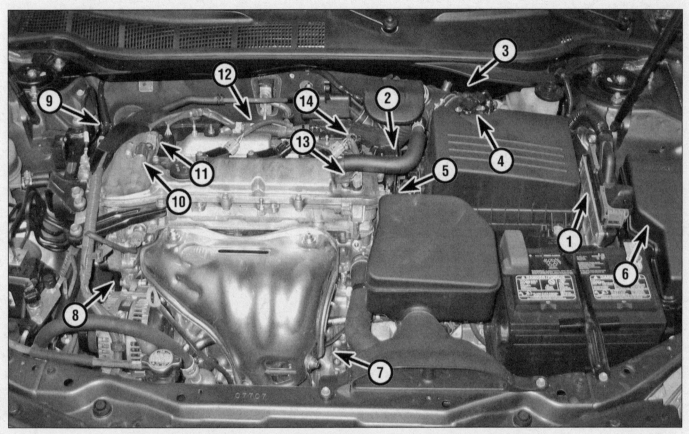

Emissions and engine control system components - 2010 and later four-cylinder models

1	Powertrain Control Module (PCM)	7	Oxygen sensor/Air-fuel ratio sensor (bank 1, sensor 1)
2	Throttle body	8	Crankshaft Position (CKP) sensor
3	Canister Purge Vacuum Switching Valve (VSV)	9	Vacuum Switching Valve (VSV) for ACIS
4	Mass Air Flow (MAF) sensor	10	Camshaft Oil Control Valve assembly (exhaust camshaft)
5	Engine Coolant Temperature (ECT) sensor	11	Camshaft Oil Control Valve assembly (intake camshaft)
6	Engine compartment fuse and relay box		

12	Knock sensor (located underneath the intake manifold)
13	Camshaft Position (CMP) sensor (exhaust side)
14	Camshaft Position (CMP) sensor (intake side)

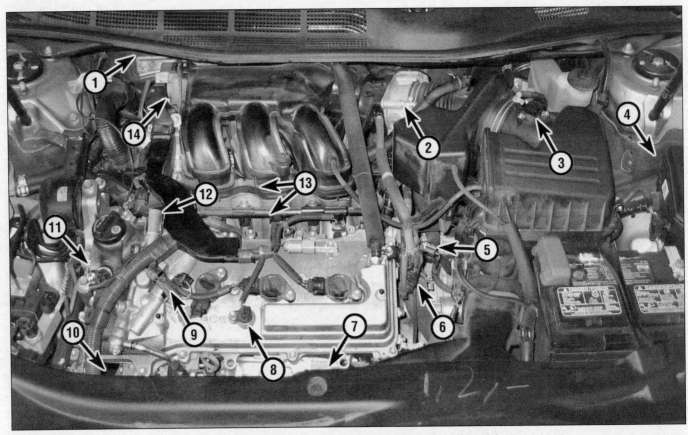

Emissions and engine control system components - V6 models

1   Powertrain Control Module (PCM)
2   Throttle body
3   Mass Air Flow (MAF) sensor
4   Engine compartment fuse and relay box
5   Engine Coolant Temperature (ECT) sensor
6   Canister Purge Vacuum Switching Valve (VSV)

7   Oxygen sensor/Air-fuel ratio sensor (bank 2, sensor 1)
8   Variable Valve Timing sensor (VVT) for the exhaust camshaft (bank 2)
9   Camshaft Timing Oil Control Valve assembly (bank 2, exhaust side)
10 Crankshaft Position (CKP) sensor

11 Variable Valve Timing sensor (VVT) for the intake camshaft (bank 2)
12 Camshaft Timing Oil Control Valve assembly (bank 2, intake side)
13 Knock sensors (located underneath the intake manifold)
14 ACIS actuator

Information Sensors

Accelerator Pedal Position (APP) sensor - as you press the accelerator pedal, the APP sensor alters its voltage signal to the PCM in proportion to the angle of the pedal, and the PCM commands a motor inside the throttle body to open or close the throttle plate accordingly

Camshaft Position (CMP) sensor - produces a signal that the PCM uses to identify the number 1 cylinder and to time the firing sequence of the fuel injectors

Crankshaft Position (CKP) sensor - produces a signal that the PCM uses to calculate engine speed and crankshaft position, which enables it to synchronize ignition timing with fuel injector timing, and to detect misfires

Engine Coolant Temperature (ECT) sensor - a thermistor (temperature-sensitive variable resistor) that sends a voltage signal to the PCM, which uses this data to determine the temperature of the engine coolant

Fuel tank pressure sensor - measures the fuel tank pressure and controls fuel tank pressure by signaling the EVAP system to purge the fuel tank vapors when the pressure becomes excessive

Intake Air Temperature (IAT) sensor - monitors the temperature of the air entering the engine and sends a signal to the PCM to determine injector pulse-width (the duration of each injector's on-time) and to adjust spark timing (to prevent spark knock)

Knock sensor - a piezoelectric crystal that oscillates in proportion to engine vibration which produces a voltage output that is monitored by the PCM. This retards the ignition timing when the oscillation exceeds a certain threshold

Manifold Absolute Pressure (MAP) sensor - monitors the pressure or vacuum inside the intake manifold. The PCM uses this data to determine engine load so that it can alter the ignition advance and fuel enrichment

Mass Air Flow (MAF) sensor - measures the amount of intake air drawn into the engine. It uses a hot-wire sensing element to measure the amount of air entering the engine

Oxygen sensors - generates a small variable voltage signal in proportion to the difference between the oxygen content in the exhaust stream and the oxygen content in the ambient air. The PCM uses this information to maintain the proper air/fuel ratio. A second oxygen sensor monitors the efficiency of the catalytic converter

Throttle Position (TP) sensor - a potentiometer that generates a voltage signal that varies in relation to the opening angle of the throttle plate inside the throttle body. Works with the PCM and other sensors to calculate injector pulse width (the duration of each injector's on-time)

Photos courtesy of Wells Manufacturing, except APP and MAF sensors.

2.4a Simple code readers are an economical way to extract trouble codes when the CHECK ENGINE light comes on

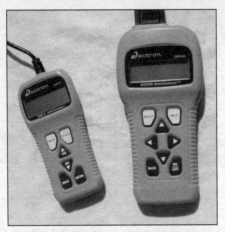

2.4b Hand-held scan tools like these can extract computer codes and also perform diagnostics

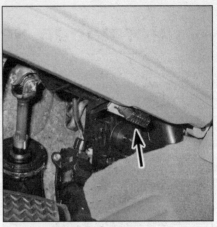

3.1 The Data Link Connector (DLC) is located under the lower edge of the dash

2   On Board Diagnosis (OBD) system

General description

1   All models are equipped with the second generation OBD-II system. This system consists of an on-board computer known as the Powertrain Control Module (PCM), and information sensors, which monitor various functions of the engine and send data to the PCM. This system incorporates a series of diagnostic monitors that detect and identify fuel injection and emissions control system faults and store the information in the computer memory. This system also tests sensors and output actuators, diagnoses drive cycles, freezes data and clears codes.

2   The PCM is the brain of the electronically controlled fuel and emissions system. It receives data from a number of sensors and other electronic components (switches, relays, etc.). Based on the information it receives, the PCM generates output signals to control various relays, solenoids (fuel injectors) and other actuators. The PCM is specifically calibrated to optimize the emissions, fuel economy and driveability of the vehicle.

3   It isn't a good idea to attempt diagnosis or replacement of the PCM or emission control components at home while the vehicle is under warranty. Because of a federally-mandated warranty which covers the emissions system components and because any owner-induced damage to the PCM, the sensors and/or the control devices may void this warranty, take the vehicle to a dealer service department if the PCM or a system component malfunctions.

Scan tool information

Refer to illustrations 2.4a and 2.4b

4   Because extracting the Diagnostic Trouble Codes (DTCs) from an engine management system is now the first step in troubleshooting many computer-controlled systems and components, a code reader, at the very least, will be required **(see illustration)**. More powerful scan tools can also perform many of the diagnostics once associated with expensive factory scan tools **(see illustration)**. If you're planning to obtain a generic scan tool for your vehicle, make sure that it's compatible with OBD-II systems. If you don't plan to purchase a code reader or scan tool and don't have access to one, you can have the codes extracted by a dealer service department or an independent repair shop. **Note:** *Some auto parts stores even provide this service.*

3   Obtaining and clearing Diagnostic Trouble Codes (DTCs)

All models covered by this manual are equipped with on-board diagnostics. When the PCM recognizes a malfunction in a monitored emission or engine control system, component or circuit, it turns on the Malfunction Indicator Light (MIL) on the dash. The PCM will continue to display the MIL until the problem is fixed and the Diagnostic Trouble Code (DTC) is cleared from the PCM's memory. You'll need a scan tool to access any DTCs stored in the PCM.

Before outputting any DTCs stored in the PCM, thoroughly inspect ALL electrical connectors and hoses. Make sure that all electrical connections are tight, clean and free of corrosion. And make sure that all hoses are correctly connected, fit tightly and are in good condition (no cracks or tears).

Accessing the DTCs

Refer to illustration 3.1

1   The Diagnostic Trouble Codes (DTCs) can only be accessed with a code reader or scan tool. Professional scan tools are expensive, but relatively inexpensive generic code readers or scan tools **(see illustrations 2.4a and 2.4b)** are available at most auto parts stores. Simply plug the connector of the scan tool into the diagnostic connector **(see illustration)**. Then follow the instructions included with the scan tool to extract the DTCs.

2   Once you have outputted all of the stored DTCs, look them up on the accompanying DTC chart.

3   After troubleshooting the source of each DTC, make any necessary repairs or replace the defective component(s).

Clearing the DTCs

4   Clear the DTCs with the code reader or scan tool in accordance with the instructions provided by the tool's manufacturer.

Diagnostic Trouble Codes

5   The accompanying tables are a list of the Diagnostic Trouble Codes (DTCs) that can be accessed by a do-it-yourselfer working at home (there are many, many more DTCs available to professional mechanics with proprietary scan tools and software, but those codes cannot be accessed by a generic scan tool). If, after you have checked and repaired the connectors, wire harness and vacuum hoses (if applicable) for an emission-related system, component or circuit, the problem persists, have the vehicle checked by a dealer service department or other qualified repair shop.

Diagnostic Trouble Codes

Code	Code identification
P0010	Camshaft position "A" actuator circuit (bank 1)
P0011	Camshaft position "A" - timing over-advanced or system performance (bank 1)
P0012	Camshaft position "A" - timing over-retarded (bank 1)
P0013	Camshaft position "B" actuator circuit open (bank 1)
P0014	Camshaft position "B" - timing over-advanced or system performance (bank 1)
P0015	Camshaft position "B" - timing over-retarded (bank 1)
P0016	Crankshaft position - camshaft position correlation (bank 1, sensor B)
P0017	Crankshaft position - camshaft position correlation (bank 1, sensor B)
P0018	Crankshaft position - camshaft position correlation (bank 2, sensor A)
P0019	Crankshaft position - camshaft position correlation (bank 2, sensor B)
P0020	Camshaft position "A" actuator circuit (bank 2)
P0021	Camshaft position "A" - timing over-advanced or system performance (bank 2)
P0022	Camshaft position "A" - timing over-retarded (bank 2)
P0023	Camshaft position "B" actuator circuit or open (bank 2)
P0024	Camshaft position "B" - timing over-advanced or system performance (bank 2)
P0025	Camshaft position "B" - timing over-retarded (bank 2)
P0031	Oxygen (A/F) sensor heater control circuit low (bank 1, sensor 1)
P0032	Oxygen (A/F) sensor heater control circuit high (bank 1, sensor 1)
P0037	Oxygen sensor heater control circuit low (bank 1, sensor 2)
P0038	Oxygen sensor heater control circuit high (bank 1, sensor 2)
P0051	Oxygen (A/F) sensor heater control circuit low (bank 2, sensor 1)
P0052	Oxygen (A/F) sensor heater control circuit high (bank 2, sensor 1)
P0057	Oxygen sensor heater control circuit low (bank 2, sensor 2)
P0058	Oxygen sensor heater control circuit high (bank 2, sensor 2)
P0100	Mass airflow sensor or circuit fault
P0101	Mass airflow sensor range or performance problem
P0102	Mass or volume air flow circuit low input
P0103	Mass or volume air flow circuit high input
P0105	Manifold absolute pressure sensor or circuit fault
P0106	Manifold absolute pressure range or performance problem

Diagnostic Trouble Codes (continued)

Code	Code identification
P0110	Intake air temperature sensor or circuit fault
P0111	2011 and earlier Camry models, 2012 Avalon and ES350 models: Intake air temperature sensor gradient too high 2012 and later Camry models, 2013 and later Avalon and ES350 models: Intake air temperature sensor 1 circuit range or performance problem
P0112	Intake air temperature circuit low input
P0113	Intake air temperature circuit high input
P0115	Engine coolant temperature sensor or circuit fault
P0116	Engine coolant temperature sensor range or performance problem
P0117	Engine coolant temperature (ECT) circuit low input
P0118	Engine coolant temperature (ECT) circuit high input
P011B	Engine coolant temperature (ECT), intake air temperature (IAT) correlation
P0120	Throttle or pedal position sensor or switch "A" circuit malfunction
P0121	Throttle or pedal position sensor or switch "A" circuit range performance problem
P0122	Throttle or pedal position sensor or switch "A" circuit low input
P0123	Throttle or pedal position sensor or switch "A" circuit high input
P0125	Insufficient coolant temperature for closed loop fuel control; oxygen sensor heater malfunction
P0128	Thermostat malfunction
P0130	Pre-converter oxygen sensor or circuit fault
P0133	Pre-converter oxygen sensor circuit slow response fault
P0135	Pre-converter oxygen sensor heater fault
P0136	2011 and earlier models: Post converter oxygen sensor or circuit failure 2012 and later models: Oxygen sensor circuit malfunction (bank 1 sensor 2)
P013A	Oxygen sensor slow response – rich to lean (bank 1 sensor 2)
P013C	Oxygen sensor slow response – rich to lean (bank 2 sensor 2)
P0137	Oxygen sensor circuit low voltage (bank 1, sensor 2)
P0138	Oxygen sensor circuit high voltage (bank 1, sensor 2)
P0139	Oxygen sensor circuit slow response (bank 1, sensor 2)
P0141	Post-converter oxygen sensor heater or circuit fault
P0156	Oxygen sensor circuit malfunction (bank 2, sensor 2)
P0157	Oxygen sensor circuit low voltage (bank 2, sensor 2)
P0158	2011 and earlier models: Post-converter circuit slow response (bank 2, sensor 2) 2012 and later models: Oxygen sensor circuit high voltage (bank 2 sensor 2)

Code	Code identification
P0159	Oxygen sensor circuit slow response (bank 2, sensor 2)
P0161	2011 and earlier models: Post-converter oxygen sensor heater or circuit fault 2012 and later models: Oxygen sensor heater circuit malfunction (bank 2 sensor 2)
P014C	A/F sensor slow response – rich to lean (bank 1 sensor 1)
P014D	A/F sensor slow response – lean to rich (bank 1 sensor 1)
P014E	A/F sensor slow response – rich to lean (bank 2 sensor 1)
P014F	A/F sensor slow response – lean to rich (bank 2 sensor 1)
P015A	A/F sensor delayed response – rich to lean (bank 1 sensor 1)
P015B	A/F sensor delayed response – lean to rich (bank 1 sensor 1)
P015C	A/F sensor delayed response – rich to lean (bank 2 sensor 1)
P015D	A/F sensor delayed response – lean to rich (bank 2 sensor 1)
P0171	Fuel injection system lean (bank 1)
P0172	Fuel injection system rich (bank 1)
P0174	Fuel injection system lean (bank 2)
P0175	Fuel injection system rich (bank 2)
P219A	Bank 1 air/fuel ratio imbalance
P219B	Bank 2 air/fuel ratio imbalance
P219C	Cylinder 1 air/fuel ratio imbalance
P219D	Cylinder 2 air/fuel ratio imbalance
P219E	Cylinder 3 air/fuel ratio imbalance
P219F	Cylinder 4 air/fuel ratio imbalance
P21A0	Cylinder 5 air/fuel ratio imbalance
P21A1	Cylinder 6 air/fuel ratio imbalance
P0220	Throttle or pedal position sensor or switch "B" circuit fault
P0222	Throttle or pedal position sensor or switch "B" circuit low input
P0223	Throttle or pedal position sensor or switch "B" circuit high input
P0230	Fuel pump primary circuit
P0300	Multiple cylinder misfire detected
P0301	Cylinder no. 1 misfire detected
P0302	Cylinder no. 2 misfire detected
P0303	Cylinder no. 3 misfire detected
P0304	Cylinder no. 4 misfire detected

Diagnostic Trouble Codes (continued)

Code	Code identification
P0305	Cylinder no. 5 misfire detected
P0306	Cylinder no. 6 misfire detected
P0325	Knock sensor or circuit fault
P0327	Knock sensor 1 circuit low input (bank 1 or single sensor)
P0328	Knock sensor 1 circuit high input (bank 1 or single sensor)
P0332	Knock sensor 2 circuit low input (bank 2)
P0333	Knock sensor 2 circuit high input (bank 2)
P0335	Crankshaft position sensor "A" circuit fault
P0336	Camshaft position sensor or range performance fault
P0339	Crankshaft position sensor "A" circuit intermittent
P0340	Camshaft position sensor or circuit fault
P0342	Camshaft position sensor "A" circuit low input (bank 1 or single sensor)
P0343	Camshaft position sensor "A" circuit high input (bank 1 or single sensor)
P0345	Camshaft position sensor "A" circuit (bank 2)
P0347	Camshaft position sensor "A" circuit low input (bank 2)
P0348	Camshaft position sensor "A" circuit high input (bank 2)
P0351	Ignition coil "A" primary or secondary circuit fault
P0352	Ignition coil "B" primary or secondary circuit fault
P0353	Ignition coil "C" primary or secondary circuit fault
P0354	Ignition coil "D" primary or secondary circuit fault
P0355	Ignition coil "E" primary or secondary circuit fault
P0356	Ignition coil "F" primary or secondary circuit fault
P0365	Camshaft position sensor "B" circuit (bank 1)
P0367	Camshaft position sensor "B" circuit low input (bank 1)
P0368	Camshaft position sensor "B" circuit high input (bank 1)
P0390	Camshaft position sensor "B" circuit (bank 2)
P0392	Camshaft position sensor "B" circuit low input (bank 2)
P0393	Camshaft position sensor "B" circuit high input (bank 2)
P0401	EGR insufficient flow detected
P0402	EGR excessive flow detected

Code	Code identification
P0420	2011 and earlier models: Catalytic converter system fault 2012 and later models: Catalyst System Efficiency Below Threshold (Bank 1)
P0430	2011 and earlier models: Catalytic converter system fault 2012 and later models Catalyst System Efficiency Below Threshold (Bank 2)
P043E	EVAP system leak detection reference orifice low flow
P043F	EVAP system reference orifice high flow
P0440	EVAP system malfunction
P0441	EVAP system incorrect purge flow – purge vacuum switch valve stuck closed or stuck open
P0442	EVAP system leak detected
P0443	EVAP system purge control valve circuit fault
P0446	EVAP canister vent control valve circuit fault
P0450	EVAP system pressure sensor or circuit fault
P0451	EVAP canister pressure sensor signal noise or signal becomes fixed/flat (pressure sensor found in canister pump module)
P0452	Canister pressure sensor voltage low
P0453	Canister pressure sensor voltage high
P0455	EVAP system gross leak
P0456	EVAP system small leak
P0500	Vehicle speed sensor "A" or circuit fault
P0504	Brake switch "A" or "B" correlation
P0505	2011 and earlier models: Idle air control valve or circuit fault 2012 and later models: Idle control system malfunction
P050A	Cold start idle air control system performance
P050B	Cold start ignition timing performance
P0560	ECM system voltage
P0604	ICM random access memory (RAM) error
P0606	ECM/PCM processor fault
P0607	Control module performance
P060A	ICM monitoring processor performance
P060B	ICM a/d processing performance
P060D	ICM accelerator pedal position performance
P060E	ICM throttle position performance
P0617	Starter relay circuit high
P062F	Internal control module EEPROM error

Diagnostic Trouble Codes (continued)

Code	Code identification
P0630	VIN not programmed or mismatch - ECM/PCM
P0657	Actuator supply voltage circuit fault or open
P0705	Transmission range sensor circuit malfunction – faulty PRNDL input
P0710	Automatic transaxle fluid temperature sensor or circuit fault
P0711	Automatic transaxle fluid temperature sensor range performance or circuit fault
P0724	Brake switch "B" circuit high
P0750	Automatic transaxle shift solenoid A stuck open or closed
P0753	Automatic transaxle shift solenoid A circuit fault
P0755	Automatic transaxle shift solenoid B stuck open or closed
P0758	Automatic transaxle shift solenoid B circuit fault
P0765	Automatic transaxle shift solenoid D stuck open or closed
P0768	Automatic transaxle shift solenoid D circuit fault
P0770	Automatic transaxle shift solenoid E stuck open or closed
P0773	Automatic transaxle shift solenoid E circuit fault
P101D	A/F sensor heater circuit performance bank 1, sensor 1 stuck on
P102D	Oxygen sensor heater circuit performance bank 1, sensor 2 stuck on
P103D	A/F sensor heater circuit performance (bank 2 sensor 1 stuck on)
P105D	O2 sensor heater circuit performance (bank 2 sensor 2 stuck on)
P1130	Air/fuel ratio sensor or range performance fault
P1133	Air/fuel ratio sensor or circuit fault
P1135	Air/fuel ratio sensor heater or circuit fault
P1153	Air/fuel ratio sensor or circuit fault
P1155	Air/fuel ratio sensor heater or circuit fault
P1300	Ignition system malfunction (no. 1 coil/igniter circuit fault)
P1305	Ignition system malfunction (no. 2 coil/igniter circuit fault)
P1310	Ignition system malfunction (no. 3 coil/igniter circuit fault)
P1315	Ignition system malfunction (no. 4 coil/igniter circuit fault)
P1335	Crankshaft position sensor or circuit fault
P1346	VVT (variable valve timing) sensor circuit fault
P1349	VVT (variable valve timing) system malfunction
P1500	Starter signal circuit malfunction

Code	Code identification
P1520	Brake light signal malfunction
P1600	ECM battery supply malfunction
P1603	Engine stall history
P1604	Startability malfunction
P1605	Rough idling
P1607	Cruise control input processor
P1656	OCV (oil control valve) circuit malfunction
P1725	Automatic transaxle input turbine speed sensor circuit fault
P1730	Automatic transaxle counter gear speed sensor circuit fault
P1780	Park/Neutral position switch or circuit fault
P2004	Intake manifold runner control stuck open (bank 1)
P2006	Intake manifold runner control stuck closed (bank 1)
P2009	Intake manifold runner control circuit low (bank 1)
P2010	Intake manifold runner control circuit high (bank 1)
P2014	Intake manifold runner position sensor or switch circuit (bank 1)
P2016	Intake manifold runner position sensor or switch circuit low (bank 1)
P2017	Intake manifold runner position sensor or switch circuit high (bank 1)
P2102	Throttle actuator control motor circuit low
P2103	Throttle actuator control motor circuit high
P2109	Throttle/pedal position sensor "A" minimum stop performance
P2111	Throttle actuator control system - stuck open
P2112	Throttle actuator control system - stuck closed
P2118	Throttle actuator control motor current range or performance
P2119	Throttle actuator control throttle body range or performance
P2120	Throttle or pedal position sensor or switch "D" circuit fault
P2121	Throttle or pedal position sensor or switch "D" circuit range or performance
P2122	Throttle or pedal position sensor or switch "D" circuit low input
P2123	Throttle or pedal position sensor or switch "D" circuit high input
P2125	Throttle or pedal position sensor or switch "E" circuit fault
P2127	Throttle or pedal position sensor or switch "E" circuit low input
P2128	Throttle or pedal position sensor or switch "E" circuit high input
P2135	Throttle or pedal position sensor or switch "A" or "B" voltage correlation

Diagnostic Trouble Codes (continued)

Code	Code identification
P2138	Throttle or pedal position sensor or switch "D" or "E" voltage correlation
P2195	Oxygen (A/F) sensor signal stuck lean (bank 1, sensor 1)
P2196	Oxygen (A/F) sensor signal stuck rich (bank 1, sensor 1)
P2197	Oxygen (A/F) sensor signal stuck lean (bank 2, sensor 1)
P2198	Oxygen (A/F) sensor signal stuck rich (bank 2, sensor 1)
P219A	Bank 1 air/fuel ratio imbalance
P219B	Bank 2 air/fuel ratio imbalance
P219C	Cylinder 1 air/fuel ration imbalance
P219D	Cylinder 2 air/fuel ration imbalance
P219E	Cylinder 3 air/fuel ration imbalance
P219F	Cylinder 4 air/fuel ration imbalance
P21A0	Cylinder 5 air/fuel ration imbalance
P21A1	Cylinder 6 air/fuel ration imbalance
P2237	Oxygen (A/F) sensor pumping current circuit or open (bank 1, sensor 1)
P2238	Oxygen (A/F) sensor pumping current circuit low (bank 1, sensor 1)
P2239	Oxygen (A/F) sensor pumping current circuit high (bank 1, sensor 1)
P2240	Oxygen (A/F) sensor pumping current circuit or open (bank 2, sensor 1)
P2241	Oxygen (A/F) sensor pumping current circuit low (bank 2, sensor 1)
P2242	Oxygen (A/F) sensor pumping current circuit high (bank 2, sensor 1)
P2252	Oxygen (A/F) sensor reference ground circuit low (bank 1, sensor 1)
P2253	Oxygen (A/F) sensor reference ground circuit high (bank 1, sensor 1)
P2255	Oxygen (A/F) sensor reference ground circuit low (bank 2, sensor 1)
P2256	Oxygen (A/F) sensor reference ground circuit high (bank 2, sensor 1)
P2401	EVAP leak detection pump stuck off
P2402	EVAP leak detection pump stuck on
P2419	EVAP switching valve control circuit low
P2420	EVAP switching valve control circuit high
P2610	ECM/PCM internal engine off timer performance
P2A00	A/F sensor circuit slow response (bank 1, sensor 1)
P2A03	A/F sensor circuit slow response (bank 2, sensor 1)
U0101	Lost communication with TCM

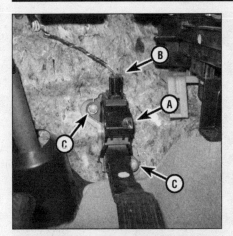

4.2 Typical Accelerator Pedal Position (APP) sensor details

A   *Accelerator Pedal Position (APP) sensor*
B   *Electrical connector*
C   *Mounting bolts*

5.2 Location of the Camshaft Position (CMP) sensor on 2009 and earlier four-cylinder models

5.6 Location of the Camshaft Position (CMP) sensors on 2010 and later four-cylinder models

A   *Intake Camshaft Position (CMP) sensor*
B   *Exhaust Camshaft Position (CMP) sensor*

4   Accelerator Pedal Position (APP) sensor - replacement

Refer to illustration 4.2
Note: *The APP sensor and the accelerator pedal are removed as a single assembly.*
1   Disconnect the cable from the negative battery terminal (see Chapter 5).
2   Working under the dash, disconnect the APP sensor electrical connector **(see illustration)**.
3   Remove the accelerator pedal/APP sensor assembly mounting bolts and sensor assembly.
4   Installation is the reverse of removal. Be sure to tighten the accelerator pedal assembly mounting bolts securely.

5   Camshaft Position (CMP) sensor(s) - replacement

Note: *CMP sensors are only used on four-cylinder models. Four VVT sensors are used on all V6 engine models. See Section 20 for more information about VVT sensors and the variable valve timing system.*
1   Disconnect the cable from the negative battery terminal (see Chapter 5).

2009 and earlier models

Refer to illustration 5.2
2   The sensor is mounted on the side of the cylinder head, just below the valve cover, near the left end of the cylinder head **(see illustration)**.

3   Remove the air filter housing (see Chapter 4).
4   Disconnect the electrical connector, remove the mounting bolt and remove the camshaft sensor from the cylinder head.
5   Installation is the reverse of removal.

2010 and later models

Refer to illustration 5.6
6   The sensor(s) are mounted on the top of the valve cover **(see illustration)**.
7   Disconnect the harness electrical connector.
8   Remove the mounting screws and remove the camshaft sensor(s) from the valve cover.
9   Installation is the reverse of removal.

6   Throttle Position (TP) sensor and throttle control motor - replacement

All models are equipped with electronic throttle bodies; the Throttle Position sensor and motor are integral components of the throttle body. If the Throttle Position sensor or motor is defective, the throttle body will have to be replaced (see Chapter 4).

7   Crankshaft Position (CKP) sensor - replacement

1   Disconnect the cable from the negative battery terminal (see Chapter 5).

2   The sensor is mounted on the timing chain cover next to the crankshaft pulley.
3   Raise the front of the vehicle and support it securely on jackstands.
4   Loosen the right-front wheel lug nuts, raise the front of the vehicle and support it securely on jackstands, then remove the wheel. Remove the inner fender splash shield (see Chapter 11).

Four-cylinder models
2009 and earlier models

Refer to illustrations 7.7 and 7.9
5   Remove the drivebelt (see Chapter 1).
6   Remove the alternator (see Chapter 5).
7   Disconnect the CKP sensor electrical connector at the harness **(see illustration)**.

7.7 Location of the CKP electrical connector on 2009 and earlier four-cylinder models

7.9 Location of the CKP sensor on 2009 and earlier four-cylinder models

7.11 Location of the CKP sensor on 2010 and later four-cylinder models

7.17 On V6 models, the CKP sensor is located at the front corner of the engine behind the air conditioning compressor. To disconnect the electrical connector (A), slide the white plastic lock to the rear and pull off the connector. (B) is the sensor mounting bolt

8.4a On four-cylinder models, the ECT sensor is located on the left end of the cylinder head

8.4b On V6 models, the ECT sensor is located on the left end of the engine on the coolant crossover between the cylinder heads

8   Remove the harness clamps and bracket.
9   Remove the bolt, detach the sensor **(see illustration)** and remove the sensor and harness.
10   Installation is the reverse of removal.

2010 and later models

Refer to illustration 7.11

11   Disconnect the CKP sensor electrical connector **(see illustration)**.
12   Remove the bolt and the sensor.
13   Installation is the reverse of removal.

V6 models

Refer to illustration 7.17

Note: *The CKP sensor is located at the front lower right corner of the engine.*

14   Remove the drivebelt (see Chapter 1).
15   Remove the alternator (see Chapter 5).
16   Remove the bolt that secures the air conditioning suction line at the front of the engine, disconnect the electrical connector from the air conditioning compressor and unbolt the compressor (see Chapter 3). **Warning:** *Do NOT disconnect the air conditioning hoses from the compressor. Move the compressor aside and support it with wire or rope.*
17   Disconnect the CKP sensor electrical connector **(see illustration)**.
18   Remove the crankshaft position sensor retaining bolt and sensor.
19   Installation is the reverse of removal. Be sure to tighten the CKP sensor retaining bolt securely.

8   Engine Coolant Temperature (ECT) sensor - replacement

Refer to illustrations 8.4a, 8.4b and 8.5

Warning: *Wait until the engine has cooled completely before beginning this procedure.*

1   Make sure the ignition key is in the OFF position.
2   Remove the engine covers and drain approximately one gallon from the cooling system.
3   Remove the air filter housing (see Chapter 4).
4   Disconnect the electrical connector and unscrew the sensor **(see illustrations)**.
5   Wrap the threads of the new sensor with Teflon sealing tape to prevent leakage and thread corrosion **(see illustration)**.

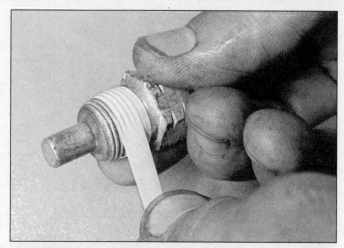

8.5 Wrap the threads of the ECT sensor with Teflon tape to prevent coolant leakage

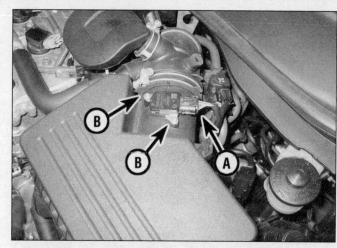

11.3 Typical Mass Airflow (MAF) sensor details

A   *Mass Airflow sensor electrical connector*
B   *Mounting screws*

6   Installation is the reverse of removal. **Caution:** *Handle the coolant sensor with care. Damage to this sensor will affect the operation of the entire fuel injection system.*

9   Intake Air Temperature (IAT) sensor - replacement

The IAT sensor is an integral component of the Mass Air Flow (MAF) sensor. See Section 11.

10   Knock sensor - replacement

Warning: *Wait for the engine to cool completely before performing this procedure.*
1   Relieve the fuel system pressure (see Chapter 4), then disconnect the cable from the negative battery terminal (see Chapter 5).
2   Drain the cooling system (see Chapter 1).

Four-cylinder models

Note: *The knock sensor is located on the backside of the engine block, directly below the cylinder head (facing toward the rear of the engine compartment) under the intake manifold.*
3   Remove the intake manifold (see Chapter 2A).
4   Disconnect the electrical connector, remove the mounting nut and slide the knock sensor off of the mounting stud.
5   Install the knock sensor onto the stud, then tighten the nut to 15 ft-lbs. Don't overtighten the sensor or the sensor won't work properly. Overtightening can also damage the sensor. **Note:** *Install the sensor in a parallel line to the engine block (no more than a 10-degree angle to the block).*

V6 models

Note: *V6 models use two knock sensors; they are located on top of the engine block, under the lower intake manifold. Both sensors must be replaced at the same time.*
6   Remove the lower intake manifold (see Chapter 2B).
7   Disconnect the knock sensor harness electrical connector.
8   Remove the mounting bolts and remove the sensors.
9   Clean the mounting surface and install the knock sensor(s).
10   Tighten the sensor(s) bolt securely (approximately 15 ft-lbs). Don't overtighten the sensor or damage may occur. **Note:** *Install the sensor(s) in a parallel line to the engine block (no more than a 10-degree angle to the block)*

All models

11   Reverse the removal procedure to reinstall all parts removed for access to the sensor(s).
12   Refill the cooling system (see Chapter 1).

11   Mass Airflow (MAF) sensor - replacement

Refer to illustration 11.3
1   The Mass Airflow (MAF) sensor is located on the air intake duct.
2   Make sure the ignition key is in the OFF position.
3   Disconnect the electrical connector from the MAF sensor **(see illustration)**.
4   Remove the two sensor retaining bolts and remove the MAF sensor.
5   Installation is the reverse of removal.

12   Oxygen sensor/air-fuel ratio sensor - replacement

Refer to illustrations 12.2a, 12.2b, 12.3 and 12.4
Note: *The manufacturer refers to the upstream (before the catalytic converter) sensor as the air-fuel ratio sensor, and the downstream sensor (after the catalytic converter) as the oxygen sensor.*
Note: *Because it is installed in the exhaust manifold or pipe, which contract when cool, the oxygen sensor may be very difficult to loosen when the engine is cold. Rather than risk damage to the sensor (assuming you are planning to reuse it in another manifold or pipe), start and run the engine for a minute or two, then shut it off. Be careful not to burn yourself during the following procedure.*
1   Disconnect the cable from the negative battery terminal (see Chapter 5).
2   If you're replacing the downstream sensor(s), raise the vehicle and support it

12.2a Downstream oxygen sensor details - four-cylinder models

A   *Sensor electrical connector*
B   *Sensor*

12.2b Downstream oxygen sensor details - V6 models

A   Bank 1, sensor 2   *B   Bank 2, sensor 2*

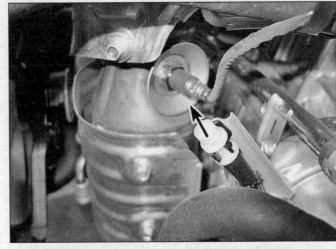

12.3 Location of the upstream oxygen sensor (or air/fuel ratio sensor) - four-cylinder models

securely on jackstands. Remove the lower engine cover. Access the oxygen sensor harness **(see illustration)** and unplug the electrical connector. **Note:** *On V6 models, Bank 1 is on the #1 cylinder side and Bank 2 is on the opposite side* **(see illustration)**.

3   The upstream sensor (also called the air-fuel ratio sensor) can be replaced without raising the vehicle **(see illustration)**. Unplug the sensor electrical connector.

4   Unscrew the sensor from the exhaust manifold(s) or exhaust pipe **(see illustration)**. **Note:** *The best tool for removing an oxygen sensor is a special slotted socket, especially if you're planning to reuse a sensor. If you don't have this tool, and you plan to reuse the sensor, be extremely careful when unscrewing the sensor.*

5   Apply anti-seize compound to the threads of the sensor to facilitate future removal. The threads of new sensors should already be coated with this compound, but if you're planning to reuse an old sensor, recoat the threads. Install the sensor and tighten it securely.

6   Reconnect the electrical connector of the pigtail lead to the main wiring harness.

13   Transaxle Speed Sensors - replacement

1   The sensor(s) is an electronic component that produces a pulsing voltage signal whenever the input and output shaft is rotated. These voltage pulses are monitored by the PCM, which uses this information to help control the fuel and ignition systems and transaxle shifting.

U250E 5-speed transaxle (2009 and earlier four-cylinder models)

Refer to illustrations 13.2a and 13.2b

2   The Transaxle Speed Sensors **(see illustrations)**, one for the turbine (input) shaft and one for the counter gear (output) shaft. On 2009 and earlier four-cylinder models, the sensors are located on top of the transaxle.

3   Disconnect the electrical connector from the sensor.

4   Unscrew the sensor from the transaxle.

5   Replace the O-ring.

6   Installation is the reverse of removal.

U660E/U760E 6-speed transaxles (all other models)

7   There is only one Transaxle Speed Sensor used on the six-speed transaxles. The speed sensor is mounted inside the transaxle on the top of the valve body. Replacement requires removing the transaxle fluid pan, filter and valve body. Due to the sensitive nature of the valve body, this job is best left to a transmission specialist.

12.4 Use a slotted socket to remove the oxygen sensors

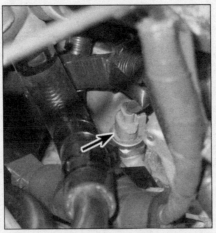

13.2a The turbine (input) shaft sensor is located on the front of the transaxle - 2009 and earlier four-cylinder models

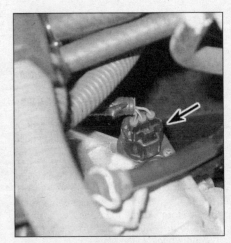

13.2b The countergear (output) shaft sensor is located on the top of the transaxle - 2009 and earlier four-cylinder models

15.6 To release the ECM connectors, rotate the levers outwards and pull the ECM connectors out of the ECM

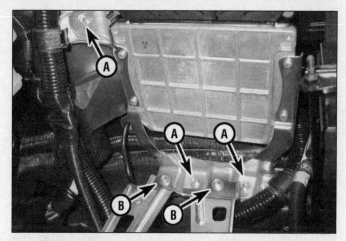

15.7 ECM mounting details - four-cylinder models

A *ECM bracket mounting fasteners*
B *Air filter housing bracket fasteners*

14 Transmission Range (TR) sensor - replacement

Even though the Society of Automotive Engineers (SAE) has recommended since 1996 that all manufacturers refer to the Park/Neutral Position (PNP) switch as the Transmission Range (TR) sensor, Toyota continues to refer to the TR sensor as the PNP switch. To avoid confusion, we have therefore included the TR sensor/PNP switch in Chapter 7B.

15 Powertrain Control Module (PCM) - removal and installation

Warning: *The models covered by this manual are equipped with Supplemental Restraint Systems (SRS), more commonly known as airbags. Always disable the airbag system before working in the vicinity of any airbag system components to avoid the possibility of accidental deployment of the airbag, which could cause personal injury (see Chapter 12).* **Caution:** *To avoid electrostatic discharge damage to the ECM, handle the ECM only by its case. Do not touch the electrical terminals during removal and installation. If available, ground yourself to the vehicle with an anti-static ground strap, available at computer supply stores.*

1   On four-cylinder models, the Electronic Control Module (ECM) is located in the engine compartment next to the driver's side inner fender panel. On V6 models it's located on the firewall in the engine compartment, on the right (passenger's) side.
2   Disconnect the cable from the negative battery terminal (see Chapter 5).

Four-cylinder models

Refer to illustrations 15.6 and 15.7

3   Remove the engine cover (see Chapter 2A).
4   Remove the air filter housing (see Chapter 4).

5   Remove the air filter housing bracket mounting bolts and bracket.
6   To release the ECM connectors, push in the lever locks (at the end of each lever), while lifting the levers outwards, and pull the ECM connectors out from the ECM **(see illustration)**. **Caution:** *The ignition switch must be turned OFF when pulling out or plugging in the electrical connectors to prevent damage to the ECM.*
7   Remove the air filter housing bracket fasteners, then the ECM bracket-to-body fasteners **(see illustration)**.
8   Carefully remove the ECM and bracket. **Caution:** *Avoid any static electricity damage to the computer by grounding yourself to the body before touching the ECM and using a special anti-static pad to store the ECM on once it is removed.*
9   Remove the bracket-to-ECM mounting screws and separate the bracket from the ECM.
10   Installation is the reverse of removal.

V6 models

11   Remove the cowl assembly (see Chapter 11).
12   Remove the ECM mounting nuts.
13   To release the ECM connectors, push in the lever locks (at the end of each lever), while lifting the levers outwards, and pull the ECM connectors out from the ECM **(see illustration 15.6)**. **Caution:** *The ignition switch must be turned OFF when pulling out or plugging in the electrical connectors to prevent damage to the ECM.*
14   Carefully remove the ECM and bracket. **Caution:** *Avoid any static electricity damage to the computer by grounding yourself to the body before touching the ECM and using a special anti-static pad to store the ECM on once it is removed.*
15   Remove the bracket-to-ECM mounting screws and separate the bracket from the ECM.
16   Installation is the reverse of removal.

16 Catalytic converter - replacement

Note: *Because of a Federally mandated extended warranty which covers emissions-related components such as the catalytic converter, check with a dealer service department before replacing the converter at your own expense.*
Note: *The catalytic converter(s) are incorporated into the exhaust manifold(s). Refer to Chapter 2A or 2B for the exhaust manifold replacement procedure.*
1   Remove the upstream oxygen sensor(s) (see Section 12).
2   Remove the exhaust manifold(s) (see Chapter 2A or 2B). The catalytic converter(s) is an integral part of the exhaust manifold and cannot be replaced separately. If the catalytic converter(s) is bad, the exhaust manifold must be replaced.
3   Installation is the reverse of removal.

17 Evaporative Emissions Control (EVAP) system - component replacement

Warning: *Gasoline and gasoline vapors are extremely flammable, so take extra precautions when you work on any part of the fuel system. Don't smoke or allow open flames or bare light bulbs near the work area, and don't work in a garage where a gas-type appliance (such as a water heater or clothes dryer) is present. Since gasoline is carcinogenic, wear fuel-resistant gloves when there's a possibility of being exposed to fuel, and, if you spill any fuel on your skin, rinse it off immediately with soap and water. Mop up any spills immediately and do not store fuel-soaked rags where they could ignite. When you perform any kind of work on the fuel system, wear safety glasses and have a Class B type fire extinguisher on hand.*

17.2a EVAP canister purge valve location - four-cylinder models

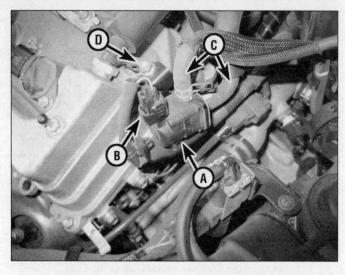

17.2b EVAP canister purge valve details - V6 models

A Canister purge valve	C Vacuum lines
B Electrical connector	D Mounting bolt

EVAP canister purge valve

Refer to illustrations 17.2a and 17.2b

Note: *On four-cylinder models, the EVAP canister purge valve is located behind the air filter housing, on the side of the intake duct; on V6 models, it's located on the left end of the front-bank cylinder head.*

1   Remove the engine cover(s).

2   Disconnect the electrical connector from the purge valve **(see illustrations)**.

3   Disconnect the EVAP hoses from the purge valve.

4   Remove the purge valve mounting bolt and remove the purge valve.

5   Installation is the reverse of removal.

EVAP canister

6   Raise the vehicle and place it securely on jackstands.

7   Remove the fuel tank (see Chapter 4).

8   Disconnect the electrical connector(s) and hoses from the EVAP canister.

9   Disconnect the electrical connector from the leak detection pump module.

10   Remove the three EVAP canister mounting bolts to detach the canister. Before removing the canister, you'll need to detach any other wiring harnesses clipped to the canister mounting bracket.

11   Installation is the reverse of removal.

Leak detection pump

12   Remove the EVAP canister (see Steps 6 through 10).

13   Disconnect the inlet hose and electrical connector.

14   Remove the pump mounting bolts and remove the leak detection pump.

15   Installation is the reverse of removal.

18   Positive Crankcase Ventilation (PCV) system

Refer to illustrations 18.1a and 18.1b

1   The Positive Crankcase Ventilation (PCV) system reduces hydrocarbon emissions by scavenging crankcase vapors. It does this by circulating fresh air from the air cleaner through the crankcase, where it mixes with blow-by gases and is then rerouted through a PCV valve to the intake manifold **(see illustrations)**.

2   The main components of the PCV system are the PCV valve, a blow-by filter and the vacuum hoses connecting these two components with the engine.

3   To maintain idle quality, the PCV valve restricts the flow when the intake manifold vacuum is high. If abnormal operating conditions (such as piston ring problems) arise, the system is designed to allow excessive amounts of blow-by gases to flow back through the crankcase vent tube into the air cleaner to be consumed by normal combustion.

4   Checking and replacement of the PCV valve is covered in Chapter 1.

19   Acoustic Control Induction System (ACIS) - description and component replacement

Description

Refer to illustration 19.2

1   The PCM-controlled Acoustic Control Induction System (ACIS) varies the effective length of the intake manifold runners in

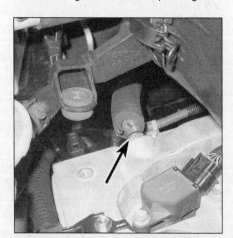

18.1a PCV valve location - 2009 and earlier four-cylinder models (on 2010 and later four-cylinder models, it's located underneath the intake manifold)

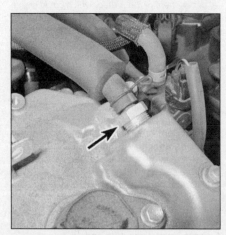

18.1b PCV valve location - V6 models

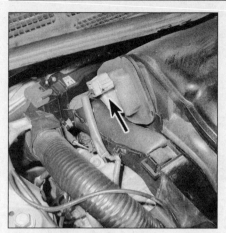

19.2 Intake air control actuator location - V6 models

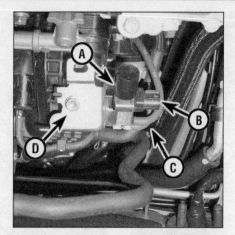

19.6a Acoustic Control Induction System Vacuum Switching Valve (ACIS VSV) from the intake manifold - four-cylinder model

A   *Vacuum Switching Valve (VSV)*
B   *Electrical connector*
C   *Vacuum hoses*
D   *Mounting fastener*

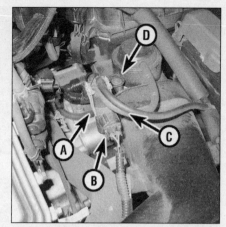

19.6b Acoustic Control Induction System Vacuum Switching Valve (ACIS VSV) from the intake manifold - V6 model

A   *Vacuum Switching Valve (VSV)*
B   *Electrical connector*
C   *Vacuum hoses*
D   *Mounting fastener*

response to engine speed and the angle of the throttle plate inside the throttle body. This capability increases efficiency and power at low and high speeds.

2   The ACIS consists of an ECM-controlled Vacuum Switching Valve (VSV), an actuator, a vacuum tank (four-cylinder models) and an intake air control valve. The VSV is an ECM controlled-device that controls the intake vacuum applied to the actuator. The actuator is a vacuum diaphragm that uses a pushrod and bellcrank to open and close the intake air control valve. The vacuum tank (four-cylinder models), is an integral part of the intake manifold, used to maintain a constant source of vacuum to keep the intake air control valve closed during deceleration (low vacuum). The intake air control valve, which is an integral part of the intake manifold, opens and closes to alter the effective length of the intake manifold runners in two stages. On four-cylinder models, there is one large intake air control valve for all four intake runners. On V6 models, there is one large intake air control valve for all six intake runners **(see illustration)**.

3   At low-to-medium speeds, the PCM activates the VSV, sending vacuum to the actuator diaphragm. The actuator closes the intake air control valve, increasing the length of the intake manifold and improving intake efficiency.

4   At higher speeds, the PCM deactivates the VSV, cutting vacuum to the actuator diaphragm. The actuator opens the intake air control valve, decreasing the length of the intake manifold and improving engine power.

Component replacement

Refer to illustrations 19.6a and 19.6b

Note: *The actuator, vacuum tank (four-cylinder models) and intake air control valve are*

integral components of the intake manifold. If any component fails, replace the intake manifold (see Chapter 2A or 2B). The VSV is the only component that you can replace at home.

Note: *On four-cylinder models, the VSV is located at the left end of the intake manifold and is accessed from below. On V6 models, the VSV is located at the upper right rear corner of the intake manifold.*

5   Remove the engine cover.

6   Disconnect the electrical connector from the VSV **(see illustrations)**.

7   Clearly label, then disconnect both hoses from the VSV.

8   Remove the VSV mounting bolt and remove the VSV.

9   Installation is the reverse of removal.

20   Variable Valve Timing-intelligent system - description and component replacement

Description

1   There are two types of system: a Variable Valve Timing-intelligent (VVT-i) system used on 2009 and earlier four-cylinder models and the dual Variable Valve Timing-intelligent (VVT-i) system used on all V6 models and 2010 and later four-cylinder models.

2   The VVT-I system varies intake and exhaust (if equipped) camshaft timing to produce valve timing that is optimized for the driving conditions. The VVT-i system achieves this by using engine oil pressure to advance or retard the controller on the front end of each intake camshaft(s) and exhaust camshaft(s) on all V6 models and 2010 and later four-cylinder models.

2009 and earlier four-cylinder models: 40 degrees (intake and exhaust)
2010 and later four-cylinder models: 50 degrees (intake camshaft); 40 degrees (exhaust camshaft)
V6 models: 40 degrees (intake camshaft); 35 degrees (exhaust camshaft)

3   The VVT-i system on the 2009 and earlier four-cylinder models consists of a CMP sensor, CKP sensor, camshaft timing oil control valve, Electronic Control Module (ECM) and one controller (intake camshaft sprocket/actuator assembly). The dual VVT-i system on 2010 and later four-cylinder models consists of two CMP sensors, a CKP sensor, two camshaft timing oil control valves, Electronic Control Module (ECM) and two controllers (intake and exhaust camshaft sprocket/actuator assemblies). The dual VVT-I system on V6 models consists of four VVT sensors, a CKP sensor, four camshaft timing oil control valves, Electronic Control Module (ECM) and four controllers (two intake and two exhaust camshaft sprocket/actuator assemblies). The VVT-i systems on V6 and four-cylinder models are virtually identical except for the design of the oil control valves.

4   Each controller consists of a timing rotor (for the VVT-i sensor), a housing with an impeller-type vane inside it, a lock pin and the actual timing chain sprocket for the intake camshaft. The vane is fixed on the end of the camshaft.

5   The camshaft timing oil control valve is an ECM-controlled device that controls and directs the flow of oil to the advance or retard passages leading to the controller. There is one oil control valve for each camshaft. A spring-loaded spool valve inside the oil control valve directs oil pumped into the valve toward either the advance outlet or the retard outlet port, depending on the engine condition.

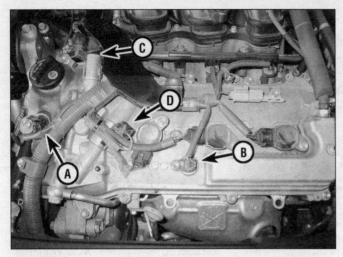

20.9 VVT sensor and camshaft timing oil control valve locations (Bank 2) - V6 models

A   *Bank 2 Intake sensor*
B   *Bank 2 Exhaust sensor*
C   *Bank 2 Intake timing oil control valve*
D   *Bank 2 Exhaust timing oil control valve*

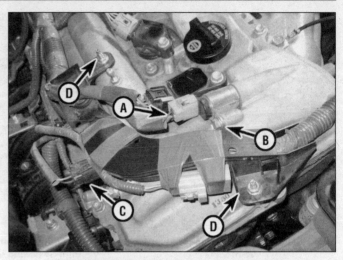

20.15 Camshaft timing oil control valve details - 2010 four-cylinder model shown

A   *Exhaust side camshaft timing oil control valve*
B   *Camshaft timing oil control valve mounting bolt*
C   *Intake side camshaft timing oil control valve*
D   *Engine harness mounting fastenersdd*

Component replacement

VVT sensors (V6 engines only)

Refer to illustration 20.9

Warning: *Wait until the engine is completely cool before beginning this procedure.*

6   Disconnect the cable from the negative battery terminal (see Chapter 5).
7   Remove the cowl assembly (see Chapter 11).
8   Refer to Chapter 2B and remove the upper intake manifold for access to the two rear VVT sensors. The two front sensors can be accessed by removing the engine cover.
9   Disconnect the electrical connector from the sensor being replaced **(see illustration)**.
10   Remove the VVT sensor mounting bolt and remove the sensor.
11   Installation is the reverse of removal.

Camshaft timing oil control valve(s)

Refer to illustration 20.15

Note: *2009 and earlier four-cylinder models use only one camshaft timing control valve. 2010 and later four-cylinder models use two control valves. All V6 engines use four timing oil control valves.*

12   Disconnect the cable from the negative battery terminal (see Chapter 5).
13   Remove the engine cover(s).
14   On V6 engines, refer to Chapter 2B and remove the upper intake manifold for access to the rear two camshaft timing oil control valves **(see illustration 20.9)**.
15   Disconnect the electrical connector from the camshaft timing oil control valve **(see illustration)**. On four-cylinder models, remove the engine harness mounting fasteners and move the harness to the side.
16   Remove the camshaft timing oil control valve mounting bolt and remove the oil control valve from the valve cover.
17   Installation is the reverse of removal.

---

21 Active Control Engine Mount (V6 models) – description and component replacement

---

Description

1   The Active Control Engine Mount generates vibrations that cancel engine vibration and reduces noise at idle. When engine speed is below 900 rpm, the PCM operates a vacuum switching valve (VSV) that uses engine vacuum to vibrate a diaphragm within the mount. The diaphragm transfers the vibration to a liquid inside the mount, which transfers the vibration to the mount's rubber pad and the engine vibration is cancelled out.

Vacuum Switching Valve (VSV) replacement

Note: *The VSV sits in front of the engine cooling fans.*
2   Disconnect the two vacuum hoses and the large hose from the VSV. Label each hose to ensure proper reassembly.
3   Remove the valve's mounting bolt and disconnect the electrical connector.
4   Disconnect the remaining hose and remove the VSV.
5   Installation is the reverse of removal.

Chapter 7 Part A
Manual transaxle

Contents

Specifications

Torque specifications

Ft-lbs (unless otherwise indicated)

Note: *One foot-pound (ft-lb) of torque is equivalent to 12 inch-pounds (in-lbs) of torque. Torque values below approximately 15 foot-pounds are expressed in inch-pounds, because most foot-pound torque wrenches are not accurate at these smaller values.*

Back-up light switch	30
Shift cable-to-firewall mounting bolts	44 in-lbs
Shift lever mounting bolts	108 in-lbs
Transaxle case protector mounting bolts	156 in-lbs
Transaxle-to-engine bolts	
2009 and earlier (5-speed) models **(see illustration 5.5a)**	
Bolts A	47
Bolts B	34
Bolts C	32
Bolt D	34
Bolt E	47
2010 and later (6-speed) models **(see illustration 5.5b)**	
Bolts A (in sequence)	47
Bolts B	34
Bolt C	34
Bolts D	32

1   General information

The vehicles covered by this manual are equipped with either a 5-speed or 6-speed manual or a 5-speed or 6-speed automatic transaxle. The E351 5-speed manual transaxle is used on 2009 and earlier models, and the EB62 6-speed is used on 2010 and later models. Information on the manual transaxle is included in this Part of Chapter 7. Service procedures for the automatic transaxles are contained in Chapter 7, Part B.

The manual transaxles are a compact, two-piece, lightweight aluminum alloy housing containing both the transmission and differential assemblies.

Because of the complexity, unavailability of replacement parts and special tools necessary, internal repair procedures for the manual transaxle are not recommended for the home mechanic. The bulk of information in this Chapter is devoted to removal and installation procedures.

2   Shift and select cables - replacement

Warning: *The models covered by this manual are equipped with Supplemental Restraint Systems (SRS), more commonly known as airbags. Always disarm the airbag system before working in the vicinity of any airbag system component to avoid the possibility of accidental deployment of the airbag, which could cause personal injury (see Chapter 12).*
1   Disconnect the negative cable from the battery (see Chapter 5).
2   Raise the front of the vehicle and place it securely on jackstands.
3   Remove the center console (see Chapter 11).
4   Remove the center console mounting bracket fasteners and bracket.
5   Remove the floor shift lever assembly mounting fasteners and lift the shift lever assembly up.
6   Remove the clips and washers that attach the shift and select cables to the shift lever.
7   Remove the large clip-type cable retainers that attach the cables to the bracket at the forward end of the shift lever base.
8   Remove the center airbag sensor mounting bolts and move the sensor to the side (see Chapter 12). **Caution:** *Do not disconnect the electrical connector or allow the sensor to be hit or dropped.*
9   From inside of the engine compartment, remove the retaining clips and washers from the cable ends at the transaxle.
10   Remove the large clips and washers that retain the shift and select cables to the bracket on the transaxle.
11   Remove the bolts that attach the cable retainer to the firewall. Remove the outer retainer and grommet.
12   Remove the inner retainer and grommet

from the firewall.
13   Pull the cable(s) out through the firewall.
14   Installation is the reverse of removal. When attaching cables to the front of the shifter assembly, the wider part of the cable end flange should face Up. When attaching the shift cable ends to the shifter with the clips and washers, the toothed edge of the cable eyes should face Up.

3   Shift lever assembly - removal and installation

1   Remove the center console (see Chapter 11).
2   Remove the shift and select cable retainers and disconnect both cables from the shift lever (see Section 2).
3   Remove the retaining bolts and detach the shift lever assembly.
4   Installation is the reverse of removal.

4   Back-up light switch - check and replacement

Refer to illustration 4.1
1   The back-up light switch is mounted on the transaxle **(see illustration)**. With the ignition key in the On position, place the shift lever in Reverse. The back-up lights should come on.

  a) *If the lights don't come on, check the ignition switch, the GAUGE fuse, the bulbs and the wire harness (see Chapter 12).*
  b) *If the lights remain on all the time, even when the shift lever is not in REVERSE, check the wire harness.*
  c) *If only one light comes on, but not the other, check the bulb for that light and check the harness.*

2   To check the operation of the back-up light switch itself, remove the air filter housing and the air inlet (see Chapter 4) to access the switch. Disconnect the electrical connector and unscrew the switch from the top

of the transaxle, then use an ohmmeter to verify that there's continuity when the plunger is depressed, and no continuity when the plunger is released.
3   If the switch doesn't operate as described, replace it. Disconnect the electrical connector from the switch and unscrew it from the case.
4   Test the new switch before installation by depressing the plunger with an ohmmeter connected across the switch terminals. There should be continuity only when the plunger is depressed.
5   Install the new switch and tighten it securely.

5   Manual transaxle - removal and installation

Removal

Refer to illustrations 5.5a and 5.5b
Note: *The manufacturer requires the engine and transaxle to be removed as a unit, then separated once they are out of the vehicle (see Chapter 2C for the engine/transaxle removal procedure).*
1   Disconnect the negative cable from the battery and remove the battery (see Chapter 5).
2   Remove the engine and transaxle as a unit (see Chapter 2C). **Caution:** *Do not depress the clutch pedal while the transaxle is removed from the vehicle.* **Warning:** *Do not place any part of your body under the transaxle assembly when it's supported only by a hoist or other lifting device.*
3   With the engine and transaxle lowered, support the transaxle with a floor jack. Place a block of wood on the jack head to prevent damage to the transaxle. Safety chains will help steady the transaxle on the jack.
4   Remove the transaxle case protector fasteners and lift the case protector from the transaxle.
5   Remove the transaxle-to-engine bolts **(see illustrations)**.

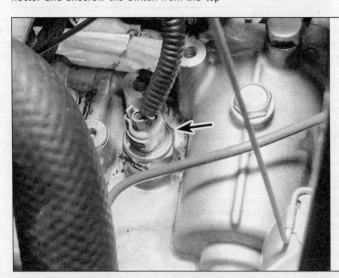

4.1 The backup light switch is threaded into the top of the transaxle case

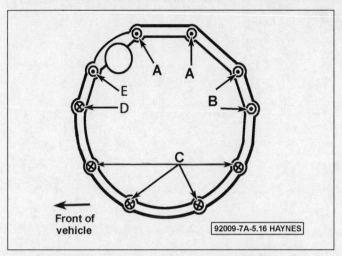

5.5a 2009 and earlier manual transaxle mounting bolts (refer to letters for torque specs when installing)

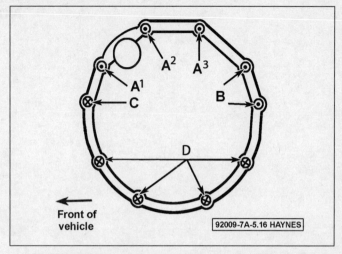

5.5b 2010 and later manual transaxle mounting bolts (refer to letters for torque specs when installing)

6   Recheck to be sure nothing is connecting the engine or the transaxle. Disconnect and label anything still remaining.

7   Move the transaxle assembly away from the engine and carefully place the transaxle assembly on the floor onto wood blocks. Leave enough room for a floor jack underneath the transaxle.

8   The clutch components can now be inspected (see Chapter 8). In most cases, new clutch components should be routinely installed whenever the transaxle is removed.

9   Check the engine and transaxle mounts and the engine control rod. If any of these components are worn or damaged, replace them.

Installation

10   If removed, install the clutch components (see Chapter 8).

11   With the transaxle secured to the jack as on removal, raise it into position and carefully slide it forward, engaging the input shaft with the clutch disc splines. Do not use excessive force to install the transaxle - if the input shaft does not slide into place, readjust the angle of the transaxle so it is level and/or turn the input shaft so the splines engage properly with the clutch. **Caution:** *Do NOT use transaxle-to-engine bolts to force the engine and transaxle into alignment. Doing so could crack or damage major components. If you experience difficulties, have an assistant help you line up the dowel pins on the block with the transaxle.*

Some wiggling of the engine and/or the transaxle will probably be necessary to secure proper alignment of the two.

12   Install the transaxle-to-engine bolts and the engine-to-transaxle bolt. Tighten the bolts to the torque listed in this Chapter's Specifications **(see illustrations 5.5a and 5.5b)**.

13   Install the engine and transaxle unit (see Chapter 2C) and tighten all mounting bolts and nuts securely.

14   Reinstall the remaining components in the reverse order of removal.

15   Tighten the wheel lug nuts to the torque listed in the Chapter 1 Specifications.

16   Add the specified amounts of coolant, oil and transaxle fluid (see Chapter 1).

17   Connect the negative battery cable. Start the engine and check for proper operation and leaks.

18   Shut off the engine and recheck the fluid levels. Road test the vehicle to check for proper transaxle operation and check for leakage.

6   Manual transaxle overhaul - general information

1   Overhauling a manual transaxle is a difficult job for the do-it-yourselfer. It involves the disassembly and reassembly of many small parts. Numerous clearances must be precisely measured and, if necessary, changed with select fit spacers and snap-rings. As a result, if transaxle problems arise, it can be removed and installed by a competent do-it-yourselfer, but overhaul should be left to a transmission repair shop. Rebuilt transaxles may be available - check with your dealer parts department and auto parts stores. At any rate, the time and money involved in an overhaul is almost sure to exceed the cost of a rebuilt unit.

2   Nevertheless, it's not impossible for an inexperienced mechanic to rebuild a transaxle if the special tools are available and the job is done in a deliberate step-by-step manner so nothing is overlooked.

3   The tools necessary for an overhaul include internal and external snap-ring pliers, a bearing puller, a slide hammer, a set of pin punches, a dial indicator and possibly a hydraulic press. In addition, a large, sturdy workbench and a vise or transaxle stand will be required.

4   During disassembly of the transaxle, make careful notes of how each component was removed, where it fits in relation to other components and what holds it in place.

5   Before taking the transaxle apart for repair, it will help if you have some idea what area of the transaxle is malfunctioning. Certain problems can be closely tied to specific areas in the transaxle, which can make component examination and replacement easier. Refer to the *Troubleshooting* Section at the front of this manual for information regarding possible sources of trouble.

Notes

Chapter 7 Part B
Automatic transaxle

Contents

Specifications

Torque specifications

Ft-lbs

Note: *One foot-pound (ft-lb) of torque is equivalent to 12 inch-pounds (in-lbs) of torque. Torque values below approximately 15 foot-pounds are expressed in inch-pounds, because most foot-pound torque wrenches are not accurate at these smaller values.*

Back-up light switch (2011 and earlier models)	33
Park/Neutral position switch (2012 and later models)	48 in-lbs
Transaxle-to-engine bolts **(see illustrations 7.15a and 7.15b)**	
Four-cylinder models	
Bolts A	47
Bolts B	34
Bolts C	32
V6 models	
Bolts A and B	47
Bolt C	34
Bolts D	32
Driveplate-to-torque converter bolts	30

1   General information

Four-cylinder engine models are equipped with either the U250E, 5-speed transaxle (2009 and earlier models), or the U760E, 6-speed transaxle (2010 and later models). Models with V6 engines are equipped with the U660E 6-speed transaxles. The transaxles vary in fluid capacity, bearing and gear size to compensate for the engine horsepower and torque. Information on the automatic transaxle is included in this Part of Chapter 7. Service procedures for the manual transaxles are contained in Chapter 7, Part A.

Due to the complexity of the automatic transaxles covered in this manual and to the specialized equipment necessary to perform most service operations, this Chapter contains only those procedures related to general diagnosis, routine maintenance, adjustment and removal and installation.

If the transaxle requires major repair work, it should be left to a dealer service department or an automotive or transmission shop. You can, however, remove and install the transaxle yourself and save the expense, even if a transmission shop does the repair work.

2   Diagnosis - general

Automatic transaxle malfunctions may be caused by five general conditions:

a) *Poor engine performance*
b) *Improper adjustments*
c) *Hydraulic malfunctions*
d) *Mechanical malfunctions*
e) *Malfunctions in the computer or its signal network*

Diagnosis of these problems should always begin with a check of the easily repaired items: fluid level and condition (see Chapter 1), shift linkage adjustment and throttle linkage adjustment. Next, perform a road test to determine if the problem has been corrected or if more diagnosis is necessary. If the problem persists after the preliminary tests and corrections are completed, additional diagnosis should be done by a dealer service department or transmission shop. Refer to the "Troubleshooting" Section at the front of this manual for information on symptoms of transaxle problems.

Preliminary checks

1   Drive the vehicle to warm the transaxle to normal operating temperature.
2   Check the fluid level as described in Chapter 1:

a) *If the fluid level is unusually low, add enough fluid to bring the level within the designated area of the dipstick, then check for external leaks (see below).*
b) *If the fluid level is abnormally high, drain off the excess, then check the drained fluid for contamination by coolant. The presence of engine coolant in the automatic transaxle fluid indicates that a failure has occurred in the internal radiator walls that separate the coolant from the transaxle fluid (see Chapter 3).*
c) *If the fluid is foaming, drain it and refill the transaxle, then check for coolant in the fluid, or a high fluid level.*

3   Check for any stored Diagnostic Trouble Codes (see Chapter 6). **Note:** *If the engine is malfunctioning, do not proceed with the preliminary checks until it has been repaired and runs normally.*
4   Inspect the shift control cable (see Section 3). Make sure that it's properly adjusted and that the linkage operates smoothly.

Fluid leak diagnosis

5   Most fluid leaks are easy to locate visually. Repair usually consists of replacing a seal or gasket. If a leak is difficult to find, the following procedure may help.
6   Identify the fluid. Make sure it's transmission fluid and not engine oil or brake fluid (automatic transmission fluid is a deep red color).
7   Try to pinpoint the source of the leak. Drive the vehicle several miles, then park it over a large sheet of cardboard. After a minute or two, you should be able to locate the leak by determining the source of the fluid

dripping onto the cardboard.
8   Make a careful visual inspection of the suspected component and the area immediately around it. Pay particular attention to gasket mating surfaces. A mirror is often helpful for finding leaks in areas that are hard to see.
9   If the leak still cannot be found, clean the suspected area thoroughly with a degreaser or solvent, then dry it.
10   Drive the vehicle for several miles at normal operating temperature and varying speeds. After driving the vehicle, visually inspect the suspected component again.
11   Once the leak has been located, the cause must be determined before it can be properly repaired. If a gasket is replaced but the sealing flange is bent, the new gasket will not stop the leak. The bent flange must be straightened.
12   Before attempting to repair a leak, check to make sure that the following conditions are corrected or they may cause another leak. **Note:** *Some of the following conditions cannot be fixed without highly specialized tools and expertise. Such problems must be referred to a transmission shop or a dealer service department.*

Gasket leaks

13   Check the pan periodically. Make sure the bolts are tight, no bolts are missing, the gasket is in good condition and the pan is flat (dents in the pan may indicate damage to the valve body inside).
14   If the pan gasket is leaking, the fluid level or the fluid pressure may be too high, the vent may be plugged, the pan bolts may be too tight, the pan sealing flange may be warped, the sealing surface of the transaxle housing may be damaged, the gasket may be damaged or the transaxle casting may be cracked or porous. If sealant instead of gasket material has been used to form a seal between the pan and the transaxle housing, it may be the wrong sealant.

Seal leaks

15   If a transaxle seal is leaking, the fluid level or pressure may be too high, the vent may be plugged, the seal bore may be damaged, the seal itself may be damaged or improperly fitted, the surface of the shaft protruding through the seal may be damaged or a loose bearing may be causing excessive shaft movement.
16   Make sure the dipstick tube seal is in good condition and the tube is properly seated. Periodically check the area around the speedometer gear or transmission speed sensors for leakage. If fluid is evident, check the O-ring for damage.

Case leaks

17   If the case itself appears to be leaking, the casting is porous and will have to be repaired or replaced.
18   Make sure the oil cooler hose fittings are tight and in good condition.

Fluid comes out vent pipe or fill tube

19   If this condition occurs, the transaxle is overfilled, there is coolant in the fluid, the case is porous, the dipstick is incorrect, the vent is plugged or the drain-back holes are plugged.

3   Shift cable - adjustment and replacement

Adjustment

Refer to illustrations 3.3, 3.5 and 3.6

1   When the shift lever inside the vehicle is moved from the Neutral position to other positions, it should move smoothly and accurately to each position and the shift indicator should indicate the correct gear position. If the indicator isn't aligned with the correct position, adjust the shift cable as follows:
2   Remove the battery and battery tray (see Chapter 5).
3   Remove the nut that attaches the shift cable to the manual lever on the transaxle **(see accompanying illustration and illustration 3.6)**.
4   Move the shift lever inside the vehicle to the Neutral position.
5   Ensure the manual lever on the transaxle is in Neutral.

a) *On 2009 and earlier four-cylinder models, move the manual lever into Park, then return it two clicks into the Neutral position* **(see illustration)**.
b) *On V6 models and 2010 and later four-cylinder models, Neutral can be found in a similar manner, but can also be verified by removing the manual lever from the shaft and confirming that the projections on the switch body and the switch hub are in alignment* **(see illustration 4.19)**.

6   Carefully slide the boot back **(see illustration)** from the end of the cable.
7   Move the slider towards the end of the cable and lift the lock upwards.
8   Install the cable to the manual lever, tighten the nut securely and push the lock

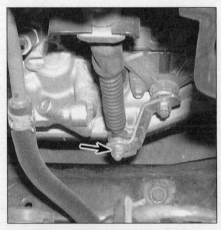

3.3 Remove the nut that connects the shift cable to the manual lever on the transaxle (2009 and earlier four-cylinder model shown)

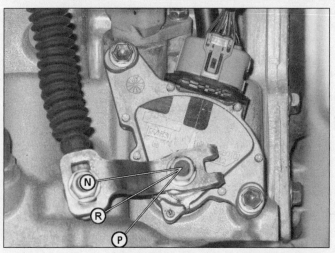

3.5 The Neutral position can be confirmed by placing the manual lever into Park, then returning it two clicks in the other direction

3.6 On V6 models and 2010 and later four-cylinder models, slide the boot (A) back from the end of the cable (B) to expose the adjusting slider. (C) is the cable-to-manual lever nut

down, locking the slider piece into the new position.

9 Check the operation of the transaxle in each shift lever position (try to start the engine in each gear - the starter should operate in the Park and Neutral positions only). If the starter doesn't operate or it is hard to shift, readjust the cable.

10 Slide the boot cover back over the adjuster assembly.

Replacement

Refer to illustrations 3.11, 3.13 and 3.14

11 Disconnect the cable from the manual lever (**see illustration 3.3 and 3.6**) and remove the large C-clip cable retainer (**see illustration**) from the bracket above the manual lever.

12 Remove the center console (see Chapter 11).

13 Pull the carpet flap back and remove the bolts from the cable housing retainer on the floor inside the vehicle (**see illustration**).

14 Pry off the cable end from the shift housing (**see illustration**).

15 Disconnect the cable eye from the shift lever pin.

16 Pull the cable through the floor.

17 Installation is the reverse of removal.

18 Adjust the cable (see Steps 1 through 10).

4 Park/Neutral Position (PNP) switch - removal, installation and adjustment

1 The Park/Neutral Position switch incorporates the Park/Neutral function as well as the backup light switch and transmission gear position information, which it sends to the PCM. The Park/Neutral function of the switch

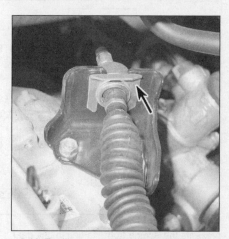

3.11 To disconnect the shift cable from the transaxle, remove the large C-clip retainer from the bracket on the top of the transaxle

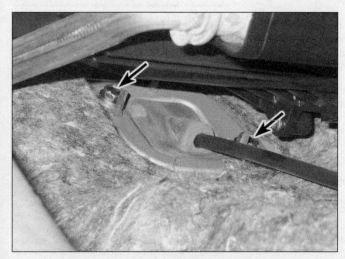

3.13 To detach the cable boot seal from the floor under the heat/ AC housing, remove the mounting bolts

3.14 To detach the shift cable from the shift lever base, twist the flange (A) to release its clips, then pry the cable eye (B) from the shifter pin (early model shown)

4.4 Remove the manual shift-lever retaining nut

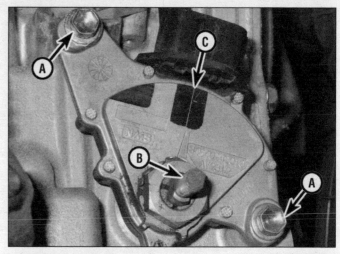

4.17 Detach the manual lever and remove the switch retaining bolts (A) - the groove on the shaft (B) should align with the Neutral line on the switch (C) when installing the switch

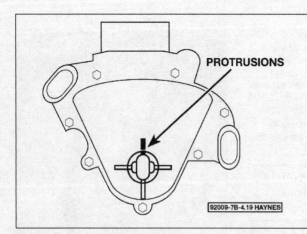

PROTRUSIONS

92009-7B-4.19 HAYNES

4.19 On V6 models and 2010 and later four-cylinder models, align the protrusion on the switch hub with the protrusion on the switch body

prevents the engine from starting in any gear other than Park or Neutral. If the engine starts with the shift lever in any position other than Park or Neutral, adjust the switch. The Park/Neutral Position switch is also an information sensor for the Electronic Controlled Transaxle (ECT) Electronic Control Unit (ECU). When the shift lever is placed in position, the Park/Neutral position switch sends a voltage signal to the ECU.

Replacement

2009 and earlier four-cylinder models (U250E)

Refer to illustration 4.4

2   Raise the front of the vehicle and place it securely on jackstands.
3   Disconnect the electrical connector.
4   Remove the manual lever retaining nut and its lock plate **(see illustration)**. **Note:** *Bend the tabs flat on the lock plate before removing it (if equipped).*
5   Remove the switch retaining bolts **(see illustration 4.17)**.
6   Remove the switch.
7   Installation is the reverse of removal. Be sure to adjust the switch.

All V6 models and 2010 and later four-cylinder models (U660E and U760E)

8   Remove the engine cover (see Chapter 2).
9   Remove the air filter housing and air inlet (see Chapter 4).
10   Remove the transaxle cable bracket clip.
11   Remove the transaxle control cable retaining nut and remove the cable from the lever.
12   Disconnect the wiring harness clamp and electrical connector from the switch.
13   Remove the control shaft lever nut, washer and lever from the switch assembly.
14   Remove the switch retaining bolts and clean any dirt from the switch area.
15   Remove the switch.
16   Installation is the reverse of removal. Be sure to adjust the switch.

Adjustment

2009 and earlier four-cylinder models (U250E)

Refer to illustration 4.17

17   Loosen the switch retaining bolts and

rotate the switch until the groove and the neutral basic line on the switch are aligned **(see illustration)**. Hold the switch in this position and tighten the bolts. **Note:** *The pointer on the sheetmetal lock plate will indicate the alignment of the groove on the shaft with the Neutral line on the body of the switch.*
18   Refer to Section 3 for the cable adjustment procedure.

All V6 models and 2010 and later four-cylinder models (U660E and U760E)

Refer to illustration 4.19

19   Loosen the switch retaining bolts and rotate the switch until the protrusion on the hub of the switch is aligned with the protrusion on the switch body **(see illustration)**. Hold the switch in this position and tighten the bolts.
20   Refer to Section 3 for the cable adjustment procedure.

5   Shift lock system - description and component replacement

Description

1   The shift lock system prevents the shift lever from being shifted out of Park until the brake pedal is applied and the key is turned to the "ON" position. The system consists of the brake light switch, a key interlock solenoid, a shift lock override button, a shift lock motor, and a shift lock control computer that incorporates a switch operated by the shift lever.

Component replacement

2   Remove the center console (see Chapter 11).
3   The shift lock control computer is located at the bottom of the shift lever base on the left side. Disconnect the electrical connector and unclip the shift-lock computer from the shifter assembly.

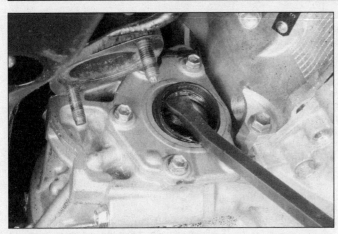

6.4 Carefully pry out the old driveaxle seal with a prybar, screwdriver or a special seal removal tool; make sure you don't gouge or nick the surface of the seal bore

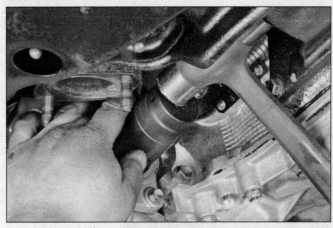

6.6 Drive in the new driveaxle seal with a large socket or a special seal installer

4   The key interlock solenoid is located near the ignition switch (see Chapter 12, Section 9).

6   Oil seal replacement

1   Fluid leaks frequently occur due to wear of the driveaxle oil seals and/or the speed sensor O-rings. Replacement of these seals is relatively easy, since the repairs can usually be performed without removing the transaxle from the vehicle.

Driveaxle seals

Refer to illustrations 6.4 and 6.6

2   The driveaxle oil seals are located in either sides of the transaxle, where the driveaxle shaft is splined into the differential. If leakage at the seal is suspected, raise the vehicle and support it securely on jackstands. If the seal is leaking, fluid will be found on the side of the transaxle.
3   Remove the driveaxle (see Chapter 8). If you're replacing the right side driveaxle seal,

remove the intermediate shaft and the driveaxle assembly as a single unit.
4   Using a screwdriver or prybar, carefully pry the oil seal out of the transaxle bore **(see illustration)**.
5   If the oil seal cannot be removed with a screwdriver or prybar, a special oil seal removal tool (available at auto parts stores) will be required.
6   Using a seal driver or a large deep socket as a drift, install the new oil seal. Drive it into the bore squarely and make sure that it is completely seated **(see illustration)**. Lubricate the lip of the new seal with multi-purpose grease.
7   Install the driveaxle assembly (see Chapter 8). Be careful not to damage the lip of the new seal.

Speed sensors (5-speed transaxles only)

Refer to illustrations 6.9 and 6.10

8   The transaxle speed sensors are located on the case of the transaxle. Look for lubricant around the sensor housings to determine if an

O-ring is leaking. **Note:** *All 6-speed transaxle speed sensors are mounted internally to the valve body in the transmission pan.*
9   Disconnect the electrical connector from the vehicle or transmission speed sensor and remove it from the transaxle **(see illustration)**.
10   Remove the O-ring **(see illustration)**.
11   Install a new O-ring on the driven gear housing. Reinstall the speedometer driven gear and vehicle speed sensor housing. Tighten the hold-down bolt securely.

7   Automatic transaxle - removal and installation

Removal

Refer to illustrations 7.2, 7.5a and 7.5b

Note: *The manufacturer requires the engine and transaxle to be removed as a unit, then separated once they are out of the vehicle (see Chapter 2C for the engine/transaxle removal procedure).*

6.9 To remove the vehicle speed sensor from the transaxle, disconnect the electrical connector and remove the sensor hold-down bolt (two sensors shown here)

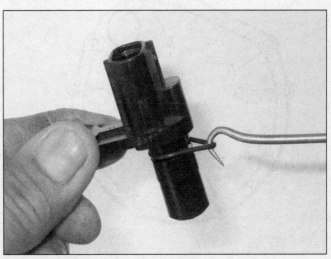

6.10 Remove the O-ring from the speed sensor

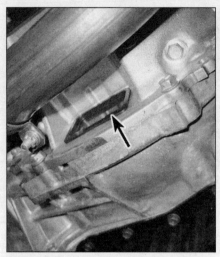

7.2 Carefully pry the torque converter access cover out to expose the converter bolts

1   Disconnect the negative cable from the battery and remove the battery (see Chapter 5).

2   With the vehicle raised on a hoist, remove the torque converter access cover **(see illustration)**, then remove the driveplate-to-torque converter bolts. **Note:** *Rotate the engine using the crankshaft pulley bolt to gain access to each bolt.* Take note of the bolts as they are removed; on some models, one of the bolts is color coded and must be reinstalled in the same location.

3   Remove the engine and transaxle as a unit (see Chapter 2C). **Caution:** *Do not depress the clutch pedal while the transaxle is removed from the vehicle.* **Warning:** *Do not place any part of your body under the transaxle assembly when it's supported only by a hoist or other lifting device.*

4   With the engine and transaxle lowered, support the transaxle with a floor jack. Place a block of wood on the jack head to prevent damage to the transaxle. Safety chains will help steady the transaxle on the jack.

5   Remove the transaxle-to-engine bolts **(see illustrations)**.

6   Recheck to be sure nothing is connecting the engine or the transaxle. Disconnect and label anything still remaining.

7   Move the transaxle assembly away from the engine and carefully place the transaxle assembly on the floor onto wood blocks. Leave enough room for a floor jack underneath the transaxle.

8   Check the engine and transaxle mounts and the engine control rod. If any of these components are worn or damaged, replace them.

Installation

9   If removed, install the torque converter on the transaxle input shaft. Make sure the converter hub splines are properly engaged with the splines on the input shaft and front pump. Apply a coat of multi-purpose grease to the hub of the torque converter

10   With the transaxle secured to the jack as on removal, raise it into position and then carefully slide it forward. Do not use excessive force to install the transaxle - if it does not slide into place, readjust the angle of the transaxle so it is level. **Caution:** *Do NOT use transaxle-to-engine bolts to force the engine and transaxle into alignment. Doing so could crack or damage major components. If you experience difficulties, have an assistant help you line up the dowel pins on the block with the transaxle. Some wiggling of the engine and/or the transaxle will probably be necessary to secure proper alignment of the two.*

11   Install the transaxle-to-engine bolts. Tighten the bolts to the torque listed in this Chapter's Specifications **(see illustrations 7.5a and 7.5b)**.

12   Install the engine and transaxle unit (see Chapter 2C) and tighten all mounting bolts and nuts securely. Tighten the driveplate-to-torque converter bolts to the torque listed in this Chapter's Specifications.

13   Reinstall the remaining components in the reverse order of removal.

14   Remove the jack and hoist and lower the vehicle. Tighten the wheel lug nuts to the torque listed in the Chapter 1 Specifications.

15   Add the specified amounts of coolant, oil and transaxle fluid (see Chapter 1).

16   Connect the negative battery cable. Start the engine and check for proper operation and leaks.

17   Shut off the engine and recheck the fluid levels. Road test the vehicle to check for proper transaxle operation and check for leakage.

---

8   Electronic control system

Trouble codes

1   The electronic control system for the transaxle has some self-diagnostic capabilities. If certain kinds of system malfunctions occur, the PCM stores the appropriate diagnostic trouble code in its memory and the CHECK ENGINE indicator light illuminates to inform the driver. The diagnostic trouble codes can only be extracted from the PCM using a SCAN tool that can be linked to the On Board Diagnostic (OBD II) computer via the Data Link connector (DLC). Codes are listed below for reference, but can only be extracted with the correct scan tool connected to the Data Link connector (DLC) under the left side of the instrument panel (refer to Chapter 6 for additional information).

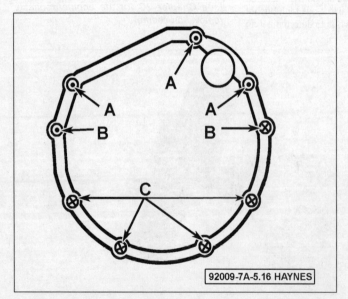

7.5a Transaxle mounting bolt locations - four-cylinder models

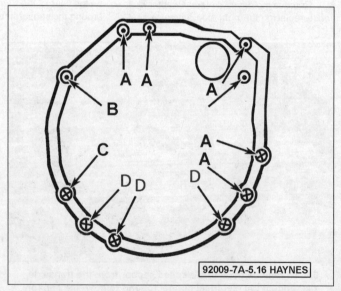

7.5b Transaxle mounting bolt locations - V6 models

Trouble codes

Code	Code identification
P0500	Vehicle speed sensor "A" or circuit fault
P0705	Transmission Range Sensor Circuit (PRNDL input)
P0560	System Voltage
P0617	Starter Relay circuit (high)
P062F	Internal Control Module EEPROM Error
P0711	Transmission fluid temperature sensor, range or performance fault
P0712	Transmission Fluid Temperature Sensor "A" Circuit (low) input
P0713	Transmission Fluid Temperature Sensor "A" Circuit (high) input
P0715	Input / Turbine Speed Sensor Circuit Malfunction
P0717	Turbine Speed Sensor Circuit No Signal
P0724	Brake Switch "B" Circuit High
P0741	Torque Converter Clutch Solenoid performance malfunction
P0746	Pressure Control Solenoid "A" performance malfunction
P0748	Pressure Control Solenoid "A" electrical malfunction
P0766	Shift Solenoid "D" performance malfunction
P0771	Shift Solenoid "E" performance malfunction
P0776	Pressure Control Solenoid "B" performance malfunction
P0778	Pressure Control Solenoid "B" electrical malfunction
P0791	Intermediate Shaft Speed Sensor "A" circuit malfunction
P0793	Intermediate Shaft Speed Sensor "A" circuit malfunction
P0796	Pressure Control Solenoid "C" performance malfunction
P0798	Pressure Control Solenoid "C" electrical malfunction

Code	Code identification
P0872	Transmission Fluid Pressure Sensor/Switch "C" circuit (low) problem
P0873	Transmission Fluid Pressure Sensor/Switch "C" circuit (high) problem
P0877	Transmission Fluid Pressure Sensor/Switch "D" circuit (low) problem
P0878	Transmission Fluid Pressure Sensor/Switch "D" circuit (high) problem
P0982	Shift Solenoid "D" Control circuit (low) problem
P0983	Shift Solenoid "D" Control circuit (high) problem
P0985	Shift Solenoid "E" Control circuit (low) problem
P0986	Shift Solenoid "E" Control circuit (high) problem
P0989	Transmission Fluid Pressure Sensor/Switch "E" circuit (low) problem
P0990	Transmission Fluid Pressure Sensor/Switch "E" circuit (high) problem
P2714	Pressure Control Solenoid "D" performance malfunction
P2716	Pressure Control Solenoid "D" electrical malfunction
P2757	Torque Converter Clutch Pressure Control Solenoid performance malfunction
P2759	Torque Converter Clutch Pressure Control Solenoid Control, circuit electrical malfunction
P2769	Torque Converter Clutch Solenoid, circuit (low) problem
P2770	Torque Converter Clutch Solenoid, circuit (high) problem
P2808	Pressure Control Solenoid "G" performance malfunction
P2810	Pressure Control Solenoid "G" " electrical malfunction
U0100	Lost Communication with ECM/PCM "A"

Other Electronic Control System checks

Preliminary checks

2   Check the fluid level and condition. If the fluid smells burned, replace it (see Chapter 1).
3   Check for fluid leaks (see Section 2).
4   Check and, if necessary, adjust the shift cable (see Section 3).
5   Check and, if necessary, adjust the PNP switch (see Section 4).

O/D OFF indicator light check

6   Turn the ignition switch to ON.
7   Verify that the O/D OFF indicator light comes on when the O/D main switch is in the Off (up) position, and goes out when the O/D main switch is pushed to the On position.
8   If the O/D OFF indicator light does not light up, or remains on all the time, have the circuit checked out by a dealer service department.

Notes

Chapter 8
Clutch and driveaxles

Contents

Specifications

Clutch

Fluid type	See Chapter 1
Pedal freeplay	See Chapter 1
Pedal height	See Chapter 1

Torque specifications

Ft-lbs (unless otherwise indicated)

Note: *One foot-pound (ft-lb) of torque is equivalent to 12 inch-pounds (in-lbs) of torque. Torque values below approximately 15 foot-pounds are expressed in inch-pounds, because most foot-pound torque wrenches are not accurate at these smaller values.*

Clutch master cylinder mounting nuts	132 in-lbs
Clutch accumulator	
Bracket bolts	108 in-lbs
Bolts at housing	29
Clutch pressure plate-to-flywheel bolts	168 in-lbs
Clutch release cylinder	
2009 and earlier models	108 in-lbs
2010 and later models	17
Driveaxle/hub nut	217
Right driveaxle center bearing lock bolt	24
Wheel lug nuts	See Chapter 1

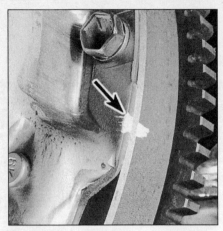

3.4 Mark the relationship of the pressure plate to the flywheel (in case you are going to re-use the same pressure plate)

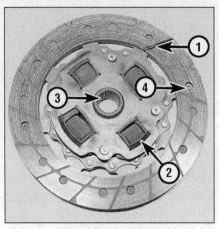

3.8 The clutch disc

1   **Lining** - *this will wear down in use*
2   **Springs or dampers** - *check for cracking and deformation*
3   **Splined hub** - *the splines must not be worn and should slide smoothly on the transaxle input shaft splines*
4   **Rivets** - *these secure the lining and will damage the flywheel or pressure plate if allowed to contact the surfaces*

1   General information

The information in this Chapter deals with the components from the rear of the engine to the front wheels, except for the transaxle, which is dealt with in Chapters 7A and 7B. For the purposes of this Chapter, these components are grouped into two categories: clutch and driveaxles. Separate Sections within this Chapter offer general descriptions and checking procedures for both groups.

Since nearly all the procedures covered in this Chapter involve working under the vehicle, make sure it's securely supported on sturdy jackstands or a hoist where the vehicle can be easily raised and lowered.

2   Clutch - description and check

1   All vehicles with a manual transaxle use a single dry plate, diaphragm spring type clutch. The clutch disc has a splined hub that allows it to slide along the splines of the transaxle input shaft. The clutch and pressure plate are held in contact by spring pressure exerted by the diaphragm in the pressure plate.
2   The clutch release system is operated by hydraulic pressure. The hydraulic release system consists of the clutch pedal, a master cylinder and fluid reservoir, the hydraulic line, an accumulator, a release (or slave) cylinder which actuates the clutch release lever and the clutch release (or throw-out) bearing. **Note:** *On 2010 and later models, the release bearing and release cylinder are an assembly and no lever is used.*
3   When pressure is applied to the clutch pedal to release the clutch, hydraulic pressure is exerted against the outer end of the clutch release lever. As the lever pivots, the shaft fingers push against the release bearing. The bearing pushes against the fingers of the diaphragm spring of the pressure plate assembly, which in turn releases the clutch plate.

4   Terminology can be a problem regarding the clutch components because common names have in some cases changed from that used by the manufacturer. For example, the driven plate is also called the clutch plate or disc, the pressure plate assembly is sometimes referred to as the clutch cover, the clutch release bearing is sometimes called a throw-out bearing, and the release cylinder is sometimes called the operating or slave cylinder.
5   Other than replacing components that have obvious damage, some preliminary checks should be performed to diagnose a clutch system failure.

a)   *The first check should be of the fluid level in the clutch master cylinder (see Chapter 1). If the fluid level is low, add fluid as necessary and inspect the hydraulic clutch system for leaks. If the master cylinder reservoir has run dry, bleed the system (see Section 7) and re-test the clutch operation.*
b)   *To check clutch spin-down time, run the engine at normal idle speed with the transaxle in Neutral (clutch pedal up - engaged). Disengage the clutch (pedal down), wait several seconds and shift the transaxle into Reverse. No grinding noise should be heard. A grinding noise would most likely indicate a problem in the pressure plate or the clutch disc.*
c)   *To check for complete clutch release, run the engine (with the parking brake applied to prevent movement) and hold the clutch pedal approximately 1/2-inch from the floor. Shift the transaxle between 1st gear and Reverse several times. If the shift is not smooth, com-*

ponent failure is indicated. Check the release cylinder pushrod travel. With the clutch pedal depressed completely the release cylinder pushrod should extend substantially. If it doesn't, check the fluid level in the clutch master cylinder.
d)   *Visually inspect the clutch pedal bushing at the top of the clutch pedal to make sure there is no sticking or excessive wear.*
e)   *Under the vehicle, check that the clutch release lever is solidly mounted on the ballstud.*

3   Clutch components - removal, inspection and installation

Warning: *Dust produced by clutch wear and deposited on clutch components is hazardous to your health. DO NOT blow it out with compressed air and DO NOT inhale it. DO NOT use gasoline or petroleum based solvents to remove the dust. Brake system cleaner should be used to flush the dust into a drain pan. After the clutch components are wiped clean with a rag, dispose of the contaminated rags and cleaner in a labeled, covered container.*

Removal

Refer to illustration 3.4

1   Access to the clutch components is accomplished by removing the transaxle and engine assembly as a unit (see Chapter 2C).
2   Separate the transaxle from the engine (see Chapter 7A). The release fork (2009 and earlier models) and release bearing can remain attached to the transaxle for the time being.
3   To support the clutch disc during removal, install a clutch alignment tool through the clutch disc hub.
4   Carefully inspect the flywheel and pressure plate for indexing marks. The marks are usually an X, an O or a white letter. If they cannot be found, scribe marks yourself so the pressure plate and the flywheel will be in the same alignment during installation **(see illustration)**.
5   Slowly loosen the pressure plate-to-flywheel bolts. Work in a diagonal pattern and loosen each bolt a little at a time until all spring pressure is relieved. Then hold the pressure plate securely and completely remove the bolts, followed by the pressure plate and clutch disc.

Inspection

Refer to illustrations 3.8, 3.10a and 3.10b

6   Ordinarily, when a problem occurs in the clutch, it can be attributed to wear of the clutch driven plate assembly (clutch disc). However, all components should be inspected at this time.
7   Inspect the flywheel for cracks, heat checking, score marks and other damage. If the imperfections are slight, a machine shop

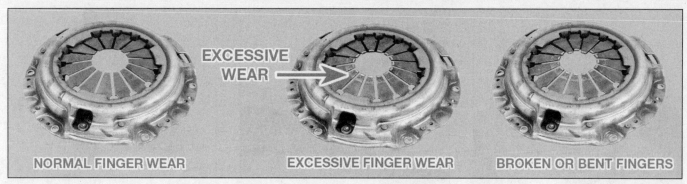

3.10a Replace the pressure plate if any of these conditions are noted

can resurface it to make it flat and smooth. Refer to Chapter 2 for the flywheel removal procedure.

8   Inspect the lining on the clutch disc. There should be at least 1/16-inch of lining above the rivet heads. Check for loose rivets, distortion, cracks, broken springs and other obvious damage **(see illustration)**. As mentioned above, ordinarily the clutch disc is replaced as a matter of course, so if in doubt about the condition, replace it with a new one.

9   The release bearing should be replaced along with the clutch disc (see Section 4).

10   Check the machined surface and the diaphragm spring fingers of the pressure plate **(see illustrations)**. If the surface is grooved or otherwise damaged, replace the pressure plate assembly. Also check for obvious damage, distortion, cracking, etc. Light glazing can be removed with emery cloth or sandpaper. If a new pressure plate is indicated, new or factory rebuilt units are available.

Installation

Refer to illustration 3.12

11   Before installation, carefully wipe the flywheel and pressure plate machined surfaces

clean. It's important that no oil or grease is on these surfaces or the lining of the clutch disc. Handle these parts only with clean hands.

12   Position the clutch disc and pressure plate with the clutch held in place with an alignment tool **(see illustration)**. Make sure it's installed properly (most replacement clutch plates will be marked "flywheel side" or something similar - if not marked, install the clutch disc with the damper springs or cushion toward the transaxle).

13   Tighten the pressure plate-to-flywheel bolts only finger-tight, working around the pressure plate.

14   Center the clutch disc by ensuring the alignment tool is through the splined hub and into the recess in the crankshaft. Wiggle the tool up, down or side-to-side as needed to bottom the tool. Tighten the pressure plate-to-flywheel bolts a little at a time, working in a crisscross pattern to prevent distortion of the cover. After all of the bolts are snug, tighten them to the torque listed in this Chapter's Specifications. Remove the alignment tool.

15   Using high-temperature grease, lubricate the inner groove of the release bearing (see Section 4). Also place grease on the release lever contact areas and the transaxle input-shaft bearing retainer.

16   Install the clutch release bearing (see Section 4).

17   Install the transaxle and all components removed previously, tightening all fasteners to the proper torque specifications.

4   Clutch release bearing and lever - removal, inspection and installation

Warning: *Dust produced by clutch wear and deposited on clutch components is hazardous to your health. DO NOT blow it out with compressed air and DO NOT inhale it. DO NOT use gasoline or petroleum-based solvents to remove the dust. Brake system cleaner should be used to flush it into a drain pan. After the clutch components are wiped clean with a rag, dispose of the contaminated rags and cleaner in a labeled, covered container.*

Removal

Note: *This procedure applies to 2009 and earlier models only. On 2010 and later models, the clutch release bearing and release cylin-*

3.10b Examine the pressure plate friction surface for score marks, cracks and evidence of overheating (blue spots)

3.12 Center the clutch disc in the pressure plate with a clutch alignment tool

4.4 To check the operation of the bearing, hold it by the outer race and rotate the inner race while applying pressure; the bearing should turn smoothly - if it doesn't, replace it

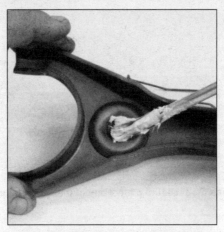

4.6a On 2009 and earlier models, use high-temperature grease to lubricate the ballstud socket in the back of the release lever . . .

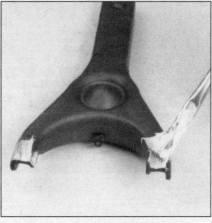

4.6b . . . the lever ends and the depression for the cylinder pushrod

der are an assembly and cannot be replaced separately. *See Section 6 for removal and installation.*

1   Disconnect the negative cable from the battery (see Chapter 5).

2   Remove the transaxle (see Chapter 7A).

3   Reach behind the release lever and disengage the lever from the ballstud by pulling on the retention spring, then remove the lever and bearing.

Inspection

Refer to illustration 4.4

4   Hold the bearing by the outer race and rotate the inner race while applying pressure **(see illustration)**. If the bearing doesn't turn smoothly or if it's noisy, replace the bearing/hub assembly with a new one. Wipe the bearing with a clean rag and inspect it for damage, wear and cracks. Don't immerse the bearing in solvent - it's sealed for life and to do so would ruin it. Also check the release lever for cracks and bends.

Installation

Refer to illustrations 4.6a and 4.6b

5   Fill the inner groove of the release bearing with high-temperature grease. Also apply a light coat of the same grease to the transaxle input shaft splines and the sleeve of the transaxle front bearing retainer.

6   Lubricate the release lever ball socket, lever ends and release cylinder pushrod socket with high-temperature grease **(see illustrations)**.

7   Attach the release bearing to the release lever.

8   Slide the release bearing onto the transaxle input shaft front bearing retainer while passing the end of the release lever through the opening in the clutch housing.

Push the clutch release lever onto the ballstud until it's firmly seated.

9   Apply a light coat of high-temperature grease to the face of the release bearing where it contacts the pressure plate diaphragm fingers.

10   The remainder of installation is the reverse of removal.

5   Clutch master cylinder - removal and installation

Removal

Refer to illustration 5.4

1   Disconnect the negative cable from the battery (see Chapter 5).

2   Remove the power brake booster (see Chapter 9).

3   Working inside the engine compartment, use pliers to remove the clutch reservoir tube clamp from the clutch master cylinder. Have rags handy as some fluid will be lost as the line is removed. **Caution:** *Don't allow brake fluid to come into contact with paint, as it will damage the finish.*

4   Remove the knee bolster (see Chapter 11) and disconnect the pushrod from the top of the clutch pedal. It's held in place with a clevis pin **(see illustration)**.

5   From under the dash, disconnect the clutch hydraulic line. Use a flare-nut wrench on the fitting, which will prevent the fitting from being rounded off. Have a small can and rags handy, as fluid will be spilled as the line is removed.

6   Remove the master cylinder mounting nuts. Remove the master cylinder and gasket, again being careful not to spill any of the fluid.

Installation

7   Position the master cylinder on the pedal assembly and firewall, installing the mounting nuts finger-tight.

8   Connect the hydraulic line to the master cylinder, moving the cylinder slightly as necessary to thread the fitting properly into the bore. Don't cross-thread the fitting as it's installed.

9   Tighten the mounting nuts to the torque listed in this Chapter's Specifications. Tighten the hydraulic line fitting securely.

10   Connect the pushrod to the clutch pedal.

11   Connect the clutch reservoir tube and fill the clutch master cylinder reservoir with brake fluid conforming to DOT 3 specifications and bleed the clutch system (see Section 7).

12   Check the clutch pedal height and free-play and adjust if necessary, following the procedure in Chapter 1.

13   The remainder of installation is the reverse of removal.

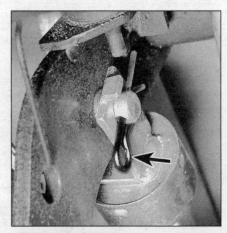

5.4 To release the clutch pushrod from the clutch pedal, remove the clip and clevis pin from the clutch pedal

6 Clutch release cylinder and accumulator - removal and installation

Clutch release cylinder

2009 and earlier models

Removal

1 Disconnect the negative cable from the battery (see Chapter 5).

2 Remove the air filter housing (see Chapter 4).

3 To disconnect the hydraulic line from the release cylinder, unscrew the threaded fitting. If available, use a flare-nut wrench on the fitting, which will prevent the fitting from being rounded off. Have a small can and rags handy, as some fluid will be spilled as the line is removed.

4 Remove the mounting bolts and separate the release cylinder from the accumulator bracket.

Installation

5 Connect the hydraulic line to the release cylinder. Install the release cylinder on the bracket, making sure the pushrod is seated in the release fork pocket. Tighten the nuts to the torque listed in this Chapter's Specifications.

6 Tighten the hydraulic line threaded fitting securely.

7 Fill the clutch master cylinder with brake fluid (conforming to DOT 3 specifications).

8 Bleed the system (see Section 7).

9 Install the air filter housing and reconnect the battery.

2010 and later models

Removal

10 Remove the engine/transaxle assembly (see Chapter 2C), then separate the transaxle from the engine (see Chapter 7A).

11 Disconnect the hydraulic line from the release cylinder. If available, use a flare-nut wrench on the fitting, which will prevent the fitting from being rounded off.

12 Remove the release cylinder mounting bolts and slide the release cylinder off of the transaxle input shaft bearing retainer.

Installation

13 Clean the inside of the clutch housing area with brake system cleaner.

14 Apply a small amount of high temperature grease to the input shaft retainer and slide the release bearing cylinder on to the input shaft retainer. **Note:** *Clean off any extra grease, making sure none gets on the input shaft splines.*

15 Connect the hydraulic line to the release cylinder, but don't tighten the fitting yet. Install the release cylinder and **new** mounting bolts, then tighten the bolts to the torque listed in this Chapter's Specifications.

16 Tighten the hydraulic line threaded fitting securely.

17 Install the transaxle to the engine, then reinstall the engine/transaxle assembly.

18 Fill the clutch master cylinder with brake fluid (conforming to DOT 3 specifications).

19 Bleed the system (see Section 7).

Accumulator

2009 and earlier models

Removal

20 Disconnect the negative cable from the battery (see Chapter 5).

21 Remove the air filter housing (see Chapter 4) and the air inlet duct.

22 Remove the accumulator bracket mounting fasteners and bracket.

23 Remove the release cylinder heat insulator mounting fasteners and heat insulator.

24 Unscrew the hydraulic line fittings from the accumulator and release cylinder, then remove the mounting bolts from the accumulator. If available, use a flare-nut wrench on the fitting, which will prevent the fitting from being rounded off. Have a small can and rags handy, as some fluid will be spilled as the line is removed.

Installation

25 Connect the hydraulic lines to the accumulator, but don't tighten them completely yet. Install the accumulator mounting bolts and tighten them to the torque listed in this Chapter's Specifications. Tighten the hydraulic line fittings securely.

26 The remainder of installation is the reverse of removal.

27 Bleed the hydraulic system (see Section 7).

2010 and later models

Removal

28 Disconnect the negative cable from the battery (see Chapter 5).

29 Loosen the left-front wheel lug nuts, raise the front of the vehicle and support it securely on jackstands, then remove the wheel. Remove the inner fender splash shield (see Chapter 11).

30 Remove the air filter housing (see Chapter 4) and the air inlet duct.

31 Unscrew the hydraulic line fittings from the accumulator and release cylinder. If available, use a flare-nut wrench on the fitting, which will prevent the fitting from being rounded off. Have a small can and rags handy, as some fluid will be spilled as the line is removed.

32 Remove the clutch orifice assembly mounting fasteners and the U-clip from the bracket with a pair of pliers and separate the clutch hose.

33 Remove the accumulator mounting bolts and accumulator assembly.

Installation

34 Install the accumulator mounting bolts and tighten them to the torque listed in this Chapter's Specifications. Connect the hydraulic lines to the accumulator and tighten the hydraulic line fittings securely.

35 The remainder of installation is the reverse of removal.

36 Bleed the hydraulic system (see Section 7).

7 Clutch hydraulic system - bleeding

1 The hydraulic system should be bled of all air whenever any part of the system has been removed or if the fluid level has been allowed to fall so low that air has been drawn into the master cylinder. The procedure is very similar to bleeding a brake system.

2 Fill the master cylinder with new brake fluid conforming to DOT 3 specifications. **Caution:** *Do not re-use any of the fluid coming from the system during the bleeding operation or use fluid which has been inside an open container for an extended period of time.*

3 Remove the air filter housing and fresh air inlet duct (see Chapter 4).

4 Remove the dust cap that fits over the bleeder valve and push a length of plastic hose over the valve. **Note:** *On 2009 and earlier models, the bleeder valve is located on the clutch release cylinder. On 2010 and later models, the bleeder valve is located on the junction block between the tube leading from the clutch orifice assembly and the tube that goes into the bellhousing (to the clutch release cylinder).* Place the other end of the hose into a clear container with about two inches of brake fluid in it. The hose end must be submerged in the fluid.

5 Have an assistant depress the clutch pedal and hold it. Open the bleeder valve, allowing fluid to flow through the hose. Close the bleeder valve when fluid stops flowing from the hose. Once closed, have your assistant release the pedal.

6 Continue this process until all air is evacuated from the system, indicated by a full, solid stream of fluid being ejected from the bleeder valve each time and no air bubbles in the hose or container. Keep a close watch on the fluid level inside the clutch master cylinder reservoir; if the level drops too low, air will be sucked back into the system and the process will have to be started all over again.

7 Check carefully for proper operation before placing the vehicle in normal service.

8 Clutch start switch - replacement

1 Check the pedal height, pedal freeplay and pushrod play (see Chapter 1).

2 Verify that the engine will not start when the clutch pedal is released.

3 Verify that the engine will start when the clutch pedal is depressed all the way.

4 The clutch start switch is located on a bracket forward of the clutch pedal (under the dash).

5 If the switch fails either of the tests, replace it. This is accomplished by removing the nut nearest the plunger end of the switch

10.3 Using a hammer and punch or chisel, unstake the driveaxle/hub nut

10.4 Use a large prybar to immobilize the hub while loosening the driveaxle/hub nut (typical)

and unscrewing the switch. Disconnect the wire harness. Installation is the reverse of removal.

6   To adjust the clutch start switch, depress the clutch pedal completely and turn the switch in or out to achieve the spacing of the original switch.

7   Verify that the switch operates properly by performing Steps 2 and 3 again.

9   Driveaxles - general information and inspection

1   Power is transmitted from the transaxle to the front wheels through a pair of driveaxles. The inner end of each driveaxle is connected to the transaxle, directly splined to the differential side gears. The outer ends of the driveaxles are splined to the front hubs and locked in place by a large nut. The left side driveaxle is shorter while the right side driveaxle is longer and equipped with an intermediate shaft that is supported in the middle by a support bearing.

10.6 Using a hammer and a brass punch, sharply strike the end of the driveaxle - it should move noticeably (don't push it in too far, though, only until it's loose)

2   The inner ends of the driveaxles are equipped with sliding constant velocity joints, which are capable of both angular and axial motion. Each inner joint assembly consists of a tripod bearing and a joint tulip (housing) constant velocity joint in which the joint is free to slide in-and-out as the driveaxle moves up-and-down with the wheel. The joints can be disassembled and cleaned in the event of a boot failure, but if any parts are damaged, the joints must be replaced as a unit (see Section 11).

3   Each outer joint, which consists of ball bearings running between an inner race and an outer race (housing), is capable of angular but not axial movement.

4   The boots should be inspected periodically for damage and leaking lubricant. Torn CV joint boots must be replaced immediately or the joints can be damaged. Boot replacement involves removal of the driveaxle (see Section 10). The most common symptom of worn or damaged CV joints, besides lubricant leaks, is a clicking noise in turns, a clunk when accelerating after coasting and vibration at highway speeds. To check for wear in the CV joints and driveaxle shafts, grasp each

axle (one at a time) and rotate it in both directions while holding the CV joint housings, feeling for play indicating worn splines or sloppy CV joints. Also check the driveaxle shafts for cracks, dents and distortion.

10   Driveaxle - removal and installation

Note: *Obtain a new driveaxle/hub nut before starting this procedure.*

Removal

Refer to illustrations 10.3, 10.4, 10.6, 10.9, 10.10a, 10.10b, 10.10c and 10.14

Note: *Not all of the steps in this procedure apply to all models. Read through the procedure carefully and determine which steps apply to the vehicle being worked on before actually beginning any work.*

1   Disconnect the cable from the negative terminal of the battery (see Chapter 5).

2   Loosen the front wheel lug nuts, raise the vehicle and support it securely on jackstands. Remove the wheel.

3   Unstake the driveaxle/hub nut **(see illustration)**.

4   Remove the driveaxle/hub nut. To prevent the hub from turning, brace a prybar between two of the wheel studs and allow the prybar to rest against the floor **(see illustration)**.

5   Disconnect the stabilizer bar link at the suspension strut and disconnect the tie-rod end from the steering knuckle. Remove the nuts and bolt securing the balljoint to the control arm, then pry the control arm down to separate the components (see Chapter 10). Disconnect the ABS wheel speed sensor from the steering knuckle and the ABS harness clamp at the suspension strut.

6   To loosen the driveaxle from the hub splines, tap the end of the driveaxle with a soft-faced hammer or a hammer and a brass

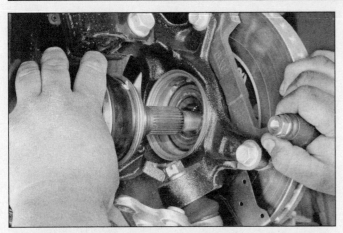

10.9 Pull the steering knuckle out and slide the end of the driveaxle out of the hub. There is a sharp ring around the CV joint just behind the stub axle - wrap a rag around it so you don't cut your hand

10.10a To release the intermediate shaft bearing from the bearing support bracket, remove this lock bolt

punch **(see illustration)**. If the driveaxle is stuck in the hub splines and won't move, it may be necessary to remove the brake disc (see Chapter 9) and push it from the hub with a two-jaw puller.

7   Place a drain pan underneath the transaxle in case lubricant leaks out.

8   If the transaxle has a case protector (the small plastic cover bolted to the transaxle) over the inner CV joint, remove it.

9   Pull out on the steering knuckle and detach the driveaxle from the hub **(see illustration)**.

10   On right driveaxle assemblies, the intermediate shaft and driveaxle assembly must be removed as a single unit. If you're removing the right driveaxle on any model, remove the center bearing lock bolt **(see illustration)**, remove the snap-ring **(see illustration)**, grasp the intermediate shaft and pull the splined inner end of the shaft out of the differential side gear **(see illustration)**.

11   If you're removing the left driveaxle, care-fully pry the inner CV joint out of the transaxle **(see illustration)**.

12   Should it become necessary to move the vehicle while the driveaxle is out, place a large bolt with two large washers (one on each side of the hub) through the hub and tighten the nut securely.

13   Refer to Chapter 7B for the driveaxle oil seal replacement procedure.

Installation

14   Installation is the reverse of the removal procedure, but with the following additional points:

a) *When installing the left driveaxle, push the driveaxle sharply inward to seat the retaining ring on the inner CV joint in the groove in the differential side gear. To ease insertion of the driveaxle, position the retaining ring with the ends of the ring at the bottom (6 o'clock).*

b) *When installing the right driveaxle/ intermediate shaft assembly, be sure to*

10.10b To remove the snap-ring from the bearing support bracket, pinch the ends together as shown and pull it out of its groove in the bracket (driveaxle assembly and bearing support bracket removed from the vehicle for clarity)

10.10c To detach the intermediate shaft from the differential side gear, grasp the shaft firmly and pull

10.11 Pry the splined end of the left driveaxle from the transaxle using a screwdriver or crowbar

11.3 Cut the old boot clamps off and discard them

11.4 Remove the boot from the inner CV joint and slide the tripod from the joint housing

tighten the center bearing lock bolt to the torque listed in this Chapter's Specifications.

c) Use a **new** driveaxle/hub nut and tighten it to the torque listed in this Chapter's Specifications, then stake the collar of the nut into the groove in the driveaxle.

d) Install the wheel and lug nuts, lower the vehicle and tighten the lug nuts to the torque listed in the Chapter 1 Specifications.

e) Check the transaxle lubricant and add, if necessary, to bring it to the proper level (see Chapter 1).

15   Check the intermediate shaft bearing for smooth operation. If it feels rough or sticky it should be replaced. Take it to a dealer service department or other repair shop, as special tools are needed to perform this job.

11   Driveaxle boot replacement

Note: Complete rebuilt driveaxles are available on an exchange basis, which eliminates much time and work. Check on the cost and availability of parts before disassembling the vehicle.

1   Remove the driveaxle (see Section 10).
2   Mount the driveaxle in a vise with wood lined jaws (to prevent damage to the axleshaft). Check the CV joint for excessive play in the radial direction, which indicates worn parts. Check for smooth operation throughout the full range of motion for each CV joint. If a boot is torn, the recommended procedure is to disassemble the joint, clean the components and inspect for damage due to loss of lubrication and possible contamination by foreign matter.

Disassembly

Refer to illustrations 11.3, 11.4, 11.6 and 11.7

3   Using diagonal cutters, cut the boot clamps **(see illustration)**, remove the clamps and discard them.
4   Using a screwdriver, carefully pry up on the edge of the outer boot and push it away from the CV joint. Old and worn boots can be cut off. Pull the inner CV joint boot back from the housing and slide the housing from the tripod **(see illustration)**.
5   Mark the tripod and axleshaft to ensure that they are reassembled properly.
6   Remove the tripod joint snap-ring with a pair of snap-ring pliers **(see illustration)**.
7   Use a hammer and a brass punch to drive the tripod joint from the driveaxle **(see illustration)**. **Note:** *The tripod joint must be removed from the driveaxle to be able to slide the inner and outer driveaxle boots over the driveaxle. Do not remove the outer CV joint from the driveaxle.*
8   If you haven't already cut them off, remove both boots.

Check

Refer to illustrations 11.9a and 11.9b

9   Thoroughly clean all components, including the outer CV joint assembly, with solvent until the old CV joint grease is completely removed. Inspect the bearing surfaces of the inner tripods and housings for cracks, pitting, scoring and other signs of wear. It's not possible to inspect the bearing surfaces of the inner and outer races of the outer CV joint, but you can at least check the surfaces of the ball bearings themselves **(see illustration)**. If they're in good shape, the races probably are, too; if they're not, neither are the races. If the inner CV joint is worn, you can buy a new inner CV joint and install it on the old axleshaft; if the outer CV joint is worn, you'll have to purchase a new outer CV joint *and* axleshaft (they're sold pre-assembled). Check

11.6 Remove the snap-ring with a pair of snap-ring pliers

11.7 Drive the tripod joint from the driveaxle with a brass punch and hammer; be careful not to damage the bearing surfaces or the splines on the shaft

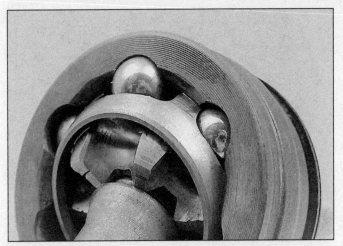

11.9a Clean the outer CV joint thoroughly with solvent and, working the joint through its entire range of motion, inspect the bearing surfaces of the balls; if they're worn or damaged, so are the bearing races

11.9b Check the condition of the support bearing on the intermediate shaft. Make sure it turns freely, quietly and smoothly; if the bearing is hard to turn, is noisy or feels rough, have it replaced by an automotive machine shop (be sure to have a pair of new dust covers installed too)

the condition of the bearing for the intermediate shaft (see illustration). It should turn freely and smoothly. If it's difficult to turn, or makes a grinding noise when rotated, take the intermediate shaft to an automotive machine shop and have a new bearing installed on the shaft.

Reassembly

Refer to illustrations 11.10a, 11.10b, 11.10c, 11.12a and 11.12b

10   Wrap the splines on the inner end of the axleshaft with electrical or duct tape to protect the boots from the sharp edges of the splines (see illustration). Slide the clamps and boots onto the axleshaft, outer boot first, then place the tripod on the shaft and install a new snap-ring. Apply grease to the tripod assembly and inside the housing. Insert the tripod into the housing and pack the remainder of the grease around the tripod (see illustrations). If you're

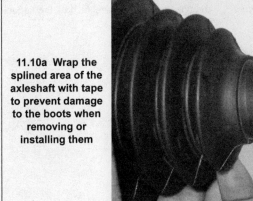

11.10a Wrap the splined area of the axleshaft with tape to prevent damage to the boots when removing or installing them

11.10b Install the tripod with the recessed portion of the splines facing the axleshaft, then install a new snap-ring

11.10c Install the boot and clamps onto the axleshaft, then insert the tripod into the housing, followed by the rest of the grease

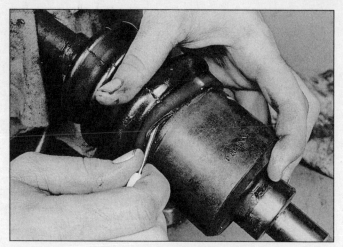

11.12a With the inner CV joint positioned half-way through its in-out travel, equalize the pressure inside the boot by inserting a small, dull screwdriver between the boot and the outer race

11.12b You'll need a special boot clamp installation tool like this one to tighten the new clamps; follow the instructions provided by the tool manufacturer

repacking the outer joint, be sure to work the entire tube of CV joint grease (included with the boot kit) into the bearing assembly.

11   Slide the boots into place, making sure the ends of both boots seat in their respective grooves in the axleshaft.

12   Position the inner CV joint mid-way through its range of travel (in/out), then equalize the pressure in the boot and tighten the boot clamps **(see illustrations)**. The driveaxle is now ready for installation (see Section 10).

Chapter 9   Brakes

Contents

Specifications

General

Brake fluid type	See Chapter 1
Brake pedal specifications	See Chapter 1
Brake light switch plunger (dimension A in **illustration 14.9**)	
All except 2013 and later ES350 models	0.059 to 0.098 inch
2013 and later ES350 models	0.024 to 0.102 inch

Disc brakes

Minimum brake pad thickness	1/8-inch
Disc minimum thickness	Cast into disc
Disc runout limit	
Front	0.0020 inch
Rear	0.006 inch
Parking brake shoe minimum thickness	1/32-inch

Torque specifications

Ft-lbs (unless otherwise indicated)

Note: *One foot-pound (ft-lb) of torque is equivalent to 12 inch-pounds (in-lbs) of torque. Torque values below approximately 15 foot-pounds are expressed in inch-pounds, because most foot-pound torque wrenches are not accurate at these smaller values.*

Caliper mounting bolts	
Front caliper	25
Rear caliper	
All models (except 2007 Avalon)	20
2007 Avalon	32
Caliper mounting bracket bolts	
Front	79
Rear	
2011 and earlier models	46
2012 and later models (except 2012 Avalon and ES350)	58
2012 Avalon and ES350	46
Brake hose-to-caliper banjo bolt	
Front	21
Rear	24
Master cylinder-to-brake booster nuts	
All 2011 and earlier models and 2012 Avalon and ES350 models	120 in-lbs
2012 and later models (except 2012 Avalon and ES350 models)	108 in-lbs
Power brake booster mounting nuts	120 in-lbs
Wheel lug nuts	See Chapter 1

1 General information

General

The vehicles covered by this manual are equipped with hydraulically operated front and rear brake systems. Both front and rear brakes are disc-type and are self-adjusting.

Hydraulic system

The hydraulic system consists of two separate circuits. The master cylinder has separate reservoirs for the two circuits, and, in the event of a leak or failure in one hydraulic circuit, the other circuit will remain operative and a warning indicator will light up on the instrument panel when a substantial amount of brake fluid is lost, showing that a failure has occurred.

Power brake booster

The power brake booster uses engine manifold vacuum to provide assistance to the brakes. It is mounted on the firewall in the engine compartment, directly behind the master cylinder.

Parking brake

Control cables are routed to the rear axle, where they operate small drum brake shoes that apply pressure to the inner diameter of the rear brake discs.

Service

After completing any operation involving disassembly of any part of the brake system, always test drive the vehicle to check for proper braking performance before resuming normal driving. When testing the brakes, perform the tests on a clean, dry, flat surface. Conditions other than these can lead to inaccurate test results.

Test the brakes at various speeds with both light and heavy pedal pressure. The vehicle should stop evenly without pulling to one side or the other. Under hard braking, the ABS system may engage, resulting in brake pedal pulsation. This is considered normal operation.

Tires, vehicle load and wheel alignment are factors which also affect braking performance.

Precautions

There are some general cautions and warnings involving the brake system on this vehicle:

a) *Use only brake fluid conforming to DOT 3 specifications.*

b) *The brake pads and linings contain fibers which are hazardous to your health if inhaled. Whenever you work on brake system components, clean all parts with brake system cleaner. Do not allow the fine dust to become airborne. Also, wear an approved filtering mask.*

c) *Safety should be paramount whenever any servicing of the brake components is performed. Do not use parts or fasteners which are not in perfect condition, and be sure that all clearances and torque specifications are adhered to. If you are at all unsure about a certain procedure, seek professional advice. Upon completion of any brake system work, test the brakes carefully in a controlled area before putting the vehicle into normal service. If a problem is suspected in the brake system, don't drive the vehicle until it's fixed.*

d) *Used brake fluid is considered a hazardous waste and it must be disposed of in accordance with federal, state and local laws.* **DO NOT pour it down the sink, into septic tanks or storm drains, or on the ground.**

e) *Clean up any spilled brake fluid immediately and then wash the area with large amounts of water. This is especially true for any finished or painted surfaces.*

2 Troubleshooting

PROBABLE CAUSE	CORRECTIVE ACTION

No brakes - pedal travels to floor

PROBABLE CAUSE	CORRECTIVE ACTION
1 Low fluid level 2 Air in system	1 and 2 Low fluid level and air in the system are symptoms of another problem - a leak somewhere in the hydraulic system. Locate and repair the leak
3 Defective seals in master cylinder	3 Replace master cylinder
4 Fluid overheated and vaporized due to heavy braking	4 Bleed hydraulic system (temporary fix). Replace brake fluid (proper fix)

Brake pedal slowly travels to floor under braking or at a stop

PROBABLE CAUSE	CORRECTIVE ACTION
1 Defective seals in master cylinder	1 Replace master cylinder
2 Leak in a hose, line, caliper or wheel cylinder	2 Locate and repair leak
3 Air in hydraulic system	3 Bleed the system, inspect system for a leak

Brake pedal feels spongy when depressed

PROBABLE CAUSE	CORRECTIVE ACTION
1 Air in hydraulic system	1 Bleed the system, inspect system for a leak
2 Master cylinder or power booster loose	2 Tighten fasteners
3 Brake fluid overheated (beginning to boil)	3 Bleed the system (temporary fix). Replace the brake fluid (proper fix)
4 Deteriorated brake hoses (ballooning under pressure)	4 Inspect hoses, replace as necessary (it's a good idea to replace all of them if one hose shows signs of deterioration)

PROBABLE CAUSE

CORRECTIVE ACTION

Brake pedal feels hard when depressed and/or excessive effort required to stop vehicle

1 Power booster faulty	1 Replace booster
2 Engine not producing sufficient vacuum, or hose to booster clogged, collapsed or cracked	2 Check vacuum to booster with a vacuum gauge. Replace hose if cracked or clogged, repair engine if vacuum is extremely low
3 Brake linings contaminated by grease or brake fluid	3 Locate and repair source of contamination, replace brake pads or shoes
4 Brake linings glazed	4 Replace brake pads or shoes, check discs and drums for glazing, service as necessary
5 Caliper piston(s) or wheel cylinder(s) binding or frozen	5 Replace calipers or wheel cylinders
6 Brakes wet	6 Apply pedal to boil-off water (this should only be a momentary problem)
7 Kinked, clogged or internally split brake hose or line	7 Inspect lines and hoses, replace as necessary

Excessive brake pedal travel (but will pump up)

1 Drum brakes out of adjustment	1 Adjust brakes
2 Air in hydraulic system	2 Bleed system, inspect system for a leak

Excessive brake pedal travel (but will not pump up)

1 Master cylinder pushrod misadjusted	1 Adjust pushrod
2 Master cylinder seals defective	2 Replace master cylinder
3 Brake linings worn out	3 Inspect brakes, replace pads and/or shoes
4 Hydraulic system leak	4 Locate and repair leak

Brake pedal doesn't return

1 Brake pedal binding	1 Inspect pivot bushing and pushrod, repair or lubricate
2 Defective master cylinder	2 Replace master cylinder

Brake pedal pulsates during brake application

1 Brake drums out-of-round	1 Have drums machined by an automotive machine shop
2 Excessive brake disc runout or disc surfaces out-of-parallel	2 Have discs machined by an automotive machine shop
3 Loose or worn wheel bearings	3 Adjust or replace wheel bearings
4 Loose lug nuts	4 Tighten lug nuts

Brakes slow to release

1 Malfunctioning power booster	1 Replace booster
2 Pedal linkage binding	2 Inspect pedal pivot bushing and pushrod, repair/lubricate
3 Malfunctioning proportioning valve	3 Replace proportioning valve
4 Sticking caliper or wheel cylinder	4 Repair or replace calipers or wheel cylinders
5 Kinked or internally split brake hose	5 Locate and replace faulty brake hose

Brakes grab (one or more wheels)

1 Grease or brake fluid on brake lining	1 Locate and repair cause of contamination, replace lining
2 Brake lining glazed	2 Replace lining, deglaze disc or drum

Troubleshooting (continued)

PROBABLE CAUSE	CORRECTIVE ACTION

Vehicle pulls to one side during braking

PROBABLE CAUSE	CORRECTIVE ACTION
1 Grease or brake fluid on brake lining	1 Locate and repair cause of contamination, replace lining
2 Brake lining glazed	2 Deglaze or replace lining, deglaze disc or drum
3 Restricted brake line or hose	3 Repair line or replace hose
4 Tire pressures incorrect	4 Adjust tire pressures
5 Caliper or wheel cylinder sticking	5 Repair or replace calipers or wheel cylinders
6 Wheels out of alignment	6 Have wheels aligned
7 Weak suspension spring	7 Replace springs
8 Weak or broken shock absorber	8 Replace shock absorbers

Brakes drag (indicated by sluggish engine performance or wheels being very hot after driving)

PROBABLE CAUSE	CORRECTIVE ACTION
1 Brake pedal pushrod incorrectly adjusted	1 Adjust pushrod
2 Master cylinder pushrod (between booster and master cylinder) incorrectly adjusted	2 Adjust pushrod
3 Obstructed compensating port in master cylinder	3 Replace master cylinder
4 Master cylinder piston seized in bore	4 Replace master cylinder
5 Contaminated fluid causing swollen seals throughout system	5 Flush system, replace all hydraulic components
6 Clogged brake lines or internally split brake hose(s)	6 Flush hydraulic system, replace defective hose(s)
7 Sticking caliper(s) or wheel cylinder(s)	7 Replace calipers or wheel cylinders
8 Parking brake not releasing	8 Inspect parking brake linkage and parking brake mechanism, repair as required
9 Improper shoe-to-drum clearance	9 Adjust brake shoes
10 Faulty proportioning valve	10 Replace proportioning valve

Brakes fade (due to excessive heat)

PROBABLE CAUSE	CORRECTIVE ACTION
1 Brake linings excessively worn or glazed	1 Deglaze or replace brake pads and/or shoes
2 Excessive use of brakes	2 Downshift into a lower gear, maintain a constant slower speed (going down hills)
3 Vehicle overloaded	3 Reduce load
4 Brake drums or discs worn too thin	4 Measure drum diameter and disc thickness, replace drums or discs as required
5 Contaminated brake fluid	5 Flush system, replace fluid
6 Brakes drag	6 Repair cause of dragging brakes
7 Driver resting left foot on brake pedal	7 Don't ride the brakes

Brakes noisy (high-pitched squeal)

PROBABLE CAUSE	CORRECTIVE ACTION
1 Glazed lining	1 Deglaze or replace lining
2 Contaminated lining (brake fluid, grease, etc.)	2 Repair source of contamination, replace linings
3 Weak or broken brake shoe hold-down or return spring	3 Replace springs
4 Rivets securing lining to shoe or backing plate loose	4 Replace shoes or pads
5 Excessive dust buildup on brake linings	5 Wash brakes off with brake system cleaner
6 Brake drums worn too thin	6 Measure diameter of drums, replace if necessary
7 Wear indicator on disc brake pads contacting disc	7 Replace brake pads
8 Anti-squeal shims missing or installed improperly	8 Install shims correctly

Note: *Other remedies for quieting squealing brakes include the application of an anti-squeal compound to the backing plates of the brake pads, and lightly chamfering the edges of the brake pads with a file. The latter method should only be performed with the brake pads thoroughly wetted with brake system cleaner, so as not to allow any brake dust to become airborne.*

PROBABLE CAUSE	CORRECTIVE ACTION

Brakes noisy (scraping sound)

1 Brake pads or shoes worn out; rivets, backing plate or brake shoe metal contacting disc or drum	1 Replace linings, have discs and/or drums machined (or replace)

Brakes chatter

1 Worn brake lining	1 Inspect brakes, replace shoes or pads as necessary
2 Glazed or scored discs or drums	2 Deglaze discs or drums with sandpaper (if glazing is severe, machining will be required)
3 Drums or discs heat checked	3 Check discs and/or drums for hard spots, heat checking, etc. Have discs/drums machined or replace them
4 Disc runout or drum out-of-round excessive	4 Measure disc runout and/or drum out-of-round, have discs or drums machined or replace them
5 Loose or worn wheel bearings	5 Adjust or replace wheel bearings
6 Loose or bent brake backing plate (drum brakes)	6 Tighten or replace backing plate
7 Grooves worn in discs or drums	7 Have discs or drums machined, if within limits (if not, replace them)
8 Brake linings contaminated (brake fluid, grease, etc.)	8 Locate and repair source of contamination, replace pads or shoes
9 Excessive dust buildup on linings	9 Wash brakes with brake system cleaner
10 Surface finish on discs or drums too rough after machining (especially on vehicles with sliding calipers)	10 Have discs or drums properly machined
11 Brake pads or shoes glazed	11 Deglaze or replace brake pads or shoes

Brake pads or shoes click

1 Shoe support pads on brake backing plate grooved or excessively worn	1 Replace brake backing plate
2 Brake pads loose in caliper	2 Loose pad retainers or anti-rattle clips
3 Also see items listed under Brakes chatter	

Brakes make groaning noise at end of stop

1 Brake pads and/or shoes worn out	1 Replace pads and/or shoes
2 Brake linings contaminated (brake fluid, grease, etc.)	2 Locate and repair cause of contamination, replace brake pads or shoes
3 Brake linings glazed	3 Deglaze or replace brake pads or shoes
4 Excessive dust buildup on linings	4 Wash brakes with brake system cleaner
5 Scored or heat-checked discs or drums	5 Inspect discs/drums, have machined if within limits (if not, replace discs or drums)
6 Broken or missing brake shoe attaching hardware	6 Inspect drum brakes, replace missing hardware

Rear brakes lock up under light brake application

1 Tire pressures too high	1 Adjust tire pressures
2 Tires excessively worn	2 Replace tires
3 Defective proportioning valve	3 Replace proportioning valve

Troubleshooting (continued)

PROBABLE CAUSE	CORRECTIVE ACTION

Brake warning light on instrument panel comes on (or stays on)

1 Low fluid level in master cylinder reservoir (reservoirs with fluid level sensor)	1 Add fluid, inspect system for leak, check the thickness of the brake pads and shoes
2 Failure in one half of the hydraulic system	2 Inspect hydraulic system for a leak
3 Piston in pressure differential warning valve not centered	3 Center piston by bleeding one circuit or the other (close bleeder valve as soon as the light goes out)
4 Defective pressure differential valve or warning switch	4 Replace valve or switch
5 Air in the hydraulic system	5 Bleed the system, check for leaks
6 Brake pads worn out (vehicles with electric wear sensors - small probes that fit into the brake pads and ground out on the disc when the pads get thin)	6 Replace brake pads (and sensors)

Brakes do not self adjust

Disc brakes

1 Defective caliper piston seals	1 Replace calipers. Also, possible contaminated fluid causing soft or swollen seals (flush system and fill with new fluid if in doubt)
2 Corroded caliper piston(s)	2 Same as above

Drum brakes

1 Adjuster screw frozen	1 Remove adjuster, disassemble, clean and lubricate with high-temperature grease
2 Adjuster lever does not contact star wheel or is binding	2 Inspect drum brakes, assemble correctly or clean or replace parts as required
3 Adjusters mixed up (installed on wrong wheels after brake job)	3 Reassemble correctly
4 Adjuster cable broken or installed incorrectly (cable-type adjusters)	4 Install new cable or assemble correctly

Rapid brake lining wear

1 Driver resting left foot on brake pedal	1 Don't ride the brakes
2 Surface finish on discs or drums too rough	2 Have discs or drums properly machined
3 Also see Brakes drag	

---

3   Anti-lock Brake System (ABS) - general information

1   The Anti-lock Brake System (ABS) is designed to maintain vehicle steerabilty, directional stability and optimum deceleration under severe braking conditions and on most road surfaces. It does so by monitoring the rotational speed of each wheel and controlling the brake line pressure to each wheel during braking. This prevents the wheel from locking up. The ABS system is primarily designed to prevent wheel lockup during heavy braking, but the information provided by the wheel speed sensors of the ABS system is shared with several optional systems that use the data to control vehicle handling. EBD (Electronic Brakeforce Distribution), varies the front-to-rear and side-to-side braking balance under different vehicle loads. The Trac system controls only the front (driving) wheels, and is designed to automatically adjust front wheel speed when starting or accelerating on slippery surfaces. The VSC system (Vehicle Skid Control) affects your car's handling during cornering, using information from the ABS sensors and the yaw-rate sensor (which senses the side-to-side tilt of the vehicle). When the skid-control ECU senses oversteer or understeer, it reduces engine power and selectively applies the brakes.

Components

Actuator assembly

2   The actuator assembly is mounted in the right front corner of the engine compartment, and consists of an electric hydraulic pump and four solenoid valves.

a) *The electric pump provides hydraulic pressure to charge the reservoirs in the actuator, which supplies pressure to the braking system. The pump and reservoirs are housed in the actuator assembly.*

b) *The solenoid valves modulate brake line pressure during ABS operation. The body contains four valves - one for each wheel.*

Speed sensors

Refer to illustration 3.5

3   These sensors are located at each wheel and generate small electrical pulsations when the toothed sensor rings are turning, sending a signal to the electronic controller indicating wheel rotational speed.

4   The front speed sensors are mounted to the front steering knuckle in close relationship to the toothed sensor rings, which are integral with the front driveaxle outer CV joints.

5   The rear wheel sensors are mounted to the rear of hub **(see illustration)**. The sensor rings are integral with the rear hub assemblies.

ABS computer

6   The ABS computer is mounted with the actuator and is the brain of the ABS system. The function of the computer is to accept and process information received from the wheel speed sensors to control the hydraulic line pressure, avoiding wheel lock up. The computer also constantly monitors the system,

even under normal driving conditions, to find faults within the system.

Diagnosis and repair

7   If a problem develops within the system, an "ABS" light will glow on the dashboard. If the dashboard warning light comes on and stays on while the vehicle is in operation, the ABS system requires attention and should be examined for stored trouble codes. Before checking for trouble codes, however, you should perform a few simple checks.

a) Check the brake fluid level in the master cylinder reservoir.
b) Check that all electrical connectors are securely connected.
c) Check all the applicable fuses.

If the above preliminary checks do not rectify the problem, or if any stored trouble codes don't lead you to the problem, the vehicle should be diagnosed and repaired by a dealer service department or other repair shop.

Trouble code retrieval

Refer to illustration 3.10

8   The ABS system control unit (computer) has a built-in self-diagnosis system which detects malfunctions in the system sensors and alerts the driver by illuminating an ABS warning light in the instrument panel. The computer stores the failure code until the diagnostic system is cleared or the malfunction is repaired.

9   The ABS warning light should come on when the ignition switch is placed in the ON position. When the engine is started, the warning light should go out. If the light remains on, the diagnostic system has detected a malfunction or abnormality in the system.

10   The codes for the ABS can be accessed by turning the ignition key to the OFF position (engine not running). Install a jumper wire onto terminals TC and CG of the diagnostic link connector and turn the ignition key ON (engine not running) **(see illustration)**. Observe the codes on the ABS warning light or the slip indicator light (on 2012 and later models with vehicle stability control).

11   The diagnostic code is the number of flashes indicated on the ABS or slip indicator lights. If any malfunction has been detected, the light will blink the first digit(s) of the code, pause 1.5 seconds, then blink the second digit of the code. For example, a code 34 (left rear wheel sensor) will first blink three flashes, pause 1.5 seconds and blink four flashes. If there is more than one code stored in the ECM, the ECM will pause 2.5 seconds before flashing the next code. If the system is operating normally (no malfunctions), the warning light will blink once every 0.5 seconds.

12   The accompanying list indicates the diagnostic code along with the system specific areas.

13   After the diagnosis check, clear the trouble codes. First, jump terminals TC and CG on the data link connector. Turn the ignition key ON (engine not running) and clear the codes by depressing the brake pedal eight or more times within five seconds. Remove the jumper wire and reinstall the cap on the data link connector. Check the indicated system or component or take the vehicle to a dealer service department to have the malfunction repaired.

ABS Trouble Codes – ABS warning light display (2011 and earlier models)

Trouble code	Code identification
Code 11	Open circuit in solenoid relay circuit
Code 12	Short to B+ in ABS solenoid relay circuit
Code 13	Open circuit in ABS motor relay circuit
Code 14	Short to B+ in ABS motor relay circuit
Code 21	Problem in right front wheel solenoid circuit
Code 22	Problem in left front wheel solenoid circuit
Code 23	Problem in right rear wheel solenoid circuit
Code 24	Problem in left rear wheel solenoid circuit
Code 25	SM circuit open or shorted
Code 31*	Sensor signal problem - right front wheel
Code 32*	Sensor signal problem - left front wheel
Code 33*	Sensor signal problem - right rear wheel
Code 34*	Sensor signal problem - left rear wheel
Code 35	Open circuit - right front speed sensor or circuit (2007 through 2009 Camry models)
Code 35	Foreign object is attached on the tip of the right front speed sensor (all models except 2007 through 2009 Camry models)
Code 36	Open circuit - left front speed sensor or circuit (2007 through 2009 Camry models)
Code 36	Foreign object is attached on the tip of the left front speed sensor (all models except 2007 through 2009 Camry models)

ABS Trouble Codes (continued) – ABS warning light display (2011 and earlier models)

Trouble code	Code identification
Code 37	Speed sensor rotor has incorrect number of teeth
Code 38	Open circuit - right rear speed sensor or circuit (2007 through 2009 Camry models)
Code 38	Foreign object is attached on the tip of the right rear speed sensor (all models except 2007 through 2009 Camry models)
Code 39	Open circuit - left rear speed sensor or circuit (2007 through 2009 Camry models)
Code 39	Foreign object is attached on the tip of the left rear speed sensor (all models except 2007 through 2009 Camry models)
Code 41	Abnormally low or high battery voltage
Code 43*	Acceleration sensor stuck malfunction
Code 44	Open or short in the acceleration sensor circuit
Code 44	Invalid data received from acceleration sensor
Code 45*	Acceleration sensor output malfunction
Code 46**	Master cylinder pressure sensor malfunction
Code 49	Open circuit - brake light switch or circuit
Code 51*	Open in pump motor circuit
Code 62	Skid control ECU malfunction
Code 71	Low output signal from right front speed sensor or circuit
Code 72	Low output signal from left front speed sensor or circuit
Code 73	Low output signal from right rear speed sensor or circuit
Code 74	Low output signal from left rear speed sensor or circuit
Code 75	Abnormal change in output signal from right front speed sensor or circuit
Code 76	Abnormal change in output signal from left front speed sensor or circuit
Code 77	Abnormal change in output signal from right rear speed sensor or circuit
Code 78	Abnormal change in output signal from left rear speed sensor or circuit
Code 91	Short in ABS motor failsafe relay
Code 94	Control module communication malfunction
Code 95	Lost communication with lateral acceleration sensor module or circuit
Code 97	Acceleration sensor power supply voltage malfunction

* Trouble code will not go off until the following steps are performed:

   a) *Drive the vehicle at 12 mph for 30 seconds or more and check to see that the ABS warning light goes off.*

   b) *Clear the trouble code (see Step 13).*

** Trouble code will not go off until the following steps are performed:

   a) *Do not move the vehicle for 5 seconds or more and depress the brake pedal lightly 2 or 3 times.*

   b) *Drive the vehicle at 31 mph and keep depressing the brake pedal strongly for approximately 3 seconds.*

   c) *Repeat the above steps 3 times or more and check that the ABS warning light goes off.*

   d) *Clear the trouble code (see Step 13).*

ABS Trouble codes – ABS warning light display (2012 and later models)

Trouble code	Code identification
Code 11	Open in ABS solenoid relay circuit
Code 12	Short in ABS solenoid relay circuit
Code 13	Open in ABS motor relay circuit
Code 14	Short in ABS motor relay circuit
Code 21	SFR solenoid circuit
Code 22	SFL solenoid circuit
Code 23	SRR solenoid circuit
Code 24	SRL solenoid circuit
Code 25	SM solenoid circuit
Code 26	SA2 solenoid circuit
Code 27	SA3 solenoid circuit
Code 28	STR solenoid circuit
Code 31	2012 and later Camry and Avalon models and 2012 ES350 models • Right front speed sensor malfunction[1] 2013 and later ES350 models • Right front speed sensor malfunction[2] • Open or short in right front speed sensor circuit[2]
Code 32	2012 and later Camry and Avalon models and 2012 ES350 models • Left front speed sensor malfunction 2013 and later ES350 models • Left front speed sensor malfunction[2] • Open or short in Left front speed sensor circuit[2]
Code 33	2012 and later Camry and Avalon models and 2012 ES350 model • Right rear speed sensor malfunction[1] 2013 and later ES350 models • Right rear speed sensor malfunction[2] • Open or short in right rear speed sensor circuit[2]
Code 34	2012 and later Camry and Avalon models and 2012 ES350 models • Left rear speed sensor malfunction[1] 2013 and later ES350 models • Left rear speed sensor malfunction[2] • Open or short in left rear speed sensor circuit[2]
Code 35	2012 and later Camry and Avalon models and 2012 ES350 models • Open in right front speed sensor 2013 and later ES350 models • Right front speed sensor output malfunction[2]
Code 36	2012 and later Camry and Avalon models and 2012 ES350 models • Open in left front speed sensor 2013 and later ES350 models • Left front speed sensor output malfunction[2]
Code 37	Speed sensor rotor faulty

ABS Trouble codes – ABS warning light display (2012 and later models)

Trouble code	Code identification
Code 38	2012 and later Camry and Avalon models and 2012 ES350 models • Open in right rear speed sensor 2013 and later ES350 models • Right rear speed sensor output malfunction[2]
Code 39	2012 and later Camry and Avalon models and 2012 ES350 models • Open in left rear speed sensor 2013 and later ES350 models • Left rear speed sensor output malfunction[2]
Code 41	• Low power supply voltage malfunction • High power supply voltage malfunction
Code 43	2013 and later ES350 models • Acceleration sensor stuck malfunction[2]
Code 44	2013 and later ES350 models • Acceleration sensor malfunction[2] • Invalid date received from acceleration sensor
Code 45	2013 and later ES350 models • Acceleration sensor output malfunction[2]
Code 46	2012 and later Camry and Avalon models and 2012 ES350 models • Master cylinder pressure sensor malfunction 2013 and later ES350 models • Open or short in master cylinder pressure sensor[3] • Master cylinder pressure sensor zero point high malfunction[3] • Master cylinder pressure sensor zero point low manfunction[3] • Master cylinder pressure sensor output malfunction[3]
Code 49	• Open in stop light switch circuit • Stop light switch stuck-off malfunction On 2013 and later ES350 models refer to note 4
Code 51	Motor circuit malfunction On 2013 and later ES350 models refer to note 2
Code 62	Skid control ECU malfunction
Code 67	• Open or short in brake pedal load sensing switch • Brake pedal load sensing switch stuck-off malfunction • Brake pedal load sensing switch stuck-on malfunction
Code 91	2013 and later ES350 models • Short in ABS motor fail safe relay circuit
Code 94	Control module communication buss off
Code 95	2013 and later ES350 models • Lost communication with lateral acceleration sensor module
Code 97	2013 and later ES350 models • Acceleration sensor power supply voltage malfunction

1- After this problem is repaired, the ABS warning light not turn off until the following steps are performed:

   a) Drive the vehicle at 34 mph for 3 seconds or more and confirm and check that the ABS warning light turns off.

   b) Clear the trouble codes (see Step 13).

2- After this problem is repaired, the ABS warning light will not turn off until the following steps are performed:

   a) Drive the vehicle at 12 mph for 3 seconds or more and confirm and check that the ABS warning light turns off.

   b) Clear the trouble codes (see Step 13) performed:

3- After this problem is repaired, the ABS warning light not turn off until the following steps are performed:

  a) *Turn the ignition switch on.*
  b) *Keep the vehicle stationary for 5 seconds or more and depress the brake pedal lightly 2 or 3 times.*
  c) *Drive the vehicle as a speec of 31 mph and depress and hold the brake pedal firmly for approximately 3 seconds.*
  d) *Repeat the above step 3 time or more and check that the ABS warning light turns off.*
  e) *Clear the DTCs.*

4- After this problem is repaired, the ABS warning light not turn off until the following steps are performed:

  a) *Turn the ignition switch on.*
  b) *Depress the brake pedal.*
  c) *Clear the DTCs.*

VSC Trouble Codes – Slip indicator light display (2012 and later models)

Trouble code	Code identification
Code 28	Accelerator sensor
Code 31	All models • Steering angle sensor output malfunction 2012 and later Camry and Avalon models and 2012 ES350 models • Steering angle sensor initialization incomplete • Vehicle driven with steering angle sensor not initialized
Code 32	• Acceleration sensor internal circuit • Acceleration sensor malfunction
Code 34	• Yaw rate sensor internal circuit • Yaw rate sensor malfunction
Code 36	Zero point calibration of yaw rate sensor undone
Code 39	Zero point calibration of acceleration sensor undone
Code 43	• This DTC displayed when the VSC system detects a malfunction in the ABS system
Code 44	NE signal
Code 51	Engine control system malfunction
Code 53	ECM communication circuit malfunction
Code 62	Lost communication with the yaw rate sensor module
Code 63	Lost communication with steering angle sensor module
Code 65	Lost communication with ECM/PCM
Code 66	• Steering angle sensor zero point malfunction • Steering angle sensor initialization incomplete
Code 6A*	Acceleration sensor power supply voltage malfunction
Code 88	Error in matching of ECUs Performance decline of brake function
Code 99	• Unusual bank angle detected • Performance decline of brake function

** The light blinks 6 times, turns off for 1.5 seconds and then blinks 10 times.

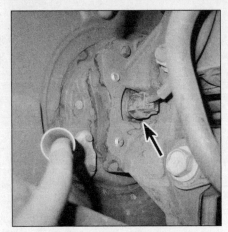

3.5 Typical rear wheel speed sensor location

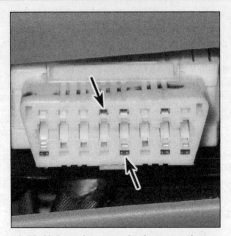

3.10 Using a jumper wire between these terminals on the diagnostic connector allows the ABS light to display trouble codes (the connector is located under the driver's side of the dash)

4.5 Before removing the caliper, be sure to depress the piston into its bore in the caliper with a large C-clamp to make room for the new pads

4.6a Always wash the brakes with brake cleaner before disassembling anything

4.6b To remove the caliper, remove the bolts indicated by the upper and lower arrows (the center arrow points to the brake hose banjo bolt, which shouldn't be unscrewed unless the caliper is being completely removed from the vehicle)

4.6c Remove the caliper . . .

4   Disc brake pads - replacement

Refer to illustrations 4.5 and 4.6a through 4.6o

Warning: *Disc brake pads must be replaced on both front or rear wheels at the same time - never replace the pads on only one wheel. Also, the dust created by the brake system is harmful to your health. Never blow it out with compressed air and don't inhale any of it. An approved filtering mask should be worn when working on the brakes. Do not, under any circumstances, use petroleum-based solvents to clean brake parts. Use brake system cleaner only!*

Note: *The following procedure applies to the front and rear brake pads.*

Note: *The manufacturer recommends replacing the pad shims and wear indicators whenever the pads are replaced.*

1   Remove the cap from the brake fluid reservoir.

2   Loosen the wheel lug nuts, raise the front

or rear of the vehicle and support it securely on jackstands. Block the wheels at the opposite end.

3   Remove the wheels. Work on one brake assembly at a time, using the assembled brake for reference if necessary.

4   Inspect the brake disc carefully as outlined in Section 6. If machining is necessary, follow the information in that Section to remove the disc, at which time the pads can be removed as well.

5   Push the piston back into its bore to provide room for the new brake pads. A C-clamp can be used to accomplish this **(see illustration)**. As the piston is depressed to the bottom of the caliper bore, the fluid in the master cylinder will rise. Make sure that it doesn't overflow. If necessary, siphon off some of the fluid.

6   Follow the accompanying photos, beginning with **illustration 4.6a**. Be sure to stay in order and read the caption under each illustration.

4.6d . . . and hang it from the strut coil spring with a piece of wire; do not allow the caliper to hang by the flexible brake hose

4.6e Remove the upper and lower anti-squeal springs (if equipped)

4.6f Remove the outer brake pad and shims, noting the arrangement of the shims

4.6g Remove the inner brake pad and shims

4.6h Remove the upper and lower pad support plates; inspect them for damage and replace as necessary (if they're weak or distorted, they should be replaced)

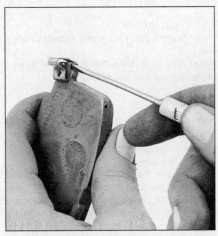

4.6i Pry the wear indicator off the old inner brake pad and transfer it to the new inner pad (if the wear indicator is worn or bent, replace it)

4.6j Install the upper and lower pad support plates, the new inner brake pad and the shims; make sure the ears on the pad are properly engaged with the pad support plates as shown

4.6k Install the outer pad and the shims, engaging the pad with the support plates

4.6l Install the upper and lower anti-squeal springs (if equipped); make sure both springs are properly engaged with the pads

4.6m Pull out the upper and lower sliding pins and clean them off (if either rubber boot is damaged, remove it by levering the flange of the metal bushing that retains the boot)

4.6n Apply a coat of high-temperature grease to the pins and install them

4.6o Install the caliper and tighten the caliper bolts to the torque listed in this Chapter's Specifications

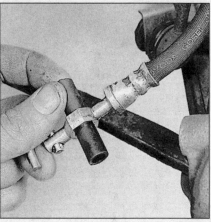

5.2 Using a piece of rubber hose of the appropriate size, plug the brake line banjo fitting to prevent brake fluid from leaking out and to prevent dirt and moisture from contaminating the fluid in the hose

7   When reinstalling the caliper, be sure to tighten the mounting bolts to the torque listed in this Chapter's Specifications. After the job has been completed, firmly depress the brake pedal a few times to bring the pads into contact with the disc. Check the level of the brake fluid, adding some if necessary. Check the operation of the brakes carefully before placing the vehicle into normal service.

5   Disc brake caliper - removal and installation

Warning: *Dust created by the brake system is harmful to your health. Never blow it out with compressed air and don't inhale any of it. An approved filtering mask should be worn when working on the brakes. Do not, under any circumstances, use petroleum-based solvents to*

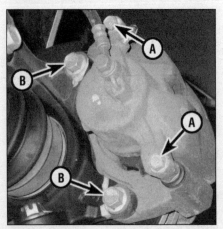

5.3 Front brake caliper details (rear caliper similar)

A   *Caliper mounting bolts*
B   *Caliper mounting bracket mounting bolts*

clean brake parts. Use brake system cleaner only!
Note: *Always replace the calipers in pairs - never replace just one of them.*

Removal
Refer to illustrations 5.2 and 5.3

1   Loosen the wheel lug nuts, raise the vehicle and support it securely on jackstands. Remove the wheels.
2   Remove the brake hose banjo bolt and disconnect the hose from the caliper. Plug the hose to keep contaminants out of the brake system and to prevent losing any more brake fluid than is necessary **(see illustration)**.
Note: *If you're only removing the caliper for access to other components, don't detach the hose.*
3   Remove the caliper mounting bolts **(see illustration)**.

6.3 The brake pads on this vehicle were obviously neglected, as they wore down completely and cut deep grooves into the disc - wear this severe means the disc must be replaced

4   Remove the caliper. If necessary, remove the caliper mounting bracket from the steering knuckle or rear axle carrier **(see illustrations 6.2a and 6.2b)**.

Installation
5   Install the caliper by reversing the removal procedure. Install **new** sealing washers on either side of the brake hose banjo fitting. Tighten the caliper mounting bolts (and caliper mounting bracket bolts, if removed) to the torque listed in this Chapter's Specifications.
6   Bleed the brake system (see Section 10).
7   Install the wheels and lug nuts. Lower the vehicle and tighten the lug nuts to the torque listed in the Chapter 1 Specifications.

6   Brake disc - inspection, removal and installation

Inspection
Refer to illustrations 6.3, 6.4a, 6.4b, 6.5a and 6.5b

1   Loosen the wheel lug nuts, raise the vehicle and support it securely on jackstands. Remove the wheel and install the lug nuts to hold the disc in place. If the rear brake disc is being worked on, release the parking brake.
2   Remove the brake caliper as outlined in Section 5. It isn't necessary to disconnect the brake hose. After removing the caliper bolts, suspend the caliper out of the way with a piece of wire **(see illustration 4.6d)**. Remove the caliper mounting bracket bolts and detach the caliper mounting bracket **(see illustration 5.3)**.
3   Visually inspect the disc surface for score marks and other damage. Light scratches and shallow grooves are normal after use and may not always be detrimental to brake operation, but deep scoring requires disc removal and refinishing by an automotive machine shop. Be sure to check both sides of the disc **(see illustration)**. If pulsating has been noticed during application of the brakes, suspect disc runout.

6.4a Use a dial indicator to check disc runout; if the reading exceeds the maximum allowable runout limit, the disc will have to be machined or replaced

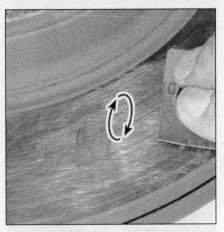

6.4b Using a swirling motion, remove the glaze from the disc surface with sandpaper or emery cloth

6.5a The minimum wear dimension is cast into the back side of the disc (typical)

4   To check disc runout, place a dial indicator at a point about 1/2-inch from the outer edge of the disc **(see illustration)**. Set the indicator to zero and turn the disc. The indicator reading should not exceed the specified allowable runout limit. If it does, the disc should be refinished by an automotive machine shop. **Note:** *Professionals recommend resurfacing the discs whenever the pads are replaced regardless of the dial indicator reading, as this will impart a smooth finish and ensure a perfectly flat surface, eliminating any brake pedal pulsation or other undesirable symptoms. At the very least, if you elect not to have the discs resurfaced, remove the glaze from the surface with sandpaper or emery cloth using a swirling motion* **(see illustration)**.

5   It's absolutely critical that the disc not be machined to a thickness under the specified minimum allowable refinish thickness. The minimum wear (or discard) thickness is cast into the inside of the disc **(see illustration)**. The disc thickness can be checked with a micrometer **(see illustration)**.

Removal

Refer to illustrations 6.6a and 6.6b

6   Remove the lug nuts that were put on to hold the disc in place and slide the disc off the hub. If the rear disc won't come off, it may be interfering with the parking brake shoes; remove the plug **(see illustration)** and rotate the adjuster to back the parking brake shoes away from the drum surface within the disc **(see illustration)**. Rotate the adjuster wheel in a clockwise direction (as seen from the front of the vehicle) to back off the parking brake shoes.

Installation

7   Place the disc in position over the threaded studs.

8   Install the caliper mounting bracket, tightening the bolts to the torque listed in this Chapter's Specifications.

9   Install the caliper, tightening the bolts to the torque listed in this Chapter's Specifications. Bleeding won't be necessary unless the

brake hose was disconnected from the caliper.

10   Install the wheel and lug nuts. Lower the vehicle and tighten the lug nuts to the torque listed in the Chapter 1 Specifications. Depress the brake pedal a few times to bring the brake pads into contact with the disc. Check the operation of the brakes carefully before driving the vehicle.

---

7   Parking brake shoes - replacement

Refer to illustrations 7.4 and 7.5a through 7.5u

Warning: *Dust created by the brake system is hazardous to your health. Never blow it out with compressed air and don't inhale any of it. An approved filtering mask should be worn when working on the brakes. Do not, under any circumstances, use petroleum-based solvents to clean brake parts. Use brake system cleaner only!*

6.5b Use a micrometer to measure disc thickness

6.6a If the rear disc is difficult to remove, remove this plug . . .

6.6b . . . insert a screwdriver through the hole (the hole must be at the 6 o'clock position, because that's where the adjuster is located) and rotate the adjuster

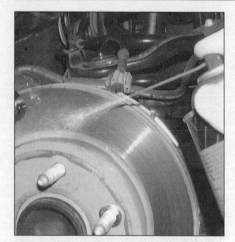

7.4 Before disassembling it, be sure to wash the parking brake assembly with brake cleaner

7.5a Remove the rear parking brake shoe return spring from the anchor pin . . .

7.5b . . . and unhook it from the rear shoe

7.5c Remove the front parking brake shoe return spring from the anchor pin . . .

7.5d . . . and unhook it from the front shoe

7.5e Remove the rear shoe hold-down spring and pull out the pin

Warning: *Parking brake shoes must be replaced on both wheels at the same time - never replace the shoes on only one wheel.*

1   Remove the brake disc (see Section 6).

2   Inspect the thickness of the lining material on the shoes. If the lining has worn down to 1/32-inch or less, the shoes must be replaced.

3   Remove the hub and bearing assembly (see Chapter 10). **Note:** *It is possible to perform the shoe replacement procedure without removing the hub and bearing assembly, although working room is limited.*

4   Wash off the brake parts with brake system cleaner **(see illustration)**.

5   Follow the accompanying illustrations for the brake shoe replacement procedure **(see illustrations 7.5a through 7.5u)**. Be sure to stay in order and read the caption under each illustration.

7.5f Remove the shoe strut from between the shoes

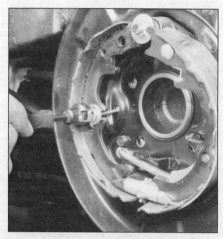

7.5g Remove the front shoe hold-down spring and pull out the pin

7.5h Remove the adjuster and the tension spring (the tension spring, which is not visible in this photo, is behind the adjuster and is attached to both shoes)

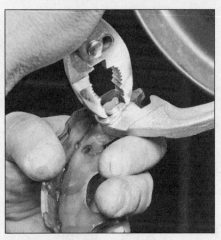

7.5i Pop the C-washer off the pivot pin on the back of the rear shoe . . .

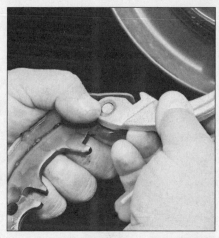

7.5j . . . and pull the parking brake lever off the pivot pin

7.5k Apply a thin coat of high-temperature grease to the contact surfaces of the backing plate

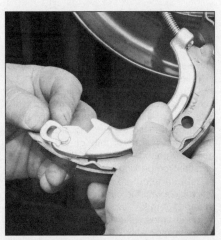

7.5l Slide the parking brake lever onto the pivot pin and install a new C-washer

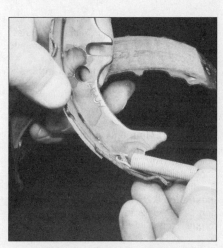

7.5m Attach the tension spring to the back side of the rear shoe . . .

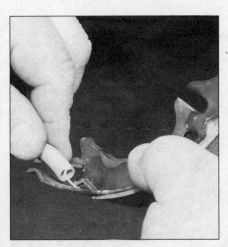

7.5n . . . and to the back side of the front shoe

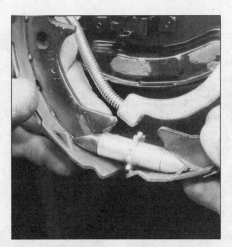

7.5o Flip the shoes around and install the adjuster; make sure both ends of the adjuster are properly engaged with the shoes as shown

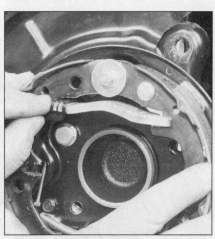

7.5p Place the shoes in position and install the strut and spring as shown; make sure the ends of the strut are properly engaged with the shoes as shown

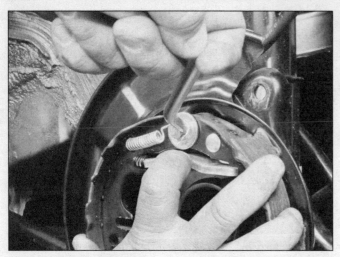

7.5q Install the front shoe return spring . . .

7.5r . . . and the rear shoe return spring

6   Install the brake disc. Temporarily thread three of the wheel lug nuts onto the studs to hold the disc in place.

7   Remove the hole plug from the brake disc. Adjust the parking brake shoe clearance by turning the adjuster star wheel with a brake adjusting tool or screwdriver until the shoes contact the disc and the disc can't be turned **(see illustrations 6.6a and 6.6b)**. Back off the adjuster eight notches, then install the hole plug. Turn the disc and verify that the shoes don't drag.

8   Install the caliper mounting bracket **(see illustration 6.2b)** and brake caliper (see Section 5). Be sure to tighten the bolts to the torque listed in this Chapter's Specifications.

9   Install the wheel and tighten the lug nuts to the torque specified in Chapter 1.

10   If the vehicle is equipped with a parking brake lever, pull up on the lever and count the number of clicks that it travels. It should be between five and eight clicks - if it's not, adjust the parking brake as described in Section 12.

11   To bed the shoes to the drum, drive the vehicle at approximately 30 mph on a dry, level road. If the vehicle has a parking brake lever, push in on the parking brake release button and pull up slightly on the lever with about 20 pounds of force; if the vehicle has a pedal-type parking brake system, apply the pedal with about 33 pounds of force. Drive the vehicle with the parking brake applied like this for 1/4-mile. Repeat this procedure two or three times, allowing the brakes to cool between applications.

7.5s Install the rear shoe hold-down spring . . .

7.5t . . . and the front shoe hold-down spring

7.5u This is how the parking brake assembly should look when you're done

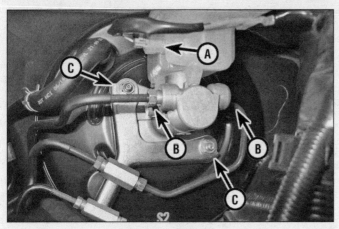

8.5 Master cylinder details

A   Electrical connector   C   Mounting nuts
B   Brake line fittings

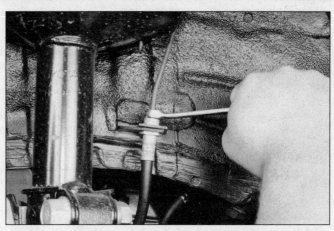

9.3 Unscrew the brake line threaded fitting with a flare-nut wrench to protect the fitting corners from being rounded off

8   Master cylinder - removal and installation

Warning: *Do not drop or hit the master cylinder. If the master cylinder is dropped it may not be reused.*
Caution: *The master cylinder is designed to allow the piston to pop out and be exposed. Hold the master cylinder by the body not the piston or the master cylinder may be damaged. Do not try to remove the piston or allow the piston to be scratched or damaged.*

Removal

Refer to illustration 8.5

1   Remove the engine covers (see Chapter 1).
2   Remove the windshield wiper assembly (see Chapter 12).
3   Remove the cowl assembly (see Chapter 11).
4   Depress the brake pedal several times and release the vacuum from the booster.
5   Unplug the electrical connector for the brake fluid level warning switch **(see illustration)**.
6   Remove as much fluid as possible from the reservoir with a syringe.
7   Place rags under the fittings and prepare caps or plastic bags to cover the ends of the lines once they're disconnected. **Caution:** *Brake fluid will damage paint. Cover all body parts and be careful not to spill fluid during this procedure.*
8   Loosen the fittings at the ends of the brake lines where they enter the master cylinder. To prevent rounding off the flats, use a flare-nut wrench, which wraps around the fitting hex.
9   Pull the brake lines away from the mas-

ter cylinder and plug the ends to prevent contamination.
10   Remove the nuts attaching the master cylinder to the power booster. Pull the master cylinder off the studs and keep the master cylinder level to prevent the piston from coming out. Again, be careful not to spill the fluid as this is done.

Installation

Note: *When installing the master cylinder, remove the piston and port protective caps.*
Note: *If the piston gets dirty, clean it with a rag or cloth and apply lithium soap based glycol grease evenly around the sliding portion of the piston. Do not use any other type of grease.*
11   Install the reservoir cover, then install the master cylinder over the studs on the power brake booster and tighten the attaching nuts only finger tight at this time. **Caution:** *Keep the master cylinder level or piston end up as much as possible to prevent the piston from falling out.*
12   Attach a pair of master cylinder bleeder tubes to the outlet ports of the master cylinder.
13   Fill the reservoir with brake fluid of the recommended type (see Chapter 1).
14   Slowly push the brake pedal down inside the vehicle - air will be expelled from the pressure chambers and into the reservoir. Because the tubes are submerged in fluid, air can't be drawn back into the master cylinder when you release the pedal. **Caution:** *Have plenty of rags on hand to catch the fluid - brake fluid will ruin painted surfaces.*
15   Repeat the procedure until no more air bubbles are present.
16   Remove the bleed tubes, one at a time, and thread the brake line fittings into the master cylinder. Since the master cylinder is finger tight, the nuts can be easily loosened and moved slightly in order for the fittings to

thread in easily. Do not strip the threads as the fittings are tightened.
17   Fully tighten the mounting nuts, then the brake line fittings.
18   Fill the master cylinder reservoir with fluid, then bleed the master cylinder and the brake system as described in Section 10.
19   Installation is the reverse of removal. Test the operation of the brake system carefully before placing the vehicle into normal service. **Warning:** *Do not operate the vehicle if you are in doubt about the effectiveness of the brake system.*

9   Brake hoses and lines - inspection and replacement

Inspection

1   About every six months, with the vehicle raised and supported securely on jackstands, the rubber hoses which connect the steel brake lines with the front and rear brake assemblies should be inspected for cracks, chafing of the outer cover, leaks, blisters and other damage. These are important and vulnerable parts of the brake system and inspection should be complete. A light and mirror will be helpful for a thorough check. If a hose exhibits any of the above conditions, replace it with a new one.

Replacement
Flexible hoses

Refer to illustrations 9.3 and 9.4

2   Loosen the wheel lug nuts, raise the vehicle and support it securely on jackstands. Remove the wheel.
3   At the frame bracket, unscrew the brake line fitting from the hose **(see illustration)**. Use a flare-nut wrench to prevent rounding off the corners.

9.4 Remove the brake hose-to-bracket U-clip with a pair of pliers

4   Remove the U-clip from the female fitting at the bracket with a pair of pliers **(see illustration)**, then pass the hose through the bracket.

5   At the caliper end of the hose, remove the banjo fitting bolt **(see illustration 4.6b)**, then separate the hose from the caliper. Note that there are two copper sealing washers on either side of the fitting - they should be replaced with new ones during installation.

6   Remove the U-clip from the strut bracket, then feed the hose through the bracket.

7   To install the hose, pass the caliper fitting end through the strut bracket, then connect the fitting to the caliper with the banjo bolt and copper washers. Make sure the locating lug on the fitting is engaged with the hole in the caliper, then tighten the bolt to the torque listed in this Chapter's Specifications.

8   Push the metal support into the strut bracket and install the U-clip. Make sure the hose isn't twisted between the caliper and the strut bracket.

9   Route the hose into the frame bracket, again making sure it isn't twisted, then connect the brake line fitting, starting the threads by hand. Install the clip and E-ring, if equipped, then tighten the fitting securely.

10   Bleed the caliper (see Section 10).

11   Install the wheel and lug nuts, lower the vehicle and tighten the lug nuts to the torque specified in Chapter 1.

Metal brake lines

12   When replacing brake lines, be sure to use the correct parts. Don't use copper tubing for any brake system components. Purchase genuine steel brake lines from a dealer or auto parts store.

13   Prefabricated brake line, with the tube ends already flared and fittings installed, is available at auto parts stores and dealer parts departments.

14   When installing the new line, make sure it's securely supported in the brackets and has plenty of clearance between moving or hot components.

15   After installation, check the master cylinder fluid level and add fluid as necessary. Bleed the brake system (see Section 10) and test the brakes carefully before driving the vehicle in traffic.

10   Brake hydraulic system - bleeding

Refer to illustration 10.8

Warning: *Wear eye protection when bleeding the brake system. If the fluid comes in contact with your eyes, immediately rinse them with water and seek medical attention.*

Caution: *If after bleeding the hydraulic system, the correct pedal height or feel can't be made, the brake actuator must be bleed. A factory scan tool or equivalent will be needed, which will necessitate taking the vehicle to a dealer service department or other properly equipped repair facility after service work has been performed.*

Note: *Bleeding the hydraulic system is necessary to remove any air that manages to find its way into the system when it's been opened during removal and installation of a hose, line, caliper or master cylinder.*

1   You'll probably have to bleed the system at all four brakes if air has entered it due to low fluid level, or if the brake lines have been disconnected at the master cylinder.

2   If a brake line was disconnected only at a wheel, then only that caliper or wheel cylinder must be bled.

3   If a brake line is disconnected at a fitting located between the master cylinder and any of the brakes, that part of the system served by the disconnected line must be bled.

4   Remove any residual vacuum from the brake power booster by applying the brake several times with the engine off.

5   Remove the master cylinder reservoir cover and fill the reservoir with brake fluid. Reinstall the cover. **Note:** *Check the fluid level often during the bleeding operation and add fluid as necessary to prevent the fluid level from falling low enough to allow air bubbles into the master cylinder.*

6   Have an assistant on hand, as well as a supply of new brake fluid, a clear container partially filled with clean brake fluid, a length of tubing to fit over the bleeder valve and a wrench to open and close the bleeder valve.

10.8 When bleeding the brakes, a hose is connected to the bleeder valve at the caliper, then submerged in brake fluid. Air will be seen as bubbles in the tube and container. All air must be expelled before moving to the next wheel

7   Beginning at the right rear wheel, loosen the bleeder valve slightly, then tighten it to a point where it's snug but can still be loosened quickly and easily.

8   Place one end of the tubing over the bleeder valve and submerge the other end in brake fluid in the container **(see illustration)**.

9   Have the assistant depress the brake pedal slowly, then hold the pedal down firmly.

10   While the pedal is held down, open the bleeder valve just enough to allow a flow of fluid to leave the valve. Watch for air bubbles to exit the submerged end of the tube. When the fluid flow slows after a couple of seconds, close the valve and have your assistant release the pedal.

11   Repeat Steps 9 and 10 until no more air is seen leaving the tube, then tighten the bleeder valve and proceed to the left rear wheel, the right front wheel and the left front wheel, in that order, and perform the same procedure. Be sure to check the fluid in the master cylinder reservoir frequently.

12   Never use old brake fluid. It contains moisture that will deteriorate the brake system components.

13   Refill the master cylinder with fluid at the end of the operation.

14   Check the operation of the brakes. The pedal should feel solid when depressed, with no sponginess. If necessary, repeat the entire process. **Warning:** *Do not operate the vehicle if you're in doubt about the effectiveness of the brake system.*

11   Power brake booster - check, removal and installation

Operating check

1   Depress the brake pedal several times with the engine off and make sure there's no change in the pedal reserve distance.
2   Depress the pedal and start the engine. If the pedal goes down slightly, operation is normal.

Airtightness check

3   Start the engine and turn it off after one or two minutes. Depress the brake pedal slowly several times. If the pedal depresses less each time, the booster is airtight.
4   Depress the brake pedal while the engine is running, then stop the engine with the pedal depressed. If there's no change in the pedal reserve travel after holding the pedal for 30 seconds, the booster is airtight.

Removal

5   Power brake booster units shouldn't be disassembled. They require special tools not normally found in most automotive repair stations or shops. They're fairly complex, and because of their critical relationship to brake performance, should be replaced with a new or rebuilt one.
6   Remove the engine covers (see Chapter 1).
7   Remove the windshield wiper assembly (see Chapter 12).
8   Remove the cowl assembly (see Chapter 11).
9   Remove the brake master cylinder (see Section 8).
10   Remove the air cleaner assembly (see Chapter 4).
11   Disconnect the vacuum hose or hoses from the brake booster. Be careful not to damage the hose when removing it from the booster fitting. **Note:** *On 2010 and later V6 models, the metal vacuum line retaining clips and line must be removed.*

12   Inside the vehicle, remove the driver's kick panel, knee bolster and the knee bolster reinforcement brace (see Chapter 11).
13   Disconnect the pedal return spring.
14   Locate the clevis which connects the booster pushrod to the top of the brake pedal. Remove the clevis pin-retaining clip with pliers and pull out the pin.
15   Remove the four nuts and washers holding the brake booster to the firewall (you may need a light to see them). Slide the booster straight out from the firewall until the studs clear the holes.

Installation

16   Installation procedures are basically the reverse of removal. Tighten the clevis locknut securely and the booster mounting nuts to the torque listed in this Chapter's Specifications.
17   After the final installation of the master cylinder and brake hoses and lines, the brake pedal height, freeplay and pedal reserve distance must be adjusted (see Chapter 1) and the system must be bled (see Section 10).

12   Parking brake - adjustment

Lever type

Refer to illustration 12.3

1   The parking brake lever, when properly adjusted, should travel seven to nine clicks when a moderate pulling force is applied. If it travels less than five clicks, there's a chance the parking brake might not be releasing completely. If the lever can be pulled up more than eight clicks, the parking brake may not hold adequately on an incline, allowing the car to roll.
2   To gain access to the parking brake cable adjuster, remove the center console (see Chapter 11).
3   Loosen the locknut (the upper nut) while holding the adjusting nut (lower nut) with a wrench **(see illustration)**. Tighten the adjusting nut until the desired travel is attained.

Tighten the locknut.
4   Install the console.

Pedal type

5   Slowly depress the parking brake pedal all the way and count the number of clicks. It should take about nine to eleven clicks to apply the parking brake on Camry and Avalon models and seven to ten on Lexus models. If it travels less than the specified clicks, there's a chance the parking brake might not be releasing completely. If it travels more than the specified clicks, the parking brake may not hold adequately on an incline, allowing the car to roll. vRelease the pedal.
6   To gain access to the parking brake cable adjuster, remove the lower instrument panels (see Chapter 11).
7   Loosen the locknut (the upper nut) while holding the adjusting nut (lower nut) with a wrench. Tighten the adjusting nut until the desired travel is attained. Tighten the locknut
8   Install the console.

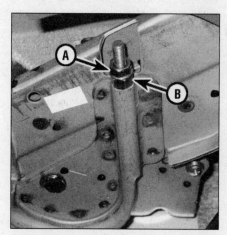

12.3 Parking brake cable locknut (A) and adjuster nut (B) for lever-type parking brake system

13   Parking brake cables - replacement

Rear parking brake cables-to-equalizer

Refer to illustrations 13.4, 13.5, 13.6a and 13.6b

1   Loosen the rear wheel lug nuts, raise the rear of the vehicle and support it securely on jackstands. Block the front wheels. Remove the wheel.

2   Make sure the parking brake is completely released, then remove the brake disc.

3   Remove the parking brake shoes and disconnect the parking brake lever (see Section 7).

4   Unbolt the cable housing from the backing plate **(see illustration)**.

5   Unbolt all cable brackets **(see illustration)**.

6   Disconnect the exhaust and lower the pipe. Remove the exhaust heat shield for access to the cable clamps **(see illustration)**. Trace the cable forward and locate the cable clamp **(see illustration)**. Loosen the clamp bolt and slide the cable housing out of the clamp.

7   Using locking pliers, remove the clip securing the cable end to the bracket. **Note:** *Before removing, mark the mounting configurations for the cable end.*

8   Disconnect the cable end from the equalizer by aligning the cable with the slot in the top of the equalizer. Slide the cable end out of the hole **(see illustration 13.6b)**. **Note:** *On Lexus models, remove the floor crossmember mounting fasteners and lift the crossmember out to access the equalizer.*

9   Installation is the reverse of removal. Adjust the parking brake (see Section 12).

13.4 To detach either parking brake cable housing from the brake backing plate, remove these two bolts

Parking brake lever-to-equalizer cable

Refer to illustration 13.12

10   Remove the center console (see Chapter 11).

11   With the parking brake cable released, remove the locknut and the adjusting nut (see Section 12), then detach the cable from the lever.

12   Inside the console area, remove the two bolts securing the cable flange to the floor **(see illustration)**. Twist the flange 90-degrees and push it out through the hole in the floorpan.

13   Installation is the reverse of the removal procedure. Apply a light coat of grease to the portion of the cable end that contacts the equalizer. Adjust the parking brake cable (see Section 12).

13.5 This parking brake cable bracket is located near the forward end of the strut rod (but there may be others, depending on the year and model)

Parking brake pedal-to-intermediate lever cable (pedal-type models)

14   Remove the front seats, console and shift lever assembly (see Chapter 11).

15   Remove the two nuts securing the cable to the rear of the turnbuckle (see Section 12). Twist the turnbuckle off the front cable end.

16   On Lexus models with VSC, you'll have to remove the yaw rate sensor from the console for access to the cable. Disconnect the electrical connector at the sensor, remove the two sensor bracket-to-floor bolts and remove the sensor. **Caution:** *Do not separate the sensor from its bracket; remove them as an assembly only.*

17   Remove the driver's kick panel, knee bolster and knee bolster reinforcement (see

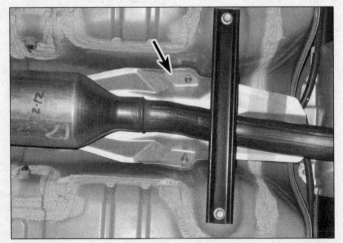

13.6a Remove the bolts and the exhaust heat shield that protects the cables (you may have to drop the exhaust pipe)

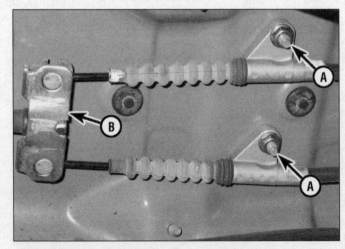

13.6b To release either parking brake cable from its cable clamp, loosen the clamp bolts (A) and slide the cable housing out of the clamp - (B) indicates the equalizer

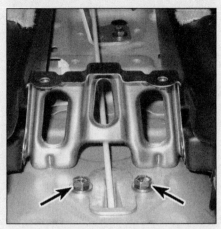

13.12 The cable flange is secured to the floorpan by these two bolts

Chapter 11) to access the parking brake pedal bracket sub-assembly.

18 Loosen and remove the locknut and adjuster nut on the cable end at the pedal assembly. Using locking pliers, remove the clip securing the cable end to the front of the parking brake pedal assembly and pull the cable out of the assembly **(see illustration 12.3)**.

19 Pull back the carpeting between the pedal assembly and the console area to locate the clamps securing the cable to the floor. Remove the clamps and the cable.

20 Installation is the reverse of removal. Adjust the parking brake (see Section 12).

14 Brake light switch - check and replacement

Check

1 The brake light switch is located on the brake pedal bracket. You'll need to remove the trim panel beneath the steering column to get to the switch and connector (see Chapter 11).

2 With the brake pedal in the fully released position, the switch opens the brake light circuit. When the brake pedal is depressed, the switch closes the circuit and sends current to the brake lights.

3 If the brake lights are inoperative, check the fuse and the bulbs (see Chapter 12).

4 If the fuse and bulbs are okay, verify that voltage is available at the switch.

5 If there's no voltage to the switch, search for an open circuit condition between the fuse block and the switch. If there is voltage to the switch, close the switch (depress the brake pedal) and verify that there's voltage on the other side of the switch.

6 If there's no voltage on the other side of the switch, replace the switch. If there is voltage but the brake lights still don't work, look for an open circuit condition between the switch and the brake lights. **Note:** *There is always the remote possibility that all of the brake light bulbs are burned out, but this is not very likely.*

Replacement

Refer to illustration 14.9

7 Disconnect the electrical connector from the brake light switch.

8 Rotate the switch counterclockwise 90-degrees, so that it unlocks from its holder, then pull it directly out of the holder.

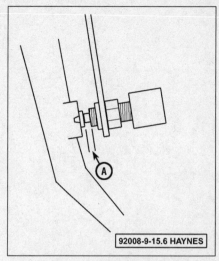

14.9 When installed, the plunger should protrude the distance given in this Chapter's Specifications

9 To install the switch, insert it into its holder and push it in until the switch body contacts the rubber stop on the brake pedal bracket. Hold the brake pedal up while placing the switch in position. Rotate the switch 90-degrees clockwise to lock it into place. It will achieve the proper clearance to the rubber stop automatically **(see illustration)**. **Caution:** *Do not press in on the switch while turning it.*

10 Plug the electrical connector into the switch.

11 Confirm that the brake lights work properly before placing the vehicle into normal service.

Notes

Chapter 10
Suspension and steering systems

Contents

Specifications
Torque specifications

Ft-lbs (unless otherwise indicated)

Note: *One foot-pound (ft-lb) of torque is equivalent to 12 inch-pounds (in-lbs) of torque. Torque values below approximately 15 foot-pounds are expressed in inch-pounds, because most foot-pound torque wrenches are not accurate at these smaller values.*

Front suspension
Balljoint
Balljoint-to-steering knuckle nut 91
Balljoint-to-control arm nuts and bolt
2011 and earlier Camry models/2012 and
earlier Avalon and ES350 models 55
2012 and later Camry models/2013 and later Avalon models
Nuts
With 20 mm flange 55
With 22 mm flange 68
Bolt .... Same as measured nut
2013 and later ES350 models 68
Control arm-to-subframe bolts
Front bolts 148
Rear bolts
2011 and earlier models 152
2012 and later models 100
Stabilizer bar
Stabilizer bar link nuts
Upper
2011 and earlier models (except 2007 Avalon models) 52
2007 Avalon models 36
2012 Camry/Avalon, 2012 and later ES350 models 55
2013 and later Camry/Avalon models 92
Lower 55
Stabilizer bushing/retainer bolts 20

Torque specifications (continued)

Ft-lbs (unless otherwise indicated)

Note: *One foot-pound (ft-lb) of torque is equivalent to 12 inch-pounds (in-lbs) of torque. Torque values below approximately 15 foot-pounds are expressed in inch-pounds, because most foot-pound torque wrenches are not accurate at these smaller values.*

Front suspension (continued)

Strut

Strut upper mounting nuts	63
Strut-to-suspension support (damper shaft) nut	
All except 2007 Avalon models	52
2007 Avalon models	36
Strut-to-steering knuckle bolts/nuts	
ES350	
2012 and earlier models	155
2013 and later models	214
Avalon	
2010 and earlier models	155
2011 and later models	214
Camry	
2010 and earlier models	155
2011 models	
TMC manufacture	155
Non-TMC manufacture	214
2012 and later models	214

Rear suspension

Hub and bearing assembly-to-axle carrier bolts	
2011 and earlier models	59
2012 and later models	44
Strut	
Strut upper mounting nuts	29
Strut-to-suspension support (damper shaft) nut	41
Strut-to-axle carrier nuts/bolts	
New nut	
2011 and earlier models	133
2012 and later models	214
Stabilizer bar	
Stabilizer bar link-to-strut assembly	29
Stabilizer bar bushing/retainer bolts	
All except 2013 and later ES350 models	23
2013 and later ES350 models	156 in-lbs
Suspension arms	
No. 1/No. 2 arm-to-suspension member through-bolt nut	74
No. 1/No. 2 arm-to-axle carrier through-bolt nut	74
Strut rod-to-body bolt	
2011 and earlier models	88
2012 and later models	63
Strut rod-to-axle carrier bolt	
2011 and earlier models	83
2012 and later models	59
Rear crossmember bolts	41

Steering system

Airbag module retaining screws (2011 and earlier models)	78 in-lbs
Steering wheel nut	37
Steering gear mounting bolts/nuts	52
Steering shaft universal joint pinch bolt	26
Tie-rod end-to-steering knuckle	36
Power steering pump	
Pressure line banjo bolt	37
Feed line fitting bolt	108 in-lbs
Wheel lug nuts	See Chapter 1

1.1 Front suspension and steering components

1	Steering gear assembly	3	Strut and spring assembly	5	Steering knuckle
2	Control arm	4	Balljoint	6	Tie-rod end

1   General information

Refer to illustrations 1.1 and 1.2

The front suspension is a MacPherson strut design. The upper end of each strut is attached to the vehicle's body strut support. The lower end of the strut is connected to the upper end of the steering knuckle. The steering knuckle is attached to a balljoint mounted on the outer end of the suspension control arm **(see illustration)**.

The rear suspension also utilizes strut/coil spring assemblies. The upper end of each strut is attached to the vehicle body by a strut support. The lower end of the strut is attached to an axle carrier. The carrier is located by a pair of suspension arms on each side, and a

1.2 Rear suspension components

1	Stabilizer bar	3	Strut rod	5	Strut assembly
2	Suspension arm (no. 1)	4	Rear axle carrier	6	Suspension arm (no. 2)

longitudinally mounted strut rod between the body and each knuckle **(see illustration)**.

The power-assisted rack-and-pinion steering gear, which is located behind the engine/transaxle assembly, is mounted on the engine cradle. The steering gear actuates the tie-rods, which are attached to the steering knuckles. The steering column is designed to collapse in the event of an accident.

Frequently, when working on the suspension or steering system components, you may come across fasteners that seem impossible to loosen. These fasteners on the underside of the vehicle are continually subjected to water, road grime, mud, etc., and can become rusted or frozen, making them extremely difficult to remove. In order to unscrew these stubborn fasteners without damaging them (or other components), be sure to use lots of penetrating oil and allow it to soak in for a while. Using a wire brush to clean exposed threads will also ease removal of the nut or bolt and prevent damage to the threads. Sometimes a sharp blow with a hammer and punch will break the bond between nut and bolt threads, but care must be taken to prevent the punch from slipping off the fastener and ruining the

threads. Heating the stuck fastener and surrounding area with a torch sometimes helps too, but isn't recommended because of the obvious dangers associated with fire. Long breaker bars and extension, or cheater, pipes will increase leverage, but never use an extension pipe on a ratchet - the ratcheting mechanism could be damaged. Sometimes tightening the nut or bolt first will help to break it loose. Fasteners that require drastic measures to remove should always be replaced with new ones.

Since most of the procedures dealt with in this Chapter involve jacking up the vehicle and working underneath it, a good pair of jackstands will be needed. A hydraulic floor jack is the preferred type of jack to lift the vehicle, and it can also be used to support certain components during various operations. **Warning:** *Never, under any circumstances, rely on a jack to support the vehicle while working on it. Whenever any of the suspension or steering fasteners are loosened or removed they must be inspected and, if necessary, replaced with new ones of the same part number or of original equipment quality and design. Torque specifications must be followed for proper*

reassembly and component retention. Never attempt to heat or straighten any suspension or steering components. Instead, replace any bent or damaged part with a new one.

2 Stabilizer bar and bushings (front) - removal and installation

Removal

Refer to illustrations 2.4 and 2.5

1   Loosen the front wheel lug nuts. Raise the front of the vehicle and support it securely on jackstands. Apply the parking brake and block the rear wheels to keep the vehicle from rolling off the stands. Remove the front wheels.

2   Remove the left and right fender apron seals. Each seal is retained by two bolts.

3   Disconnect the left and right tie-rod ends from the steering knuckles (see Section 17).

4   Disconnect the stabilizer bar links from the bar **(see illustration)**. If the ballstud turns with the nut, use an Allen wrench to hold the stud.

2.4 To detach the stabilizer bar link from the bar, remove the lower nut; if you're removing the strut, remove the upper nut

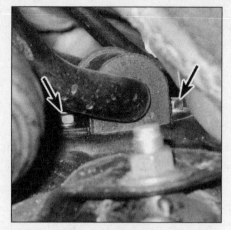

2.5 To detach the stabilizer bar from the subframe, remove these bushing retainer bolts and remove the retainer

3.3 Detach the brake hose from the strut bracket

5   Detach both stabilizer bar bushing retainers from the subframe **(see illustration)**.
6   Remove the front exhaust pipe (see Chapter 4).
7   Remove the steering gear mounting bolts (see Section 19).
8   Lift the steering gear assembly and remove the stabilizer bar by working it out through the left wheel housing.
9   While the stabilizer bar is off the vehicle, slide off the retainer bushings and inspect them. If they're cracked, worn or deteriorated, replace them. It's also a good idea to inspect the stabilizer bar link. To check it, flip the balljoint stud side-to-side five or six times as shown, then install the nut. Using an inch-pound torque wrench, turn the nut continuously one turn every two to four seconds and note the torque reading on the fifth turn. It should be about 0.4 to 17 in-lbs. If it isn't, replace the link assembly.
10   Clean the bushing area of the stabilizer bar with a stiff wire brush to remove any rust or dirt.

Installation

11   Lubricate the inside and outside of the new bushings with vegetable oil (used in cooking) to simplify reassembly. **Caution:** *Don't use petroleum or mineral-based lubricants or brake fluid - they will lead to deterioration of the bushings.*
12   Installation is the reverse of removal.

3   Strut assembly (front) - removal, inspection and installation

Removal

Refer to illustrations 3.3, 3.5 and 3.7

1   Loosen the wheel lug nuts, raise the vehicle and support it securely on jackstands. Remove the wheel. Support the control arm with a floor jack.
2   Disconnect the stabilizer bar link end

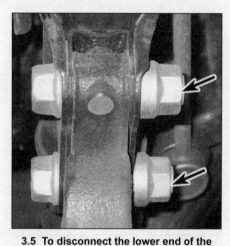

3.5 To disconnect the lower end of the strut from the steering knuckle, remove these two nuts and knock out the bolts with a hammer and punch

from the strut **(see illustration 2.4)**.
3   Remove the brake hose bracket and the speed sensor wiring harness from the strut **(see illustration)**.
4   On models equipped with electronic modulated suspension, remove the shock absorber cap and disconnect the shock absorber wiring harness. If the strut is to be disassembled, loosen, but do not remove, the damper shaft (center) nut (this will require a special socket if the vehicle is equipped with electronic modulated suspension; check with your local auto parts store or tool dealer).
5   Remove the strut-to-knuckle nuts **(see illustration)** and knock the bolts out with a hammer and punch.
6   Separate the strut from the steering knuckle. Be careful not to overextend the inner CV joint. Also, don't let the steering knuckle fall outward, as the brake hose could be damaged.
7   Support the strut and spring assembly with one hand and remove the three strut-to-shock tower nuts (this is only if the strut is

3.7 To disconnect the upper end of the strut from the vehicle body, remove these three nuts - do not lose the two spacer washers under the shock tower brace (if equipped) at the inner stud. Warning: *Don't remove the large nut in the center*

going to be disassembled) **(see illustration)**. On models equipped with electronic modulated suspension, loosen (but do not remove) the nut in the center of the strut (this is only necessary if the strut is going to be disassembled). Remove the assembly out from the fenderwell. **Note:** *Some models have a front suspension brace between the tops of the two shock towers that is retained by the same nuts that secure the strut to the body. At the inner stud, there are two spacer washers under the brace that are easy to lose when removing the strut.*

Inspection

8   Check the strut body for leaking fluid, dents, cracks and other obvious damage that would warrant repair or replacement.
9   Check the coil spring for chips or cracks in the spring coating (this can cause premature spring failure due to corrosion). Inspect the spring seat for cuts, hardness and general deterioration.

4.3 Install the spring compressor in accordance with the tool manufacturer's instructions and compress the spring until all pressure is relieved from the upper spring seat

4.4 Remove the damper shaft nut

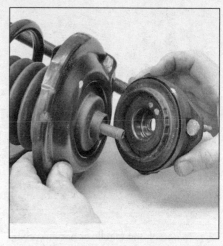

4.5 Lift the suspension support off the damper shaft

10   If any undesirable conditions exist, proceed to the strut disassembly procedure (see Section 4).

Installation

11   Guide the strut assembly up into the fenderwell and insert the three upper mounting studs through the holes in the shock tower. Once the three studs protrude from the shock tower, install the nuts so the strut won't fall back through. This is most easily accomplished with the help of an assistant, as the strut is quite heavy and awkward.
12   Slide the steering knuckle into the strut flange and insert the two bolts. Install the nuts and tighten them to the torque listed in this Chapter's Specifications.
13   Reattach the brake hose bracket to the strut. If equipped, install the speed sensor wiring harness bracket.
14   Install the wheel and lug nuts, then lower the vehicle and tighten the lug nuts to the torque listed in the Chapter 1 Specifications.

15   Tighten the three upper mounting nuts to the torque listed in this Chapter's Specifications.
16   If you're working on a model equipped with electronic modulated suspension and the strut had been disassembled, tighten the nut in the center of the strut to the torque listed in this Chapter's Specifications, using a special tool (check with your local auto parts store, dealer parts department or tool dealer regarding tool availability). Connect the electrical connector and install the cap.

4   Strut/coil spring assembly - replacement

1   If the struts or coil springs exhibit the telltale signs of wear (leaking fluid, loss of damping capability, chipped, sagging or cracked coil springs) explore all options before beginning any work. The strut/shock absorber assemblies are not serviceable and must be replaced if a problem develops. However, strut assemblies complete with springs may

be available on an exchange basis, which eliminates much time and work. Whichever route you choose to take, check on the cost and availability of parts before disassembling your vehicle. **Warning:** *Disassembling a strut is potentially dangerous and utmost attention must be directed to the job, or serious injury may result. Use only a high-quality spring compressor and carefully follow the manufacturer's instructions furnished with the tool. After removing the coil spring from the strut assembly, set it aside in a safe, isolated area.*

Disassembly

Refer to illustrations 4.3, 4.4, 4.5 and 4.7
2   Remove the strut and spring assembly (see Section 3 [front] or Section 10 [rear]). Mount the strut assembly in a vise. Line the vise jaws with wood or rags to prevent damage to the unit and don't tighten the vise excessively.
3   Following the tool manufacturer's instructions, install the spring compressor (which can be obtained at most auto parts stores or equipment yards on a daily rental basis)

4.7 Remove the compressed spring assembly - keep the ends of the spring pointed away from your body

4.11 When installing the spring, make sure the end fits into the recessed portion of the lower seat

4.12 The flats on the damper shaft must match up with the flats in the spring seat

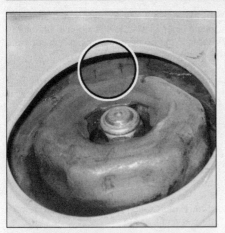

4.14 Make sure the arrows on the upper spring seat face toward the outside of the vehicle

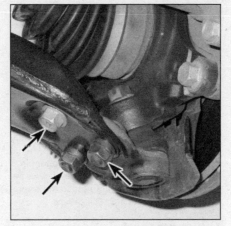

5.3a Remove these nuts and this bolt to disconnect the control arm from the balljoint

5.3b Separate the control arm from the balljoint with a prybar

on the spring and compress it sufficiently to relieve all pressure from the upper spring seat **(see illustration)**. This can be verified by wiggling the spring.

4   Loosen the damper shaft nut **(see illustration)**.

5   Remove the nut and suspension support **(see illustration)**. Inspect the bearing in the suspension support for smooth operation. If it doesn't turn smoothly, replace the suspension support. Check the rubber portion of the suspension support for cracking and general deterioration. If there is any separation of the rubber, replace it.

6   Remove the upper spring seat from the damper shaft. Check the spring seat for cracking and hardness; replace it if necessary. Remove the upper insulator from the damper shaft.

7   Carefully lift the compressed spring from the assembly **(see illustration)** and set it in a safe place. **Warning:** *Never place your head near the end of the spring!*

8   Slide the rubber bumper off the damper shaft.

9   Check the lower insulator for wear, cracking and hardness and replace it if necessary.

Reassembly

Refer to illustrations 4.11, 4.12 and 4.14

10   If the lower insulator is being replaced, set it into position with the dropped portion seated in the lowest part of the seat. Extend the damper rod to its full length and install the rubber bumper.

11   Carefully place the coil spring onto the lower insulator, with the end of the spring resting in the lowest part of the insulator **(see illustration)**.

12   Install the upper insulator and spring seat, making sure that the flats in the hole in the seat match up with the flats on the damper shaft **(see illustration)**.

13   Align the OUT mark of the spring upper seat with the mark of the upper insulator.

14   If you're working on a front strut, make sure the arrow on the spring seat faces toward the lower bracket, where the steering knuckle fits **(see illustration)**.

15   Install the dust seal and suspension support to the damper shaft.

16   Install the nut and, if you're working on a model without electronic modulated suspension, tighten it to the torque listed in this Chapter's Specifications (on models with electronic modulated suspension, final tightening of this nut is carried out when the strut is installed on the vehicle). Remove the spring compressor tool.

17   Install the strut/spring assembly (see Section 3 [front] or 10 [rear]). If you're working on a model with electronic modulated suspension, tighten the damper shaft nut to the torque listed in this Chapter's Specifications (see Section 3).

5   Control arm - removal, inspection and installation

Removal

Refer to illustrations 5.3a, 5.3b, 5.4 and 5.5

1   Loosen the wheel lug nuts on the side to be dismantled, raise the front of the vehicle, support it securely on jackstands and remove the wheel.

2   The transverse engine mount at the subframe interferes with removal of the rear bolts of the control arms. The procedure is difficult and requires the use of an engine lifting hoist or support fixture (refer to Chapter 2 for engine mount removal/installation).

3   Remove the balljoint retaining bolt and nuts **(see illustration)**. Use a prybar to disconnect the balljoint from the control arm **(see illustration)**.

4   Remove the two bolts that attach the front of the control arm to the subframe **(see illustration)**.

5   Remove the bolt and nut that attach the rear of the control arm to the subframe **(see illustration)**.

6   Remove the control arm.

5.4 To detach the front end of the control arm from the subframe, remove these two bolts

5.5 To detach the rear end of the control arm from the subframe, remove this nut and bolt

6.12 To separate the balljoint from the steering knuckle, install a small puller and pop the balljoint stud loose

Inspection

7   Make sure the control arm is straight. If it's bent, replace it. Do not attempt to straighten a bent control arm.
8   Inspect the bushings. If they're cracked, torn or worn out, replace the control arm.

Installation

9   Installation is the reverse of removal. Be sure to tighten all fasteners to the torque listed in this Chapter's Specifications.
10   Install the wheel and lug nuts, lower the vehicle and tighten the lug nuts to the torque listed in the Chapter 1 Specifications.
11   It's a good idea to have the front wheel alignment checked, and if necessary, adjusted after this job has been performed.

6   Balljoints - replacement

1   Loosen the wheel lug nuts, raise the vehicle and support it securely on jackstands. Remove the wheel. **Note:** *If you're going to remove the balljoint using a puller (as described in Steps 9 through 13), loosen the driveaxle/hub nut before raising the vehicle (see Chapter 8).*

Picklefork method

Caution: *The following procedure is the quickest way to detach a balljoint from the steering knuckle, but it will very likely damage the balljoint boot. If you want to save the boot, proceed to Step 9.*
2   Remove the cotter pin from the balljoint stud and loosen the nut (but don't remove it yet).
3   Separate the balljoint from the steering knuckle with a picklefork-type balljoint separator. Lubricate the rubber boot with grease and work carefully so as not to tear the boot. Remove the balljoint stud nut.
4   Remove the bolt and nuts securing the balljoint to the control arm **(see illustration 5.3a)**. Separate the balljoint from the control

arm with a prybar **(see illustration 5.3b).**
5   To install the balljoint, position it on the steering knuckle and install the nut, but don't tighten it yet.
6   Attach the balljoint to the control arm and install the bolt and nuts, tightening them to the torque listed in this Chapter's Specifications.
7   Tighten the balljoint stud nut to the torque listed in this Chapter's Specifications and install a new cotter pin. If the cotter pin hole doesn't line up with the slots on the nut, tighten the nut additionally until it does line up - don't loosen the nut to insert the cotter pin.
8   Install the wheel and lug nuts. Lower the vehicle and tighten the lug nuts to the torque listed in the Chapter 1 Specifications.

Puller method

Refer to illustration 6.12

9   Separate the control arm from the balljoint (see Section 5).
10   Pull the outer end of the driveaxle from the steering knuckle (see Chapter 8) and suspend the driveaxle with a piece of wire.
11   Remove the cotter pin from the balljoint stud and loosen the nut (but don't remove it yet).
12   Install a small puller **(see illustration)** and pop the balljoint stud from the steering knuckle.
13   Remove the nut and remove the balljoint.
14   Install the new balljoint into the steering knuckle and tighten the nut to the torque listed in this Chapter's Specifications. Install a new cotter pin. If the cotter pin hole doesn't line up with the slots on the nut, tighten the nut until it does - don't loosen the nut to insert the cotter pin.
15   Insert the outer end of the driveaxle through the steering knuckle and install the nut. Tighten it securely, but don't attempt to tighten it completely yet.
16   Connect the balljoint to the lower arm and tighten the fasteners to the torque listed in this Chapter's Specifications.
17   Install the wheel and lug nuts, lower the vehicle and tighten the lug nuts to the torque listed in the Chapter 1 Specifications.
18   Tighten the driveaxle/hub nut to the torque listed in the Chapter 8 Specifications. Install the lock washer and cotter pin.

7   Steering knuckle and hub - removal and installation

Warning: *Dust created by the brake system is harmful to your health. Never blow it out with compressed air and don't inhale any of it. Do not, under any circumstances, use petroleum-based solvents to clean brake parts. Use brake system cleaner only.*

Removal

1   Loosen the driveaxle/hub nut (see Chapter 8). Loosen the wheel lug nuts, raise the vehicle and support it securely on jackstands. Remove the wheel.

2   Remove the brake caliper and support it with a piece of wire as described in Chapter 9. Remove the caliper torque plate and separate the brake disc from the hub.
3   Loosen, but do not remove the strut-to-steering knuckle bolts **(see illustration 3.5)**.
4   Separate the tie-rod end from the steering knuckle arm (see Section 17).
5   Remove the balljoint-to-lower arm bolt and nuts **(see illustration 5.3a and 5.3b)**. The strut-to-knuckle bolts can now be removed.
6   Push the driveaxle from the hub as described in Chapter 8. Support the end of the driveaxle with a piece of wire.
7   Separate the steering knuckle from the strut. If necessary, detach the balljoint from the steering knuckle.

Installation

8   Guide the knuckle and hub assembly into position, inserting the driveaxle into the hub.
9   Push the knuckle into the strut flange and install the bolts and nuts, but don't tighten them yet.
10   Connect the balljoint to the control arm and install the bolt and nuts (don't tighten them yet).
11   Attach the tie-rod to the steering knuckle arm (see Section 17). Tighten the strut bolt nuts, the balljoint-to-control arm bolt and nuts and the tie-rod nut to the torque values listed in this Chapter's Specifications.
12   Place the brake disc on the hub and install the caliper as outlined in Chapter 9.
13   Install the driveaxle/hub nut and tighten it securely (final tightening will be carried out when the vehicle is lowered).
14   Install the wheel and lug nuts.
15   Lower the vehicle and tighten the lug nuts to the torque listed in the Chapter 1 Specifications. Tighten the driveaxle/hub nut to the torque listed in the Chapter 8 Specifications.

8   Hub and bearing assembly (front) - removal and installation

Due to the special tools and expertise required to press the hub and bearing from the steering knuckle, this job should be left to a professional shop. However, the steering knuckle and hub may be removed and the assembly taken to a dealer service department or other repair shop. See Section 7 for the steering knuckle and hub removal procedure.

9   Stabilizer bar and bushings (rear) - removal and installation

Refer to illustrations 9.3 and 9.4

1   Loosen the rear wheel lug nuts. Raise the rear of the vehicle and place it securely on jackstands. Remove the rear wheels.
2   Remove the heat insulator from the exhaust system.

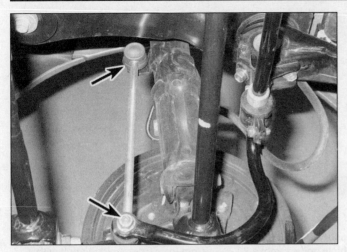

9.3 To detach the stabilizer bar link from the bar, remove the lower nut; if you're removing the strut, remove the upper nut

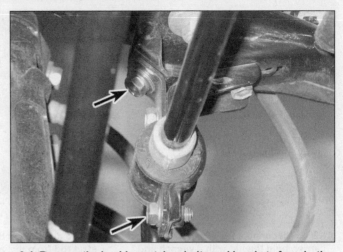

9.4 Remove the bushing retainer bolts and brackets from both the left and right retainers (left retainer shown)

3   Disconnect the stabilizer bar links from the bar **(see illustration)**. If the ballstud turns with the nut, use an Allen wrench to hold the stud.

4   Unbolt the stabilizer bar bushing retainers and the two brackets (at each side) from the body **(see illustration)**. **Note:** *On Camry Solara convertible models, there is a floor reinforcement subassembly of braces that must be removed to allow stabilizer bar removal.*

5   The stabilizer bar can now be removed from the vehicle. Pull the retainers off the stabilizer bar (if they haven't fallen off already) using a rocking motion.

6   Check the bushings for wear, hardness, distortion, cracking and other signs of deterioration, replacing them if necessary. Check the stabilizer bar links as described in Section 2, Step 9.

7   Using a wire brush, clean the areas of the bar where the bushings ride. Installation is the reverse of the removal procedure. If necessary, use a light coat of vegetable oil to ease bushing and U-bracket installation (don't use petroleum-based products or brake fluid, as these will damage the rubber).

8   Installation is the reverse of removal. On Solara convertible models, tighten the floor reinforcement brace bolts to 38 ft-lbs.

10   Strut assembly (rear) - removal, inspection and installation

Removal

Refer to illustrations 10.7 and 10.8

Note: *When removing/replacing any rear suspension arms, loosely tighten all the bolts, move the suspension to its normal ride-height angle and position, then fully tighten the bolts.*

1   Remove the rear seat and package tray trim panel (see Chapter 11).

2   Loosen the rear wheel lug nuts, raise the rear of the vehicle and support it securely on jackstands. Remove the wheel.

3   Remove the flexible hose and ABS speed sensor from the shock absorber.

4   Detach the brake hose from the strut **(see illustration 3.3)**. Detach the ABS sensor wire from the strut. On models equipped with electronic modulated suspension, remove the clip and clamp and disconnect the shock absorber wiring harness.

5   Disconnect the stabilizer bar link from the strut **(see illustration 9.3)**.

6   Support the axle carrier with a floor jack.

7   Loosen the strut-to-axle carrier bolt nuts **(see illustration)**.

8   Remove the three upper strut-to-body mounting nuts **(see illustration)**. On models equipped with electronic modulated suspension, loosen but do not remove the damper shaft (center) nut (this is only necessary if the strut is going to be disassembled, and will require a special socket; check with your local auto parts store or tool dealer) (see Section 3). Remove the assembly out from the fenderwell.

9   Lower the axle carrier with the jack and remove the two strut-to-axle carrier bolts.

10   Remove the strut assembly.

10.7 To disconnect the lower end of the strut from the rear axle carrier, unbolt the brake hose from the strut, then remove these nuts and knock out the bolts (but don't remove the bolts until after the upper strut nuts are removed and the axle carrier is supported by a floor jack)

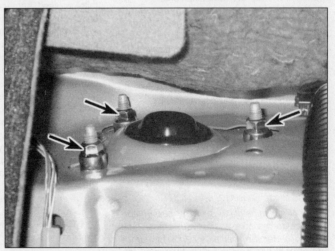

10.8 To disconnect the upper end of the strut from the vehicle, remove these three nuts

11.2 To disconnect the strut rod from the carrier, hold the nut with a wrench and remove the bolt

11.3 To disconnect the forward end of the strut rod from the vehicle body, remove this bolt

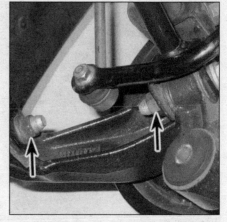

12.4 To disconnect the suspension arms from the carrier, hold the bolt with a wrench and remove the nut.

Inspection

11   Follow the inspection procedures described in Section 3. If you determine that the strut assembly must be disassembled for replacement of the strut or the coil spring, refer to Section 4.

Installation

12   Maneuver the assembly up into the fenderwell and insert the mounting studs through the holes in the body. Install the nuts, but don't tighten them yet.
13   Push the axle carrier into the strut lower bracket and install the bolts and nuts, tightening them to the torque listed in this Chapter's Specifications.
14   Connect the stabilizer bar link to the strut bracket.
15   Attach the brake hose bracket to the strut. Attach the ABS wire to the strut.
16   Install the wheel and lug nuts, lower the vehicle and tighten the lug nuts to the torque listed in the Chapter 1 Specifications.
17   Tighten the three strut upper mounting nuts to the torque listed in this Chapter's Specifications.
18   If you're working on a model equipped with electronic modulated suspension and the strut has been disassembled, tighten the strut center nut to the torque listed in this Chapter's Specifications. Connect the electrical connector.
19   Install the package tray trim and seat.

11   Strut rod - removal and installation

Refer to illustrations 11.2 and 11.3

Note: *When reinstalling any rear suspension arms, raise the suspension with a floor jack (placed under the rear axle carrier) to simulate normal ride-height before tightening the fasteners.*

1   Loosen the wheel lug nuts, raise the vehicle and support it securely on jackstands. Remove the wheel.

2   Remove the strut rod-to-axle carrier bolt **(see illustration).**
3   Remove the strut rod-to-body bracket bolt **(see illustration)** and detach the rod from the vehicle. **Note:** *The parking brake cable bracket may have to be unbolted to allow removal of the strut bolt.*
4   Installation is the reverse of the removal procedure. Be sure to tighten the bolts to the torque listed in this Chapter's Specifications.

12   Suspension arms (rear) - removal and installation

Removal

Refer to illustrations 12.4 and 12.5

1   Raise the rear of the vehicle and support it securely on jackstands. Block the front wheels.
2   Disconnect the strut rod from the axle carrier **(see illustration 11.2).**
3   Remove the exhaust center section and tailpipe (see Chapter 4). Remove the rear stabilizer bar (see Section 9).
4   Remove the suspension arm-to-rear axle carrier bolt and nut **(see illustration).**
5   To access the bolts at the inner ends of the suspension arms, the rear suspension crossmember must be lowered. Position a floor jack under the center of the crossmember, then loosen and remove the crossmember-to-body bolts **(see illustration).** Lower the rear suspension crossmember with the jack (do not place any part of your body under the suspension while it is supported only by the jack) until the suspension arm bolts are accessible. Remove the bolts.
6   Remove the No. 2 (rear) suspension arm.
7   Remove the No. 1 (front) suspension arm.

Installation

Note: *When reinstalling any rear suspension arms, raise the suspension with a floor jack (placed under the rear axle carrier) to simu-*

late normal ride-height before tightening the fasteners.

8   Installation is the reverse of removal. Be sure to tighten all fasteners to the torque listed in this Chapter's Specifications. **Note:** *When reinstalling the suspension arms, the factory paint marks on the arms should face the rear of the vehicle.*
9   Install the wheel and lug nuts, then lower the vehicle to the ground. Tighten the wheel lug nuts to the torque listed in the Chapter 1 Specifications.
10   Have the rear wheel alignment checked by a dealer service department or an alignment shop.

13   Hub and bearing assembly (rear) - removal and installation

Warning: *Dust created by the brake system is harmful to your health. Never blow it out with compressed air and don't inhale any of it. Do not, under any circumstances, use petroleum-based solvents to clean brake parts. Use brake system cleaner only.*
Note: *The rear hub and bearing assembly is not serviceable. If found to be defective, it must be replaced as a unit.*

Removal

Refer to illustration 13.3

1   Loosen the wheel lug nuts, raise the vehicle and support it securely on jackstands. Remove the wheel.
2   Remove the brake drum or disc from the hub (see Chapter 9). If equipped, disconnect the wheel speed sensor.
3   Remove the four hub-to-axle carrier bolts, accessible by turning the hub flange so that the large circular cutout exposes each bolt **(see illustration).**
4   Remove the hub and bearing assembly from its seat, maneuvering it out through the brake assembly.

12.5 Rear suspension crossmember mounting bolts

13.3 To remove the four bolts that attach the hub and bearing assembly to the rear axle carrier, rotate the hub flange and align one of the holes in the flange with each of the bolts

5   Remove the old O-ring from the hub seat and install a new one. Wheel bearing grease may be used to keep the O-ring in place before installing the hub-and-bearing assembly.

Installation

6   Position the hub and bearing assembly on the axle carrier and align the holes in the backing plate. Install the bolts. A magnet is useful in guiding the bolts through the hub flange and into position. After all four bolts have been installed, tighten them to the torque listed in this Chapter's Specifications.
7   Install the brake drum, or disc and caliper, and the wheel. Lower the vehicle and tighten the lug nuts to the torque listed in Chapter 1 Specifications.

14   Rear axle carrier - removal and installation

Warning: *Dust created by the brake system is harmful to your health. Never blow it out with compressed air and don't inhale any of it. Do not, under any circumstances, use petroleum-based solvents to clean brake parts. Use brake system cleaner only.*

Removal

1   Loosen the wheel lug nuts, raise the vehicle and support it securely on jackstands. Block the front wheels and remove the rear wheel.
2   Remove the rear brake disc (see Chapter 9). Don't detach the brake hose from the caliper; hang it with a length of wire.
3   Remove the rear hub and bearing assembly (see Section 13).
4   It isn't necessary to disassemble the brake shoe assembly or disconnect the parking brake cable from the backing plate. Detach the backing plate and rear parking brake assembly from the axle carrier. Suspend the backing plate and brake assembly

from the coil spring with a piece of wire.
5   Remove the wheel speed sensor from the axle carrier.
6   Loosen, but don't remove the strut-to-axle carrier bolts **(see illustration 10.7).**
7   Detach the strut rod and suspension arms from the axle carrier (see Sections 11 and 12).
8   Remove the loosened strut-to-axle carrier bolts while supporting the carrier so it doesn't fall and detach the axle carrier from the strut bracket.

Installation

9   Inspect the carrier bushing for cracks, deformation and signs of wear. If it is worn out, take the carrier to a dealer service department or other repair shop to have the old one pressed out and a new one pressed in.
10   Push the axle carrier into the strut bracket, aligning the two bolt holes. Insert the two strut-to-carrier bolts and tighten them to the torque listed in this Chapter's Specifications.
11   Connect the suspension arms to the axle carrier, but don't tighten the nut(s) yet.
12   Connect the strut rod to the axle carrier, but don't tighten the nut yet.
13   Place a jack under the carrier and raise it to simulate normal ride height.
14   Tighten the suspension arm bolt(s)/nut(s) and the strut rod bolt/nut to the torque listed in this Chapter's Specifications.
15   Reattach the wheel speed sensor to the axle carrier.
16   Attach the brake backing plate to the axle carrier, install the hub and tighten the four bolts to the torque listed in this Chapter's Specifications.
17   Install the rear brake disc and caliper (see Chapter 9).
18   Install the wheel and lug nuts.
19   Bleed the wheel cylinder (see Chapter 9).
20   Lower the vehicle and tighten the lug nuts to the torque listed in the Chapter 1 Specifications.

15   Steering system - general information

1   All models are equipped with rack-and-pinion steering. The steering gear is bolted to the subframe and operates the steering knuckles via tie-rods. The inner ends of the tie-rods are protected by rubber boots that should be inspected periodically for secure attachment, tears and leaking lubricant.
2   On 2011 and earlier models, the power assist system consists of a belt-driven pump and the associated lines and hoses. The fluid level in the power steering pump reservoir should be checked periodically (see Chapter 1). On 2012 and later models, power assist is provided by an electric power assist motor that is mounted onto the steering column.
3   The steering wheel operates the steering shaft, which actuates the steering gear through universal joints. Looseness in the steering can be caused by wear in the steering shaft universal joints, the steering gear, the tie-rod ends and loose retaining bolts.

16   Steering wheel - removal and installation

Warning: *The models covered by this manual are equipped with Supplemental Restraint Systems (SRS), more commonly known as airbags. Always disable the airbag system before working in the vicinity of any airbag system component to avoid the possibility of accidental deployment of the airbag(s), which could cause personal injury (see Chapter 12).*

Removal

Refer to illustrations 16.2a, 16.2b, 16.3a, 16.3b, 16.4 and 16.6

1   Turn the ignition key to Off, then disconnect the cable from the negative terminal of the battery (see Chapter 5).

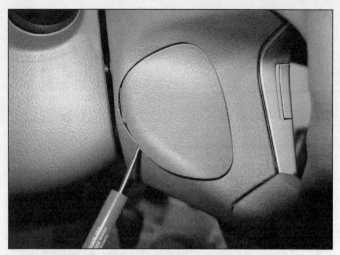

16.2   Pry off the small covers on both sides of the steering wheel . . .

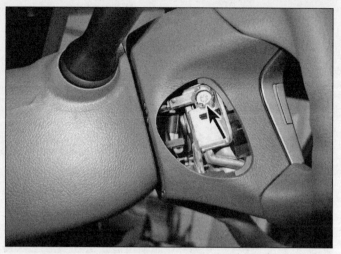

16.3   . . . then loosen the airbag module Torx screw from each side

2   Turn the steering so that the wheels are pointing straight ahead. Pry off the small covers on either side of the steering wheel **(see illustrations)**. On 2012 and later models, also remove the small cover from beneath the steering wheel.

3   On 2011 and earlier models, loosen the Torx screws that attach the airbag module to the steering wheel **(see illustration)**. Loosen each screw until the groove in the circumference of the screw catches on the screw case. **Note:** *The screws do not need to be removed completely.*

4   On 2012 and later models, insert a screwdriver into each cover opening and disengage the torsion spring from each of the three pins that secure the airbag module to the steering wheel.

5   Pull the airbag module off the steering wheel and disconnect the module electrical connectors **(see illustrations)**. **Warning:** *Carry the airbag module with the trim side facing away from you and set it down in an isolated area with the trim side facing up.*

6   Unplug the electrical connector for the horn and cruise control system **(see illustration)**.

7   Remove the steering wheel retaining nut, then mark the relationship of the steering shaft to the hub (if marks don't already exist or don't line up) to simplify installation and ensure steering wheel alignment.

8   Use a puller to disconnect the steering wheel from the shaft **(see illustration)**. **Caution:** *Don't hammer on the shaft in an attempt to remove the wheel.* If it's necessary to remove the spiral cable, remove the steering column covers (see Chapter 11), unplug the electrical connector and disengage the three claws, then remove it from the column.

Installation

Refer to illustration 16.9

9   Make sure that the front wheels are facing straight ahead. Turn the spiral cable coun-

terclockwise by hand until it becomes harder to turn the cable. Rotate the cable clockwise about two and a half turns and align the two pointers **(see illustration)**.

10   To install the wheel, align the mark on the steering wheel hub with the mark on the shaft and slip the wheel onto the shaft. Install the nut and tighten it to the torque listed in this Chapter's Specifications.

11   Plug in the horn and cruise control connector.

12   Plug in the electrical connectors for the airbag module. Make sure the connector locks are pushed back into position.

13   Install the airbag module and tighten the Torx retaining screws to the torque listed in this Chapter's Specifications.

14   Connect the negative battery cable.

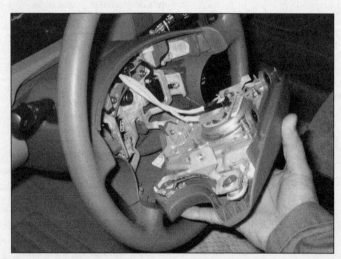

16.5a   Remove the airbag module . . .

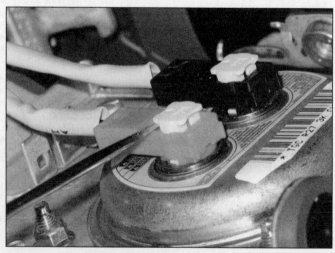

16.5b   . . . pry up the locks for the module electrical connectors, then unplug the electrical connectors

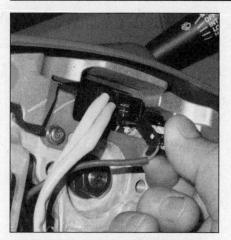

16.6 Unplug the electrical connector for the horn and cruise control

16.8 Use a steering wheel puller to remove the steering wheel

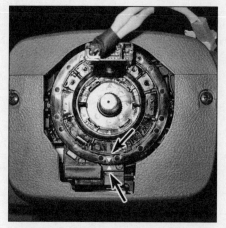

16.9 To center the spiral cable, turn the cable counterclockwise until it's harder to turn, rotate the cable clockwise two and a half turns and align the two red marks (the cable should be able to rotate about two and a half turns in either direction when it's properly centered)

17 Tie-rod ends - removal and installation

Removal

Refer to illustrations 17.2a, 17.2b and 17.4

1   Loosen the wheel lug nuts. Raise the front of the vehicle, support it securely on jackstands, block the rear wheels and set the parking brake. Remove the front wheel.

2   Hold the tie-rod with a pair of locking pliers or wrench and loosen the jam nut enough to mark the position of the tie-rod end in relation to the threads **(see illustrations)**.

3   Remove the cotter pin and loosen the nut on the tie-rod end stud.

4   Disconnect the tie-rod from the steering knuckle arm with a puller **(see illustration)**. Remove the nut and separate the tie-rod.

5   Unscrew the tie-rod end from the tie-rod.

Installation

6   Thread the tie-rod end on to the marked position and insert the tie-rod stud into the steering knuckle arm. Tighten the jam nut securely.

7   Install the castle nut on the stud and tighten it to the torque listed in this Chapter's Specifications. Install a new cotter pin.

8   Install the wheel and lug nuts. Lower the vehicle and tighten the lug nuts to the torque listed in the Chapter 1 Specifications.

9   Have the alignment checked and, if necessary, adjusted.

18 Steering gear boots - replacement

Refer to illustration 18.3

1   Loosen the lug nuts, raise the vehicle and support it securely on jackstands. Remove the wheel.

2   Remove the tie-rod end and jam nut (see Section 17).

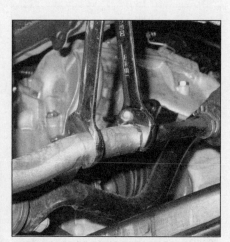

17.2a Hold the tie rod end with a wrench and break the jam nut loose with another wrench

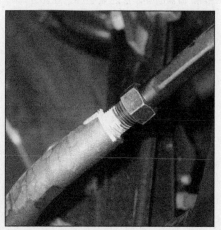

17.2b Back off the jam nut and mark the exposed threads to ensure that the new tie-rod end is threaded on the same number of turns

17.4 Install a small puller as shown to separate the tie-rod end from the steering knuckle

18.3 Remove the outer clamp from the steering gear boot with a pair of pliers; the inner clamp (not visible in this photo) must be cut or pried off

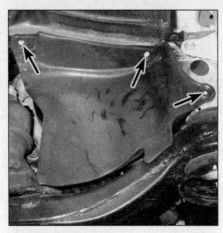

20.4 Remove the three screws and the plastic inner seal from the fenderwell

20.6 Installation details of the power steering pump (four-cylinder engine). Remove the banjo bold (A) and the feed line fitting bolt (B)

3   Remove the steering gear boot clamps **(see illustration)** and slide off the boot.
4   Before installing the new boot, wrap the threads and serrations on the end of the steering rod with a layer of tape so that the small end of the new boot isn't damaged.
5   Slide the new boot into position on the steering gear until it seats in the groove in the steering rod and install new clamps.
6   Remove the tape and install the tie-rod end (see Section 17).
7   Install the wheel and lug nuts. Lower the vehicle and tighten the lug nuts to the torque listed in the Chapter 1 Specifications.

19   Steering gear - removal and installation

Warning: *Make sure the steering shaft is not turned while the steering gear is removed or you could damage the spiral cable for the air-bag system. To prevent the shaft from turning, place the ignition key in the lock position or thread the seat belt through the steering wheel and clip it into place.*
Note: *Toyota requires the engine and transaxle assembly be removed to gain access to the steering gear.*

Removal

1   Remove the engine and transaxle assembly (see Chapter 2C).
2   Detach the pressure and return lines from the steering gear. Remove the steering gear mounting fasteners.
3   Pull the steering gear assembly out.
4   Check the steering gear mounting grommets for excessive wear or deterioration, replacing them if necessary.

Installation

5   Place the steering gear into position, install the mounting fasteners and tighten them to the torque listed in this Chapter's Specifications.

6   Install the engine and transaxle assembly (see Chapter 2C).
7   Connect the U-joint, aligning the marks, then attach the tie-rod ends to the steering knuckle arms (see Section 17).
8   Install the U-joint pinch bolt and tighten it to the torque listed in this Chapter's Specifications.
9   Connect the power steering pressure and return hoses to the steering gear and fill the power steering pump reservoir with the recommended fluid (see Chapter 1). Reattach the bracket to the top of the steering gear assembly.
10   Lower the vehicle and bleed the steering system (see Section 22).

20   Power steering pump (2011 and earlier models) - removal and installation

Removal

Refer to illustrations 20.4, 20.6 and 20.8

1   Disconnect the cable from the negative battery terminal (see Chapter 5).
2   Using a large syringe or suction gun, siphon as much fluid out of the power steering fluid reservoir as possible. Place a drain pan under the vehicle to catch any fluid that spills out when the hoses are disconnected.
3   Loosen the right front wheel lug nuts, raise the vehicle and support it securely on jackstands. Remove the right front wheel.
4   Remove the right front fender apron seal **(see illustration)**.
5   Remove the drivebelt (see Chapter 1).
6   Detach the fluid feed hose from the pump **(see illustration)**. Disconnect the electrical connector from the Power Steering Pressure (PSP) switch (see Section 21).
7   Remove the pressure line-to-pump union bolt and separate the line from the pump **(see illustration 20.6)**. Use two wrenches,

one to hold the pressure port fitting and one to hold the union bolt. Remove the sealing washers on each side of the fitting - these should be replaced when installing the pump.
8   Working through the power steering pulley, loosen the pump mounting bolts completely **(see illustration)**.
9   Lower the pump and remove the mounting bolts, then remove the pump.

Installation

10   Installation is the reverse of removal. Be sure to tighten the pressure line banjo bolt and the feed line fitting bolt. Adjust the drive-belt tension (see Chapter 1).
11   Top up the fluid level in the reservoir (see Chapter 1) and bleed the system (see Section 22).

20.8 Power steering pump pivot bolt (four-cylinder engine) - turn the pulley until an opening is over the upper bolt for access

21 Power Steering Pressure (PSP) switch (2011 and earlier models) - check and replacement

Check

Refer to illustration 21.4

1   The power steering pressure (PSP) switch is located at the high pressure line outlet fitting of the power steering pump.
2   When steering system pressure reaches a high-pressure setpoint, the PSP switch closes and sends a signal to the PCM that the PCM uses to maintain engine idle speed during parking maneuvers.
3   Check the operation of the PSP switch if the engine stalls during parking or if the engine idles continuously at high rpm.
4   Loosen the right front wheel lug nuts, raise the vehicle and support it securely on jackstands. Remove the right front wheel and the right front fender apron seal **(see illustration 20.4)**. Disconnect the PSP switch connector and connect an ohmmeter to the terminal and the switch body **(see illustration)**.
5   Start the engine and let it idle.
6   Turn the steering wheel to point the front wheels straight ahead and read the ohmmeter. It should indicate no continuity (infinite resistance).
7   Turn the steering wheel to each side and watch the ohmmeter. The PSP switch should close as the wheel nears the steering stop on each side, and the meter should indicate continuity (zero ohms).
8   If the switch fails either test, replace it.

Replacement

9   Raise the vehicle and support it securely on jackstands.
10   Disconnect the cable from the negative battery terminal (see Chapter 5).
11   Disconnect the electrical connector from the switch and unscrew the switch from the fitting on the steering pump. Remove the old O-ring on the switch and install a new O-ring.
12   Install and connect the new switch and lower the vehicle to the ground.
13   Bleed air from the power steering system (see Section 22). Add fluid as required (see Chapter 1).

22 Power steering system (2011 and earlier models) - bleeding

1   Following any operation in which the power steering fluid lines have been disconnected, the power steering system must be bled to remove all air and obtain proper steering performance.
2   With the front wheels in the straight ahead position, check the power steering fluid level and, if low, add fluid until it reaches the Cold mark on the dipstick.
3   Start the engine and allow it to run at fast idle. Recheck the fluid level and add more if necessary to reach the Cold mark on the dipstick.
4   Bleed the system by turning the wheels from side to side, without hitting the stops. This will work the air out of the system. Keep the reservoir full of fluid as this is done. **Note:** *This procedure can be done with the front of the vehicle raised with a jack and supported on jackstands. This makes it easier to turn the wheels back and forth during the bleeding process.*
5   When the air is worked out of the system, return the wheels to the straight-ahead position and leave the vehicle running for several more minutes before shutting it off.
6   Road test the vehicle to be sure the steering system is functioning normally and noise free.
7   Recheck the fluid level to be sure it is up to the Hot mark on the dipstick while the engine is at normal operating temperature. Add fluid if necessary (see Chapter 1).

23 Electric Power Steering (EPS) (2012 and later models) – general information

1   The EPS system consists of a power steering ECU, torque sensor, power steering motor and a motor rotation angle sensor. During operation, the ECU monitors vehicle speed as well as input from the torque sensor and motor rotation angle sensor. It then operates the power steering motor and reduction gear to generate torque and provide an appropriate level of steering assist for current operating conditions. The system increases steering assist during low-speed operation, and it decreases assist at high speeds.

2   If the electric power steering unit requires service, take the vehicle to a dealership or other qualified repair shop. Calibrating the unit after repair requires tools not available to most home mechanics.

24 Wheels and tires - general information

Refer to illustration 24.1

1   All vehicles covered by this manual are equipped with metric-sized fiberglass or steel belted radial tires **(see illustration)**. Use of other size or type of tires may affect the ride and handling of the vehicle. Don't mix different types of tires, such as radials and bias belted, on the same vehicle as handling may be seriously affected. It's recommended that tires be replaced in pairs on the same axle, but if only one tire is being replaced, be sure it's the same size, structure and tread design as the other.
2   Because tire pressure has a substantial effect on handling and wear, the pressure on all tires should be checked at least once a month or before any extended trips (see Chapter 1). **Note:** *All models are equipped with tire pressure sensors incorporated into the valve stem inside the wheel.*
3   Wheels must be replaced if they are bent, dented, leak air, have elongated bolt holes, are heavily rusted, out of vertical symmetry or if the lug nuts won't stay tight. Wheel repairs that use welding or peening are not recommended.
4   Tire and wheel balance is important in the overall handling, braking and performance of the vehicle. Unbalanced wheels can adversely affect handling and ride characteristics as well as tire life. Whenever a tire is installed on a wheel, the tire and wheel should be balanced by a shop with the proper equipment.

21.4 Location of the Power Steering Pressure (PSP) switch

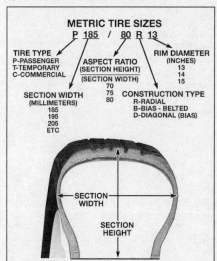

24.1 Metric tire size code

25   Wheel alignment - general information

Refer to illustration 25.1

A wheel alignment refers to the adjustments made to the wheels so they are in proper angular relationship to the suspension and the ground. Wheels that are out of proper alignment not only affect vehicle control, but also increase tire wear. The alignment angles normally measured are camber, caster and toe-in **(see illustration)**. Toe-in is the only adjustable angle on the front or the rear. The other angles should be measured to check for bent or worn suspension parts.

Getting the proper wheel alignment is a very exacting process, one in which complicated and expensive machines are necessary to perform the job properly. Because of this, you should have a technician with the proper equipment perform these tasks. We will, however, use this space to give you a basic idea of what is involved with a wheel alignment so you can better understand the process and deal intelligently with the shop that does the work.

Toe-in is the turning in of the wheels. The purpose of a toe specification is to ensure parallel rolling of the wheels. In a vehicle with zero toe-in, the distance between the front edges of the wheels will be the same as the distance between the rear edges of the wheels. The actual amount of toe-in is normally only a fraction of an inch. On the front end, toe-in is controlled by the tie-rod end position on the tie-rod. On the rear end, it's controlled by a threaded adjuster on the rear (number two) suspension arm. Incorrect toe-in will cause the tires to wear improperly by making them scrub against the road surface.

Camber is the tilting of the wheels from vertical when viewed from one end of the vehicle. When the wheels tilt out at the top, the camber is said to be positive (+). When the wheels tilt in at the top the camber is negative (-). The amount of tilt is measured in degrees from vertical and this measurement is called the camber angle. This angle affects the amount of tire tread which contacts the road and compensates for changes in the suspension geometry when the vehicle is cornering or traveling over an undulating surface.

Caster is the tilting of the front steering axis from the vertical. A tilt toward the rear is positive caster and a tilt toward the front is negative caster. Too little caster will make the front end wander, while too much caster can make the steering effort higher.

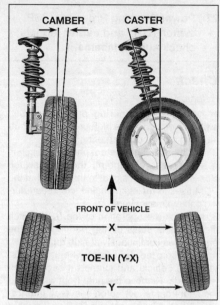

25.1 Camber, caster and toe-in angle

Notes

Notes

Chapter 11 Body

Contents

1   General information

Warning: *The models covered by this manual are equipped with Supplemental Restraint Systems (SRS), more commonly known as airbags. Always disable the airbag system before working in the vicinity of any airbag system components to avoid the possibility of accidental deployment of the airbags, which could cause personal injury (see Chapter 12).*

Certain body components are particularly vulnerable to accident damage and can be unbolted and repaired or replaced. Among these parts are the hood, doors, tailgate, liftgate, bumpers and front fenders.

Only general body maintenance practices and body panel repair procedures within the scope of the do-it-yourselfer are included in this Chapter.

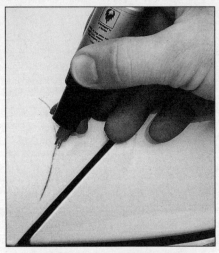

Make sure the damaged area is perfectly clean and rust free. If the touch-up kit has a wire brush, use it to clean the scratch or chip. Or use fine steel wool wrapped around the end of a pencil. Clean the scratched or chipped surface only, not the good paint surrounding it. Rinse the area with water and allow it to dry thoroughly

Thoroughly mix the paint, then apply a small amount with the touch-up kit brush or a very fine artist's brush. Brush in one direction as you fill the scratch area. Do not build up the paint higher than the surrounding paint

2   Repair minor paint scratches

No matter how hard you try to keep your vehicle looking like new, it will inevitably be scratched, chipped or dented at some point. If the metal is actually dented, seek the advice of a professional. But you can fix minor scratches and chips yourself. Buy a touch-up paint kit from a dealer parts department or an auto parts store. To ensure that you get the right color, you'll need to have the specific make, model and year of your vehicle and, ideally, the paint code, which is located on a special metal plate under the hood or in the door jamb.

3   Body repair - minor damage

Plastic body panels

The following repair procedures are for minor scratches and gouges. Repair of more serious damage should be left to a dealer service department or qualified auto body shop. Below is a list of the equipment and materials necessary to perform the following repair procedures on plastic body panels.

Wax, grease and silicone removing solvent
Cloth-backed body tape
Sanding discs
Drill motor with three-inch disc holder
Hand sanding block
Rubber squeegees
Sandpaper
Non-porous mixing palette
Wood paddle or putty knife
Curved-tooth body file
Flexible parts repair material

Flexible panels (bumper trim)

1   Remove the damaged panel, If necessary or desirable. In most cases, repairs can be car-

If the vehicle has a two-coat finish, apply the clear coat after the color coat has dried

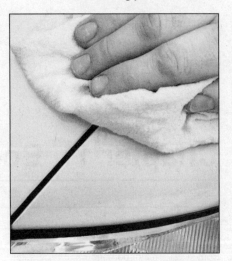

Wait a few days for the paint to dry thoroughly, then rub out the repainted area with a polishing compound to blend the new paint with the surrounding area. When you're happy with your work, wash and polish the area

ried out with the panel installed.
2   Clean the area(s) to be repaired with a wax, grease and silicone removing solvent applied with a water-dampened cloth.
3   If the damage is structural, that is, if it extends through the panel, clean the backside of the panel area to be repaired as well. Wipe dry.
4   Sand the rear surface about 1-1/2 inches beyond the break.
5   Cut two pieces of fiberglass cloth large enough to overlap the break by about 1-1/2 inches. Cut only to the required length.
6   Mix the adhesive from the repair kit according to the instructions included with the kit, and apply a layer of the mixture approximately 1/8-inch thick on the backside of the panel. Overlap the break by at least 1-1/2 inches.
7   Apply one piece of fiberglass cloth to the adhesive and cover the cloth with additional adhesive. Apply a second piece of fiberglass

cloth to the adhesive and immediately cover the cloth with additional adhesive in sufficient quantity to fill the weave.
8   Allow the repair to cure for 20 to 30 minutes at 60-degrees to 80-degrees F.
9   If necessary, trim the excess repair material at the edge.
10   Remove all of the paint film over and around the area(s) to be repaired. The repair material should not overlap the painted surface.
11   With a drill motor and a sanding disc (or a rotary file), cut a "V" along the break line approximately 1/2-inch wide. Remove all dust and loose particles from the repair area.
12   Mix and apply the repair material. Apply a light coat first over the damaged area; then continue applying material until it reaches a level

slightly higher than the surrounding finish.

13   Cure the mixture for 20 to 30 minutes at 60-degrees to 80-degrees F.

14   Roughly establish the contour of the area being repaired with a body file. If low areas or pits remain, mix and apply additional adhesive.

15   Block sand the damaged area with sandpaper to establish the actual contour of the surrounding surface.

16   If desired, the repaired area can be temporarily protected with several light coats of primer. Because of the special paints and techniques required for flexible body panels, it is recommended that the vehicle be taken to a paint shop for completion of the body repair.

Steel body panels

See photo sequence

Repair of dents

17   When repairing dents, the first job is to pull the dent out until the affected area is as close as possible to its original shape. There is no point in trying to restore the original shape completely as the metal in the damaged area will have stretched on impact and cannot be restored to its original contours. It is better to bring the level of the dent up to a point that is about 1/8-inch below the level of the surrounding metal. In cases where the dent is very shallow, it is not worth trying to pull it out at all.

18   If the backside of the dent is accessible, it can be hammered out gently from behind using a soft-face hammer. While doing this, hold a block of wood firmly against the opposite side of the metal to absorb the hammer blows and prevent the metal from being stretched.

19   If the dent is in a section of the body which has double layers, or some other factor makes it inaccessible from behind, a different technique is required. Drill several small holes through the metal inside the damaged area, particularly in the deeper sections. Screw long, self-tapping screws into the holes just enough for them to get a good grip in the metal. Now pulling on the protruding heads of the screws with locking pliers can pull out the dent.

20   The next stage of repair is the removal of paint from the damaged area and from an inch or so of the surrounding metal. This is easily done with a wire brush or sanding disk in a drill motor, although it can be done just as effectively by hand with sandpaper. To complete the preparation for filling, score the surface of the bare metal with a screwdriver or the tang of a file or drill small holes in the affected area. This will provide a good grip for the filler material. To complete the repair, see the Section on filling and painting.

Repair of rust holes or gashes

21   Remove all paint from the affected area and from an inch or so of the surrounding metal using a sanding disk or wire brush mounted in a drill motor. If these are not available, a few sheets of sandpaper will do the job just as effectively.

22   With the paint removed, you will be able to determine the severity of the corrosion and decide whether to replace the whole panel, if possible, or repair the affected area. New body panels are not as expensive as most people think and it is often quicker to install a new panel than to repair large areas of rust.

23   Remove all trim pieces from the affected area except those which will act as a guide to the original shape of the damaged body, such as headlight shells, etc. Using metal snips or a hacksaw blade, remove all loose metal and any other metal that is badly affected by rust. Hammer the edges of the hole in to create a slight depression for the filler material.

24   Wire-brush the affected area to remove the powdery rust from the surface of the metal. If the back of the rusted area is accessible, treat it with rust inhibiting paint.

25   Before filling is done, block the hole in some way. This can be done with sheet metal riveted or screwed into place, or by stuffing the hole with wire mesh.

26   Once the hole is blocked off, the affected area can be filled and painted. See the following subsection on filling and painting.

Filling and painting

27   Many types of body fillers are available, but generally speaking, body repair kits which contain filler paste and a tube of resin hardener are best for this type of repair work. A wide, flexible plastic or nylon applicator will be necessary for imparting a smooth and contoured finish to the surface of the filler material. Mix up a small amount of filler on a clean piece of wood or cardboard (use the hardener sparingly). Follow the manufacturer's instructions on the package, otherwise the filler will set incorrectly.

28   Using the applicator, apply the filler paste to the prepared area. Draw the applicator across the surface of the filler to achieve the desired contour and to level the filler surface. As soon as a contour that approximates the original one is achieved, stop working the paste. If you continue, the paste will begin to stick to the applicator. Continue to add thin layers of paste at 20-minute intervals until the level of the filler is just above the surrounding metal.

29   Once the filler has hardened, the excess can be removed with a body file. From then on, progressively finer grades of sandpaper should be used, starting with a 180-grit paper and finishing with 600-grit wet-or-dry paper. Always wrap the sandpaper around a flat rubber or wooden block, otherwise the surface of the filler will not be completely flat. During the sanding of the filler surface, the wet-or-dry paper should be periodically rinsed in water. This will ensure that a very smooth finish is produced in the final stage.

30   At this point, the repair area should be surrounded by a ring of bare metal, which in turn should be encircled by the finely feathered edge of good paint. Rinse the repair area with clean water until all of the dust produced by the sanding operation is gone.

31   Spray the entire area with a light coat of primer. This will reveal any imperfections in the surface of the filler. Repair the imperfections with fresh filler paste or glaze filler and once more smooth the surface with sandpaper. Repeat this spray-and-repair procedure until you are satisfied that the surface of the filler and the feathered edge of the paint are perfect. Rinse the area with clean water and allow it to dry completely.

32   The repair area is now ready for painting. Spray painting must be carried out in a warm, dry, windless and dust free atmosphere. These conditions can be created if you have access to a large indoor work area, but if you are forced to work in the open, you will have to pick the day very carefully. If you are working indoors, dousing the floor in the work area with water will help settle the dust that would otherwise be in the air. If the repair area is confined to one body panel, mask off the surrounding panels. This will help minimize the effects of a slight mismatch in paint color. Trim pieces such as chrome strips, door handles, etc., will also need to be masked off or removed. Use masking tape and several thickness of newspaper for the masking operations.

33   Before spraying, shake the paint can thoroughly, then spray a test area until the spray painting technique is mastered. Cover the repair area with a thick coat of primer. The thickness should be built up using several thin layers of primer rather than one thick one. Using 600-grit wet-or-dry sandpaper, rub down the surface of the primer until it is very smooth. While doing this, the work area should be thoroughly rinsed with water and the wet-or-dry sandpaper periodically rinsed as well. Allow the primer to dry before spraying additional coats.

34   Spray on the top coat, again building up the thickness by using several thin layers of paint. Begin spraying in the center of the repair area and then, using a circular motion, work out until the whole repair area and about two inches of the surrounding original paint is covered. Remove all masking material 10 to 15 minutes after spraying on the final coat of paint. Allow the new paint at least two weeks to harden, then use a very fine rubbing compound to blend the edges of the new paint into the existing paint. Finally, apply a coat of wax

4   Body repair - major damage

1   Major damage must be repaired by an auto body shop specifically equipped to perform body and frame repairs. These shops have the specialized equipment required to do the job properly.

2   If the damage is extensive, the frame must be checked for proper alignment or the vehicle's handling characteristics may be adversely affected and other components may wear at an accelerated rate.

3   Due to the fact that all of the major body components (hood, fenders, etc.) are separate and replaceable units, any seriously damaged components should be replaced rather than repaired. Sometimes the components can be found in a wrecking yard that specializes in used vehicle components, often at considerable savings over the cost of new parts.

These photos illustrate a method of repairing simple dents. They are intended to supplement *Body repair - minor damage* in this Chapter and should not be used as the sole instructions for body repair on these vehicles.

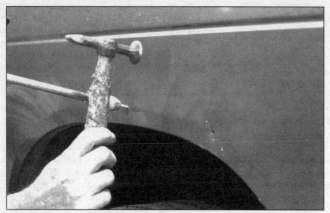

1 If you can't access the backside of the body panel to hammer out the dent, pull it out with a slide-hammer-type dent puller. Tap with a hammer near the edge of the dent to help 'pop' the metal back to its original shape, about 1/8-inch below the surface of the surrounding metal

2 Using coarse-grit sandpaper, remove the paint down to the bare metal. Clean the repair area with wax/silicone remover.

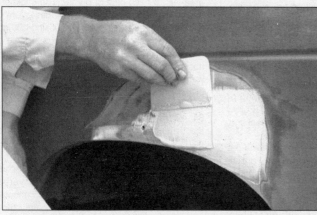

3 Following label instructions, mix up a batch of plastic filler and hardener, then quickly press it into the metal with a plastic applicator. Work the filler until it matches the original contour and is slightly above the surrounding metal

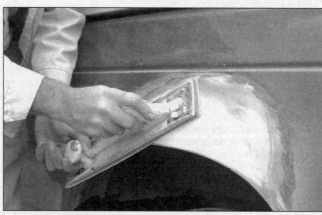

4 Let the filler harden until you can just dent it with your fingernail. File, then sand the filler down until it's smooth and even. Work down to finer grits of sandpaper - always using a board or block - ending up with 360 or 400 grit

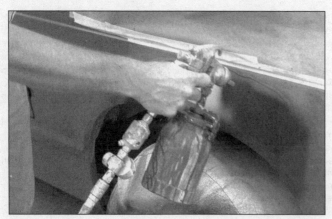

5 When the area is smooth to the touch, clean the area and mask around it. Apply several layers of primer to the area. A professional-type spray gun is being used here, but aerosol spray primer works fine

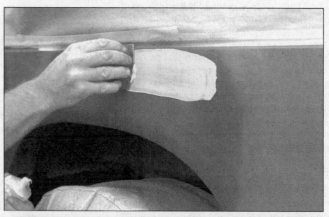

6 Fill imperfections or scratches with glazing compound. Sand with 360 or 400-grit and re-spray. Finish sand the primer with 600 grit, clean thoroughly, then apply the finish coat. Don't attempt to rub out or wax the repair area until the paint has dried completely (at least two weeks)

5 Upholstery, carpets and vinyl trim - maintenance

Upholstery and carpets

1 Every three months remove the floormats and clean the interior of the vehicle (more frequently if necessary). Use a stiff whiskbroom to brush the carpeting and loosen dirt and dust, then vacuum the upholstery and carpets thoroughly, especially along seams and crevices.

2 Dirt and stains can be removed from carpeting with basic household or automotive carpet shampoos available in spray cans. Follow the directions and vacuum again, then use a stiff brush to bring back the "nap" of the carpet.

3 Most interiors have cloth or vinyl upholstery, either of which can be cleaned and maintained with a number of material-specific cleaners or shampoos available in auto supply stores. Follow the directions on the product for usage, and always spot-test any upholstery cleaner on an inconspicuous area (bottom edge of a backseat cushion) to ensure that it doesn't cause a color shift in the material.

4 After cleaning, vinyl upholstery should be treated with a protectant. **Note:** *Make sure the protectant container indicates the product can be used on seats - some products may make a seat too slippery.* **Caution:** *Do not use protectant on vinyl-covered steering wheels.*

5 Leather upholstery requires special care. It should be cleaned regularly with saddle-soap or leather cleaner. Never use alcohol, gasoline, nail polish remover or thinner to clean leather upholstery.

6 After cleaning, regularly treat leather upholstery with a leather conditioner, rubbed in with a soft cotton cloth. Never use car wax on leather upholstery.

7 In areas where the interior of the vehicle is subject to bright sunlight, cover leather seating areas of the seats with a sheet if the vehicle is to be left out for any length of time.

Vinyl trim

8 Don't clean vinyl trim with detergents, caustic soap or petroleum-based cleaners. Plain soap and water works just fine, with a soft brush to clean dirt that may be ingrained. Wash the vinyl as frequently as the rest of the vehicle.

9 After cleaning, application of a high-quality rubber and vinyl protectant will help prevent oxidation and cracks. The protectant can also be applied to weather-stripping, vacuum lines and rubber hoses, which often fail as a result of chemical degradation, and to the tires.

6 Fastener and trim removal

Refer to illustration 6.4

1 There is a variety of plastic fasteners used to hold trim panels, splash shields and other parts in place in addition to typical screws, nuts and bolts. Once you are familiar with them, they can usually be removed without too much difficulty.

2 The proper tools and approach can prevent added time and expense to a project by minimizing the number of broken fasteners and/or parts.

3 The following illustration shows various types of fasteners that are typically used on most vehicles and how to remove and install them **(see illustration)**. Replacement fasten-

Fasteners

This tool is designed to remove special fasteners. A small pry tool used for removing nails will also work well in place of this tool

A Phillips head screwdriver can be used to release the center portion, but light pressure must be used because the plastic is easily damaged. Once the center is up, the fastener can easily be pried from its hole

Here is a view with the center portion fully released. Install the fastener as shown, then press the center in to set it

This fastener is used for exterior panels and shields. The center portion must be pried up to release the fastener. Install the fastener with the center up, then press the center in to set it

This type of fastener is used commonly for interior panels. Use a small blunt tool to press the small pin at the center in to release it . . .

. . . the pin will stay with the fastener in the released position

Reset the fastener for installation by moving the pin out. Install the fastener, then press the pin flush with the fastener to set it

This fastener is used for exterior and interior panels. It has no moving parts. Simply pry the fastener from its hole like the claw of a hammer removes a nail. Without a tool that can get under the top of the fastener, it can be very difficult to remove

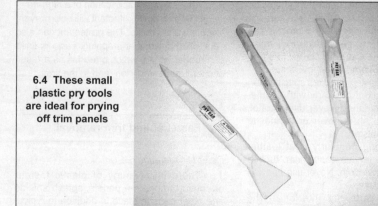

6.4 These small plastic pry tools are ideal for prying off trim panels

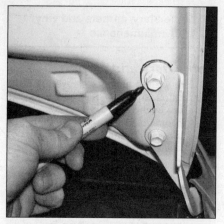

9.3 Draw alignment marks around the hood hinges to ensure proper alignment of the hood when it's reinstalled

ers are commonly found at most auto parts stores, if necessary.

4   Trim panels are typically made of plastic and their flexibility can help during removal. The key to their removal is to use a tool to pry the panel near its retainers to release it without damaging surrounding areas or breaking-off any retainers. The retainers will usually snap out of their designated slot or hole after force is applied to them. Stiff plastic tools designed for prying on trim panels are available at most auto parts stores **(see illustration)**. Tools that are tapered and wrapped in protective tape, such as a screwdriver or small pry tool, are also very effective when used with care.

7   Hinges and locks - maintenance

Once every 3000 miles, or every three months, the hinges and latch assemblies on the doors, hood and trunk should be given a few drops of light oil or lock lubricant. The door latch strikers should also be lubricated with a thin coat of grease to reduce wear and ensure free movement. Lubricate the door and trunk locks with spray-on graphite lubricant.

8   Windshield and fixed glass - replacement

Replacement of the windshield and fixed glass requires the use of special fast-setting adhesive/caulk materials and some specialized tools and techniques. These operations should be left to a dealer service department or a shop specializing in glass work.

9   Hood - removal, installation and adjustment

Note: *The hood is somewhat awkward to remove and install; at least two people should perform this procedure.*

Removal and installation

Refer to illustrations 9.3, 9.4 and 9.5

1   Open the hood, then place blankets or pads over the fenders and cowl area of the body. This will protect the body and paint as the hood is lifted off.

2   Disconnect any cables or wires that will

interfere with removal.

3   Make marks around the hood hinge to ensure proper alignment during installation **(see illustration)**.

4   Detach the support struts by prying out the clips at the top **(see illustration)**.

5   Grasp the lower corner of the hood and use your shoulder to support the hood while an assistant does the same on the other side, then unscrew the bolts **(see illustration)**.

6   Installation is the reverse of removal. Align the hinges with the marks made in Step 3.

Adjustment

Refer to illustrations 9.10 and 9.11

7   Fore-and-aft and side-to-side adjustment of the hood is done by moving the hinge plate slot after loosening the bolts or nuts. **Note:** *The factory bolts are centering type that will not allow adjustment. To adjust the hood in relation to the hinges, these bolts must be replaced with standard bolts with flat washers and lock washers.*

9.4 On models so equipped, detach the hood support struts by prying out the clip and pulling the strut from the stud

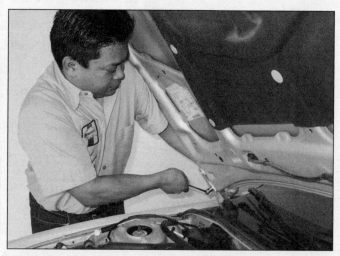

9.5 Support the hood with your shoulder while removing the hood bolts

9.10 To adjust the hood latch horizontally or vertically, loosen these bolts

9.11 To adjust the vertical height of the leading edge of the hood so that it's flush with the fenders, turn each edge cushion clockwise to lower the hood or counterclockwise to raise the hood

10.2 Pry out the cable retainer from the backside of the hood latch assembly, then disengage the cable

8   Mark around the entire hinge plate so you can determine the amount of movement.

9   Loosen the bolts and move the hood into correct alignment. Move it only a little at a time. Tighten the hinge bolts and carefully lower the hood to check the position.

10   If necessary after installation, the entire hood latch assembly can be adjusted up-and-down as well as from side-to-side on the radiator support so the hood closes securely and flush with the fenders. On Avalon models, remove the front grille (see Section 11). Scribe a line or mark around the hood latch mounting bolts to provide a reference point, then loosen them and reposition the latch assembly, as necessary **(see illustration)**. Following adjustment, retighten the mounting bolts. **Note:** *On all models except Avalon, the front bumper cover must be removed (see Section 11) to gain access to the latch assembly.*

11   Finally, adjust the hood bumpers on the ends of the fender so the hood, when closed, is flush with the fenders **(see illustration)**.

12   The hood latch assembly, as well as the hinges, should be periodically lubricated with white, lithium-base grease to prevent binding and wear.

---

10   Hood latch and release cable - removal and installation

Warning: *The models covered by this manual are equipped with Supplemental Restraint Systems (SRS), more commonly known as airbags. Always disarm the airbag system before working in the vicinity of any airbag system component to avoid the possibility of accidental deployment of the airbag, which could cause personal injury (see Chapter 12).*

Latch

Refer to illustration 10.2

1   On all models except Avalon, remove the front bumper assembly; on Avalon models,

remove the radiator grille (see Section 11). Scribe a line around the latch to aid alignment when installing, then (on models so equipped) remove the plastic cover over the latch, retained by plastic pins. Remove the retaining bolts securing the hood latch to the radiator support **(see illustration 9.10)**. Remove the latch.

2   Disconnect the hood release cable by disengaging the cable from the latch assembly **(see illustration)**.

3   Installation is the reverse of removal. **Note:** *Adjust the latch so the hood engages securely when closed and the hood bumpers are slightly compressed.*

Cable

Refer to illustration 10.10

4   Raise the vehicle, support it securely on jackstands and remove the front wheel.

5   Remove the lower opening extension pad from the bottom of the fender.

6   Remove the inner fender liner (see Section 12).

7   Disconnect the hood release cable from the latch assembly **(see illustration 10.2)**.

8   Attach a piece of thin wire or string to the end of the cable and unclip all remaining cable retaining clips at the radiator support, fender and firewall.

9   Working in the passenger compartment, remove the driver's side door sill cover and kick panel.

10   Remove the driver's knee bolster panel (see Section 23). The hood latch release lever is attached to the panel **(see illustration)**.

11   Pull the cable and grommet rearward into the passenger compartment until you can see the wire or string. Ensure that the new cable has a grommet attached, then remove the wire or string from the old cable and fasten it to the new cable.

12   With the new cable attached to the wire or string, pull the wire or string back through

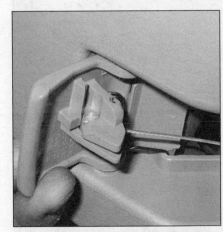

10.10 Remove the knee bolster and detach the cable end from the release lever assembly

the firewall until the new cable reaches the latch assembly.

13   Working in the passenger compartment, reinstall the new cable into the hood release lever, making sure the cable housing fits snugly into the notch in the handle bracket.

14   The remainder of the installation is the reverse of removal. **Note:** *Push on the grommet with your fingers from the passenger compartment to seat the grommet in the firewall correctly.*

---

11   Bumper covers - removal and installation

Warning: *The models covered by this manual are equipped with Supplemental Restraint Systems (SRS), more commonly known as airbags. Always disarm the airbag system before working in the vicinity of any airbag system component to avoid the possibility of*

11.3 On V6 models remove the radiator support cover retaining clips and cover

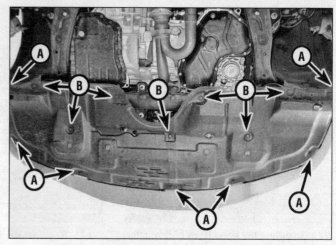

11.4a Remove the screws (A) and clips (B) retaining the splash apron and the bottom edge of the front bumper cover (Avalon shown)

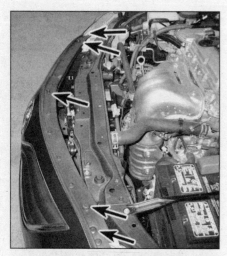

11.4b Remove the screws/pushpins along the top edge of the bumper cover (Camry shown)

accidental deployment of the airbag, which could cause personal injury (see Chapter 12).

Front bumper

Refer to illustrations 11.3, 11.4a, 11.4b, 11.5 and 11.6

1   Pull back the front portion of the fender-well liner (see Section 12). Apply the parking brake, raise the vehicle and support it securely on jackstands.

2   Disconnect the cable from the negative battery terminal (see Chapter 5). On models equipped with fog lights, disconnect the electrical connectors at the fog lights on the back of the bumper cover. On Avalon models, the grille may be removed separately by removing the grille retaining bolts and clip. Carefully pull the grille out and disengage the remaining mounting clips.

3   Remove the radiator support cover mounting clips and cover **(see illustration)**.

4   Detach the screws and/or push-pins securing the top, bottom and sides of the bumper cover **(see illustrations)**. **Note:** *Use a small screwdriver to pop the center button up on the plastic fasteners, but do not try to remove the center buttons. They stay in the ferrules.* **Note:** *The number and location of the cover screws varies among the different models. Don't try to remove the cover until all fasteners have been located and removed.*

5   There are two locking pins located at the front portion of the fenderwell liner where it meets the bumper. The pins must be rotated 90-degrees **(see illustration)**, then removed.

6   Pull the fenderwell liner back and remove the bumper cover-to-fender mounting bolt **(see illustration)**.

7   There are four clips where the cover meets the front of the fenders. Pull outward on the ends of the cover to release the clips.

8   Installation is the reverse of removal. Make sure the tabs on the back of the bumper cover fit into the corresponding clips on the

11.5 To remove the front portion of the inner fenderwell liner, rotate the lock pin (A) 90-degrees and pull it out, and remove the mounting screw (B)

11.6 With the inner fenderwell liner pulled back, remove the one fender-to-bumper cover bolt at each side

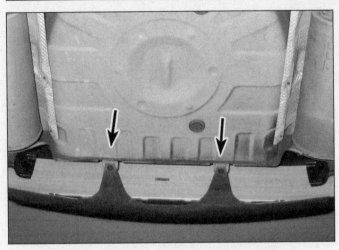

11.9 Remove the plastic pins at the bottom of the rear bumper cover

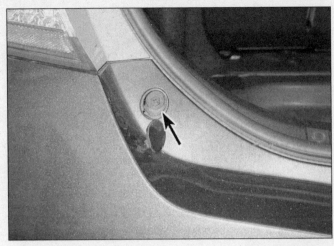

11.11 Inside the trunk, remove the corner mounting fasteners

body before attaching the bolts and screws. An assistant would be helpful at this point.

Rear bumper

Refer to illustrations 11.9 and 11.11

9   Working under the vehicle, detach the plastic pins securing the lower edge of the bumper cover **(see illustration)**.

10   In the rear fenderwells, remove the screw(s) securing the front edge of the cover to the fenderwell. On some models, the plastic fenderwell liner must be released for access.

11   Open the trunk lid and remove the fasteners securing the bumper cover in each corner **(see illustration)**.

12   Disconnect the electrical connectors to the parking system and/or back up camera, if equipped.

13   From under the vehicle, remove the screws securing the lower edge of the bumper cover. Pull the bumper cover out and away from the vehicle. **Note:** *Use a small screwdriver to pop the center button up on*

the plastic fasteners, but do not try to remove the center buttons - they stay in the ferrules. Where studs/bolts stick through the body, use a plastic hammer to tap them out of the body.

14   Installation is the reverse of removal.

12   Front fender - removal and installation

Refer to illustration 12.3a, 12.3b, 12.4, 12.5a, 12.5b, 12.8a and 12.8b

1   Raise the vehicle, support it securely on jackstands and remove the front wheel.

2   On 2009 and earlier Lexus models, remove the front turn signal side light (see Chapter 12).

3   Detach the inner fenderwell screws and clips, then remove the inner fenderwell and mud shield **(see illustrations)**.

4   Open the front door and remove the upper fender-to-body bolt **(see illustration)**.

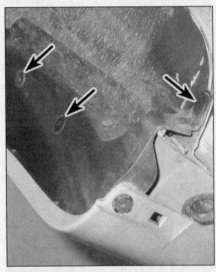

12.3a Remove the bolts at the front lower portion of the inner fenderwell

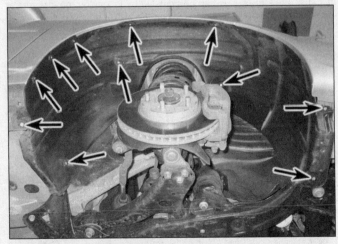

12.3b Detach the main portion of the inner fenderwell, secured by bolts, screws and plastic clips

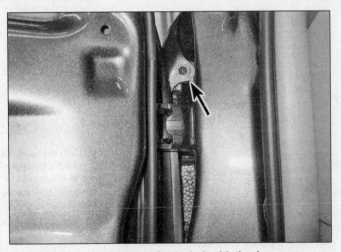

12.4 Remove the upper fender bolt with the door open

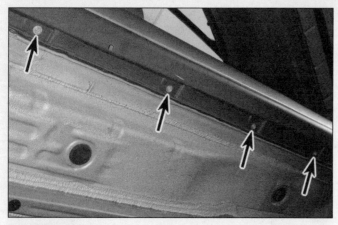

12.5a Remove the bolts securing the rocker trim panel

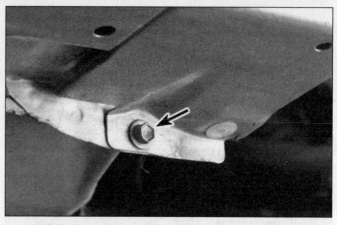

12.5b Remove the lower fender-to-rocker panel bolt

5   Unbolt and lower the rocker trim panel to access the lower fender bolt **(see illustrations)**.

6   Remove the front bumper cover (see Chapter 11).

7   Remove the headlight housing (see Chapter 12).

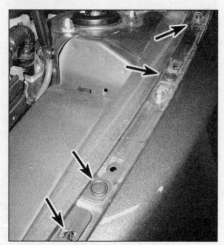

12.8a Remove the fender trim mounting clips and trim panel

12.8b Remove the mounting bolts along the top of the fender

8   Remove the cowl cover (see Section 26), and the rubber hood weatherseal and fender trim fasteners along the top of the fender **(see illustration)**, then remove the remaining fender mounting bolts **(see illustration)**.

9   Lift off the fender. It's a good idea to have an assistant support the fender while it's being moved away from the vehicle to prevent damage to the surrounding body panels.

10   Installation is the reverse of removal. Check the alignment of the fender to the hood and front edge of the door before final tightening of the fender fasteners.

13   Trunk lid - removal, installation and adjustment

Note: *The trunk lid is heavy and somewhat awkward to remove and install - at least two people should perform this procedure.*

Removal and installation

Refer to illustrations 13.1, 13.3a and 13.3b

1   Open the trunk lid and cover the edges of the trunk compartment with pads or cloths to protect the painted surfaces when the lid is removed. Remove the trim fasteners all around the trunk lid trim panel **(see illustration)** and remove the trim panel. **Note:** *Slide the emergency trunk release handle*

through the trim panel.

2   Disconnect the electrical connectors from the backup lights, license plate lights, taillights and back up camera (if equipped), then unplug the harness at the front of the trunk lid.

3   Remove the hinge trim cover fasteners **(see illustration)** and covers (if equipped). Scribe or draw alignment marks around the trunk hinges **(see illustration)**.

4   With the help of an assistant, remove the hinge-to-trunk lid bolts from both sides and lift off the trunk lid.

5   Installation is the reverse of removal. Be sure to align the hinge flanges with the marks made on the trunk lid during removal.

Adjustment

Refer to illustration 13.7

6   After installation, close the lid and see if it's in proper alignment with the adjacent body surfaces. Fore-and-aft and side-to-side adjustments of the lid are controlled by the position of the hinge bolts in the slots. To adjust it, loosen the hinge bolts, reposition the lid and retighten the bolts.

7   The height of the rear of the lid in relation to the surrounding body panels when closed can be adjusted by loosening the lock striker bolts, moving the striker up/down or left/right, then re-tightening the bolts **(see illustration)**.

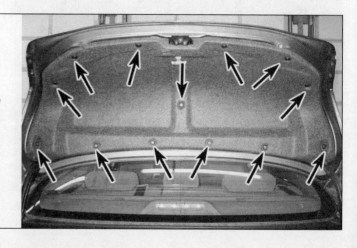

13.1 Remove the plastic fasteners that secure the trunk trim panel

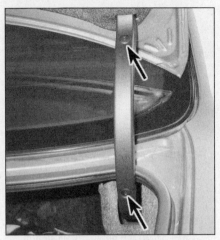

13.3a Remove the plastic hinge
trim fasteners

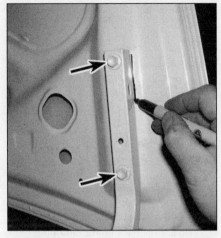

13.3b Draw around the trunk hinges with
a marking pen before loosening the bolts
to ensure proper alignment of the trunk lid
when it's reinstalled

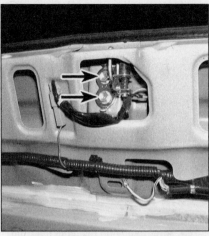

13.7 Loosen the bolts and move the
striker as necessary to adjust the trunk lid
flush with the body in the closed position

Note: *Make a reference mark around the striker before making adjustments.*

14 Trunk lid latch and lock assembly - removal and installation

Trunk lid latch

Refer to illustration 14.2

1   Remove the trunk lid trim panel **(see illustration 13.1)** and latch trim cover.
2   Scribe a line around the trunk lid latch assembly for a reference point to aid the installation procedure **(see illustration)**.
3   Detach the two retaining bolts and remove the latch.
4   Disconnect the latch release cable and/or actuator rod and the electrical connector from the latch.
5   Installation is the reverse of removal.

Trunk lock assembly

Refer to illustration 14.6

6   Open the trunk and remove the trunk lid trim panel **(see illustration 13.1)**. Remove the lock cylinder rod from its clip and remove the lock cylinder mounting bolts **(see illustration)**. On models so equipped, disconnect the electrical connector from the lock.
7   Remove the cylinder from the trunk.
8   Installation is the reverse of removal.

15 Trunk release and fuel door release - removal and installation

Trunk release switch

1   Remove the trunk lid trim panel (see Section 13).
2   Remove the trunk latch and lock assem-

bly (see Section 14).
3   From inside the trunk lid, remove the trim mounting nuts. From the outside of the trunk lid, carefully pry the trim piece off of the lid. **Note:** *Put tape against the trunk lid to prevent the lid from being scratched.*
4   Remove the trunk release switch mounting screws, disconnect the harness clips and remove the switch from the trim panel.
5   Installation is the reverse of removal.

Fuel door release

Note: *On some models, the fuel door release is electrically operated - there is no cable.*

Motor

Refer to illustrations 15.7 and 15.8

6   Inside the trunk, remove the floor mat, spare tire and left-side trim panel for access to the fuel door release motor.
7   Open the fuel door and remove the nut.

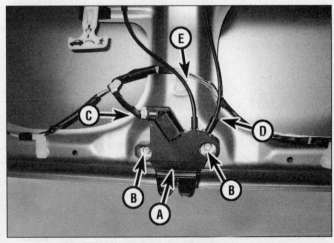

14.2 Trunk latch details

A	Truck latch cover	C	Electrical connector
B	Trunk latch mounting	D	Release cable
	bolts	E	Emergency release cable

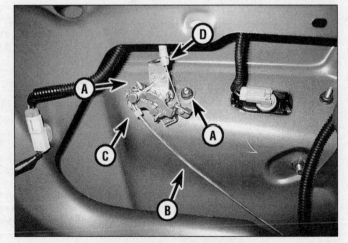

14.6 Trunk lock cylinder details

A	Truck lock cylinder	C	Actuating rod retaining
	mounting nuts		clip
B	Actuating rod	D	Emergency release cable

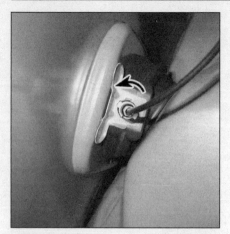

15.7 After removing the jamb nut from the fuel door side, rotate the cable lock housing counterclockwise to release the cable end

15.8 Fuel door motor mounting nut location

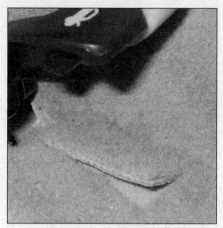

15.14 Open the slit in the carpeting and remove the bolt holding the release mechanism to the floor

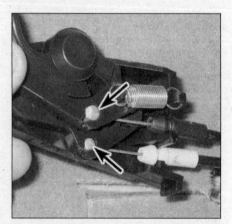

15.15 Remove the cables from the clips and the cable eyes from the slots in the levers

Remove the motor lock-to-door cable by turning the sleeve at the end of the cable counterclockwise and pulling back on the sleeve **(see illustration)**.

8　Disconnect the electrical connector and remove the mounting nut **(see illustration)**. Remove the motor and fuel door as an assembly.

9　Installation is the reverse of removal.

Cable

Refer to illustrations 15.14 and 15.15

10　Inside the trunk, remove the floor mat and left-side panel for access to the fuel door cable end. Push in the tabs of the fuel door latch cable end (white plastic part) and pull it from the fuel door housing **(see illustration 15.7)**. To remove the cable end retainer (black plastic), twist it out of the bracket.

11　Remove the rear seat bottom (see Section 27).

12　Remove the center door pillar's lower trim panel.

13　Peel back the carpeting to access the release cable. Open all of the clips holding the cable to the body.

14　Remove the bolt holding the release han-

dle assembly to the floor **(see illustration)**.

15　Turn the housing over and remove the cable housings from the clips and the eyes from the levers **(see illustration)**.

16　Attach a piece of thin wire to the end of the cable.

17　Working in the trunk compartment, pull the cable towards the rear of the vehicle until you can see the wire.

18　Attach the wire to the front of the new cable and fish it back through the body until it can be attached to the lever. The remainder of installation is the reverse of removal.

---

16 Door trim panels - removal and installation

Warning: *The models covered by this manual are equipped with Supplemental Restraint Systems (SRS), more commonly known as airbags. Always disarm the airbag system before working in the vicinity of any airbag system component to avoid the possibility of accidental deployment of the airbag, which could cause personal injury (see Chapter 12).*
Caution: *Wear gloves when working inside the door openings to protect against cuts from sharp metal edges.*

Removal

Refer to illustrations 16.3, 16.4, 16.5, 16.7 and 16.9

1　Disconnect the cable from the negative battery terminal (see Chapter 5).

2　Using a trim tool, pry out the outside mirror trim plate (see Section 21).

3　Use a trim tool to pry out the cover from the inside door handle, then remove the mounting screw **(see illustration)**.

4　On Avalon models, pry up the window switch plate to access one panel mounting screw underneath and disconnect the electrical connectors **(see illustration)**.

5　On Camry and Lexus models, pry out the trim cover in the armrest and remove the mounting screw **(see illustration)**.

6　Pry the courtesy light assembly out from the bottom of the panel and disconnect the electrical connector (if equipped).

7　Remove the remaining door trim panel retaining plastic push pins or screws, then carefully pry the panel out until the clips disengage. Work slowly and carefully around the outer edge of the trim panel until it's free **(see illustration)**.
Note: *Most of the screws on the door panel are covered by small plastic discs, which must be pried out before removing the screws.*

8　Once all of the clips are disengaged, pull the trim panel up from the door, unplug any wiring harness connectors, disconnect the inside door handle cables and remove the panel.

9　For access to the door outside handle or the door window regulator inside the door, raise the window fully, remove the power window control unit (if equipped), the door panel bracket and the speaker assembly (see Chapter 12), then carefully peel back the plastic watershield **(see illustration)**.

Installation

10　Prior to installation of the door trim panel, be sure to reinstall any clips in the panel which may have come out when you removed the panel.

11　Plug in the wire harness connectors for the power door lock switch and the power window switch, and place the panel in position in the door. Press the door panel into place until the clips are seated. Install the inner door handle and its screw and connect the two cables. Install the power door lock switch assembly, if equipped. Install the power window switch assembly.

---

17 Door - removal, installation and adjustment

Warning: *The models covered by this manual are equipped with Supplemental Restraint Systems (SRS), more commonly known as airbags. Always disarm the airbag system before working in the vicinity of any airbag system component to avoid the possibility of*

16.3 Remove the decorative cover to reveal the screw, remove the screw and pry the bezel from the door panel

16.4 On Avalon models, pry up the power window switch plate, disconnect the electrical connectors and remove the one screw through the door panel (if present)

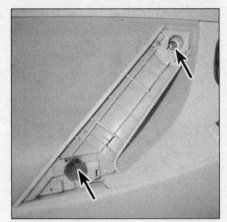

16.5 On Camry and Lexus models, pry the armrest support handle cover off and remove the mounting screws

accidental deployment of the airbag, which could cause personal injury (see Chapter 12) **Warning:** *Wear gloves when working inside the door openings to protect against cuts from sharp metal edges.*
Note: *The door is heavy and somewhat awkward to remove and install - at least two people should perform this procedure.*

Removal and installation

Refer to illustrations 17.6, 17.8a and 17.8b

1   Lower the window completely in the door, then disconnect the cable from the negative battery terminal (see Chapter 5).
2   Open the door all the way and support it from the ground on jacks or blocks covered with rags to prevent damaging the paint.
3   Remove the door trim panel and watershield (see Section 16).
4   Disconnect all electrical connections, ground wires and harness retaining clips from the door. **Note:** *It is a good idea to label all connections to aid the reassembly process.*
5   From the door side, detach the rubber conduit between the body and the door. Pull the wiring harness through the conduit hole

16.7 Carefully use a trim panel tool to pry all around the panel and release the clips

and remove it from the door.
6   Remove the door stop strut bolt **(see illustration)**.
7   Mark around the door hinges with a pen or a scribe to facilitate realignment during reassembly. **Note:** *On Lexus models, pry the hinge*

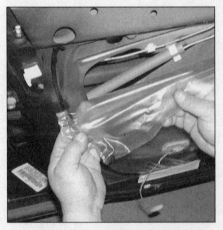

16.9 Carefully peel back the plastic watershield for access to the inner door

trim cover out using a screwdriver or trim tool.
8   With an assistant holding the door, remove the hinge-to-door bolts **(see illustrations)** and lift the door off.
9   Installation is the reverse of removal.

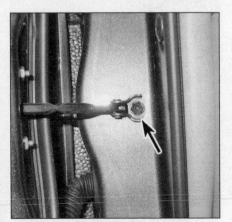

17.6 Remove the bolt retaining the door stop strut

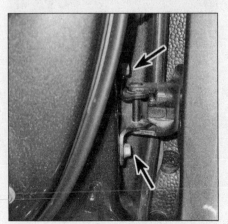

17.8a Remove the door hinge bolts with the door supported (bottom hinge bolts indicated, top hinge similar)

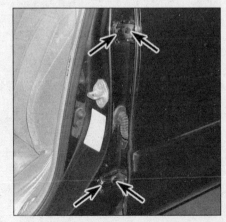

17.8b Open the front door to access the rear door hinge-to-body bolts

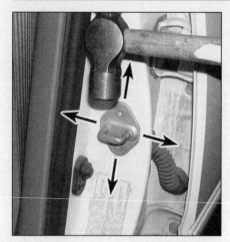

17.13 Adjust the door lock striker by loosening the mounting screws and gently tapping the striker in the desired direction

Adjustment

Refer to illustration 17.13

10   Having proper door-to-body alignment is a critical part of a well-functioning door assembly. First check the door hinge pins for excessive play. Fully open the door and lift up and down on the door without lifting the body. If a door has 1/16-inch or more excessive play, the hinges should be replaced.

11   Door-to-body alignment adjustments are made by loosening the hinge-to-body bolts or hinge-to-door bolts and moving the door. Proper body alignment is achieved when the top of the doors are parallel with the roof section, the front door is flush with the fender, the rear door is flush with the rear quarter panel and the bottom of the doors are aligned with the lower rocker panel. If these goals can't be reached by adjusting the hinge-to-body or hinge-to-door bolts, body alignment shims may have to be purchased and inserted behind the hinges to achieve correct alignment.

12   To adjust the door-closed position, scribe

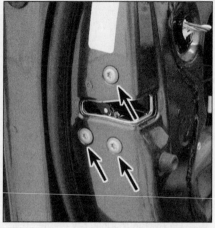

18.4 The latch is secured to the door with three screws

a line or mark around the striker plate to provide a reference point, then check that the door latch is contacting the center of the latch striker. If not, adjust the up and down position first. **Note:** *On Lexus models, remove the plastic cover over the striker before making adjustments.*

13   Finally, adjust the latch striker sideways position, so that the door panel is flush with the center pillar or rear quarter panel and provides positive engagement with the latch mechanism **(see illustration)**.

---

18   Door latch, lock cylinder and handle - removal and installation

---

Warning: *Wear gloves when working inside the door openings to protect against cuts from sharp metal edges.*

Door latch

Refer to illustration 18.4

1   Raise the window, then remove the door trim panel and watershield (see Section 16).

2   Working through the large access hole, disengage the rod to the outside handle and the lock cylinder.

3   The door lock rod is attached by plastic clips. The plastic clips can be removed by unsnapping the portion engaging the connecting rod and pulling the rod out of its locating hole.

4   Remove the screws securing the latch to the door **(see illustration)** and pull the latch back enough to disconnect the electrical connector at the latch. Remove the latch assembly through the door opening with the two cables from the inside door handle still attached to the latch.

5   Installation is the reverse of removal.

Door lock cylinder

Refer to illustrations 18.8a and 18.8b

6   To remove the outside handle and lock cylinder assembly, raise the window and remove the door trim panel and watershield (see Section 16). **Caution:** *Take care not to scratch the paint on the outside of the door. Wide masking tape applied around the handle opening before beginning the procedure can help avoid scratches.*

7   Remove an access plug at the rear of the door (jamb side).

8   Working through the access hole, loosen the TORX screw **(see illustration)** and remove the lock cylinder cover and the door lock key cylinder as a unit **(see illustration)**. **Note:** *The TORX screw can't be fully removed, it is a part of the outside handle.*

9   Once the lock cylinder is out, disengage the lock cover clips using a screwdriver and separate the cover from the lock cylinder.

10   Installation is the reverse of removal.

Door handle

Outside handle

Refer to illustration 18.11

11   Once the lock cylinder has been removed, slide the exterior handle rearward

18.8a Remove the rubber plug at the end of the door and use a Torx tool through the hole to loosen the lock cylinder bolt (the bolt does not come out)

18.8b Slide the lock cylinder out

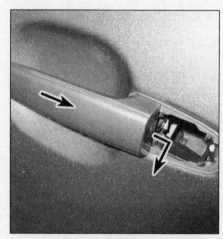

18.11 Remove the exterior door handle by sliding the handle rewards and out

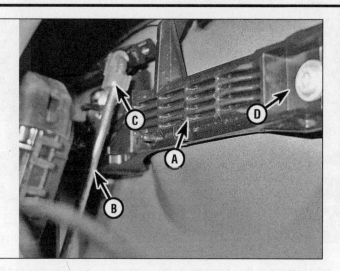

18.13 Outside door handle details

A   Outside door handle frame assembly
B   Actuating rod
C   Actuating rod retaining clip
D   Mounting screw

18.14 Squeeze the clip at the outside and remove the door handle assembly from inside the door

and out to remove it **(see illustration)**. **Note:** *On models with Smart Key Systems, disconnect the electrical connector to the handle then slide the handle back, then pull out and remove the handle with the harness.*

Outside handle assembly

Refer to illustrations 18.13 and 18.14

12   Working from the outside of the door, remove the handle assembly exterior mounting screw.

13   From inside of the door, disconnect the electrical connector, remove the mounting screw, disconnect the lock rod clip and move the lock rod away from the handle **(see illustration)**. **Note:** *If the door latch was removed, leave the lock rod attached to the door handle assembly. If the latch is not being removed, disconnect the rod and move it away from the door handle.*

14   Disengage the door handle assembly mounting clips and remove the handle assembly from the vehicle **(see illustration)**. **Note:** *On models with Smart Key Systems, remove the door electrical key solenoid mounting screw and solenoid, then the handle assembly.*

15   Installation is the reverse of removal.

19 Door window glass - removal and installation

Warning: *Wear gloves when working inside the door openings to protect against cuts from sharp metal edges.*

Front door glass

Refer to illustration 19.6

1   Remove the door trim panel and the plastic watershield (see Section 16).

2   Using a screwdriver, disengage the four weatherstrip mounting clips and lift the weatherstrip out. **Note:** *On Lexus models, remove the window frame trim mounting clips and pry the trim out of the window frame.*

3   Remove the outer mirror plastic watershield (if equipped).

4   On Avalon models, remove the door armrest trim bracket

5   Lower the window glass all the way down into the door.

6   Raise the window just enough to access the window retaining bolts through the holes in the door frame **(see illustration)**.

7   Place a rag over the glass to help prevent scratching the glass and remove the glass mounting bolts. **Caution:** *Once the window retaining bolts have been removed, the window may fall and break.*

8   Rotate the front end of the glass slightly down, then lift the window up and out.

9   Installation is the reverse of removal. When installing the glass in Avalon models, make sure the glass is level in the door opening before tightening the bolts.

Rear door glass

10   Remove the door panel and watershield (see Section 16). Remove the rear run channel bolts located at the top of the door and the lower portion of the channel.

11   Pull the rear quarter glass weatherstripping out and slide the quarter glass forward and out.

12   Lower the window enough to see the regulator bar. Push the glass guide arms back and out of the regulator, then remove the glass through the window opening.

13   Installation is the reverse of removal.

20 Door window glass regulator - removal and installation

Warning: *Wear gloves when working inside the door openings to protect against cuts from sharp metal edges.*

Front

Refer to illustration 20.5

1   Remove the door trim panel and the plastic watershield (see Section 16).

2   Remove the door speaker fasteners and disconnect the electrical connector (see Chapter 12).

3   Remove the window glass (see Section 19).

4   Disconnect the electrical connector from the window regulator motor.

5   Loosen the temporary locking bolt, but

19.6 Raise the window to access the glass retaining bolts through the holes in the door frame - Camry model shown

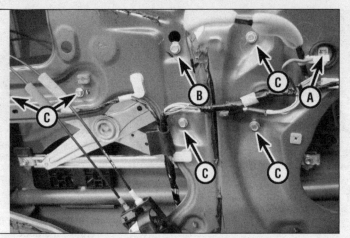

20.5 Window regulator mounting details

A   Power window motor electrical connector
B   Temporary locking bolt
C   Regulator mounting bolts

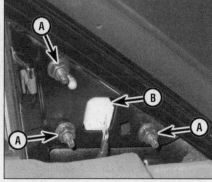

21.2 Disconnect the electrical connector (A) and remove the three mirror mounting nuts (B)

do not remove it **(see illustration)**. **Caution:** *If the temporary bolt is removed before the regulator assembly is removed, the regulator may fall and be damaged.*

6   Remove the regulator/motor assembly mounting bolts and remove the regulator assembly through the service hole in the door frame.

7   Once the regulator is out of the vehicle, remove the temporary locking bolt.

8   Installation is the reverse of removal. Lubricate the rollers and wear points on the regulator with white grease before installation.

Rear

9   Remove the door trim panel and the plastic watershield (see Section 16).

10   Remove the quarter glass and window glass assembly (see Section 19).

11   Reconnect the power window switch and raise the window regulator to the up position.

12   Disconnect the power window switch and the electrical connector from the window regulator motor.

13   Loosen the temporary locking bolt until the bolt contacts the gear. **Caution:** *If the temporary bolt is removed before the regulator assembly is removed, the regulator may fall and be damaged.*

14   Remove the regulator/motor assembly mounting bolts and remove the regulator assembly through the service hole in the door frame.

15   Once the regulator is out of the vehicle, remove the temporary locking bolt.

16   Installation is the reverse of removal. Lubricate the rollers and wear points on the regulator with white grease before installation.

---

21   Mirrors - removal and installation

Outside mirrors
Toyota models

Refer to illustration 21.2

1   Pry off the mirror trim cover on the inside of the door.

2   Disconnect the electrical connector from the mirror (if equipped) **(see illustration)**.

3   Remove the three mirror retaining nuts and detach the mirror from the vehicle.

4   Installation is the reverse of removal.

Lexus models

5   Remove the door trim panel and window frame trim (see Section 17).

6   Remove the three mirror retaining nuts and disconnect the electrical connector.

7   Carefully pull the mirror up to disengage the retaining clip and remove the mirror.

8   Installation is the reverse of removal.

Inside mirror

9   Disengage the sensor cover clips, then remove the cover(s) and electrical connector.

10   To remove/install the mirror, remove/install the Torx screw at the base on the windshield.

11   If the mount plate itself has come off the windshield, adhesive kits are available at auto parts stores to re-secure it. Follow the instructions included with the kit.

---

22   Center console and armrest - removal and installation

Refer to illustrations 22.3, 22.5, 22.8, 22.9 and 22.12

Warning: *The models covered by this manual are equipped with Supplemental Restraint Systems (SRS), more commonly known as airbags. Always disarm the airbag system*

22.3 Use a trim tool to pry out the upper, center and side trim panels

22.5 Use a trim tool to pry up the shift indicator panel

22.8 Pry up the trim panel from the top of the console

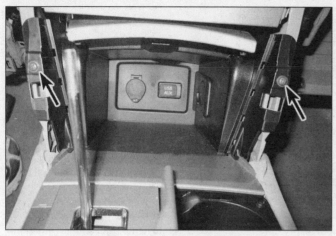

22.9 Lower storage box mounting screws

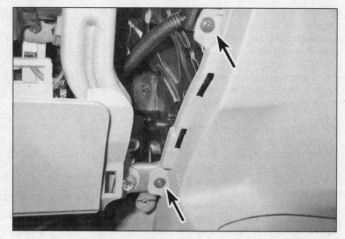

22.12 Remove the console side panel upper mounting screws

before working in the vicinity of any airbag system component to avoid the possibility of accidental deployment of the airbag, which could cause personal injury (see Chapter 12).

1 Disconnect the cable from the negative battery terminal (see Chapter 5).

2 Remove the knee bolster, driver's side trim panel and passenger's side trim panel (see Section 23). **Note:** *On models equipped with the Smart Key system, pry the panel out and disconnect the electrical connector to the "Power" button.*

3 Carefully pry the upper, center and side trim panels out from the instrument panel until the clips disengage **(see illustration)**, then remove the panels.

4 Twist the shift lever knob counterclockwise and remove the knob.

5 On automatic transaxle models, carefully pry the floor shift indicator up from the console until the clips disengage **(see illustration)**, disconnect any electrical connectors and remove the indicator assembly.

6 On manual transaxle models, open the cup holder lid and carefully pry the floor shift cover up from the console until the clips disengage and remove the boot and cover.

7 On Avalon and Lexus models, pry the seat heater switch panel up to disengage the four mounting clips, then disconnect the electrical connector and remove the switch assembly.

8 Pry the top trim panel from the floor console until the mounting clips disengage and remove the panel **(see illustration)**. **Note:** *On Avalon models, the top trim panel is also attached with several mounting fasteners that must be removed before disengaging the mounting clips.*

9 Remove the lower storage box mounting screws **(see illustration)** and pry the box out far enough to disconnect the electrical connectors.

10 On Camry and Lexus models, pry up the center register panel above the center trim panel and disconnect the electrical connector (see Chapter 3). **Note:** *The radio unit and trim are an assembly and must be removed together (see Chapter 12).*

11 On Avalon models, remove the center

register and A/C heater control panel assembly (see Chapter 3) and audio unit (see Chapter 12).

12 Remove the upper and lower mounting screws **(see illustration)** at the front of console side pieces and remove the sides. **Note:** *On Lexus models, disengage the mounting clips next to the mounting screws. On Avalon models, the console is a long one-piece unit.*

13 On Lexus models, pry the rear end panel of the center console outwards to disengage the panel from the console and remove the two mounting bolts from the end of the console.

14 Open the armrest, remove the console pocket (if equipped) and lift the carpet out from the bottom of the console. Remove the mounting fasteners and lift the console out. **Note:** *Some models have a mounting clip at the bottom of the console that must be disengaged before the console can be removed.*

15 Installation is the reverse of removal.

23 Dashboard trim panels - removal and installation

Warning: *The models covered by this manual are equipped with Supplemental Restraint Systems (SRS), more commonly known as airbags. Always disarm the airbag system before working in the vicinity of any airbag system component to avoid the possibility of accidental deployment of the airbag, which could cause personal injury (see Chapter 12). The yellow wiring harnesses and connectors are for this system. Do not use electrical test equipment on any of the airbag system wiring or tamper with it in any way.*

Note: *Several types and designs of mounting clips and hooks are used to secure the trim panels to the instrument panel. Care should be taken when trying to remove the panel.*

1 Disconnect the cable from the negative battery terminal (see Chapter 5).

Instrument cluster bezel

Camry and Lexus models

Refer to illustration 23.4

2 If equipped with a tilt steering column, tilt the column all the way down.

3 Remove the steering column covers (see Section 24) and driver's side trim panels (see Steps 18 through 21).

4 Remove the cluster bezel mounting fasteners **(see illustration)**.

5 Starting at the bottom of the bezel, carefully pry the outer edges of the bezel away from the instrument panel until the clips are released. Take care not to scratch the surrounding trim on the instrument panel.

6 Installation is the reverse of removal. Make sure the clips are engaged properly before pushing the bezel firmly into place.

Avalon models

Refer to illustration 23.9

7 Remove the steering wheel (see Chapter 10) and the steering column covers (see Section 24)

8 Remove the driver's side trim panels (see Steps 18 through 21).

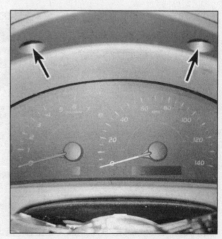

23.4 Cluster bezel mounting fasteners - Camry shown

9   Pry the driver's side center trim strip **(see illustration 23.21a)** and the passenger's side center trim strip out from the instrument panel **(see illustration)**.

10   Remove the center panel.

11   Remove the cluster bezel mounting screws. **Note:** *There are two separate instrument clusters, both are removed the same way.*

12   Starting at the top of the bezel and working from left to right, carefully pry the outer edges of the bezel away from the instrument panel until the clips are released. Take care not to scratch the surrounding trim on the instrument panel.

13   Installation is the reverse of removal. Make sure the clips are engaged properly before pushing the bezel firmly into place.

Knee bolster

Refer to illustrations 23.15, 23.16a and 23.16b

14   Remove the driver's kick panel (see Steps 28 and 29) for access to the left side bolster bolt.

15   Remove the right-hand bolster screw, then remove the bolt at the lower left side and disengage the bolster from the clips **(see illustration)**.

16   Carefully pry the knee bolster out, disen-

gaging the mounting clips **(see illustrations)**. Disconnect the electrical connector at the back of the bolster, then disconnect the hood release cable and remove the panel. **Caution:** *Do not pry on the knee airbag when removing*

23.9 On Avalon models, pry the passenger's side center trim strip out to disengage the clips and remove

23.15 Remove the right and left mounting screws from the knee bolster

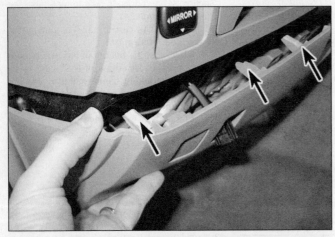

23.16a Carefully pry the knee bolster outwards to disengage the retaining clips along the perimeter of the panel

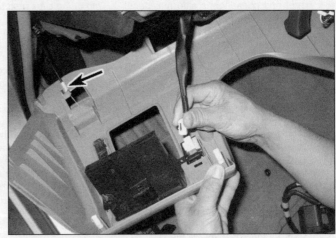

23.16b Once the bolster is pulled away from the instrument panel, disconnect the electrical connector and hood release cable

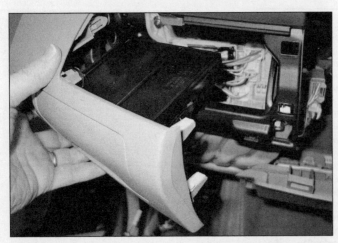

23.19a Carefully pry out the left driver's side trim panel . . .

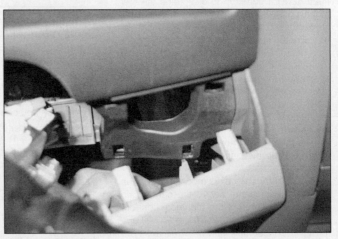

23.19b . . . and the right driver's side trim panel - Camry and Lexus models

23.21a On Avalon models, pry the center trim strip out . . .

23.21b . . . then pry the one-piece driver's side trim panel out, working all of the edges to release the retaining clips

the knee bolster.

17   Installation is the reverse of removal.

Driver's side trim panel

Refer to illustrations 23.19a, 23.19b, 23.21a and 23.21b

18   Remove the knee bolster (see Steps 14 through 16). **Note:** *On Avalon models, the steering column covers must be removed (see Section 24).*

19   On Camry and Lexus models, the driver's side panel is two pieces The panels are held in place under the side vent and instrument cluster area by clips **(see illustrations)**. Pry the edges straight out to release it.

20   Pull the panel back and disconnect the electrical connectors and remove the panel.

21   On Avalon models, pry out the center trim strip **(see illustration)**, then carefully pry the trim panel out **(see illustration)** far enough to disconnect any electrical connectors and remove the panel.

22   Installation is the reverse of removal.

Passenger's side lower panel and glove box

Refer to illustrations 23.24, 23.25 and 23.26

23   Disengage the mounting clips of the insulator panel and remove the panel (if equipped) and passenger's side kick panel.

24   Open the glove box, squeeze the strut locking tabs together **(see illustration)** and slide the strut off of the glove box tab.

25   Squeeze the glove box stops in and allow the glove box to come down enough to disengage the glove box from the lower panel **(see illustration)** and remove the glove box.

26   With the glove box removed, remove the lower passenger's side trim panel mounting screws and panel **(see illustration)**.

27   Installation is the reverse of removal.

Kick panels

28   Using a trim tool, pry up the door scuff plate.

29   Unscrew the kick panel-to-firewall fastener from the stud, then carefully pull the panel out to release the remaining two clips.

30   Installation is the reverse of removal.

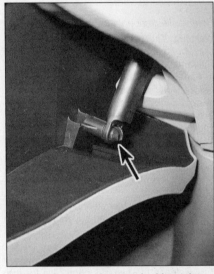

23.24 Squeeze the strut locking tabs together and slide the strut off of the tabs, then squeeze the sides past their stops and lower the glove box

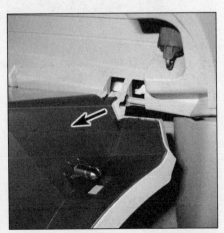

23.25 With the glove box in a 90-degree position, pull the bottom of the glove box outwards to unclip it from the trim panel

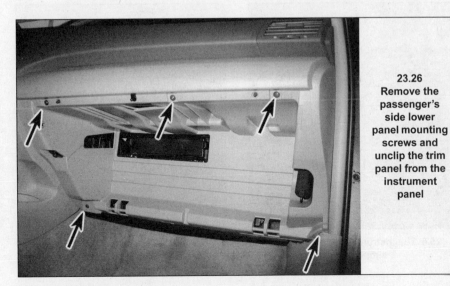

23.26 Remove the passenger's side lower panel mounting screws and unclip the trim panel from the instrument panel

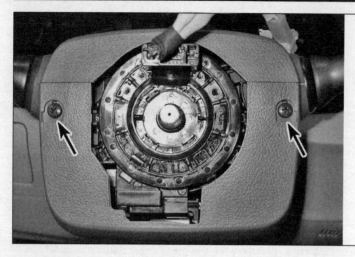

24.2 Remove the screws, then remove the steering column covers

24 Steering column covers - removal and installation

Refer to illustration 24.2

Warning: *The models covered by this manual are equipped with Supplemental Restraint Systems (SRS), more commonly known as airbags. Always disarm the airbag system before working in the vicinity of any airbag system component to avoid the possibility of accidental deployment of the airbag, which could cause personal injury (see Chapter 12).*

1   Disconnect the cable from the negative battery terminal (see Chapter 5). On tilt steering columns, move the column to the lowest position. Remove the steering wheel (see Chapter 10).

2   Remove the lower steering cover screws at the ends of the column covers **(see illustration)**.

2011 and earlier models

3   Release the two mounting clips for the lower cover, and remove the lower cover. Release the mounting clip in the center of the upper cover, and remove the cover.

4   Installation is the reverse of removal.

2012 and later models

5   The upper mounting clips of the lower steering cover sit just beneath the instrument stalk on each side of the cover. Release these two upper mounting clips by pressing each side of the cover inward.

6   Insert a finger into the column's tilt lever opening, release the lower mounting clip, and then remove the lower steering column cover.

7   Release the four mounting clips across the top of the upper steering column cover. Press the edges of the cover inward to release the clips, and remove the upper steering column cover.

8   Installation is the reverse of removal.

25 Instrument panel - removal and installation

Refer to illustrations 25.9, 25.10a, 25.10b, 25.11a, 25.11b and 25.12

Warning: *Models covered by this manual are equipped with a Supplemental Restraint System (SRS), more commonly known as*

airbags. Always disable the airbag system before working in the vicinity of any airbag system component to avoid the possibility of accidental deployment of the airbag, which could cause personal injury (see Chapter 12).

Note: *This is a difficult procedure for the home mechanic. There are many hidden fasteners, difficult angles to work in and many electrical connectors to tag and disconnect/connect. We recommend that this procedure be done only by an experienced do-it-yourselfer.*

Note: *During removal of the instrument panel, make careful notes of how each piece comes off, where it fits in relation to other pieces and what holds it in place. If you note how each part is installed before removing it, getting the instrument panel back together again will be much easier.*

Note: *It is not necessary, but it is suggested to remove both front seats to allow additional working space and lessen the chance of damage to the seats during this procedure.*

1   Disconnect the cable from the negative battery terminal (see Chapter 5).

2   Remove the dashboard trim panels (see Section 23) and the center floor console (see Section 22).

3   Remove the instrument cluster (see Chapter 12) and the glove box (see Section 23).

4   Carefully pry out the instrument panel lower side console trim and remove the trim panels. **Note:** *On Lexus models, the corner trim for the lower side console trim must be removed first before the side console trim panels can be removed.*

5   Disconnect the passenger's side airbag and remove the mounting fasteners and airbag (see Chapter 12).

6   Remove the audio unit from the center of the dashboard (see Chapter 12).

7   Remove the air conditioning control panel (see Chapter 3).

8   Remove the driver's knee bolster (see Section 23). **Note:** *If equipped, disconnect the driver's side knee airbag, remove the mounting bolts and remove the airbag (see Chapter 12).*

9   Pry off the end cap trim panels **(see**

25.9 The instrument panel end caps simply pry off

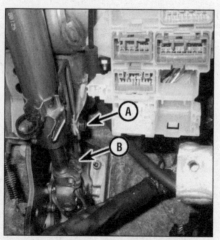

25.10a Remove the lower bolt (A) (and the pinch bolt [B] if removing the column entirely) . . .

25.10b . . . then the two upper bolts

25.11a Label and disconnect the main instrument panel electrical connectors at the left . . .

25.11b . . . and the right sides, below the instrument panel

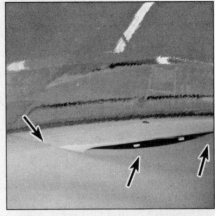

25.12 Carefully pry up the defrost panel starting from the left side and working around to the right side

illustration) for access to the reinforcement tube mounting bolts.

10   Remove the bolts securing the steering column and lower it away from the instrument panel **(see illustrations)**.

11   A number of electrical connectors must be disconnected in order to remove the instrument panel. Most are designed so that they will only fit on the matching connector (male or female), but if there is any doubt, mark the connectors with masking tape and a marking pen before disconnecting them **(see illustrations)**.

12   Pry up the speaker trim covers, defroster trim panel (at the top of the instrument panel) **(see illustration)** and disconnect the optical sensor electrical connector.

13   Remove all of the fasteners (bolts, screws and nuts) holding the instrument panel to the body. Once all are removed, lift the panel, then pull it away from the windshield and take it out through the door opening. **Note:** *This is a two-person job.*

14   If you're also removing the instrument panel reinforcement tube, disconnect any electrical connectors that might interfere with the removal of the reinforcement tube. Detach

the wire harness and remove the fasteners securing the tube, then take it out through the door opening.

15   Installation is the reverse of removal.

26 Cowl cover - removal and installation

Refer to illustrations 26.3, 26.5a and 26.5b

1   Remove the wiper arms (see Chapter 12).

2   Remove the side cowl seals from both ends of the cowl.

3   Remove the two pushpins, one at each end near the fender. Using a small screwdriver, release the four mounting clips and remove the louvered cowl cover by sliding it forward and out **(see illustration)**.

4   Remove the wiper motor and linkage (see Chapter 12).

5   Remove the cowl mounting fasteners **(see illustrations)** and remove the cowl from athe vehicle.

6   Installation is the reverse of removal.

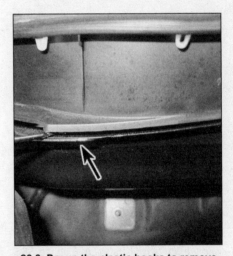

26.3 Pry up the plastic hooks to remove the cowl cover and slide the cowl cover forward to remove it

26.5a Passenger's side lower cowl cover mounting fasteners

26.5b Driver's side lower cowl cover mounting fasteners

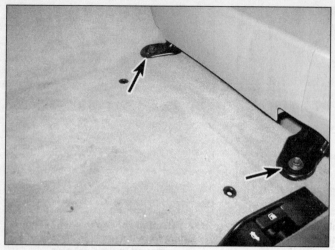

27.2 Typical front seat track retaining bolts; two of the four are indicated here (the track covers have been removed)

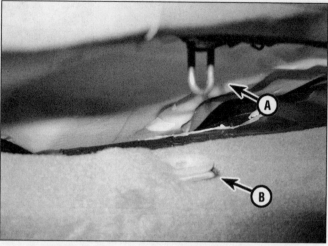

27.5 Lift the seat up to release the mounting bar (A) from the lock (B)

27 Seats - removal and installation

Front seat

Refer to illustration 27.2

Warning: *The front seat belts on some models are equipped with pre-tensioners, which are pyrotechnic (explosive) devices designed to retract the seat belts in the event of a collision. On models equipped with pre-tensioners, do not remove the front seat belt retractor assemblies, and do not disconnect the electrical connectors leading to the assemblies. Problems with the pre-tensioners will turn on the SRS (airbag) warning light on the dash. If any pretensioner problems are suspected, take the vehicle to a dealer service department.*

Warning: *On models with side-impact airbags, be sure to disarm the airbag system before beginning this procedure (see Chapter 12).*

1   Disconnect the cable from the negative battery terminal (see Chapter 5). Pry out the plastic covers to access the seat tracks and their mounting bolts.

2   Slide the seat back and remove the front retaining bolts **(see illustration)**, then slide the seat forward and remove the rear retaining bolts.

3   Tilt the seat upward to access the underside, then disconnect any electrical connectors and lift the seat from the vehicle.

4   Installation is the reverse of removal.

Rear seat

Bottom cushion

Refer to illustration 27.5

5   Slide your hands under one side of the rear bottom cushion and lift up on the front edge of the cushion to release the mounting

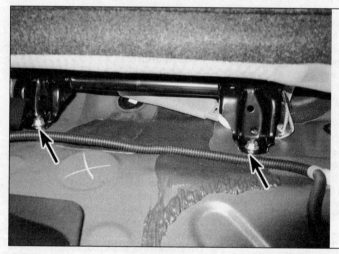

27.15 Flip the seat backs down and remove the bolts at the hinge, then remove the seat backs

bar from the lock **(see illustration)**. Use the same procedure for the opposite side, then remove the rear cushion from the vehicle.

6   Slide the seat belts out of the guides.

Seat back cushion

Refer to illustration 27.15

7   Pull the rear headrests up and out while holding the release clip and remove the headrests from the seat.

Fixed type

8   Remove the four mounting bolts for the one-piece seatback at the bottom of the cushion and remove the seat cushion.

9   Installation is the reverse of removal.

Reclining type

10   With the headrests removed, carefully pry the seat back mounting nut cover out from the seat.

11   Remove the upper mounting nuts (now

visible) and the lower bolts from the seat back.

12   Pull the seat back in at the top to release the mounting clips and remove the seat back. Repeat the same procedure for the remaining seat back.

13   Remove the center seat back mounting bolts and slide the center section up and out.

14   Installation is the reverse of removal.

Folding type

15   Fold one of the two rear seat backs down, then remove the mounting fasteners and seat back **(see illustration)**. Repeat the same procedure for the remaining seat back.

16   Remove the side rear seat back mounting fasteners and remove the seat back. Repeat the same procedure for the remaining side seat back.

17   Installation is the reverse of removal.

28 Rear package shelf - removal and installation

Warning: *The models covered by this manual are equipped with Supplemental Restraint Systems (SRS), more commonly known as airbags. Always disable the airbag system before working in the vicinity of any airbag system components to avoid the possibility of accidental deployment of the airbags, which could cause personal injury (see Chapter 12).*

1   Disconnect the cable from the negative battery terminal (see Chapter 5).

2   Remove the rear seat backs (see Section 27).

3   Remove the rear scuff plate and side trim. **Note:** *If equipped, disconnect the reclining remote control connector from the side trim panels.*

4   Carefully pry the rear side trim panels from the pillars and remove the side trim panels.

5   Carefully pry out the rear seat belt shoulder covers from the package shelf.

6   Remove the bolts from the shoulder belts.

7   Flip up the covers over the child safety belt hooks and unbolt the hooks.

8   Starting from the front and working towards the rear of the package shelf, pry the retaining clips up and remove the tray and sunshade (if equipped) assembly up and over the seat belt assemblies.

9   Disconnect the high-mount brake light electrical connector and remove the package shelf from the vehicle.

10   Installation is the reverse of removal. If removed, torque the lower seat belt bolts to 31 ft-lbs.

Notes

Chapter 12
Chassis electrical system

Contents

1 General information

The electrical system is a 12-volt, negative ground type. Power for the lights and all electrical accessories is supplied by a lead/acid-type battery that is charged by the alternator.

This Chapter covers repair and service procedures for the various electrical components not associated with the engine. Information on the battery, alternator, ignition system and starter motor can be found in Chapter 5.

It should be noted that when portions of the electrical system are serviced, the negative cable should be disconnected from the battery to prevent electrical shorts and/or fires.

2 Electrical troubleshooting - general information

Refer to illustrations 2.5a, 2.5b, 2.6 and 2.9

A typical electrical circuit consists of an electrical component, any switches, relays, motors, fuses, fusible links or circuit breakers related to that component and the wiring and connectors that link the component to both the battery and the chassis. To help you pinpoint an electrical circuit problem, wiring diagrams are included at the end of this Chapter.

Before tackling any troublesome electrical circuit, first study the appropriate wiring diagrams to get a complete understanding of what makes up that individual circuit. Trouble spots, for instance, can often be narrowed down by noting if other components related to the circuit are operating properly. If several components or circuits fail at one time, chances are the problem is in a fuse or ground connection, because several circuits are often routed through the same fuse and ground connections.

Electrical problems usually stem from simple causes, such as loose or corroded connections, a blown fuse, a melted fusible link or a failed relay. Visually inspect the condition of all fuses, wires and connections in a problem circuit before troubleshooting the circuit.

If test equipment and instruments are going to be utilized, use the diagrams to plan ahead of time where you will make the necessary connections in order to accurately pinpoint the trouble spot.

The basic tools needed for electrical

troubleshooting include a circuit tester or voltmeter (a 12-volt bulb with a set of test leads can also be used), a continuity tester, which includes a bulb, battery and set of test leads, and a jumper wire, preferably with a circuit breaker incorporated, which can be used to bypass electrical components **(see illustrations)**. Before attempting to locate a problem with test instruments, use the wiring diagram(s) to decide where to make the connections.

Voltage checks

Voltage checks should be performed if a circuit is not functioning properly. Connect one lead of a circuit tester to either the negative battery terminal or a known good ground. Connect the other lead to a connector in the circuit being tested, preferably nearest to the battery or fuse **(see illustration)**. If the bulb of the tester lights, voltage is present, which means that the part of the circuit between the connector and the battery is problem free. Continue checking the rest of the circuit in the same fashion. When you reach a point at which no voltage is present, the problem lies between that point and the last test point with voltage. Most of the time the problem can be traced to a loose connection. **Note:** *Keep in mind that some circuits receive voltage only when the ignition key is in the Accessory or Run position.*

Finding a short

One method of finding shorts in a circuit is to remove the fuse and connect a test light or voltmeter in place of the fuse terminals. There should be no voltage present in the circuit. Move the wiring harness from side-to-side while watching the test light. If the bulb goes on, there is a short to ground somewhere in that area, probably where the insulation has rubbed through. The same test can be performed on each component in the circuit, even a switch.

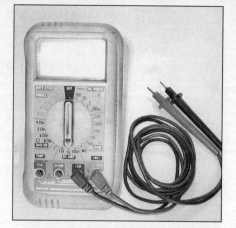

2.5a The most useful tool for electrical troubleshooting is a digital multimeter that can check volts, amps, and test continuity

Ground check

Perform a ground test to check whether a component is properly grounded. Disconnect the battery and connect one lead of a continuity tester or multimeter (set to the ohms scale), to a known good ground. Connect the other lead to the wire or ground connection being tested. If the resistance is low (less than 5 ohms), the ground is good. If the bulb on a self-powered test light does not go on, the ground is not good.

Continuity check

A continuity check is done to determine if there are any breaks in a circuit - if it is passing electricity properly. With the circuit off (no power in the circuit), a self-powered continuity tester or multimeter can be used to check the circuit. Connect the test leads to both ends of the circuit (or to the power end and a good ground), and if the test light comes on the circuit is passing current properly **(see illus-**

2.5b A test light is a very handy tool for checking voltage

tration)**. If the resistance is low (less than 5 ohms), there is continuity; if the reading is 10,000 ohms or higher, there is a break somewhere in the circuit. The same procedure can be used to test a switch, by connecting the continuity tester to the switch terminals. With the switch turned On, the test light should come on (or low resistance should be indicated on a meter).

Finding an open circuit

When diagnosing for possible open circuits, it is often difficult to locate them by sight because the connectors hide oxidation or terminal misalignment. Merely wiggling a connector on a sensor or in the wiring harness may correct the open circuit condition. Remember this when an open circuit is indicated when troubleshooting a circuit. Intermittent problems may also be caused by oxidized or loose connections.

Electrical troubleshooting is simple if you keep in mind that all electrical circuits

2.6 In use, a basic test light's lead is clipped to a known good ground, then the pointed probe can test connectors, wires or electrical sockets - if the bulb lights, the part being tested has battery voltage

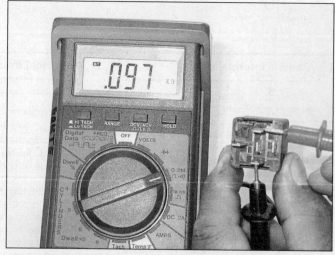

2.9 With a multimeter set to the ohms scale, resistance can be checked across two terminals - when checking for continuity, a low reading indicates continuity, a high reading indicates lack of continuity

3.1a The interior fuse box is located under the left (driver's) side of the instrument panel, above the parking brake pedal

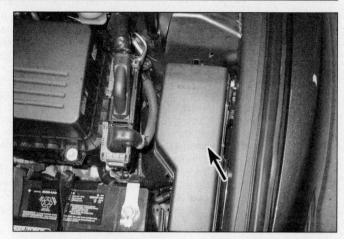

3.1b The engine compartment fuse/relay box is located along the left inner fender panel, by the battery

are basically electricity running from the battery, through the wires, switches, relays, fuses and fusible links to each electrical component (light bulb, motor, etc.) and to ground, from which it is passed back to the battery. Any electrical problem is an interruption in the flow of electricity to and from the battery.

3 Fuses and fusible links - general information

Fuses

Refer to illustrations 3.1a, 3.1b and 3.3

The electrical circuits of the vehicle are protected by a combination of fuses, circuit breakers and fusible links. The main fuse/relay panel is in the engine compartment **(see Illustration)**, while the interior fuse/relay panel is located inside the passenger compartment **(see illustration)**. Each of the fuses is designed to protect a specific circuit, and the various circuits are identified on the fuse panel itself.

Several sizes of fuses are employed in the fuse blocks. There are small, medium and large sizes of the same design, all with the same blade terminal design. The medium and large fuses can be removed with your fingers, but the small fuses require the use of pliers or the small plastic fuse-puller tool found in most fuse boxes.

If an electrical component fails, always check the fuse first. The best way to check the fuses is with a test light. Check for power at the exposed terminal tips of each fuse. If power is present at one side of the fuse but not the other, the fuse is blown. A blown fuse can also be identified by visually inspecting it **(see illustration)**.

Be sure to replace blown fuses with the correct type. Fuses (of the same physical size) of different ratings may be physically interchangeable, but only fuses of the proper rating should be used. Replacing a fuse with one of a higher or lower value than specified is not recommended. Each electrical circuit needs a specific amount of protection. The amperage value of each fuse is molded into the top of the fuse body.

If the replacement fuse immediately fails, don't replace it again until the cause of the problem is isolated and corrected. In most cases, this will be a short circuit in the wiring caused by a broken or deteriorated wire.

Fusible links

Some circuits are protected by fusible links. The links are used in circuits which are not ordinarily fused, or which carry high current, such as the circuit between the alternator and the starter motor. Fusible links, which are usually several wire gauges smaller in size than the circuit that they protect, are designed to melt if the circuit is subjected to more current than it was designed to carry. If you have to replace a blown fusible link, make sure that you replace it with one of the same specification. If the replacement fusible link blows in the same circuit, make sure that you troubleshoot the circuit in which the fusible link melted BEFORE installing another fusible link.

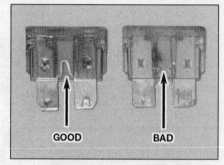

3.3 When a fuse blows, the element between the terminals melts

For a basic check, pull the circuit breaker up out of its socket on the fuse panel, but just far enough to probe with a voltmeter. The breaker should still contact the sockets. With the voltmeter negative lead on a good chassis ground, touch each end prong of the circuit breaker with the positive meter probe. There should be battery voltage at each end. If there is battery voltage only at one end, the circuit breaker must be replaced.

Some circuit breakers must be reset manually.

4 Circuit breakers - general information

Circuit breakers protect certain circuits, such as the power windows or heated seats. Depending on the vehicle's accessories, there may be one or two circuit breakers, located in the fuse/relay box in the engine compartment.

Because the circuit breakers reset automatically, an electrical overload in a circuit breaker-protected system will cause the circuit to fail momentarily, then come back on. If the circuit does not come back on, check it immediately.

5 Relays - general information

Several electrical accessories in the vehicle, such as the fuel injection system, horns, starter, and fog lamps use relays to transmit the electrical signal to the component. Relays use a low-current circuit (the control circuit) to open and close a high-current circuit (the power circuit). If the relay is defective, that component will not operate properly. Most relays are mounted in the engine compartment and interior fuse/relay boxes **(see illustrations 3.1a and 3.1b)**.

6   Electrical connectors - general information

Most electrical connections on these vehicles are made with multiwire plastic connectors. The mating halves of many connectors are secured with locking clips molded into the plastic connector shells. The mating halves of some large connectors, such as some of those under the instrument panel, are held together by a bolt through the center of the connector.

To separate a connector with locking clips, use a small screwdriver to pry the clips apart carefully, then separate the connector halves. Pull only on the shell, never pull on the wiring harness as you may damage the individual wires and terminals inside the connectors. Look at the connector closely before trying to separate the halves. Often the locking clips are engaged in a way that is not immediately clear. Additionally, many connectors have more than one set of clips.

Each pair of connector terminals has a male half and a female half. When you look at the end view of a connector in a diagram, be sure to understand whether the view shows the harness side or the component side of the connector. Connector halves are mirror images of each other, and a terminal shown on the right side end-view of one half will be on the left side end-view of the other half.

It is often necessary to take circuit voltage measurements with a connector connected. Whenever possible, carefully insert a small straight pin (not your meter probe) into the rear of the connector shell to contact the terminal inside, then clip your meter lead to the pin. This kind of connection is called "back-probing." When inserting a test probe into a terminal, be careful not to distort the terminal opening. Doing so can lead to a poor connection and corrosion at that terminal later. Using the small straight pin instead of a meter probe results in less chance of deforming the terminal connector.

Electrical connectors

Most electrical connectors have a single release tab that you depress to release the connector

Some electrical connectors have a retaining tab which must be pried up to free the connector

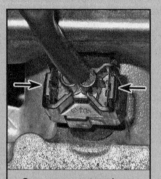

Some connectors have two release tabs that you must squeeze to release the connector

Some connectors use wire retainers that you squeeze to release the connector

Critical connectors often employ a sliding lock (1) that you must pull out before you can depress the release tab (2)

Here's another sliding-lock style connector, with the lock (1) and the release tab (2) on the side of the connector

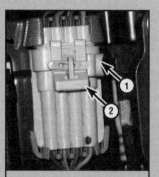

On some connectors the lock (1) must be pulled out to the side and removed before you can lift the release tab (2)

Some critical connectors, like the multi-pin connectors at the Powertrain Control Module employ pivoting locks that must be flipped open

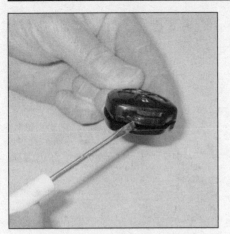

7.7 Use a small screwdriver or coin to separate the transmitter halves . . .

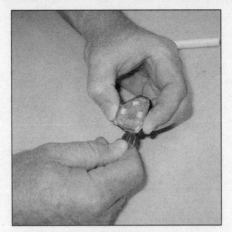

7.9 . . . then carefully pry open the module cover

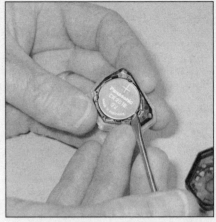

7.10 Remove the lithium battery, and install a new one with the positive (+) side of the battery facing up

7 Remote keyless entry fob - battery replacement

1   The keyless entry system consists of a remote control transmitter that sends a coded infrared signal to a receiver which then operates the door lock system. On models so equipped, the transmitter may also engage the alarm system and provide a panic button which flashes the lights and blows the horn for emergencies.
2   Replace the key battery when the smart key or wireless remote does not work properly. As the batteries deteriorate with age, the distance at which the remote transmitter operates will diminish.

Smart key models
3   Remove the mechanical key from the fob body.
4   Insert and twist a small screwdriver carefully between the case halves and separate the two halves for battery replacement.
5   Replace the lithium battery with the same type as originally installed, observing the polarity diagram on the case.
6   Snap the case halves together.

Non-smart key models
Refer to illustration 7.7, 7.9 and 7.10
7   Insert and twist a small screwdriver carefully between the case halves and separate the two halves for battery replacement **(see illustration)**.
8   Remove the module from the key.
9   Use a small coin to separate the module cover **(see illustration)**.
10   Replace the lithium battery with the same type as originally installed, observing the polarity diagram on the case **(see illustration)**.
11   Snap the cover on to the module and insert the module back into the key.
12   Snap the case halves together.

8 Steering column switches - replacement

Warning: *The models covered by this manual are equipped with Supplemental Restraint Systems (SRS), more commonly known as airbags. Always disable the airbag system before working in the vicinity of any airbag system components to avoid the possibility of accidental deployment of the airbag(s), which could cause personal injury (see Section 26).*
1   Disconnect the cable from the negative battery terminal (see Chapter 5).
2   Remove the steering wheel (see Chapter 10).
3   Remove the steering column covers (see Chapter 11).

Windshield wiper switch
Refer to illustration 8.5
4   Unplug the electrical connectors from the combination switch.
5   Lift the locking tab up and slide the switch out from the combination switch assembly **(see illustration)**.
6   Installation is the reverse of removal.

Headlight/turn signal switch
7   Unplug the electrical connectors from the combination switch. **Note:** *On models equipped with a telescopic steering column, disconnect the electrical connector to the telescopic switch, then disconnect the mounting clips and remove the switch.*
8   Remove the windshield wiper switch **(see illustration 8.5)**.
9   Using pliers, squeeze the spring mounting clip at the top of the combination switch and pull the combination switch and clockspring as an assembly from the column.
10   Installation is the reverse of removal.

8.5 Pry the mounting clip back and slide the windshield wiper switch off the combination switch assembly

9 Ignition switch and key lock cylinder - replacement

Warning: *The models covered by this manual are equipped with Supplemental Restraint Systems (SRS), more commonly known as airbags. Always disable the airbag system before working in the vicinity of any airbag system components to avoid the possibility of accidental deployment of the airbag(s), which could cause personal injury (see Section 26).*
1   Disconnect the cable from the negative battery terminal (see Chapter 5).
2   Place the ignition key in the ACC position.
3   Remove the steering wheel (see Chapter 10).
4   Remove the steering column covers (see Chapter 11).
5   Remove the steering column switches (see Section 8).

9.7 Remove the interlock solenoid mounting screws and solenoid

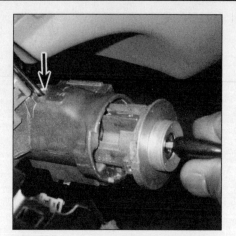

9.12 With the lock cylinder in the ACC position, depress the retaining pin with a small screwdriver, then pull the cylinder straight out

10.2 Carefully pry the center register assembly out of the instrument panel

Ignition switch

Refer to illustration 9.7

6   Unplug the ignition switch wiring harness connector and key light connector (if equipped).

7   Remove the interlock solenoid mounting screws **(see illustration)** and disengage the ignition switch mounting clips, then pull the switch from the housing.

8   Installation is reverse of removal.

Lock cylinder - without Smart Key System

Refer to illustration 9.12

9   Carefully pry the transponder key amplifier switch mounting clips outwards and slide the transponder forward to detach it and the bracket from the steering column.

10   Turn the ignition switch to ON (ACC).

11   Use a small screwdriver or punch inserted into the hole in the top of the steering column bracket, to depress the locking claw and pull the ignition switch lock cylinder out until its claw comes into contact with the stopper of the steering column bracket.

10.4 Hazard flasher switch screws

12   Insert the tip of a screwdriver into the hole inside of the steering column bracket and tilt it downward to disengage the claw. Pull the ignition switch lock cylinder out **(see illustration)**.

13   The remainder of installation is the reverse of removal.

Lock Actuator - with Smart Key System

Note: *After replacing the steering lock actuator assembly, perform the key ID code registration by opening and closing the driver's door. The engine may not start until the driver's door has been opened and closed.*

14   Remove the steering column (see Chapter 10) and place the column in a soft jaw vise.

15   Using a grinder or small hacksaw blade, cut a slot into the steering lock shear bolt heads.

16   Use a screwdriver to back the bolts out and remove the actuator.

17   Install the steering lock actuator and steering column clamp with new steering lock shear-head bolts, then tighten the bolts until their heads break off.

---

10   Instrument panel switches - replacement

Warning: *The models covered by this manual are equipped with Supplemental Restraint Systems (SRS), more commonly known as airbags. Always disable the airbag system before working in the vicinity of any airbag system components to avoid the possibility of accidental deployment of the airbag(s), which could cause personal injury (see Section 26).*

Hazard warning switch

1   Disconnect the cable from the negative battery terminal (see Chapter 5).

Camry models

Refer to illustrations 10.2 and 10.4

2   Using a trim tool, carefully pry the registers from the center of the instrument panel **(see illustration)**.

3   Disconnect the electrical connector from the back of the switch.

4   Remove the screws and detach the switch from the panel **(see illustration)**.

5   Installation is the reverse of removal.

Avalon models

6   Carefully remove the center trim panel (see Chapter 11).

7   Disconnect the electrical connector and remove the switch from in between the A/C heater registers. Depress the tabs and push the switch out of the panel.

8   Installation is the reverse of removal.

Lexus models

9   Remove the center cluster finish panel (see Chapter 11) from the instrument panel.

10   Remove the radio unit (see Section 13) and separate the radio from the heater/air conditioning control panel assembly.

11   The hazard warning switch is integrated into the control panel and must be serviced as a unit.

12   Installation is the reverse of removal.

Power mirror control switch

Refer to illustration 10.16

13   On Avalon and Lexus models, remove the knee bolster trim panel (see Chapter 11).

14   On Avalon and Lexus models, remove the driver's side trim panel from the instrument panel (see Chapter 11, Section 23).

15   On Avalon and Lexus models, disconnect the electrical connector and disengage the mounting clips from the back side.

16   On Camry models, pry the switch from the trim panel **(see illustration)** and disconnect the electrical connector.

17   Installation is the reverse of removal.

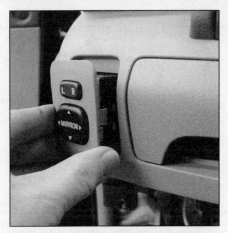

10.16 Use a screwdriver or trim tool to pry out the mirror switch (Camry models)

11.3 Instrument cluster mounting screws

Defogger control switch

18   The defogger control switch and A/C control switch is one unit and must be replaced as an assembly (see Chapter 3).

Instrument panel illumination rheostat

19   Remove the driver's side trim panel (see Chapter 11) and carefully pry the switch from the instrument panel, using tape on the screwdriver tip to prevent scratching the instrument panel.
20   Disconnect the electrical connector and remove the switch.
21   Installation is the reverse of removal.

Power outlets

22   On Avalon and Lexus models, carefully pry the switch base from the center console (see Chapter 11). **Note:** *On models equipped with a seat heater, pry the heater switch base up and out to access the power outlets. On Camry models, remove the lower storage box (see Chapter 11, Section 22).*
23   Disconnect the electrical connector. Depress the tabs and push the outlet through the panel.
24   Installation is the reverse of removal.

Engine switch (smart key models)

25   Carefully remove the driver's side trim panel (see Chapter 11).
26   Unplug the engine switch wiring harness connectors.
27   Pull the two retaining clips back and pull the switch from the control assembly.
28   Installation is reverse of the removal.

---

11   Instrument cluster - removal and installation

Refer to illustration 11.3

Warning: *The models covered by this manual are equipped with Supplemental Restraint Systems (SRS), more commonly known as airbags. Always disable the airbag system before working in the vicinity of any airbag system components to avoid the possibility of accidental deployment of the airbag(s), which could cause personal injury (see Section 26).*
Note: *On Avalon models, there are two separate instrument clusters under one instrument cluster trim panel; both are removed the same way.*
1   Disconnect the cable from the negative battery terminal (see Chapter 5).
2   Remove the steering column covers and the instrument cluster trim panel (see Chapter 11).

12.2 Make a reference mark before removing the wiper arm

3   Remove the cluster mounting screws **(see illustration)** and pull the instrument cluster towards the steering wheel.
4   Disconnect any electrical connectors that would interfere with removal.
5   Cover the steering column with a cloth to protect the trim covers, then remove the instrument cluster from the vehicle.
6   Installation is the reverse of removal.

---

12   Wiper motor - replacement

Refer to illustrations 12.2, 12.4 and 12.7

1   Disconnect the cable from the negative battery terminal (see Chapter 5).
2   Mark the positions of the wiper arm(s) on the windshield and the studs, then remove the wiper arm(s) **(see illustration)**.
3   Remove the windshield cowl cover (see Chapter 11).
4   Disconnect the wiper motor harness connector and remove the windshield wiper motor/linkage assembly mounting nuts **(see illustration)**.
5   Lift the windshield wiper motor assembly from the cowl area.
6   Using needle nose pliers, pull the wiper linkage from the ballstud.

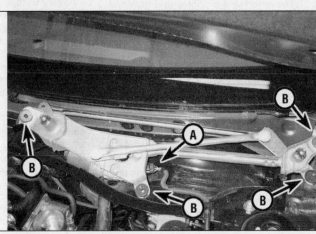

12.4 Wiper motor and linkage details

A   *Wiper motor electrical connector*
B   *Wiper linkage mounting bolts*

12.7　Wiper motor mounting bolts and linkage crank arm nut (A)

13.5a　Remove the upper mounting fasteners . . .

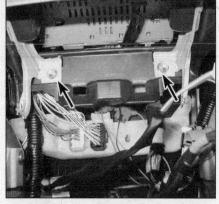

13.5b　. . . and the lower mounting fasteners and pull the audio/navigation unit outwards

7　Remove the wiper motor mounting nuts and separate the motor from the assembly **(see illustration)**.
8　Installation is the reverse of removal.

13　Radio and speakers - removal and installation

Warning: *The models covered by this manual are equipped with Supplemental Restraint Systems (SRS), more commonly known as airbags. Always disable the airbag system before working in the vicinity of any airbag system components to avoid the possibility of accidental deployment of the airbag(s), which could cause personal injury (see Section 26).*
1　Disconnect the cable from the negative battery terminal (see Chapter 5).

Radio/Navigation unit

Refer to illustrations 13.5a and 13.5b
2　On Camry and Lexus models, pry out the center register above the radio using a trim tool (see Chapter 11).
3　On Avalon models, remove the center trim panel (see Chapter 11).
4　On Camry models, pry off the side center trim panels (see Chapter 11).
5　Remove the retaining fasteners and pull the radio/navigation unit outward to access the backside, then disconnect the electrical connectors and the antenna lead **(see illustrations)**.
6　Remove the mounting bracket fasteners and brackets, then separate the radio/navigation unit from the heater and A/C control panel assembly. Separate the radio unit from the navigation unit.
7　Installation is the reverse of removal.

Door speakers

Refer to illustration 13.9
8　Remove the door trim panel (see Chapter 11).
9　Remove the mounting fasteners and pull

the speaker out of the door. Disconnect the electrical connector and remove the speaker from the vehicle **(see illustration)**.
10　Installation is the reverse of removal.

Instrument panel speakers

11　Carefully pry the speaker covers out using a trim tool.
12　Remove the mounting fasteners and pull the speaker up.
13　Disconnect the electrical connector and remove the speaker from the instrument panel.
14　Installation is the reverse of removal.

Rear package shelf speakers

15　Remove the rear seats (see Chapter 11).
16　Remove the rear package shelf (see Chapter 12).
17　Remove the mounting fasteners and pull the speaker up.
18　Disconnect the electrical connector and remove the speaker from the shelf.
19　Installation is the reverse of removal.

14　Antenna - removal and installation

1　The antenna is a printed grid type and is located in the rear window, at the top. The only way to replace the antenna is to replace this window.
2　However, you can repair a grid-type antenna the same way that you would repair the rear window defogger grid (see Section 15).

15　Rear window defogger - check and repair

1　The rear window defogger consists of a number of horizontal elements baked onto the glass surface.
2　Small breaks in the element can be repaired without removing the rear window.

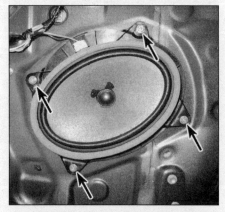

13.9　Remove the speaker mounting screws and disconnect the electrical connector to remove the speaker from the vehicle

Check

Refer to illustrations 15.4, 15.5 and 15.7
3　Turn the ignition switch and defogger system switches to the ON position. Using a voltmeter, place the positive probe against the defogger grid positive terminal and the negative probe against the ground terminal. If battery voltage is not indicated, check the fuse, defogger switch and related wiring. If voltage is indicated, but all or part of the defogger doesn't heat, proceed with the following tests.
4　When measuring voltage during the next two tests, wrap a piece of aluminum foil around the tip of the voltmeter positive probe and press the foil against the heating element with your finger **(see illustration)**. Place the negative probe on the defogger grid ground terminal.
5　Check the voltage at the center of each heating element **(see illustration)**. If the voltage is 5 or 6-volts, the element is okay (there is no break). If the voltage is 0-volts, the element is broken between the center of the element and the positive end. If the voltage is 10

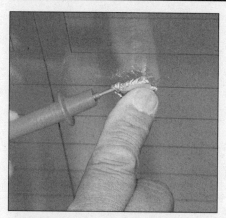

15.4 When measuring the voltage at the rear window defogger grid, wrap a piece of aluminum foil around the positive probe of the voltmeter and press the foil against the wire with your finger

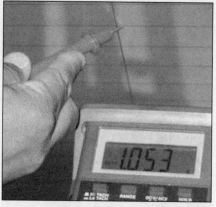

15.5 To determine if a heating element has broken, check the voltage at the center of each element - if the voltage is 5 or 6-volts, the element is unbroken; if the voltage is 10 or 12-volts, the element is broken between the center and the ground side; if there is no voltage, the element is broken between the center and the positive side

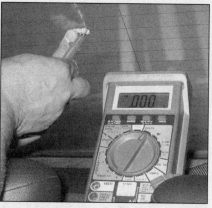

15.7 To find the break, place the voltmeter negative lead against the defogger ground terminal, place the voltmeter positive lead with the foil strip against the heating element at the positive terminal end and slide it toward the negative terminal end - the point at which the voltmeter reading changes abruptly is the point at which the element is broken

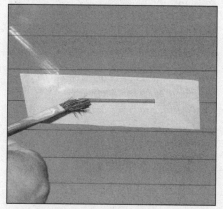

15.13 To use a defogger repair kit, apply masking tape to the inside of the window at the damaged area, then brush on the special conductive coating

10   Lightly buff the element area with fine steel wool, then clean it thoroughly with rubbing alcohol.
11   Use masking tape to mask off the area being repaired.
12   Thoroughly mix the epoxy, following the instructions provided with the repair kit.
13   Apply the epoxy material to the slit in the masking tape, overlapping the undamaged area about 3/4-inch on either end (see illustration).
14   Allow the repair to cure for 24 hours before removing the tape and using the system.

16 Headlight bulb - replacement

Warning: *Halogen gas filled bulbs are under pressure and may shatter if the surface is scratched or the bulb is dropped. Wear eye protection and handle the bulbs carefully, grasping only the base whenever possible. Do not touch the surface of the bulb with your fingers because the oil from your skin could cause it to overheat and fail prematurely. If you do touch the bulb surface, clean it with rubbing alcohol.*

Halogen headlights

Refer to illustration 16.2

Note: *The inner headlight bulbs are the high-beam bulbs and the outer bulbs are the low-beam bulbs.*

1   Reach behind the headlight assembly, depress the release tab and disconnect the electrical connector from the headlight bulb socket.
2   Turn the bulb socket counterclockwise and pull it out of the headlight housing (see illustration). **Caution:** *Don't touch the bulb with your fingers. If you do, clean it with rubbing alcohol (the oil from your skin can cause the bulb to overheat and fail).*

3   When installing the bulb, make sure that the three lugs on the mounting base of the bulb socket are aligned with their corresponding cutouts in the headlight housing, then insert the bulb socket into the housing and turn it clockwise until it stops. Installation is otherwise the reverse of removal.

Xenon (HID) headlights

Warning: *Some models use High Intensity Discharge (HID) bulbs instead of conventional halogen bulbs. According to the manufacturer, the high voltages produced by this system can be fatal in the event of shock. Also, the voltage can remain in the circuit even after the headlight switch has been turned to OFF and the ignition key has been removed. Therefore, for your safety, we don't recommend that you try to replace one of these bulbs yourself.*

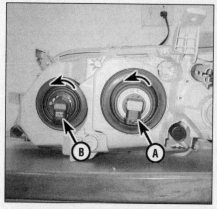

16.2 Rotate the headlight bulb(s) counterclockwise to remove the bulb from the housing

A   *Low beam bulb*
B   *High beam bulb*

to 12-volts the element is broken between the center of the element and ground. Check each heating element.
6   Connect the negative lead to a good body ground. The reading should stay the same. If it doesn't, the ground connection is bad.
7   To find the break, place the voltmeter negative probe against the defogger ground terminal. Place the voltmeter positive probe with the foil strip against the heating element at the positive terminal end and slide it toward the negative terminal end. The point at which the voltmeter deflects from several volts to zero is the point at which the heating element is broken (see illustration).

Repair

Refer to illustration 15.13

8   Repair the break in the element using a repair kit specifically recommended for this purpose, available at most auto parts stores. Included in this kit is plastic conductive epoxy.
9   Prior to repairing a break, turn off the system and allow it to cool off for a few minutes.

17.2a Models with halogen bulbs have only one vertical adjuster that can be accessed from above using a long Phillips screwdriver

17.2b On models with Xenon bulbs, there are two adjusters that can be accessed from the back of the headlight housing

Instead, have this service performed by a dealer service department or other qualified repair shop.
Warning: *Never attempt to check for voltage at the bulb socket of an HID headlight.*

17   Headlights - adjustment

Refer to illustrations 17.2a, 17.2b and 17.4
Note: *The headlights must be aimed correctly. If adjusted incorrectly they could blind the driver of an oncoming vehicle and cause a serious accident or seriously reduce your ability to see the road. The headlights should be checked for proper aim every 12 months and any time a new headlight is installed or front end body work is performed. It should be emphasized that the following procedure is only an interim step which will provide temporary adjustment until the headlights can be adjusted by a properly equipped shop.*
Note: *Some models are equipped with a headlight leveling system. This adjustment procedure will not apply. Have the headlights adjusted by a dealer service department or other qualified repair shop.*
1   These models have one adjustment screw located on the back of each headlight housing.
2   Insert a Phillips screwdriver into the gear-drive mechanism to turn the screw **(see illustrations)**.
3   There are several methods of adjusting the headlights. The simplest method requires masking tape, a blank wall and a level floor.
4   Position masking tape vertically on the wall in reference to the vehicle centerline and the centerlines of both headlights **(see illustration)**.
5   Position a horizontal tape line in reference to the centerline of all the headlights.
Note: *It may be easier to position the tape on the wall with the vehicle parked only a few inches away.*

6   Adjustment should be made with the vehicle parked 25 feet from the wall, sitting level, the gas tank half-full and no unusually heavy load in the vehicle.
7   Starting with the low beam adjustment, position the high intensity zone so it is two inches below the horizontal line and two inches to the side of the headlight vertical line,

away from oncoming traffic. Adjustment is made by turning the vertical adjusting screw to raise or lower the beam. The horizontal adjusting screw should be used in the same manner to move the beam left or right.
8   With the high beams on, the high intensity zone should be vertically centered with the exact center just below the horizontal line.
Note: *It may not be possible to position the headlight aim exactly for both high and low beams. If a compromise must be made, keep in mind that the low beams are the most used and have the greatest effect on driver safety.*
9   Have the headlights adjusted by a dealer service department or service station at the earliest opportunity.

18   Headlight housing - replacement

Refer to illustration 18.3
Warning: *Some models use High Intensity Discharge (HID) bulbs instead of conventional halogen bulbs. According to the manufacturer, the high voltages produced by this system can be fatal in the event of shock. Also, the voltage can remain in the circuit even after the headlight switch has been turned to OFF and the ignition key has been removed. Therefore,*

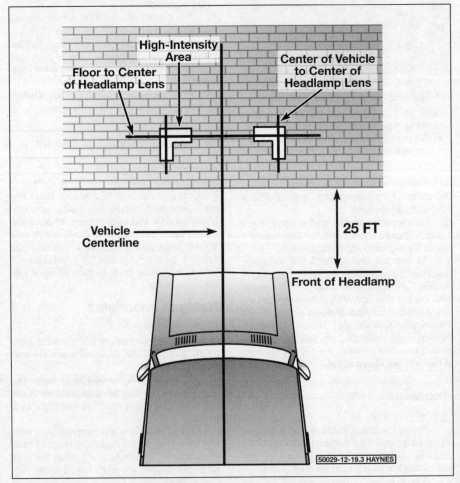

17.4 Headlight adjustment details

18.3 Headlight housing mounting fasteners - Camry shown, other models similar

19.3 Horn details (left side shown, right side is the same)

A   Horn
B   Bumper cover (pulled forward)
C   Horn mounting bolt
D   Electrical connector

for your safety, we don't recommend that you try to replace a headlight housing yourself. Instead, have this service performed by a dealer service department or other qualified repair shop.

1   Remove the front bumper cover (see Chapter 11).
2   Disconnect the electrical connectors to the bulbs.
3   Remove the retaining screws, detach the housing and withdraw it from the vehicle **(see illustration)**.
4   Installation is the reverse of removal. Be sure to check headlight adjustment (see Section 17).

19 Horn - replacement

Refer to illustration 19.3
Warning: *The models covered by this manual*

are equipped with Supplemental Restraint Systems (SRS), more commonly known as airbags. Always disable the airbag system before working in the vicinity of any airbag system components to avoid the possibility of accidental deployment of the airbag(s), which could cause personal injury (see Section 26).

1   Remove the radiator support trim cover mounting fasteners and remove the trim panel (see Chapter 3).
2   To access the horns on Camry and Lexus models, remove the front bumper cover upper mounting fasteners (see Chapter 11), then pull and hold the cover outwards.
Note: *On Avalon models, remove the grill section of the bumper cover (see Chapter 11).*
3   To replace the horn(s), disconnect the electrical connector and remove the bracket bolt **(see illustration)**.
4   Installation is the reverse of removal.

20 Bulb replacement

Front park/turn signal lights

Refer to illustration 20.1
1   Reach behind the headlight assembly, rotate the bulb holder counterclockwise and pull the bulb out **(see illustration)**.
2   Remove the bulb from the holder.
3   Installation is the reverse of removal.

Rear taillight/brake light/turn signal

Refer to illustration 20.5
4   To access the taillight bulbs, working in the trunk area, lift the taillight access cover (carpet) back.
5   Rotate the bulb holders counterclockwise and pull the bulbs out to remove them **(see illustration)**.
6   Installation is the reverse of removal.

20.1 Rotate the turn signal and marker light bulb holders counterclockwise to remove them from the housing

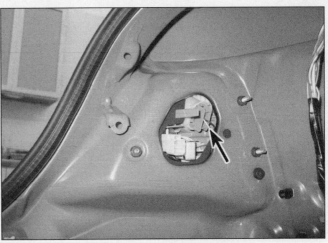

20.5 Rotate the bulb holder counterclockwise to remove it

High-mounted brake light

7   Remove the rear package shelf (see Chapter 11).

8   Twist the bulb holder counterclockwise to remove it, then pull the bulb straight out of the holder.

9   Installation is the reverse of removal.

Instrument cluster lights

10   To gain access to the instrument cluster illumination bulbs, the instrument cluster will have to be removed (see Section 11). The bulbs can then be removed and replaced from the rear of the cluster.

11   Rotate the bulb counterclockwise to remove it.

12   Installation is the reverse of removal.

Interior light

Refer to illustrations 20.13 and 20.14

13   Pry the interior lens off the interior light housing **(see illustration)**.

14   Detach the bulb from the terminals **(see**

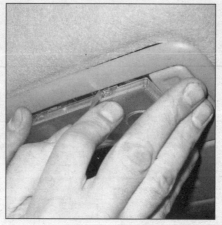

20.13 Carefully pry off the dome light lens using a flat-bladed screwdriver . . .

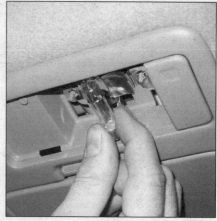

20.14 . . . then remove the bulb from the terminals

illustration). It may be necessary to pry the bulb out - if this is the case, pry only on the ends of the bulb (otherwise the glass may shatter).

15   Installation is the reverse of removal.

License plate light

16   Press the release clip from left to right. While holding the clip, push the light housing towards the center and rotate the left side of the housing out, then the right side out.

Bulb removal

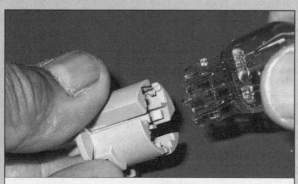

To remove many modern exterior bulbs from their holders, simply pull them out

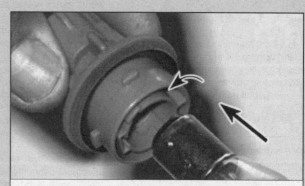

On bulbs with a cylindrical base ("bayonet" bulbs), the socket is spring-loaded; a pair of small posts on the side of the base hold the bulb in place against spring pressure. To remove this type of bulb, push it into the holder, rotate it 1/4-turn counterclockwise, then pull it out

If a bayonet bulb has dual filaments, the posts are staggered, so the bulb can only be installed one way

To remove most overhead interior light bulbs, simply unclip them

17   Twist the bulbholder counterclockwise to remove it and replace the bulb.

18   Installation is the reverse of removal.

Fog light

19   Raise the vehicle and secure it on jackstands.

20   Remove the front wheels and remove the inner fender covers to access the fog light assembly. Remove the lower splash shield to access the fog light bulbs.

21   Twist the bulbholder from the housing and replace the bulb.

Side turn signal light (Lexus models)

22   Carefully pry the outer cover off of the side view mirror(s) housing.

23   Remove the turn signal mounting fasteners and detach the signal housing from the mirror.

24   Rotate the bulb counterclockwise to remove it.

25   Installation is the reverse of removal.

21   Power mirror control system - description and check

1   Electric rear view mirrors use two motors to move the glass; one for up and down adjustments and one for left-right adjustments.

2   The control switch has a selector portion which sends voltage to the left or right side mirror. With the ignition ON but the engine OFF, roll down the windows and operate the mirror control switch through all functions (left-right and up-down) for both the left and right side mirrors.

3   Listen carefully for the sound of the electric motors running in the mirrors.

4   If the motors can be heard but the mirror glass doesn't move, there's probably a problem with the drive mechanism inside the mirror.

5   If the mirrors do not operate and no sound comes from the mirrors, check the fuse (see Section 3).

6   If the fuse is OK, remove the mirror control switch from its mounting without disconnecting the wires attached to it. Turn the ignition ON and check for voltage at the switch. There should be voltage at one terminal. If there's no voltage at the switch, check for an open or short in the circuit between the fuse panel and the switch.

7   If the mirror motor fails to operate as described, replace the mirror assembly (see Chapter 11).

22   Cruise control system - description and check

1   All models have an electronically controlled throttle body - there is no accelerator cable or cruise control cable. When you select the speed that you want to maintain, the PCM controls vehicle speed by opening and clos-

ing the throttle plate by means of a computer-controlled solenoid (motor) inside the throttle body.

2   The diagnostic procedures for troubleshooting the cruise control system are beyond the scope of this manual, but if the system can't be set, or the set speed doesn't cancel when the brake pedal is depressed, check the fuses. Start with the fuses in the engine compartment fuse and relay box, then check the fuses in the under-dash fuse and relay box. If the set speed doesn't cancel when the CANCEL button is depressed, check the fuse for that circuit.

3   Other than checking the fuses, the diagnostic procedures for troubleshooting the cruise control system on these models are beyond the scope of this manual. A dealer service department should handle any further testing.

23   Power window system - description and check

1   The power window system operates electric motors, mounted in the doors, which lower and raise the windows. The system consists of the control switches, relays, the motors, regulators, glass mechanisms and associated wiring.

2   The power windows can be lowered and raised from the master control switch by the driver or by remote switches located at the individual windows. Each window has a separate motor which is reversible. The position of the control switch determines the polarity and therefore the direction of operation.

3   The circuit is protected by a fuse and a circuit breaker. Each motor is also equipped with an internal circuit breaker; this prevents one stuck window from disabling the whole system.

4   The power window system will only operate when the ignition switch is ON. In addition, many models have a window lockout switch at the master control switch which, when activated, disables the switches at the rear windows and, sometimes, the switch at the passenger's window also. Always check these items before troubleshooting a window problem.

5   These procedures are general in nature, so if you can't find the problem using them, take the vehicle to a dealer service department or other properly equipped repair facility.

6   If the power windows won't operate, always check the fuse and circuit breaker first.

7   If only the rear windows are inoperative, or if the windows only operate from the master control switch, check the rear window lockout switch for continuity in the unlocked position. Replace it if it doesn't have continuity.

8   Check the wiring between the switches and fuse panel for continuity. Repair the wiring, if necessary.

9   If only one window is inoperative from

the master control switch, try the other control switch at the window. **Note:** *This doesn't apply to the driver's door window.*

10   If voltage is reaching the motor, disconnect the glass from the regulator (see Chapter 11). Move the window up and down by hand while checking for binding and damage. Also check for binding and damage to the regulator. If the regulator is not damaged and the window moves up and down smoothly, replace the motor. If there's binding or damage, lubricate, repair or replace parts, as necessary.

11   If voltage isn't reaching the motor, check the wiring in the circuit for continuity between the switches and motors. You'll need to consult the wiring diagram for the vehicle. If the circuit is equipped with a relay, check that the relay is grounded properly and receiving voltage.

12   Test the windows after you are done to confirm proper repairs.

24   Power door lock system - description and check

1   A power door lock system operates the door lock actuators mounted in each door. The system consists of the switches, actuators, the Body Control Module and associated wiring. Diagnosis can usually be limited to simple checks of the wiring connections and actuators for minor faults that can be easily repaired.

2   Power door lock systems are operated by bi-directional solenoids located in the doors. The lock switches have two operating positions: Lock and Unlock. When activated, the switch sends a ground signal to the door lock control unit to lock or unlock the doors. Depending on which way the switch is activated, the control unit reverses polarity to the solenoids, allowing the two sides of the circuit to be used alternately as the feed (positive) and ground side.

3   Some vehicles may have an anti-theft system incorporated into the power locks. If you are unable to locate the trouble using the following general Steps, consult a dealer service department or other qualified repair shop.

4   Always check the circuit protection first. Some vehicles use a combination of circuit breakers and fuses.

5   Operate the door lock switches in both directions (Lock and Unlock) with the engine off. Listen for the click of the solenoids operating.

6   Test the switches for continuity (refer to the wiring diagrams at the end of this Chapter).

7   Check the wiring between the switches, control unit and solenoids for continuity. Repair the wiring if there's no continuity.

8   Check for a bad ground at the switches or the control unit.

9   If all but one of the lock solenoids operate, remove the trim panel from the affected

door (see Chapter 11) and check for voltage at the solenoid while the lock switch is operated. One of the wires should have voltage in the Lock position; the other should have voltage in the Unlock position.

10   If the inoperative solenoid is receiving voltage, replace the solenoid.

11   If the inoperative solenoid isn't receiving voltage, check for an open-circuit condition in the wire between the switch and the Body Control Module, and between the lock solenoid and the Body Control Module (see the wiring diagrams at the end of this Chapter).

25   Daytime Running Lights (DRL) - general information

The Daytime Running Lights (DRL) system used on some models illuminates the headlights whenever the engine is running. The only exception is with the engine running and the parking brake engaged. Once the parking brake is released, the lights will remain on as long as the ignition switch is on, even if the parking brake is later applied.

The DRL system supplies reduced power to the headlights during daylight operation, prolonging headlight life.

26   Airbag system - general information

These models are equipped with a Supplemental Restraint System (SRS), more commonly known as airbags. This system is designed to protect the driver and the front seat passenger from serious injury in the event of a head-on or frontal collision. It consists of an airbag module in the center of the steering wheel and another airbag module on the right side of the instrument panel, a pair of impact sensors that are located at the front of the vehicle, and a sensing/diagnostic module, which is mounted in the center of the vehicle below the instrument panel. Plus, on some later models, driver knee airbags, side airbags and curtain shield airbags designed to protect the occupants in a side impact.

Some models are equipped with seatbelt pre-tensioners, also part of the airbag system. The pre-tensioners are pyrotechnic (explosive) devices designed to retract the seat belts in the event of a collision.

On models equipped with pre-tensioners, do not remove the front seat belt retractor assemblies. Problems with the pre-tensioners will turn on the SRS (airbag) warning light on

the dash. If any pre-tensioner problems are suspected, take the vehicle to a dealer service department.

Airbag module
Steering wheel-mounted

The airbag inflator module contains a housing incorporating the cushion (airbag) and inflator unit, mounted in the center of the steering wheel. The inflator assembly is mounted on the back of the housing over a hole through which gas is expelled, inflating the bag almost instantaneously when an electrical signal is sent from the system. A spiral cable assembly on the steering column under the module carries this signal to the module. This spiral cable assembly can transmit an electrical signal regardless of steering wheel position.

Instrument panel-mounted

The passenger side airbag is mounted above the glove compartment and designated by the letters SRS (Supplemental Restraint System). It consists of an inflator containing an igniter, a bag assembly, a reaction housing and a trim cover.

The passenger airbag is considerably larger than the steering wheel-mounted unit and is supported by the steel reaction housing. The trim cover has a molded seam which splits when the bag inflates.

Sensing and diagnostic module

The sensing and diagnostic module supplies the current to the airbag system in the event of the collision, even if battery power is cut off. It checks this system every time the vehicle is started, causing the AIRBAG light to go on then off, if the system is operating properly. If there is a fault in the system, the light will go on and stay on, flash, or the dash will make a beeping sound. If this happens, the vehicle should be taken to your dealer immediately for service.

Side and curtain airbags

The passenger side airbag and inflator modules are mounted on the sides of the front seats and contain an inflator containing an igniter and bag assembly. The curtain shield airbag assemblies run along the interior of the roof from the front A-pillar to the rear of the passenger compartment. In the event of a side impact, both airbag assemblies are activated by the sensors mounted at the base of the center pillar behind the seats.

Precautions
Disabling the SRS system

Warning: *Failure to follow these precautions could result in accidental deployment of the airbag and personal injury.*

Warning: *Never install a memory-saver device, used to preserve PCM memory and radio station presets, when working on or around any of the airbag system components.*

Whenever working in the vicinity of the steering wheel, instrument panel or any of the other SRS system components, the system must be disarmed. To disarm the system:

a) *Point the wheels straight ahead and turn the ignition key to the LOCK position.*

b) *Disconnect the cable from the negative terminal of the battery.*

c) *Wait at least two minutes for the back-up power supply capacitor to be depleted.*

Whenever handling an airbag module, always keep the airbag opening (trim side) pointed away from your body. Never place the airbag module on a bench or other surface with the airbag opening facing the surface. Always place the airbag module in a safe location with the airbag opening (trim side) facing up.

Never measure the resistance of any SRS component. An ohmmeter has a built-in battery supply that could accidentally deploy the airbag.

Never use electrical welding equipment on a vehicle equipped with an airbag without first disconnecting the negative battery cable.

Never dispose of a live airbag module. Return it to your dealer for safe deployment, using special equipment, and disposal.

27   Wiring diagrams - general information

Since it isn't possible to include all wiring diagrams for every year covered by this manual, the following diagrams are those that are typical and most commonly needed.

Prior to troubleshooting any circuits, check the fuse and circuit breakers (if equipped) to make sure they're in good condition. Make sure the battery is properly charged and check the cable connections (see Chapter 1).

When checking a circuit, make sure that all connectors are clean, with no broken or loose terminals. When unplugging a connector, do not pull on the wires. Pull only on the connector housings themselves.

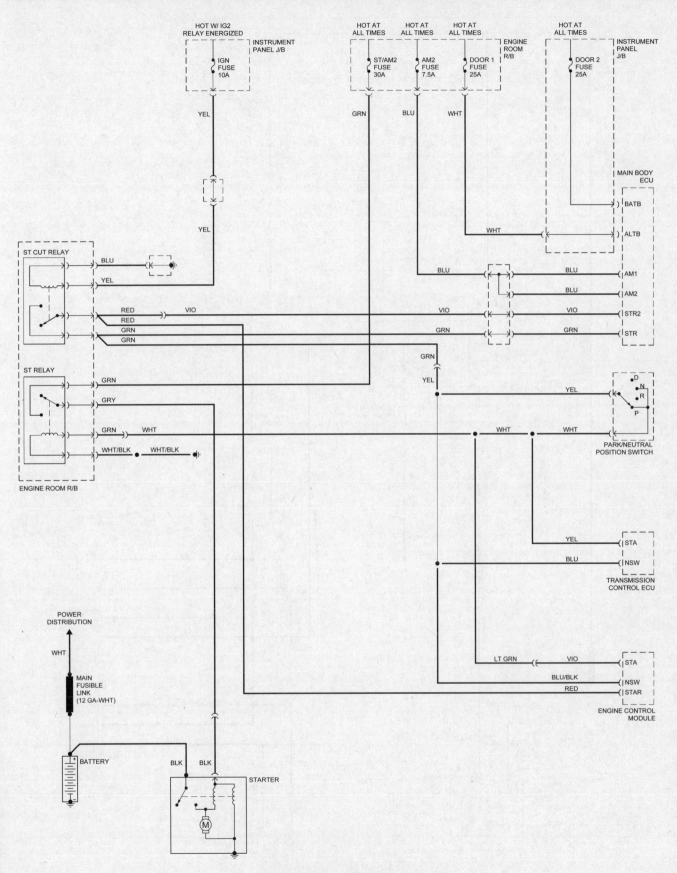

Starting system - with Smart Key system

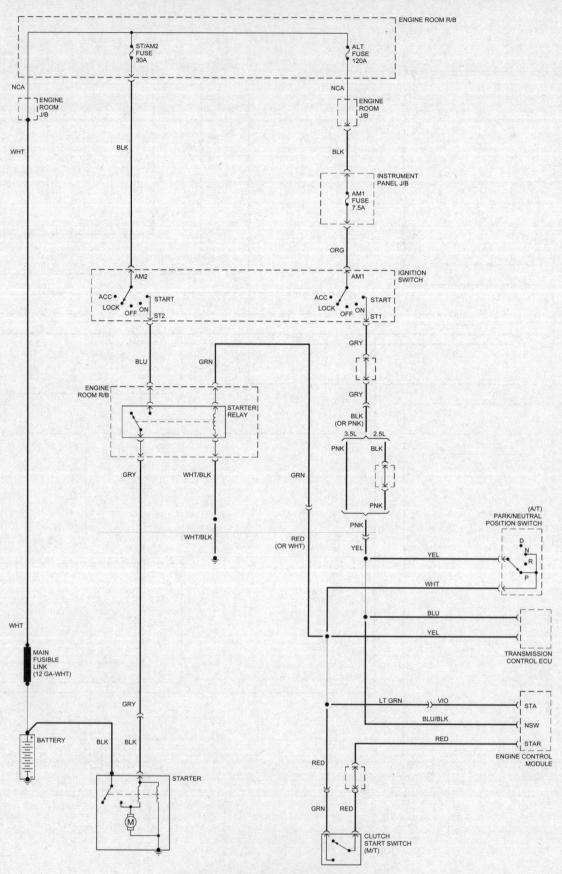

Starting system - without Smart Key system

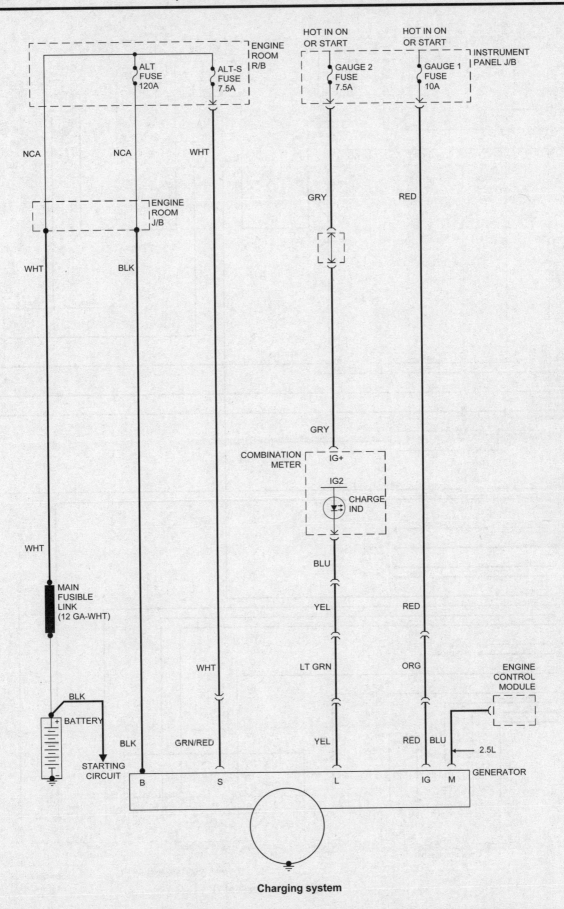

Charging system

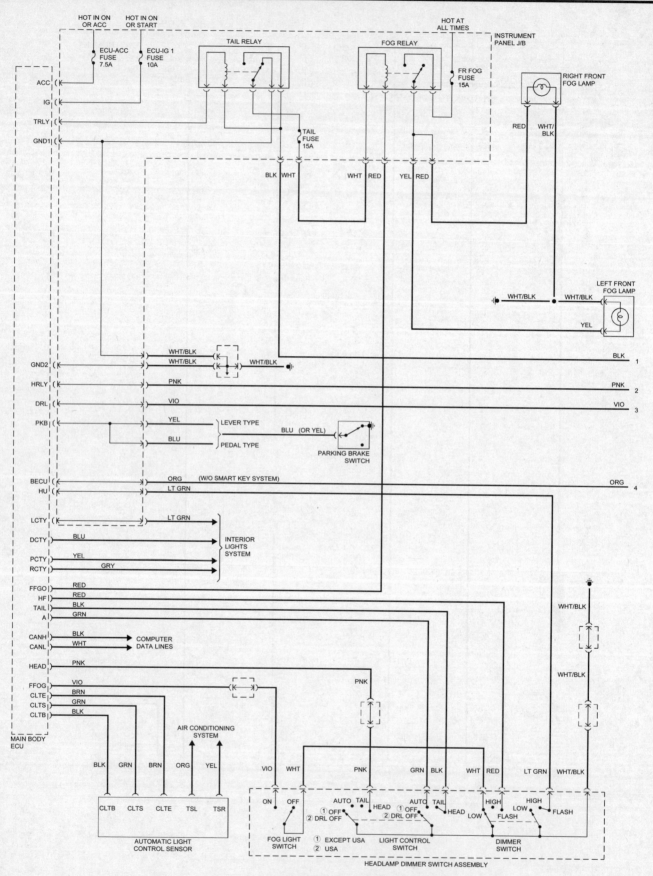

Headlight system (1 of 2)

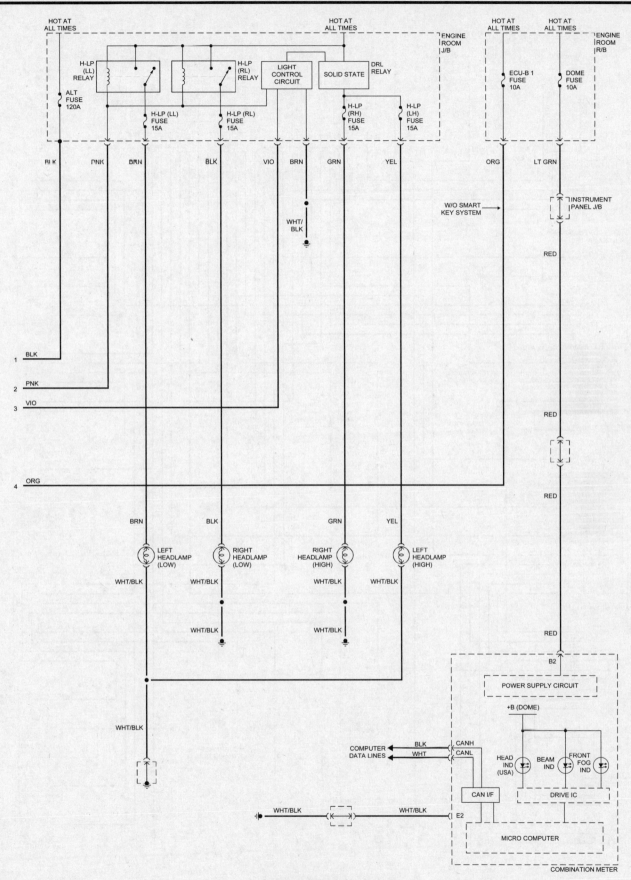

Headlight system (2 of 2)

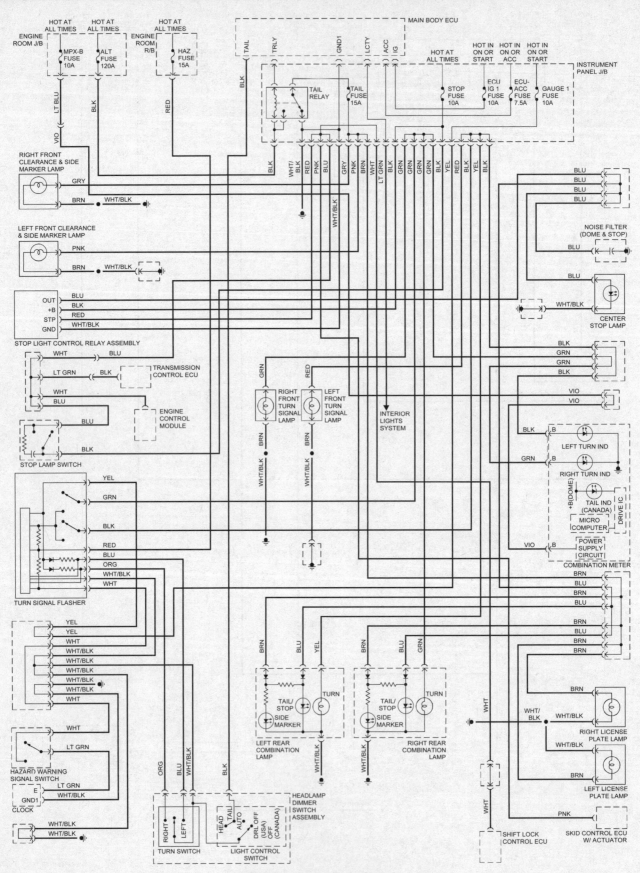

Exterior lighting system - 2010 and 2011 models

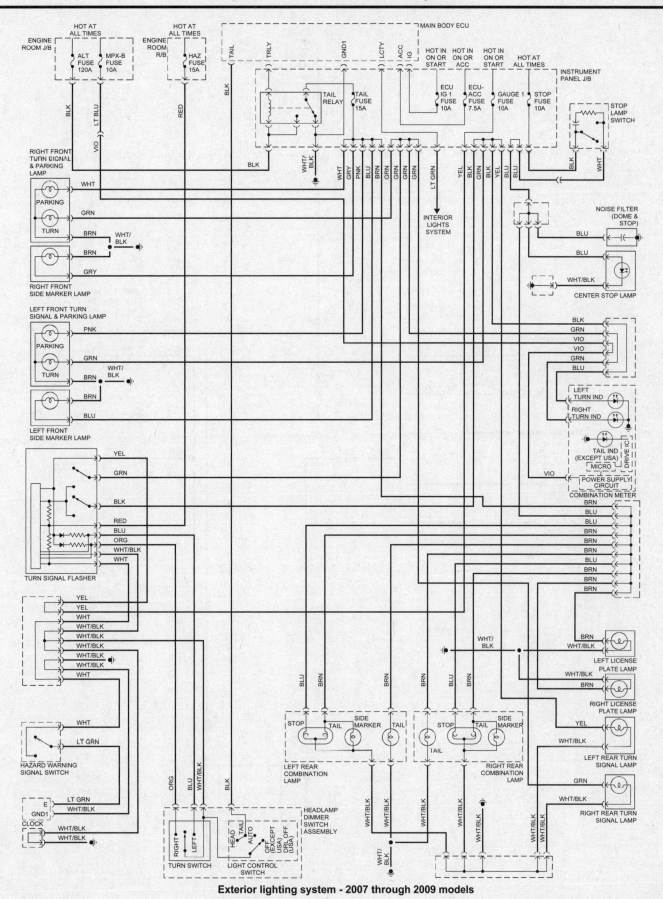

Exterior lighting system - 2007 through 2009 models

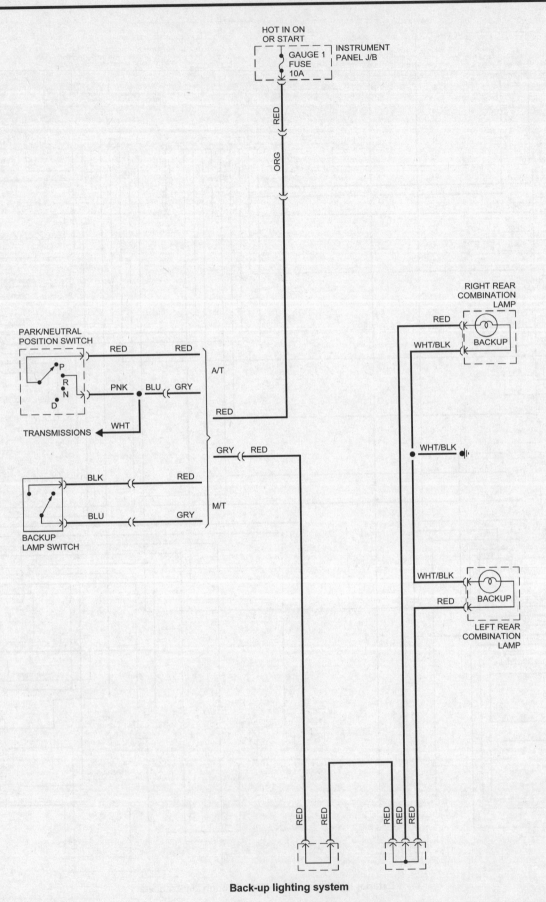

Back-up lighting system

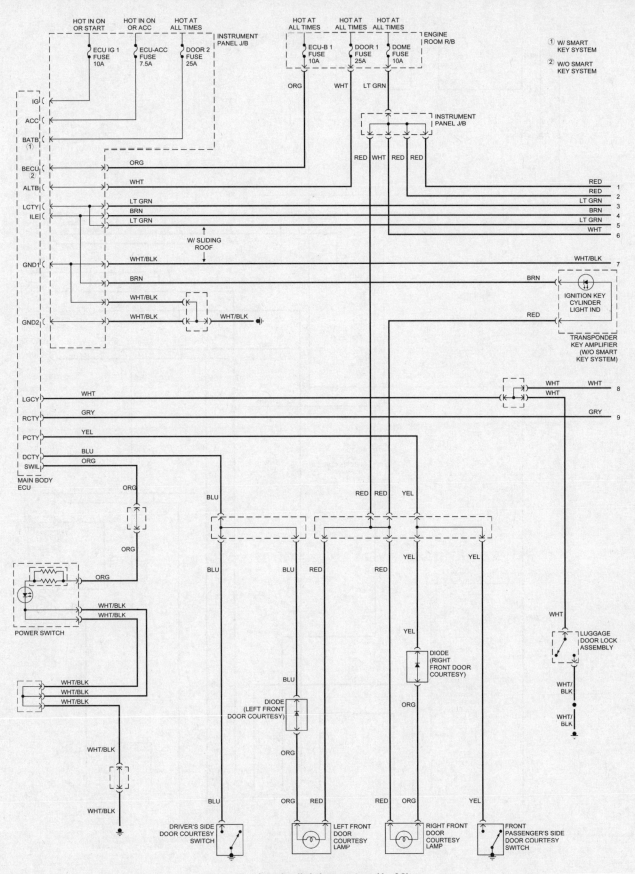

Interior lighting system (1 of 2)

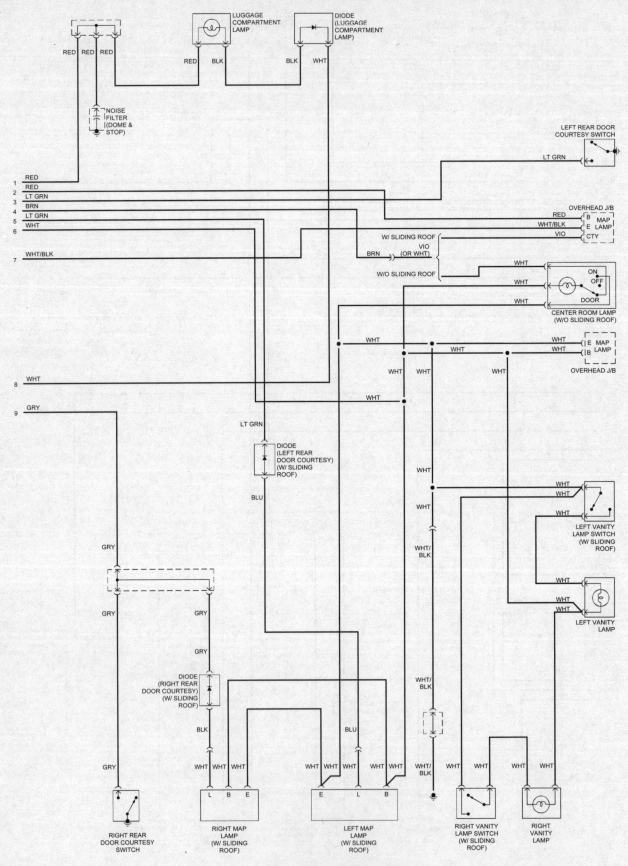

Interior lighting system (2 of 2)

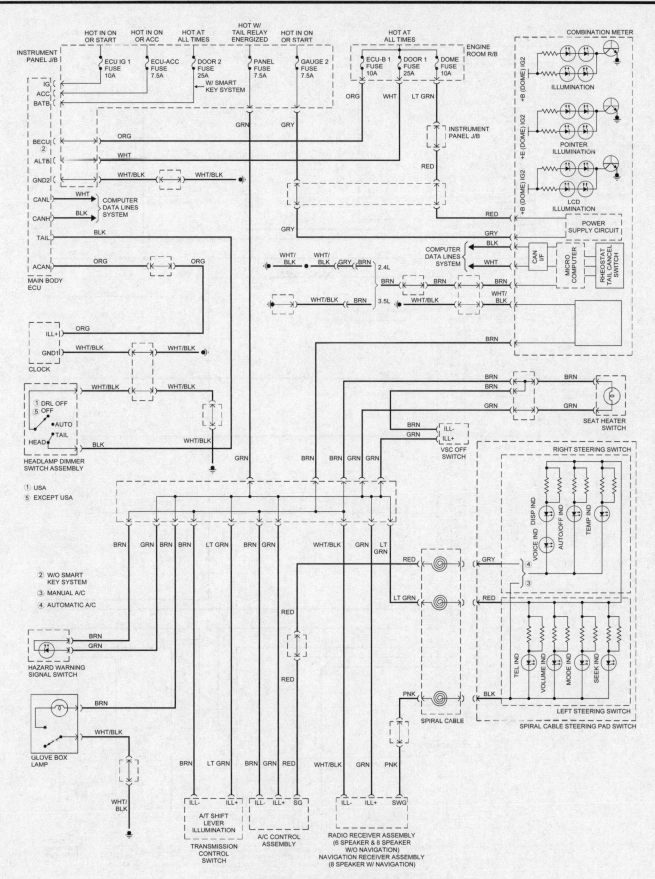

Instrument panel and switch illumination

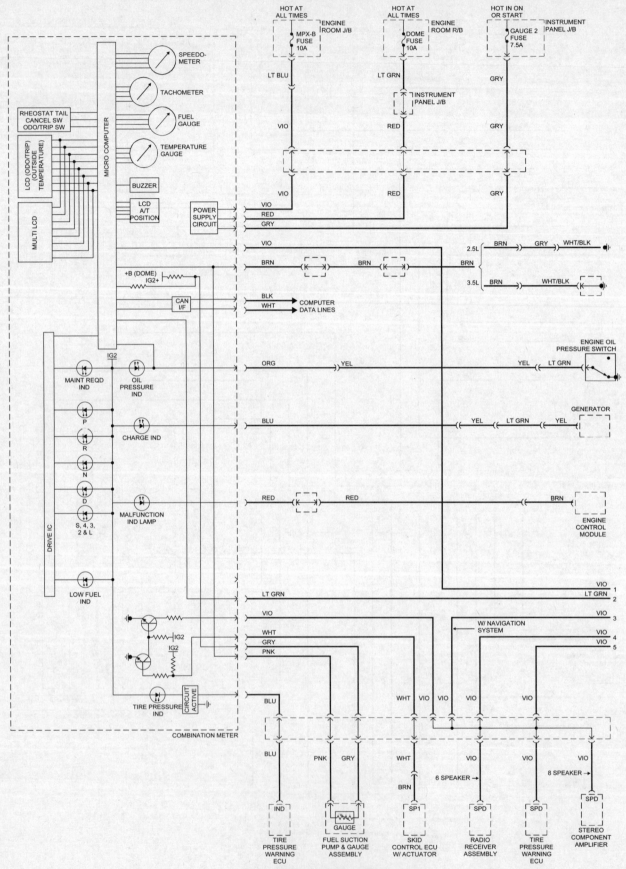

Warning lights and gauges (1 of 2)

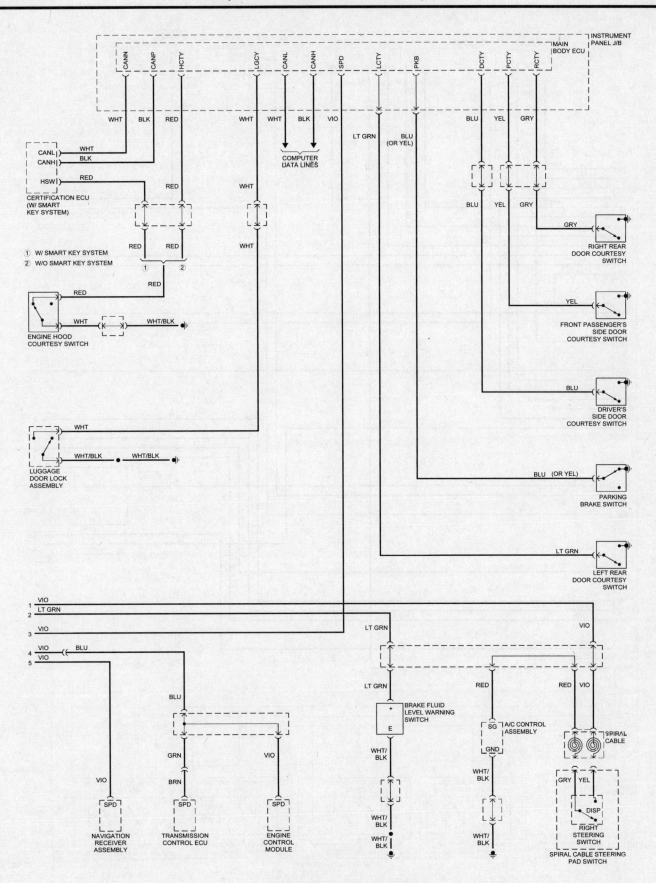

Warning lights and gauges (2 of 2)

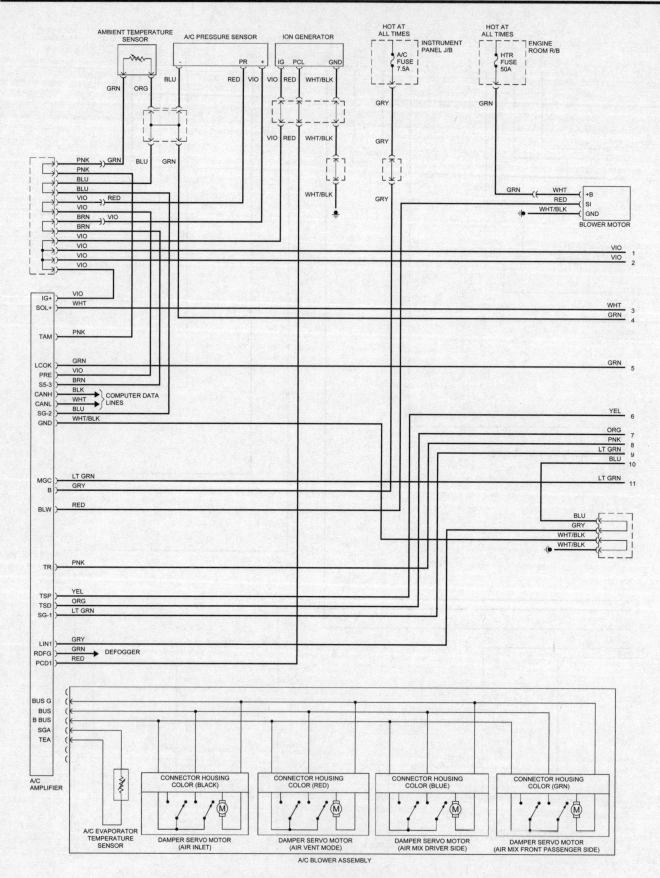

Air conditioning/heating (automatic) and engine cooling fan system - V6 models (1 of 2)

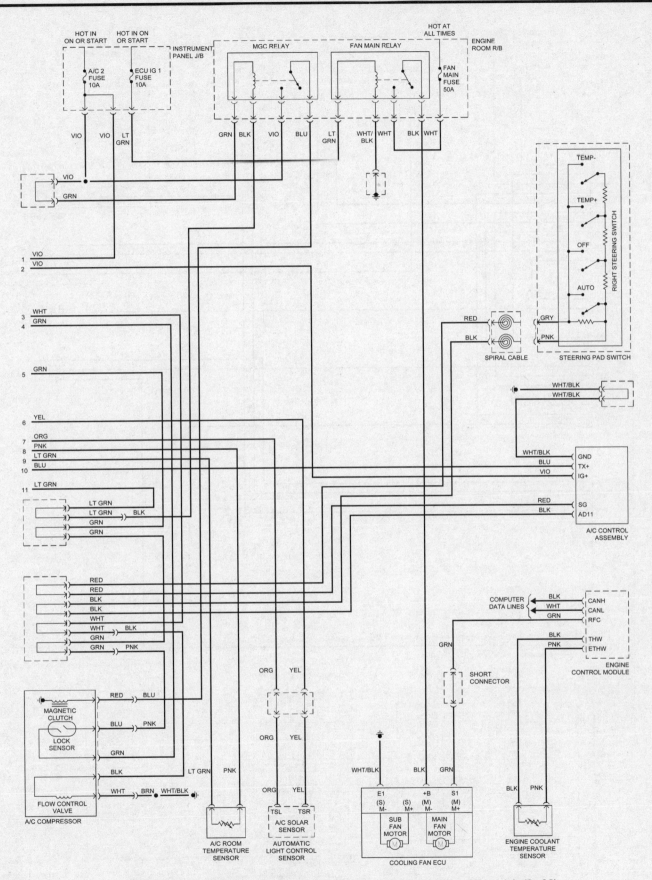

Air conditioning/heating (automatic) and engine cooling fan system - V6 models (2 of 2)

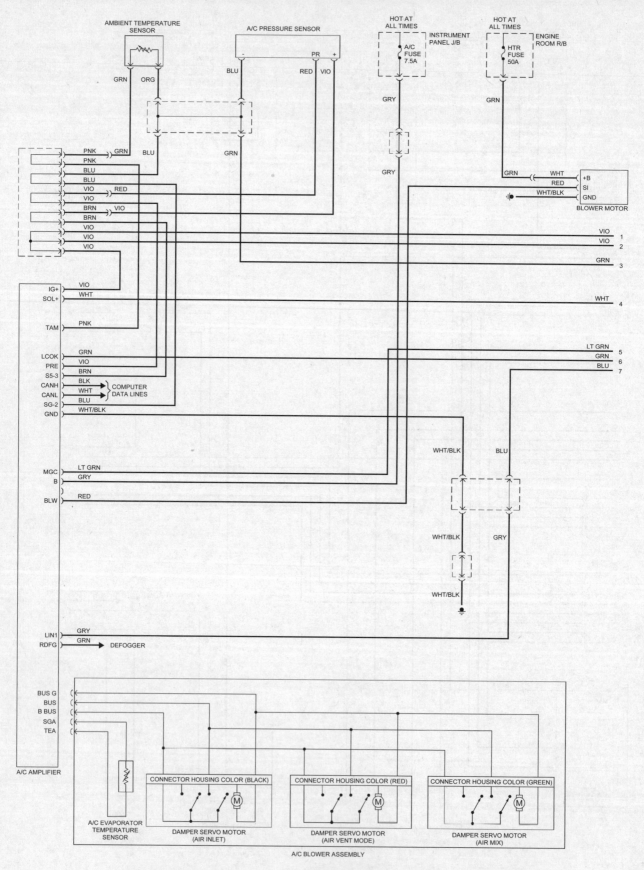

Air conditioning/heating (manual) and engine cooling fan system - V6 models (1 of 2)

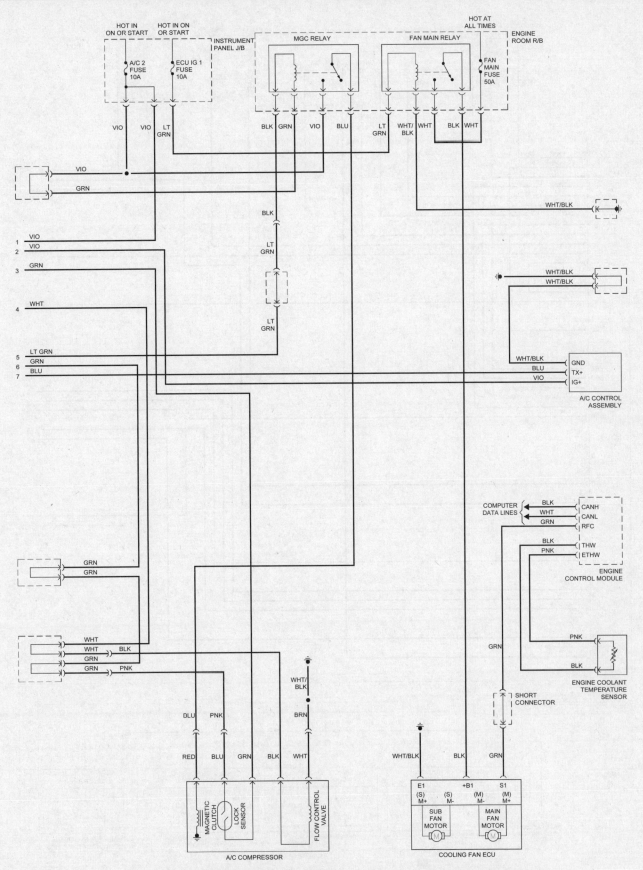

Air conditioning/heating (manual) and engine cooling fan system - V6 models (2 of 2)

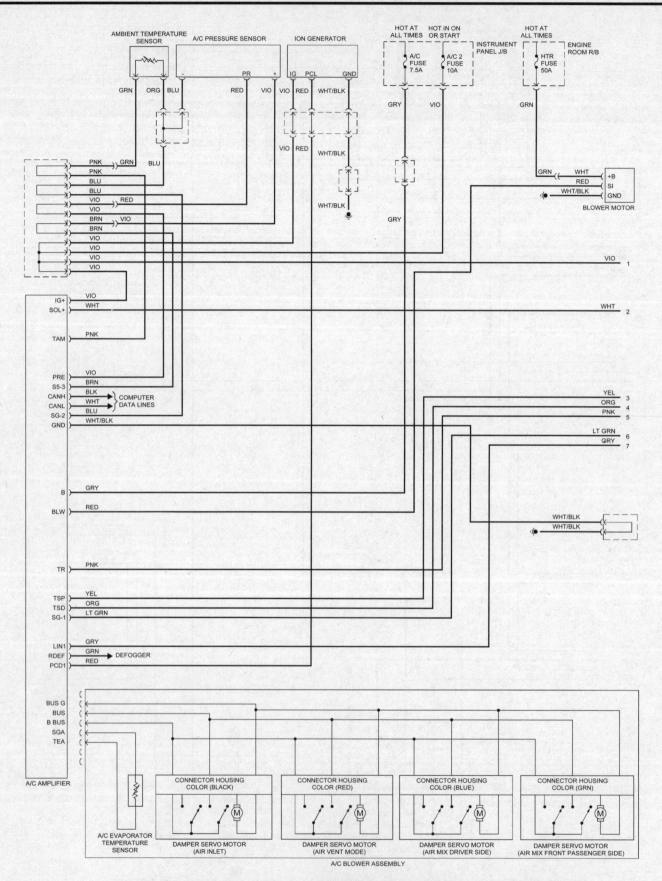

Air conditioning/heating (automatic) and engine cooling fan system - four-cylinder models (1 of 2)

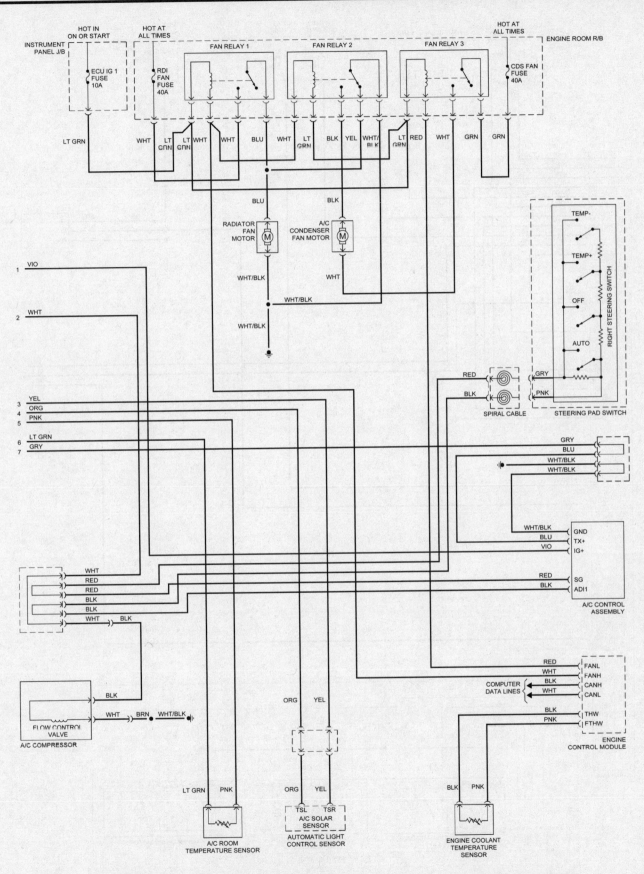

Air conditioning/heating (automatic) and engine cooling fan system - four-cylinder models (2 of 2)

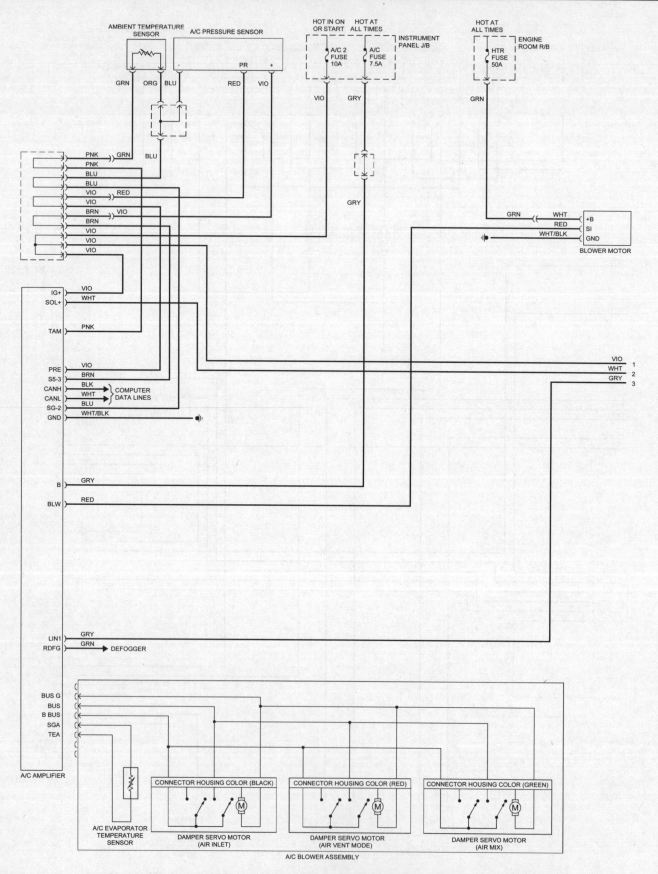

Air conditioning/heating (manual) and engine cooling fan system - four-cylinder models (1 of 2)

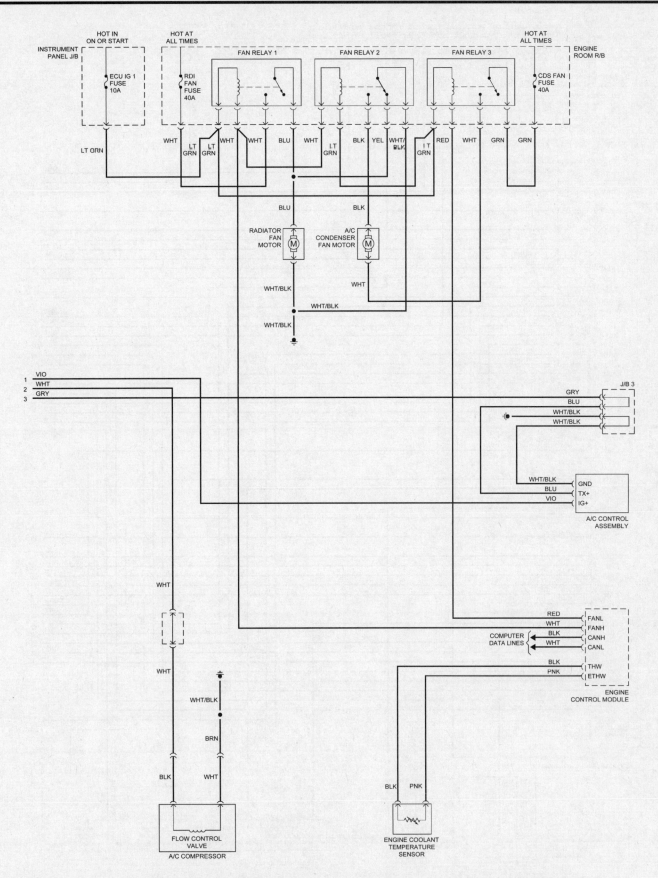

Air conditioning/heating (manual) and engine cooling fan system - four-cylinder models (2 of 2)

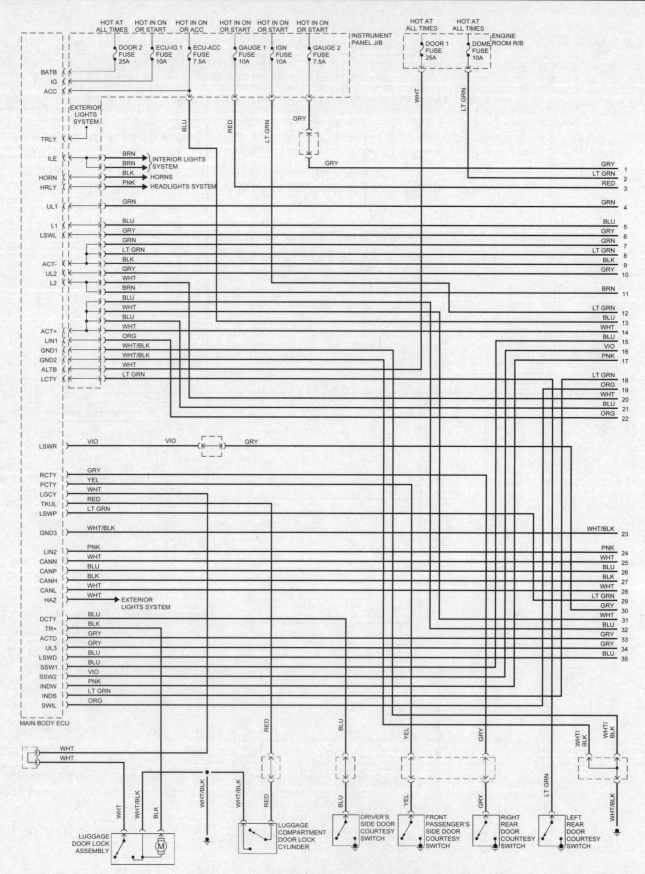

Power door lock system - with Smart Key system (1 of 4)

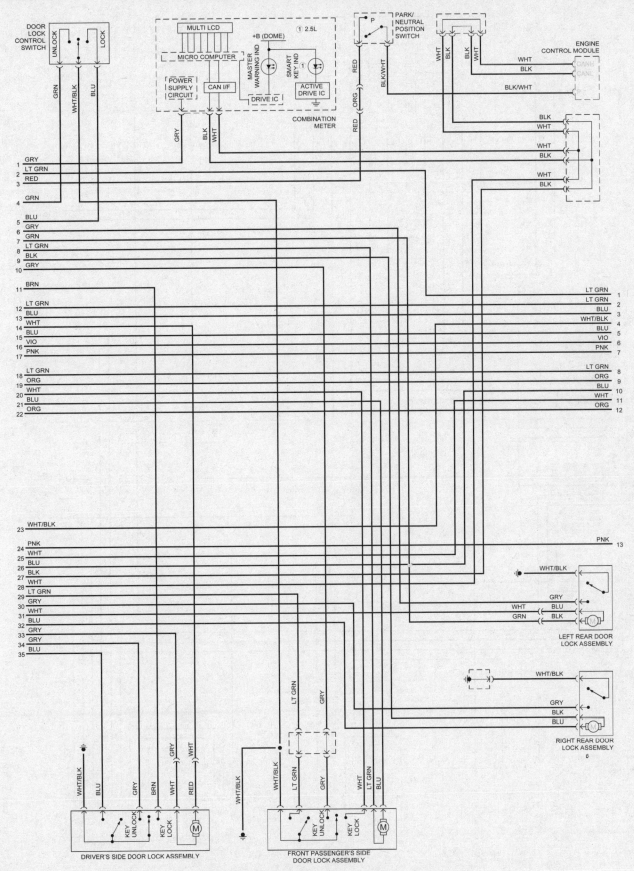

Power door lock system - with Smart Key system (2 of 4)

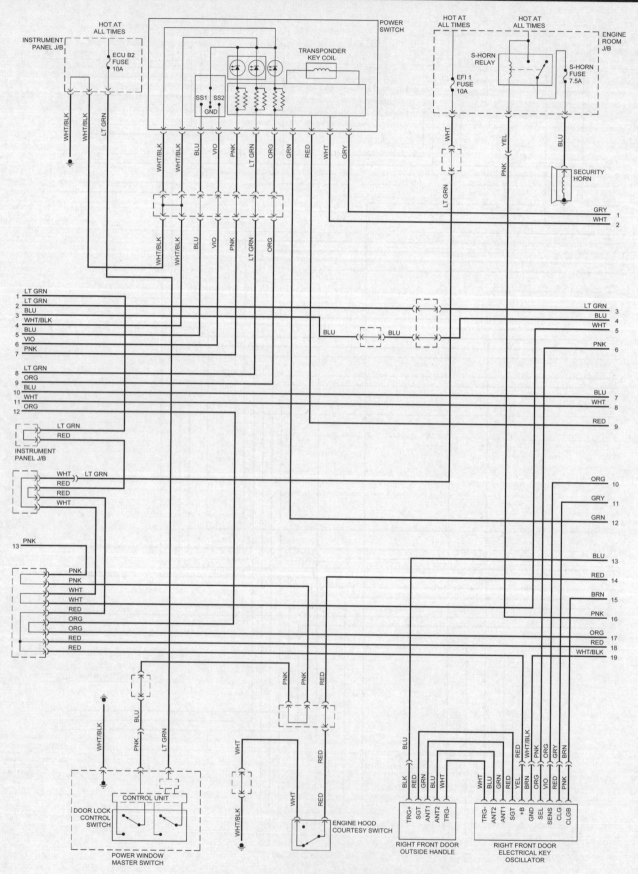

Power door lock system - with Smart Key system (3 of 4)

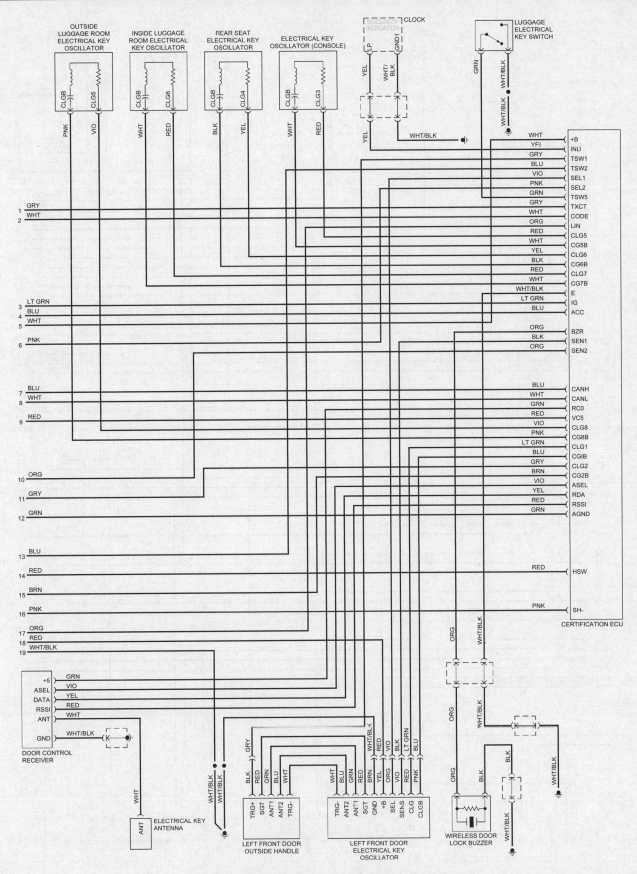

Power door lock system - with Smart Key system (4 of 4)

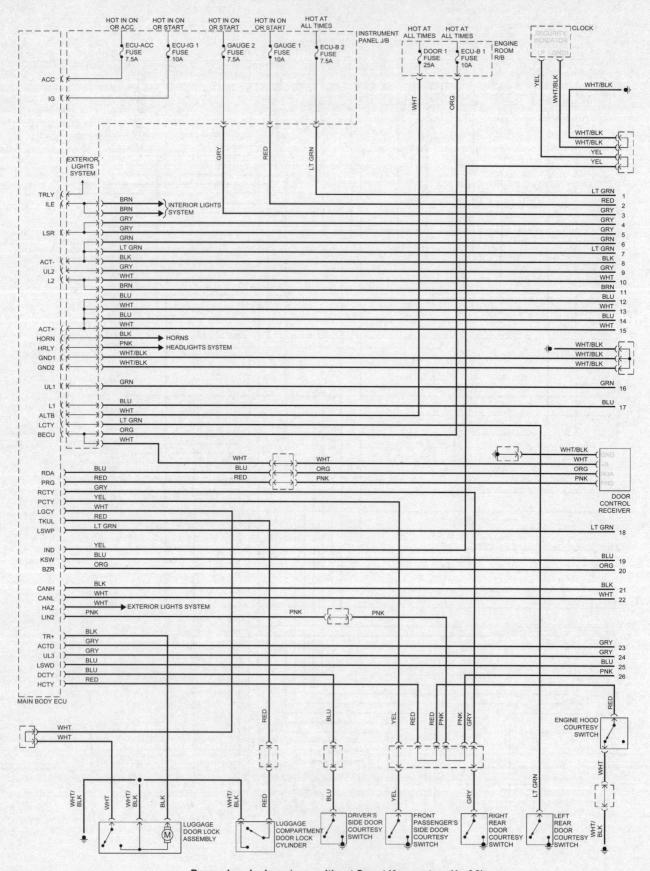

Power door lock system - without Smart Key system (1 of 2)

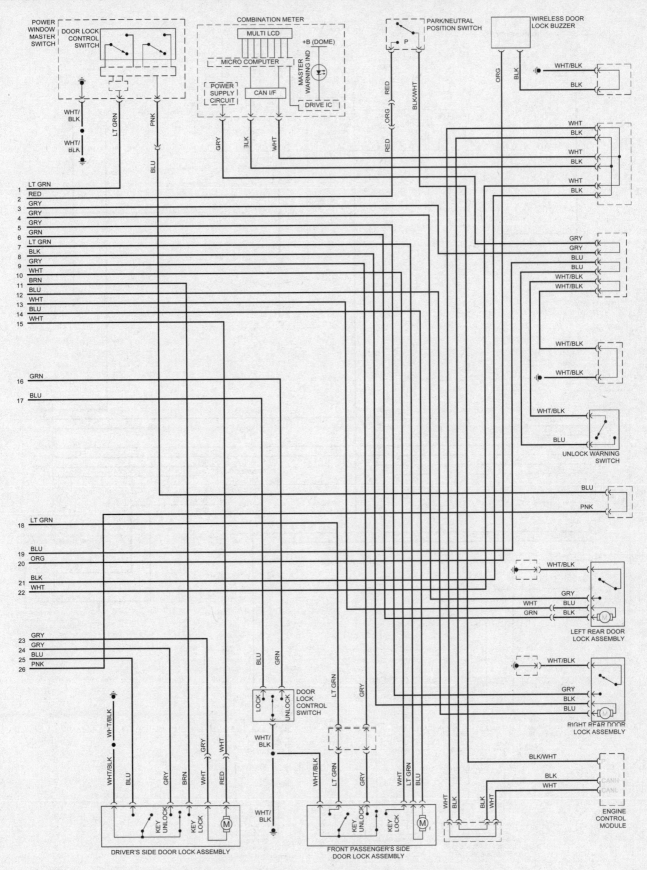

Power door lock system - without Smart Key system (2 of 2)

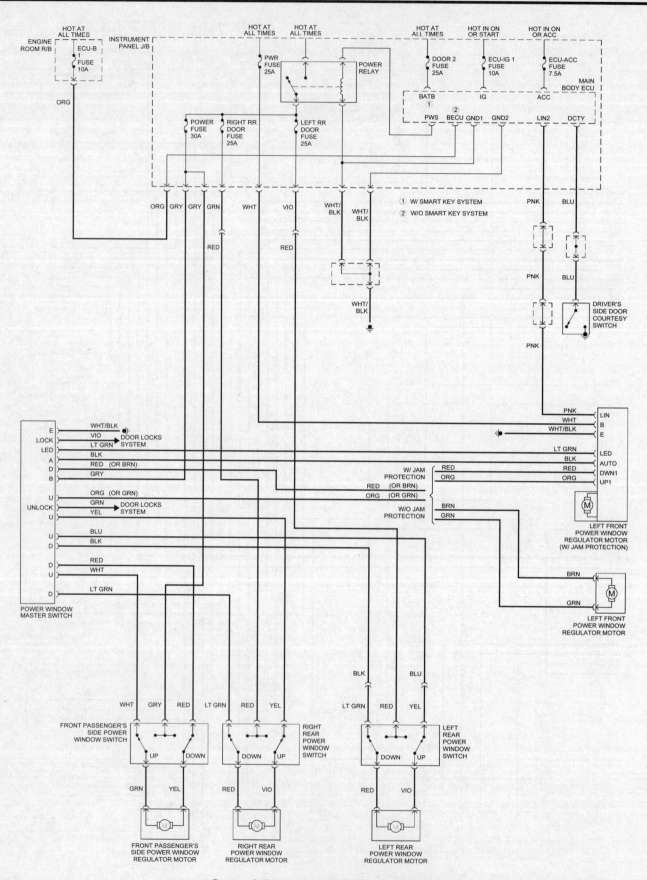

Power window system - 2007 through 2009 models

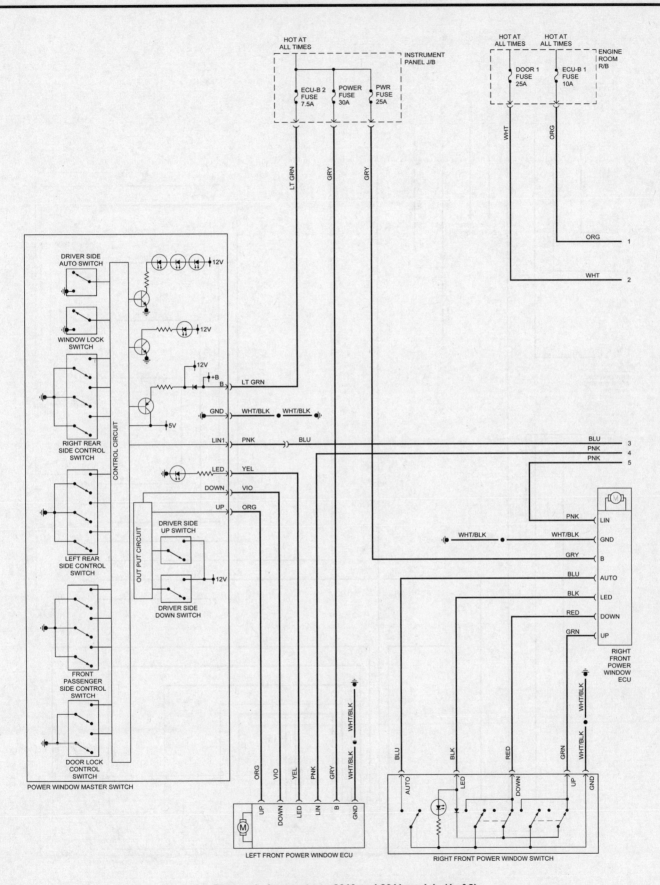

Power window system - 2010 and 2011 models (1 of 2)

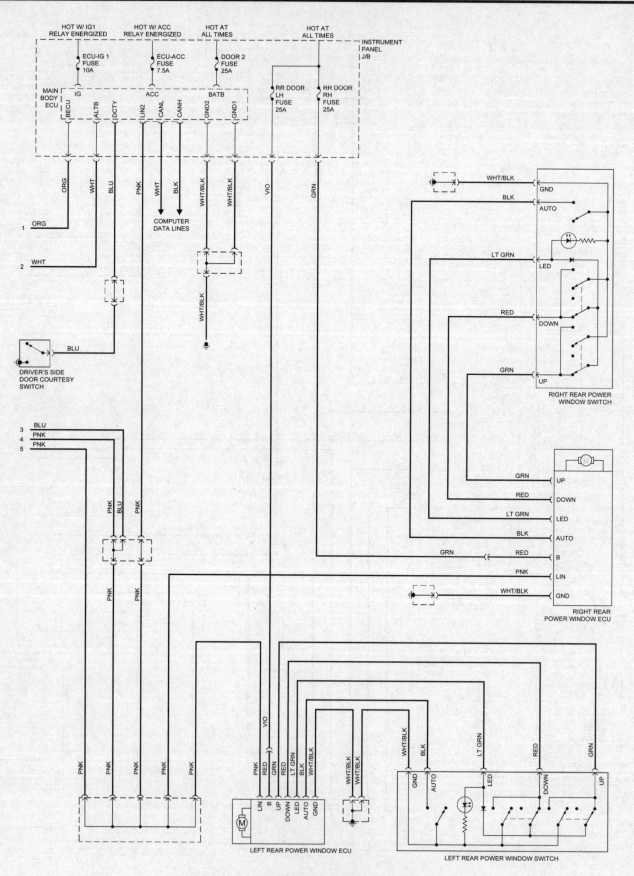

Power window system - 2010 and 2011 models (2 of 2)

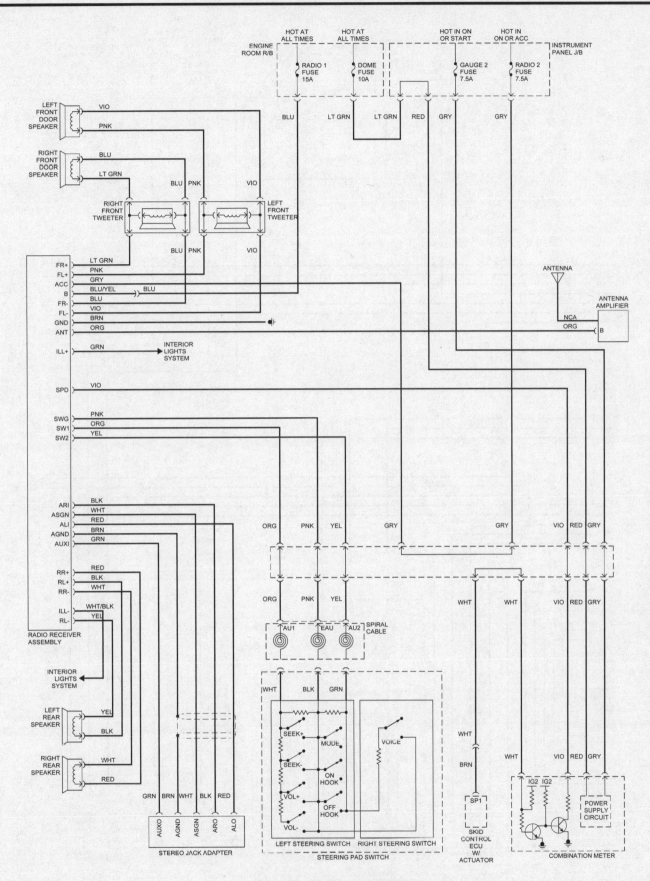

Audio system - 2007 through 2009 models

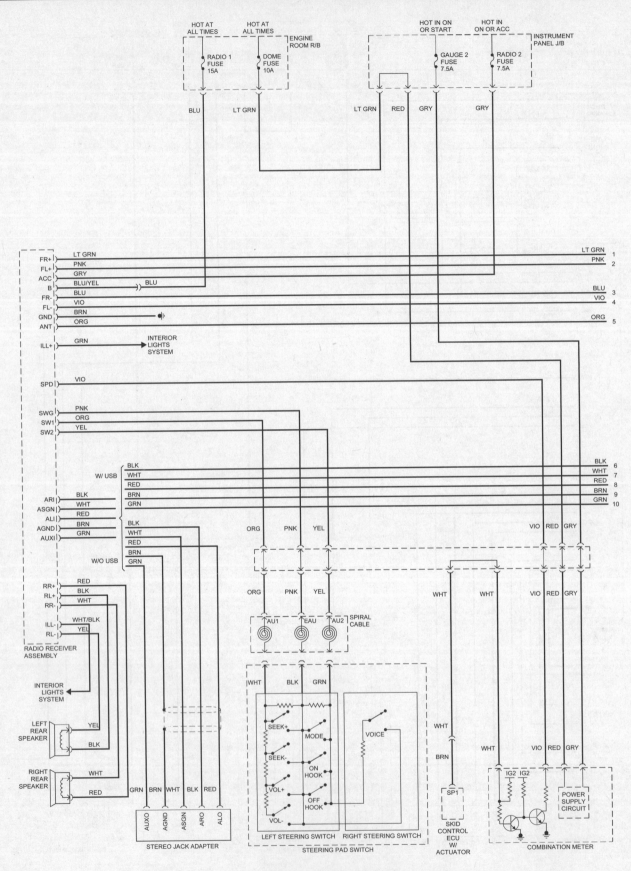

Audio system - 2010 and 2011 models (1 of 2)

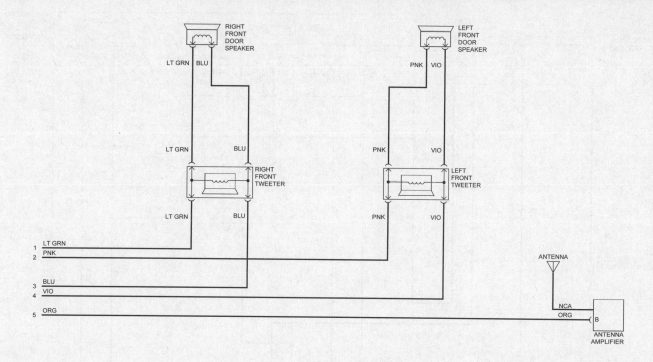

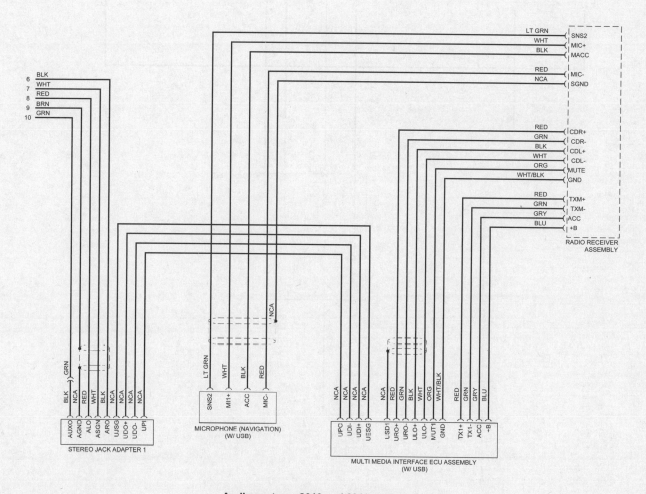

Audio system - 2010 and 2011 models (2 of 2)

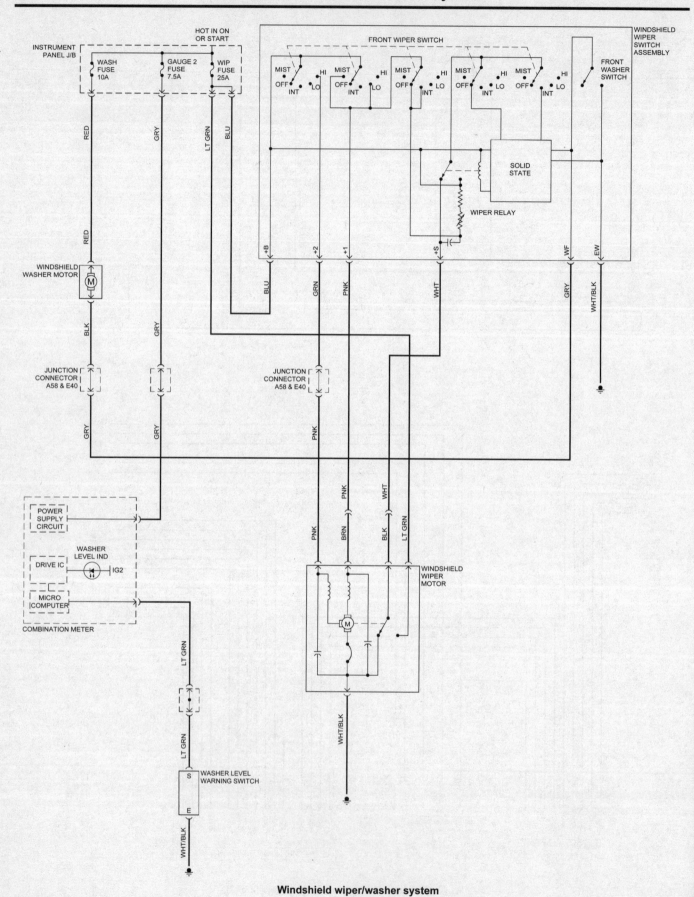

Windshield wiper/washer system

Index

Notes

Haynes Automotive Manuals

NOTE: If you do not see a listing for your vehicle, consult your local Haynes dealer for the latest product information.

ACURA
- 12020 **Integra** '86 thru '89 **& Legend** '86 thru '90
- 12021 **Integra** '90 thru '93 **& Legend** '91 thru '95
  Integra '94 thru '00 - see HONDA Civic (42025)
  MDX '01 thru '07 - see HONDA Pilot (42037)
- 12050 **Acura TL** all models '99 thru '08

AMC
- **Jeep CJ** - see JEEP (50020)
- 14020 **Mid-size models** '70 thru '83
- 14025 **(Renault) Alliance & Encore** '83 thru '87

AUDI
- 15020 **4000** all models '80 thru '87
- 15025 **5000** all models '77 thru '83
- 15026 **5000** all models '84 thru '88
  Audi A4 '96 thru '01 - see VW Passat (96023)
- 15030 **Audi A4** '02 thru '08

AUSTIN-HEALEY
- **Sprite** - see MG Midget (66015)

BMW
- 18020 **3/5 Series** '82 thru '92
- 18021 **3-Series** incl. Z3 models '92 thru '98
- 18022 **3-Series** incl. Z4 models '99 thru '05
- 18023 **3-Series** '06 thru '10
- 18025 **320i** all 4 cyl models '75 thru '83
- 18050 **1500 thru 2002** except Turbo '59 thru '77

BUICK
- 19010 **Buick Century** '97 thru '05
  Century (front-wheel drive) - see GM (38005)
- 19020 **Buick, Oldsmobile & Pontiac Full-size
  (Front-wheel drive)** '85 thru '05
  Buick Electra, LeSabre and Park Avenue;
  Oldsmobile Delta 88 Royale, Ninety Eight
  and Regency; **Pontiac** Bonneville
- 19025 **Buick, Oldsmobile & Pontiac Full-size
  (Rear wheel drive)** '70 thru '90
  Buick Estate, Electra, LeSabre, Limited,
  Oldsmobile Custom Cruiser, Delta 88,
  Ninety-eight, **Pontiac** Bonneville,
  Catalina, Grandville, Parisienne
- 19030 **Mid-size Regal & Century** all rear-drive
  models with V6, V8 and Turbo '74 thru '87
  Regal - see GENERAL MOTORS (38010)
  Riviera - see GENERAL MOTORS (38030)
  Roadmaster - see CHEVROLET (24046)
  Skyhawk - see GENERAL MOTORS (38015)
  Skylark - see GM (38020, 38025)
  Somerset - see GENERAL MOTORS (38025)

CADILLAC
- 21015 **CTS & CTS-V** '03 thru '12
- 21030 **Cadillac Rear Wheel Drive** '70 thru '93
  Cimarron - see GENERAL MOTORS (38015)
  DeVille - see GM (38031 & 38032)
  Eldorado - see GM (38030 & 38031)
  Fleetwood - see GM (38031)
  Seville - see GM (38030, 38031 & 38032)

CHEVROLET
- 10305 **Chevrolet Engine Overhaul Manual**
- 24010 **Astro & GMC Safari Mini-vans** '85 thru '05
- 24015 **Camaro V8** all models '70 thru '81
- 24016 **Camaro** all models '82 thru '92
- 24017 **Camaro & Firebird** '93 thru '02
  Cavalier - see GENERAL MOTORS (38016)
  Celebrity - see GENERAL MOTORS (38005)
- 24020 **Chevelle, Malibu & El Camino** '69 thru '87
- 24024 **Chevette & Pontiac T1000** '76 thru '87
  Citation - see GENERAL MOTORS (38020)
- 24027 **Colorado & GMC Canyon** '04 thru '10
- 24032 **Corsica/Beretta** all models '87 thru '96
- 24040 **Corvette** all V8 models '68 thru '82
- 24041 **Corvette** all models '84 thru '96
- 24045 **Full-size Sedans** Caprice, Impala, Biscayne,
  Bel Air & Wagons '69 thru '90
- 24046 **Impala SS & Caprice and Buick Roadmaster**
  '91 thru '96
  Impala '00 thru '05 - see LUMINA (24048)
- 24047 **Impala & Monte Carlo** all models '06 thru '11
  Lumina '90 thru '94 - see GM (38010)
- 24048 **Lumina & Monte Carlo** '95 thru '05
  Lumina APV - see GM (38035)
- 24050 **Luv Pick-up** all 2WD & 4WD '72 thru '82
  Malibu '97 thru '00 - see GM (38026)
- 24055 **Monte Carlo** all models '70 thru '88
  Monte Carlo '95 thru '01 - see LUMINA (24048)
- 24059 **Nova** all V8 models '69 thru '79
- 24060 **Nova and Geo Prizm** '85 thru '92
- 24064 **Pick-ups** '67 thru '87 - Chevrolet & GMC
- 24065 **Pick-ups** '88 thru '98 - Chevrolet & GMC

- 24066 **Pick-ups** '99 thru '06 - Chevrolet & GMC
- 24067 **Chevrolet Silverado & GMC Sierra** '07 thru '12
- 24070 **S-10 & S-15 Pick-ups** '82 thru '93,
  Blazer & Jimmy '83 thru '94,
- 24071 **S-10 & Sonoma Pick-ups** '94 thru '04, including **Blazer, Jimmy & Hombre**
- 24072 **Chevrolet TrailBlazer, GMC Envoy &
  Oldsmobile Bravada** '02 thru '09
- 24075 **Sprint** '85 thru '88 **& Geo Metro** '89 thru '01
- 24080 **Vans - Chevrolet & GMC** '68 thru '96
- 24081 **Chevrolet Express & GMC Savana**
  Full-size Vans '96 thru '10

CHRYSLER
- 10310 **Chrysler Engine Overhaul Manual**
- 25015 **Chrysler Cirrus, Dodge Stratus,
  Plymouth Breeze** '95 thru '00
- 25020 **Full-size Front-Wheel Drive** '88 thru '93
  K-Cars - see DODGE Aries (30008)
  Laser - see DODGE Daytona (30030)
- 25025 **Chrysler LHS, Concorde, New Yorker,
  Dodge** Intrepid, **Eagle** Vision, '93 thru '97
- 25026 **Chrysler LHS, Concorde, 300M,
  Dodge** Intrepid, '98 thru '04
- 25027 **Chrysler 300, Dodge Charger &
  Magnum** '05 thru '09
- 25030 **Chrysler & Plymouth Mid-size**
  front wheel drive '82 thru '95
  Rear-wheel Drive - see Dodge (30050)
- 25035 **PT Cruiser** all models '01 thru '10
- 25040 **Chrysler** Sebring '95 thru '06, **Dodge** Stratus
  '01 thru '06, **Dodge** Avenger '95 thru '00

DATSUN
- 28005 **200SX** all models '80 thru '83
- 28007 **B-210** all models '73 thru '78
- 28009 **210** all models '79 thru '82
- 28012 **240Z, 260Z & 280Z** Coupe '70 thru '78
- 28014 **280ZX** Coupe & 2+2 '79 thru '83
  300ZX - see NISSAN (72010)
- 28018 **510 & PL521 Pick-up** '68 thru '73
- 28020 **510** all models '78 thru '81
- 28022 **620 Series Pick-up** all models '73 thru '79
  720 Series Pick-up - see NISSAN (72030)
- 28025 **810/Maxima** all gasoline models '77 thru '84

DODGE
- **400 & 600** - see CHRYSLER (25030)
- 30008 **Aries & Plymouth Reliant** '81 thru '89
- 30010 **Caravan & Plymouth Voyager** '84 thru '95
- 30011 **Caravan & Plymouth Voyager** '96 thru '02
- 30012 **Challenger/Plymouth Saporro** '78 thru '83
- 30013 **Caravan, Chrysler Voyager, Town &
  Country** '03 thru '07
- 30016 **Colt & Plymouth Champ** '78 thru '87
- 30020 **Dakota Pick-ups** all models '87 thru '96
- 30021 **Durango** '98 & '99, **Dakota** '97 thru '99
- 30022 **Durango** '00 thru '03 **Dakota** '00 thru '04
- 30023 **Durango** '04 thru '09, **Dakota** '05 thru '11
- 30025 **Dart, Demon, Plymouth Barracuda,
  Duster & Valiant** 6 cyl models '67 thru '76
- 30030 **Daytona & Chrysler Laser** '84 thru '89
  Intrepid - see CHRYSLER (25025, 25026)
- 30034 **Neon** all models '95 thru '99
- 30035 **Omni & Plymouth Horizon** '78 thru '90
- 30036 **Dodge and Plymouth Neon** '00 thru '05
- 30040 **Pick-ups** all full-size models '74 thru '93
- 30041 **Pick-ups** all full-size models '94 thru '01
- 30042 **Pick-ups** full-size models '02 thru '08
- 30045 **Ram 50/D50 Pick-ups & Raider and
  Plymouth Arrow Pick-ups** '79 thru '93
- 30050 **Dodge/Plymouth/Chrysler RWD** '71 thru '89
- 30055 **Shadow & Plymouth Sundance** '87 thru '94
- 30060 **Spirit & Plymouth Acclaim** '89 thru '95
- 30065 **Vans - Dodge & Plymouth** '71 thru '03

EAGLE
- **Talon** - see MITSUBISHI (68030, 68031)
- **Vision** - see CHRYSLER (25025)

FIAT
- 34010 **124 Sport Coupe & Spider** '68 thru '78
- 34025 **X1/9** all models '74 thru '80

FORD
- 10320 **Ford Engine Overhaul Manual**
- 10355 **Ford Automatic Transmission Overhaul**
- 11500 **Mustang** '64-1/2 thru '70 Restoration Guide
- 36004 **Aerostar Mini-vans** all models '86 thru '97
- 36006 **Contour & Mercury Mystique** '95 thru '00
- 36008 **Courier Pick-up** all models '72 thru '82
- 36012 **Crown Victoria & Mercury Grand
  Marquis** '88 thru '10
- 36016 **Escort/Mercury Lynx** all models '81 thru '90
- 36020 **Escort/Mercury Tracer** '91 thru '02

- 36022 **Escape & Mazda Tribute** '01 thru '11
- 36024 **Explorer & Mazda Navajo** '91 thru '01
- 36025 **Explorer/Mercury Mountaineer** '02 thru '10
- 36028 **Fairmont & Mercury Zephyr** '78 thru '83
- 36030 **Festiva & Aspire** '88 thru '97
- 36032 **Fiesta** all models '77 thru '80
- 36034 **Focus** all models '00 thru '11
- 36036 **Ford & Mercury Full-size** '75 thru '87
- 36044 **Ford & Mercury Mid-size** '75 thru '86
- 36045 **Fusion & Mercury Milan** '06 thru '10
- 36048 **Mustang V8** all models '64-1/2 thru '73
- 36049 **Mustang II** 4 cyl, V6 & V8 models '74 thru '78
- 36050 **Mustang & Mercury Capri** '79 thru '93
- 36051 **Mustang** all models '94 thru '04
- 36052 **Mustang** '05 thru '10
- 36054 **Pick-ups & Bronco** '73 thru '79
- 36058 **Pick-ups & Bronco** '80 thru '96
- 36059 **F-150 & Expedition** '97 thru '09, **F-250** '97
  thru '99 **& Lincoln Navigator** '98 thru '09
- 36060 **Super Duty Pick-ups, Excursion** '99 thru '10
- 36061 **F-150 full-size** '04 thru '10
- 36062 **Pinto & Mercury Bobcat** '75 thru '80
- 36066 **Probe** all models '89 thru '92
  Probe '93 thru '97 - see MAZDA 626 (61042)
- 36070 **Ranger/Bronco II** gasoline models '83 thru '92
- 36071 **Ranger** '93 thru '10 **& Mazda Pick-ups** '94 thru '09
- 36074 **Taurus & Mercury Sable** '86 thru '95
- 36075 **Taurus & Mercury Sable** '96 thru '05
- 36078 **Tempo & Mercury Topaz** '84 thru '94
- 36082 **Thunderbird/Mercury Cougar** '83 thru '88
- 36086 **Thunderbird/Mercury Cougar** '89 thru '97
- 36090 **Vans** all V8 Econoline models '69 thru '91
- 36094 **Vans** full size '92 thru '10
- 36097 **Windstar Mini-van** '95 thru '07

GENERAL MOTORS
- 10360 **GM Automatic Transmission Overhaul**
- 38005 **Buick Century, Chevrolet Celebrity,
  Oldsmobile Cutlass Ciera & Pontiac 6000**
  all models '82 thru '96
- 38010 **Buick Regal, Chevrolet Lumina,
  Oldsmobile Cutlass Supreme &
  Pontiac Grand Prix** (FWD) '88 thru '07
- 38015 **Buick Skyhawk, Cadillac Cimarron,
  Chevrolet Cavalier, Oldsmobile Firenza &
  Pontiac J-2000 & Sunbird** '82 thru '94
- 38016 **Chevrolet Cavalier &
  Pontiac Sunfire** '95 thru '05
- 38017 **Chevrolet Cobalt & Pontiac G5** '05 thru '11
- 38020 **Buick Skylark, Chevrolet Citation,
  Olds Omega, Pontiac Phoenix** '80 thru '85
- 38025 **Buick Skylark & Somerset,
  Oldsmobile Achieva & Calais and
  Pontiac Grand Am** all models '85 thru '98
- 38026 **Chevrolet Malibu, Olds Alero & Cutlass,
  Pontiac Grand Am** '97 thru '03
- 38027 **Chevrolet Malibu** '04 thru '10
- 38030 **Cadillac Eldorado, Seville, Oldsmobile
  Toronado, Buick Riviera** '71 thru '85
- 38031 **Cadillac Eldorado & Seville, DeVille, Fleetwood
  & Olds Toronado, Buick Riviera** '86 thru '93
- 38032 **Cadillac DeVille** '94 thru '05 **& Seville** '92 thru '04
  Cadillac DTS '06 thru '10
- 38035 **Chevrolet Lumina APV, Olds Silhouette
  & Pontiac Trans Sport** all models '90 thru '96
- 38036 **Chevrolet Venture, Olds Silhouette,
  Pontiac Trans Sport & Montana** '97 thru '05
  **General Motors Full-size
  Rear-wheel Drive** - see BUICK (19025)
- 38040 **Chevrolet Equinox** '05 thru '09 **Pontiac
  Torrent** '06 thru '09
- 38070 **Chevrolet HHR** '06 thru '11

GEO
- **Metro** - see CHEVROLET Sprint (24075)
- **Prizm** - '85 thru '92 see CHEVY (24060),
  '93 thru '02 see TOYOTA Corolla (92036)
- 40030 **Storm** all models '90 thru '93
  Tracker - see SUZUKI Samurai (90010)

GMC
- **Vans & Pick-ups** - see CHEVROLET

HONDA
- 42010 **Accord CVCC** all models '76 thru '83
- 42011 **Accord** all models '84 thru '89
- 42012 **Accord** all models '90 thru '93
- 42013 **Accord** all models '94 thru '97
- 42014 **Accord** all models '98 thru '02
- 42015 **Accord** '03 thru '07
- 42020 **Civic 1200** all models '73 thru '79
- 42021 **Civic 1300 & 1500 CVCC** '80 thru '83
- 42022 **Civic 1500 CVCC** all models '75 thru '79

(Continued on other side)

<del>---</del>

Haynes North America, Inc., 859 Lawrence Drive, Newbury Park, CA 91320-1514 • (805) 498-6703 • http://www.haynes.com

Haynes Automotive Manuals (continued)

NOTE: If you do not see a listing for your vehicle, consult your local Haynes dealer for the latest product information.

42023 **Civic** all models '84 thru '91
42024 **Civic & del Sol** '92 thru '95
42025 **Civic** '96 thru '00, **CR-V** '97 thru '01,
  Acura Integra '94 thru '00
42026 **Civic** '01 thru '10, **CR-V** '02 thru '09
42035 **Odyssey** all models '99 thru '10
  Passport - see ISUZU Rodeo (47017)
42037 **Honda Pilot** '03 thru '07, **Acura MDX** '01 thru '07
42040 **Prelude CVCC** all models '79 thru '89

HYUNDAI
43010 **Elantra** all models '96 thru '10
43015 **Excel & Accent** all models '86 thru '09
43050 **Santa Fe** all models '01 thru '06
43055 **Sonata** all models '99 thru '08

INFINITI
  G35 '03 thru '08 - see NISSAN 350Z (72011)

ISUZU
  Hombre - see CHEVROLET S-10 (24071)
47017 **Rodeo, Amigo & Honda Passport** '89 thru '02
47020 **Trooper & Pick-up** '81 thru '93

JAGUAR
49010 **XJ6** all 6 cyl models '68 thru '86
49011 **XJ6** all models '88 thru '94
49015 **XJ12 & XJS** all 12 cyl models '72 thru '85

JEEP
50010 **Cherokee, Comanche & Wagoneer Limited**
  all models '84 thru '01
50020 **CJ** all models '49 thru '86
50025 **Grand Cherokee** all models '93 thru '04
50026 **Grand Cherokee** '05 thru '09
50029 **Grand Wagoneer & Pick-up** '72 thru '91
  Grand Wagoneer '84 thru '91, Cherokee &
  Wagoneer '72 thru '83, Pick-up '72 thru '88
50030 **Wrangler** all models '87 thru '11
50035 **Liberty** '02 thru '07

KIA
54050 **Optima** '01 thru '10
54070 **Sephia** '94 thru '01, **Spectra** '00 thru '09,
  Sportage '05 thru '10

LEXUS
  ES 300/330 - see TOYOTA Camry (92007) (92008)
  RX 330 - see TOYOTA Highlander (92095)

LINCOLN
  Navigator - see FORD Pick-up (36059)
59010 **Rear-Wheel Drive** all models '70 thru '10

MAZDA
61010 **GLC Hatchback (rear-wheel drive)** '77 thru '83
61011 **GLC (front-wheel drive)** '81 thru '85
61012 **Mazda3** '04 thru '11
61015 **323 & Protegé** '90 thru '03
61016 **MX-5 Miata** '90 thru '09
61020 **MPV** all models '89 thru '98
  Navajo - see Ford Explorer (36024)
61030 **Pick-ups** '72 thru '93
  Pick-ups '94 thru '00 - see Ford Ranger (36071)
61035 **RX-7** all models '79 thru '85
61036 **RX-7** all models '86 thru '91
61040 **626 (rear-wheel drive)** all models '79 thru '82
61041 **626/MX-6 (front-wheel drive)** '83 thru '92
61042 **626, MX-6/Ford Probe** '93 thru '02
61043 **Mazda6** '03 thru '11

MERCEDES-BENZ
63012 **123 Series Diesel** '76 thru '85
63015 **190 Series** four-cyl gas models, '84 thru '88
63020 **230/250/280** 6 cyl sohc models '68 thru '72
63025 **280** 123 Series gasoline models '77 thru '81
63030 **350 & 450** all models '71 thru '80
63040 **C-Class:** C230/C240/C280/C320/C350 '01 thru '07

MERCURY
64200 **Villager & Nissan Quest** '93 thru '01
  All other titles, see FORD Listing.

MG
66010 **MGB** Roadster & GT Coupe '62 thru '80
66015 **MG Midget, Austin Healey Sprite** '58 thru '80

MINI
67020 **Mini** '02 thru '11

MITSUBISHI
68020 **Cordia, Tredia, Galant, Precis &**
  Mirage '83 thru '93
68030 **Eclipse, Eagle Talon & Ply. Laser** '90 thru '94
68031 **Eclipse** '95 thru '05, **Eagle Talon** '95 thru '98
68035 **Galant** '94 thru '10
68040 **Pick-up** '83 thru '96 & **Montero** '83 thru '93

NISSAN
72010 **300ZX** all models including Turbo '84 thru '89
72011 **350Z & Infiniti G35** all models '03 thru '08
72015 **Altima** all models '93 thru '06
72016 **Altima** '07 thru '10
72020 **Maxima** all models '85 thru '92
72021 **Maxima** all models '93 thru '04
72025 **Murano** '03 thru '10
72030 **Pick-ups** '80 thru '97 **Pathfinder** '87 thru '95
72031 **Frontier Pick-up, Xterra, Pathfinder** '96 thru '04
72032 **Frontier & Xterra** '05 thru '11
72040 **Pulsar** all models '83 thru '86
  Quest - see MERCURY Villager (64200)
72050 **Sentra** all models '82 thru '94
72051 **Sentra & 200SX** all models '95 thru '06
72060 **Stanza** all models '82 thru '90
72070 **Titan pick-ups** '04 thru '10 **Armada** '05 thru '10

OLDSMOBILE
73015 **Cutlass** V6 & V8 gas models '74 thru '88
  For other OLDSMOBILE titles, see BUICK,
  CHEVROLET or GENERAL MOTORS listing.

PLYMOUTH
  For PLYMOUTH titles, see DODGE listing.

PONTIAC
79008 **Fiero** all models '84 thru '88
79018 **Firebird** V8 models except Turbo '70 thru '81
79019 **Firebird** all models '82 thru '92
79025 **G6** all models '05 thru '09
79040 **Mid-size Rear-wheel Drive** '70 thru '87
  Vibe '03 thru '11 - see TOYOTA Matrix (92060)
  For other PONTIAC titles, see BUICK,
  CHEVROLET or GENERAL MOTORS listing.

PORSCHE
80020 **911** except Turbo & Carrera 4 '65 thru '89
80025 **914** all 4 cyl models '69 thru '76
80030 **924** all models including Turbo '76 thru '82
80035 **944** all models including Turbo '83 thru '89

RENAULT
  Alliance & Encore - see AMC (14020)

SAAB
84010 **900** all models including Turbo '79 thru '88

SATURN
87010 **Saturn** all S-series models '91 thru '02
87011 **Saturn Ion** '03 thru '07
87020 **Saturn** all L-series models '00 thru '04
87040 **Saturn VUE** '02 thru '07

SUBARU
89002 **1100, 1300, 1400 & 1600** '71 thru '79
89003 **1600 & 1800** 2WD & 4WD '80 thru '94
89100 **Legacy** all models '90 thru '99
89101 **Legacy & Forester** '00 thru '06

SUZUKI
90010 **Samurai/Sidekick & Geo Tracker** '86 thru '01

TOYOTA
92005 **Camry** all models '83 thru '91
92006 **Camry** all models '92 thru '96
92007 **Camry, Avalon, Solara, Lexus ES 300** '97 thru '01
92008 **Toyota Camry, Avalon and Solara and**
  Lexus ES 300/330 all models '02 thru '06
92009 **Camry** '07 thru '11
92015 **Celica Rear Wheel Drive** '71 thru '85
92020 **Celica Front Wheel Drive** '86 thru '99
92025 **Celica Supra** all models '79 thru '92
92030 **Corolla** all models '75 thru '79
92032 **Corolla** all rear wheel drive models '80 thru '87
92035 **Corolla** all front wheel drive models '84 thru '92
92036 **Corolla & Geo Prizm** '93 thru '02
92037 **Corolla** models '03 thru '11
92040 **Corolla Tercel** all models '80 thru '82
92045 **Corona** all models '74 thru '82
92050 **Cressida** all models '78 thru '82
92055 **Land Cruiser** FJ40, 43, 45, 55 '68 thru '82
92056 **Land Cruiser** FJ60, 62, 80, FZJ80 '80 thru '96
92060 **Matrix & Pontiac Vibe** '03 thru '11
92065 **MR2** all models '85 thru '87
92070 **Pick-up** all models '69 thru '78
92075 **Pick-up** all models '79 thru '95
92076 **Tacoma, 4Runner, & T100** '93 thru '04
92077 **Tacoma** all models '05 thru '09
92078 **Tundra** '00 thru '06 & **Sequoia** '01 thru '07
92079 **4Runner** all models '03 thru '09
92080 **Previa** all models '91 thru '95
92081 **Prius** all models '01 thru '08
92082 **RAV4** all models '96 thru '10
92085 **Tercel** all models '87 thru '94
92090 **Sienna** all models '98 thru '09
92095 **Highlander & Lexus RX-330** '99 thru '07

TRIUMPH
94007 **Spitfire** all models '62 thru '81
94010 **TR7** all models '75 thru '81

VW
96008 **Beetle & Karmann Ghia** '54 thru '79
96009 **New Beetle** '98 thru '11
96016 **Rabbit, Jetta, Scirocco & Pick-up** gas
  models '75 thru '92 & Convertible '80 thru '92
96017 **Golf, GTI & Jetta** '93 thru '98, **Cabrio** '95 thru '02
96018 **Golf, GTI, Jetta** '99 thru '05
96019 **Jetta, Rabbit, GTI & Golf** '05 thru '11
96020 **Rabbit, Jetta & Pick-up** diesel '77 thru '84
96023 **Passat** '98 thru '05, **Audi A4** '96 thru '01
96030 **Transporter 1600** all models '68 thru '79
96035 **Transporter 1700, 1800 & 2000** '72 thru '79
96040 **Type 3 1500 & 1600** all models '63 thru '73
96045 **Vanagon** all air-cooled models '80 thru '83

VOLVO
97010 **120, 130 Series & 1800 Sports** '61 thru '73
97015 **140 Series** all models '66 thru '74
97020 **240 Series** all models '76 thru '93
97040 **740 & 760 Series** all models '82 thru '88
97050 **850 Series** all models '93 thru '97

TECHBOOK MANUALS
10205 **Automotive Computer Codes**
10206 **OBD-II & Electronic Engine Management**
10210 **Automotive Emissions Control Manual**
10215 **Fuel Injection Manual** '78 thru '85
10220 **Fuel Injection Manual** '86 thru '99
10225 **Holley Carburetor Manual**
10230 **Rochester Carburetor Manual**
10240 **Weber/Zenith/Stromberg/SU Carburetors**
10305 **Chevrolet Engine Overhaul Manual**
10310 **Chrysler Engine Overhaul Manual**
10320 **Ford Engine Overhaul Manual**
10330 **GM and Ford Diesel Engine Repair Manual**
10333 **Engine Performance Manual**
10340 **Small Engine Repair Manual,** 5 HP & Less
10341 **Small Engine Repair Manual,** 5.5 - 20 HP
10345 **Suspension, Steering & Driveline Manual**
10355 **Ford Automatic Transmission Overhaul**
10360 **GM Automatic Transmission Overhaul**
10405 **Automotive Body Repair & Painting**
10410 **Automotive Brake Manual**
10411 **Automotive Anti-lock Brake (ABS) Systems**
10415 **Automotive Detailing Manual**
10420 **Automotive Electrical Manual**
10425 **Automotive Heating & Air Conditioning**
10430 **Automotive Reference Manual & Dictionary**
10435 **Automotive Tools Manual**
10440 **Used Car Buying Guide**
10445 **Welding Manual**
10450 **ATV Basics**
10452 **Scooters 50cc to 250cc**

SPANISH MANUALS
98903 **Reparación de Carrocería & Pintura**
98904 **Manual de Carburador Modelos**
  Holley & Rochester
98905 **Códigos Automotrices de la Computadora**
98906 **OBD-II & Sistemas de Control Electrónico**
  del Motor
98910 **Frenos Automotriz**
98913 **Electricidad Automotriz**
98915 **Inyección de Combustible** '86 al '99
99040 **Chevrolet & GMC Camionetas** '67 al '87
99041 **Chevrolet & GMC Camionetas** '88 al '98
99042 **Chevrolet & GMC Camionetas**
  Cerradas '68 al '95
99043 **Chevrolet/GMC Camionetas** '94 al '04
99048 **Chevrolet/GMC Camionetas** '99 al '06
99055 **Dodge Caravan & Plymouth Voyager** '84 al '95
99075 **Ford Camionetas y Bronco** '80 al '94
99076 **Ford F-150** '97 al '09
99077 **Ford Camionetas Cerradas** '69 al '91
99088 **Ford Modelos de Tamaño Mediano** '75 al '86
99089 **Ford Camionetas Ranger** '93 al '10
99091 **Ford Taurus & Mercury Sable** '86 al '95
99095 **GM Modelos de Tamaño Grande** '70 al '90
99100 **GM Modelos de Tamaño Mediano** '70 al '88
99106 **Jeep Cherokee, Wagoneer & Comanche**
  '84 al '00
99110 **Nissan Camioneta** '80 al '96, **Pathfinder** '87 al '08
99118 **Nissan Sentra** '82 al '94
99125 **Toyota Camionetas y 4Runner** '79 al '95

Over 100 Haynes
motorcycle manuals
also available

7-12

Haynes North America, Inc., 859 Lawrence Drive, Newbury Park, CA 91320-1514 • (805) 498-6703 • http://www.haynes.com